Rick Steves®

PARIS

Rick Steves, Steve Smith &
Gene Openshaw

2017

CONTENTS

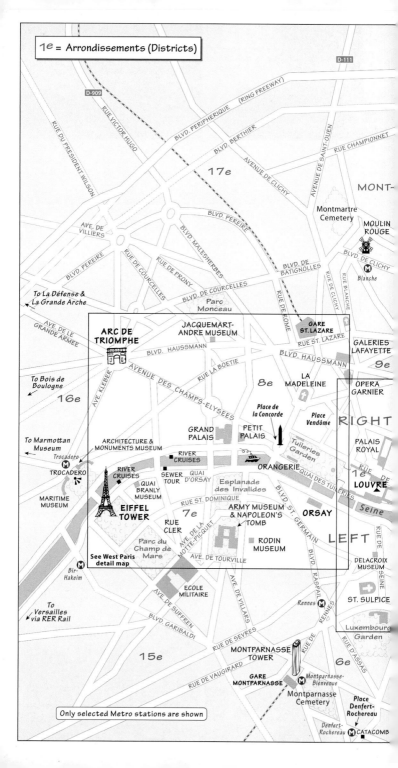

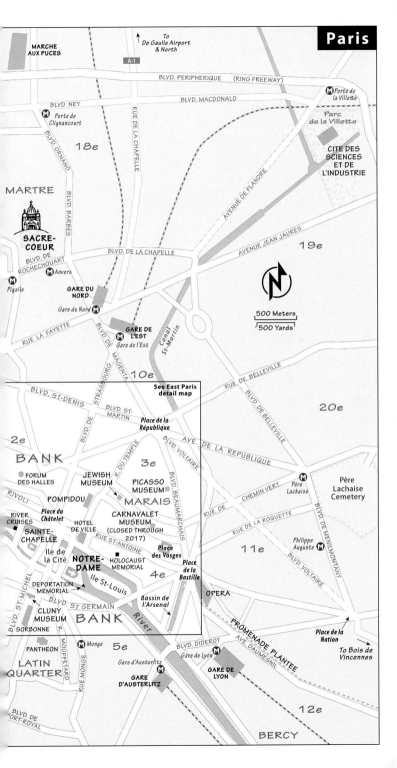

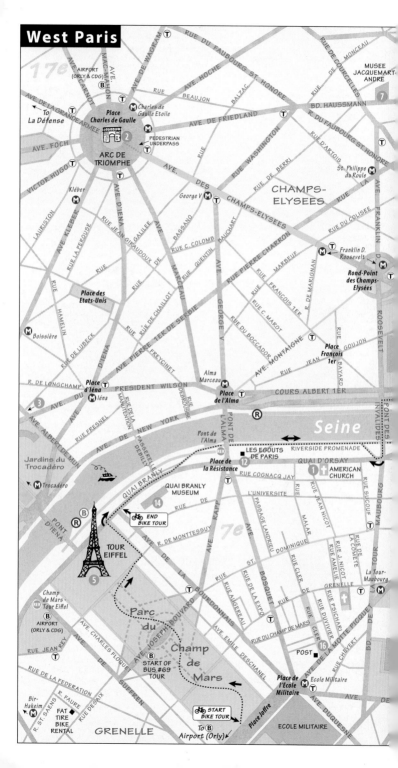

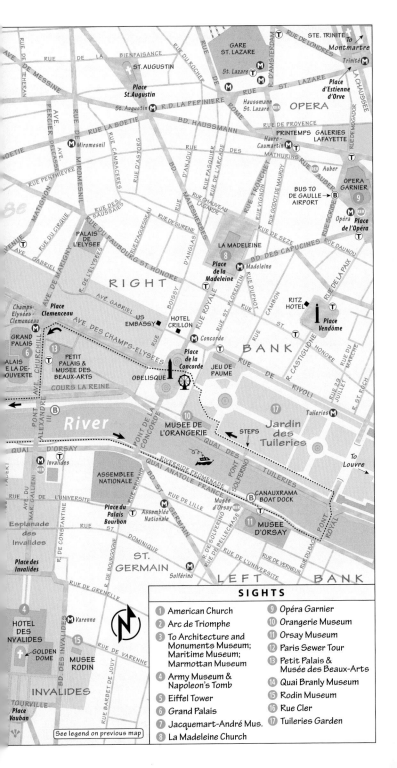

SIGHTS

1. American Church
2. Arc de Triomphe
3. To Architecture and Monuments Museum; Maritime Museum; Marmottan Museum
4. Army Museum & Napoleon's Tomb
5. Eiffel Tower
6. Grand Palais
7. Jacquemart-André Mus.
8. La Madeleine Church
9. Opéra Garnier
10. Orangerie Museum
11. Orsay Museum
12. Paris Sewer Tour
13. Petit Palais & Musée des Beaux-Arts
14. Quai Branly Museum
15. Rodin Museum
16. Rue Cler
17. Tuileries Garden

See legend on previous map

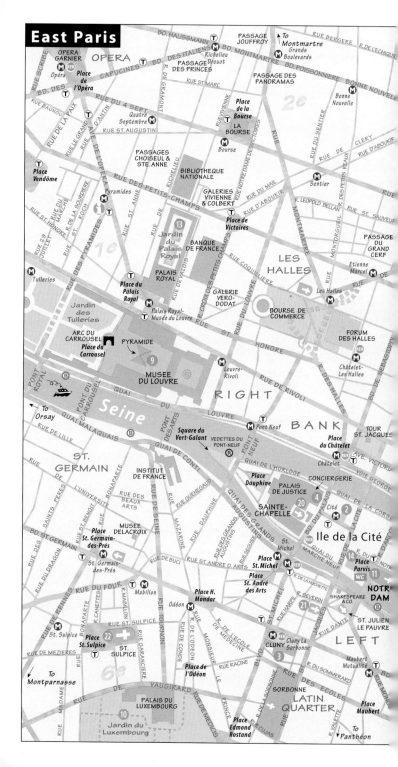

East Paris

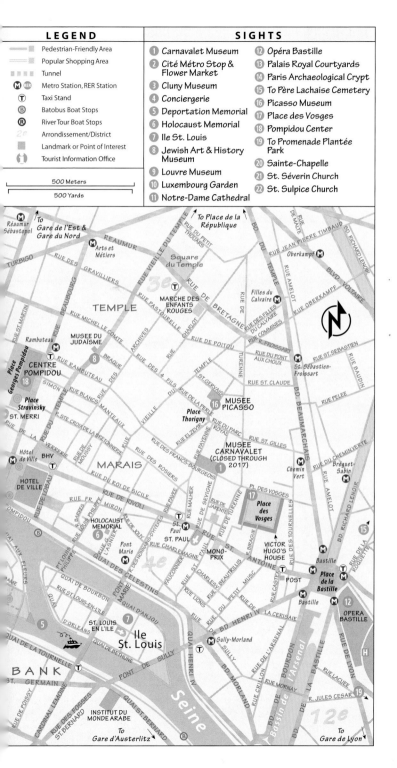

LEGEND	SIGHTS

LEGEND

- ——— Pedestrian-Friendly Area
- ------ Popular Shopping Area
- ■ ■ ■ ■ Tunnel
- Ⓜ Ⓡ Metro Station, RER Station
- Ⓣ Taxi Stand
- Ⓑ Batobus Boat Stops
- Ⓡ River Tour Boat Stops
- 2e Arrondissement/District
- ■ Landmark or Point of Interest
- 👫 Tourist Information Office

500 Meters
500 Yards

SIGHTS

1. Carnavalet Museum
2. Cité Métro Stop & Flower Market
3. Cluny Museum
4. Conciergerie
5. Deportation Memorial
6. Holocaust Memorial
7. Ile St. Louis
8. Jewish Art & History Museum
9. Louvre Museum
10. Luxembourg Garden
11. Notre-Dame Cathedral
12. Opéra Bastille
13. Palais Royal Courtyards
14. Paris Archaeological Crypt
15. To Père Lachaise Cemetery
16. Picasso Museum
17. Place des Vosges
18. Pompidou Center
19. To Promenade Plantée Park
20. Sainte-Chapelle
21. St. Séverin Church
22. St. Sulpice Church

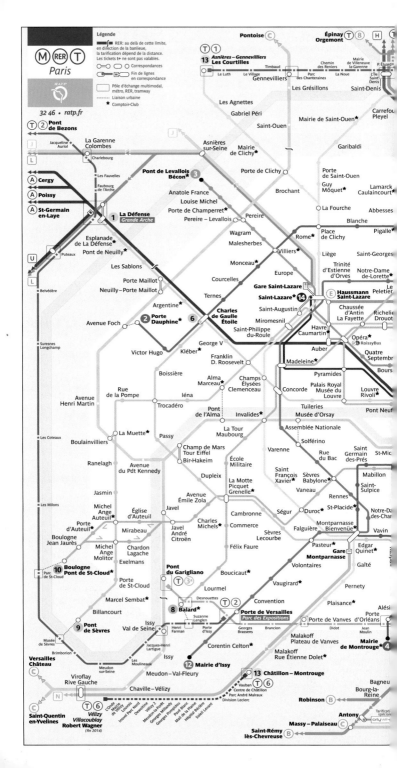

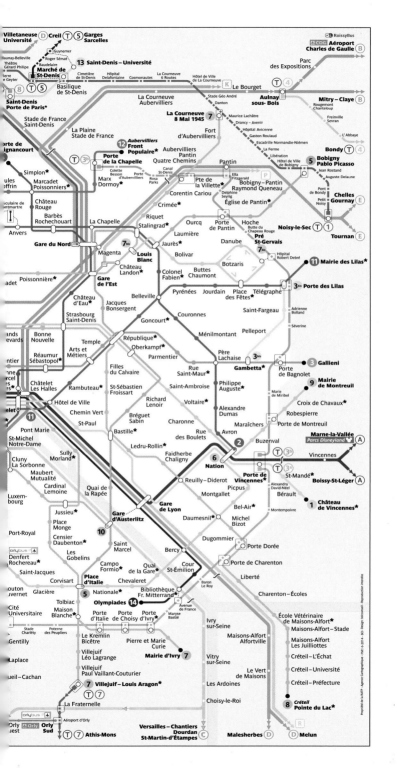

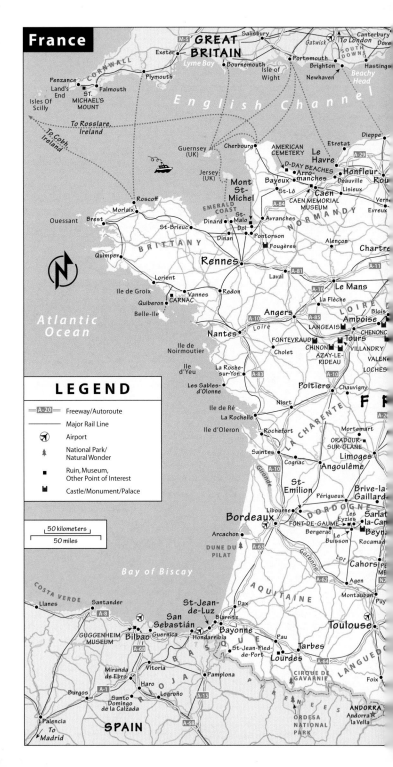

France

GREAT BRITAIN

Canterbury
Dover
Salisbury
Gatwick
To London
SOUTH DOWNS
Exeter
Portsmouth
Brighton
Hastings
CORNWALL
Lyme Bay
Bournemouth
Newhaven
Beachy Head
Penzance
Plymouth
Isle of Wight
Land's End
Falmouth
ST. MICHAEL'S MOUNT
Isles Of Scilly

E n g l i s h   C h a n n e l

To Rosslare, Ireland
To Cobh Ireland
Guernsey (UK)
Cherbourg
Dieppe
AMERICAN CEMETERY
Le Havre
Etretat
A-29
Honfleur
Rou
Jersey (UK)
Mont St-Michel
D-DAY BEACHES
Bayeux
Arromanches
Deauville
Lisieux
Roscoff
EMERALD COAST
St-Lô
Caen
Vern
Morlaix
St-Malo
Avranches
A-84
CAEN MEMORIAL MUSEUM
Evreux
Ouessant
Brest
Dinard
Dol
NORMANDY
Alençon
Chartre
St-Brieuc
Dinan
Pontorson
Fougères
BRITTANY
Rennes
A-81
A-11
Quimper
Laval
Le Mans
A-10
Lorient
Redon
La Flèche
LOIRE
Ile de Groix
Vannes
Angers
A-85
Blois
Amboise
Quiberon
CARNAC
A-10
LANGEAIS
CHENONC
Belle-Ile
Nantes
Loire
FONTEVRAUD
Tours
CHINON
VILLANDRY
Atlantic Ocean
Cholet
AZAY-LE-RIDEAU
VALEN
Ile de Noirmoutier
LOCHES
Ile d'Yeu
La Roche-sur-Yon
A-83
Poitiers
Chauvigny
A-10
F
F

LEGEND

A-20 — Freeway/Autoroute
—— Major Rail Line
✈ Airport
🌲 National Park/Natural Wonder
■ Ruin, Museum, Other Point of Interest
🏰 Castle/Monument/Palace

50 kilometers
50 miles

Les Sables-d'Olonne
Niort
Ile de Ré
La Rochelle
Rochefort
LA CHARENTE
A-2
Ile d'Oleron
Mortemart
ORADOUR-SUR-GLANE
Limoges
Saintes
Cognac
Angoulême
Gironde
A-10
St-Emilion
Périgueux
Brive-la-Gaillard
DORDOGNE
Libourne
Les Eyzies
Sarlat-la-Car
Bordeaux
FONT-DE-GAUME
Beyn
Arcachon
Le Buisson
Bergerac
Rocamad
DUNE DU PILAT
A-63
Lot
Cahors
PE
Gatonne
ME
AQUITAINE
A-62
Agen
N2
Bay of Biscay
Montauban
Puy
COSTA VERDE
Dax
Toulouse
Llanes
Santander
St-Jean-de-Luz
A-8
San Sebastián
Biarritz
Bayonne
Pau
LANGUEDO
GUGGENHEIM MUSEUM
Bilbao
Guernica
Hondarribia
St-Jean-Pied-de-Port
Tarbes
A-64
A-68
Lourdes
Foix
Miranda de Ebro
Vitoria
Pamplona
CIRQUE DE GAVARNIE
ANDORRA
Burgos
Haro
Logroño
Andorra la Vella
A-1
Santo Domingo de la Calzada
A-15
PYRENEES
ORDESA NATIONAL PARK
Palencia
To Madrid
SPAIN
A-68

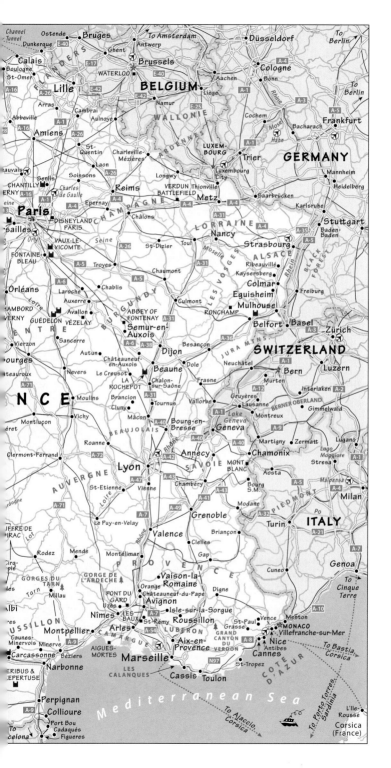

Arc de Triomphe

Versailles Gardens

Typical crêperie

Sacré-Cœur

Montmartre

Rick Steves®

PARIS

2017

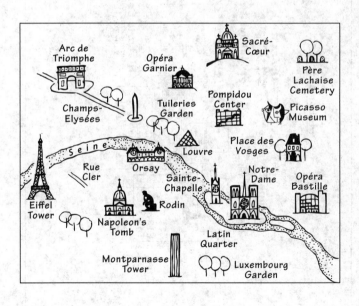

Arc de Triomphe · Opéra Garnier · Sacré-Cœur · Père Lachaise Cemetery · Champs-Elysées · Tuileries Garden · Pompidou Center · Picasso Museum · Seine · Louvre · Place des Vosges · Eiffel Tower · Rue Cler · Orsay · Sainte-Chapelle · Notre-Dame · Opéra Bastille · Napoleon's Tomb · Rodin · Latin Quarter · Montparnasse Tower · Luxembourg Garden

Paris Map Overview

Legend:
- ★ Sleeping & Eating Area (as described in text)
- ■ Self-Guided Tour
- Ⓑ Bus Tour
- ···· Walk
- ▢ District Map

N

1 Kilometer
1 Mile

Montmartre
Montmartre Walk ★

Opéra
Place de la Madeleine Shopping Walk

Major Museums
Louvre, Orsay & Orangerie

Marais & Nearby
Pompidou
Picasso
Carnavalet (Closed through 2017)
Marais Walk ★

Champs-Elysées
Champs-Elysées Walk

Historic Core
Historic Paris Walk, Notre-Dame & Sainte-Chapelle

Left Bank
Left Bank Walk
Cluny
Sèvres-Babylone Shopping Walk ★

Eiffel Tower
Rodin ★
Army Museum & Napoleon's Tomb
Rue Cler Walk
Bus #69 Tour Starts Ⓑ
Marmottan

Bus #69 Tour Ends Ⓑ
Père Lachaise Cemetery

PÉRIPHÉRIQUE (RING FREEWAY)

Seine River

Bois de Boulogne
Bois de Vincennes

To Giverny & Rouen →
To Auvers-sur-Oise →
To Charles de Gaulle Airport & Chantilly →
To Disneyland Paris & Reims →
To Orly Airport, Vaux-le-Vicomte, Fontainebleau & Chartres →
To Versailles →

INTRODUCTION

Paris—the City of Light—has been a beacon of culture for centuries. As a world capital of art, fashion, food, literature, and ideas, it stands as a symbol of all the fine things human civilization can offer. Come prepared to celebrate this, rather than judge our cultural differences, and you'll capture the romance and *joie de vivre* that this city exudes.

Paris offers sweeping boulevards, chatty crêpe stands, chic boutiques, and world-class art galleries. Sip decaf with deconstructionists at a sidewalk café, then step into an Impressionist painting in a tree-lined park. Climb Notre-Dame and rub shoulders with a gargoyle. Cruise the Seine, zip to the top of the Eiffel Tower, and saunter down Avenue des Champs-Elysées. Master the Louvre and Orsay museums. Save some after-dark energy for one of the world's most romantic cities.

ABOUT THIS BOOK

Rick Steves Paris 2017 is a personal tour guide in your pocket. Better yet, it's actually three tour guides in your pocket: The co-authors of this book are Steve Smith and Gene Openshaw. Steve has been traveling to France—as a guide, researcher, homeowner, and devout Francophile—every year since 1985. Gene and I have been exploring the wonders of the Old World since our first "Europe through the gutter" trip together as high school buddies in the 1970s. An inquisitive historian and lover of European culture, Gene wrote most of this book's self-guided museum tours and neighborhood walks. Together, Steve, Gene, and I keep this book current (though, for simplicity, from this point "we" will shed our respective egos and become "I").

The book divides Paris into convenient neighborhoods (shown

Map Legend

⅃ Viewpoint	🚲 Bike Rental/Bike Route	——— Pedestrian Zone
↑ Entrance	ⓣ Taxi Stand	------- Railway
❿ Tourist Info	Ⓑ Bus Stop	.... Ferry/Boat Route
�📱 Restroom	ⓟ Parking	✈ Airport
▮ Castle	ⓡ RER Train	⬛⬛⬛ Stairs
⌂ Church	ⓣ Tourist Train	- - - - Walk/Tour Route
▪ Statue/Point of Interest	Ⓑ Batobus Stop	
⌣ Park	Ⓜ Métro Stop	- - - - - Trail
◎ Fountain		

Use this legend to help you navigate the maps in this book.

on "Paris Map Overview" on page XVIII). In this book, you'll find the following chapters:

Orientation to Paris has specifics on public transportation, helpful hints, local tour options, easy-to-read maps, and tourist information. The "Planning Your Time" section suggests a schedule for how to best use your limited time.

Sights in Paris describes the top attractions and includes their cost and hours.

The **Self-Guided Walks** cover six of Paris' most intriguing neighborhoods: Historic Paris (including Notre-Dame and Sainte-Chapelle), Rue Cler (near the Eiffel Tower), the Left Bank, the Champs-Elysées, the Marais, and Montmartre.

The **Self-Guided Tours** lead you through Paris' most fascinating museums and sights: the Louvre, Orsay, Orangerie, Eiffel Tower, Rodin Museum, Army Museum and Napoleon's Tomb, Marmottan, Cluny, Picasso Museum, Pompidou Center, and Père Lachaise Cemetery. The Bus #69 Sightseeing Tour gives you an inexpensive overview of the city.

Sleeping in Paris describes my favorite hotels in five appealing neighborhoods (plus hotels convenient to Paris' two main airports), from good-value deals to cushy splurges.

Eating in Paris serves up a buffet of options, from inexpensive cafés to romantic bistros, arranged by neighborhood, plus a listing of historic cafés.

Paris with Children includes my top recommendations for keeping your kids (and you) happy, along with information for visiting Disneyland Paris.

Shopping in Paris gives you tips for shopping painlessly and enjoyably, without letting it overwhelm your vacation or ruin your budget. Read up on Paris' great department stores, neighborhood boutiques, flea markets, outdoor food markets, and arcaded, Old World shopping streets. Try the suggested boutique strolls on Place de la Madeleine, in the Left Bank, and on Rue des Martyrs.

Entertainment in Paris is your guide to fun, including live music, driving tours, and the best night walks and river cruises. You'll also find information on how to translate *Pariscope*, the weekly entertainment guide.

Paris in Winter provides tips on how to enjoy the City of Light during the wonderfully untouristy holiday season and beyond.

Paris Connections lays the groundwork for your arrival and departure, covering transportation by train (including the Eurostar to London) and plane, with detailed information on Paris' two major airports (Charles de Gaulle and Orly), a remote airport (Beauvais), and Paris' seven train stations.

Day Trips include the great châteaux of Versailles (with a self-guided tour), Vaux-le-Vicomte, Fontainebleau, and Chantilly; Chartres' majestic cathedral (with a self-guided tour and a town walk); and the Impressionist retreats of Claude Monet's Giverny and Vincent van Gogh's Auvers-sur-Oise. For those who like to linger, I list accommodations near most of these sights.

France: Past & Present gives you a quick overview of the country's tumultuous history and contemporary challenges.

The **Practicalities** chapter near the end of this book is a traveler's tool kit, with my best advice about money, sightseeing, sleeping, eating, staying connected, and transportation.

The **appendix** has the nuts and bolts: useful phone numbers and websites, a holiday and festival list, recommended books and films, a climate chart, a handy packing checklist, a guide to pronouncing Parisian landmarks, and French survival phrases.

Throughout this book, you'll find money- and time-saving tips for sightseeing, transportation, and more. Some businesses—especially hotels and walking tour companies—offer special discounts to my readers, indicated in their listings.

Browse through this book and select your favorite sights. Then have a trip that's truly *formidable!* Traveling like a temporary local, you'll get the absolute most out of every mile, minute, and dollar. As you visit places I know and love, I'm happy that you'll be meeting my favorite Parisians.

Planning

This section will help you get started planning your trip—with advice on trip costs, when to go, and what you should know before you take off.

Key to This Book

Updates

This book is updated every year—but things change. For the latest, visit www.ricksteves.com/update.

Abbreviations and Times

I use the following symbols and abbreviations in this book:

Sights are rated:

▲▲▲   Don't miss

▲▲   Try hard to see

▲   Worthwhile if you can make it

No rating   Worth knowing about

Tourist information offices are abbreviated as **TI,** and bathrooms are **WC**s. Accommodations are categorized with a **Sleep Code** (described on page 387); eateries are classified with a **Restaurant Price Code** (page 642). To indicate discounts for my readers, I include **RS%** in the listings.

Like Europe, this book uses the **24-hour clock.** It's the same through 12:00 noon, then keeps going: 13:00, 14:00, and so on. For anything over 12, subtract 12 and add p.m. (14:00 is 2:00 p.m.).

When giving **opening times,** I include both peak season and off-season hours if they differ. So, if a museum is listed as "May-Oct daily 9:00-18:00," it should be open from 9 a.m. until 6 p.m. from the first day of May until the last day of October (but expect exceptions).

A □ symbol in a sight listing means that the sight is described in greater detail elsewhere—either with its own self-guided tour, or as part of a self-guided walk. A ∩ symbol indicates that a free, downloadable self-guided audio tour is available.

For **transit** or **tour departures,** I first list the frequency, then the duration. So, a train connection listed as "2/hour, 1.5 hours" departs twice each hour and the journey lasts an hour and a half.

TRAVEL SMART

Your trip to Paris is like a complex play—it's easier to follow and really appreciate on a second viewing. While no one does the same trip twice to gain that advantage, reading this book in its entirety before your trip accomplishes much the same thing.

Design an itinerary that enables you to visit sights at the best possible times. Note festivals, holidays, street-market days, specifics on sights, and days when sights are closed or most crowded (all covered in this book). You can wait in line at the Louvre, or—with a Paris Museum Pass and some planning ahead—zip through without breaking a sweat. Day-tripping to Versailles on Monday is bad, since it's closed—but it's not recommended on Tuesday either, when the Louvre is closed and tourist mobs storm the palace. Designing a smart trip is a puzzle—a fun, doable, and worthwhile challenge.

Make your itinerary a mix of intense and relaxed stretches. Every trip—and every traveler—needs slack time (laundry, picnics, café-sitting, and so on). Pace yourself. Assume you will return.

Even with the best-planned itinerary, you'll need to be flexible. Update your plans as you travel. Though I encourage you to disconnect from life back home and immerse yourself in the French experience, you can get online or call ahead to learn the latest on sights (special events, tour schedules, and so on), book tickets and tours, make reservations, reconfirm hotels, and research transportation connections.

Enjoy the friendliness of the French people. Connect with the culture. Learn a new French expression each day and practice it. Cheer for your favorite bowler at a *boules* match, leave no chair unturned in your quest for the best café, find that perfect Eiffel Tower view, and make friends with a crêpe stand. Slow down to appreciate the sincerity of your Parisian hosts, and be open to unexpected experiences. Ask questions—most locals are eager to point you in their idea of the right direction. Keep a notepad in your pocket for confirming prices, noting directions, and organizing your thoughts. Wear your money belt, learn the currency, and figure out how to estimate prices in dollars. Those who expect to travel smart, do.

TRIP COSTS

Five components make up your trip costs: airfare to Europe, transportation in Europe, room and board, sightseeing and entertainment, and shopping and miscellany.

Airfare to Europe: A basic round-trip flight from the US to Paris can cost, on average, about $1,000-2,000 total, depending on where you fly from and when (cheaper in winter). If Paris is part of a longer European trip, consider saving time and money by flying into one city and out of another; for instance, into Paris and out of Rome. Overall, Kayak.com is the best place to start searching for flights on a combination of mainstream and budget carriers.

Transportation in Europe: For a typical one-week visit, allow about $65 for Métro tickets and a couple of day trips by train. To get between Paris and either major airport, figure $30-125 round-trip, depending on which option you choose.

Room and Board: You can manage comfortably in Paris in 2017 on $195 a day per person for room and board. This allows $15 for breakfast, $20 for lunch with a drink, $50 for dinner with drinks, and $110 for lodging (based on two people splitting the cost of a $220 double room). If you've got more money, I've listed great

The Language Barrier and That French Attitude

You've no doubt heard that Parisians are "mean and cold and re-fuse to speak English." This is an out-of-date preconception left over from the days of Charles de Gaulle. Parisians are as friendly as any other people, and no more disagreeable than New York-ers. Like many big cities, Paris is a melting pot of international cultures; your evening hotel receptionist is just as likely to speak French with an accent as not. Without any doubt, Parisians speak more English than Americans speak French. Be reasonable in your expectations: French waiters are paid to be efficient, not chatty. And Parisian postal clerks are every bit as speedy, cheery, and multilingual as ours are back home.

My best advice? Slow down. The biggest mistake most Americans make when traveling in France is trying to do too much with limited time. Hurried, impatient travelers who miss the subtle pleasures of people-watching from a sun-dappled café often mis-interpret French attitudes. By slowing your pace and making an effort to understand French culture by living it, you're more likely to have a richer experience. With the five weeks of paid vacation and 35-hour work week that many French workers consider as nonnegotiable rights, your hosts can't fathom why anyone would rush through their vacation.

Parisians take great pride in their customs, clinging to the sense of their own cultural superiority. Let's face it: It's tough to keep on smiling when you've been crushed by a Big Mac, Mickey-Moused by Disney, and drowned in Starbucks coffee. Your hosts are cold only if you decide to see them that way. Polite and for-mal, the French respect the fine points of culture and tradition. In Paris, strolling down the street with a big grin on your face and saying hello to strangers is a sign of senility, not friendliness (seri-ously). Parisians think that Americans, while friendly, are hesitant

ways to spend it. Students and tightwads can enjoy Paris for as little as $70 a day ($35 for a bed, $35 for meals and snacks).

Sightseeing and Entertainment: Get the Paris Museum Pass, which covers most sights in the city (for more information, see page 49). You'll pay about $55 for a two-day pass. Without a Museum Pass, figure about $15 per major sight, $10 for others. Add $20-60 for bus tours and splurge experiences (such as walking tours and concerts in Sainte-Chapelle). An overall average of $40 a day works for most people. Don't skimp here. After all, this category is the driving force behind your trip—you came to sightsee, enjoy, and experience Paris.

Shopping and Miscellany: Figure $4 per ice cream cone, cof-fee, or soft drink. Shopping can vary in cost from nearly nothing to

to pursue more serious friendships. Recognize sincerity and look for kindness. Give them the benefit of the doubt.

Communication difficulties are exaggerated. To hurdle the language barrier, start with the French survival phrases in this book (see the appendix). Bring a small English/French dictionary and/or a phrase book (look for mine, which contains a dictionary and menu decoder), a menu reader, and a good supply of patience. In transactions, a small notepad and pen minimize misunderstandings about prices; have vendors write the price down.

Though many French people—especially those in the tourist trade and in big cities—speak English, you'll get better treatment if you use French pleasantries. If you learn only five phrases, try these: *bonjour* (good day), *pardon* (pardon me), *s'il vous plaît* (please), *merci* (thank you), and *au revoir* (good-bye). The French value politeness. Begin every encounter with "*Bonjour* (or *S'il vous plaît*), *madame* (or *monsieur*)," and end every encounter with "*Au revoir, madame* (or *monsieur*)." When spelling out your name, you'll find that most letters are pronounced very differently in French: *a* is pronounced "ah," *e* is pronounced "eh," and *i* is pronounced "ee." To avoid confusion, say "*a*, Anne," "*e*, euro," and "*i*, Isabelle."

When you do make an effort to speak French, you may be politely corrected—*c'est normal.* The French are linguistic perfectionists—they take their language (and other languages) seriously. Often they speak more English than they let on. This isn't a tourist-baiting tactic, but timidity on their part about speaking another language less than fluently. To ask a French person to speak English, say, "*Bonjour, madame* (or *monsieur*). *Parlez-vous anglais?*" They may say "*non*," but as you continue you'll probably find they speak more English than you speak French.

a small fortune. Good budget travelers find that this category has little to do with assembling a trip full of lifelong memories.

WHEN TO GO

Late spring and fall bring the best weather and the biggest crowds. May, June, September, and October are the toughest months for hotel-hunting—don't expect many hotel deals. Summers are generally hot and dry; if you wilt in the heat, look for a room with air-conditioning. Rooms are easy to land in August (some hotels offer deals), and though many French businesses close in August, you'll hardly notice.

Paris makes a great winter getaway (see the Paris in Winter chapter). Airfare costs less, cafés are cozy, and the city feels lively but not touristy. The only problem—weather—is solved by dressing

∩ Rick Steves Audio Europe ∩

My free **Rick Steves Audio Europe app** is a great tool for enjoying Europe. This app makes it easy to download my audio tours of top attractions, plus hours of travel interviews, all organized into destination-specific playlists.

My self-guided **audio tours** of major sights and neighborhoods are free, user-friendly, fun, and informative. Among the sights in this book, these audio tours include the Historic Paris Walk, Louvre Museum, Orsay Museum, and Versailles Palace. Sights covered by my audio tours are marked with this symbol: ∩. You can choose whether to follow the written tour in this book, or pop in your headphones and listen to essentially the same information—freeing up your eyes to appreciate the sights. These audio tours are hard to beat: Nobody will stand you up, the quality is reliable, you can take the tour exactly when you like, and the price is right.

The Rick Steves Audio Europe app also offers a far-reaching library of insightful **travel interviews** from my public radio show with experts from around the globe—including many of the places in this book.

This app and all of its content are entirely free. (And new content is added about twice a year.) You can download Rick Steves Audio Europe from Apple's App Store, Google Play, or the Amazon Appstore. For more information, see www.ricksteves.com/audioeurope.

warmly, with layers. Expect cold (even freezing lows) and rain (hats, gloves, scarves, umbrellas, and thick-soled shoes are essential). For specific temperatures, see the climate chart in the appendix.

KNOW BEFORE YOU GO

Check this list of things to arrange while you're still at home.

You need a **passport**—but no visa or shots—to travel in France. You may be denied entry into certain European countries if your passport is due to expire within six months of your ticketed date of return. Get it renewed if you'll be cutting it close. It can take up to six weeks to get or renew a passport (for more on passports and requirements for France, see www.travel.state.gov). Pack a photocopy of your passport in your luggage in case the original is lost or stolen.

Book rooms well in advance if you'll be traveling during peak season (April through October) or any major holidays (see page 677). Some famous restaurants (but not ones I recommend) require reservations several weeks in advance.

Call your **debit- and credit-card companies** to let them know

Paris Almanac

Population: About 2.3 million in the city center, 10 million in the greater Paris region.

Currency: Euro.

Nickname: The City of Light.

City Layout: Paris is the capital and largest city in France. The Seine River slices through the city, with the Right Bank to the north and the Left Bank to the south (orient yourself by looking downstream—the Left Bank is to your left, the Right Bank to your right). The city is divided into 20 municipal boroughs, called arrondissements.

Transportation Basics: The Métro is the most-used public transportation in Paris, with 16 colored lines, 300 stations, and nearly 5 million passengers riding each day. The mayor of Paris, Anne Hidalgo, is continuing a trend to reduce vehicular traffic by calling for diesel cars to be banned from Paris streets by 2020, expanding traffic-free areas, and doubling the number of bike lanes. Today 60 percent of Parisians do not own cars compared to 40 percent in 2001.

Tourist Tracks: Paris is the world's top tourist destination, attracting more than 30 million visitors a year. Of its 3,800 historical monuments, the most popular draws within the city are the Louvre (more than 9 million people tour it each year) and the Eiffel Tower (more than 7 million). But Mona doesn't hold a candle to Mickey—Disneyland Paris gets 16 million visitors a year.

Culture Count: Most Parisians, including those of French ancestry, were born outside of the city—and roughly one in five residents of greater Paris was born outside France (and one in three has at least one immigrant parent). The city has significant populations of people from Africa, China, Eastern Europe, and the Middle East.

Famous Residents: Brigitte Bardot, Juliette Binoche, Carla Bruni, Sofia Coppola, Catherine Deneuve, Jean-Luc Godard, Rickie Lee Jones, Diane Kruger, Tony Parker, Roman Polanski, Mick Jagger, Kristin Scott Thomas, Audrey Tautou, and one of the researchers for this book, Mary Bouron.

Average Parisian: Compared to the average Frenchman or Frenchwoman, the average Parisian is younger (since so many people retire in the countryside), makes more money, and is more likely to live alone or with just one other person. That said, the city has experienced a baby boom in the last several years, with French families averaging two children per household.

Cheap Tricks in Paris

Book good-value rooms early. I list several well-located and comfortable hotels with rooms under €140, but you'll need to beat others to the punch.

Enjoy picnic lunches and dinners. You'll find tasty €5 sandwiches, to-go salads, quiches, crêpes, and high-quality takeout at bakeries, charcuteries, and stands. Wine merchants sell chilled, picnic-friendly bottles that they'll happily open for you. Scenic picnic sites are everywhere.

In cafés, stand at the bar to sip your drink, and you'll get the lowest prices. Before ordering at a table, check out the price list *(Les Prix de Consommation),* which is always prominently displayed. This shows the price of the most commonly ordered drinks *au comptoir* (at the counter) and *en salle* (seated at a table). I use the price of *un café* (shot of espresso) at the counter as my barometer—if the price is €1.50 or less, the place is likely to be reasonable. If given a choice between small-, medium-, or large-size beverage, be aware that small is usually the norm and that medium drinks can be crazy pricey.

Order only a *plat* (main course) for dinner on some nights. And at cafés (as opposed to restaurants), it's fine to order only a soup or salad for dinner.

Shop at grocery stores for bottled water, drinks, and snacks, not at expensive snack stands. Refill bottles from the tap.

Visit sights on free days (see sidebar on page 64).

Buy a Paris Museum Pass and use it wisely (see page 49 for advice).

the countries you'll be visiting, ask about fees, to request your PIN if you don't already know it, and more. See page 625 for details.

Do your homework if you're considering **travel insurance.** Compare the cost of the insurance to the cost of your potential loss. Also check whether your existing insurance (health, homeowners, or renters) covers you and your possessions overseas. For more tips, see www.ricksteves.com/insurance.

High-speed trains (TGVs) in France require a seat reservation; book as early as possible, as these trains fill fast, and some routes use TGV trains almost exclusively. This is especially true if you're traveling with a rail pass, as TGV pass-holder reservations are limited, and usually sell out well before other seat reservations do (look also for online deals for individual ticket purchases at http://en.voyages-sncf.com). For more on train travel, see page 518.

To avoid long ticket-buying lines at the **Eiffel Tower,** book an entry time several months in advance using its online reservation system (see page 212).

If seeing the City of Light at night from a taxi or Uber appeals

How Was Your Trip?

Were your travels fun, smooth, and meaningful? You can share tips, concerns, and discoveries at www.ricksteves.com/feedback. I value your feedback. Thanks in advance.

to you, photocopy the **"Floodlit Paris Driving Tour"** (in the Entertainment in Paris chapter) to bring along and give to your driver.

If you plan to hire a **local guide,** reserve ahead by email. Popular guides can get booked up. For suggestions see page 43.

If you're bringing a **mobile device,** consider signing up for an international plan for cheaper calls, texts, and data (see page 659). Download any apps you might want to use on the road, such as translators, maps, transit schedules, and **Rick Steves Audio Europe** (see page 8).

If you'll be **traveling with children,** read over the list of pretrip suggestions on page 451.

Check for recent updates to this book at www.ricksteves.com/update.

Traveling as a Temporary Local

We travel all the way to France to enjoy differences—to become temporary locals. You'll experience frustrations. Certain truths that we find "God-given" or "self-evident," such as cold beer, ice in drinks, bottomless cups of coffee, "the customer is king," and bigger being better, are suddenly not so true. One of the benefits of travel is the eye-opening realization that there are logical, civil, and even better alternatives.

Paris is an understandably proud city. To enjoy its people, you need to celebrate the differences. A willingness to go local ensures that you'll enjoy a full dose of Parisian hospitality. And with an eagerness to go local, you'll have even more fun.

Europeans generally like Americans. But if there is a negative aspect to the French image of Americans, it's that we are loud, wasteful, ethnocentric, too informal (which can seem disrespectful), and a bit naive.

The French (and Europeans in general) place a high value on speaking quietly in public places. Listen while on the bus or in a restaurant—the place can be packed, but the decibel level is low. Try to adjust your volume accordingly to show respect for the culture.

While the French look bemusedly at some of our Yankee excesses—and worriedly at others—they nearly always afford us individual travelers all the warmth we deserve.

Judging from all the happy feedback I receive from travelers who have used this book, it's safe to assume you'll enjoy a great, affordable vacation—with the finesse of an independent, experienced traveler.

Thanks, and *bon voyage!*

Rick Steves

Back Door Travel Philosophy

From *Rick Steves Europe Through the Back Door*

Travel is intensified living—maximum thrills per minute and one of the last great sources of legal adventure. Travel is freedom. It's recess, and we need it.

Experiencing the real Europe requires catching it by surprise, going casual..."through the Back Door."

Affording travel is a matter of priorities. (Make do with the old car.) You can eat and sleep—simply, safely, and enjoyably—anywhere in Europe for $100 a day plus transportation costs. In many ways, spending more money only builds a thicker wall between you and what you traveled so far to see. Europe is a cultural carnival, and time after time, you'll find that its best acts are free and the best seats are the cheap ones.

A tight budget forces you to travel close to the ground, meeting and communicating with the people. Never sacrifice sleep, nutrition, safety, or cleanliness to save money. Simply enjoy the local-style alternatives to expensive hotels and restaurants.

Connecting with people carbonates your experience. Extroverts have more fun. If your trip is low on magic moments, kick yourself and make things happen. If you don't enjoy a place, maybe you don't know enough about it. Seek the truth. Recognize tourist traps. Give a culture the benefit of your open mind. See things as different, but not better or worse. Any culture has plenty to share. When an opportunity presents itself, make it a habit to say "yes."

Of course, travel, like the world, is a series of hills and valleys. Be fanatically positive and militantly optimistic. If something's not to your liking, change your liking.

Travel can make you a happier American, as well as a citizen of the world. Our Earth is home to seven billion equally precious people. It's humbling to travel and find that other people don't have the "American Dream"—they have their own dreams. Europeans like us, but with all due respect, they wouldn't trade passports.

Thoughtful travel engages us with the world. It reminds us what is truly important. By broadening perspectives, travel teaches new ways to measure quality of life.

Globetrotting destroys ethnocentricity, helping us understand and appreciate other cultures. Rather than fear the diversity on this planet, celebrate it. Among your most prized souvenirs will be the strands of different cultures you choose to knit into your own character. The world is a cultural yarn shop, and Back Door travelers are weaving the ultimate tapestry. Join in!

ORIENTATION TO PARIS

Paris is magnificent, but it's also super-sized, crowded, and fast-paced. Take a deep breath, then use this orientation to the City of Light to help illuminate your trip. The day plans—for visits of one to seven days—will help you prioritize the many sights. You'll tap into Paris' information sources for current events. Most important, you'll learn to navigate Paris by Métro, bus, taxi, bicycle, or on foot. With the proper approach and a measure of patience, you'll fall head over heels for Europe's cultural capital.

PARIS: A VERBAL MAP

Central Paris (population 2.3 million) is circled by a ring road and split in half by the Seine River, which runs east-west. If you were on a boat floating downstream, the Right Bank (Rive Droite) would be on your right, and the Left Bank (Rive Gauche) on your left. The bull's-eye on your map is Notre-Dame, on an island in the middle of the Seine and ground zero in Paris.

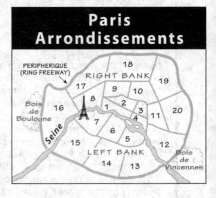

Twenty arrondissements (administrative districts) spiral out from the center, like an escargot shell. If your hotel's zip code is 75007, you know (from the last two digits) that it's in the 7th arrondissement. The city is peppered with Métro stops, and most Parisians locate addresses by the closest stop. So in Parisian jargon, the Eiffel Tower is on *la Rive Gauche* (the Left Bank) in the *7ème*

(7th arrondissement), zip code 75007, Mo: Trocadéro (the nearest Métro stop).

As you're tracking down addresses, these words and pronunciations will help: arrondissement (ah-roh<u>n</u>-dees-mah<u>n</u>), Métro (may-troh), *place* (plahs; square), *rue* (rew; road), *avenue* (ah-vuh-new), *boulevard* (bool-var), *pont* (pohn; bridge), and *carrefour* (kah-ruh-foor; intersection).

ORIENTATION

PARIS BY NEIGHBORHOOD

Paris is a big city, but its major sights cluster in convenient zones. Grouping your sightseeing, walks, dining, and shopping thoughtfully can save you lots of time and money.

Historic Core: This area centers on the Ile de la Cité ("Island of the City"), located in the middle of the Seine. On the Ile de la Cité, you'll find Paris' oldest sights, from Roman ruins to the medieval Notre-Dame and Sainte-Chapelle churches. Other sights in this area: Archaeological Crypt, Deportation Memorial, Conciergerie, flower market, Paris *Plages*, and the lovely island of Ile St. Louis, with appealing shops, cafés, and restaurants. Paris' most historic riverside vendors, *les bouquinistes*, line both sides of the Seine as it passes Ile de la Cité.

Major Museums Neighborhood: Located just west of the historic core, this is where you'll find the Louvre, Orsay, and Orangerie. Other sights are the Tuileries Garden and Palais Royal's courtyards.

Champs-Elysées: The greatest of the many grand, 19th-century boulevards on the Right Bank, the Champs-Elysées runs northwest from Place de la Concorde to the Arc de Triomphe. Sights in this area include the Petit and Grand Palais, Hôtel Hyatt Regency (for its great city view), and La Défense with La Grande Arche.

Eiffel Tower Neighborhood: Dominated by the Eiffel Tower, this area also boasts the colorful Rue Cler (with many recommended hotels and restaurants), Army Museum and Napoleon's Tomb, Rodin Museum, and the thriving outdoor

ORIENTATION

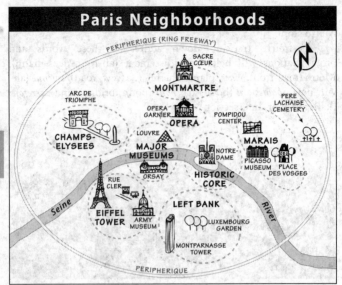

Paris Neighborhoods

PERIPHERIQUE (RING FREEWAY)

SACRE CŒUR

MONTMARTRE

ARC DE TRIOMPHE

OPERA GARNIER

OPERA

POMPIDOU CENTER

PERE LACHAISE CEMETERY

CHAMPS-ELYSEES

LOUVRE

MAJOR MUSEUMS

ORSAY

NOTRE-DAME

MARAIS

PICASSO MUSEUM

PLACE DES VOSGES

RUE CLER

HISTORIC CORE

LEFT BANK

Seine

EIFFEL TOWER

ARMY MUSEUM

LUXEMBOURG GARDEN

River

MONTPARNASSE TOWER

PERIPHERIQUE

market Marché Boulevard de Grenelle. Other sights are the Quai Branly Museum, National Maritime Museum, Architecture and Monuments Museum, and Sewer Tour. The Marmottan Museum and Museum of Wine are west of the Eiffel Tower on the Right Bank.

Opéra Neighborhood: Surrounding the Opéra Garnier, this classy area on the Right Bank is home to a series of grand boulevards and monuments. In the 19th century, it was modernized by Baron Haussmann into a neighborhood of wide roads lined with stately buildings (see sidebar on page 89). Though these days it's busy with traffic, there are still hints of Paris, circa 1870, when it was the capital of the world. Along with elegant sights such as the Opéra Garnier, Jacquemart-André Museum, and Fragonard Perfume Museum, the neighborhood also offers high-end shopping: at Galeries Lafayette department store, around Place de la Madeleine and Place Vendôme, and at the covered *passages* of Choiseul and Ste. Anne.

Left Bank: The Left Bank is home to...the Left Bank. Anchored by the large Luxembourg Garden (near numerous recommended hotels and eateries), the Left Bank is the traditional neighborhood of Paris' intellectual, artistic, and café life. Other sights: the Latin Quarter, Cluny Museum, St. Germain-des-Prés and St. Sulpice churches, Panthéon, Montparnasse Tower,

Catacombs, Delacroix Museum, and the Jardin des Plantes park. This is also one of Paris' best shopping areas (see the Sèvres-Babylone to St. Sulpice shopping stroll on page 475).

Marais: Stretching eastward to Bastille along Rue de Rivoli/ Rue St. Antoine, this neighborhood has lots of recommended restaurants and hotels, shops, the delightful Place des Vosges, and artistic sights such as the Pompidou Center and Picasso Museum. The area is known for its avant-garde boutiques and residents. Other Marais sights: Jewish Art and History Museum, Carnavalet Museum (closed for renovation through 2017 and beyond), Victor Hugo's House, Holocaust Memorial, Promenade Plantée park, Père Lachaise Cemetery, the Marché des Enfants Rouges covered market, and the outdoor markets at Bastille and Place d'Aligre.

Montmartre: This hill, topped by the bulbous white domes of Sacré-Cœur, hovers on the northern fringes of your Paris map. Home to many recommended hotels and restaurants, it still retains some of the untamed charm that once drew Impressionist painters and turn-of-the-century bohemians. Other sights are the Dalí and Montmartre museums, Moulin Rouge, Pigalle, and nearby Puces St. Ouen flea market.

PLANNING YOUR TIME

In the planning sections that follow, I've listed sights in descending order of importance. If you have only one day, just do Day 1; for two days, add Day 2; and so on. When deciding where to plug in Versailles, remember that the main palace is closed on Mondays and especially crowded on Sundays, Tuesdays, and Saturdays (in that order). For other itinerary considerations on a day-by-day basis, check the "Daily Reminder" on page 20.

Paris in One, Two, or Three Busy Days

To fit in Versailles on a three-day visit, plan it for the morning of the third day.

Day 1
Morning: Follow my Historic Paris Walk, featuring Ile de la Cité, Notre-Dame, the Latin Quarter, and Sainte-Chapelle.
Afternoon: Tour the Louvre.
Evening: Enjoy the Place du Trocadéro scene and a twilight ride up the Eiffel Tower.

ORIENTATION

Day 2

Morning: Follow my Champs-Elysées Walk from the Arc de Triomphe down the grand Avenue des Champs-Elysées to the Tuileries Garden.

Midday: Cross the pedestrian bridge from the Tuileries Garden, then tour the Orsay Museum.

Afternoon: Tour the Rodin Museum, or the Army Museum and Napoleon's Tomb.

Evening: Take one of the tours by bus, taxi/Uber, or retro-chic Deux Chevaux car (see page 496). (If you're staying more than two days, save this for your last-night finale.)

Day 3

Morning: Catch the RER suburban train by 8:00 to arrive early at Versailles (before it opens at 9:00), then tour the château and sample the gardens.

Afternoon: Versailles can take up a full sightseeing day, so be realistic. If you plan to do anything once back in Paris, consider a sight near one of the RER-C stations: the Army Museum and Napoleon's Tomb or Rodin Museum (near RER-C stop: Invalides), or the Orsay Museum or this book's Left Bank Walk (near RER-C stop: St. Michel).

Evening: Cruise the Seine River or have dinner on Ile St. Louis, then take a floodlit walk by Notre-Dame.

Paris in Five to Seven Days Without Going In-Seine

Day 1

Morning: Follow this book's Historic Paris Walk, featuring Ile de la Cité, Notre-Dame, the Latin Quarter, and Sainte-Chapelle. If you enjoy medieval art, visit the Cluny Museum. If you prefer parks, pause for a break in Luxembourg Garden.

Afternoon: Tour the Opéra Garnier, and end your day enjoying the glorious rooftop views at the Galeries Lafayette or Printemps department stores.

Evening: Cruise the Seine River.

Day 2

Morning: Tour the Louvre (arrive 30 minutes before opening).

Afternoon: Follow this book's Champs-Elysées Walk from the Arc de Triomphe downhill along the incomparable Avenue des Champs-Elysées to the Tuileries Garden, and possibly the Orangerie Museum. Reversing the morning and afternoon activities on this day could also work well.

Evening: Enjoy dinner on Ile St. Louis, then a floodlit walk by Notre-Dame.

Day 3

Morning: Tour the Orsay Museum.

Midday: Tour the Rodin Museum (café lunch in gardens).

Afternoon: Visit the Army Museum and Napoleon's Tomb, then take this book's Rue Cler Walk and relax at a café. If it's balmy, consider walking the Left Bank riverside promenade that runs between the Orsay and Pont de l'Alma (near the Eiffel Tower).

Evening: Take one of the nighttime tours by taxi/Uber, bus, or retro-chic Deux Chevaux car.

Day 4

Morning: Ride the RER suburban train to arrive early at Versailles and tour the palace's interior.

Midday: Have lunch in the gardens at Versailles.

Afternoon: Spend the afternoon touring the gardens, Trianon Palaces, and Domaine de Marie-Antoinette. (Late risers should reverse this plan and tour the palace's interior in the afternoon to minimize crowd frustrations.) Or return to Paris and do this book's Montmartre Walk.

Evening: Dine in Versailles town or back in Paris.

Day 5

Morning: Follow this book's Marais Walk and tour the Picasso Museum. Have lunch on Place des Vosges or Rue des Rosiers.

Afternoon: Choose from these Marais sights—Pompidou Center, Jewish Art and History Museum, or Père Lachaise Cemetery.

Evening: Enjoy the Place du Trocadéro scene and a twilight ride up the Eiffel Tower.

Day 6

Morning: Spend most of your day at Chartres or a half-day touring the château of Vaux-le-Vicomte.

Afternoon: Enjoy the balance of your day exploring the shopping districts of Paris (follow the Left Bank Walk or seek out what appeals to you from the many options in the Shopping in Paris chapter).

Evening: Join the parade along the Champs-Elysées (which offers a different scene at night than the daytime walk you enjoyed on Day 2). If you haven't hiked to the top of the Arc de Triomphe yet, consider doing it by twilight. Or ride the Paris Ferris Wheel, if it's spinning.

Day 7

Choose from:

Θ More shopping and cafés

Θ Luxembourg Garden

Θ Bus #69 tour followed by Père Lachaise Cemetery

Θ Montmartre and Sacré-Cœur

Daily Reminder

Sunday: Many sights are free on the first Sunday of the month, including the Orsay, Cluny, Pompidou, Picasso, Quai Branly, and Delacroix museums. Several sights are free on the first Sunday, but only during winter, including the Louvre, Rodin Museum, and Arc de Triomphe (Oct-March), and all the sights at Versailles (Nov-March). These free days at popular sights attract hordes of visitors. Versailles is more crowded than usual on Sunday in any season, and when the garden's fountains run (April-Oct).

Look for organ concerts at St. Sulpice and other churches. The American Church often hosts a free concert (generally Sept-June at 17:00—but not every week and not in Dec). Luxembourg Garden has puppet shows today.

Most of Paris' stores are closed on Sunday, but shoppers will find relief along the Champs-Elysées, at flea markets, and in the Marais neighborhood's lively Jewish Quarter, where many boutiques are open. Many recommended restaurants in the Rue Cler neighborhood are closed for dinner.

Monday: These sights are closed today: Orsay, Rodin, Marmottan, Picasso, Catacombs, Petit Palais, Victor Hugo's House, Quai Branly, Paris Archaeological Crypt, Jewish Art and History Museum, and Deportation Memorial. Outside of Paris, all sights in Auvers-sur-Oise and at Versailles are closed (but the gardens are open). The Louvre is far more crowded because of these closings. From October through June, the Army Museum is closed the first Monday of the month, though Napoleon's Tomb remains open.

Market streets such as Rue Cler, Rue des Martyrs, and Rue Mouffetard are dead today.

Tuesday: Many sights are closed today, including the Louvre, Orangerie, Cluny, Pompidou, National Maritime, Delacroix, and Architecture and Monuments museums, as well as the châteaux of Chantilly and Fontainebleau and many sights in Auvers-sur-Oise. The Orsay and Versailles are crazy busy today. The fountains at

Marmottan or Jacquemart-André museums
Day trip to Vaux-le-Vicomte and/or Fontainebleau
Day trip to Disneyland Paris
Evening: Night bus or boat tour (whichever you have yet to do)

Overview

TOURIST INFORMATION

Paris' tourist offices (abbreviated as "TI" in this book) can provide useful information but may have long lines (www.parisinfo.com). While TIs sell Museum Passes and individual tickets to sights, they charge a small fee and may have longer lines than the museums (see "Sightseeing Strategies" on page 48).

Versailles run today from mid-May until late June; music (no fountains) fills the gardens on Tuesdays from April to mid-May, and from July through October. Napoleon's Tomb is open until 21:00 (April-Sept).

Wednesday: All sights are open, and some have late hours, including the Louvre (until 21:45, last entry 21:00), the Rodin (until 20:45), Sainte-Chapelle (until 21:30 mid-May-mid-Sept), and the Jewish Art and History Museum (until 21:00 during special exhibits only). The weekly *Pariscope* magazine comes out today. Most schools are closed, so kids' sights are busy, and puppet shows play in Luxembourg Garden. Some cinemas offer discounts.

Thursday: All sights are open except the Sewer Tour. Some sights are open late, including the Orsay (until 21:45, last entry 21:00), Marmottan (until 21:00), the Architecture and Monuments Museum (21:00), the Quai Branly (21:00), and the Holocaust Memorial (22:00). Some department stores are open late.

Friday: All sights are open except the Sewer Tour. The Louvre is open until 21:45 (last entry 21:00), Notre-Dame's tower is open until 23:00 (July-Aug), and the Quai Branly closes at 21:00. The Picasso Museum is open until 21:00 on the third Friday of every month. Afternoon trains and roads leaving Paris are crowded. Restaurants are busy—it's smart to book ahead at popular places.

Saturday: All sights are open except the Holocaust Memorial. The fountains run at Versailles (April-Oct), and Vaux-le-Vicomte hosts candlelight visits tonight (early May-early Oct); otherwise, avoid weekend crowds at area châteaux and Impressionist sights. Notre-Dame's tower is open until 23:00 (July-Aug), and the Quai Branly is open until 21:00. Department stores are jammed today. Restaurants throughout Paris get packed; reserve in advance if you have a particular place in mind. Luxembourg Garden hosts puppet shows today.

Paris has several TI locations, including **Pyramides** (daily May-Oct 9:00-19:00, Nov-April 10:00-19:00, free Wi-Fi, 25 Rue des Pyramides—at Pyramides Métro stop between the Louvre and Opéra), **Paris Rendez-Vous** (a city-sponsored souvenir shop and TI combined, Mon-Sat 10:00-19:00, closed Sun, 29 Rue de Rivoli—located within the Hôtel de Ville city hall), **Gare du Nord** (daily 8:00-18:00), **Gare de l'Est** (Mon-Sat 8:00-19:00, closed Sun), and two in **Montmartre** (21 Place du Tertre, daily 10:00-18:00, covers only Montmartre sights and doesn't sell Museum Passes, tel. 01 42 62 21 21; and at the Anvers Métro stop, full-service office, daily 10:00-18:00). In summer, TI kiosks may pop up in the squares in front of Notre-Dame and Hôtel de Ville.

Both **airports** have handy TIs with long hours and short lines.

Event Listings: Several French-only but easy-to-decipher periodicals list the most up-to-date museum hours, art exhibits, concerts, festivals, plays, movies, and nightclubs (for tips on deciphering the listings, see page 488). The best is the weekly *Pariscope* magazine; *L'Officiel des Spectacles* is similar (available at any newsstand). The *Paris Voice,* with snappy English-language reviews of concerts, plays, and current events, is available online only at www.parisvoice.com.

ARRIVAL IN PARIS

For a comprehensive rundown of the city's train stations and airports, and for information on parking a car, see the Paris Connections chapter.

HELPFUL HINTS

Theft Alert: Paris is safe in terms of violent crime but is filled with thieves and scammers who target tourists. Don't be paranoid; just be smart. Wherever there are crowds (especially of tourists) there are thieves at work. They thrive near famous monuments and on Métro and train lines that serve airports and high-profile tourist sights. Pickpockets work busy lines (e.g., at ticket windows at train stations). Look out for groups of young girls who swarm around you (be very firm—even forceful—and walk away).

It's smart to wear a money belt, put your wallet in your front pocket, loop your day bag over your shoulders, and keep a tight hold on your purse or shopping bag. Watch out for your electronics; pickpockets snatch smartphones and tablets too.

Muggings are rare, but they do occur. If you're out late, avoid the dark riverfront embankments and any place where the lighting is dim and pedestrian activity is minimal.

Paris has taken action to combat crime by stationing police at monuments, on streets, and on the Métro, and installing security cameras at key sights.

Tourist Scams: Be aware of the latest tricks, such as the "found ring" scam (a con artist pretends to find a "pure gold" ring on the ground and offers to sell it to you) or the "friendship bracelet" scam (a vendor asks you to help with a demo, makes a bracelet on your arm that seems like it can't easily be removed, and then asks you to pay for it). Don't be intimidated. They are removed with the pull of a string.

Distractions by a stranger can all be tricks that function as a smokescreen for theft. As you try to wriggle away from the pushy stranger, an accomplice picks your pocket. Be wary of a "salesman" monopolizing your attention, an "activist" asking you to sign a petition (and then bullying you into a contribution), someone posing as a deaf person to show you a small note to read, or a sidewalk hawker inviting you to play shell games (his thuggish accomplices are likely lurking nearby). Be skeptical of anything too good to be true, such as overly friendly people inviting you into impossibly friendly (or sexy) bars late at night.

To all these scammers, simply say "no" firmly and step away purposefully. For reports from my readers on the latest scams, go to https://community.ricksteves.com/travel-forum/tourist-scams.

Pedestrian Safety: Parisian drivers are notorious for ignoring pedestrians. Look both ways and be careful of seemingly quiet bus/taxi lanes. Don't assume you have the right of way, even in a crosswalk. When crossing a street, keep your pace constant and don't stop suddenly. By law, drivers are allowed to miss pedestrians by up to just one meter—a little more than three feet (1.5 meters in the countryside). Drivers calculate your speed so they won't hit you, provided you don't alter your route or pace.

Watch out for bicyclists and electric cars. Cyclists ride in specially marked bike lanes on wide sidewalks and can also use lanes reserved for buses and taxis. Bikes commonly go against traffic, so always look both ways, even on one-way streets. Paris' popular and cheap short-term electric-car rental program (Autolib') has put many of these small, silent machines on the streets—pay attention.

Busy Parisian sidewalks are like freeways, so conduct yourself as if you were a foot-fueled car: Stick to your lane, look to the left before passing a slow-moving pedestrian, and if you need to stop, look for a safe place to pull over.

Medical Help: There are a variety of English-speaking resources for medical help in Paris, including doctors who will visit your hotel. For a list, see page 675.

Avoiding Lines at Sights: Lines at Paris' major sights can be long. Consider the worthwhile Paris Museum Pass, which covers most sights in the city and allows you to skip ticket lines. You can also buy tickets in advance for certain sights. For more on these options, see page 49.

Free Wi-Fi: You'll find free wireless hotspots at many cafés and in many public areas (including the TI office at Pyramides, parks, squares, and museums). In a café, order something, then ask the waiter for the Wi-Fi ("wee-fee") password (*"mot de passe"*; moh duh pahs).

Select Métro stations offer 20 minutes of free Wi-Fi, and most public parks offer two hours of free Wi-Fi (look for purple *Zone Wi-Fi* signs). The one-time registration process is

ORIENTATION

easy, with English instructions: The Wi-Fi network is usually called "Paris_WIFI" plus a number.

The Orange network also has many hotspots and offers a free two-hour pass. If you come across one, click "Select Your Pass" to register.

Useful Apps: Gogo Paris reviews trendy places to eat, drink, relax, and sleep in Paris (www.gogocityguides.com/paris). The **RATP** app can help you plan Métro trips (see page 27).

∩ For free audio versions of some of the self-guided tours in this book (the Historic Paris Walk, and tours of the Louvre Museum, Orsay Museum, and Versailles Palace), get the **Rick Steves Audio Europe** app (for details, see page 8).

Bookstores: Paris has several English-language bookstores. My favorites include **Shakespeare and Company** (some used travel books, daily 10:00-23:00, 37 Rue de la Bûcherie, across the river from Notre-Dame, Mo: St. Michel, tel. 01 43 25 40 93; described on page 120); **W. H. Smith** (Mon-Sat 9:00-19:00, Sun 12:30-19:00, 248 Rue de Rivoli, Mo: Concorde, tel. 01 44 77 88 99); and **San Francisco Book Company** (used books only, Mon-Sat 11:00-21:00, Sun 14:00-19:30, 17 Rue Monsieur le Prince, Mo: Odéon, tel. 01 43 29 15 70).

Baggage Storage: Lockers are available at several **City Locker** locations in central Paris (€10-16/day, daily 8:00-22:00, book ahead or take your chances and drop in, details and locations at www.city-locker.com).

Public WCs: Most public toilets are free. If it's a pay toilet, the price will be clearly indicated. If the toilet is free but there's an attendant, it's polite to leave a tip of €0.20-0.50. Booth-like toilets on the sidewalks provide both relief and a memory (don't leave small children inside unattended). The restrooms in museums are free and the best you'll find. Bold travelers can walk into any sidewalk café like they own the place and find the toilet downstairs or in the back. Or do as the locals do—order a shot of espresso *(un café)* while standing at the café bar (then use the WC with a clear conscience). Keep toilet paper or tissues with you, as some WCs are poorly stocked.

Tobacco Stands *(Tabacs):* These little kiosks—usually just a counter inside a café—are handy and very local. Most sell public-transit tickets, cards for parking meters, postage stamps (though not all sell international postage), and... oh yeah, cigarettes. (For more on this slice of Parisian life, see page 211. For details on parking cards, see page 530.) To find a kiosk, just look for a *Tabac* sign and the red cylinder-shaped symbol above certain cafés. A *tabac* can be a godsend for avoiding long ticket lines at the Métro, especially at the end of the month when ticket booths get crowded with locals buying next month's pass.

GETTING AROUND PARIS

Paris is easy to navigate. Your basic choices are Métro (in-city subway), RER (suburban rapid transit tied into the Métro system), public bus, and taxi. There are also nine tram (light rail) lines running at street level, using the same tickets as the bus and Métro, but few travelers will use these heavily suburban routes (except from Orly Airport—see page 516). Also consider the hop-on, hop-off bus and boat tours (described under "Tours in Paris," later).

You can buy tickets and passes at Métro stations and at many *tabacs*. Staffed ticket windows in stations are being phased out in favor of ticket machines, so expect some stations to have only machines and an information desk. Most machines accept only credit cards and coins, though there's usually one that will take small bills of €20 or less, and chip-and-PIN cards (no American magnetic-stripe or chip-and-signature cards). If a ticket machine is out of order or if you're out of change, buy tickets at a *tabac*.

Public-Transit Tickets: The Métro, RER, tramways, and buses all work on the same tickets. You can make as many transfers as you need on a single ticket, except when transferring between the bus or tramway systems and the Métro/RER system (an additional ticket is required). A **single ticket** costs €1.80. To save money, buy a *carnet* (kar-nay) of 10 tickets for €14.10 (cheaper for ages 4-10). *Carnets* can be shared among travelers. Kids under four ride free.

Passe Navigo: This chip-embedded card costs a one-time €5 fee (plus another €5 for the required photo; photo booths are in major Métro stations). The weekly unlimited pass (Navigo Semaine) costs €21.25 and covers all forms of transit from Monday to Sunday (expiring on Sunday, even if you buy it on, say, a Thursday). The pass is good for all zones in the Paris region, which means that you can travel anywhere within the city center, out to the châteaux of Versailles, Vaux-le-Vicomte, and Fontainebleau, and to Charles de Gaulle and Orly airports (except on Orlyval trains—see page 516). A monthly pass covering the same area is also available. To use the Navigo, touch the card to the purple pad, wait for the green validation light and the "ding," and you're on your way. You can buy your Passe Navigo at any Métro station in Paris (for more details, visit www.ratp.fr).

Navigo or *Carnet*? The Navigo covers a far greater area than *carnet* tickets, but cannot be shared. It is most worthwhile for visitors who use it for regional trips, or stay a full week (and start their trip early in the week) or month (and start their trip near the beginning of the month). Two 10-packs of *carnets*—enough for most travelers staying a week—cost €28.20, are shareable, and don't expire, but are only valid in the center of Paris.

Other Passes: A handy one-day bus/Métro pass (called **Mobilis**) is available for €7 (zones 1-2). The even more handy regional Mobilis ticket (zones 1-5, €16.60) works well for some day trips, as it includes regional train travel, some local transportation at day-trip destinations, and 24 hours of travel on the Paris bus/Métro system (see page 567 for specifics). Mobilis tickets are not valid for airport trips.

If you are under 26 and in Paris on a Saturday or Sunday, you can buy an unlimited daily transit pass called **Ticket Jeunes Weekend** for the unbeatable price of €3.85. The **Paris Visite** travel card, on the other hand, is only a good choice over *carnets* if you travel around the city extensively, though they do offer minor discounts at minor sights (1 day-€11.15, 2 days-€18.15, 3 days-€24.80, 5 days-€35.70).

By Métro

In Paris, you're never more than a 10-minute walk from a Métro station. Europe's best subway system allows you to hop from sight to sight quickly and cheaply (runs 5:30-1:00 in the morning, Fri-Sat until 2:00 in the morning, www.ratp.fr). Learn to use it. Begin by studying the color Métro map at the beginning of this book.

Using the Métro System: To get to your destination, determine the closest "Mo" stop and which line or lines will get you there. The lines are color-coded and numbered. You can tell their direction by the end-of-the-line stops. For example, the La Défense/Château de Vincennes line, also known as line 1 (yellow), runs between La Défense, on its west end, and Vincennes on its east end. Once in the Métro station, you'll  see the color-coded line numbers and/or blue-and-white signs directing you to the train going in your direction (e.g., *direction: La Défense*). Insert your ticket in the turnstile, reclaim your ticket, pass through, and keep it until you exit the system (some stations require you to pass your ticket through a turnstile to exit). Smaller stations are unstaffed but have ticket machines (coins are essential unless you have a chip-and-PIN card). Fare inspectors regularly check for cheaters, accept absolutely no excuses, and have portable credit card machines to fine you on the spot: Keep that ticket or pay a minimum fine of €45.

Be prepared to walk significant distances within Métro stations (especially when you transfer). Transfers are free and can be made wherever lines cross, provided you do so within 1.5 hours and don't exit the station. When you transfer, follow the appropriately colored line number and end-of-the-line stop to find your next train, or look for *correspondance* (connection) signs that lead to your next line.

When you reach your destination, blue-and-white *sortie* signs point you to the exit. Before leaving the station, check the helpful *plan du quartier* (map of the neighborhood) to get your bearings. At stops with several *sorties,* you can save time by choosing the best exit.

After you finish your trip and exit onto the street, toss or tear your used ticket so you don't confuse it with unused tickets.

Métro Resources: Métro maps are free at Métro stations and included on freebie Paris maps at your hotel. Several good online tools can also help you navigate the public-transit system. The website Metro.Paris provides an interactive map of Paris' sights and Métro lines, with a trip-planning feature and information about each sight and station's history (www.metro.paris). The free RATP mobile app can estimate Métro travel times, help you locate the best station exit, and tell you when the next bus will arrive, among other things (in English, download from Apple's App Store, Google Play, or the Amazon App Store).

Beware of Pickpockets: Thieves dig the Métro and RER. If your pocket is picked as you pass through a turnstile, you end up stuck on the wrong side while the thief gets away. Stand away from Métro doors to avoid being a target for a theft-and-run just before the doors close. Any jostling or commotion—especially when boarding or leaving trains—is likely the sign of a thief or a team of thieves in action. Make any fare inspector show proof of identity (ask locals for help if you're not certain). Keep your bag close, hang on to your smartphone, and never show anyone your wallet. For more tips, see page 22.

By RER

The RER (Réseau Express Régionale; ehr uh ehr) is the suburban arm of the Métro, serving outlying destinations such as Versailles, Disneyland Paris, and the airports. These routes are indicated by thick lines on your subway map and identified by the letters A, B, C, and so on.

Within the city center, the RER works like the Métro and can be speedier if it serves your destination directly, because it makes fewer stops. Métro tickets are good on the RER when traveling

Transit Basics

- The same tickets are good on the Métro, RER trains (within the city), and city buses.
- Save money by buying a *carnet* of 10 discounted tickets or a Passe Navigo.
- Beware of pickpockets, and don't buy tickets from people roaming the stations.
- Find your train by its end-of-the-line stop.
- Insert your ticket into the turnstile, retrieve it, and keep it until the end of your journey.
- Safeguard your belongings; avoid standing near the train doors with luggage.

- At a stop, the door may open automatically. If it doesn't, open the door by either pushing a square button (green or black) or lifting a metal latch.
- Transfers *(correspondances)* between the Métro and RER system are free (but not between Métro/RER and bus).
- Trash or tear used tickets after you complete your ride and leave the station (not before) to avoid confusing them with fresh ones.

Etiquette

- When your train arrives, board only after everyone leaving the car has made it out the door.
- Avoid using the hinged seats near the doors when the car is crowded; they take up valuable standing space.
- Always offer your seat to the elderly, those with disabilities,

in the city center. You can transfer between the Métro and RER systems with the same ticket. But to travel outside the city (to Versailles or the airport, for example), you'll need a separate, more expensive ticket. The Passe Navigo card covers all RER trips, including to the airport and Versailles. Unlike the Métro, not every train stops at every station along the way; check the sign or screen over the platform to see if your destination is listed as a stop (*"toutes les gares"* means it makes all stops along the way), or confirm with a local before you board.

and pregnant women.

- Talk softly in cars. Listen to how quietly Parisians communicate (if at all) and follow their lead.
- When standing, hold on to the bar with one hand, leaving room for others while stabilizing yourself so you don't tumble or step on neighboring toes.
- If you find yourself blocking the door at a stop, step out of the car to let others off, then get back on.
- Métro doors close automatically. Don't try to hold open the door for late-boarding passengers.
- On escalators and stairs, keep to the right and pass on the left.

Key Words for the Métro and RER

French	English
station de Métro (stah-see-ohn duh may-troh)	Métro stop/station
direction (dee-rehk-see-ohn)	direction
ligne (leen-yuh)	line
correspondance (koh-rehs-pohn-dahns)	connection/transfer
sortie (sor-tee)	exit
carnet (kar-nay)	discounted set of 10 tickets
Pardon, madame/monsieur. (par-dohn, mah-dahm/muhs-yuh)	Excuse me, ma'am/sir.
Je descends. (zhuh day-sahn)	I'm getting off.
Rendez-moi mon porte-monnaie! (rahn-day-mwah mohn porte-moh-nay)	Give me back my wallet!

For RER trains, you may need to insert your ticket in a turnstile to exit the system.

By City Bus

Paris' excellent bus system is worth figuring out (www.ratp.fr). Buses require less walking and fewer stairways than the Métro, and

you can see Paris unfold as you travel. Sure they don't seem as romantic as the famous Métro and are subject to traffic jams—but savvy travelers know that buses can have you swinging through the city like Tarzan in an urban jungle.

Bus Stops: Stops are everywhere, and most come with all the information you need. This includes a good city bus map, route maps for each bus that stops there, a frequency chart and schedule, live screens showing the time the next two buses will arrive, a *plan du quartier* map of the immediate neighborhood, and a *soirées* map explaining night service, if available (there are even phone chargers at some locations). Bus-system maps are also available in any Métro station (and in the *Paris Pratique* map book sold at newsstands). For longer stays, consider buying the *Paris Urbain* book of transit info, including bus routes.

Using the Bus System: Buses use the same tickets and passes as the Métro and RER. One Zone 1 ticket buys you a bus ride

anywhere in central Paris within the freeway ring road *(le périphérique)*. Use your Métro ticket or buy one on board for €0.20 more, these tickets are *sans correspondance,* which means you can't use them to transfer to another bus. (The ticket system has a few quirks—see "More Bus Tips," later.)

When a bus approaches, it's wise to wave to the driver to indicate that you want to be picked up. Board your bus through the front door. (Families with strollers can use any doors—the ones in the center of the bus are wider. To open the middle or back doors on long buses, push the green button located by those doors.) Validate your ticket in the machine (stripe up) and reclaim it. With a Passe Navigo, scan it on the purple touchpad. Keep track of which stop is coming up next by following the on-board diagram or listening to recorded announcements. When you're ready to get off, push the red button to signal you want a stop, then exit through the central or rear door. Even if you're not certain you've figured out the system, do some joyriding.

More Bus Tips: Avoid rush hour (Mon-Fri 8:00-9:30 & 17:30-19:30), when buses are jammed and traffic doesn't move. While the Métro shuts down at about 1:00 in the morning (even later Fri-Sat), some buses continue much later (called *Noctilien* lines, www.vianavigo.com). Not all city buses are air-conditioned, so they can become rolling greenhouses on summer days. *Carnet* ticket holders—but not those buying individual tickets on the bus—can transfer from one bus to another on the same ticket (within 1.5 hours, revalidate your ticket on the next bus). However you can't do a round-trip or hop on and off on the same line using the same ticket. You can use the same ticket to transfer between

Hop on the Bus, Gus

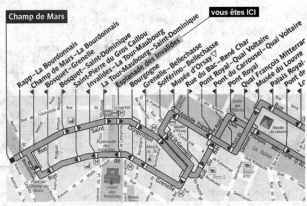

Just like the Métro, every bus stop has a name, and every bus is headed to one end-of-the-line stop or the other. This graphic shows the route map posted at the Esplanade des Invalides #69 bus stop. First, find the stop on the chart—it says *"vous êtes ICI"* ("you are HERE") at Esplanade des Invalides. Next, find your destination stop—let's say Bosquet-Grenelle, located a few stops to the west. Now, find out exactly where to catch the bus going in that direction. On the route map, notice the triangle-shaped arrows pointing in the direction the bus is headed. You'll see that Esplanade des Invalides has two different bus stops—one for buses headed east, one for those going west. If you want to go west to Bosquet-Grenelle, head for that street corner to catch the bus. (With so many one-way streets in Paris, it's easy to get on the bus in the wrong direction.) When the bus pulls up, double-check that the sign on the front of the bus has the end-of-the-line stop going in your direction—to "Champ de Mars," in this case.

buses and tramways, but you can't transfer between the bus and Métro/RER systems (it'll take two tickets).

For a list of Paris' most scenic and convenient routes, see page 32.

By Uber

Uber works in Paris like it does at home, and in general works better than taxis in Paris (www.uber.com). Drivers are nicer and more flexible than taxi drivers, it's a bit cheaper than a taxi (be warned that peak hour rates are higher), and you can generally get a car wherever you are within five minutes. Uber drivers can pick you up anywhere so you don't have to track down a taxi stand, and you can text them if you don't see the car. There's no language problem giving directions, as you can type your destina-

ORIENTATION

Scenic Buses for Tourists

Of Paris' many bus routes, these are some of the most scenic. They provide a great, cheap, and convenient introduction to the city.

Bus #69 runs east-west between the Eiffel Tower and Père Lachaise Cemetery by way of Rue Cler, Quai d'Orsay, the Louvre, and the Marais. ⌘ See the Bus #69 Sightseeing Tour chapter.

Bus #24 runs east-west along the Seine riverbank from Gare St.

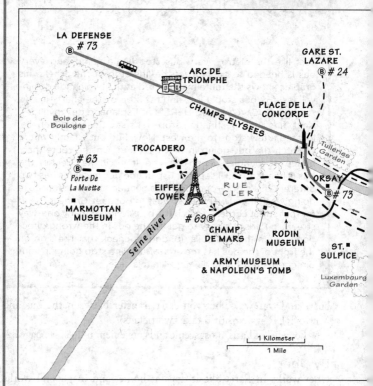

Lazare to Madeleine, Place de la Concorde, Orsay Museum, the Louvre, St. Michel, Notre-Dame, and Jardin des Plantes, all the way to Bercy Village (cafés and shops).

Bus #63 is another good east-west route, connecting the Marmottan Museum, Trocadéro (Eiffel Tower), Pont de l'Alma, Orsay Museum, St. Sulpice Church, Luxembourg Garden, Latin Quarter/Panthéon, and Gare de Lyon.

Bus #73 is one of Paris' most scenic lines, starting at the Orsay Museum and running westbound around Place de la Concorde, then up the Champs-Elysées, around the Arc de Triomphe, and down Avenue Charles de Gaulle to La Défense.

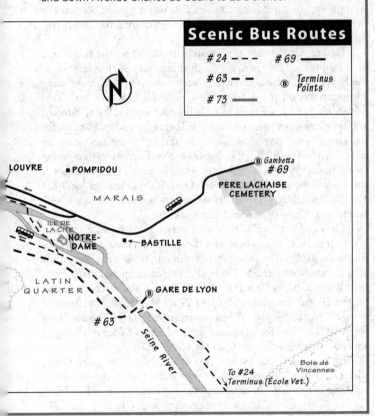

Scenic Bus Routes

#24 – – –   #69 ———
#63 – –   Ⓑ Terminus Points
#73 ———

tion into the app. Your US app and US Uber accounts will work in Paris as long as you have access to cellular data. The only downside is that Uber drivers can't use the taxi/bus lanes during rush hour, so your trip may take longer at busy times than it would in a cab.

By Taxi

Parisian taxis are reasonable, especially for couples and families. The meters are tamper-proof. Fares and supplements (described in English on the rear windows) are straightforward and tightly regulated.

A taxi can fit four people. Cabbies are legally required to accept four passengers, though they don't always like it. If you have five in your group, you can book a larger taxi in advance (your hotelier can call), or try your luck at a taxi stand. A surcharge may be applied for a fifth rider.

Rates: All Parisian taxis start with €2.60 on the meter and have a minimum charge of €7. A 20-minute ride (such as Bastille to the Eiffel Tower) costs about €25 (versus about €1.40/person using a *carnet* ticket on the Métro or bus, or about €15 via Uber). Taxi drivers charge higher rates at rush hour, at night, all day Sunday, and for extra passengers (see above). There's a standard flat rate for the airport—see page 514. To tip, round up to the next euro (at least €0.50). The A, B, or C lights on a taxi's rooftop sign correspond to hourly rates, which vary with the time of day and day of the week (for example, the A rate of €32.50/hour applies Mon-Sat 10:00-17:00). Tired travelers need not bother with the subtle differences in fares—if you need a cab, take it.

How to Catch *un Taxi:* You can try waving down a taxi, but it's often easier to ask someone for the nearest taxi stand (*"Où est une station de taxi?"*; oo ay ewn stah-see-ohn duh tahk-see). Taxi stands are indicated by a circled "T" on good city maps and on many maps in this book. To order a taxi in English, call the reservation line for the G7 cab company (tel. 01 41 27 66 99), or ask your hotelier or waiter to call for you. When you summon a taxi by phone, a set fee of €4 is applied for an immediate booking or €7 for reserving in advance (this fee will appear on the meter when they pick you up). Smartphone users can book a taxi using the cab company's app, which also provides approximate wait times (surcharge similar to booking by phone). To download an app, search for either "Taxi G7" or "Taxis Bleus" (the two major companies, both available in English).

Taxis are tough to find during rush hour, when it's raining, on weekend nights, or on any night after the Métro closes. If you need to catch a train or flight early in the morning, book a taxi the day before (especially for weekday departures). Some taxi companies require a €5 reservation fee by credit card for weekday morning rush-hour departures (7:00-10:00) and only have a limited number of reservation spots.

By Bike

Paris is surprisingly easy by bicycle. The city is flat, and riders have access to more than 370 miles of bike lanes and many of the priority lanes for buses and taxis (be careful on these). You can rent from a bike-rental shop or use the city-operated Vélib' bikes. Though I wouldn't use bikes to get around routinely (traffic is a bit too intense), they're perfect for a joyride away from busy streets. Bike-rental shops have good route suggestions. I biked along the river from Notre-Dame to the Eiffel Tower in 15 wonderfully scenic minutes. The Left Bank riverside promenade between the Orsay Museum and Pont de l'Alma is magnificent for biking. For a self-guided ride combining the Eiffel Tower and the riverside promenade, see page 68. For information on bike tours—a safe way to sightsee with a group—see page 44.

Urban bikers will find Paris a breeze. First-timers will get the hang of it quickly enough by following some simple rules. Always

stay to the right in your lane, bike single-file, stay off sidewalks, watch out for opening doors on parked cars, signal with your arm before making turns, and use bike paths when available. Obey the traffic laws as if you were driving a car. Parisians use the same road rules as Americans, with two exceptions: When passing vehicles or other bikes, always pass on the left (it's illegal to pass on the right); and where there is no stoplight, always yield to traffic merging from the right, even if you're on a major road and the merging driver is on a side street. You'll find a bell on your bike; use it like a horn to warn pedestrians who don't see you.

Sundays are peaceful for pedaling, when the city's "Paris Respire" program opens up some streets to cyclists and rollerbladers (cars are banned) from 9:00 to 17:00. Participating neighborhoods include the Marais, Montmartre, the Rue Mouffetard area east of Luxembourg Garden, and the Rue Daguerre area (near the Denfert-Rochereau Métro station). Also open are sections of the small roads directly bordering the Seine—on the Left Bank from the Eiffel Tower to the Orsay and also outside of the Paris *Plages* (see page 57), on the Right Bank between the Louvre and Gare de Lyon. Neighborhood bike-path maps are available at www.paris. fr/parisrespire. The TIs have a helpful "Paris à Vélo" map, which shows all the dedicated bike paths. Many other versions are available for sale at newsstand kiosks, some bookstores, and department stores.

Rental Bikes: The following companies rent bikes to individuals and offer organized bike tours (see "Bike Tours," later) and general tips about cycling in Paris. **Bike About Tours** is your best bet for bike rental, with good information and kid-friendly solutions such as baby seats, tandem attachments, and kid-sized bikes. Their office/coffee shop, called Le Peloton Café, offers bikes, tours, and artisan coffee (bike rental-€15/day during office hours, €20/24 hours, includes lock and helmet; daily 9:00-17:00, closed Dec-mid-Feb; shop/café at 17 Rue du Pont Louis Philippe, Mo: Hôtel de Ville, tel. 06 18 80 84 92, www.bikeabouttours.com). **Fat Tire Bike Tours** has a limited supply of bikes for rent, so call ahead to check availability (€4/hour, €25/24 hours, includes lock and helmet, photo ID and credit-card imprint required for deposit, €2/day rental discount with this book, maximum 2 discounts per book; office open daily 9:00-18:30, May-Aug bike rental only after 11:00 as priority is given to those taking a tour, 24 Rue Edgar Faure—see map on page 63, Mo: Dupleix, tel. 01 82 88 80 96, www.fattiretours.com/paris).

Vélib' Bikes: The city's Vélib' program (from *vélo* + *libre* = "bike freedom") gives residents and foreigners alike access to more than 20,000 bikes at nearly 1,500 stations scattered around the city at great rates. Use these bikes only for short-term rental (a few hours or less), as pricing is structured to discourage longer use. If you want a bike for longer, rent from one of the companies I list above. Vélib' bikes are also very heavy—avoid hills and stairs or rent elsewhere. See the sidebar on page 37 for step-by-step rental instructions.

Tours in Paris

♫ To sightsee on your own, download my **free audio tours** that illuminate some of Paris' top sights and neighborhoods, including the Historic Paris Walk, Louvre Museum, Orsay Museum, and Versailles Palace (see sidebar on page 8 for details).

BY BUS OR PETIT TRAIN
Bus Tours
City Vision offers bus tours of Paris, day and night. I'd consider them only for their nighttime tour (see page 497) or for tricky-to-reach day trips (such as Vaux-le-Vicomte). During the day, you'll get a better value and more versatility by taking a hop-on, hop-off tour by bus (described next) or Batobus boat (see "By Boat," later), which provide transportation between sights.

Guide to Vélib' Bike Rental

It's easy to borrow a Vélib' bike and ride like the locals. With a debit card, a chip-and-PIN card, or an American Express credit card, you should be able to follow these instructions and rent a bike at any rack in Paris. Should you have trouble you can also register online at http://en.velib.paris.fr. The subscription process is in English and easy to follow.

First locate a station near you. They are everywhere (or use the Vélib' app, which shows how many bikes and parking slots are available at the nearest stations). Once you find a rack, locate the screen meant for registration. Touch any key to activate, and select English language. Touch "1" to buy a 24-hour ticket (€1.70) or a 7-day ticket (€8), or use a Navigo Métro pass. You can check out a bike as many times as you want while your ticket is valid. There's no extra charge for taking a bike for less than 30 minutes. After the first 30 minutes of each session, added charges start racking up: €1 for the first half-hour, €2 for a second half-hour, and €4 for each half-hour after that. So a two-hour rental would cost €7 (in addition to the initial €1.70 ticket cost).

Next, insert your card and authorize a €150 hold on your account (to be released once the bike is returned). You'll be asked to choose a four-digit PIN; then you'll receive an 8- to 10-digit number.

Switch to the screen meant for bike rental (sometimes on the other side), and click "Use pre-purchased ticket" (or similar wording). Insert the 8- to 10-digit number on the machine, then follow with your four-digit PIN. Select the bike you want, find the bike station number, and enter this number. Do not select a bike with a seat turned backwards, which means the bike needs maintenance. Unlock your bike by pushing on the gray button next to the bike.

To return the bike, wheel it to any available station and plug it in appropriately. Wait 10 seconds and you should see the red light on the station turn green and hear two beeps. This means you have returned the bike successfully.

ORIENTATION

Hop-On, Hop-Off Bus Tours

Double-decker buses connect Paris' main sights, giving you an easy once-over of the city with a basic recorded commentary, punctuated with vintage French folk songs. You can hop off at any stop, tour a sight, then hop on a later bus. It's dang scenic, but only if you get a top-deck seat and the weather's decent. Because of traffic and stops, these buses can be dreadfully slow. (Busy sightseers will do better using the Métro to connect sights.) On the plus side, because the buses move so slowly, you have time to read my sight descriptions, making this a decent orientation tour.

Of the several different hop-on, hop-off bus companies,

Rollerblading with Parisians

Inline skaters take to the streets most Sunday afternoons and Friday evenings. It's serious skaters only on Fridays (they meet at 21:30 and are ready to roll at 22:00), but anyone can join in on Sundays (at 14:30). Police close off different routes each week to keep locals engaged, but the starting points are always the same. On Sunday, skaters leave from the south side of Place de la Bastille (for the route, see www.rollers-coquillages. org, click on *"Randonnées du Dimanches,"* then your date); on Fridays it's from Place Raoul Dautry (Mo: Montparnasse; see route at www.pari-roller.com). You can rent skates near Sunday's starting point at Nomades (€6/half-day, €9/day, Tue-Fri 11:00-13:30 & 14:30-19:30, Sat 10:00-19:00, Sun 12:00-18:00, closed Mon, 37 Boulevard Bourdon, near Place de la Bastille, Mo: Bastille, tel. 01 44 54 07 44).

L'OpenTour is best. They offer frequent service on four routes covering central Paris. You can even transfer between routes with one ticket. Look up the various routes and stops either on their website or by picking up a brochure (available at any TI or on one of their bright yellow-and-green buses). Their Paris Grand Tour (green route) offers the best introduction and most frequent buses (every 10 minutes). Other routes run a bit less frequently (every 15-30 minutes). You can catch the bus at just about any major sight (look for the Open Bus icon on public transit bus shelters and signs). Buy tickets from the driver or online and download directly to your smartphone (1 day-€33, 2 days-€37, 3 days-€41, kids 4-11 pay €17 for 1, 2, or 3 days, days must be consecutive, allow 2 hours per route, tel. 01 42 66 56 56, www.paris.opentour. com). A combo-ticket covers the Batobus boats, described later (2 days-€46, 3 days-€50, kids 4-11-€21). L'OpenTour also runs night illumination tours (see page 497).

Big Bus Paris runs a fleet of buses around Paris on a route with just 10 stops and recorded narration (1 day-€33, 2 days-€37, kids 4-12-€16, 10 percent cheaper if you book online, tel. 01 53 95 39 53, www.bigbustours.com).

Paris' cheapest "bus tour" is simply to hop on **city bus #69** and follow my commentary. ☐ See the Bus #69 Sightseeing Tour chapter.

Petit Train Tour

For a relaxing cultural overview of Paris that requires no walking, **"Another Paris" Mini-train Tours** offers five neighborhood itineraries, with simple yet informative audio commentary, on their blue *petit train*. With see-through roofs (covered in the peak heat of summer) and huge view windows, passengers enjoy a leisurely ride through streets that large buses can't access. Tours cover neighborhoods such as the Marais, the Latin Quarter, St. Germain-des-Prés, and Montparnasse. See their website for itinerary and departure details (daily Mon-Fri, 1.5 hours, reservations required; tel. 06 31 99 29 38, www.another-paris.com, contact@another-paris.com).

BY BOAT
Seine Cruises

Several companies run one-hour boat cruises on the Seine. A typical cruise loops back and forth between the Eiffel Tower and the

Pont d'Austerlitz, and drops you off where you started. For the best experience, cruise at twilight or after dark. (To dine while you cruise, see "Dinner Cruises" on page 447.) Two of the companies—Bateaux-Mouches and Bateaux Parisiens—are convenient to Rue Cler hotels, and both run daily year-round (April-Oct 10:00-22:30, 2-3/hour; Nov-March shorter hours, runs hourly). Some offer discounts for early online bookings.

Bateaux-Mouches, the oldest boat company in Paris, departs from Pont de l'Alma's right bank and has the biggest open-top, double-decker boats (higher up means better views). But this company caters to tour groups, making their boats jammed and noisy (€13.50, kids 4-12-€5.50, tel. 01 42 25 96 10, www.bateaux-mouches.fr).

Bateaux Parisiens has smaller covered boats with audioguides, fewer crowds, and only one deck. I'd pass on this cruise, as you're stuck inside the boat. It leaves from right in front of the Eiffel Tower (€15, kids 3-12-€7, tel. 01 76 64 14 45, www.bateauxparisiens.com).

Vedettes du Pont Neuf offers essentially the same one-hour tour as the other companies, but starts and ends at Pont Neuf, closer to recommended hotels in the Marais and Luxembourg Garden neighborhoods. The boats feature a live guide whose delivery (in English and French) is as stiff as a recorded narration—and as hard to understand, given the quality of their sound system (€14, €12 if you book directly with this book in 2017, discounts for online bookings, kids 4-12-€7, tip requested, nearly 2/hour, daily 10:30-22:30, tel. 01 46 33 98 38, www.vedettesdupontneuf.com).

ORIENTATION

Connecting with the Culture

Paris hosts more visitors than any other city in the world, and with such a robust tourism industry, many travelers feel cut off from "real life" in the City of Light. Fortunately, Paris offers *beaucoup* ways for you to connect with locals—and thereby make your trip more personal...and more memorable.

Staying with a family is a simple way to experience everyday Parisian life firsthand. Several agencies set up **bed-and-breakfast** stays in private homes (listed on page 419). Other opportunities abound:

Meeting the Locals

I'm amazed at the number of groups that help travelers meet locals. These get good reviews:

Meeting the French puts travelers in touch with Parisians who offer bed-and-breakfast listings, conversations groups, specialty tours, and more (fees vary by activity, tel. 01 42 51 19 80, www. meetingthefrench.com).

Paris Greeter is an all-volunteer organization that connects travelers with English-speaking Parisians who want to share their knowledge of the city. These volunteer "guides" act as informal companions who can show you "their Paris"—it's like seeing Paris through the eyes of a friend. The tours are free (though donations are welcome); you must sign up five weeks before your visit (www. greeters.paris).

The American Church and Franco-American Center, an interdenominational church in the Rue Cler neighborhood, offers many services for travelers wanting to connect with Parisian culture. The Thursday-evening English/French language exchange (18:00-19:30) is a handy way to meet locals who want to improve their English. It's free and relaxed—just show up. You'll chat with Parisians, who will respond in their best English. English-language worship services are held every Sunday (at 9:00 and 11:00, contemporary service at 13:30). The coffee hour after each service and the free Sunday concerts (generally Sept-June at 17:00, but not every week and not in Dec) are a good way to meet the very international congregation (church reception open Mon-Sat 9:00-12:30 & 13:30-22:00, Sun 8:30-19:00, 65 Quai d'Orsay, Mo: Invalides, tel. 01 40 62 05 00, www.acparis.org).

Cooking Schools and Wine Tastings: It's easy to hook up with small cooking schools and wine-tasting classes that provide an unthreatening and personal experience (see page 434).

Language Classes: You're at *Kilomètre Zéro* of the French language—where better to take a class? You'll have no problem finding French-language classes for any level, and class size is usually small. **Alliance Francaise** has the best reputation and good variety of courses (101 Boulevard Raspail, tel. 01 42 84 90 00, www.alliancefr.org). **France Langue** provides intensive classes on a weekly basis, some focusing on topics like wine, sports, business, or culture (tel. 01 45 00 40 15 or 01 42 66 18 08, www.france-langue.fr). **Le Français Face à Face** runs one-on-one intensive French courses with total immersion (based in Angers, tel. 06 66 60 00 63, www.lefrancaisfaceaface.com).

Conversation Swap: Parler Parlor is a free-form conversation group organized for native French and English speakers who want to practice in a relaxed environment. In a small group, you'll discuss interesting topics—45 minutes in French, then 45 minutes in English. Your first visit is free; after that it's €12 a session (several meetings per week, none in summer, tel. 01 48 42 26 10, www.parlerparlor.com, info@parlerparlor.com). Their monthly Après-Midi meet-ups provide another chance to exchange conversation.

Meeting the Americans

Long-term American residents can give you surprisingly keen insight into life in Paris.

The American Church and Franco-American Center is the community center for Americans living in Paris (see previous page).

The American Library, in the Rue Cler neighborhood, offers free programs and events for adults and children (10 Rue du Général Camou, Mo: Ecole Militaire, tel. 01 53 59 12 60, www.americanlibraryinparis.org).

WICE (Women in Continuing Education) is a nonprofit association that provides an impressive array of cultural and educational programs in English for those eager to master the art of living in France. Check their schedule at www.wice-paris.org, or call 01 45 66 75 50.

Meetup connects people in cities around the world, whether they are in town for a day or longer. Sponsored events include picnics, museum tours, cocktail evenings, and more. This is a particularly good tool for the 20-something traveler (www.meetup.com, search "Paris" to find groups according to your interests).

ORIENTATION

Hop-On, Hop-Off Boat Tour

Batobus allows you to get on and off as often as you like at any of eight popular stops along the Seine. The boats, which make a continuous circuit, stop in this order: Eiffel Tower, Orsay Museum, St. Germain-des-Prés, Notre-Dame, Jardin des Plantes, Hôtel de Ville, the Louvre, and Pont Alexandre III, near the Champs-Elysées (1 day-€16, 2 days-€18, April-Aug boats run every 20 minutes 10:00-21:30, Sept-March every 25 minutes 10:00-19:00, 45 minutes one-way, 1.5-hour round-trip, www.batobus.com). If you use this for getting around—sort of a scenic, floating alternative to the Métro—it can be worthwhile, but if you just want a guided boat tour, the Seine cruises described earlier are a better choice. Combo-tickets covering the L'OpenTour hop-on, hop-off buses (described earlier) are available, but skip the one-day ticket—you'll feel rushed trying to take full advantage of the bus and boat routes in a single day.

Low-Key Cruise on a Tranquil Canal

Canauxrama runs a lazy three-hour cruise connecting the Orsay Museum and the Bassin de la Villette (near Mo: Stalingrad). You'll pass Notre-Dame and Ile de la Cité along the Seine, then float on the Canal St. Martin through a long tunnel (built by order of Napoleon in the early 19th century, when canal boats were vital for industrial transport). You'll glide—not much faster than you can walk—through sleepy Parisian neighborhoods and slowly pass through four double locks as a guide narrates in French and English (adults-€20, kids 12 and under-€13, check online for discounts for advance booking, departs at 9:45 from the riverbank below the Orsay Museum and in the opposite direction at 14:45 from Bassin de la Villette, tel. 01 42 39 15 00, www.canauxrama.com). It's OK to bring a picnic on board.

ON FOOT
Walking Tours

For food-oriented walking tours, see page 434.

Paris Walks offers a variety of thoughtful and entertaining two-hour walks, led by British and American guides (€15-20, generally 2/day—morning and afternoon, private tours available, family-friendly and Louvre tours are a specialty, best to check current offerings on their website, tel. 01 48 09 21 40, www.paris-walks.com, paris@paris-walks.com). Tours focus on the Marais, Montmartre, St. Germain-des-Prés and the medieval Latin Quarter, Ile de la Cité/Notre-Dame, the "Two Islands" (Ile de la Cité and Ile St. Louis), the Revolution, and Hemingway's Paris. They also run less-frequent tours to the Puces St. Ouen flea market, in addition to tours on WWI and WWII topics. Reservations aren't necessary for most tours, but specialty tours—such as the Louvre, fashion, or chocolate tours—require advance reservations and prepayment with credit card (deposits are nonrefundable).

Context Travel offers "intellectual by design" walking tours geared for serious learners. The tours are led by well-versed docents (historians, architects, and academics) and cover both museums and specific neighborhoods. They range from traditional topics such as French art history in the Louvre and the Gothic architecture of Notre-Dame to more thematic explorations like immigration and the changing face of Paris, jazz in the Latin Quarter, and the history of the baguette. It's best to book in advance—groups are limited to six participants and can fill up fast (€70-105/person, admission to sights extra, generally 3 hours, tel. 09 75 18 04 15, US tel. 800-691-6036, www.contexttravel.com). They also offer private tours and excursions outside Paris.

Fat Tire Tours offers lowbrow, lighter-on-information but high-on-fun walking tours (run by Fat Tire Bike Tours). Their three-hour Classic Paris Walking Tour covers most major sights and has an option that includes a Louvre ticket (usually Mon, Wed, and Fri at 10:00 or 14:00). They also offer neighborhood walks of Montmartre, the Marais, and the Latin Quarter, as well as a themed walk on the French Revolution. Fat Tire also offers a range of "Skip the Line" tours of major sights, including the Louvre, Notre-Dame Tower, Catacombs, Eiffel Tower, Sainte-Chapelle, and Versailles. Paying more to visit a sight this way is most worthwhile at Sainte-Chapelle, the Eiffel Tower (if you were not able to reserve ahead), and Notre-Dame Tower. Reservations are required and can be made online, by phone, or in person at their office near the Eiffel Tower (€20-40/person for walking tours, €40-90/person for Skip the Line tours, €2 discount per person with this book—two-discount maximum per book; office open daily 9:00-19:00, shorter hours off-season, 36 Avenue de la Bourdonnais, Mo: Ecole Militaire, tel. 01 82 88 80 96, www.fattiretours.com/paris).

Local Guides

For many, Paris merits hiring a Parisian as a personal guide. **Thierry Gauduchon** is a terrific guide and a gifted teacher (€230/half-day, €450/day, tel. 06 19 07 30 77, tgauduchon@gmail.com). **Sylvie Moreau** also leads good tours in Paris (€200 for 3 hours, €320 for 7 hours, tel. 01 74 30 27 46, mobile 06 87 02 80 67, sylvie.ja.moreau@gmail.com). **Arnaud Servignat** is a top guide who has taught me much about Paris (private tours starting at €200, also does minivan tours of the countryside around Paris for more, mobile 06 68 80 29 05, www.french-guide.com, arnotour@me.com). **Elisabeth Van Hest** is another likable and very capable guide (€200/half-day, tel. 01 43 41 47 31, mobile 06 77 80 19 89, elisa.guide@gmail.com).

Sylviane Ceneray is gentle and knowledgeable (€200/half-day, tel. 06 84 48 02 44, www.paris-asyoulikeit.com).

ON WHEELS
Bike Tours

A bike tour is a fun way to see Paris. Two companies—Bike About Tours and Fat Tire Bike Tours—offer tours and bike maps of Paris, and give good advice on cycling routes in the city. Their tour routes cover different areas of the city, so avid cyclists could do both without much repetition.

Run by Christian (American) and Paul (New Zealander), **Bike About Tours** offers easygoing tours with a focus on the eastern half of the city. Their four-hour tours run daily year-round at 10:00 (also at 15:00 May-Sept). You'll meet at the statue of Charlemagne in front of Notre-Dame, then walk nearby to get your bikes. The tour includes a good back-street visit of the Marais, Rive Gauche outdoor sculpture park, Ile de la Cité, heart of the Latin Quarter (with a lunch break), Louvre, Les Halles, and Pompidou Center. Group tours have a 12-person maximum—reserve online to guarantee a spot, or show up and take your chances (€30, 10 percent discount on this tour with this book, includes helmets upon request, private group tours available). Their private family tours of Paris include fun activities like scavenger hunts (€200 for 2 people, €25/person after that, complimentary boat-tour tickets—a €14 value—included, see listing on page 36). They also offer a day-trip bike tour of Versailles.

Over at **Fat Tire Bike Tours,** a gang of Anglophone expats offers an extensive program of bike, Segway (see next), and walking tours (see earlier). Their young guides run four-hour bike tours of Paris day and night (adults-€34, kids-€32 but must weigh at least 100 pounds, €4 discount per person with this book—two-discount maximum per book, reservations recommended but not required, especially in off-season). Kid-size bikes are available, as are tandem attachments that hook on to a parent's bike. On the day tour, you'll pedal with a pack of 10 to 20 riders, mostly in parks and along bike lanes, with a lunch stop in the Tuileries Garden (tours leave daily rain or shine at 10:30, April-Oct also at 14:30). Livelier night tours follow a route past floodlit monuments and include a boat cruise on the Seine (€44, April-Oct daily at 18:30, less frequent in winter). Both tours meet at the exit of the Dupleix Métro station near the Eiffel Tower; from there you'll walk to the nearby Fat Tire office to pick up bikes (helmets available on request at no extra charge; see listing on page 36). They also run bike tours to Versailles and Giverny (reservations required, see website for details).

Segway Tour

Fat Tire offers pricey three-hour **City Segway Tours.** Learn to ride these stand-up motorized scooters while exploring Paris (you'll get

the hang of it after about a half-hour). These tours take no more than eight people at a time, so reservations are required. Kids must be at least 12 years old or 100 pounds (€80, daily at 9:30, April-Oct also at 13:30 and 17:30, off-season tours are shorter, cheaper, and colder, tel. 01 82 88 80 96, www.fattiretours.com/paris).

Wheelchair Tour

Paris on Wheels provides services for travelers with disabilities, including city wheelchair tours, excursions from Paris, and transportation within the city—a terrific service, as public transportation is not wheelchair-accessible (tel. 06 68 23 74 38, www.parisonwheels. com, derek@parisonwheels.com).

WEEKEND TOUR PACKAGES FOR STUDENTS

Andy Steves (Rick's son) runs **Weekend Student Adventures** (WSA Europe), offering three-day and 10-day budget travel packages across Europe including accommodations, skip-the-line sightseeing, and unique local experiences. Locally guided and DIY unguided options are available for student and budget travelers in 12 of Europe's most popular cities, including Paris (guided trips from €199, see www.wsaeurope.com for details).

EXCURSIONS FROM PARIS

You'll never run out of things to do in Paris, but the outlying areas may lure you out of the city. The grand châteaux at **Versailles, Vaux-le-Vicomte,** and **Fontainebleau,** the cathedral at **Chartres,** Monet's garden at **Giverny,** and the artist town of **Auvers-sur-Oise** are all within reach as day trips. You can go on your own (for details, see the Day Trips from Paris chapter), or go with a local guide—most of the guides listed earlier will do excursion tours from Paris using your rental car.

Farther from Paris

It's easy to arrange day trips from Paris to places around northern France, such as Reims, the Loire Valley, and the D-Day beaches of Normandy (all beyond the scope of this book, but well covered in *Rick Steves France*). Thanks to bullet trains and good local guides who can help you maximize your time, well-coordinated blitz-tour trips to these places are doable (though hardly relaxing). To see these places in a day, I recommend using a guide from the region who will meet you at the train station (most have cars) and show you the highlights before getting you back on your return train to Paris. Book well in advance, especially for the D-Day beaches.

Reims: The wine gurus at **Ô Château** in Paris offer day trips and tastings to Reims and Champagne (see page 435 for contact info).

Loire Valley: Pascal Accolay runs **Acco-Dispo,** which offers good all-day château tours from the city of Tours—an hour from Paris by train (tel. 06 82 00 64 51, www.accodispo-tours.com).

D-Day Beaches: An army of small companies offers all-day excursions to the D-Day beaches from Bayeux or Caen, both reachable by train from Paris in 2.5 hours or less. These guides are top notch: **Dale Booth Normandy Tours** (Dale Booth, tel. 02 33 71 53 76, www.dboothnormandytours.com, dboothholidays@sfr.fr), **D-Day Historian Tours** (Paul Woodadge, mobile 07 88 02 76 57, www.ddayhistorian.com, paul@ddayhistorian.com), **Normandy American Heroes Tours** (Rodolphe Passera, tel. 06 30 55 63 39, www.normandyamericanheroes.com, normandyamericanheroes@gmail.com), **First Normandy Battlefield Tours** (Allan Bryson, www.firstnormandybattlefieldtours.com, firstnormandy@sfr.fr), and **Normandy Battle Tours** (Stuart Robertson, tel. 02 33 41 28 34, www.normandybattletours.com, stuart@normandybattletours.com).

Bayeux Shuttle takes individual signups for their minivan tours and has an easy booking calendar online (tel. 06 59 70 72 55, www.bayeuxshuttle.com). The **Caen Memorial Museum**'s "D-Day Tour" package includes pickup from the Caen train station, a guided tour through the WWII exhibits at the Memorial Museum, lunch, and then a five-hour afternoon tour in English (and French) of the major Anglo-American or Canadian beaches. Your day ends with a drop-off at the Caen train station in time to catch a train back to Paris (tel. 02 31 06 06 44, www.memorial-caen.fr).

Other Day-Trip Options

If you'd be happier letting someone else arrange the logistics, the following companies offer convenient transportation and a smidgeon of guiding to destinations outside Paris.

Paris Webservices, a reliable outfit, offers day trips with English-speaking chauffeur-guides in cushy minivans for private groups to Giverny, Versailles, Mont St-Michel, D-Day Beaches, and more (figure €90-140/person for groups of 4 or more, use promo code "PWSRS08" and show current edition of this book for discounts of 5 percent—discount valid only for their tours, tel.

01 45 56 91 67, or 09 52 06 02 59, www.pariswebservices.com, contactpws@pariswebservices.com).

City Vision runs tours to several popular regional destinations, including the Loire Valley, Champagne region, D-Day beaches, and Mont St-Michel (tel. 01 42 60 30 01, www.pariscityvision.com). Their minivan tours are pricier, but more personal and given in English, and most offer convenient pickup at your Paris hotel (half-day tour about €100/person, all-day tour about €200/person). Their full-size bus tours are multilingual, mass-marketed, and mediocre at best, but can be worthwhile for some travelers simply for the ease of transportation to the sights (about €80-170, destinations include Versailles, Giverny, Mont St-Michel, and more).

ORIENTATION

SIGHTS IN PARIS

Paris is blessed with world-class museums and monuments—more than anyone could see in a single visit. To help you prioritize your limited time and money, I've chosen what I think are the best of Paris' many sights. I've clustered them into walkable neighborhoods for more efficient sightseeing.

When you see a 📖 in a listing, it means the sight is described in greater detail in one of my self-guided walks or tours. A 🎧 means the walk or tour is available as a free audio tour (via my Rick Steves Audio Europe app—see page 8). Some walks and tours are available in both formats—take your pick.

This is why some of Paris' greatest sights get less coverage in this chapter—we'll explore them later in the book, where you'll also find crucial info on avoiding lines, saving money, and finding a decent bite to eat nearby.

For general tips on sightseeing, see page 629. For advice on saving money, see "Affording Paris' Sights" on page 64. Also, be sure to check www.ricksteves.com/update for any significant changes that may have occurred since this book was printed.

Sightseeing Strategies

If you plan ahead, you can avoid many of the lines that tourists suffer through in Paris. For most sightseers, the best single way to avoid long lines is to buy a Paris Museum Pass. If you decide to forego the pass—or for sights not covered by the pass—you have other options. Note, though, that because of heightened terrorism concerns, there are likely to be slow security checks at most tourist-oriented sights.

PARIS MUSEUM PASS

In Paris there are two classes of sightseers—those with a Paris Museum Pass, and those who stand in line. The pass admits you to many of Paris' most popular sights, and it allows you to skip ticket-buying lines (but not security lines). You'll save time and money by getting this pass. Pertinent details about the pass are outlined here—for more info, visit www.parismuseumpass.com.

Buying the Pass

The pass pays for itself with four key admissions in two days (for example, the Louvre, Orsay, Sainte-Chapelle, and Versailles), and it lets you skip the ticket line at most sights (2 days-€48, 4 days-€62, 6 days-€74, no youth or senior discounts). It's sold at participating museums, monuments, TIs (small fee added; includes TIs at Paris airports), and at some souvenir stores located near major sights. Try to avoid buying the pass at a major museum (such as the Louvre), where the supply can be spotty and lines long. It's not worth the cost or hassle to buy the pass online—you have to either pay dearly for shipping, or print vouchers and redeem them in person at a Paris TI.

To determine whether the pass is a good value for your trip, tally up what you want to see from the list below. Remember, with the pass you skip to the front of most (but not all) lines, which can save hours of waiting, especially in summer. Another benefit is that you can pop into lesser sights that otherwise might not be worth the expense.

Families: The pass isn't worth buying for children and teens, as most museums are free or discounted for those under age 18 (teenagers may need to show ID as proof of age). If parents have a Museum Pass, kids can usually skip the ticket lines as well. A few places, such as the Arc de Triomphe and Army Museum, require everyone—even pass holders—to stand in line to collect your child's free ticket.

What the Paris Museum Pass Covers

Here's a list of key sights and their admission prices without the pass:

Louvre (€15)	Notre-Dame Tower (€10)
Orsay Museum (€11)	Paris Archaeological Crypt (€7)
Orangerie Museum (€9)	Paris Sewer Tour (€4.40)
Sainte-Chapelle (€8.50)	Cluny Museum (€8)
Arc de Triomphe (€9.50)	Pompidou Center (€14)
Rodin Museum (€10)	Picasso Museum (€11)
Army Museum (€11)	Conciergerie (€8.50)
Panthéon (€8.50)	Château Chantilly (€16)
Château Fontainebleau (€11)	Versailles (€25 total)

SIGHTS

1e = Arrondissements (Districts)

Notable sights that are *not* covered by the pass include the Eiffel Tower, Montparnasse Tower, Marmottan Museum, Opéra Garnier, Notre-Dame Treasury, Jacquemart-André Museum, Grand Palais, Catacombs, Montmartre Museum, Sacré-Cœur's dome, and the ladies of Pigalle. The pass also does not cover these recommended sights outside Paris: Vaux-le-Vicomte, Château d'Auvers in Auvers-sur-Oise, and Monet's Garden and House in Giverny.

Using the Pass

Plan carefully to make the most of your pass. Validate it only when you're ready to tackle the covered sights on consecutive days. Activating it is simple—just write the start date you want (and your name) on the pass. But first make sure the sights you want to visit will be open when you want to go (many museums are closed on either a Mon or Tue).

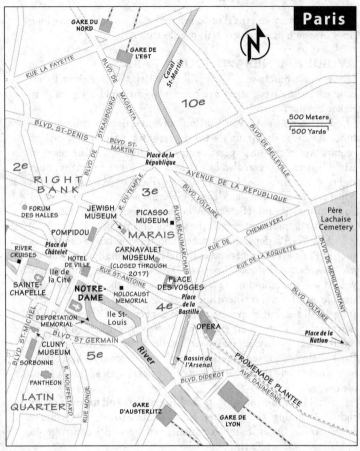

The pass provides the best value on days when sights close later, letting you extend your sightseeing day. Take advantage of late hours on selected evenings or times of year at the Arc de Triomphe, Pompidou Center, Notre-Dame Tower, Sainte-Chapelle, Louvre, Orsay, Rodin Museum, and Napoleon's Tomb. On days that you don't have pass coverage, plan to visit free sights and those not covered by the pass (see page 64 for a list of free sights).

You can't skip the security lines, though at a few sights (including the Louvre), pass holders may be able to skip to the front. Once past security, look for signs designating the entrance for reserved ticket holders. If it's not obvious, boldly walk to the front of the ticket line, hold up your pass, and ask the ticket taker: *"Entrez, pass?"* (ahn-tray pahs). You'll either be allowed to enter at that point, or you'll be directed to a special entrance. For major sights, such as the Louvre and Orsay museums, I've identified pass holder entrances on the maps in this book. Don't be shy—some places (the Orsay and the Arc de Triomphe, in particular) have long lines in which pass holders wait needlessly.

AVOIDING LINES WITHOUT A PASS

If you don't purchase a Paris Museum Pass, or if a sight is not covered by the pass, there are other ways to avoid long waits in ticket-buying lines.

For some sights, you can buy **advance tickets** either at the official website or through a third party (for a fee). Some tickets require you to choose a specific entry time, like at the line-plagued Eiffel Tower. You can also buy tickets in advance for many other sights (including the Louvre, Orsay, Picasso Museum, Rodin Museum, and Monet's gardens at Giverny) as well as for activities and cultural events (Bateaux-Mouches cruises, Sainte-Chapelle concerts, and performances at the Opéra Garnier).

TIs, FNAC department stores, and travel-services companies such as Paris Webservices and Fat Tire Tours sell individual *"coupe-file"* **tickets** (pronounced "koop feel") for some sights, which allow you to use the Museum Pass entrance (worth the extra cost and trouble only for sights where lines are longest). TIs sell these tickets for a small fee, but elsewhere you can expect a surcharge of 10-20 percent. FNAC stores are everywhere (www.fnactickets.com), even on the Champs-Elysées (ask your hotelier for the nearest one); for Paris Webservices, see page 388. Despite the surcharges and often-long lines to buy them, getting *coupe-file* tickets can still be a good idea.

Fat Tire Tours offers **Skip the Line tickets and tours** of major sights, including the Louvre, Notre-Dame Tower, Catacombs, Eiffel Tower, Orsay, Sainte-Chapelle, and Versailles (see page 43 or visit www.fattiretours.com/paris).

Some sights, such as the Louvre, have **ticket-vending machines** that save time in line. These accept cash (usually no bills larger than €20) or chip-and-PIN cards (so many American credit cards won't work). And at certain sights, including the Louvre and Orsay, **nearby shops** sell tickets, allowing you to avoid the main ticket lines (for details, see the Louvre and Orsay tour chapters).

Sights

HISTORIC CORE OF PARIS

Many of these sights—Notre Dame, Sainte-Chapelle, and more—are covered in detail in my Historic Paris Walk. If a sight is covered in the walk, I've listed only its essentials here. 📖 See my Historic Paris Walk or 🎧 download my free audio tour.

▲▲▲Notre-Dame Cathedral
(Cathédrale Notre-Dame de Paris)

This 850-year-old cathedral is packed with history and tourists. With a pair of 200-foot-tall bell towers, a facade studded with

ornate statuary, beautiful stained-glass rose windows, famous gargoyles, a picture-perfect Seine-side location, and textbook flying buttresses, there's a good reason that this cathedral of "Our Lady" *(Notre-Dame)* is France's most famous church.

Check out the facade: Mary with the Baby Jesus (in rose window) above the 28 Kings of Judah (statues that were beheaded during the Revolution). Stroll the interior, which echoes with history. Then wander around the exterior, through a forest of frilly buttresses, watched over by a fleet of whimsical gargoyles. The long line to the left is to climb the famous tower.

Cost and Hours: Cathedral—free, Mon-Sat 7:45-18:45, Sun 7:15-19:15; **Tower**—€10, covered by Museum Pass but no bypass line, daily April-Sept 10:00-18:30, Fri-Sat until 23:00 in July-Aug, Oct-March 10:00-17:30, last entry 45 minutes before closing, avoid the worst lines by arriving before 10:00 or after 17:00 (after 16:00 in winter); **Treasury**—€5, not covered by Museum Pass, Mon-Fri 9:30-18:00, Sat 9:30-18:30, Sun 13:30-18:40; audioguide-€5, free English tours—normally Mon, Tue, and Sat at 14:30, Wed and Thu at 14:00; Mo: Cité, Hôtel de Ville, or St. Michel; tel. 01 42 34 56 10, www.notredamedeparis.fr.

For a detailed tour of Notre-Dame Cathedral, 📖 see page 108 of my Historic Paris Walk or 🎧 download my free audio tour.

Paris Archaeological Crypt

This intriguing 20-minute stop lets you view Roman ruins from Emperor Augustus' reign (when this island became ground zero in Paris), trace the street plan of the medieval village, and see diagrams of how early Paris grew. It's all thoughtfully explained in English (pick up the floor plan with some background info) and well presented with videos and touchscreens.

Cost and Hours: €7, covered by Museum Pass, Tue-Sun 10:00-18:00, closed Mon, enter 100 yards in front of cathedral, tel. 01 55 42 50 10, www.crypte.paris.fr.

Visiting the Crypt: The first few displays put the ruins in historical context. Three models show the growth of Paris—from an uninhabited riverside plot to the grid-planned Roman town of Lutèce, then to an early medieval city with an enclosing wall and the church that preceded Notre-Dame. A fourth model (off to the left)

Paris at a Glance

▲▲▲**Notre-Dame Cathedral** Paris' most beloved church, with towers and gargoyles. **Hours:** Cathedral—Mon-Sat 7:45-18:45, Sun 7:15-19:15; Tower—daily April-Sept 10:00-18:30, Fri-Sat until 23:00 in July-Aug, Oct-March 10:00-17:30; Treasury—Mon-Fri 9:30-18:00, Sat 9:30-18:30, Sun 13:30-18:40. See page 53.

▲▲▲**Sainte-Chapelle** Gothic cathedral with peerless stained glass. **Hours:** Daily March-Oct 9:30-18:00, Wed until 21:30 mid-May-mid-Sept, Nov-Feb 9:00-17:00. See page 56.

▲▲▲**Louvre** Europe's oldest and greatest museum, starring *Mona Lisa* and *Venus de Milo*. **Hours:** Wed-Mon 9:00-18:00, Wed and Fri until 21:45, closed Tue. See page 58.

▲▲▲**Orsay Museum** Nineteenth-century art, including Europe's greatest Impressionist collection. **Hours:** Tue-Sun 9:30-18:00, Thu until 21:45, closed Mon. See page 60.

▲▲▲**Eiffel Tower** Paris' soaring exclamation point. **Hours:** Daily mid-June-Aug 9:00-24:45, Sept-mid-June 9:30-23:45. See page 61.

▲▲▲**Champs-Elysées** Paris' grand boulevard. **Hours:** Always open. See page 80.

▲▲▲**Versailles** The ultimate royal palace (Château), with a Hall of Mirrors, vast gardens, a grand canal, plus a queen's playground (Trianon Palaces and Domaine de Marie-Antoinette). **Hours:** Château April-Oct Tue-Sun 8:30-19:00, Nov-March 9:00-17:30; Trianon/Domaine April-Oct Tue-Sun 12:00-18:30, Nov-March until 17:30; gardens generally April-Oct daily 8:00-20:30, Nov-March until 18:00; entire complex closed Mon year-round except the Gardens. See the Versailles chapter.

▲▲▲**Picasso Museum** World's largest collection of Picasso's works. **Hours:** Tue-Fri 11:30-18:00 (until 21:00 third Fri of month), Sat-Sun 9:30-18:00, closed Mon. See page 95.

▲▲**Orangerie Museum** Monet's water lilies and modernist classics in a lovely setting. **Hours:** Wed-Mon 9:00-18:00, closed Tue. See page 61.

▲▲**Rue Cler** Ultimate Parisian market street. **Hours:** Stores open Tue-Sat 8:30-13:00 & 15:00-19:30, Sun 8:30-12:00, dead on Mon. See page 67.

▲▲**Army Museum and Napoleon's Tomb** The emperor's imposing tomb, flanked by museums of France's wars. **Hours:** Daily 10:00-18:00, Nov-March until 17:00; tomb also open July-Aug until 19:00 and April-Sept Tue until 21:00; museum (except for tomb) closed first Mon of month Oct-June; Charles de Gaulle exhibit closed Mon year-round. See page 67.

▲▲**Rodin Museum** Works by the greatest sculptor since Michelangelo, with many statues in a peaceful garden. **Hours:** Tue-Sun 10:00-17:45, closed Mon. See page 68.

▲▲**Marmottan Museum** Art museum focusing on Monet. **Hours:** Tue-Sun 10:00-18:00, Thu until 21:00, closed Mon. See page 70.

▲▲**Cluny Museum** Medieval art with unicorn tapestries. **Hours:** Wed-Mon 9:15-17:45, closed Tue. See page 71.

▲▲**Arc de Triomphe** Triumphal arch marking start of Champs-Elysées. **Hours:** Always viewable; interior daily 10:00-23:00, Oct-March until 22:30. See page 80.

▲▲**Opéra Garnier** Grand belle époque theater with a modern ceiling by Chagall. **Hours:** Generally daily 10:00-16:30, mid-July-Aug until 18:00. See page 88.

▲▲**Jacquemart-André Museum** Art-strewn 19th-century mansion. **Hours:** Daily 10:00-18:00, Mon until 20:30 during special exhibits. See page 93.

▲▲**Pompidou Center** Modern art in colorful building with city views. **Hours:** Permanent collection open Wed-Mon 11:00-21:00, closed Tue. See page 99.

▲▲**Sacré-Cœur and Montmartre** White basilica atop Montmartre with spectacular views. **Hours:** Daily 6:00-22:30; dome climb daily May-Sept 8:30-20:00, Oct-April 9:00-17:00. See page 101.

▲**Panthéon** Neoclassical monument and burial place of the famous. **Hours:** Daily 10:00-18:30, Oct-March until 18:00. See page 75.

▲**Ile St. Louis** Residential island behind Notre-Dame known for its restaurants. **Hours:** Always open. See page 56.

▲**Jewish Art and History Museum** History of Judaism in Europe. **Hours:** Tue-Fri 11:00-18:00, Sat-Sun 10:00-18:00, open later during special exhibits—Wed until 21:00 and Sat-Sun until 19:00, closed Mon year-round. See page 95.

▲**Père Lachaise Cemetery** Final home of Paris' illustrious dead. **Hours:** Mon-Fri 8:00-18:00, Sat 8:30-18:00, Sun 9:00-18:00, until 17:30 in winter. See page 100.

SIGHTS

shows the current Notre-Dame surrounded by buildings, along with the old, straight road—Rue Neuve de Notre-Dame—that led up to the church and now runs right down the center of the museum. The ruins in the middle of the museum are a confusing mix of foundations from all these time periods, including parts of the old Rue Neuve.

As you circle the ruins counter-clockwise, here are some highlights: Along the right side of the museum, you can see big stone blocks from the old Roman wall. At the back, you can step onto the remains of a Roman dock. Further along is a chance to build Notre-Dame Cathedral with a touchscreen, and a view of the Rue Neuve ruins. On the museum's far side, find the thermal baths, where you can see a Roman building with "hypocaustal" heating—narrow passages pumped full of hot air to heat the room.

▲Deportation Memorial (Mémorial de la Déportation)

Climb down the steps into this memorial dedicated to the 200,000 French victims of the Nazi concentration camps. As Paris disappears above you, this monument draws you into the victims' experience. Once underground you enter a one-way hallway studded with tiny lights commemorating the dead, leading you to an eternal flame.

Cost and Hours: Free, Tue-Sun 10:00-19:00, Oct-March until 17:00, closed Mon year-round, may randomly close at other times, free but boring audioguide; at the east tip of Ile de la Cité, behind Notre-Dame and near Ile St. Louis (Mo: Cité); tel. 01 46 33 87 56.

▲Ile St. Louis

The residential island behind Notre-Dame is known for its restaurants (see the Eating in Paris chapter), great ice cream, and shops (along Rue St. Louis-en-l'Ile).

For a detailed description of Ile St. Louis, 📖 see page 118 of my Historic Paris Walk chapter or 🎧 download my free audio tour.

▲▲▲Sainte-Chapelle

The interior of this 13th-century chapel is a triumph of Gothic church architecture. Built to house Jesus' Crown of Thorns, Sainte-Chapelle is jam-packed with stained-glass windows, bathed in colorful light, and slippery with the drool of awestruck tourists. Ignore the humdrum exterior and climb the stairs into the sanctuary, where more than 1,100 Bible scenes—from the Creation to the Passion to Judgment Day—are illustrated by light and glass.

Cost and Hours: €8.50, €13.50 combo-ticket with Conciergerie, free for those under age 18, covered by Museum Pass; daily March-Oct 9:30-18:00, Wed until 21:30 mid-May–mid-Sept, Nov-Feb 9:00-17:00; be prepared for long lines (for tips on avoiding them, see page 23), audioguide-€4.50 (€6 for two), evening concerts—see page 491, 4 Boulevard du Palais, Mo: Cité, tel. 01 53 40 60 80, www.sainte-chapelle.fr.

For a detailed tour of the cathedral's interior, 🕮 see page 124 of my Historic Paris Walk or 🎧 download my free audio tour.

▲Conciergerie

Marie-Antoinette was imprisoned here, as were Louis XVI, Robespierre, Danton, and many others on their way to the

guillotine. Exhibits with good English descriptions trace the history of the building and give some insight into prison life. You can also relive the drama in Marie-Antoinette's cell on the day of her execution—complete with dummies and period furniture.

Cost and Hours: €8.50, €13.50 combo-ticket with Sainte-Chapelle, covered by Museum Pass, daily 9:30-18:00, 2 Boulevard du Palais, Mo: Cité, tel. 01 53 40 60 80, www.paris-conciergerie.fr.

For a detailed description of the Conciergerie, 🕮 see page 130 of my Historic Paris Walk or 🎧 download my free audio tour.

▲Paris *Plages* (Paris Beaches)

The Riviera it's not, but this string of fanciful faux beaches—assembled in summer along a one-mile stretch of the Right Bank of the Seine—is a fun place to stroll, play, and people-watch on a sunny day. Each summer, the Paris city government closes the embankment's highway and trucks in potted palm trees, hammocks, lounge chairs, and 2,000 tons of sand to create colorful urban beaches. You'll also find "beach cafés," climbing walls, prefab pools, trampolines, *boules,* a library, beach volleyball, badminton, and Frisbee areas in three zones: sandy, grassy, and wood-tiled. (Other less-central areas of town, such as Bassin de la Vilette, have their own *plages.*)

Cost and Hours: Free, mid-July–mid-Aug daily 8:00-24:00, on Right Bank of Seine, just north of Ile de la Cité, between Pont des Arts and Pont de Sully; for information, go to www.quefaire.paris.fr/parisplages.

SIGHTS

MAJOR MUSEUMS NEIGHBORHOOD

Paris' grandest park, the Tuileries Garden, was once the private property of kings and queens. Today it links the Louvre, Orangerie, and Orsay museums. And across from the Louvre are the tranquil, historic courtyards of the Palais Royal.

▲▲▲Louvre (Musée du Louvre)

This is Europe's oldest, biggest, greatest, and second-most-crowded museum (after the Vatican). Housed in a U-shaped, 16th-century palace (accentuated by a 20th-century glass pyramid), the Louvre is Paris' top museum and one of its key landmarks. It's home to *Mona Lisa, Venus de Milo,* and hall after hall of Greek and Roman masterpieces, medieval jewels, Michelangelo statues, and paintings by the greatest artists from the Renaissance to the Romantics.

Touring the Louvre can be overwhelming, so be selective. Focus on the Denon wing, with Greek sculptures, Italian paintings (by Raphael and da Vinci), and—

of course—French paintings (Neoclassical and Romantic), and the adjoining Sully wing, with Egyptian artifacts and more French paintings. For extra credit, tackle the Richelieu wing, displaying works from ancient Mesopotamia, as well as French, Dutch, and Northern art.

Cost and Hours: €15, includes special exhibits, free on first Sun of month Oct-March, covered by Museum Pass, tickets good all day, reentry allowed; Wed-Mon 9:00-18:00, Wed and Fri until 21:45 (except on holidays), closed Tue, galleries start shutting 30 minutes before closing, last entry 45 minutes before closing; crowds worst in the morning (arrive 30 minutes before opening) and all day Sun, Mon, and Wed; videoguide-€5, guided tours available—see page 136, several cafés, tel. 01 40 20 53 17, recorded info tel. 01 40 20 51 51, www.louvre.fr.

Getting There: It's at the Palais Royal-Musée du Louvre Métro stop. (The old Louvre Métro stop, called Louvre-Rivoli, is farther from the entrance.) Bus #69 also runs past the Louvre.

📖 See the Louvre Tour chapter or 🎧 download my free audio tour.

Major Museums Neighborhood

Palais Royal Courtyards

Across from the Louvre are the lovely courtyards of the stately Palais Royal. Although the palace is closed to the public, the courtyards are open.

Cost and Hours: Free and always open. The Palais Royal is directly north of the Louvre on Rue de Rivoli (Mo: Palais Royal-Musée du Louvre).

Visiting the Courtyards: Enter through a whimsical (locals say tacky) courtyard filled with stubby, striped columns and playful

fountains (with fun, reflective metal balls). Next, you'll pass into another, perfectly Parisian garden. This is where in-the-know Parisians come to take a quiet break, walk their poodles and kids, or enjoy a rendezvous—amid flowers and surrounded by a serene arcade and a handful of historic restaurants. Bring a picnic and create your own quiet break, or have a drink at one of the outdoor cafés at the courtyard's northern end. This is Paris.

Though tranquil today, this was once a hotbed of political activism. The palace was built in the 17th century by Louis XIII and eventually became the headquarters of the powerful Dukes of Orléans. Because the Dukes' digs were off-limits to the police, some shocking free-thinking took root here. This was the meeting place for the debating clubs—the precursors to modern political parties. During the Revolution, palace resident Duke Philippe (nicknamed Philippe Egalité for his progressive ideas) advocated a constitutional monarchy, and voted in favor of beheading Louis XVI—his own cousin. Philippe hoped his liberal attitudes would spare him from the Revolutionaries, but he, too, was guillotined. His son, Louis-Philippe, became France's first constitutional monarch (r. 1830-1848). The palace's courtyards were backdrops for a riotous social and political scene, filled with lively café culture, revolutionaries, rabble-rousers, scoundrels, and...Madame Tussaud's first wax shop (she used the severed heads of guillotine victims to model her sculptures).

Nearby: Exiting the courtyard at the side facing away from the Seine brings you to the Galeries Colbert and Vivienne, attractive examples of shopping arcades from the early 1800s (see page 487).

▲▲▲Orsay Museum (Musée d'Orsay)

The Orsay boasts Europe's greatest collection of Impressionist works. It might be less important than the Louvre—but it's more purely enjoyable.

The Orsay, housed in an atmospheric old train station, picks up where the Louvre leaves off: the second half of the 19th century. This is art from the tumultuous time that began when revolutions swept across Europe in 1848 and ended when World War I broke out in 1914. Begin with the conservative art of the mid-1800s—careful, idealized Neoclassicism (with a few rebels mixed in). Then tour the late 1800s, when the likes of Manet, Monet, Degas, and Renoir jolted the art world with their colorful, lively new invention, Impressionism. (Somewhere in there, *Whistler's Mother* sits quietly.) The Orsay also displays the works of their artistic descendants, the Post-Impressionists: Cézanne, Van Gogh, Gauguin, Seurat, and Toulouse-Lautrec. On the mezzanine level, waltz through Rodin sculptures and Art Nouveau exhibits, and finish in the Grand Ballroom, which shows the chandeliered elegance of this former train station.

Cost and Hours: €11, €8.50 Tue-Wed and Fri-Sun after 16:30 and Thu after 18:00, free on first Sun of month and often right when the ticket booth stops selling tickets (Tue-Wed and Fri-Sun at 17:00, Thu at 21:00; they won't let you in much after that), covered by Museum Pass, combo-ticket with Orangerie Museum (€16) or Rodin Museum (€18). Museum open Tue-Sun 9:30-18:00, Thu until 21:45, closed Mon, last entry one hour before closing (45 minutes before on Thu), Impressionist galleries start shutting 45 minutes before closing. For line-avoiding tips, see page 168; museum especially crowded on Sun and Tue; audioguide-€5, guided tours available—see page 168; cafés and a restaurant, tel. 01 40 49 48 14, www.musee-orsay.fr.

Getting There: The museum, at 1 Rue de la Légion d'Honneur, sits above the RER-C stop called Musée d'Orsay; the nearest Métro stop is Solférino, three blocks southeast of the Orsay. Bus #69 also stops at the Orsay. From the Louvre, it's a lovely 15-minute walk through the Tuileries Garden and across the pedestrian bridge to the Orsay.

 See the Orsay Museum Tour chapter or download my free audio tour.

▲▲Orangerie Museum (Musée de l'Orangerie)

Located in the Tuileries Garden and drenched by natural light from skylights, the Orangerie (oh-rahn-zhuh-ree) is the closest you'll

ever come to stepping right into an Impressionist painting. Start with the museum's claim to fame: Monet's *Water Lilies*. Then head downstairs to enjoy the manageable collection of select works by Utrillo, Cézanne, Renoir, Matisse, and Picasso.

Cost and Hours: €9, €6.50 after 17:00, free for those under age 18, €16 combo-ticket with Orsay Museum, covered by Museum Pass; Wed-Mon 9:00-18:00, closed Tue; audioguide-€5, English guided tours usually Mon and Thu at 14:30 and Sat at 11:00, located in Tuileries Garden near Place de la Concorde (Mo: Concorde or scenic bus #24), 15-minute stroll from the Orsay, tel. 01 44 77 80 07, www.musee-orangerie.fr.

 See the Orangerie Museum Tour chapter.

EIFFEL TOWER AND NEARBY
▲▲▲Eiffel Tower (La Tour Eiffel)

Built on the 100th anniversary of the French Revolution (and in the spirit of the Industrial Revolution), the tower was the centerpiece of a World Expo designed simply to show off what people could

build in 1889. For decades it was the tallest structure the world had ever known, and though it's since been eclipsed, it's still the most visited monument. Ride the elevators to the top of its 1,063 feet for expansive views that stretch 40 miles. Then descend to the two lower levels, where the views are arguably even better, since the monuments are more recognizable.

Cost and Hours: €17 to ride all the way to the top, €11.50 for just the two lower levels, €5 to climb the stairs to the first or second level, not covered by Museum Pass; daily mid-June-Aug 9:00-24:45, last ascent to top at 23:00 and to lower levels at 24:00 (elevator or stairs); Sept-mid-June 9:30-23:45, last ascent to top at 22:30 and to lower levels at 23:00 (elevator) or at 18:00 (stairs); cafés and great view restaurants, Mo: Bir-Hakeim or Trocadéro, RER: Champ de Mars-Tour Eiffel (all stops about a 10-minute walk away). Recorded information tel. 08 92 70 12 39, www.toureiffel.paris.

Reservations: Since long waits are common, it's wise to make a reservation well in advance of your visit. At www.toureiffel. paris, you can book a time slot to begin your ascent; this allows you to skip the long initial entry line. Tickets go on sale about three months in advance and sell out quickly for visits from April through September, so don't dally.

📖 See the Eiffel Tower Tour chapter (which includes more tips on getting in).

▲Quai Branly Museum (Musée du Quai Branly)

This is the best collection I've seen anywhere of non-Western art from Africa, Oceania, Asia, and the Americas. Because art illustrates the ways in which a people organizes and delineates its culture and beliefs, viewing this collection offers a richer appreciation of traditions from around the world. The exhibits are presented in a wild, organic, and strikingly modern building. It's well worth a look if you have a Museum Pass and are near the Eiffel Tower.

Cost and Hours: €10, free on first Sun of the month, covered by Museum Pass; museum—Tue-Sun 11:00-19:00, Thu-Sat until 21:00, closed Mon, ticket office closes one hour before closing; gardens—Tue-Sun 9:15-19:30, Thu-Sat until 21:15, closed Mon; audioguide-€5, 37 Quai Branly, 10-minute walk east (upriver) of

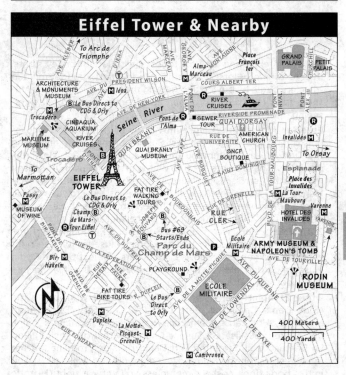

Eiffel Tower & Nearby

SIGHTS

Eiffel Tower, along the river (RER: Champ de Mars-Tour Eiffel or Pont de l'Alma), tel. 01 56 61 70 00, www.quaibranly.fr.

Visiting the Museum: After passing the security check and the ticket taker, pick up the museum map, then follow a ramp upstream along a projected river of the 1,657 names of the peoples covered in the museum. The permanent collection occupies the first floor up. Masks, statuettes, musical instruments, textiles, clothes, voodoo dolls, and a variety of temporary exhibitions and activities are artfully presented and exquisitely lit (the dim lighting also helps to preserve the fragile works). There's no need to follow a route: Wander at whim. Helpful English explanations are posted in most rooms and provide sufficient description for most visitors, though serious students will want to rent the audioguide.

Eiffel Tower Views: Even if you skip the museum, drop by its peaceful garden café for fine Eiffel Tower views (closes 30 minutes before museum) and enjoy the intriguing gardens. The pedestrian bridge that crosses the river and runs up to the museum also has sensational tower views.

▲Paris Sewer Tour (Les Egouts de Paris)

Discover what happens after you flush. This quick, interesting, and slightly stinky visit (a perfumed hanky helps) takes you along a few

Affording Paris' Sights

Paris is an expensive city for tourists, with lots of pricey sights, but—fortunately—lots of freebies, too. Smart, budget-minded travelers begin by buying and getting the most out of a **Paris Museum Pass** (see page 49), then considering these frugal sightseeing options.

Free (or Almost Free) Museums: Many of Paris' famous museums offer free entry on the first Sunday of the month, including the Orsay, Cluny, Pompidou Center, Quai Branly, and Delacroix museums. These sights are free on the first Sunday of off-season months: the Louvre, Rodin Museum, and Arc de Triomphe (all Oct-March), and Versailles (Nov-March). Expect big crowds on free days. Some museums are always free (with the possible exception of special exhibits), including the Carnavalet Museum (closed in 2017), Petit Palais, Victor Hugo's House, and Fragonard Perfume Museum. You can usually visit the Orsay Museum for free right when the ticket booth stops selling tickets. For just €4, the Rodin Museum garden lets you enjoy many of Rodin's finest works in a lovely outdoor setting.

Other Freebies: Many sights don't charge entry, including the Notre-Dame Cathedral, Père Lachaise Cemetery, Deportation Memorial, Holocaust Memorial, Paris *Plages* (summers only), Sacré-Cœur Basilica, St. Sulpice Church (with organ recital), and La Défense mall. Stroll the Left Bank riverside promenade from the Orsay to Pont de l'Alma. The neighborhood walks described in this book don't cost a dime unless you enter a sight (Historic Paris, Left Bank, Champs-Elysées, Marais, Rue Cler, and Montmartre).

hundred yards of water tunnels in the world's first underground sewer system.

Cost and Hours: €4.40, covered by Museum Pass, Sat-Wed 11:00-17:00, Oct-April until 16:00, closed Thu-Fri year-round, located where Pont de l'Alma greets the Left Bank—on the right side of the bridge as you face the river, Mo: Alma-Marceau, RER: Pont de l'Alma, tel. 01 53 68 27 81.

Visiting the Sewer: Pick up the helpful English self-guided tour, then drop down into Jean Valjean's world of tunnels, rats, and manhole covers. (Victor Hugo was friends with the sewer inspector when he wrote *Les Misérables*.) You'll pass well-organized displays with extensive English information explaining the history of water distribution and collection in Paris, from Roman times to the present.

The evolution of this amazing network

Paris' glorious, entertaining parks are free, *bien sûr.* These include Luxembourg Garden, Champ de Mars (under the Eiffel Tower), Tuileries Garden (between the Louvre and Place de la Concorde), Palais Royal Courtyards, Jardin des Plantes, Parc Monceau, the Promenade Plantée walk, and Versailles' gardens (except when the fountains perform on weekends April-Oct and many Tue).

Reduced Prices: Several sights offer a discount if you enter later in the day, including the Orsay, the Orangerie, and the Army Museum and Napoleon's Tomb (after 17:00 or 16:00 off-season). The Eiffel Tower costs less if you're willing to restrict your visit to the two lower levels—and even less if you're willing to use the stairs.

Free Concerts: Venues offering free or cheap (€8) concerts include the American Church, Army Museum, St. Sulpice Church, La Madeleine Church, and Notre-Dame Cathedral. For a listing of free concerts, check *Pariscope* magazine (under the "Musique" section) and look for events marked *entrée libre.*

Good-Value Tours: At €15-20, Paris Walks' tours are a good value. The Seine River cruises (around €14), best after dark, are also worthwhile. My Bus #69 Sightseeing Tour, which costs only the price of a transit ticket, could be the best deal of all.

Pricey...but worth it? Certain big-ticket items—primarily the top of the Eiffel Tower, the Louvre, and Versailles—are expensive and crowded, but offer once-in-a-lifetime experiences. All together they amount to less than the cost of a ticket to Disneyland—only these are real.

of sewers is fascinating. More than 1,500 miles of tunnels carry 317 million gallons of water daily through this underworld. It's the world's longest sewer system—so long, they say, that if it were laid out straight, it would stretch from Paris all the way to Istanbul.

It's enlightening to see how much work goes into something we take for granted. Sewage didn't always disappear so readily. In the Middle Ages, wastewater was tossed from windows to a center street gutter, then washed into the river (which also supplied locals' drinking water). In castles, sewage ended up in the moat (enhancing the moat's defensive role). In the 1500s, French Renaissance King François I moved from château to château (he had several) when the moat-muck became too much. This tour illustrates how, over time, sewage became separated from drinking water and explains the intricate systems in place today that sustain that separation.

▲Riverside Promenade (Les Berges du Seine)

This one-time busy expressway turned riverfront park runs along the Left Bank of the Seine from the Pont de l'Alma (near the Eiffel Tower) to the Orsay Museum, allowing walkers to experience the Seine at water level. Distractions abound, with loads of kid-friendly activities, gardens, lively cafés, sling chairs, *crêperies,* and more. It's part of Paris's grand 21st-century plan to rid the city center of cars and create pedestrian-friendly areas. It's hugely popular in good weather, and a fun place to rub shoulders with Parisians.

National Maritime Museum (Musée National de la Marine)

This fun museum anchors a dazzling collection of ship models, submarine models, torpedoes, cannonballs, *beaucoup* bowsprits, and naval you-name-it. It's a kid-friendly place filled with *Pirates of the Caribbean*-like ship models, some the size of small cars. Start with the full-sized party barge made for Napoleon in 1810, then look up to see the elaborate stern of the 1694 *Réale de France* royal galley (don't miss the scale model in the glass case). From here you can follow a more or less chronological display of ship construction, from Roman vessels to modern cruise ships to aircraft carriers. Few English explanations make the free audioguide essential.

Cost and Hours: €8.50, includes audioguide, free for those age 26 and under, covered by Museum Pass; Mon and Wed-Fri 11:00-18:00, Sat-Sun 11:00-19:00, closed Tue; on left side of Place du Trocadéro with your back to Eiffel Tower, tel. 01 53 65 69 69, www.musee-marine.fr.

Architecture and Monuments Museum (Cité de l'Architecture et du Patrimoine)

This museum, on the east side of Place du Trocadéro, takes you through 1,000 years of French architecture, starring some of France's greatest Gothic churches—all brought to life through full-sized casts and scale models. Pick up the museum plan, augment it with the English info sheets in the rooms, and focus most of your time on the ground floor. Walk the length of the floor, passing under tympanum arches and pondering how many ways you can envision the Last Judgment. Gaze into the eyes of medieval statues from the abbey of Cluny, Chartres Cathedral, Château de Chambord, and much more. A U-turn at the end of the hall leads to the Renaissance and the screaming passion of the Revolution.

Take the elevator up a floor to see thought-provoking designs for modern projects, including for low-income housing. You can walk into a room from Le Corbusier's 1952 Habitation Unit from Marseille and appreciate what a forward thinker this man was. Farther along, you'll see how colorfully painted the chapels were in medieval churches. The views to the Eiffel Tower are sensational.

Cost and Hours: €8, includes audioguide, covered by Museum

Pass, Wed-Mon 11:00-19:00, Thu until 21:00, closed Tue, 1 Place du Trocadéro, Mo: Trocadéro, RER: Champ de Mars-Tour Eiffel, tel. 01 58 51 52 00, www.citechaillot.fr.

Museum of Wine (Musée du Vin)

Wine enthusiasts may want to stop into this 15th-century cellar for a musty, atmospheric, wine-fueled experience. The museum displays tools and items used for harvesting and winemaking, collected over the years by the *Confrérie des Echansons*. The role of this order is to protect and promote French wines. Started in 1954, it has thousands of members worldwide. Follow your visit with a wine tasting (€5 for one glass, €25 to taste three wines with a *sommelier*) and/or lunch at the restaurant (open 12:00-15:00, free aperitif with lunch if you show this book).

Cost and Hours: €10, €8 with this book, includes dry audioguide, Tue-Sat 10:00-18:00, closed Sun-Mon, 5 Square Charles Dickens, Mo: Passy, 15-minute walk from Eiffel Tower, tel. 01 45 25 63 26, www.museeduvinparis.com.

▲▲Rue Cler

Paris is changing quickly, but a stroll down this market street introduces you to a thriving, traditional Parisian neighborhood and offers insights into the local culture. Although this is a wealthy district, Rue Cler retains the workaday charm still found in most neighborhoods throughout Paris. The shops lining the street are filled with the freshest produce, the stinkiest cheese, the tastiest chocolate, and the finest wines (markets generally open Tue-Sat 8:30-13:00 & 15:00-19:30, Sun 8:30-12:00, dead on Mon). I'm still far from a gourmet eater, but my time spent tasting my way along Rue Cler has substantially bumped up my appreciation of good cuisine (as well as the French knack for good living).

📖 See Rue Cler Walk chapter.

▲▲Army Museum and Napoleon's Tomb (Musée de l'Armée)

Europe's greatest military museum, in the Hôtel des Invalides, provides interesting coverage of several wars, particularly World Wars I and II. At the center of the complex, Napoleon lies majestically dead inside several coffins under a grand dome—a goose-bump inducing pilgrimage for historians. The dome overhead glitters with 26 pounds of thinly pounded gold leaf.

Cost and Hours: €11, €9 after 17:00 (16:00 in Nov-March), free for military personnel in uniform, free for kids but they must wait in line for ticket, covered by Museum Pass, special exhibits are extra; open daily 10:00-18:00, Nov-March until 17:00; tomb also open July-Aug until 19:00 and April-Sept Tue until 21:00; museum (except for tomb) closed first Mon of month Oct-June; Charles de Gaulle exhibit closed Mon year-round; videoguide-€6, cafeteria, tel. 08 10 11 33 99, www.musee-armee.fr.

Getting There: The Hôtel des Invalides is at 129 Rue de Grenelle, a 10-minute walk from Rue Cler (Mo: La Tour Maubourg, Varenne, or Invalides). You can also take bus #69 (from the Marais and Rue Cler), bus #87 (from Rue Cler and Luxembourg Garden area), or bus #63 from the St. Germain-des-Prés area.

📖 See the Army Museum and Napoleon's Tomb Tour chapter.

SIGHTS

▲▲Rodin Museum (Musée Rodin)

This recently renovated, user-friendly museum is filled with passionate works by the greatest sculptor since Michelangelo. You'll see *The Kiss, The Thinker, The Gates of Hell,* and many more. Well-displayed in the mansion where the sculptor lived and worked, exhibits trace Rodin's artistic development, explain how his bronze statues were cast, and show some of the studies he created to work up to his masterpiece, the unfinished *Gates of Hell.* Learn about Rodin's tumultuous relationship with his apprentice and lover, Camille Claudel. Mull over what makes his sculptures some of the most evocative since the Renaissance. And stroll the beautiful gardens, packed with  many of his greatest works (including *The Thinker*) and ideal for artistic reflection.

Cost and Hours: €10, free for those under age 18, free on first Sun of the month Oct-March, €4 for just the garden (with several important works on display), €18 combo-ticket with Orsay Museum, both museum and garden covered by Museum Pass; Tue-Sun 10:00-17:45, closed Mon; gardens close at 18:00, Oct-March at 17:00; audioguide-€6, mandatory baggage check, self-service café in garden, 77 Rue de Varenne, Mo: Varenne, tel. 01 44 18 61 10, www.musee-rodin.fr.

📖 See the Rodin Museum Tour chapter.

▲Self-Guided Bike Loop from Champ de Mars Park

This easy, level one-hour bike tour is designed as a loop trip. It starts at the Champ de Mars, follows the riverside promenade, and heads into the Tuileries Garden, across Place de la Concorde, and along the Champs-Elysées before returning to the park.

Your main obstacle when riding this route will be pedestrian

Paris for Early Birds and Night Owls

Many major sights in Paris are open between 9:00 and 18:00, but some open even earlier and/or stay open late.

Sights Open Early

Sacré-Cœur: Basilica daily at 6:00 (dome opens at 8:30 May-Sept, 9:00 Oct-April)

St. Sulpice Church: Daily at 7:30

Notre-Dame Cathedral: Mon-Sat at 7:45, Sun at 7:15

Paris *Plages* (Paris Beaches): Mid-July-mid-Aug daily at 8:00

Père Lachaise Cemetery: Mon-Fri at 8:00, Sat at 8:30, Sun at 9:00

Gardens at Versailles: Tue-Sun at 8:00

Sights Open Late

Every night in Paris, at least one sight is open late. Keep in mind that many of them stop admitting visitors well before their posted closing times.

Jacquemart-André Museum: Mon until 20:30 during special exhibits

Gardens at Versailles: April-Oct daily until 20:30 (may close earlier for special events)

Marmottan Museum: Thu until 21:00

Napoleon's Tomb: April-Sept Tue until 21:00

Pompidou Center: Wed-Mon until 21:00, special exhibits until 22:00 and Thu until 23:00

Architecture and Monuments Museum: Thu until 21:00

Jewish Art and History Museum: Wed until 21:00 during special exhibits

Quai Branly: Thu-Sat until 21:00 (gardens until 21:15)

Sainte-Chapelle: Mid-May-mid-Sept Wed until 21:30

Louvre: Wed and Fri until 21:45

Orsay Museum: Thu until 21:45

Sacré-Cœur: Basilica daily until 22:30

Tower at Notre-Dame: July-Aug Fri-Sat until 23:00

Arc de Triomphe: Daily April-Sept until 23:00, Oct-March until 22:30

Paris *Plages* (Paris Beaches): Mid-July-mid-Aug daily until 24:00

Eiffel Tower: Daily mid-June-Aug until 24:45, Sept-mid-June until 23:45

traffic—try to avoid weekends when locals flock to the riverside. Feel free to linger longer when the spirit moves you. Respect one-way bike lanes—travel only in the direction indicated. For information on where to pick up a bike, see page 35. If using a Vélib' bike (explained on page 37), you could do a one-way trip and drop your bike at any rack (you'll find a rack near the Pont de l'Alma bridge, before you reach the tower).

The Route: Find your way to the south side of the Champ de Mars (near Ecole Militaire). Zig-zag your way back and forth across the park for views as you ride toward the river. Brake for *pétanque* games and Eiffel Tower views (prepare to walk the bike through tourist crowds as you approach the tower).

Turn right onto Quai Branly (the street running along the river below the tower) and join the bike lane. Cross Quai Branly at the first traffic light (just after passing the Quai Branly Museum). Ride into the riverside parkway, then drop down the ramp to the riverside promenade (Les Berges du Seine, described on page 66). Take oodles of time to savor the riverside activities, cafés, and people-watching.

Follow the riverside path to its end at the Orsay Museum. Exit up the ramp, then walk your bike across the bridge (Pont Royal) and turn left into the Tuileries Garden (do not ride into the underpass tunnel). You can't ride down the center of the Tuileries, but you can on the elevated section just above the river. On your way down the path, find a good place to park your bike and enjoy a deserved break in a chair by a pond.

Carry your bike down a flight of steps and continue at street level, still hugging the river side of the park. Exit the park through its main exit, cross Place de la Concorde, then ride along the path that leads straight ahead along the Champs-Elysées. Turn left on Avenue Winston Churchill, passing between the Grand Palais and Petit Palais.

Ride back to the river, but do not cross it. Enjoy views of the beautiful Alexandre III Bridge from the riverbank, then reverse about 10 yards to find the bike lane in the parkway and follow it toward the Eiffel Tower. Cross the next bridge (Pont des Invalides), return to the riverside promenade, and pedal back to the Champ de Mars and Eiffel Tower.

▲▲Marmottan Museum (Musée Marmottan Monet)

In this private, intimate, and untouristy museum, you'll find the best collection anywhere of works by Impressionist headliner Claude Monet. Follow Monet's life through more than a hundred works, from simple sketches to the *Impression: Sunrise* painting that gave his artistic movement its start—and a name. The museum also displays some of the enjoyable large-scale canvases featuring the water lilies from his garden at Giverny.

Cost and Hours: €11, not covered by Museum Pass, €18.50 combo-ticket with Monet's garden and house at Giverny (see page 603; lets you skip the line at Giverny); Tue-Sun 10:00-18:00, Thu until 21:00, closed Mon; audioguide-€3, 2 Rue Louis-Boilly, Mo: La Muette, tel. 01 44 96 50 33, www.marmottan.fr.

☐ See the Marmottan Museum Tour chapter.

LEFT BANK

☐ For more information on many of these sights, see the Left Bank Walk and the "Sèvres-Babylone to St. Sulpice" stroll in the Shopping in Paris chapter. My Historic Paris Walk chapter and 🎧 audio tour also dip into the Latin Quarter.

▲Latin Quarter (Quartier Latin)

This Left Bank neighborhood, immediately across the river from Notre-Dame, was the center of Roman Paris. But the Latin Quar-

ter's touristy fame relates to its intriguing, artsy, bohemian character. This was perhaps Europe's leading university district in the Middle Ages, when Latin was the language of higher education. The neighborhood's main boulevards (St. Michel and St. Germain) are lined with cafés—once the haunts of great poets and philosophers, now the hangouts of tired tourists. Though still youthful and artsy, much of this area has become a tourist ghetto filled with cheap North African eateries. Exploring a few blocks up or downriver from here gives you a better chance of feeling the pulse of what survives of Paris' classic Left Bank.

☐ See the Left Bank Walk chapter.

▲▲Cluny Museum (Musée National du Moyen Age)

This treasure trove of Middle Ages (Moyen Age) art fills old Roman baths, offering close-up looks at stained glass, Notre-Dame carvings, fine goldsmithing and jewelry, and rooms of tapestries. The star here is the exquisite series of six Lady and the Unicorn tapestries: A delicate, as-medieval-as-can-be noble lady introduces a delighted unicorn to the senses of taste, hearing, sight, smell, and touch.

Cost and Hours: €8, includes audioguide, free on first Sun of month, covered by Museum Pass (though pass holders pay €1 for audioguide); Wed-Mon 9:15-17:45, closed Tue; near corner of Boulevards St. Michel and St. Germain at 6 Place Paul Painlevé; Mo: Cluny-La Sorbonne, St. Michel, or Odéon; tel. 01 53 73 78 16, www.musee-moyenage.fr.

📖 See the Cluny Museum Tour chapter.

St. Germain-des-Prés

A church was first built on this site in A.D. 558. The church you see today was constructed in 1163 and is all that's left of a once sprawling and influential monastery. The colorful interior reminds us that medieval churches were originally painted in bright colors. The surrounding area hops at night with venerable cafés, fire-eaters, mimes, and scads of artists.

Cost and Hours: Free, daily 8:00-20:00, Mo: St. Germain-des-Prés.

📖 For more on St. Germain-des-Prés, see page 286 of the Left Bank Walk chapter.

▲St. Sulpice Church

For pipe-organ enthusiasts, a visit here is one of Europe's great musical treats. The Grand Orgue at St. Sulpice Church has a rich history, with a succession of 12 world-class organists—including Charles-Marie Widor and Marcel Dupré—that goes back 300 years.

Patterned after St. Paul's Cathedral in London, the church has a Neoclassical arcaded facade and two round towers. Inside, in the first chapel on the right, are three murals of fighting angels by Delacroix: *Jacob Wrestling the Angel, Heliodorus Chased from the Temple,* and *The Archangel Michael* (on the ceiling). The fourth chapel on the right has a statue of Joan of Arc and wall plaques listing hundreds from St. Sulpice's congregation who died during World War I. The north transept wall features an Egyptian-style obelisk used as a gnomon on a sundial. The last chapel before the exit has a display on the Shroud of Turin.

Cost and Hours: Free, daily 7:30-19:30, Mo: St. Sulpice or Mabillon. See www.stsulpice.com for special concerts.

Sunday Organ Recitals: You can hear the organ played at Sunday Mass (10:30-11:30, come appropriately dressed) followed by a high-powered 25-minute recital, usually performed by talented organist Daniel Roth.

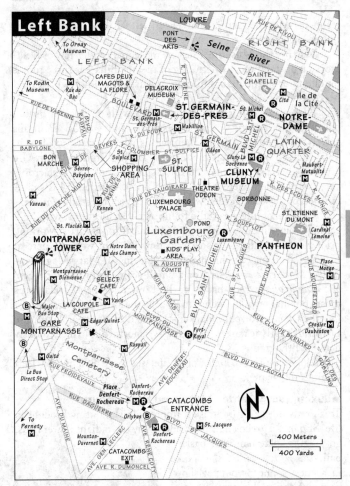

Nearby: Tempting boutiques surround the church (see the Shopping in Paris chapter), and Luxembourg Garden is nearby.

📖 For more on St. Sulpice, see page 287 of the Left Bank Walk chapter.

Delacroix Museum (Musée National Eugène Delacroix)

This museum celebrating the Romantic artist Eugène Delacroix (1798-1863) was once his home and studio. A friend of bohemian artistic greats—including George Sand and Frédéric Chopin—Delacroix is most famous for his monumental flag-waving *Liberty Leading the People* (displayed at the Louvre).

Cost and Hours: €7, free on first Sun of the month, covered by Museum Pass; Wed-Mon 9:30-17:30, closed Tue; 6 Rue de Furstenberg, Mo: St. Germain-des-Prés, tel. 01 44 41 86 50, www. musee-delacroix.fr.

Visiting the Museum: The tiny museum—with a few of Delacroix's paintings and a smattering of memorabilia—is three rooms on one floor in the main building, the artist's studio in back, and his oasis-like garden.

Delacroix's living room is decorated with original furniture, paintings and exotic keepsakes (swords and gourds) from his travels. The bedroom (with fireplace) is where Delacroix died in 1863, nursed by his longtime servant, Lucile Virginie "Jenny" Le Guillou (her portrait may be on display). Look for Delacroix's small worktable (where he kept his paints). Outside is his small-but-peaceful walled garden where you can visit his studio *(atelier)*.

Delacroix built the studio to his own specifications, with high ceilings, big windows, and a skylight, ideal for an artist working prior to electric lights. It's easy to imagine him working here at his easel. You may see his haunting painting of Mary Magdalene (titled *Madeleine au Desert*) or a small-scale study for *The Death of Sardanapalus,* which hangs in the Louvre. Some of Delacroix's most popular works were book illustrations (lithographs for Goethe's *Faust,* Revolutionary history, and Shakespeare). Admire Delacroix's artistic range—from messy, colorful oils to meticulously detailed lithographs.

📖 For more on Delacroix's life, see page 283 in the Left Bank Walk chapter.

▲Luxembourg Garden (Jardin du Luxembourg)

This lovely 60-acre garden is an Impressionist painting brought to life. Slip into a green chair pondside, enjoy the radiant flower beds, go jogging, play tennis or basket-  ball, sail a toy sailboat, or take in a chess game or puppet show. Some of the park's prettiest (and quietest) sections lie around its pe- rimeter. Notice any pigeons? The story goes that a very poor Ernest Hemingway used to hand-hunt (read: strangle) them here.

Cost and Hours: Free, daily dawn until dusk, Mo: Odéon, RER: Luxembourg.

📖 For more on the garden and nearby sights, see page 288 in the Left Bank Walk chapter. Also see the kid-friendly activities in the garden (Paris with Children chapter) and cafés listed in "Les Grands Cafés de Paris" (Eating in Paris chapter).

Other Parks: If you enjoy Luxembourg Garden and want to see more green spaces, you could visit the more elegant **Parc**

Monceau (Mo: Monceau), the colorful **Jardin des Plantes** (Mo: Jussieu or Gare d'Austerlitz, RER: Gare d'Austerlitz), or the hilly and bigger **Parc des Buttes-Chaumont** (Mo: Buttes-Chaumont).

▲Panthéon

This state-capitol-style Neoclassical monument celebrates France's illustrious history and people, balances a Foucault pendulum, and is the final home of many French VIPs.

In 1744, an ailing King Louis XV was miraculously healed by St. Geneviève, the city's patron saint, and he thanked her by replacing her ruined church with a more fitting tribute. By the time the church was completed (1791), however, the secular-minded Revolution was in full swing, and the church was converted into a nonreligious mausoleum honoring the "Champions of French liberty": Voltaire, Rousseau, Descartes, and others. On the entrance pediment (inspired by the ancient Pantheon in Rome), the Revolutionaries carved the inscription, "To the great men of the Fatherland."

Cost and Hours: €8.50, free for those under age 18, covered by Museum Pass, €2 for dome climb (not covered by Museum Pass); daily 10:00-18:30, Oct-March until 18:00, last entry 45 minutes before closing; audioguide-€5, Mo: Cardinal Lemoine, tel. 01 44 32 18 00, http://pantheon.monuments-nationaux.fr.

Dome Climb: From the main floor, you can climb 206 steps to the colonnade at the base of the dome for views of the interior and a 360-degree view of the city. You're not so much high above Paris—it feels like you're in the middle of it. To visit, join the queue at the meeting spot near the nave. An escort takes groups of about 50 at a time. Visits leave about every hour until 17:30 (or earlier—confirm the schedule as you go in) and take 40 minutes.

❷ Self-Guided Tour: Stand in the **❶ nave** and take in the vast, evenly lit space—360 feet long, 280 feet wide, and 270 feet high. On the left wall, find the mural of **St. Geneviève** dressed in white, saving the fledgling city from Attila the Hun, the event that marks the birth of an independent Paris. When Geneviève died (A.D. 512), she was buried here atop what was at the time the city's highest hill (elevation 200 feet). When Louis XV rebuilt her

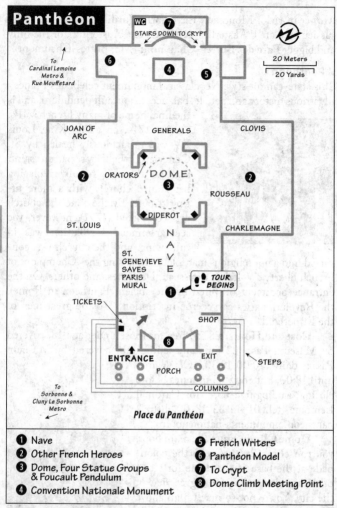

Panthéon

- **1** Nave
- **2** Other French Heroes
- **3** Dome, Four Statue Groups & Foucault Pendulum
- **4** Convention Nationale Monument
- **5** French Writers
- **6** Panthéon Model
- **7** To Crypt
- **8** Dome Climb Meeting Point

church to make the domed structure we see today (1791), her relics were placed directly beneath the dome. Even when Revolutionaries stripped the church of Christian elements and publicly burned Geneviève's relics, the French still honored Geneviève as their champion. You can see Geneviève immortalized high in the frescoed dome and in the mosaic over the altar wall—always depicted as the lady in white.

The Panthéon's murals also honor **2** other French heroes. In the right transept (left wall) is Clovis, the father of the Franks and contemporary of Geneviève. He's the guy in winged helmet and Asterix-style mustache amid the chaos of battle, having a vision of Christ that leads him to victory. In the next panel, he kneels to be baptized a Christian (and was subsequently buried here on Geneviève's hill). On the opposite wall is Charlemagne being crowned Emperor of the Franks (c. 800), marking the symbolic birth of France. In the left transept are scenes of Joan of Arc, who rallied the French in the 1420s to rid the country of the English.

The 15,000-ton ❸ **dome** is made of a core of iron ribs covered with stone. Under the dome stand **four statue groups,** marking

the next phase of French history, the Revolution. The most striking statue (of a bold, forward-facing woman) is dedicated to Denis Diderot, whose *Encyclopédie* championed secular knowledge. Jean-Jacques Rousseau (find his portrait in the low-profile round relief on the base) promoted the idea of a social contract between government and the people. The statue of men in business suits depicts the orators and bureaucrats who served the state. Finally, there are the generals, including Napoleon on horseback.

A **Foucault pendulum** swings gracefully at the end of a cable suspended from the towering dome. It was here in 1851 that the scientist Léon Foucault first demonstrated the rotation of the earth. The great length of the cable (220 feet) produces a slow enough oscillation to make the rotation more obvious. Stand a few minutes and watch the pendulum's arc (appear to) shift as you and the earth rotate beneath it. (It's easier to visualize if you picture the pendulum suspended directly above the North Pole, with the earth spinning beneath it. Every time the pendulum swings back to the same spot, the earth will have shifted. If there was a bowling pin on the earth, the pendulum would eventually knock it over.) The pendulum can also be used to tell time: Check your watch against the 24-hour dial that surrounds the pendulum.

At the altar end of the church stands the massive ❹ **Convention Nationale Monument.** "Marianne," the fictional woman who symbolized the Revolution, stands in the center, flanked by soldiers who fight for her and citizens who pledge allegiance to her. The inscription below reads "Live free or die." Marianne embodies liberty, reason, and the nation of France. Above her is a mosaic in which Christ (accompanied by Geneviève and Joan of Arc) seems to give his blessing. From Geneviève to Joan of Arc to Marianne, France has always incarnated its national spirit in the female form.

To the right of the monument, ❺ **French writers** have their names inscribed onto the walls.

To the left of the monument is a room displaying a ❻ **model of the Panthéon.** This cross-section model allows you to look inside and see the structural elements. The dome is actually made of three

SIGHTS

domes-within-a-dome, and it's supported by flying buttresses. Also, notice that there's no patriotic inscription over the entrance, as the model was built before the Revolution.

A staircase behind the monument leads down to the ❼ **crypt,** where a panoply of greats is buried. Rousseau is along the right wall as you enter, while Voltaire faces him impishly from across the hall. A little farther on the left is Soufflot, the architect who built the Panthéon, and Marat, the Revolutionary murdered in his bathtub. From the small central rotunda, straight ahead are more greats: Victor Hugo *(Les Misérables, The Hunchback of Notre-Dame),* Alexandre Dumas *(The Three Musketeers, The Count of Monte Cristo),* and Louis Braille, who invented the script for the blind. To the right of the central rotunda you'll find scientist Marie Curie (follow the glow), and various WWII dead, from Holocaust victims to the hero of the resistance, Jean Moulin. This building is truly a pantheon of all those who've forged France's freedom and defended freedom of thought.

From here, if you're planning to do the ❽ **dome climb,** return to the entrance and find the meeting point.

Montparnasse Tower

This sadly out-of-place 59-story superscraper has one virtue: If you can't make it up the Eiffel Tower, the sensational views from this tower are cheaper, far easier to access, and make for a fair consolation prize. Come early in the day for clearest skies and shortest lines, and be treated to views from a comfortable interior and from up on the rooftop (consider their €5 breakfast with a view). Sunset is great but views are disappointing after dark. Some say it's the very best view in Paris, as you can see the Eiffel Tower clearly...and you can't see the Montparnasse Tower at all.

Cost and Hours: €16, 30 percent discount with this book, not covered by Museum Pass; daily 9:30-23:30, Oct-March until 22:30; entrance on Rue de l'Arrivée, Mo: Montparnasse-Bienvenüe—from the Métro, stay inside the station and follow sparse Tour signs to exit #4; tel. 01 45 38 52 56, www.tourmontparnasse56.com.

Visiting the Tower: Find the view elevator entrance near the skyscraper's main entry (under the awning marked *Panoramique*). Exit the elevator at the 56th floor, passing the eager photographer (they'll superimpose your group's image with the view). Here you can marvel at the views of *tout Paris* (good even if cloudy), have a drink or a light lunch (reasonable prices), and peruse the gift shop. Take time to explore every corner of the floor. Exhibits identify highlights of the star-studded vista. Many find the view from this level better than from the 59th floor, as there are no railings blocking the sightlines.

Next, climb three flights of steps (behind the photogra-

pher) to the open terrace on the 59th floor to enjoy magnificent views in all directions (and a surprise champagne bar). Here, 690 feet above Paris, you can scan the city through glass panels that limit wind. The view over Luxembourg Garden is terrific, as is the view up the Champ de Mars to the Eiffel Tower. Montparnasse Cemetery is right below, and the high-rise suburbs lie immediately to the west. From this vantage, it's easy to admire Baron Georges-Eugène Haussmann's grand-boulevard scheme (see sidebar on page 89). Notice the lush courtyards hiding behind grand street fronts.

SIGHTS

Sightseeing Tip: The tower is an efficient stop when combined with a day trip to Chartres, which begins at the Montparnasse train station (see the Chartres chapter for details).

▲Catacombs

Descend 60 feet below the street and walk a one-mile (one-hour) route through tunnels containing the anonymous bones of six million permanent Parisians.

In 1786, health-conscious Parisians looking to relieve congestion and improve the city's sanitary conditions emptied the church cemeteries and moved the bones here, to former limestone quarries. For decades, priests led ceremonial processions of black-veiled, bone-laden carts into the quarries, where the bones were stacked in piles five feet high and as much as 80 feet deep. Descend 130 steps and ponder the sign announcing, "Halt, this is the empire of the dead." Shuffle through passageways of skull-studded tibiae, admire 300-year-old sculptures cut into the walls of the catacombs, and see more cheery signs: "Happy is he who is forever faced with the hour of his death and prepares himself for the end every day." Then climb 86 steps to emerge far from where you entered, with white-limestone-covered toes, telling everyone you've been underground gawking at bones. Note to wannabe Hamlets: An attendant checks your bag at the exit for stolen souvenirs.

Cost and Hours: €12, not covered by Museum Pass, Tue-Sun 10:00-20:30, closed Mon; lines can be long, between 10:00 and 16:00; arrive by 9:30 to minimize the wait; ticket booth closes at 19:30, come no later than 19:00 or risk not getting in; audioguide—€5, tel. 01 43 22 47 63, www.catacombes.paris.fr.

Getting There: 1 Place Denfert-Rochereau. Take the Métro to Denfert-Rochereau, then find the lion in the big traffic circle; if he looked left rather than right, he'd stare right at the green entrance to the Catacombs.

After Your Visit: You'll likely exit at 36 Rue Rémy Dumoncel, far from where you started (though this may change in 2017). Turn right out of the exit and walk to Avenue du Général Leclerc, where you'll be equidistant from Métro stops Alésia (walk left) and Mouton Duvernet (walk right). Traffic-free Rue Daguerre, a pleasing pedestrian street (see the Shopping in Paris chapter), is four blocks to the right on Avenue du Général Leclerc (a block from where you entered the Catacombs).

CHAMPS-ELYSEES AND NEARBY
▲▲▲Champs-Elysées

This famous boulevard is Paris' backbone, with its greatest concentration of traffic. From the Arc de Triomphe down Avenue des Champs-Elysées, all of France seems to converge on Place de la Concorde, the city's largest square. And though the Champs-Elysées has become as international as it is Parisian, a walk here is still a must.

To reach the top of the Champs-Elysées, take the Métro to the Arc de Triomphe (Mo: Charles de Gaulle-Etoile), then saunter down the grand boulevard (Métro stops every few blocks, including George V and Franklin D. Roosevelt).

📖 See the Champs-Elysées Walk chapter.

▲▲Arc de Triomphe

Napoleon had the magnificent Arc de Triomphe commissioned to commemorate his victory at the 1805 battle of Austerlitz. The foot of the arch is a stage on which the last two centuries of Parisian history have played out—from the funeral of Napoleon to the goose-stepping arrival of the Nazis to the triumphant return of Charles de Gaulle after the Allied liberation. Examine the carvings on the pillars, featuring a mighty Napoleon and excitable Lady Liberty. Pay your respects at the Tomb of the Unknown Soldier. Then climb the 284 steps to the observation deck up top, with sweeping skyline panoramas and a mesmerizing view down onto the traffic that swirls around the arch.

Cost and Hours: Free and always viewable; steps to rooftop—€9.50, free for those under age 18, free on first Sun of month Oct-March, covered by Museum Pass; daily 10:00-23:00, Oct-March until 22:30, last entry 45 minutes before closing; lines are slow—see page 299 for advice; Place Charles de Gaulle, use underpass to reach arch, Mo: Charles de Gaulle-Etoile, tel. 01 55 37 73 77, www.paris-arc-de-triomphe.fr.

📖 See the Champs-Elysées Walk chapter.

▲Petit Palais (and the Musée des Beaux-Arts)

This free museum displays a broad collection of paintings and sculpture from the 1600s to the 1900s on its ground floor, and

an easy-to-appreciate collection of art from Greek antiquities to Art Nouveau in its basement. Though it houses mostly second-tier art, there are a few diamonds in the rough (including pieces by Rembrandt, Courbet, and Monet). The building itself is impressive, and the museum's classy café merits the detour. If it's raining and your Museum Pass has expired, the Petit Palais is a worthwhile stop.

Cost and Hours: Free, Tue-Sun 10:00-18:00, Fri until 21:00 for special exhibits (fee), closed Mon; audioguide-€5; across from Grand Palais on Avenue Winston Churchill, a looooong block west of Place de la Concorde, Mo: Champs-Elysées Clemenceau; lovely café, tel. 01 53 43 40 00, www.petitpalais.paris.fr.

Visiting the Museum: Enter the museum, ask for a ticket to the permanent collection (free but may be required), and head down the main hall. Soak up turn-of-the-century ambience, with Art Nouveau vases and portraits of well-dressed, belle époque-era Parisians. Find the occasional printed information in English.

Turn right, entering the large painting gallery that features Romantics and Realists from the late 19th century. Midway down the main hall on the left, Courbet's soft-porn *The Sleepers* (*Le Sommeil*, 1866) captures two women nestled in post-climactic bliss. His large, dark *Firefighters (Pompiers courant à un incendie)* is a Realist's take on an everyday scene—firefighters rushing to put out a blaze.

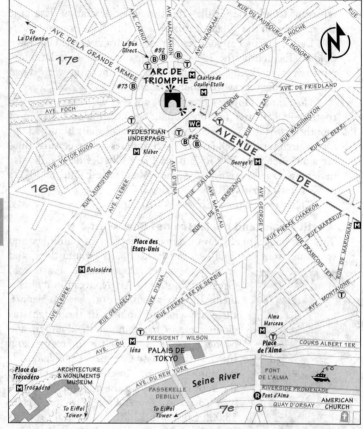

Turning the corner, you'll find artwork by Gustave Doré (1832-1883), best known as the 19th-century's greatest book illustrator. In his enormous *La Vallée de larmes* (1883), Christ and the cross are the only salvation from this "vale of tears."

At the end of the main hall, enter the smaller room to find Claude Monet's *Sunset on the Seine at Lavacourt* (*Soleil couchant sur la Seine a Lavacourt,* 1880). Painted the winter after his wife died, it looks across the river from Monet's home to two lonely boats in the distance, with the hazy town on the far bank. The sun's reflection is a vertical smudge down the water. Nearby are works by Alfred Sisley, the American painter Mary Cassatt, and other Impressionists. Before heading downstairs, check out the side rooms adjoining the large painting gallery, with exquisite furniture in the Louis XIV, XV, and XVI styles.

The museum's basement features a surprising collection of art, from Greek antiquities to Art Nouveau, including paintings by the Dutch masters Rembrandt and Jan Steen.

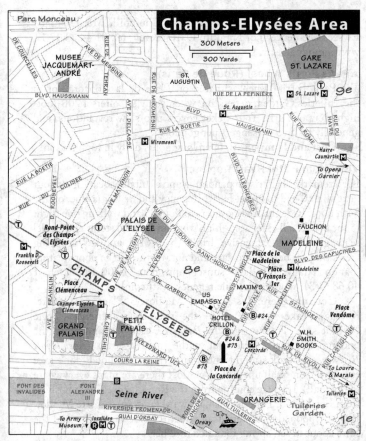

Champs-Elysées Area

Parc Monceau

MUSEE JACQUEMART-ANDRÉ

GARE ST. LAZARE

300 Meters
300 Yards

BLVD. HAUSSMANN

ST. AUGUSTIN

St. Lazare 9e

RUE DE LA PEPINIÈRE

St. Augustin

BLVD

RUE LA BOETIE

HAUSSMANN

Havre-Caumartin

Miromesnil

To Opera Garnier

Rond-Point des Champs-Elysées

PALAIS DE L'ELYSEE

FAUCHON

MADELEINE

Franklin D. Roosevelt

BLVD. DES CAPUCINES

Place de la Madeleine

Madeleine

CHAMPS

8e

Place François 1er

Place Clémenceau

ELYSEES

MAXIM'S

Place Vendôme

Champs-Elysées Clémenceau

US EMBASSY

#24

GRAND PALAIS

PETIT PALAIS

HOTEL CRILLON

W.H. SMITH BOOKS

#24 & #73

Concorde

To Louvre & Marais

COURS LA REINE

#73

Place de la Concorde

Tuileries

PONT DES INVALIDES

PONT ALEXANDRE III

Seine River

RIVERSIDE PROMENADE

ORANGERIE

Tuileries Garden

To Army Museum

Invalides

QUAI D'ORSAY

To Orsay

1e

SIGHTS

Grand Palais

This grand exhibition hall, built for the 1900 World's Fair, is used for temporary exhibits. The building's Industrial Age, erector-set,

iron-and-glass exterior is striking, but the steep entry price is only worthwhile if you're interested in any of the exhibitions currently on view. Many areas are undergoing renovation, which may still be underway during your visit. Get details on the current schedule from a TI, in *Pariscope,* or from the website.

Cost and Hours: Admission prices and hours vary with each exhibition; major exhibitions usually €11-15, not covered by Museum Pass; generally open daily 10:00-20:00, Wed until 22:00, some parts of building closed Mon, other parts closed Tue, closed between exhibitions; Avenue Winston Churchill, Mo: Champs-Elysées Clemenceau or Franklin D. Roosevelt, tel. 01 44 13 17 17, www.grandpalais.fr.

▲Paris Ferris Wheel (Roue de Paris)

The Paris Ferris Wheel, situated on Place de la Concorde or in the Tuileries Garden, depending when you visit, offers a 200-foot-high view of Paris. Your ticket covers two slow revolutions, and generally it's two passengers per gondola.

Cost and Hours: €12, open long hours daily in high season.

View from Hôtel Hyatt Regency

For a remarkable Parisian panorama and a suitable location for your next affair, head to Hôtel Hyatt Regency and its Bar la Vue, on the 34th floor. Ride the free elevators to floor 33 and walk up one flight to the bar. You'll enter a sky-high world of colorful stools and swivel seats, glass walls, expensive drinks (beer-€15), and jaw-dropping views that are best before dark and not worthwhile in poor weather (bar open daily 17:00-late, "sunset happy hour" 17:00-19:00, tel. 01 40 68 51 31, www.parisetoile.regency.hyatt.com).

Getting There: It's at Porte Maillot (3 Place du Général Koenig). Take the Métro to the pedestrian-unfriendly Porte Maillot stop. Follow signs to *Palais des Congrès,* and enter the underground mall, turn right at the small sign for *Hôtel Hyatt Regency,* and walk straight until you arrive at the hotel (don't take escalator from mall up—if you get lost there are maps everywhere in the mall). If you're coming from the Rue Cler area, take RER-C from Invalides or Pont de l'Alma toward Pontoise to Porte Maillot. If you're pooped or strapped for time, the skies are clear, and the sun's about to set, spring for a taxi or Uber.

La Défense and La Grande Arche

Though Paris keeps its historic center classic and skyscraper-free, this district, nicknamed *"le petit Manhattan,"* offers an impressive excursion into a side of Paris few tourists see: that of a modern-day economic superpower. La Défense was first conceived more than 60 years ago as a US-style forest of skyscrapers that would accommodate the business needs of the modern world. Today La Défense is a thriving commercial and shopping center, home to 150,000 employees and 55,000 residents.

For a worthwhile visit, take the Métro to the La Défense Grande Arche stop, follow *Sortie Grande Arche* signs, and climb the steps of La Grande Arche for distant city views. Then stroll about three-quarters of a mile gradually downhill among the glass buildings to the Esplanade de la Défense Métro station, and return home from there. Mall stores are open every day.

Visiting La Défense: The centerpiece of this ambitious complex is the mammoth **La Grande Arche de la Fraternité.** Inaugurated in 1989 on the 200th anniversary of the French Revolution, it was, like the Revolution, dedicated to human rights and brotherhood. The place is big—Notre-Dame Cathedral could fit under its

arch. The four-sided structure sits on enormous underground pillars and is covered with a veneer of beautiful white Carrara marble. The arch is a 38-story office building for 30,000 people on more than 200 acres. The left side houses government ministries, the right side corporate offices, and the top is dedicated to human

rights. The "cloud"—a huge canvas canopy under the arch—is an attempt to cut down on the wind-tunnel effect this gigantic building creates.

Wander behind the arch, past freestanding glass sheets that help to deflect wind, to see an unusual mix of glassy skyscrapers and a cemetery (in the orchard). Study the Le Corbusier-style planning, where motor traffic (the freeway and trains that tunnel underneath) are separated from pedestrian traffic (the skybridges).

Back on the mall side, notice the Arc de Triomphe in the distance, bull's-eye down the Esplanade. La Grande Arche aligns perfectly with the Arc de Triomphe, the Obelisk on Place de la Concorde, and the Arc de Triomphe du Carrousel in front of the Louvre.

Survey the skyscraping scene. La Défense is much more than its eye-catching arch—it's an international power broker. Check out the skyscrapers from left to right: Engie deals in electricity, Areva is a global energy company that is big into nuclear power, and EDF is France's national gas company. Back to the left, that tall brass thing is one of French artist César Baldaccini's famous thumb statues (40 feet high).

Wander down the **Esplanade** (a.k.a. "le Parvis"), back toward the city center (and to the next Métro stop). Take in the monumental structures around you: Les Quatre Temps is a giant shopping mall of 250 stores, and like malls at home, it's a teenage wasteland when school is out and eerily quiet at night.

Facing Les Quatre Temps, the half-dome Center of New Industries and Technologies (better known as CNIT) was built in 1958 and looks like it. It's now a congress center and is a feat of

Best Views over the City of Light

Your trip to Paris is played out in the streets, but the brilliance of the City of Light can only be fully appreciated by rising above it all. Invest time to marvel at all the man-made beauty, seen best in the early morning or around sunset. Many of the viewpoints I've listed are free or covered by the Museum Pass; otherwise, expect to pay €8-15. Here are some prime locations for soaking in the views:

Eiffel Tower: It's hard to find a grander view of Paris than from the tower's second level. Go around sunset and stay after dark to see the tower illuminated; or go in the early morning to avoid the midday haze and crowds (not covered by Museum Pass, see page 61).

Paris Ferris Wheel: The Roue de Paris offers a 200-foot-high view of Paris from Place de la Concorde or the Tuileries Garden (not covered by Museum Pass, high season only, two slow and scenic loops, see page 84).

Arc de Triomphe: Without a doubt, this is the perfect place to see the glamorous Champs-Elysées (if you can manage the 284 steps). It's great during the day, but even greater at night, when the boulevard positively glitters (covered by Museum Pass, see page 80).

Notre-Dame's Tower: This viewpoint is brilliant—it couldn't be more central—but it requires climbing 400 steps and is usually crowded with long lines (try to arrive early or late). Up high on the tower, you'll get an unobstructed view of gargoyles, the river, the Latin Quarter, and the Ile de la Cité (covered by Museum Pass, see page 53).

Steps of Sacré-Cœur: Join the party on Paris' only hilltop. Walk

architecture: It's the largest concrete vault anywhere that rests on only three points. Enter the vault to see a semicircle of dazzling offices and shops that recede as they rise, like the seating in an opera house.

In France, getting a building permit often comes with a requirement to dedicate two percent of the construction cost to art. Hence the Esplanade is a virtual open-air modern art gallery, sporting pieces by Joan Miró (blue, red, and yellow), Alexander Calder (red), and Yaacov Agam (the fountain with colorful stripes and rhythmically dancing spouts), among others. Near Yaacov's fountain, find *La Défense de Paris,* the statue that gave the area its name; it recalls the 1870 Franco-Prussian war—a rare bit of old Paris out here in the 'burbs.

As you descend the Esplanade, notice how the small gardens and *boules* courts (reddish dirt areas) are designed to integrate tra-

uphill, or take the funicular or Montmartrobus, then hunker down on Sacré-Cœur's steps to enjoy the sunset and territorial views over Paris. Stay in Montmartre for dinner, then see the view again after dark (free, see page 101).

Galeries Lafayette or Printemps: Take the escalator to the top floor of either department store (they sit side by side) for a stunning overlook of the old Opéra district (free, see page 467).

Montparnasse Tower: The top of this solitary skyscraper has some of the best views in Paris, though they're too high to be worthwhile after dark. Zip up 56 floors on the elevator, then walk to the rooftop (not covered by Museum Pass, see page 78).

Pompidou Center: Take the escalator up and admire the beautiful cityscape along with the exciting modern art. There may be better views over Paris, but this is the best one from a museum (covered by Museum Pass, see page 99).

Place du Trocadéro: This square, a 20-minute walk from the Eiffel Tower, is *the* place to see the tower. Come for a look at Monsieur Eiffel's festive creation day or night (when the tower is lit up), before or after your tower visit.

Arab World Institute (Institut du Monde Arabe): This building near Ile St. Louis has free, 180-degree views over the river from its roof terrace (Tue-Sun 10:00-18:00, closed Mon, don't wait in special exhibit line—ask for entrance for *"la terrasse,"* 1 Rue des Fossés Saint-Bernard, Place Mohammed V, Mo: Jussieu, www.imarabe.org).

Bar at Hôtel Hyatt Regency: This otherwise unappealing hotel is noteworthy for its razzle-dazzle 34th-floor Bar la Vue, where you can sip wine and enjoy a stunning Parisian panorama (free elevator but pricey drinks, see page 84).

SIGHTS

dition into this celebration of modern commerce. Note also how the buildings tend to decrease in height and increase in age as you approach Paris' center. Your walk ends at the amusing fountain of Bassin Takis, where you'll find the Esplanade de la Défense Métro station that zips you out of all this modernity and directly back into town.

OPERA NEIGHBORHOOD

The glittering Garnier opera house anchors this neighborhood of broad boulevards and grand architecture. This area is also nirvana for high-end shoppers, with the opulent Galeries Lafayette, the delicate Fragonard Perfume Museum, and the sumptuous shops that line Place Vendôme and Place de la Madeleine (see page 471 for my self-guided shopping walk of this area). Key

SIGHTS

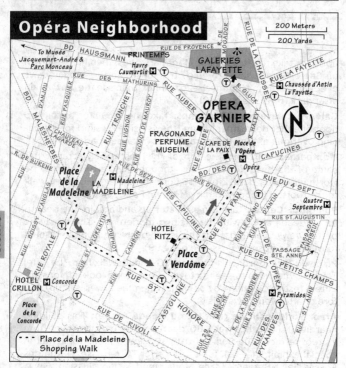

Métro stops include Opéra, Madeleine, and Havre Caumartin (RER: Auber).

▲▲Opéra Garnier
(Opéra National de Paris—Palais Garnier)

A gleaming grand theater of the belle époque, the Palais Garnier was built for Napoleon III and finished in 1875. From Avenue de l'Opéra, once lined with Paris' most fashionable haunts, the facade suggests "all power to the wealthy." In the 1980s, that elitism prompted the call for a new opera house built for the people, and the larger Opéra Bastille was situated symbolically on Place de la Bastille, where the French Revolution started in 1789. The smaller Opéra Garnier is now home to ballet, some opera, and other performances.

To see the interior, you have several choices: Take a guided tour (your best look), tour the public areas on your own (using the audioguide and/or my self-guided tour, below), or attend a performance. Note that the auditorium is sometimes off-limits due to performances and rehearsals. Highlights of the interior include the Grand Staircase, the various chandeliered reception halls, the 2,000-seat auditorium, and a few exhibits on the building and opera.

Baron Georges-Eugène Haussmann
(1809-1891)

The elegantly uniform streets that make Paris so Parisian are the work of Baron Haussmann, who oversaw the modernization of the city in the mid-19th century. He cleared out the cramped, higgledy-piggledy, unhygienic medieval cityscape and replaced it with broad, straight boulevards lined with stately buildings and linked by modern train stations.

The quintessential view of Haussmann's work is from the pedestrian island immediately in front of the Opéra Garnier. You're surrounded by Paris circa 1870, when it was the capital of the world. Gaze down the surrounding boulevards to find the column of Place Vendôme in one direction, and the Louvre in another. Haussmann's uniform, cohesive buildings are all five stories tall, with angled, black slate roofs and formal facades. The balconies on the second and fifth floors match those of their neighbors, creating strong lines of perspective as the buildings stretch down the boulevard.

But there was more than aesthetics to the plan. In pre-Haussmann Paris, angry rioters would take to the narrow streets, setting up barricades to hold back government forces (as made famous in Victor Hugo's *Les Misérables*). With Haussmann's new design, government troops could circulate easily and fire cannons down the long, straight boulevards. A whiff of "grapeshot"—chains, nails, and other buckshot-type shrapnel—could clear out any revolutionaries in a hurry.

The 19th century was a great time to be wealthy, thanks to the city's fancy covered market halls, civilized sidewalks, and even elevators. With the coming of elevators, the wealthy took the higher floors and enjoyed the view.

SIGHTS

Cost and Hours: €11, not covered by Museum Pass, generally daily 10:00-16:30, mid-July-Aug until 18:00, 8 Rue Scribe, Mo: Opéra, RER: Auber, www.operadeparis.fr/en/visits/palais-garnier.

Tours: The €5 audioguide gives a good self-guided tour. Guided tours in English run at 11:30 and 14:30 July-Aug daily, Sept-June Wed, Sat, and Sun only—call to confirm schedule (€14.50, includes entry, 1.5 hours, tel. 01 40 01 17 89 or 08 25 05 44 05).

Ballet and Concert Tickets: To find out about upcoming performances, ask for a schedule at the information booth, consult *Pariscope* magazine (see page 488), or look on the Paris Opera website (www.operadeparis.fr). There are usually no performances mid-July-mid-Sept. It's easiest to reserve online. To buy tickets by phone, call 08 92 89 90 90 (toll call) within France or 01 71 25 24 23 from outside France (office closed Sun). You can also go directly to the ticket office (open Mon-Sat 11:30–18:30 and an hour before the show, closed Sun).

⊃ Self-Guided Tour: For the best exterior view, stand in front of the Opéra Métro stop. (To better understand what you're seeing, read the "Baron Georges-Eugène Haussmann" sidebar on page 89.) The building is huge. Its massive foundations straddle an underground lake (inspiring the mysterious world of *The Phantom of the Opera*). It's the masterpiece of architect Charles Garnier, who oversaw every element, from laying the foundations to what color the wallpaper should be. His cohesive design was so admired that the building came to be known as the Palais Garnier.

Take in the ❶ **facade.** Garnier's classically inspired facade is a celebration of opera—the art form that combines all the arts. Atop the green dome, a shimmering Apollo, the God of Music, holds aloft his shining bronze lyre, as if to declare, "This is a temple of the highest arts." (You'll see lyres and Apollos all over the building, outside and in.) Running across the middle of the facade are (smallish) bronze busts of famous composers. The medallions with "E" and "N" honor the Emperor Napoleon III. On the lower right (second statue from the right) is a copy of the well-known *Dance* by Carpeaux (whose original is in the Orsay).

The ❷ **tourist entrance** is around the left side of the building, between the two curved ramps. In fact, this was once the rich patrons' entrance, as they could drive their carriages right up the ramps and slip in, away from the riff-raff. Before the entrance stands a bust of Garnier and a bronze plaque showing the building's footprint. Find the horseshoe-shaped seating area (in the center), the rectangular stage (to the left), and the rectangular Grand Staircase (to the right). Notice how little space was given to the seating area itself—the public spaces were paramount.

Enter, buy your ticket, and make your way (up a small curving staircase) to the foot of the ❸ **Grand Staircase.** Gaze up into this vast hall, where the whole building is united by the set of stairs that branches into a Y midway up. Take in the columns, statues, railings, lanterns, chandeliers, and the different colors of marble, as your eye goes up to a ceiling fresco featuring Apollo. Check out the Grand Staircase from all angles: from the bottom looking up, from the landing as you ascend, and looking back from above. This staircase was the Opera House's real "stage," for the evening's real show: the grand spectacle of elite Parisians—out to see and be seen—strutting their elegant stuff. Mentally populate the space with *fin de siècle* ladies in flowing satin gowns and white-gloved gentlemen in top hats and tuxes.

Ascend to the top of the stairs, where you'll find the numbered doors of the ❹ **box seats.** These were where the rich people watched the opera. Before entering, note the busts between the boxes,

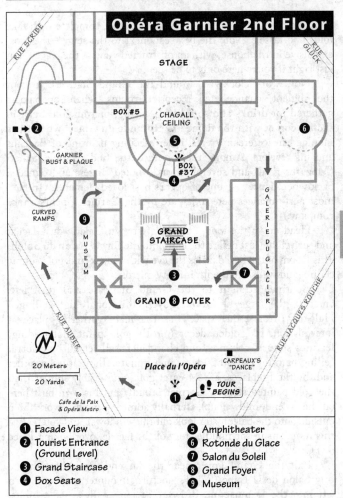

Opéra Garnier 2nd Floor

RUE SCRIBE

RUE GLUCK

STAGE

BOX #5

CHAGALL CEILING

5

2

GARNIER BUST & PLAQUE

BOX #37

4

6

CURVED RAMPS

9

MUSEUM

GALERIE DU GLACIER

GRAND STAIRCASE

3

7

GRAND **8** FOYER

RUE AUBER

RUE JACQUES ROUCHE

20 Meters

20 Yards

CARPEAUX'S "DANCE"

Place du l'Opéra

TOUR BEGINS

1

To Cafe de la Paix & Opéra Metro

SIGHTS

1 Facade View
2 Tourist Entrance (Ground Level)
3 Grand Staircase
4 Box Seats

5 Amphitheater
6 Rotonde du Glace
7 Salon du Soleil
8 Grand Foyer
9 Museum

honoring great librettists, set designers, dancers, and composers, like Hector Berlioz (near box #37). The famous box #5 (around the left) honors the (fictional) Phantom of the Opera, who always sat here. The novel and musical are based on two historical facts: the building's underground cistern, and a real incident in which the chandelier fell and killed someone.

Now enter an open box and take in the view of the **5** **amphitheater.** The red-velvet performance hall seats 2,000. Admire Marc Chagall's colorful ceiling (1964) playfully dancing around the seven-ton chandelier. If Chagall's modern depiction of famous operas feels out of place, we'll soon see the original painting it replaced. The stage curtain is made of canvas, painted to look like...a curtain, seemingly made of velvet, complete with fake folds and tassels. Note the box seats next to the stage—the most expensive in the house, with an obstructed view of the stage—but just right if you're here only to be seen.

Now work clockwise around the Grand Staircase to tour the opulent, chandeliered reception rooms, where operagoers gathered for drinks and socializing during intermission. Start in the far corner with the domed ❻ **Rotonde du Glace,** where they indulged in ice cream treats under a ceiling painting of Bacchus and his revelers. Among the room's busts, find Antonio Salieri (Mozart's rival) and several "divas"—noted singers and dancers, back when dance was one of opera's best-loved elements. (In fact, most performances here today are by the Garnier Opéra's dance company.)

Head down the long, chandelier-strewn Galerie du Glacier, and turn right (just before the end) into the tiny ❼ **Salon du Soleil.** This Room of the Sun dazzles the eye with a black-and-gold sunray ceiling and walls fitted with infinity mirrors.

Continue straight to the Grand Staircase and turn left, entering the large ❽ **Grand Foyer.** This long, high-ceilinged Hall-of-Mirrors-esque space was the main gathering place at intermission. Its golden decor (mostly gold paint, not gilding) features statues, columns, and chandeliers, all set off by colorful ceiling paintings. Find 20 lyres in a minute. The statues at either end, by the fireplaces, are 24-carat gold, and visibly shinier than the gold-painted statues. Garnier proudly put his own bust here (at the far end, midway up), eternally admiring his fine work. Step outside onto the balcony (or look out the windows), and you realize this room sits in the middle story of the facade, overlooking Place de l'Opéra.

Exit the Grand Foyer near the far end, pass through the tiny Salon de la Lune (Soleil's nocturnal counterpart), and turn left into the ❾ **museum.** Browse the long hallway of exhibits, seeing a cutaway model of the stage (with two subterranean levels below and elaborate pulleys above) and many paintings of famous singers, dancers, composers, and set designers. Near the far end is a round gold-framed work depicting the original ceiling painting that graced the auditorium before Chagall came along. Muses spin and cavort among the fluffy clouds of heaven. The museum leads into the library, with dioramas of set designs for famous operas, including *Faust,* by Paris's hometown boy Charles Gounod.

Head downstairs (where there are often other exhibits), and enjoy one more view from the foot of the Grand Staircase.

Nearby: Across the street, the illustrious Café de la Paix has been a meeting spot for the local glitterati for generations. If you can afford the coffee, this spot offers a delightful break.

Fragonard Perfume Museum

Near Opéra Garnier, this perfume shop masquerades as a museum. Housed in a beautiful 19th-century mansion, it's the best-smelling museum in Paris—and you'll learn a little about how perfume is made, too (ask for the English handout).

Cost and Hours: Free, daily 9:00-17:30, 9 Rue Scribe, Mo: Opéra, RER: Auber, tel. 01 47 42 04 56, http://nouveaumuseefragonard.com.

High-End Shopping

The upscale Opéra neighborhood hosts some of Paris' best shopping. Even window shoppers can appreciate this as a ▲ "sight." Just behind the Opéra, the **Galeries Lafayette** department store is a magnificent cathedral to consumerism, under a stunning stained-glass dome (for more, see page 467 of the Shopping in Paris chapter). The area between **Place de la Madeleine,** dominated by the Madeleine Church (looking like a Roman temple), and the octagonal **Place Vendôme,** is filled with pricey shops and boutiques, giving travelers a whiff of the exclusive side of Paris (for a boutique-to-boutique stroll through this area, see page 471).

▲▲Jacquemart-André Museum (Musée Jacquemart-André)

This thoroughly enjoyable museum-mansion (with an elegant café) showcases the lavish home of a wealthy, art-loving, 19th-century Parisian couple. After visiting the Opéra Garnier and wandering Paris' grand boulevards, get inside for an intimate look at the lifestyles of the Parisian rich and fabulous. Edouard André and his wife Nélie Jacquemart—who had no children—spent their lives and fortunes designing, building, and then decorating this sumptuous mansion. What makes the visit so rewarding is the excellent audioguide tour (included with admission, plan on spending an hour with the audioguide). The place is strewn with paintings by Rembrandt, Botticelli, Uccello, Mantegna, Bellini, Boucher, and Fragonard. Though there are no must-see masterpieces, the art gathered here would still be enough to make any gallery famous.

Cost and Hours: €12, includes audioguide, not covered by Museum Pass; daily 10:00-18:00, Mon until 20:30 during special exhibits (which are common); can avoid lines (worst during the first week of special exhibits and weekends generally) by purchasing tickets online (€2 fee), 158 Boulevard Haussmann, Mo: St. Philippe-du-Roule, bus #80 connects conveniently with Ecole Militaire; tel. 01 45 62 11 59, www.musee-jacquemart-andre.com.

Visiting the Museum: While you follow the audioguide, keep an eye out for these highlights.

The **Antechamber** introduces you to the museum's winning formula: opulent decor (chandeliers, red velvet walls, gilded trim)

+ semi-famous paintings (two Boucher nudes and two Canaletto scenes of Venice) + the lifestyle of Edouard and Nélie (who received visitors here) = an immersive aesthetic experience. Next, you enter the Versailles-like **Grand Salon,** the central focus for their parties, with a guest list of up to 1,000.

After passing through several rooms of Edouard's collection of beautiful things—furniture, tapestries, exotic curios, and Tiepolo paintings on the ceiling—you'll reach the **Library,** displaying portraits by Rembrandt, Hals, and Van Dyck, and Rembrandt's *Supper at Emmaus.*

Backtracking, you reach the spacious **Music Room,** used for candlelit parties and concerts. (The band was perched on the balconies above, so the music seemed to waft down from heaven.) Find the bronze bust of Edouard, age 57, done by his wife, Nélie. They'd met when he hired her to do his portrait. The **Winter Room** is fitted with skylights and exotic plants, to brighten a sunny day. It leads into the **Smoking Room,** the belle époque man cave.

Upstairs, you enter the world of Italian art. You pass a mural by Tiepolo and enter the **Studio,** which Edouard made for his artist wife to work in. Among the many (minor) sculptures displayed now, locate Luca della Robbia's ceramic Madonna and Donatello's small bronze torchbearer. The **Florentine and Venetian Painting Rooms** have Botticelli's *Virgin and Child,* a Giovanni Bellini *Madonna,* Mantegna's *Ecce Homo,* and works by Uccello, Guardi, and Carpaccio.

Downstairs is the couple's **Private Apartments.** They kept separate bedrooms (one for "Madame," one for "Monsieur") but met in the room in between for breakfast. There you'll see the portrait that Nélie painted of Edouard when they first met—the spark that brought about their marriage, their mutual passion for art, and eventually the Jacquemart-André Museum.

After Your Visit: Consider a break in the sumptuous museum tearoom, with delicious cakes and tea (daily 11:45-17:30). From here walk north on Rue de Courcelles to see Paris' most beautiful park, Parc Monceau.

MARAIS NEIGHBORHOOD AND NEARBY

The Marais neighborhood extends along the Right Bank of the Seine, from the Bastille to the Pompidou Center. The main east-west axis is formed by Rue St. Antoine, Rue des Rosiers (the heart of Paris' Jewish community), and Rue Ste. Croix de la Bretonnerie. The centerpiece of the neighborhood is the stately Place des Vosges. Helpful Métro stops are Bastille, St-Paul, and Hôtel de Ville.

Don't waste time looking for the Bastille, the prison of Revolution fame. It's Paris' most famous non-sight. The building is long gone, and just the square remains, good only for its nightlife and as a jumping-off point for the Marais Walk or a stroll through Promenade Plantée Park.

☐ The Marais Walk chapter connects the following sights with a fun, fact-filled stroll from Bastille to the Pompidou.

▲Carnavalet Museum (Musée Carnavalet)

The tumultuous history of Paris—starring the Revolutionary years—is well portrayed in this converted Marais mansion (at 23 Rue de Sévigné, closed for renovation throughout 2017 and beyond). The museum contains models of medieval Paris, maps of the city over the centuries, paintings of Parisian scenes, French Revolution paraphernalia—including a small guillotine—and fully furnished rooms re-creating life in Paris in different eras.

▲▲Picasso Museum (Musée Picasso)

Whatever you think about Picasso the man, as an artist he was unmatched in the 20th century for his daring and productivity. The Picasso Museum has the world's largest collection of his work— some 400 paintings, sculptures, sketches, and ceramics—spread across five levels of this mansion in the Marais. A visit here walks you through the full range of this complex man's life and art.

Cost and Hours: €11, covered by Museum Pass, free on first Sun of month and for those under age 18 with ID; open Tue–Fri 11:30–18:00 (until 21:00 on third Fri of month), Sat–Sun 9:30–18:00, closed Mon, last entry 45 minutes before closing; videoguide-€4, timed-entry tickets available on museum website but lines generally aren't bad; 5 Rue de Thorigny, Mo: St. Sébastien-Froissart, St-Paul, or Chemin Vert, tel. 01 42 71 25 21, www.musee-picasso.fr.

☐ See the Picasso Museum Tour chapter.

▲Jewish Art and History Museum
(Musée d'Art et Histoire du Judaïsme)

This is a fine museum of historical artifacts and rare ritual objects spanning the Jewish people's long cultural heritage. It emphasizes the cultural unity maintained by this continually dispersed population. You'll learn about Jewish traditions, and see exquisite costumes and objects central to daily life and religious practices. Be aware that the museum is not ideal for the novice. Some visitors may find the displays beautiful and thought-provoking but not especially meaningful. However, those with a background in Judaism or who take the time with the thoughtful audioguide and information (some but not all posted info is in English) will be rewarded.

Cost and Hours: €9, includes audioguide, covered by Museum Pass; Tue-Fri 11:00-18:00, Sat-Sun 10:00-18:00, open later during special exhibits—Wed until 21:00 and Sat-Sun until 19:00, closed

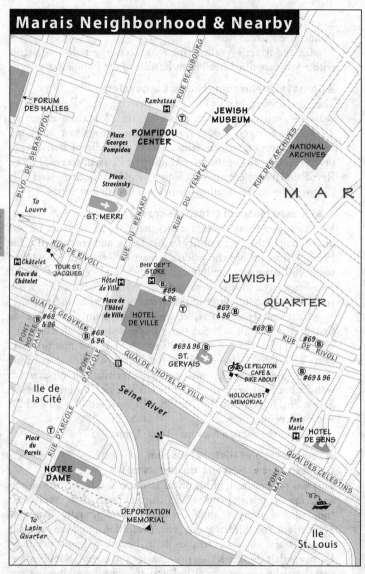

Marais Neighborhood & Nearby

FORUM DES HALLES

Rambuteau

JEWISH MUSEUM

RUE BEAUBOURG

Place Georges Pompidou

POMPIDOU CENTER

NATIONAL ARCHIVES

RUE DES ARCHIVES

BLVD DE SEBASTOPOL

To Louvre

Place Stravinsky

ST. MERRI

RUE DU RENARD

RUE DU TEMPLE

M A R

RUE DE RIVOLI

Châtelet

Place du Châtelet

TOUR ST. JACQUES

Hôtel de Ville

BHV DEP'T STORE

#69 & 96

JEWISH

QUAI DE GESVRES

Place de l'Hôtel de Ville

HOTEL DE VILLE

#69 & 96

#69 & 96

QUARTER

#69 & 96

#69 & 96

PONT NOTRE DAME

#69 & 96

#69 & 96

QUAI DE L'HOTEL DE VILLE

ST. GERVAIS

RUE DE RIVOLI

#69 & 96

PONT D'ARCOLE

Ile de la Cité

Seine River

LE PELOTON CAFÉ & BIKE ABOUT

#69 & 96

HOLOCAUST MEMORIAL

RUE D'ARCOLE

Place du Parvis

NOTRE DAME

Pont Marie

HOTEL DE SENS

QUAI DES CELESTINS

To Latin Quarter

DEPORTATION MEMORIAL

PONT MARIE

Ile St. Louis

Mon year-round, last entry 45 minutes before closing; 71 Rue du Temple, Mo: Rambuteau or Hôtel de Ville a few blocks farther away, RER: Châtelet-Les Halles; tel. 01 53 01 86 60, www.mahj. org.

Visiting the Museum: Before entering, visitors undergo a thorough security check. Once inside, a centuries-old Torah scroll introduces the exhibit. Then (in Room 2) it's the early Middle Ages (A.D. 500-1000), and Judaism is flourishing in France. A row of

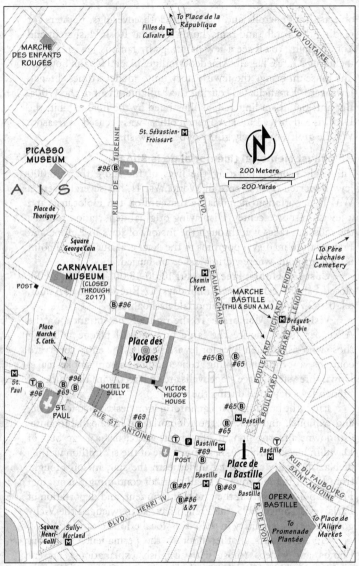

excavated gravestones attests to Jews living peacefully on the Ile de la Cité. Then came the Crusade of 1096 and several centuries of persecution, pogroms, and expulsions under Christian kings like "Saint" Louis IX. Continuing on, you'll see displays on Jewish rituals—getting married under a canopy, menorahs lit during Hanukkah, and gift-giving during Purim. There's a full-size sukkah (tabernacle), a structure for celebrating the harvest festival.

Upstairs, you'll find many exquisite silver-and-jeweled ritual objects: Torah scrolls and their rich cloth coverings, pointers for reading the Torah, and rams' horns blown at Rosh Hashanah and Yom Kippur. You'll see a few paintings by famous Jewish artists, including Marc Chagall, Amedeo Modigliani, and Chaim Soutine. The museum brings the Jewish story up to modern times. French Jews were "Emancipated" during the Enlightenment of the 1700s. But anti-Semitism lingered, as illustrated by the final exhibit: the Dreyfus Affair (c. 1900). A French officer was accused of treason. Was he guilty, or merely guilty of being Jewish?

Holocaust Memorial (Mémorial de la Shoah)

This sight, commemorating the lives of the more than 76,000 Jews deported from France in World War II, has several facets: a WWII deportation memorial, a museum on the Holocaust, and a Jewish resource center. Displaying original deportation records, the museum takes you through the history of Jews in Europe and France, from medieval pogroms to the Nazi era. But its focal point is underground, where victims' ashes are buried.

Cost and Hours: Free, Sun-Fri 10:00-18:00, Thu until 22:00, closed Sat and certain Jewish holidays, 17 Rue Geoffroy l'Asnier, tel. 01 42 77 44 72, www.memorialdelashoah.org.

Visiting the Memorial: To the right of the entrance, on the Allée des Justes, notice the large bronze wall plaque honoring those who risked their lives for Jewish people. The entry courtyard contains a cylinder evoking concentration camp smokestacks. Down three steps, large stone walls are engraved with the names of French Jews deported during the war.

Enter the building (with an information desk, bookstore, café, and exhibits), and pick up the Mémorial de la Shoah brochure. Go downstairs one floor to the crypt, which has a large Star of David in black marble. Ashes from some of the six million victims of Nazi brutality are buried underneath the star, in soil brought from Israel. Behind you is a small corridor containing the original French police files from the arrest, internment, and deportation of Paris' Jews. (Since 1995, the French have acknowledged the Vichy government's complicity in the Nazis' local ethnic cleansing.)

Go downstairs another floor to the permanent exhibition. Photos and videos (most with English explanations) present an introduction to Judaism and the history of Jews in Europe (including pogroms) and in France (including the notorious Dreyfus affair, concerning a Jewish officer unjustly imprisoned for treason). The displays trace the rise of Nazism, the deportations (12,884 Parisians were once rounded up in a single day), the death camps, and the liberation at the end of the war. The moving finale is a brightly lit collage of children lost to the Holocaust.

▲▲Pompidou Center (Centre Pompidou)

One of Europe's greatest collections of far-out modern art is housed in the Musée National d'Art Moderne, on the fourth and fifth

floors of this colorful exoskeletal building. Created ahead of its time, the modern and contemporary art in this collection is still waiting for the world to catch up. After so many Madonnas-and-children, a piano smashed to bits and glued to the wall is refreshing.

The Pompidou Center and the square that fronts it are lively, with lots of people, street theater, and activity inside and out—a perpetual street fair. Kids of any age enjoy the fun, colorful fountain (an homage to composer Igor Stravinsky) next to the Pompidou Center. Ride the escalator for a great city view from the top (ticket or Museum Pass required), and consider eating at the good café.

Cost and Hours: €14, free on first Sun of month, Museum Pass covers permanent collection and escalators to sixth-floor panoramic views (plus occasional special exhibits), €3 View of Paris ticket lets you ride to sixth floor for view but doesn't cover museum entry; permanent collection open Wed-Mon 11:00-21:00, closed Tue, ticket counters close at 20:00; rest of the building open until 22:00 (Thu until 23:00); arrive after 17:00 to avoid crowds (mainly for special exhibits); free "Pompidou Centre" app, café on mezzanine, pricey view restaurant on level 6, Mo: Rambuteau or Hôtel de Ville, tel. 01 44 78 12 33, www.centrepompidou.fr.

📖 See the Pompidou Center Tour chapter.

Promenade Plantée Park (Viaduc des Arts)

This elevated viaduct was once used for train tracks and is now a two-mile-long, narrow garden walk and a pleasing place for a refreshing stroll or run. Botanists appreciate the well-maintained and varying vegetation. From west (near Opéra Bastille) to east, the first half of the path is elevated until the midway point, the pleasant Jardin de Reuilly (a good stopping point for most, near Mo: Dugommier), then it continues at street level—with separate paths for pedestrians and cyclists—out to Paris' ring road, the *périphérique*.

Cost and Hours: Free, opens Mon-Fri at 8:00, Sat-Sun at 9:00, closes at sunset (17:30 in winter, 20:30 in summer). It runs from Place de la Bastille (Mo: Bastille) along Avenue Daumesnil to St. Mandé (Mo: Michel Bizot) or Porte Dorée, passing within a block of Gare de Lyon.

Getting There: To get to the park from Place de la Bastille (exit the Métro following *Sortie Rue de Lyon* signs), walk a looooong block down Rue de Lyon, hugging the Opéra on your left. Find the low-key entry and steps up the red-brick wall a block after the Opéra.

▲Père Lachaise Cemetery (Cimetière du Père Lachaise)

Littered with the tombstones of many of the city's most illustrious dead, this is your best one-stop look at Paris' fascinating, romantic

past residents. More like a small city, the cemetery is big and confusing, but my self-guided tour directs you to the graves of Frédéric Chopin, Molière, Edith Piaf, Oscar Wilde, Gertrude Stein, Jim Morrison, Héloïse and Abélard, and many more.

Cost and Hours: Free, Mon-Fri 8:00-18:00, Sat 8:30-18:00, Sun 9:00-18:00, until 17:30 in winter; two blocks from Mo: Gambetta (do not go to Mo: Père Lachaise) and two blocks from bus #69's last stop (see the Bus #69 Sightseeing Tour chapter); tel. 01 55 25 82 10, searchable map available at unofficial website: www.pere-lachaise.com.

📖 See the Père Lachaise Cemetery Tour chapter.

Victor Hugo's House (Maison Victor Hugo)

France's literary giant lived in this house on Place des Vosges from 1832 to 1848. (Hugo stayed in many places during his life, but he was here the longest.) He moved to this apartment after the

phenomenal success of *The Hunchback of Notre-Dame,* and it was while living here that he wrote much of *Les Misérables* (when he wasn't entertaining Paris' elite). You'll see well-decorated rooms recreating different phases of his life, from his celebrity years, to his 19-year exile during the repressive reign of Napoleon III (Hugo said "When freedom returns, I will return"),

to his final years as a national treasure. Rooms are littered with paintings of Hugo and his family and of some of his most famous character creations. The display cases show personal objects. Posted explanations in English provide sufficient context to grasp the importance of Hugo to France. The €5 audioguide adds greater depth.

Cost and Hours: Free, fee for optional special exhibits, Tue-Sun 10:00-18:00, closed Mon, audioguide-€5, 6 Place des Vosges; Mo: Bastille, St-Paul, or Chemin Vert; tel. 01 42 72 10 16, http://maisonsvictorhugo.paris.fr.

MONTMARTRE

Paris' highest hill, topped by Sacré-Cœur Basilica, is best known as the home of cabaret nightlife and bohemian artists. Struggling painters, poets, dreamers, and drunkards came here for cheap rent, untaxed booze, rustic landscapes, and views of the underwear of high-kicking cancan girls at the Moulin Rouge. These days, the hill is equal parts charm and kitsch—still vaguely village-like but mobbed with tourists and pickpockets on sunny weekends. Come for a bit of history, a getaway from Paris' noisy boulevards, and the view.

📖 Connect the following sights with the Montmartre Walk chapter (to locate the sights, see the map on page 372).

▲▲Sacré-Cœur

You'll spot Sacré-Cœur, the Byzantine-looking white basilica atop Montmartre, from most viewpoints in Paris. Though only 130 years old, it's impressive and iconic, with a climbable dome.

Cost and Hours: Church—free, daily 6:00-22:30; dome—€6, not covered by Museum Pass, daily May-Sept 8:30-20:00, Oct-April 9:00-17:00; tel. 01 53 41 89 00, www.sacre-coeur-montmartre.com.

Getting There: You have several options. You can take the Métro to the Anvers stop (to avoid the stairs up to Sacré-Cœur, use one more Métro ticket and ride up on the funicular). Alternatively, from Place Pigalle, you can take the "Montmartrobus," a city bus that drops you right by Sacré-Cœur (Funiculaire stop, costs one Métro ticket, 4/hour). A taxi from the Seine or the Bastille saves time and avoids sweat (about €15, €20 at night).

📖 See the Montmartre Walk chapter for details.

Nearby: To lose the crowd and feel Montmartre's pulse, explore a few blocks behind Place du Tertre. Go down Rue du Mont Cenis and turn left on Rue Cortot (past the Montmartre Museum). At Rue des Saules take a few steps downhill to see the vineyards that still supply cheap wine. Backtrack up Rue des Saules to the hilltop.

▲Montmartre Museum (Musée de Montmartre)

This 17th-century home recreates the traditional cancan-and-cabaret Montmartre scene, with paintings, posters, photos, music, and memorabilia. It offers the best look at the history of Montmartre and the amazing period from 1870 to 1910 when so much artistic action was percolating in this neighborhood, plus a chance to see the studio of Maurice Utrillo.

Cost and Hours: €9.50, includes good 45-minute audioguide, not covered by Museum Pass, daily 10:00-18:00, Aug-Sept until 19:00, last entry 45 minutes before closing, 12 Rue Cortot, tel. 01 49 25 89 39, www.museedemontmartre.fr.

📖 See the Montmartre Walk chapter for details.

Pigalle

Paris' red light district, the infamous "Pig Alley," is at the foot of Butte Montmartre. *Ooh la la*. It's more racy than dangerous. Walk from Place Pigalle to Place Blanche, teasing desperate barkers and fast-talking temptresses. In bars, a €150 bottle of (what would otherwise be) cheap champagne comes with a friend. Stick to the bigger streets, hang on to your wallet, and exercise good judgment. Cancan can cost a fortune, as can con artists in topless bars. After dark, countless tour buses line the streets, reminding us that tour guides make big bucks by bringing their groups to touristy nightclubs like the famous Moulin Rouge (Mo: Pigalle or Abbesses).

HISTORIC PARIS WALK

Ile de la Cité and the Latin Quarter

Paris has been the cultural capital of Europe for centuries. We'll start where it did, on Ile de la Cité, with a foray onto the Left Bank, on a walk that laces together 80 generations of history—from Celtic fishing village to Roman city, bustling medieval capital, birthplace of the Revolution, bohemian haunt of the 1920s café scene, and the working world of modern Paris. Along the way, we'll step into two of Paris' greatest sights—Notre-Dame and Sainte-Chapelle.

Orientation

Length of This Walk: Allow four hours to do justice to this three-mile walk.

Paris Museum Pass: Several sights on this walk that charge admission are covered by the time- and money-saving Museum Pass (see page 49 for details). On Ile de la Cité, you can buy a pass at the tourist-friendly *tabac*/souvenir store (5 Boulevard du Palais) across the street from the Sainte-Chapelle entrance.

Notre-Dame: Cathedral—free, Mon-Sat 7:45-18:45, Sun 7:15-19:15; **Treasury**—€5, not covered by Museum Pass, Mon-Fri 9:30-18:00, Sat 9:30-18:30, Sun 13:30-18:40; audioguide—€5, free English tours—normally Mon, Tue, and Sat at 14:30, Wed and Thu at 14:00.

The cathedral hosts **Mass** several times daily (early morning, noon, evening), plus Vespers at 17:45. The international Mass is held Sun at 11:30. The **Crown of Thorns** is venerated with a service every first Fri at 15:00. Call or check the website for a full schedule (Mo: Cité, Hôtel de Ville, or St. Michel; tel. 01 42 34 56 10, www.notredamedeparis.fr).

The entrance for Notre-Dame's **tower climb** is outside

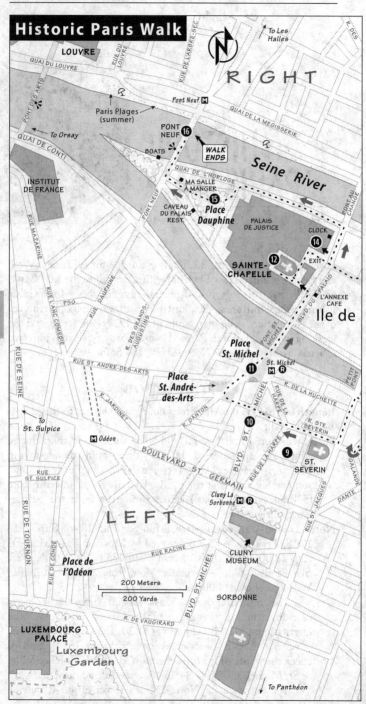

Historic Paris Walk

HISTORIC PARIS

To Les Halles

RIGHT

LOUVRE

QUAI DU LOUVRE

RUE DU LOUVRE

RUE DE L'ARBRE-SEC

R. DES

Pont Neuf Ⓜ

QUAI DE LA MEGISSERIE

PONT DES ARTS

Paris Plages
(summer)

PONT
NEUF ⓰

WALK
ENDS

Seine River

QUAI DE CONTI

To Orsay

BOATS

QUAI DE L'HORLOGE

MA SALLE
A MANGER

PONT AU
CHANGE

INSTITUT
DE FRANCE

PONT NEUF

CAVEAU
DU PALAIS
REST.

Ⓟⓛace Ⓙ
Place Ⓞⓤ
Dauphine

PALAIS
DE JUSTICE

CLOCK

Ⓓ

RUE MAZARINE

RUE DAUPHINE

PSG

R. DES GRANDS-AUGUSTINS

SAINTE-
CHAPELLE

Ⓘ

EXIT

BLVD. DU PALAIS

Ile de

L'ANNEXE
CAFE

RUE DE SEINE

RUE DE L'ANC COMEDIE

RUE ST.ANDRE-DES-ARTS

Place
St. Michel

Ⓘ

Place
St. André-
des-Arts

PONT ST. MICHEL

St. Michel
Ⓜ Ⓡ

R. JARDINET

R. DANTON

Ⓘ

BLVD. ST. MICHEL

RUE DE LA HARPE

R. DE LA HUCHETTE

PETIT PONT

To
St. Sulpice

Ⓜ Odéon

Ⓘ

R. STE.
SEVERIN

RUE DE LA HARPE

Ⓘ

ST.
SEVERIN

RUE ST. JACQUES

PANTE.

GALANDE

BOULEVARD ST. GERMAIN

RUE
ST. SULPICE

RUE DE TOURNON

LEFT

RUE RACINE

Cluny La
Sorbonne
Ⓜ Ⓡ

Place de
l'Odéon

CLUNY
MUSEUM

200 Meters

200 Yards

SORBONNE

RUE DE CONDE

LUXEMBOURG
PALACE

R. DE VAUGIRARD

BLVD. ST.-MICHEL

Luxembourg
Garden

To Panthéon

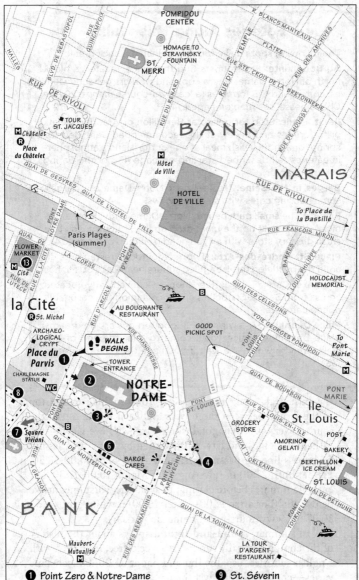

1. Point Zero & Notre-Dame
2. Notre-Dame Interior
3. Notre-Dame Side View
4. Deportation Memorial
5. Ile St. Louis
6. Left Bank Booksellers
7. Medieval Paris: St. Julien-le-Pauvre
8. Shakespeare & Co. Bookstore
9. St. Séverin
10. Boulevard St. Michel
11. Place St. Michel
12. Sainte-Chapelle
13. Cité Métro Stop
14. Conciergerie
15. Place Dauphine
16. Pont Neuf & the Seine

Eateries Along This Walk

The following spots make for a nice lunch or snack break:

Au Bougnante: Few tourists find this place, located a block north of Notre-Dame, where cops and workers get sandwiches, coffee, and €15 *formules* (a.k.a., two-course *menus;* 26 Rue Chanoinesse, see map on page 104).

Ile St. Louis: Stop for gelato at Berthillon or Amorino Gelati, or for crêpes and a view at the recommended Café Med. Or spring for a more lavish meal at one of the island's atmospheric eateries (all described starting on page 438 of the Eating in Paris chapter).

Barges in the Seine: Docked near Notre-Dame are barges, some housing cafés with stunning views.

Picnics: The small park behind Notre-Dame is idyllic for a picnic. A short walk up the main drag on Ile St. Louis leads to a small grocery store with all you need (see map on page 104).

Place St. André-des-Arts: Two nice outdoor restaurants sit amid the bustle on this tree-filled square near Place St. Michel.

L'Annexe Café: This coffee shop is conveniently located across from Sainte-Chapelle's entrance and offers reasonably priced café fare.

Place Dauphine: A few peaceful food refuges are on dreamy Place Dauphine, which you'll come to near the end of this walk—they're worth the wait if you have the time (see page 133).

the cathedral, along the left side. You can hike to the top of the facade between the towers and then to the top of the south tower (400 steps total) for a gargoyle's-eye view of the cathedral, Seine, and city (€10, covered by Museum Pass but no bypass line for passholders; daily April-Sept 10:00-18:30, Fri-Sat until 23:00 in July-Aug, Oct-March 10:00-17:30, last entry 45 minutes before closing; to avoid the worst lines arrive before 10:00 or after 17:00—after 16:00 in winter; tel. 01 53 10 07 00, www.tours-notre-dame-de-paris.fr).

In summer, **sound-and-light displays** about the history of the church generally run twice a week (free, in French with English subtitles, usually Thu and Sat at 21:00, but schedule varies—check cathedral website or call).

Paris Archaeological Crypt: €7, covered by Museum Pass, Tue-Sun 10:00-18:00, closed Mon, enter 100 yards in front of the cathedral, tel. 01 55 42 50 10, www.crypte.paris.fr.

Deportation Memorial: Free, Tue-Sun 10:00-19:00, Oct-March until 17:00, closed Mon year-round, may randomly close at other times, free but boring audioguide, Mo: Cité, tel. 01 46 33 87 56.

Shakespeare and Company Bookstore: Daily 10:00-23:00, 37 Rue de la Bûcherie, across the river from Notre-Dame, Mo: St. Michel, tel. 01 43 25 40 93.

Sainte-Chapelle: €8.50, €13.50 combo-ticket with Conciergerie, free for those under age 18, covered by Museum Pass; daily March-Oct 9:30-18:00, Wed until 21:30 mid-May-mid-Sept, Nov-Feb 9:00-17:00; audioguide-€4.50 (€6 for two), frequent evening concerts—see page 491, 4 Boulevard du Palais, Mo: Cité, tel. 01 53 40 60 80, www.sainte-chapelle.fr.

Expect long lines to get in. First comes the **security line** (all sharp objects and glass are confiscated). No one can skip this line. It can be frustrating, but it's just the way it is. Security lines are shortest first thing (be in line by 9:15, or arrive at 10:00 after the first rush subsides), and on weekends (when the courts are closed). They're longest on Tue and any day around 13:00-14:00 (when staff takes lunch). Once past security, you'll encounter the **ticket-buying line**—those with combo-tickets or Museum Passes *can* skip this queue. (L'Annexe Café, across the street from the main entry, sells cheap coffee to-go—perfect for sipping while you wait in the security line.)

If you visit Sainte-Chapelle near the end of the day, being the last person in the chapel as it closes is an experience you'll never forget.

Conciergerie: €8.50, €13.50 combo-ticket with Sainte-Chapelle, covered by Museum Pass, daily 9:30-18:00, 2 Boulevard du Palais, Mo: Cité, tel. 01 53 40 60 80, www.paris-conciergerie.fr.

Avoiding Crowds: This area is most crowded from midmorning to midafternoon, especially on Tue (when the Louvre is closed). On weekends, Notre-Dame and many sights can be packed (but, conversely, the security line for Sainte-Chapelle is often shorter). Generally, come early in the morning or as late in the day as possible (while still leaving enough time to visit all the sights). The worst bottleneck is at Sainte-Chapelle. To avoid this line, it can be worth rearranging the order in which you take this walk: See Sainte-Chapelle first thing in the morning, then walk over to Notre-Dame (five minutes away) to begin this tour.

Tours: ∩ Download my free Paris Historic Walk audio tour.

Services: A pay WC is in front of Notre-Dame near the statue of Charlemagne. Find other WCs at the Conciergerie and at cafés. A free public Wi-Fi hotspot is in Square Viviani, on the Left Bank.

HISTORIC PARIS

The Walk Begins

• *Start at Notre–Dame Cathedral on the island in the Seine River, the physical and historic bull's-eye of your Paris map. The closest Métro stops are Cité, Hôtel de Ville, and St. Michel, each a short walk away.*

NOTRE-DAME AND NEARBY

• *On the square in front of the cathedral, stand far enough back to take in the whole facade. Find the circular window in the center.*

For centuries, the main figure in the Christian pantheon has been Mary, the mother of Jesus. Catholics petition her in times of trouble to gain comfort, and to ask her to convince God to be compassionate with them. This church is dedicated to "Our Lady" *(Notre Dame),* and there she is, cradling God, right in the heart of the facade, surrounded by the halo of the rose window. Though the church is massive and imposing, it has always stood for the grace and compassion of Mary, the "mother of God."

Imagine the faith of the people who built this cathedral. They broke ground in 1163 with the hope that someday their great-

great-great-great-great-great grandchildren might attend the dedication Mass, which finally took place two centuries later, in 1345. Look up the 200-foot-tall bell towers and imagine a tiny medieval community mustering the money and energy for construction. Master masons supervised, but the people did much of the grunt work themselves for free—hauling the huge stones from distant quarries, digging a 30-foot-deep trench to lay the foundation, and treading like rats on a wheel designed to lift the stones up, one by one. This kind of backbreaking, arduous manual labor created the real hunchbacks of Notre-Dame.

• *"Walk this way" toward the cathedral, and view it from the bronze plaque on the ground (30 yards from the central doorway).*

❶ Point Zero and Notre-Dame

You're standing at the center of France, the point from which all distances are measured. It was also the center of Paris 2,300

years ago, when the Parisii tribe fished where the east-west river crossed a north-south road. The Romans conquered the Parisii and built their Temple of Jupiter where Notre-Dame stands today (52 B.C.). Then as now, the center of religious power faced the center of political power (once the Roman military, today the police station, at the far end of the square). When Rome fell, the Germanic Franks sealed their victory by replacing the temple with the Christian church of St. Etienne in the sixth century. See the outlines of the former church in the pavement (in smaller gray stones), showing what were once walls and columns, angling out from Notre-Dame to Point Zero.

In fact, much of the history of Paris is directly beneath your feet. Two thousand years of dirt and debris have raised the city's altitude. The nearby **Archaeological Crypt** has the remains of the many structures that have stood on this spot in the center of Paris: Roman buildings that surrounded the temple of Jupiter; a wall that didn't keep the Franks out; the main medieval road that once led grandly up the square to Notre-Dame; and even (wow) a 19th-century sewer. The museum entrance is 100 yards in front of Notre-Dame's entrance; for more on the crypt, see the listing on page 53.

The grand equestrian statue (to your right as you face the church) is of Charlemagne ("Charles the Great," 742-814), King

of the Franks, whose reign marked the birth of France as a nation. He briefly united Europe and was crowned the first Holy Roman Emperor in 800, but after his death, the kingdom was divided into what would become modern France and Germany.

Before its renovation 150 years ago, this square was much smaller. The church's huge bell towers rose above a tangle of small, ramshackle medieval buildings, inspiring Victor Hugo's story of a deformed bell-ringer who could look down on all of Paris.

Looking two-thirds of the way up Notre-Dame's left tower, those with binoculars or good eyes can find Paris' most photographed gargoyle (see drawing on next page). Propped on his elbows on the balcony rail, he watches all the tourists in line.

• *Now turn your attention to the rest of the...*

HISTORIC PARIS

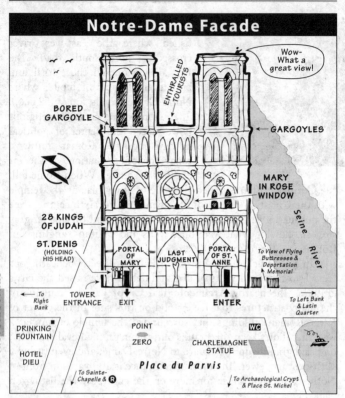

Notre-Dame Facade

• *Look at the left doorway, and to the left of the door, find the statue with his head in his hands.*

St. Denis

The man with the misplaced head is St. Denis, the city's first bishop and patron saint. He stands among statues of other early Christians who helped turn pagan Paris into Christian Paris.

Sometime in the third century, Denis came here from Italy to convert the Parisii. He settled here on the Ile de la Cité, back when there was a Roman temple on this spot and Christianity was suspect. Denis proved so successful at winning converts that the Romans' pagan priests got worried. Denis was beheaded as a warning to those forsaking the Roman gods. But those early Christians were hard to keep down. The man who would become St. Denis got up, tucked his head under his arm, headed north, paused at a fountain to wash it off, and continued until he found just the right place to meet his maker: Montmartre. The Parisians were convinced by this miracle, Christianity gained ground, and a church soon replaced the pagan temple.

Medieval art was OK if it embellished the house of God and told biblical stories. For a fine example, move as close as you can get to the base of the central column (at the foot of Mary, about where the head of St. Denis could spit if he were really good). Working around from the left, find God telling a barely created Eve, "Have fun, but no apples." Next, the sexiest serpent I've ever seen makes apples à la mode. Finally, Adam and Eve, now ashamed of their nakedness, are expelled by an angel. This is a tiny example in a church covered with meaning.

• *Above the central doorway, you'll find scenes from the Last Judgment.*

Central Portal

It's the end of the world, and Christ sits on the throne of judgment (just under the arches, holding both hands up). Beneath him an

angel and a demon weigh souls in the balance; the demon cheats by pressing down. It's a sculptural depiction of the good, the bad, and the ugly. The good souls stand to the left, gazing up to heaven. The bad souls to the right are chained up and led off to a six-hour tour of the Louvre with a lousy guide on a hot summer day. The ugly souls must be the crazy, sculpted demons just below. On the arch to the right, find the flaming cauldron with the sinner diving into it headfirst. The lower panel (beneath the chain of souls) shows angels with trumpets waking the dead from their graves. The souls are from every class of French society—knights, ladies, peasants, clergy, even royalty—reminding all who entered these doors that everyone will be judged. Fortunately, Jesus (who stands below, between the double doors) can lead the way to salvation, along with his 12 apostles—each barefoot and with his ID symbol (such as Peter with his keys).

• *Take 10 big paces back* (un, deux, trois...). *Above the arches is a row of 28 statues, known as...*

The Kings of Judah

In the days of the French Revolution (1789-1799), these biblical kings were mistaken for the hated French kings, and Notre-Dame represented the oppressive Catholic hierarchy. The citizens stormed the church, crying, "Off with their heads!" Plop—they lopped off the crowned heads of these kings with glee, creating a row of St. Denises that weren't repaired for decades.

Paris Through History

250 B.C.: Small fishing village of the Parisii, a Celtic tribe.

52 B.C.: Julius Caesar conquers the Parisii capital of Lutetia (near Paris); Romans replace it with a new capital on the Left Bank.

A.D. 497: Roman Paris falls to the Germanic Franks. King Clovis (482-511) converts to Christianity and makes Paris his capital.

885-886: Paris gets wasted in a siege by Viking Norsemen = Normans.

1163: Notre-Dame cornerstone laid.

c. 1250: Paris is a bustling commercial city with a university and new construction, such as Sainte-Chapelle and Notre-Dame.

c. 1600: King Henry IV beautifies Paris with buildings, roads, bridges, and squares.

c. 1700: Louis XIV makes Versailles his capital. Parisians grumble.

1789: Paris is the heart of France's Revolution, which condemns thousands to the guillotine.

1804: Napoleon Bonaparte crowns himself emperor in a ceremony at Notre-Dame.

1830 & 1848: Parisians take to the streets again in revolutions, fighting the return of royalty.

c. 1860: Napoleon's nephew, Napoleon III, builds Paris' wide boulevards.

1889: The centennial of the Revolution is celebrated with the Eiffel Tower. Paris enjoys wealth and middle-class prosperity in the belle époque (beautiful age).

But the story doesn't end there. A schoolteacher who lived nearby collected the heads and buried them in his backyard for safekeeping. There they slept until 1977, when they were accidentally unearthed. Today, you can stare into the eyes of the original kings in the Cluny Museum, a few blocks away (see page 291).

• *Now let's head into the...*

❷ Notre-Dame Interior

• *Enter the church at the right doorway (the line moves quickly) and find a spot where you can view the long, high central aisle. (Be careful: Pickpockets attend church here religiously.)*

Nave

Remove your metaphorical hat and become a simple bareheaded peasant, entering the dim medieval light of the church. Take a minute to let your pupils dilate, then take in the subtle, mysterious light show that God beams through the stained-glass windows. Follow

1920s: After the draining Great War, Paris is a cheap place to live, attracting expatriates such as Ernest Hemingway.

1940-1944: Occupied Paris spends the war years under gray skies and gray Nazi uniforms.

1968: In May, student protests and a general strike bring Paris to a halt.

1981: High-speed rail service (TGV) is inaugurated from Paris to Lyon, starting a trend that would change travel patterns in France (and make it easier for tourists to see more of the country).

1981-1995: Under President François Mitterrand, Paris' cityscape is enriched by the new Louvre Pyramid, Musée d'Orsay, La Grande Arche de la Défense, and Opéra Bastille.

1998: Playing at home, France wins the World Cup in soccer.

2008: All bars, cafés, and restaurants in France become smoke-free, officially ending the era of the smoky Parisian café.

2012: New French President François Hollande moves into Paris' Elysée Palace.

2014: Paris elects its first female mayor, socialist Anne Hidalgo.

2015: Terrorists attack the Paris offices of satirical magazine *Charlie Hebdo.* Free-speech supporters worldwide respond with a slogan of solidarity: *Je suis Charlie.* Another attack in November at the Bataclan Theater and several other locations around the city tests Parisian resolve once again.

2016: Great Britain's vote to leave the European Union (called "Brexit") sends business and political relations between Paris and London into a state of anxious uncertainty.

the slender columns up 10 stories to the praying-hands arches of the ceiling, and contemplate the heavens. Let's say it's dedication day for this great stone wonder. The priest intones the words of the Mass that echo through the hall: *Terribilis est locus iste...*"This place is *terribilis,*" meaning awe-inspiring or even terrifying. It's a huge, dark, earthly cavern lit with an unearthly light.

This is Gothic. Taller and filled with light, Notre-Dame was a major improvement over the earlier Romanesque style. Gothic architects needed only a few structural columns, topped by crisscrossing pointed arches, to support the weight of the roof. This let them build higher than ever, freeing up the walls for windows.

Notre-Dame has the typical basilica floor plan shared by so many Catholic churches: a long central nave lined with columns and

Notre-Dame Interior

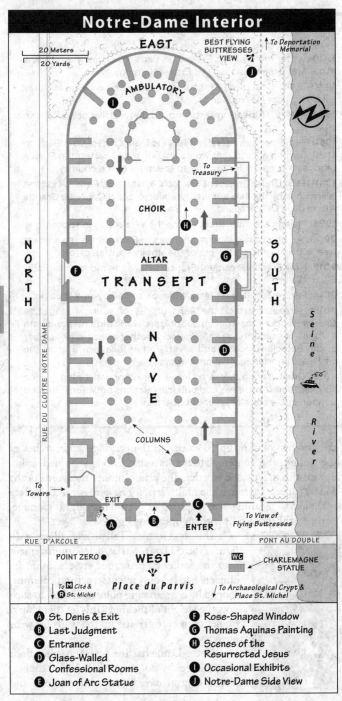

EAST

20 Meters
20 Yards

BEST FLYING BUTTRESSES VIEW **J**

↑ To Deportation Memorial

AMBULATORY

I

To Treasury

CHOIR

H

ALTAR

T R A N S E P T

G

E

F

D

N O R T H

RUE DU CLOITRE NOTRE DAME

N A V E

COLUMNS

S O U T H

Seine

River

To Towers

EXIT

A   **B**   **C**

ENTER

To View of Flying Buttresses

RUE D'ARCOLE

PONT AU DOUBLE

POINT ZERO ●

WEST

↓

Place du Parvis

To **M** Cité & **R** St. Michel

To Archaeological Crypt & Place St. Michel

WC

CHARLEMAGNE STATUE

A St. Denis & Exit

B Last Judgment

C Entrance

D Glass-Walled Confessional Rooms

E Joan of Arc Statue

F Rose-Shaped Window

G Thomas Aquinas Painting

H Scenes of the Resurrected Jesus

I Occasional Exhibits

J Notre-Dame Side View

HISTORIC PARIS

flanked by side aisles. It's designed in the shape of a cross, with the altar placed where the crossbeam intersects. The church can hold up to 10,000 faithful, and it's probably buzzing with visitors now, just as it was 600 years ago. The quiet, deserted churches we see elsewhere are in stark contrast to the busy, center-of-life places they were in the Middle Ages.

• *Follow the flow of the crowd and approach closer to the main altar.*

Altar

This marks the place where Mass is said and the bread and wine of Communion are blessed and distributed. In olden days, there were

no chairs. This was the holy spot for Romans, Christians...and even atheists. When the Revolutionaries stormed the church, they gutted it and turned it into a "Temple of Reason." A woman dressed like the Statue of Liberty held court at the altar as a symbol of the divinity of Man. France today, though nominally Catholic, remains aloof from Vatican dogmatism. Instead of traditional wooden confessional booths, there's an inviting **glass-walled room** (right aisle), where modern sinners seek counseling as much as forgiveness.

Just past the altar is the so-called choir, the area enclosed with carved-wood walls, where more intimate services can be held in this spacious building.

Right Transept (and Beyond)

A statue of **Joan of Arc** (Jeanne d'Arc, 1412-1431), dressed in armor and praying, honors the French teenager who rallied her country's soldiers to try to drive English invaders from Paris. The English and their allies burned her at the stake for claiming to hear heavenly voices. Almost immediately, Parisians rallied to condemn Joan's execution, and finally,

in 1909, here in Notre-Dame, the former "witch" was beatified.

Join the statue in gazing up to the blue-and-purple, **rose-shaped window** in the opposite transept—with teeny green Mary and baby Jesus in the center—the only one of the three rose windows still with its original medieval glass.

A large painting back down to

your right shows portly **Thomas Aquinas** (1225-1274) teaching, while his students drink from the fountain of knowledge. This Italian monk did undergrad and master's work at the multicultural University of Paris, then taught there for several years while writing his theological works. His "scholasticism" used Aristotle's logic to examine the Christian universe, aiming to fuse faith and reason.

• *Continue a few paces toward the far end of the church, pausing at the top of the three stairs.*

Circling the Choir

The back side of the choir walls feature **scenes of the resurrected Jesus** (c. 1350) appearing to his followers, starting with Mary

Magdalene. Their starry robes still gleam, thanks to a 19th-century renovation. The niches below these carvings mark the tombs of centuries of archbishops. Just ahead on the right is the **Treasury.** It contains lavish robes, golden reliquaries, and the humble tunic of King (and St.) Louis IX, but it probably isn't worth the entry fee.

As you continue around the choir, check out the chapels with their radiant stained glass, each dedicated to a particular saint and funded by a certain guild. Directly behind the choir lies one of the oldest statues in the church, a bishop of Paris from the 13th century, in his jewel-studded robe with a lion at his feet. A chapel nearby displays models of the church and an exhibit on medieval construction techniques—pulleys, wagons, hamster-wheel cranes, and lots of elbow grease. Farther along, there are often displays on the long multicentury project of constructing Notre-Dame. In the right transept, find a gilded-and-enameled reliquary dedicated to St. Geneviève (fifth century), whose prayers saved Paris from Attila the Hun. Throughout the church, the faithful can pause at any of the chapels to light a candle as an offering and meditate in the cool light of the stained glass.

• *Amble around the ambulatory, spill back outside, and make a slow U-turn left. Enter the park (named "Square Jean XXIII") through the iron gates along the riverside and walk about 50 yards until you come to a statue of Saint John Paul II.*

❸ Notre-Dame Side View

Alongside the church you'll notice many of the elements of Gothic: pointed arches, the lacy stone tracery of the windows, pinnacles, statues on rooftops, a lead roof, and a pointed steeple covered with

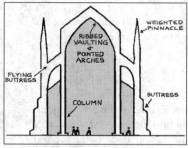

It takes 13 tourists to build a Gothic church: one steeple, six columns, and six buttresses.

the prickly "flames" (Flamboyant Gothic) of the Holy Spirit. Most distinctive of all are the flying buttresses. These 50-foot stone

"beams" that stick out of the church were the key to the complex Gothic architecture. The pointed arches we saw inside cause the weight of the roof to push outward rather than downward. The "flying" buttresses support the roof by pushing back inward. Gothic architects were masters at playing architectural forces against each other to build loftier and loftier churches, opening the walls for stained-glass windows. The Gothic style was born here in Paris.

Picture Quasimodo (the fictional hunchback) limping around along the railed balcony at the base of the roof among the "gargoyles." These grotesque beasts sticking out from pillars and buttresses represent souls caught between heaven and earth. They also function as rainspouts (from the same French root word as "gargle") when there are no evil spirits to battle.

The Neo-Gothic 300-foot spire is a product of the 1860 reconstruction of the dilapidated old church. Victor Hugo's book *The Hunchback of Notre-Dame* (1831) inspired a young architecture student named Eugène-Emmanuel Viollet-le-Duc to dedicate his career to a major renovation in Gothic style. Find Viollet-le-Duc at the base of the spire among the green apostles and evangelists (visible as you approach the back end of the church). The apostles look outward, blessing the city, while the architect (at top) looks up the spire, marveling at his fine work.

• *Behind Notre-Dame, cross the street and enter through the iron gate into the park at the tip of the island. (If this gate is closed, you can still enter the park 30 yards to the left.) Look for the stairs and head down to reach the...*

❹ Deportation Memorial (Mémorial de la Déportation)

This memorial to the 200,000 French victims of the Nazi concentration camps (1940-1945) draws you into their experience. France was quickly overrun by Nazi Germany, and Paris spent the war years under Nazi occupation. Jews and dissidents were rounded up and deported—many never returned.

As you descend the steps, the city around you disappears. Surrounded by walls, you have become a prisoner. Your only freedom is your view of the sky and the tiny glimpse of the river below. Enter the dark, single-file chamber up ahead. Inside, the circular plaque in the floor reads, "They went to the end of the earth and did not return."

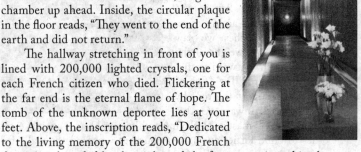

The hallway stretching in front of you is lined with 200,000 lighted crystals, one for each French citizen who died. Flickering at the far end is the eternal flame of hope. The tomb of the unknown deportee lies at your feet. Above, the inscription reads, "Dedicated to the living memory of the 200,000 French deportees shrouded by the night and the fog, exterminated in the Nazi concentration camps." The side rooms are filled with triangles—reminiscent of the identification patches inmates were forced to wear—each bearing the name of a concentration camp. Above the exit as you leave is the message you'll find at many other Holocaust sites: "Forgive, but never forget."

• *Back on street level, but before leaving the memorial park, look across the river (north) to the island called...*

❺ Ile St. Louis

If Ile de la Cité is a tugboat laden with the history of Paris, it's towing this classy little residential dinghy, laden only with high-rent apartments, boutiques, characteristic restaurants, and famous ice cream shops.

Ile St. Louis wasn't developed until much later than Ile de la Cité (17th century). What was a swampy mess is now harmonious Parisian architecture and one of Paris' most exclusive neighborhoods.

Look upstream (east) to the

bridge (Pont Tournelle) that links Ile St. Louis with the Left Bank (which is now on your right). Where the bridge meets the Left Bank, you'll find one of Paris' most exclusive restaurants, La Tour d'Argent (with a flag flying from the rooftop). This restaurant was the inspiration for the movie *Ratatouille*. Because the top floor has floor-to-ceiling windows, your evening meal comes with glittering views—and a golden price (allow €200 minimum, though you get a photo of yourself dining elegantly with Notre-Dame floodlit in the background).

It's a lovely place for an evening stroll (for details, see page 494). If you won't have time to come back, consider taking a brief detour across the pedestrian bridge, Pont St. Louis, to explore this little island.

• *From the Deportation Memorial, cross the bridge to the Left Bank. Turn right and walk along the river, toward the front end of Notre-Dame and to the next bridge. Stairs detour down to the riverbank if you need a place to picnic. This side view of the church from across the river is one of Europe's great sights and is best from river level. At times, you may find **barges** housing restaurants with great cathedral views docked here.*

LEFT BANK
❻ Left Bank Booksellers

The Rive Gauche, or the Left Bank of the Seine—"left" if you were floating downstream—still has many of the twisting lanes and narrow buildings of medieval times. The Right

Bank is more modern and business-oriented, with wide boulevards and stressed Parisians in suits. Here along the riverbank, the "big business" is secondhand books, displayed in the green metal stalls on the parapet (called *bouquinistes*). These literary entrepreneurs pride themselves on their easygoing style. With flexible hours and virtually no overhead, they run their businesses as they have since medieval times.

Bouquinistes (boo-keen-eest) have been a Parisian fixture since the mid-1500s, when such shops and stalls lined most of the bridges in Paris. In 1557, these merchants ran afoul of the authorities for selling forbidden Protestant pamphlets in then-Catholic Paris. After the Revolution, business boomed when entire libraries were liberated from rich nobles.

Today, the waiting list to become one of Paris' 250 *bouquinistes* is eight years. Each *bouquiniste* is allowed four boxes, and the most-coveted spots are awarded based on seniority. Rent is around €100 per year. *Bouquinistes* are required to paint their boxes a standard green and stay open at least four days a week, or they lose their spot. Notice how they guard against the rain by wrapping everything in plastic. And yes, they do leave everything inside when they lock up at night; metal bars and padlocks keep things safe. Though their main items may be vintage books, these days tourists prefer posters and magnets.

• *When you reach the bridge (Pont au Double) that crosses to the front of Notre-Dame, veer left across the street and find a small park called Square Viviani (fill your water bottle from fountain on left).*

Angle across the square and pass by Paris' oldest inhabitant—an acacia tree nicknamed Robinier, after the guy who planted it in 1602. Imagine that this same tree might once have shaded the Sun King, Louis XIV. Just beyond the tree you'll find the small rough-stone church of St. Julien-le-Pauvre. Leave the park, walking past the church, to tiny Rue Galande.

➐ Medieval Paris

Picture Paris in 1250, when the church of St. Julien-le-Pauvre was still new. Notre-Dame was nearly done (so they thought), Sainte-Chapelle had just opened, the university was expanding human knowledge, and Paris was fast becoming a prosperous industrial and commercial center. The area around the church and along Rue Galande gives you some of the medieval feel of ramshackle architecture and old houses leaning every which way. In medieval days, people were piled on top of each other, building at all angles, as they scrambled for this prime real estate near the main commercial artery of the day—the Seine. The smell of fish competed with the smell of neighbors in this knot of humanity.

Narrow dirt (or mud) streets sloped from here down into the mucky Seine until the 19th century, when modern quays and embankments cleaned everything up.

• *Now, return toward the river, walking past the church and park on the cobbled lane. Turn left on Rue de la Bûcherie and drop into the...*

➑ Shakespeare and Company Bookstore

In addition to hosting butchers and fishmongers, the Left Bank has been home to scholars, philosophers, and poets since medieval times. This funky bookstore—a reincarnation of the original shop

from the 1920s on Rue de l'Odéon—has picked up the literary torch. Sylvia Beach, an American with a passion for free thinking, opened Shakespeare and Company for the post-WWI Lost Generation, who came to Paris to find themselves. American writers flocked to the city for the cheap rent, fleeing the uptight, Prohibition-era United States. Beach's bookstore was famous as a meeting place for Paris' expatriate literary elite. Ernest Hemingway borrowed books from it regularly. James Joyce struggled to find a publisher for his now-classic novel *Ulysses*—until Sylvia Beach published it. George Bernard Shaw, Gertrude Stein, and Ezra Pound also got their English fix at her shop.

Today, the bookstore carries on that literary tradition—the owner, Sylvia, is named after the original store's founder. Struggling writers are given free accommodations in tiny rooms with views of Notre-Dame. Explore—the upstairs has a few seats, cots, antique typewriters, and cozy nooks. Downstairs, travelers enjoy a great selection of used English books—including my Paris and France guidebooks. Their cozy coffee shop sits next door.

Notice the green water fountain (1900) in front of the bookstore, one of the many in Paris donated by the English philanthropist Sir Richard Wallace. The hooks below the caryatids once held metal mugs for drinking the water before the age of plastic.

• *Continue to Rue du Petit-Pont and turn left. This bustling north-south boulevard (which becomes Rue St. Jacques) was the Romans' busiest street 2,000 years ago, with chariots racing in and out of the city. (Roman-iacs can view remains from the third-century baths, and a fine medieval collection, at the nearby Cluny Museum;* 📖 *see the Cluny Museum Tour chapter.)*

A block south of the Seine, turn right at the Gothic church of St. Séverin and walk into the Latin Quarter.

❾ St. Séverin

Don't ask me why, but building this church took a century longer than building Notre-Dame. This is Flamboyant, or "flame-like," Gothic, and you can see how the short, prickly spires are meant to make this building flicker in the eyes of the faithful. The church gives us a close-up look at gargoyles, the decorative drain spouts that also functioned to keep evil spirits away.

Inside you can see the final stage of Gothic, on the cusp of the Renaissance. It's also notable for carrying on the medieval tradition of stained-glass windows into more modern times, while keeping the dominant blues, greens, and reds popular in St. Séverin's heyday. Walk to the apse and admire the lone twisted Flamboyant Gothic column and the fan vaulting. The apse's windows (by Jean Bazaine, c. 1960) echo the fan-vaulting effect in a modern, abstract way. Each colorful window represents one of the seven sacraments—blue for baptism, yellow for marriage, etc. The impressive organ filling the entrance wall is a reminder that this church is still a popular venue for evening concerts (see gate for information posters, buy tickets at door).

• At #22 Rue St. Séverin, you'll find the skinniest house in Paris, two windows wide. Rue St. Séverin leads right through...

The Latin Quarter

Although it may look more like the Greek Quarter today (cheap gyros abound), this area is the Latin Quarter, named for the language you'd have heard on these streets if you walked them in the Middle Ages. The University of Paris (founded 1215), one of the leading educational institutions of medieval Europe, was (and still is) nearby.

A thousand years ago, the "crude" or vernacular local languages were sophisticated enough to communicate basic human needs, but if you wanted to get philosophical, the language of choice was Latin. Medieval Europe's class of educated elite transcended nations and borders. From Sicily to Sweden, they spoke and corresponded in Latin. Now the most "Latin" thing about this area is the beat you may hear coming from some of the subterranean jazz clubs.

Walking along Rue St. Séverin, you can still see the shadow of the medieval sewer system. The street slopes into a central channel of bricks. In the days before plumbing and toilets, when people still went to the river or neighborhood wells for their water, flushing meant throwing it out the window. At certain times of day, maids on the fourth floor would holler, *"Garde de l'eau!"* ("Watch out for the water!") and heave it into the streets, where it would eventually wash down into the Seine.

As you wander, remember that before Napoleon III commissioned Baron Haussmann to modernize the city with grand boulevards (19th century), Paris was just like this—a medieval tangle.

The ethnic feel of this area is nothing new—it's been a melting pot and university district for almost 800 years.
• *Keep wandering straight, and you'll come to...*

⑩ Boulevard St. Michel

Busy Boulevard St. Michel (or "boul' Miche") is famous as the main artery for Paris' café and arts scene, culminating a block away

(to the left) at the intersection with Boulevard St. Germain. Although nowadays you're more likely to find pantyhose at 30 percent off, there are still many cafés, boutiques, and bohemian haunts nearby.

The Sorbonne—the University of Paris' humanities department—is also nearby, if you want to make a detour, though visitors are not allowed to enter. (Turn left on Boulevard St. Michel and walk two blocks south. Gaze at the dome from the Place de la Sorbonne courtyard.) Originally founded as a theological school, the Sorbonne began attracting more students and famous professors—such as St. Thomas Aquinas and Peter Abélard—as its prestige grew. By the time the school expanded to include other subjects, it had a reputation for bold new ideas. Nonconformity is a tradition here, and Paris remains a world center for new intellectual trends.
• *Nearby is the Cluny Museum (see page 71), which brings the era of Aquinas and Abélard to life. But to continue this walk, cross Boulevard St. Michel. Just ahead is...*

Place St. André-des-Arts

This tree-filled square is lined with cafés. In Paris, most serious thinking goes on in cafés. For centuries these have been social watering holes, where you can get a warm place to sit and stimulating conversation for the price of a cup of coffee. Every great French writer—from Voltaire and Jean-Jacques Rousseau to Jean-Paul Sartre and Jacques Derrida—had a favorite haunt.

Paris honors its intellectuals. If you visit the Panthéon (described on page 75)—several blocks up Boulevard St. Michel and to the left—you'll find French writers (Voltaire, Victor Hugo, Emile Zola, and Rousseau), inventors (Louis Braille), and scientists (including Marie and Pierre Curie) buried in a setting usually reserved for warriors and politicians.
• *Adjoining this square toward the river is the triangular Place St. Michel, with a Métro stop and a statue of St. Michael killing a devil. Note:*

*If you were to continue west along Rue St. André-des-Arts, you'd find
more Left Bank action (see page 280).*

⓫ Place St. Michel

You're standing at the traditional core of the Left Bank's artsy, liberal, hippie, bohemian district of poets, philosophers, winos, and
*baba cool*s (neo-hippies). Nearby, you'll find in-
ternational eateries, far-out bookshops, street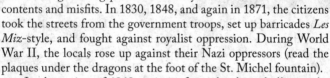
singers, pale girls in black berets, jazz clubs,
and—these days—tourists. Small cinemas
show avant-garde films, almost always in the
version originale (v.o.). For colorful wandering
and café-sitting, afternoons and evenings are
best. In the morning, it feels sleepy. The Latin
Quarter stays up late and sleeps in.

In less commercial times, Place St. Michel was a gathering point for the city's mal-
contents and misfits. In 1830, 1848, and again in 1871, the citizens
took the streets from the government troops, set up barricades *Les
Miz*-style, and fought against royalist oppression. During World
War II, the locals rose up against their Nazi oppressors (read the
plaques under the dragons at the foot of the St. Michel fountain).

In the spring of 1968, a time of social upheaval all over the
world, young students battled riot batons and tear gas by digging
up the cobblestones on the street and hurling them at police. They
took over the square and declared it an independent state. Factory
workers followed their call to arms and went on strike, challeng-
ing the de Gaulle government and forcing change. Eventually, the
students were pacified, the university was reformed, and the Latin
Quarter's original cobblestones were replaced with pavement, so
future scholars could never again use the streets as weapons. Even
today, whenever there's a student demonstration, it starts here.

• *From Place St. Michel, look across the river and find the prickly steeple
of the Sainte-Chapelle church. Head toward it. Cross the river on Pont
St. Michel and continue north along the Boulevard du Palais. On your
left, you'll see the doorway to Sainte-Chapelle.*

SAINTE-CHAPELLE AND NEARBY

Security is strict at the Sainte-Chapelle complex because this is
more than a tourist attraction: France's Supreme Court meets to
the right of Sainte-Chapelle in the Palais de Justice. Expect a long
wait (for tips on avoiding the worst lines, see page 107).

Once past security, you'll enter the courtyard outside Sainte-
Chapelle, where you'll find information about upcoming church
concerts. The ticket office is near the church entry, which is often
hidden behind a long line of ticket buyers. Remember, if you al-

ready have a Museum Pass or Conciergerie combo-ticket in hand, march up to the front, and you'll be allowed right in.

• *Enter the humble ground floor.*

⓬ Sainte-Chapelle

This triumph of Gothic church architecture is a cathedral of glass like no other. It was speedily built between 1242 and 1248 for King

Louis IX—the only French king who is now a saint—to house the supposed Crown of Thorns (now kept at Notre-Dame and shown only on Good Friday and on the first Friday of the month at 15:00). Its architectural harmony is due to the fact that it was completed under the direction of one architect and in only six years—unheard of in Gothic times. Recall that Notre-Dame took more than 200 years.

Though the inside is beautiful, the exterior is basically functional. The muscular buttresses hold up the stone roof, so the walls are essentially there to display stained glass. The lacy spire is Neo-Gothic—added in the 19th century. Inside, the layout clearly shows an *ancien régime* approach to worship. The low-ceilinged basement was for staff and other common folks—worshipping under a sky filled with painted fleurs-de-lis, a symbol of the king. Royal Christians worshipped upstairs. The paint job, a 19th-century restoration, helps you imagine how grand this small, painted, jeweled chapel was. (Imagine Notre-Dame painted like this...) Each capital is playfully carved with a different plant's leaves.

• *Climb the spiral staircase to the Chapelle Haute. Leave the rough stone of the earth and step into the light.*

The Stained Glass

Fiat lux. "Let there be light." From the first page of the Bible, it's clear: Light is divine. Light shines through stained glass like God's grace shining down to earth. Gothic architects used their new technology to turn dark stone buildings into lanterns of light. The glory of Gothic shines brighter here than in any other church.

There are 15 separate panels of stained glass (6,500 square feet—two thirds of it 13th-century original), with more than 1,100 different scenes, mostly from

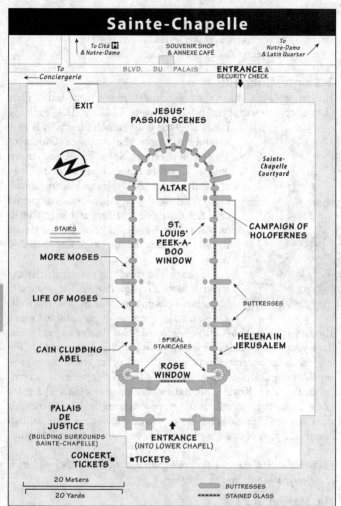

Sainte-Chapelle

To Cité **M** & Notre-Dame

SOUVENIR SHOP & ANNEXE CAFÉ

To Notre-Dame & Latin Quarter

To Conciergerie

BLVD.   DU   PALAIS

ENTRANCE & SECURITY CHECK

EXIT

JESUS' PASSION SCENES

ALTAR

Sainte-Chapelle Courtyard

STAIRS

ST. LOUIS' PEEK-A-BOO WINDOW

CAMPAIGN OF HOLOFERNES

MORE MOSES

LIFE OF MOSES

BUTTRESSES

CAIN CLUBBING ABEL

SPIRAL STAIRCASES

HELENA IN JERUSALEM

ROSE WINDOW

PALAIS DE JUSTICE (BUILDING SURROUNDS SAINTE-CHAPELLE)

ENTRANCE (INTO LOWER CHAPEL)

CONCERT TICKETS

TICKETS

20 Meters

20 Yards

BUTTRESSES

STAINED GLASS

the Bible. These cover the entire Christian history of the world, from the Creation in Genesis (first window on the left, as you face the altar), to the coming of Christ (over the altar), to the end of the world (the round "rose"-shaped window at the rear of the church). Each individual scene is interesting, and the whole effect is overwhelming. Allow yourself a few minutes to bask in the glow of the colored light before tackling the window descriptions below.

• *Working clockwise from the entrance, look for these notable scenes, using the map above as a reference. (The sun lights up different windows at various times of day. Overcast days give the most even light. On bright,*

Stained Glass Supreme

Craftsmen made glass—which is, essentially, melted sand—using this recipe:

- Melt one part sand with two parts wood ash.
- Mix in rusty metals to get different colors—iron makes red; cobalt makes blue; copper, green; manganese, purple; cadmium, yellow.
- Blow glass into a cylinder shape, cut lengthwise, and lay flat to cool.
- Cut into pieces with an iron tool, or by heating and cooling a select spot to make it crack.
- Fit pieces together to form a figure, using strips of lead to hold them in place.
- Place masterpiece so high on a wall that no one can read it.

sunny days, some sections are glorious, while others look like sheets of lead.)

Genesis—Cain Clubbing Abel (first window on the left, always dark because of a building butted up against it): On the bottom level in the third circle from the left, we see God create the round earth and hold it up. On the next level up, we catch glimpses of naked Adam and Eve. On the third level (far right circle), Cain, in red, clubs his brother Abel, committing the first murder.

Life of Moses (second window, the dark bottom row of diamond panels): The first panel shows baby Moses in a basket, placed by his sister in the squiggly brown river. Next he's found by the pharaoh's daughter. Then he grows up. And finally, he's a man, a prince of Egypt on his royal throne.

More Moses (third window, in middle and upper sections): See how many guys with bright yellow horns you can spy. Moses is shown with horns as the result of a medieval mistranslation of the Hebrew word for "rays of light," or halo.

Jesus' Passion Scenes (directly over the altar and behind the canopy): These scenes from Jesus' arrest and Crucifixion were the backdrop for the Crown of Thorns (originally displayed on the altar), which was placed on Jesus' head when the Romans were torturing and humiliating him before his execution. Stand close to the steps of the altar—about five paces away—and look through the canopy to see Jesus, tied to a green column, being whipped. Alongside is the key scene in this relic chapel—Jesus (in purple robe) being fitted with the painful Crown of Thorns. Now get right up to the altar steps and look up. Just below the top of the canopy, find Jesus in yellow shorts, carrying his cross (fifth frame up from right bottom). Finally (as high as you can see), Jesus on the cross is speared by a soldier.

Campaign of Holofernes (window to the right of the altar wall): On the bottom row are four scenes of colorful knights. The second circle from the left is a battle scene (the campaign of Holofernes), showing three soldiers with swords slaughtering three men. The background is blue. The men have different-colored clothes—red, blue, green, mauve, and white. Examine some of the details. You can see the folds in the robes, the hair, and facial features. Look at the victim in the center—his head is splotched with blood. Details like the folds in the robes (see the victim in white, lower left) came about either by scratching on the glass or by baking on paint. It was a painstaking process of finding just the right colors, fitting them together to make a scene...and then multiplying by 1,100.

Helena in Jerusalem (first window on the right wall by entrance): This window tells the story of how Christ's Crown of Thorns found its way from Jerusalem to Constantinople to this chapel. Start in the lower-left corner, where the Roman emperor Constantine (in blue, on his throne) waves goodbye to his Christian mom, Helena. She arrives at the gate of Jerusalem (next panel to the right). Her men (in the two-part medallion above Jerusalem) dig through ruins and find Christ's (tiny) cross and other relics. She returns to Constantinople with a stash of holy relics, including the Crown of Thorns. Nine hundred years later, French Crusader knights (the next double medallion above) invade the Holy Land and visit Constantinople. Finally, King Louis IX (hard to see, but he's the guy dressed in blue farther up) returns to France with the sacred relic.

Rose Window (above entrance): It's Judgment Day, with a tiny Christ in the center of the chaos and miracles. This window, from the Flamboyant period, is 200 years newer than the rest. Facing west and the sunset, it's best late in the day.

If you can't read much into the individual windows, you're not alone. (For some tutoring, a little book with color photos is on sale downstairs with the postcards.)

Altar

The altar was raised up high to better display the Crown of Thorns, the relic around which this chapel was built. Notice the staircase: Access was limited to the priest and the king, who wore the keys to the shrine around his neck. Also note that there is no high-profile image of Jesus anywhere—this chapel was all about the Crown.

King Louis IX, convinced he'd found the real McCoy, spent roughly the equivalent of €500 million for the Crown, €370 million for the gem-studded shrine to display it in (later destroyed in the French Revolution), and a mere €150 million to build Sainte-Chapelle to house it. Today, the supposed Crown of Thorns is kept by the Notre-Dame Treasury (though it's occasionally brought out for display).

Lay your camera on the ground and shoot the ceiling. Those pure and simple ribs growing out of the slender columns are the essence of Gothic structure.

• *Exit Sainte-Chapelle. Back outside, as you walk around the church exterior, look down to see the foundation and take note of how much Paris has risen in the 750 years since Sainte-Chapelle was built.*

Next door to Sainte-Chapelle is the...

Palais de Justice

Sainte-Chapelle sits within a huge complex of buildings that has housed the local government since ancient Roman times. It was

the site of the original Gothic palace of the early kings of France. The only surviving medieval parts are Sainte-Chapelle and the Conciergerie prison.

Most of the site is now covered by the giant Palais de Justice, built in 1776, home of the French Supreme Court. The motto *Liberté, Egalité, Fraternité* over the doors is a reminder that this was also the headquarters of the Revolutionary government. Here they doled out justice, condemning many to imprisonment in the Conciergerie downstairs—or to the guillotine.

• *Now pass through the big iron gate to the noisy Boulevard du Palais. Cross the street to the wide, pedestrian-only Rue de Lutèce and walk about halfway down.*

⓫ Cité "Metropolitain" Métro Stop

Of the 141 original early-20th-century subway entrances, this is one of only a few survivors—now preserved as a national art treasure. (New York's Museum of Modern Art even exhibits one.) It marks Paris at its peak in 1900—on the cutting edge of Modernism, but with an eye for beauty. The curvy, plantlike ironwork is a textbook example of Art Nouveau, the style that rebelled against the erector-set squareness of the Industrial Age. Other similar Métro stations in Paris are Abbesses and Porte Dauphine.

The flower and plant market on Place Louis Lépine is a pleasant detour. On Sundays this square flutters with a busy bird market. And across the way is the Préfecture de Police, where Inspector Clouseau of *Pink Panther* fame used to work, and where the local resistance fighters took the first building from the Nazis in August 1944, leading to the Allied liberation of Paris a week later.

• *Pause here to admire the view. Sainte-Chapelle is a pearl in an ugly architectural oyster. Double back to the Palais de Justice, turn right onto Boulevard du Palais, and enter the Conciergerie. It's free with the Museum Pass; passholders can sidestep the bottleneck created by the ticket-buying line.*

⑭ Conciergerie

Though pretty barren inside, this former prison echoes with history. Positioned next to the courthouse, the Conciergerie was the gloomy prison famous as the last stop for 2,780 victims of the guillotine, including France's last *ancien régime* queen, Marie-Antoinette. Before then, kings had used the building to torture and execute failed assassins. (One of its towers along the river was called "The Babbler," named for the pain-induced sounds that leaked from it.) When the Revolution (1789) toppled the king, the building kept its same function, but without torture. The progressive Revolutionaries proudly unveiled a modern and more humane way to execute people—the guillotine. The Conciergerie was the epicenter of the Reign of Terror—the year-long period of the Revolution (1793-94) during which Revolutionary fervor spiraled out of control and thousands were killed. It was

here at the Conciergerie that "enemies of the Revolution" were imprisoned, tried, sentenced, and marched off to Place de la Concorde for decapitation.

Inside the Conciergerie

Pick up a free map and breeze through the one-way circuit. It's well-described in English. See the spacious, low-ceilinged Hall of Men-at-Arms (Room 1), originally a guards' dining room, with

Marie-Antoinette

In 1789, as the Revolution was coming to a head, it was Queen Marie-Antoinette—even more than her husband, King Louis XVI—who became the focus of the citizens' disgust.

First off, she was foreign-born, known simply as "The Austrian." Reports flew that she spent extravagantly, plunging France into debt. She was seen as a dragon lady who'd manipulated her husband against the Revolution. Worst of all, a rumor spread (probably false) that when Marie was told that the Parisians had no bread, she sneered, "Let them eat cake!" ("Cake" was the burnt crusts of the bread oven.)

Enraged and hungry, 6,000 Parisian women (backed by armed men) marched through the rain to the royal palace at Versailles. The Revolutionaries stormed the chateau, kidnapped the royal family, and brought them back to Paris. They were placed under house arrest in the Tuileries Palace (which once stood in the Tuileries Garden).

In 1791, Marie and Louis engineered an escape to Austria to begin a counterrevolution. They had one of their servants pretend to be a German baroness, while Louis disguised himself as her servant. (The irony must have been killing him.) But someone recognized Louis from his portrait on a franc note. The family was captured, put on trial as traitors to France, and the monarchy was abolished.

Louis, Marie-Antoinette, and their eight-year-old son were tearfully split up and sent to separate prisons. Marie-Antoinette was taken to the Conciergerie.

On January 21, 1793, King Louis XVI (excuse me, that's "Citizen Capet") was led to Place de la Concorde and laid face down on a slab. *Shoop!*—a thousand years of monarchy that dated back to before Charlemagne was decapitated. On October 16, Marie-Antoinette was also carted to Place de la Concorde. Genteel to the end, she apologized to the executioner for stepping on his foot. The blade fell, the blood gushed, and her head was shown to the crowd on a stick—an exclamation point for the new rallying cry: *Vive la nation!*

four big fireplaces (look up the chimneys). During the Reign of Terror, this large hall served as a holding tank for the poorest prisoners. Then they were taken upstairs (in an area not open to visitors), where the Revolutionary tribunals grilled scared prisoners on their political correctness. Continue to the raised area at the far end of the room (Room 4, today's bookstore). In Revolutionary days, this was notorious as the walkway of the executioner, who was known affectionately as "Monsieur de Paris."

Pass through the bookstore to find the Office of the Keeper, or "Concierge" of the place (who admitted shackled prisoners, monitored torture...and recommended nearby restaurants). Next door is the *Toilette,* where condemned prisoners combed their hair or touched up their lipstick before their final public appearance—waiting for the open-air cart (tumbrel) to pull up outside. The tumbrel would carry them to the guillotine, which was on Place de la Concorde.

Upstairs is a memorial room with the names of the 2,780 citizens condemned to death by the guillotine. Here are some of the people you'll find, in alphabetical order. Anne Elisabeth Capet (a.k.a. Princess Elisabeth) was decapitated for the crime of being a "sister of the tyrant." Charlotte Corday *("dite d'Armais"),* a noblewoman, snuck into the bathroom of the revolutionary writer Jean-Paul Marat and stabbed him while he bathed. Georges Danton was a prominent revolutionary who was later condemned for being insufficiently liberal—a nasty crime. Louis XVI (called "Capet: last king of France") deserves only a modest mention, as does his wife, Marie-Antoinette (*veuve* means she's widowed). And finally—oh, the irony—there's Maximilien de Robespierre, the head of the Revolution, the man who sent so many to the guillotine. He was eventually toppled, humiliated, imprisoned here, and beheaded.

Head down the hallway. Along the way, you'll see some reconstructed cells showing how the poor slept on straw (first cell), whereas the wealthy got a cot (next cell).

Then comes a small set of displays (in French). You'll see old paintings of the Conciergerie and some of the famous prisoners.

Next, go downstairs, where—tucked behind heavy gray curtains—is a tiny chapel built on the site where Marie-Antoinette's

prison cell originally stood. The chapel was made in Marie's honor by Louis XVIII, the brother of beheaded Louis XVI and the first king to reclaim the throne after the Revolution. The chapel's three paintings tell her sad story: First, Marie (dressed in widow's black) stoically says goodbye to her grieving family as she's led off to prison. Next, still stoic, she awaits her fate. Finally, she piously kneels in her cell to receive the Last Sacrament on the night before her beheading. The chapel's walls drip with silver-embroidered tears.

The tour continues outside in the "Cour de Femmes" courtyard, where female prisoners were allowed a little fresh air (notice the spikes still guarding from above). Return indoors through the door at the opposite end of the courtyard, on your left.

The next room (immediately on the left) is a re-creation of Marie-Antoinette's cell. On August 12, 1793, the queen was brought here to be tried for her supposed crimes against the peo-

ple. Imagine the queen spending her last days—separated from her 10-year-old son, and now widowed because the king had already been executed. Mannequins, period furniture, and the real cell wallpaper set the scene. The guard stands modestly behind a screen, while the queen psyches herself up with a crucifix. In the glass display case, see her actual crucifix, rug, and small water pitcher. On October 16, 1793, the queen was awakened at 4:00 in the morning and led away. She walked the corridor, stepped onto the cart, and was slowly carried to Place de la Concorde, where she had a date with "Monsieur de Paris."

• *Back outside, turn left on Boulevard du Palais. On the corner is the city's oldest public clock. The mechanism of the present clock is from 1334, and even though the case is Baroque, it keeps on ticking.*

Turn left onto Quai de l'Horloge and walk along the river, past "The Babbler" tower. The bridge up ahead is the Pont Neuf, where we'll end this walk. At the first corner, veer left into a sleepy triangular square called...

⑮ Place Dauphine

It's amazing to find such coziness in the heart of Paris. This city of more than two million is still a city of neighborhoods, a collection of villages. The French Supreme Court building looms behind like a giant marble gavel. Enjoy the village-Paris feeling in the park. The **$$$ Caveau du Palais** restaurant is a refined spot for a drink (cool bar/café) or a fine meal, inside or out (17 Place Dauphine, tel. 01 43 26 04 28). If you feel

more like plotting a revolution (while saving some euros), try the funky **$$ Ma Salle à Manger** (across the square at #26, tel. 01 43 29 52 34).

• *Continue through Place Dauphine. As you pop out the other end, you're face-to-face with a...*

Statue of Henry IV

Henry IV (1553-1610) is not as famous as his grandson, Louis XIV, but Henry helped make Paris what it is today—a European capital of elegant buildings and quiet squares. He built the Place Dauphine (behind you), the Pont Neuf (to the right), residences (to the left, down Rue Dauphine), the Louvre's long Grand Gallery (downriver on the right), and the tree-filled Square du Vert-Galant (directly behind the statue, on the tip of the island). The square is one of Paris' make-out spots; its name comes from Henry's nickname, the Green Knight, as Henry was a notorious ladies' man. The park is a great place to relax, dangling your legs over the concrete prow of this boat-shaped island.

• *From the statue, turn right onto the old bridge. Pause at the little nook halfway across.*

⑯ Pont Neuf and the Seine

This "new bridge" is now Paris' oldest. Built during Henry IV's reign (about 1600), its arches span the widest part of the river.

Unlike other bridges, this one never had houses or buildings growing on it. The turrets were originally for vendors and street entertainers. In the days of Henry IV, who promised his peasants "a chicken in every pot every Sunday," this would have been a lively scene. From the bridge, look downstream (west) to see the next bridge, the pedestrian-only Pont des Arts. Ahead on the Right Bank is the long Louvre museum. Beyond that, on the Left Bank, is the Orsay. And what's that tall black tower in the distance?

Our walk ends where Paris began—on the **Seine River.** From Dijon to the English Channel, the Seine meanders 500 miles, cutting through the center of Paris. The river is shallow and slow within the city, but still dangerous enough to require steep stone embankments (built 1910) to prevent occasional floods.

In summer, the roads that run along the river are replaced with acres of sand, as well as beach chairs and tanned locals, creating the Paris *Plages* (see page 57). The success of the Paris *Plages* event has motivated the city to take the next step: to permanently banish vehicles from those fast lanes on the Left Bank between the Orsay and Pont de l'Alma, turning them into riverside parks instead.

Any time of year, you'll see tourist boats and the commercial barges that carry 20 percent of Paris' transported goods. And on the banks, sportsmen today cast into the waters once fished by Paris' original Celtic inhabitants.

• We're done. You can take a boat tour that leaves from near the base of Pont Neuf on the island side (Vedettes du Pont Neuf; see page 39).

Or you could take my walking tour of the Left Bank, which begins one bridge downriver (🕮 see the Left Bank Walk chapter). The nearest Métro stop is Pont Neuf, across the bridge on the Right Bank. Bus #69 heads east along Quai du Louvre (at the north end of the bridge) and west along Rue de Rivoli (a block farther north; 🕮 see the Bus #69 Sightseeing Tour chapter). In fact, you can go anywhere—you're standing in the heart of Paris.

LOUVRE TOUR

Musée du Louvre

Paris walks you through world history in three world-class museums—the Louvre (ancient world to 1850), the Orsay (1848-1914, including Impressionism), and the Pompidou (20th century to today). Start your "art-yssey" at the Louvre. With more than 30,000 works of art, the Louvre is a full inventory of Western civilization. To cover it all in one visit is impossible. Let's focus on the Louvre's specialties—Greek sculpture, Italian painting, and French painting.

We'll see "Venuses" through history, from prehistoric stick figures to the curvy *Venus de Milo* to the wind-blown *Winged Victory of Samothrace,* and from placid medieval Madonnas to the *Mona Lisa* to the symbol of modern democracy. Those with a little more time can visit some impressive chunks of stone from Mesopotamia—the "Cradle of Civilization" (modern-day Iraq). As we traverse the centuries, we'll see how each generation defined beauty differently, and gain insight into long-ago civilizations by admiring what they found beautiful.

Orientation

Cost: €15, includes special exhibits, free on first Sun of month Oct-March only, covered by Museum Pass. Tickets good all day; reentry allowed.

Hours: Wed-Mon 9:00-18:00, open Wed and Fri nights until 21:45 (except on holidays), closed Tue. Galleries start shutting down 30 minutes before closing. Last entry is 45 minutes before closing.

When to Go: Crowds can be miserably bad on Sun, Mon (the worst day), Wed, and in the morning (arrive 30 minutes before

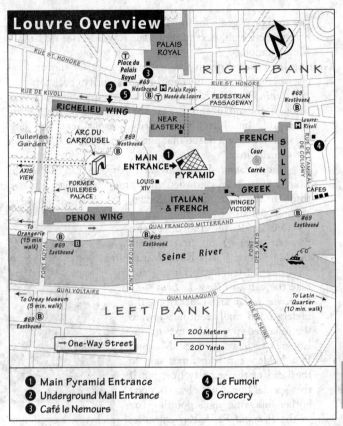

Louvre Overview

PALAIS
ROYAL

RUE ST. HONORE

T Place du
Palais
Royal

3

RIGHT BANK

RUE ST. HONORE

#69
2 Westbound **M** Palais Royal–
B **T** Musée du Louvre

RUE DE RIVOLI

5

PEDESTRIAN
PASSAGEWAY

#69
Westbound
B

RICHELIEU WING

Louvre–
M Rivoli

NEAR
EASTERN

ARC DU
CARROUSEL

Tuileries
Garden

#69
Westbound
B

FRENCH

S
U
L
L
Y

RUE DE L'AMIRAL DE COLIGNY

4

MAIN **1**
ENTRANCE ➤

Cour
Carrée

AXIS
VIEW

PYRAMID

FORMER
TUILERIES
PALACE

LOUIS
XIV

GREEK

CAFÉS

**ITALIAN
& FRENCH**

WINGED
VICTORY

To
Orangerie
(15 min.
walk)

DENON WING

QUAI FRANCOIS MITTERRAND

#69
Eastbound
B

PONT ROYAL

#69
Eastbound **B** **B**

PONT CARROUSEL

B #69
Eastbound

Seine River

PONT DES ARTS

QUAI VOLTAIRE

QUAI MALAQUAIS

To Orsay Museum
(5 min. walk)

#69
Eastbound
B

LEFT BANK

RUE DE SEINE

To Latin
Quarter
(10 min. walk)

200 Meters

200 Yards

➤ **One-Way Street**

1 Main Pyramid Entrance
2 Underground Mall Entrance
3 Café le Nemours
4 Le Fumoir
5 Grocery

opening to secure a good place in line). Evening visits are quieter, and the glass pyramid glows after dark.

Buying Tickets at the Louvre: Self-serve ticket machines located under the pyramid may be faster to use than the ticket windows (machines accept euro bills, coins, and chip-and-PIN Visa cards). A shop in the underground mall sells tickets to the Louvre, Orsay, and Versailles, plus Museum Passes, for no extra charge (cash only). To find it from the Carrousel du Louvre entrance off Rue de Rivoli (described later), turn right after the last escalator down onto Allée de France, and follow *Museum Pass* signs.

Getting There: Métro stop Palais Royal-Musée du Louvre is the closest. From the station, you can stay underground to enter the museum, or exit above ground if you want to go in through the pyramid (more details later). The eastbound bus #69 stops along the Seine River; the best stop is labeled Quai François Mitterrand. The westbound #69 stops in front of the pyramid (see map on page 33 for stop locations). You'll find a taxi stand on Rue de Rivoli, next to the Palais Royal-Musée du Louvre Métro station.

Getting In: Enter through the pyramid, or opt for shorter lines elsewhere. Everyone must go through security checkpoints.

Main Pyramid Entrance: There is no grander entry than through the main entrance at the pyramid in the central courtyard, but lines (for security reasons) can be long. Passholders have a queue that puts them closer to the head of the security line.

Underground Mall Entrance: Anyone can enter the Louvre from its less crowded underground entrance, accessed through the Carrousel du Louvre shopping mall. Enter the mall at 99 Rue de Rivoli (the door with the red awning) or directly from the Métro stop Palais Royal-Musée du Louvre (stepping off the train, take the exit to *Musée du Louvre–Le Carrousel du Louvre*). Once inside the underground mall, continue toward the inverted pyramid next to the Louvre's security entrance. Museum Pass holders can sometimes skip to the head of the security line, but if that special line is not obvious, don't bother following signs pointing you  to the *Pyramid Passholders* entrance (which is a long detour away).

Information: Pick up the free *Plan/Information* at the information desk under the pyramid as you enter. You'll find explanations throughout the museum. Tel. 01 40 20 53 17, recorded info tel. 01 40 20 51 51, www.louvre.fr.

Tours: Ninety-minute English-language **guided tours** leave twice daily (except the first Sun of the month Oct-March) from the *Accueil des Groupes* area, under the pyramid (normally at 11:15 and 14:00, possibly more often in summer; €12 plus admission, tour tel. 01 40 20 52 63). **Videoguides** (€5) provide commentary on about 700 masterpieces.

Ω Download my free Louvre Museum **audio tour,** which complements the text in this chapter.

Length of This Tour: Allow at least two hours. With less time, string together the *Venus de Milo, Winged Victory, Mona Lisa,* and *Coronation of Emperor Napoleon*...and sightsee whatever else you can along the way.

Eating at or near the Louvre

The Louvre has several cafés. The best is **$$ Café Mollien,** located near the end of our tour (on the terrace overlooking the pyramid, closes at 18:00). A self-service **$ cafeteria** is up the escalator from the pyramid in the Richelieu wing. **$$$ Le Grand Louvre Café** under the pyramid is a pricier option. For the best selection, walk to the underground shopping mall, the **Carrousel du Louvre** (daily 8:30-23:00), which has a food court upstairs with decent-value, multiethnic fast-food eateries, including—*quelle horreur*—a McDonald's. The mall also has glittering boutiques, a post office, two Starbucks, a big Apple store (*vive* globalization), a Métro entrance (Mo: Palais Royal-Musée du Louvre), and a convenient exit *(sortie)* directly into the Tuileries Garden.

Picnics are painting-perfect in the adjacent Palais Royal gardens (enter from Place du Palais Royal). Pick up all you need at the Franprix market at 165 Rue St-Honoré (see map on page 201) and take a fresh-air break a block north of the museum (see page 59 for more on the Palais Royal).

For a great post-Louvre lunch/retreat, head to the venerable **$$ Café le Nemours,** with elegant brass and Art Deco style and outdoor tables that get good afternoon sun (daily; leaving the Louvre, cross Rue de Rivoli and veer left to 2 Place Colette, adjacent to Comédie Française; tel. 01 42 61 34 14). **$$$ Le Fumoir** is another classy place, with brown leather couches perfect for kicking back with a coffee or cocktail (€23 for two-course lunch *menu,* daily, 6 Rue de l'Amiral de Coligny, near Louvre-Rivoli Métro stop, tel. 01 42 92 00 24).

Baggage Check: You can store bags for free in self-service lockers (look for the *Vestiaires* sign). Bigger bags must be checked.

Services: WCs are located under the pyramid, behind the escalators to the Denon and Richelieu wings. Once you're in the galleries, WCs are scarce.

Photography: Photography without a flash is allowed.

Starring: *Venus de Milo, Winged Victory, Mona Lisa,* Leonardo da Vinci, Raphael, Michelangelo, the French painters, and many of the most iconic images of Western civilization.

SURVIVING THE LOUVRE

Start by picking up a free map at the information desk and orienting yourself while standing underneath the **glass pyramid.**

The Louvre, the largest museum in the Western world, fills three wings of this immense, U-shaped palace. The **Richelieu wing** (north side) houses Near Eastern antiquities (covered in the last part of this tour), decorative arts, and French, German, and Northern European art. The **Sully wing** (east side) has extensive French painting and collections of ancient Egyptian and Greek art. The **Denon wing** (south side) houses Greek and Roman antiquities, as well as Italian, French, and Spanish paintings—plus an Islamic art exhibit.

We'll concentrate on the Denon and Sully wings, which hold many of the superstars, including ancient Greek sculpture, Italian Renaissance painting, and French Neoclassical and Romantic painting.

The Louvre's Map: The Louvre's free map is detailed but confusing. To get oriented, find the *Mona Lisa:* She's on level 1 (first floor), in Room 6 of the Denon wing. Our tour starts on level -1, under the pyramid; then we enter the Denon wing and turn left into Room 1.

Expect Changes: The sprawling Louvre is constantly shuffling its deck. Rooms close, and pieces can be on loan or in restoration. If you can't find the artwork you're looking for, ask the nearest guard for its new location. Point to the photo in your book and ask, *"Où est, s'il vous plaît?"* (oo ay, see voo play).

The bottom line: You could spend a lifetime here. Zero in on the biggies, and try to finish the tour with enough energy left to browse.

LOUVRE

The Tour Begins

• *From inside the big glass pyramid, head for the Denon wing. Ride the escalator up one floor. After showing your ticket, continue ahead 25 paces, take the* **first left,** *follow the* Antiquités Grecques *signs, and climb a set of stairs to the brick-ceilinged Salle (Room) 1: Grèce Préclassique. Enter prehistory.*

GREECE (3000 B.C.-A.D. 1)
Pre-Classical Greek Statues

These statues are noble but crude. In the first glass cases, find Greek Barbie dolls (3000 B.C.) that are older than the pyramids—as old as writing itself. These prerational voodoo dolls whittle women down to their life-giving traits. Halfway down the hall, a miniature woman *(Dame d'Auxerre)* pledges allegiance to stability. Nearby, another woman *(Core)* is essentially a column with breasts.

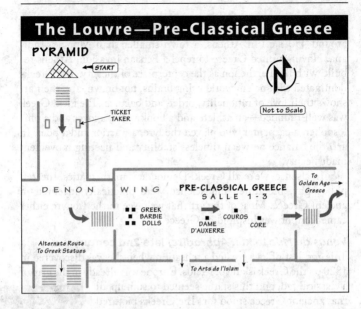

The Louvre—Pre-Classical Greece

PYRAMID

← START

TICKET TAKER

Not to Scale

DENON WING

PRE-CLASSICAL GREECE
SALLE 1 - 3

GREEK BARBIE DOLLS

COUROS

DAME D'AUXERRE

CORE

To Golden Age Greece →

Alternate Route To Greek Statues

To Arts de l'Islam

These statues stand like they have a gun to their backs—hands at sides, facing front, with sketchy muscles and mask-like faces. "Don't move."

The early Greeks, who admired statues like these, found stability more attractive than movement. Like their legendary hero Odysseus, the Greek people spent generations wandering, war-weary and longing for the comforts of a secure home. The strength and sturdiness of these works looked beautiful.

• Before moving on, note that the Islamic rooms are to the right. But we'll continue on with ancient Greece.

Exit at the far end of the pre-Classical Greece galleries, and climb the stairs one flight. At the top, veer left (toward 11 o'clock), and continue into the Sully wing. After about 50 yards, turn right into Salle 16, where you'll find Venus de Milo *floating above a sea of worshipping tourists. It's been said that among the warlike Greeks, this was the first statue to unilaterally disarm.*

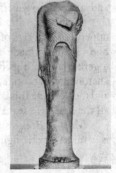

Golden Age Greece

The great Greek cultural explosion that

LOUVRE

changed the course of history unfolded over 50 years (starting around 450 B.C.) in Athens, a town smaller than Muncie, Indiana. Having united Greece to repel a Persian invasion, Athens rebuilt, with the Parthenon as the centerpiece of the city. The Greeks dominated the ancient world using brains, not brawn, and their art shows their love of rationality, order, and balance. The ideal Greek was well-rounded—an athlete and a bookworm, a lover and a philosopher, a carpenter who played the lyre, a warrior and a poet. In art, the balance between timeless stability and fleeting movement made beauty.

In a sense, we're all Greek: Democracy, mathematics, theater, philosophy, literature, and science were practically invented in ancient Greece. Most of the art that we'll see in the Louvre either came from or was inspired by Greece.

Venus de Milo, a.k.a. Aphrodite, late 2nd century B.C.

This goddess of love created a sensation when she was discovered in 1820 on the Greek island of Melos. Europe was already in the grip of a classical fad, and this statue seemed to sum up all that ancient Greece stood for. The Greeks pictured their gods in human form (meaning humans are godlike), telling us they had an optimistic view of the human race. Venus' well-proportioned body captures the balance and orderliness of the Greek universe.

Split *Venus* down the middle from nose to toes and see how the two halves balance each other. Venus rests on her right foot (a position called *contrapposto*, or "counterpoise"), then lifts her left leg, setting her whole body in motion. As the left leg rises, her right shoulder droops down. And as her knee points one way, her head turns the other. *Venus* is a harmonious balance of opposites, orbiting slowly around a vertical axis. The twisting pose gives a balanced S-curve to her body (especially noticeable from the back view) that Golden Age Greeks and succeeding generations found beautiful.

Other opposites balance as well, like the smooth skin of her upper half that sets off the rough-cut texture of her dress (size 14). She's actually made from two different pieces of stone plugged together at the hips (the seam is visible). The face is realistic and anatomically accurate, but it's also idealized, a goddess, too generic and too perfect. This isn't any particular woman, but Everywoman—all the idealized features that appealed to the Greeks.

Most "Greek" statues are actually later Roman copies. This is a rare Greek original. This "epitome of the Golden Age" was

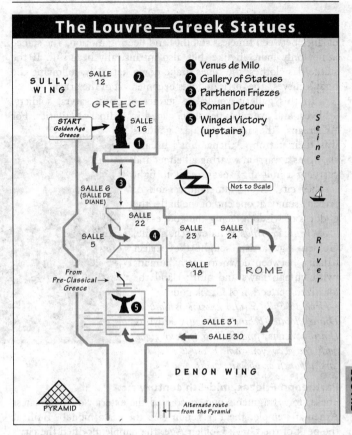

The Louvre—Greek Statues

SULLY WING

SALLE 12 ❷

GREECE

START
Golden Age
Greece →

SALLE 16 ❶

❶ Venus de Milo
❷ Gallery of Statues
❸ Parthenon Friezes
❹ Roman Detour
❺ Winged Victory (upstairs)

Seine River

SALLE 6 (SALLE DE DIANE) ❸

Not to Scale

SALLE 22

SALLE 5

❹

SALLE 23 SALLE 24

SALLE 18 **ROME**

From Pre-Classical → Greece

❺

SALLE 31

SALLE 30 ←

DENON WING

PYRAMID

||| Alternate route from the Pyramid

LOUVRE

sculpted three centuries after the Golden Age, though in a retro style.

What were her missing arms doing? Some say her right arm held her dress, while her left arm was raised. Others say she was hugging a male statue or leaning on a column. I say she was picking her navel.

• *Orbit Venus. This statue is interesting and different from every angle. Remember the view from the back—we'll see it again later. Now make your reentry to earth. Follow Venus' gaze and browse around the adjoining rooms (15, 14, and 13) of this long hall.*

Gallery of Statues

Greek statues feature the human body in all its splendor. The anatomy is accurate, and the poses are relaxed and natural. Around the fifth century B.C., Greek sculptors learned to capture people in motion and to show them from different angles, not just face-forward. The undoubted master was Praxiteles, whose lifelike statues set the tone for later sculptors. He pioneered the classic *contrapposto* pose—with the weight resting on one leg—capturing a balance between timeless stability and fleeting motion. The stance is not only more lifelike, but also intrinsically beautiful. If the statue has clothes, the robes drape down naturally, following the body's curves. The intricate folds become part of the art.

In this gallery, you'll see statues of gods, satyrs, soldiers, athletes, and everyday people engaged in ordinary activities. For Athenians, the most popular goddess was their patron, Athena. She's usually shown as a warrior, wearing a helmet and carrying a (missing) spear, ready to fight for her city. A monumental version of Athena stands at one end of the hall—the goddess of wisdom facing the goddess of love *(Venus de Milo)*. Whatever the statue, Golden Age artists sought the perfect balance between down-to-earth humans (with human flaws and quirks) and the idealized perfection of Greek gods.

• *Head to Salle 6 (also known as Salle de Diane), located behind the* Venus de Milo. *(Facing* Venus, *find Salle 6 to your right, back the way you came.) You'll find two carved panels on opposite walls.*

Parthenon Friezes, mid-5th century B.C.

These stone fragments once decorated the exterior of the greatest Athenian temple, the Parthenon (see the scale model). Built at the peak of the Greek Golden Age, the temple glorified the city's divine protector, Athena, and the superiority of the Athenians, who were feeling especially cocky, having just crushed their archrivals, the Persians. A model of the Parthenon shows where the panels might have hung. The centaur panel would have gone above the entrance. The panel of young women was placed under the covered colonnade, but above the doorway (to see it in the model, you'll have to crouch way down and look up).

The panel on the right side of the room shows a centaur (half-human/half-horse) sexually harassing a woman, telling the story of how these rude creatures crashed a party of regular people. But the humans fought back and threw the brutes out, just as Athens had defeated its Persian invaders.

The other relief shows the sacred procession of young women who marched up the temple hill every four years with an embroidered shawl for the 40-foot-high statue of Athena, the goddess of wisdom (relief pictured at bottom of previous page). Though headless, the maidens speak volumes about Greek craftsmanship. Carved in only a couple of inches of stone, they're amazingly realistic—more so than anything seen in the pre-Classical period. They glide along horizontally (their belts and shoulders all in a line), while the folds of their dresses drape down vertically. The man in the center is relaxed, realistic, and *contrapposto*. Notice the veins in his arm. The maidens' pleated dresses make them look as stable as fluted columns, but their arms and legs step out naturally—their human forms emerging gracefully from the stone.

• *Keep backtracking another 20 paces, turning left into Salle 22, the Roman Antiquities room (Antiquités Romaines), for a...*

Roman Detour (Salles 22-30)

Stroll among the Caesars and try to see the person behind the public persona. Besides the many faces of the ubiquitous Emperor *Inconnu*

("unknown"), you might spot Augustus (Auguste), the first emperor, and his wily wife, Livia (Livie). Their son Tiberius (Tibère) was the Caesar that Jesus Christ "rendered unto." Caligula was notoriously depraved, curly-haired Domitia murdered her husband, Hadrian popularized the beard, Trajan ruled the Empire at its peak, and Marcus Aurelius (Marc Aurèle) presided stoically over Rome's slow fall.

The pragmatic Romans (500 B.C.-A.D. 500) were great conquerors but bad artists. One area in which they excelled was realistic portrait busts, especially of their emperors, who were worshipped as gods on earth. Fortunately for us, the Romans also had a huge appetite for Greek statues and made countless copies. They took the Greek style and wrote it in capital letters, adding a veneer of sophistication to their homes, temples, baths, and government buildings.

You'll wander past several impressive sarcophagi while looping around a massive courtyard (Salle 31) with an impressive mosaic floor and beautiful wall-mounted mosaics from the ancient city of Antioch.

• *To reach the* Winged Victory *continue clockwise through the Roman collection, which eventually spills out at the base of the stairs leading up to the first floor and the dramatic...*

LOUVRE

Winged Victory of Samothrace (Victoire de Samothrace), c. 190 B.C.

This woman with wings, poised on the prow of a ship, once stood on an island hilltop to commemorate a naval victory. Her clothes

are windblown and sea-sprayed, clinging close enough to her body to win a wet T-shirt contest. (Look at the detail in the folds of her dress around the navel, curving down to her hips.) Originally, her right arm was stretched high, celebrating the victory like a Super Bowl champion, waving a "we're number one" finger.

This is the *Venus de Milo* gone Hellenistic, from the time after the culture of Athens was spread around the Mediterranean by Alexander the Great (c. 325 B.C.). As *Victory*

strides forward, the wind blows her and her wings back. Her feet are firmly on the ground, but her wings (and missing arms) stretch upward. She is a pillar of vertical strength, while the clothes curve and whip around her. These opposing forces create a feeling of great energy, making her the lightest two-ton piece of rock in captivity.

The earlier Golden Age Greeks might have considered this statue ugly. Her rippling excitement is a far cry from the dainty Parthenon maidens and the soft-focus beauty of *Venus*. And the statue's off-balance pose, like an unfinished melody, leaves you hanging. But Hellenistic Greeks loved these cliff-hanging scenes of real-life humans struggling to make their mark.

In the glass case nearby is *Victory*'s open right hand with an outstretched finger, found in 1950, a century after the statue itself was unearthed. When the French learned the hand was in Turkey, they negotiated with the Turkish government for the rights to it. Considering all the other ancient treasures that France had looted from Turkey in the past, the Turks thought it only appropriate to give the French the finger.

• *Enter the octagonal room to the left as you face the* Winged Victory, *with Icarus bungee-jumping from the ceiling. Find a friendly window and look out toward the pyramid.*

THE LOUVRE AS A PALACE

Formerly a royal palace, the Louvre was built in stages over eight centuries. On your right (the Sully wing) was the original medieval fortress. About 500 yards to the west, in the now-open area past the pyramid and the triumphal arch, is where the Tuileries Palace used to stand. Succeeding kings tried to connect these two palaces, each monarch adding another section onto the long, skinny north and south wings. Finally, in 1852, after three centuries of building, the two palaces were connected, creating a rectangular Louvre. Nineteen years later, the Tuileries Palace burned down during a riot, leaving the U-shaped Louvre we see today.

The glass pyramid was designed by the Chinese-born American architect I. M. Pei (1989). Many Parisians initially hated the pyramid, just as they hated another new and controversial structure 100 years earlier—the Eiffel Tower.

In the octagonal room, find the plaque at the base of the dome. The inscription reads: *"Le Musée du Louvre, fondé le 16 Septembre, 1792."* The museum was founded by France's Revolutionary National Assembly—the same people who brought you the guillotine. What could be more logical? You behead the king, inherit his palace and art collection, open the doors to the masses, and *voilà!* You have Europe's first public museum.

• *From the octagonal room, enter the Apollo Gallery (Galerie d'Apollon).*

Apollo Gallery

This gallery gives us a feel for the Louvre as the glorious home of French kings (before Versailles). Imagine a chandelier-lit party in this room, drenched in stucco and gold leaf, with tapestries of leading Frenchmen and paintings featuring mythological and symbolic themes. The crystal vases, the inlaid tables made from marble and semiprecious stones, and many other art objects show the wealth of France, Europe's number-one power for two centuries. Portraits on the walls depict great French kings: Henry IV, who built the Pont Neuf; Louis XIV, the Sun King; and François I, who brought Leonardo da Vinci (and the Italian Renaissance) to France.

Stroll past glass cases of royal dinnerware to the far end of the room. In a glass case are the crown jewels. The display varies, but you may see the jewel-studded crowns of Louis XV and the less flashy Crown of Charlemagne (the only crowns to escape destruction in the Revolution), along with the 140-carat Regent Diamond, which once graced crowns worn by Louis XV, Louis XVI, and Napoleon.

• *A rare WC is a half-dozen rooms away, near Salle 38 in the Sully wing. The Italian collection* (Peintures Italiennes) *is on the other side of*

Winged Victory. *Cross back in front of Winged Victory and enter the Denon wing and Salle 1, where you'll find...*

Two Botticelli Frescoes

Look at the paintings on the wall to the left. These pure maidens, like colorized versions of the Parthenon frieze, give us a preview of how ancient Greece would be "reborn" in the Renaissance.
• *But first, the Medieval World. Continue into the large Salle 3.*

THE MEDIEVAL WORLD (1200-1500)

Cimabue, *The Madonna and Child in Majesty Surrounded by Angels (La Vierge et l'Enfant en Majesté Entourés de Six Anges)*, c. 1280

During the Age of Faith (1200s), almost every church in Europe had a painting like this one. Mary was a cult figure—even

bigger than the late-20th-century Madonna—adored and prayed to by the faithful for bringing Baby Jesus into the world. After the collapse of the Roman Empire (c. A.D. 500), medieval Europe was a poor and violent place, with the Christian Church as the only constant in troubled times.

Altarpieces tended to follow the same formula: somber iconic faces, stiff poses, elegant folds in the robes, and generic angels. Violating the laws of perspective, the angels at the "back" of Mary's throne are the same size as those holding the front. These holy figures are laid flat on a gold background like cardboard cutouts, existing in a golden never-never land, as though the faithful couldn't imagine them as flesh-and-blood humans inhabiting our dark and sinful earth.
• *Do a 180 and find...*

Giotto, *St. Francis of Assisi Receiving the Stigmata (Saint François d'Assise Recevant les Stigmates)*, c. 1295-1300

Francis of Assisi (c. 1181-1226), a wandering Italian monk of renowned goodness, kneels on a rocky Italian hillside, pondering the pain of Christ's torture and execution. Suddenly, he looks up, startled, to see Christ himself, with

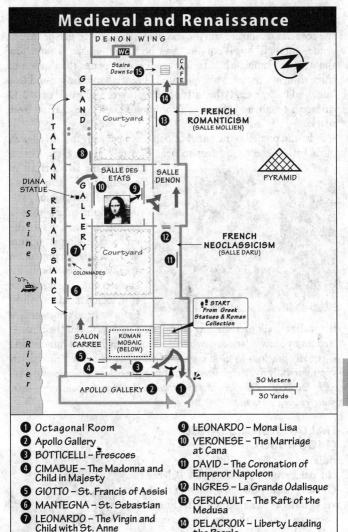

Medieval and Renaissance

DENON WING

WC

Stairs Down to ⑮

CAFE

G R A N D

Courtyard

⑭

⑬

FRENCH ROMANTICISM (SALLE MOLLIEN)

I T A L I A N   R E N A I S S A N C E

PYRAMID

DIANA STATUE

SALLE DES ETATS

SALLE DENON

⑩ ⑨

G A L L E R Y

Seine

⑫

FRENCH NEOCLASSICISM (SALLE DARU)

⑦

Courtyard

⑪

COLONNADES

⑥

🚩 START From Greek Statues & Roman Collection

River

SALON CARREE

ROMAN MOSAIC (BELOW)

⑤

④

③

APOLLO GALLERY ②

①

30 Meters
30 Yards

LOUVRE

① Octagonal Room
② Apollo Gallery
③ BOTTICELLI – Frescoes
④ CIMABUE – The Madonna and Child in Majesty
⑤ GIOTTO – St. Francis of Assisi
⑥ MANTEGNA – St. Sebastian
⑦ LEONARDO – The Virgin and Child with St. Anne
⑧ RAPHAEL – La Belle Jardinière

⑨ LEONARDO – Mona Lisa
⑩ VERONESE – The Marriage at Cana
⑪ DAVID – The Coronation of Emperor Napoleon
⑫ INGRES – La Grande Odalisque
⑬ GERICAULT – The Raft of the Medusa
⑭ DELACROIX – Liberty Leading the People
⑮ MICHELANGELO – Slaves

six wings, hovering above. Christ shoots lasers from his wounds to the hands, feet, and side of the empathetic monk, marking him with the stigmata. Francis went on to breathe the spirit of the Renaissance into medieval Europe. His humble love of man and nature inspired artists like Giotto to portray real human beings with real emotions, living in a physical world of beauty.

Like a good filmmaker, Giotto (c. 1266-1337) doesn't just

tell us what happened, he *shows* us in the present tense, freezing the scene at its most dramatic moment. Though the perspective is crude—Francis' hut is smaller than he is, and Christ is somehow shooting at Francis while facing us—Giotto creates the illusion of three dimensions, with a foreground (Francis), middle ground (his hut), and background (the hillside). Painting a 3-D world on a 2-D surface is tough, and after a millennium of Dark Ages, artists were rusty.

In the predella (the panel of paintings beneath the altarpiece), birds gather at Francis' feet to hear him talk about God. Giotto

catches the late arrivals in midflight, an astonishing technical feat for an artist working more than a century before the Renaissance. The simple gesture of Francis' companion speaks volumes about his amazement. Breaking the stiff, iconic mold for saints, Francis bends forward at the waist to talk to his fellow creatures. The diversity of the birds—"red and yellow, black and white"—symbolizes how all humankind is equally precious in God's sight. Meanwhile, the tree bends down symmetrically to catch a few words from the beloved hippie of Assisi.

• *The long Grand Gallery displays Italian Renaissance painting—some masterpieces, some not.*

ITALIAN RENAISSANCE (1400-1600)

Built in the late 1500s to connect the old palace with the Tuileries Palace, the **Grand Gallery** displays much of the Louvre's Italian Renaissance art. From the doorway, look to the far end and consider this challenge: I hold the world record for the Grand Gallery Heel-Toe-Fun-Walk-Tourist-Slalom, going end to end in 1 minute, 58 seconds (only two injured). Time yourself. Along the way, notice some of the features of Italian Renaissance painting:

• **Religious:** Lots of Madonnas, children, martyrs, and saints.
• **Symmetrical:** The Madonnas are flanked by saints—two to the left, two to the right, and so on.

Italian Renaissance

A thousand years after Rome fell, plunging Europe into the Dark Ages, the Greek ideal of beauty was reborn in 15th-cen-

tury Italy. The Renaissance—or "rebirth" of the culture of ancient Greece and Rome—was a cultural boom that changed people's thinking about every aspect of life. In politics, it meant democracy. In religion, it meant a move away from Church dominance and toward the assertion of man (humanism) and a more personal faith. Science and secular learning were revived after centuries of superstition and ignorance. In architecture, it was a return to the balanced columns and domes of Greece and Rome.

In painting, the Renaissance meant realism, and for the Italians, realism was spelled "3-D." Artists rediscovered the beauty of nature and the human body. With pictures of beautiful people in harmonious 3-D surroundings, they expressed the optimism and confidence of this new age.

- **Realistic:** Real-life human features are especially obvious in the occasional portrait.
- **Three-Dimensional:** Every scene gets a spacious setting with a distant horizon.
- **Classical:** You'll see some Greek gods and classical nudes, but even Christian saints pose like Greek statues, and Mary is a *Venus* whose face and gestures embody all that was good in the Christian world.

Andrea Mantegna, *St. Sebastian,* c. 1480

Not the patron saint of acupuncture, St. Sebastian was a Christian martyr, although here he looks more like a classical Greek statue. Notice the *contrapposto* stance (all of his weight resting on one leg) and the Greek ruins scattered around him. His executioners look like ignorant medieval brutes bewildered by this enlightened Renaissance Man. Italian artists were beginning to learn how to create human realism and earthly beauty on the canvas. Let the Renaissance begin.

• *Look for the following masterpieces by Leonardo 50 yards down the Grand Gallery, on the left.*

Leonardo da Vinci, *The Virgin and Child with St. Anne (La Vierge à l'Enfant Jésus avec Sainte-Anne),* c. 1510

Three generations—grandmother, mother, and child—are arranged in a pyramid, with Anne's face as the peak and the lamb as the lower right corner. Within this balanced structure, Leonardo sets the figures in motion. Anne's legs are pointed to our left. (Is Anne *Mona?* Hmm.) Her daughter Mary, sitting on her lap, reaches to the right. Jesus looks at her playfully while turning away. The lamb pulls away from him. But even with all the twisting and turning, this is still a placid scene. It's as orderly as the geometrically perfect universe created by the Renaissance god.

There's a psychological kidney punch in this happy painting. Jesus, the picture of childish joy, is innocently playing with a lamb—the symbol of his inevitable sacrificial death.

The Louvre has the greatest collection of Leonardos in the world—five of them. Look for the neighboring *Virgin of the Rocks* and *John the Baptist.* Leonardo was the consummate Renaissance Man; a musician, sculptor, engineer, scientist, and sometime painter, he combined knowledge from all these areas to create beauty. If he were alive today, he'd create a Unified Field Theory in physics—and set it to music.

• *You'll likely find Raphael's art on the right side of the Grand Gallery, just past the statue of Diana the Huntress.*

Raphael, *La Belle Jardinière,* c. 1507

Raphael perfected the style Leonardo pioneered. This configuration of Madonna, Child, and John the Baptist is also a balanced pyramid with hazy grace and beauty. Mary is a mountain of maternal tenderness (the title translates as "The Beautiful Gardener") as she eyes her son with a knowing look and holds his hand in a gesture of union. Jesus looks up innocently, standing *contrapposto* like a chubby Greek statue. Baby John the

LOUVRE

Baptist kneels lovingly at Jesus' feet, holding a cross that hints at his playmate's sacrificial death. The interplay of gestures and gazes gives the masterpiece both intimacy and cohesiveness, while Raphael's blended brushstrokes varnish the work with an iridescent smoothness.

With Raphael, the Greek ideal of beauty—reborn in the Renaissance—reached its peak. His work spawned so many imitators who cranked out sickly sweet, generic Madonnas that we often take him for granted. Don't. This is the real thing.

• *The* Mona Lisa (La Joconde) *is near the statue of* Diana, *in Salle 6, midway down the Grand Gallery on the right.* Mona *is alone behind glass on her own false wall. Six million heavy-breathing people crowd in each year to glimpse the most ogled painting in the world. (You can't miss her. Just follow the signs and the people...it's the only painting you can hear. With all the groveling crowds, you can even smell it.)*

Leonardo da Vinci, *Mona Lisa,* a.k.a. *La Joconde,* 1503-1506

Leonardo was already an old man when François I invited him to France. Determined to pack light, he took only a few paintings with him. One was a portrait of Lisa del Giocondo, the wife of a wealthy Florentine merchant. When Leonardo arrived, François immediately fell in love with the painting, making it the centerpiece of the small collection of Italian masterpieces that would, in three centuries, become the Louvre museum. He called it *La Gioconda* (*La Joconde* in French)—a play on both her last name and the Italian word for "happiness." We know it as the *Mona Lisa*—a contraction of the Italian for "my lady Lisa."

Mona may disappoint you. She's smaller than you'd expect, darker, engulfed in a huge room, and hidden behind a glaring

pane of glass. So, you ask, "Why all the hubbub?" Let's take a closer look. As you would with any lover, you've got to take her for what she is, not what you'd like her to be.

The famous smile attracts you first. Leonardo used a hazy technique called *sfumato,* blurring the edges of her mysterious smile. Try as you might, you can never quite see the corners of her mouth. Is she happy? Sad? Tender? Or is it a cynical supermodel's smirk? All visitors read it differently, projecting their own moods onto her enigmatic face. *Mona* is a Rorschach inkblot...so, how are you feeling?

LOUVRE

Now look past the smile and the eyes that really do follow you (most eyes in portraits do) to some of the subtle Renaissance elements that make this painting work. The body is surprisingly massive and statue-like, a perfectly balanced pyramid turned at an angle, so we can see its mass. Her arm rests lightly on the armrest of a chair, almost on the level of the frame itself, as if she's sitting in a window looking out at us. The folds of her sleeves and her gently folded hands are remarkably realistic and relaxed. The typical Leonardo landscape shows distance by getting hazier and hazier.

Though the portrait is generally accepted as a likeness of Lisa del Giocondo, other hypotheses about the sitter's identity have been suggested, including the idea that it's Leonardo himself. Or she might be the Mama Lisa. A recent infrared scan revealed that she has a barely visible veil over her dress, which may mean (in the custom of the day) that she had just had a baby.

The overall mood is one of balance and serenity, but there's also an element of mystery. *Mona*'s smile and long-distance beauty are subtle and elusive, tempting but always just out of reach, like strands of a street singer's melody drifting through the Métro tunnel. *Mona* doesn't knock your socks off, but she winks at the patient viewer.

• *Before leaving* Mona, *step back and just observe the paparazzi scene. The huge canvas opposite* Mona *is...*

Paolo Veronese, *The Marriage at Cana* (*Les Noces de Cana*), 1562-1563

Stand 10 steps away from this enormous canvas to where it just fills your field of vision, and suddenly...you're in a party! Help yourself

to a glass of wine. This is the Renaissance love of beautiful things gone hog-wild. Venetian artists like Veronese painted the good life of rich, happy-go-lucky Venetian merchants.

In a spacious setting of Renaissance architecture, colorful lords and ladies, decked out in their fanciest duds, feast on a great spread of food and drink, while the musicians fuel the fires of good fun. Servants prepare and serve the food, jesters play, and animals roam. In the upper left, a dog and his master look on. A sturdy linebacker in yellow pours wine out of a jug (right foreground). The man in white samples some and thinks, "Hmm, not bad," while nearby a ferocious cat battles a lion. The wedding couple at the far left is almost forgotten.

Believe it or not, this is a religious work showing the wedding celebration in which Jesus turned water into wine. And there's Jesus in the dead center of 130 frolicking figures, wondering if maybe wine coolers might not have been a better choice. With true Renaissance optimism, Venetians pictured Christ as a party animal, someone who loved the created world as much as they did.

Now, let's hear it for the band! On bass—the bad cat with the funny hat—Titian the Venetian! And joining him on viola—Crazy Veronese!

• *Exit behind* Mona *into the Salle Denon (Room 76). The dramatic Romantic room is to your left, and the grand Neoclassical room is to your right. These two rooms feature the most exciting French canvases in the Louvre. Turn right into the Neoclassical room (Salle Daru) and kneel before the largest canvas in the Louvre.*

FRENCH PAINTING (1780-1850)
Jacques-Louis David, *The Coronation of Emperor Napoleon (Sacre de l'Empereur Napoléon)*, 1806-1807

Napoleon holds aloft an imperial crown. This common-born son of immigrants is about to be crowned emperor of a "New Rome." He has just made his wife, Josephine, the empress, and she kneels at his feet. Seated behind Napoleon is the pope, who journeyed from Rome to place the imperial crown on his head. But Napoleon feels that no one is worthy of the task. At the last moment, he shrugs the pope aside, grabs the crown, holds it up for all to see...and crowns himself. The pope looks p.o.'d.

After the French people decapitated their king during the Revolution (1793), their fledgling democracy floundered in chaos. France was united by a charismatic, brilliant, temperamental, upstart general who kept his feet on the ground, his eyes on the horizon, and his hand in his coat—Napoleon Bonaparte. Napoleon quickly conquered most of Europe and insisted on being made emperor (not merely king). The painter David (dah-VEED) recorded the coronation for posterity.

The radiant woman in the gallery in the background center wasn't actually there. Napoleon's mother couldn't make it to see her boy become the most powerful man in Europe, but he had David paint her in anyway. (There's a key on the frame telling who's who in the picture.)

The traditional setting for French coronations was the ultra-Gothic Notre-Dame cathedral. But Napoleon wanted a location that would reflect the glories of Greece and the grandeur of Rome. So, interior decorators erected stage sets of Greek columns and Roman arches to give the cathedral the architectural political correctness you see in this painting. (The *pietà* statue on the right edge of the painting is still in Notre-Dame today.)

David was the new emperor's official painter and propagandist, in charge of color-coordinating the costumes and flags for public ceremonies and spectacles. (Find his self-portrait with curly gray hair in the *Coronation*, way up in the second balcony, peeking around the tassel directly above Napoleon's crown.) His "Neoclassical" style influenced French fashion. Take a look at his *Madame Juliet Récamier* portrait on the opposite wall, showing a modern Parisian woman in ancient garb and Pompeii hairstyle reclining on a Roman couch. Nearby paintings, such as *The Oath of the Horatii (Le Serment des Horaces)*, are fine examples of Neoclassicism, with Greek subjects, patriotic sentiment, and a clean, simple style.

• *As you double back toward the Romantic room, stop at...*

Jean-Auguste-Dominique Ingres, *La Grande Odalisque*, 1814

Take *Venus de Milo*, turn her around, lay her down, and stick a hash pipe next to her, and you have the *Grande Odalisque*. OK, maybe you'd have to add a vertebra or two.

Using clean, polished, sculptural lines, Ingres (ang-gruh) exaggerates the S-curve of a standing Greek nude. As in the *Venus de Milo,* rough folds of cloth set off her smooth skin. Ingres gave the face, too, a touch of *Venus*' idealized features, taking nature and improving on it. Contrast the cool colors of this statue-like nude with Titian's golden girls. Ingres preserves *Venus*' backside for posterior—I mean, posterity.

• *Cross back through the Salle Denon and into Room 77, gushing with French Romanticism.*

Théodore Géricault, *The Raft of the Medusa (Le Radeau de la Méduse)*, 1819

In the artistic war between hearts and minds, the heart style was known as Romanticism. Stressing motion and emotion, it was the flip side of cool, balanced Neoclassicism, though they both flourished in the early 1800s.

What better setting for an emotional work than a shipwreck? Clinging to a raft is a tangle of bodies and lunatics sprawled over

each other. The scene writhes with agitated, ominous motion—the ripple of muscles, churning clouds, and choppy seas. On the right is a deathly green corpse dangling overboard. The face of the man at left, cradling a dead body, says it all—the despair of spending weeks stranded in the middle of nowhere.

This painting was based on the actual sinking of the ship *Medusa* off the coast of Africa in 1816. About 150 people packed onto the raft. After floating in the open seas for 12 days—suffering hardship and hunger, even resorting to cannibalism—only 15 survived. The story was made to order for a painter determined to shock the public and arouse its emotions. That painter was young Géricault (ZHAIR-ee-ko). He interviewed survivors and honed his craft, sketching dead bodies in the morgue and the twisted faces of lunatics in asylums, capturing the moment when all hope is lost.

But wait. There's a stir in the crowd. Someone has spotted something. The bodies rise up in a pyramid of hope, culminating in a flag wave. They signal frantically, trying to catch the attention of the tiny ship on the horizon, their last desperate hope...which did finally save them. Géricault uses rippling movement and powerful colors to catch us up in the excitement. If art controls your heartbeat, this is a masterpiece.

Eugène Delacroix, *Liberty Leading the People* (*La Liberté Guidant le Peuple*), 1831

The year is 1830. King Charles has just issued the 19th-century equivalent of the Patriot Act, and his subjects are angry. Parisians

take to the streets once again, *Les Miz*-style, to fight royalist oppressors. The people triumph—replacing the king with Louis-Philippe, who is happy to rule within the constraints of a modern constitution. There's a hard-bitten proletarian with a sword (far left),

an intellectual with a top hat and a sawed-off shotgun, and even a little boy brandishing pistols.

Leading them on through the smoke and over the dead and dying is the figure of Liberty, a strong woman waving the French flag. Does this symbol of victory look familiar? It's the *Winged Victory,* wingless and topless.

To stir our emotions, Delacroix (del-ah-kwah) uses only three major colors—the red, white, and blue of the French flag. France is the symbol of modern democracy, and this painting has long stirred its citizens' passion for liberty. The French weren't the first to adopt democracy in its modern form (Americans were), nor are they the best working example of it, but they've had to try harder to achieve it than any other country. No sooner would they throw one king or dictator out than they'd get another. They're now working on their fifth republic.

This symbol of freedom is a fitting tribute to the Louvre, the first museum ever opened to the common rabble of humanity. The good things in life don't belong only to a small, wealthy part of society, but to everyone. The motto of France is *Liberté, Egalité, Fraternité*—liberty, equality, and brotherhood for all.

• *Exit the room at the far end (past the Café Mollien) and go downstairs, where you'll bump into the bum of a large, twisting male nude looking like he's just waking up after a thousand-year nap.*

LOUVRE

MORE ITALIAN RENAISSANCE
Michelangelo, *Slaves (Esclaves),* 1513-1515

These two statues by the earth's greatest sculptor are a bridge between the ancient and modern worlds. Michelangelo, like his fellow Renaissance artists, learned from the Greeks. The perfect anatomy, twisting poses, and idealized faces appear as if they could have been created 2,000 years earlier.

The so-called *Dying Slave* (also called the *Sleeping Slave,* looking like he should be stretched out on a sofa) twists listlessly against

his T-shirt-like bonds, revealing his smooth skin. Compare the polished detail of the rippling, bulging left arm with the sketchy details of the face and neck. With Michelangelo, the body does the talking. This is probably the most sensual nude that Michelangelo, the master of the male body, ever created.

The *Rebellious Slave* fights against his bondage. His shoulders rotate one way, his head and leg turn the other. He looks upward, straining to get free. He even seems to be trying to release himself from the rock he's made of. Michelangelo said that his purpose was to carve away the marble to reveal the figures God put inside. This slave shows the agony of that process and the ecstasy of the result.

• *Tour over! These two may be slaves of the museum, but you are free to go. You've seen the essential Louvre. (But no Louvre visit is complete without first taking a photo alongside the statue located 20 paces away, which I believe is titled "Apollo Taking Selfie.")*

To leave the museum, head for the end of the hall, turn right, and follow signs down the stairs to the Sortie.

But, of course, there's so much more. After a break (or on a second visit), consider a stroll through a few rooms of the Richelieu wing, which contain some of the Louvre's most ancient pieces. Bible students, amateur archaeologists, and Iraq War vets may find the collection especially interesting.

NEAR EASTERN ANTIQUITIES

Saddam Hussein was only the latest iron-fisted, palace-building conqueror to fall in the long history of the region that roughly corresponds with modern Iraq. Its origins stretch back to the dawn of time. Civilization began 6,000 years ago between the Tigris and Euphrates rivers, in the area called the Fertile Crescent.

In the Richelieu wing, you can quickly sweep through 2,000 years of this area's ancient history, enjoying some of the Louvre's biggest and oldest artifacts. See how each new civilization toppled the previous one—pulling down its statues, destroying its palaces, looting its cultural heritage, and replacing it with victory monuments of its own...only to be toppled again by the next wave of history.

The iconoclasm continues to this day, as Islamist militants recently vandalized ancient artifacts at Nineveh and elsewhere—making the Louvre's collection all that much more priceless.

• *From under the pyramid, enter the Richelieu wing. Show your ticket, then take the first right. Go up one flight of stairs and one escalator to the ground floor (rez-de-chaussée), where you'll find the Near Eastern antiquities. Walk straight off the escalator, enter Salle 1-a (Mesopotamie Archaïque), and come face-to-face with fragments of the broken...*

Stela of the Vultures (Stèle des Vautours), 2600-2330 B.C.

As old as the pyramids, this Sumerian stela (ceremonial stone pillar) is thought to be the world's oldest surviving historical document. Its images and words record the battle be-

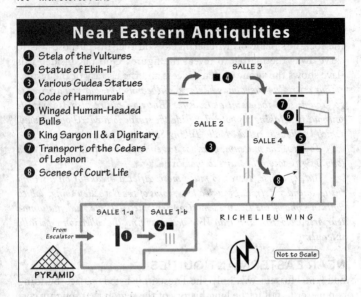

Near Eastern Antiquities

1. Stela of the Vultures
2. Statue of Ebih-il
3. Various Gudea Statues
4. Code of Hammurabi
5. Winged Human-Headed Bulls
6. King Sargon II & a Dignitary
7. Transport of the Cedars of Lebanon
8. Scenes of Court Life

SALLE 3

SALLE 2

SALLE 4

SALLE 1-a   SALLE 1-b

From Escalator

RICHELIEU WING

PYRAMID   Not to Scale

tween the city of Lagash (100 miles north of modern Basra) and its neighboring archrival, Umma.

Circle around the partition to the other side of the stela. "Read" the stela from top to bottom. Top level: Behind a wall of shields, a phalanx of helmeted soldiers advances, trampling the enemy underfoot. They pile the corpses (right), and vultures swoop down from above to pluck the remains. Middle level: Bearded King Eannatum waves to the crowd from his chariot in the victory parade. Bottom level: They dig a mass grave—one of 20 for the 36,000 enemy dead—while a priest (top of the fragment, in a skirt) gives thanks to the gods. A tethered ox (see his big head tied

to a stake) is about to become a burnt sacrifice.

The inscription on the stela is in cuneiform, the world's first written language, invented by the Sumerians.

• *Continue into Salle 1-b, with the blissful...*

Statue of Ebih-il, Superintendent of Mari (Statue de l'Intendant Ebih-il), c. 2400 B.C.

Bald, bearded, blue-eyed Ebih-il (his name is inscribed on his shoulder) sits in his fleece skirt, folds his hands reverently across his chest, and gazes rapturously into space, dreaming of...Ishtar.

A high-ranking dignitary, Ebih-il placed this statue of himself in the goddess Ishtar's temple to declare his perpetual devotion to her.

Ishtar was the chief goddess of many Middle Eastern peoples. As goddess of both love and war, she was a favorite of horny soldiers. She was a giver of life (this statue is dedicated "to Ishtar the virile"), yet also miraculously a virgin. She was also a great hunter with bow and arrow, and a great lover ("Her lips are sweet...her figure is beautiful, her eyes are brilliant...women and men adore her," sang the *Hymn to Ishtar,* c. 1600 B.C.).

Ebih-il adores her eternally with his eyes made of seashells and lapis lazuli. The smile on his face reflects the pleasure the goddess has just given him, perhaps through one of the sacred prostitutes who resided in Ishtar's temple.

• *Go up the five steps behind* Ebih-il, *and turn left into Salle 2, containing a dozen statues of the same man.*

Statue of Gudea, Prince of Lagash (Statue de Gudea, Prince de Lagash), c. 2120 B.C.

Gudea (r. 2141-2122 B.C.), in his wool stocking cap (actually a royal turban), folds his hands and prays to the gods to save his people from invading barbarians. One of Sumeria's last great rulers, the peaceful and pious Gudea (his name means "the destined") rebuilt temples (where these statues once stood) to thank the gods for their help.

• *Exit Salle 2 at the far end and enter Salle 3, with the large black stela of Hammurabi.*

Code of Hammurabi, King of Babylon (Code de Hammurabi, Roi de Babylone), 1792-1750 B.C.

King Hammurabi (r. c. 1792-1750 B.C.) extended the reach of the great Babylonian empire, which joined Sumer and Akkad (stretching from modern-day Baghdad to the Persian Gulf). He proclaimed 282 laws, all inscribed on this eight-foot black basalt stela—one of the first formal legal documents, four centuries before the Ten Commandments. Stelas such as this likely dotted Hammurabi's empire, and this one may have stood in Babylon before being moved to Susa, Iran.

At the top of the stela, Hammurabi (standing and wearing

Gudea's hat of kingship) receives the scepter of judgment from the god of justice and the sun, who radiates flames from his shoulders. The inscription begins, "When Anu the Sublime...called me, Hammurabi, by name...I did right, and brought about the well-being of the oppressed."

Next come the laws, scratched in cuneiform down the length of the stela, some 3,500 lines reading right to left. The laws cover very specific situations, everything from lying, theft, and trade to marriage and medical malpractice. The legal innovation was the immediate retribution for wrongdoing, often with poetic justice. Here's a sample:

#1: If any man ensnares another falsely, he shall be put to death.

#57: If your sheep graze another man's land, you must repay 20 *gur* of grain.

#129: If a couple is caught in adultery, they shall both be tied up and thrown in the water.

#137: If you divorce your wife, you must pay alimony and child support.

#218: A surgeon who bungles an operation shall have his hands cut off.

#282: If a slave shall say, "You are not my master," the master can cut off the slave's ear.

The most quoted laws—summing up the spirit of ancient Near Eastern justice—are #196 ("If a man put out the eye of another man, his eye shall be put out") and #200 ("a tooth for a tooth").

• *Make a U-turn to the right, entering the large Salle 4, dominated by colossal winged bulls with human heads. These sculptures—including five winged bulls and many relief panels along the walls—are from the...*

Palace of Sargon II

Sargon II, the Assyrian king (r. 721-705 B.C.), spared no expense on his palace (see various reconstructions of the palace on plaques around the room). In Assyrian society, the palace of the king—not the temple of the gods—was the focus of life, and each ruler demonstrated his authority with large residences.

Sargon II actually built a whole new city for his palace, just north of the traditional capital of Nineveh (modern-day Mosul). He called it Dur Sharrukin ("Sargonburg"), and the city's vast dimensions were 4,000 cubits by—oh, excuse me—it covered about 150 football fields pieced together. The whole city was built on

Just Enough Geography and History for This Tour

The ancient region of Mesopotamia generally matches the contours of present-day Iraq. The northern half is mountainous, and the southern half is the fertile delta of the Tigris and Euphrates rivers. Modern Baghdad sits roughly in the middle, along the Tigris. The Sumerians inhabited the south, the Assyrians the north, and the Akkadians and Babylonians the center, around Baghdad. Here's a brief timeline:

3500-2400 B.C.: Sumerian city-states flourish between the Tigris and Euphrates rivers. Sumerians invent cuneiform writing.

2300 B.C.: Akkadians invade Sumer.

1750 B.C.: Hammurabi establishes first Babylonian empire.

710 B.C.: Sargon II rules over a vast Assyrian-controlled empire, encompassing modern Iraq, Israel, Syria, and Egypt.

612 B.C.: Babylonians revolt against the Assyrians and destroy their capital of Nineveh, then build their own—Babylon.

a raised, artificial mound, and the 25-acre palace itself sat even higher, surrounded by walls, with courtyards, temples, the king's residence, and a wedding cake-shaped temple (called a ziggurat) dedicated to the god Sin.

• *Start with the two big bulls supporting a (reconstructed) arch.*

Winged Human-Headed Bulls
(Taureau Androcéphale Ailé), c. 721-704 B.C.

These 30-ton, 14-foot alabaster bulls with human faces once guarded the entrance to the throne room of Sargon II. A visitor to the palace back then could have looked over the bulls' heads and seen a 15-story zig-gurat (stepped-pyramid temple) towering overhead. The winged bulls were guardian spirits, warding off demons and intimidating liberals.

Between their legs are cuneiform in-scriptions such as: "I, Sargon, King of the Universe, built palaces for my royal residence...I had winged bulls with human heads carved from great blocks of mountain stone, and I placed them at the doors facing the four winds as powerful divine guardians...My creation amazed all who gazed upon it."

• *We'll see a few relief panels from the palace, working counterclockwise around the room. Start with the panel just to the left of the two big bulls (as you face them). Find the bearded, earringed man in whose image the bulls were made.*

King Sargon II and a Dignitary
(Le Roi Sargon II et un Haut Dignitaire), c. 710 B.C.

Sargon II, wearing a fez-like crown with a cone on the top and straps down the back, cradles his scepter and raises his staff to re-

ceive a foreign ambassador who has come to pay tribute. Sargon II controlled a vast empire, consisting of modern-day Iraq and extending westward to the Mediterranean and Egypt.

Before becoming emperor, Sargon II was a conquering general who invaded Israel (2 Kings 17:1-6). After a three-year siege, he took Jerusalem and deported much of the population, inspiring the legends of the "Lost" Ten Tribes. The prophet Isaiah saw him as God's tool to

The Assyrians

This Semitic people from the agriculturally challenged hills of northern Mesopotamia became traders and conquerors, not farmers. They conquered their southern neighbors and dominated the Near East for 300 years (c. 900-600 B.C.).

Their strength came from a superb army (chariots, mounted cavalry, and siege engines), a policy of terrorism against enemies ("I tied their heads to tree trunks all around the city," reads a royal inscription), ethnic cleansing and mass deportations of the vanquished, and efficient administration (roads and express postal service). They have been called "The Romans of the East."

punish the sinful Israelites, "to seize loot and snatch plunder, and to trample them down like mud in the streets" (Isaiah 10:6).

• *On the wall to the left of Sargon are four panels depicting the...*

Transport of the Cedars of Lebanon
(Transport du Bois de Cèdre du Liban), c. 713-706 B.C.

Boats carry the finest quality logs for Sargon II's palace, crossing a wavy sea populated with fish, turtles, crabs, and mermen. The transport process is described in the Bible (1 Kings 5:9): "My men will haul them down from Lebanon to the sea, and I will float them in rafts to the place you specify."

• *Continue counterclockwise around the room—past more big, winged animals, past the huge hero, Gilgamesh, crushing a lion—until you reach more relief panels. These depict...*

Scenes of Court Life

The brown, eroded gypsum panels we see here were originally painted and varnished. Placed side by side, they would have stretched over a mile. The panels read like a comic strip, showing the king's men parading in to serve him.

First, soldiers sheathe their swords and fold their hands reverently. A winged spirit prepares them to enter the king's presence by shaking a pinecone to anoint them with holy perfume. Next, servants hurry to the throne room with the king's dinner, carrying his table, chair, and bowl. Other servants ready the king's horses and chariots. They all proceed forward, ready to serve their master—the all-powerful ruler of the civilized world.

From Sargon to Saddam

Sargon II's palace remained unfinished and was later burned and buried. Sargon's great Assyrian empire dissolved over the next few generations. When the Babylonians revolted and conquered their northern neighbors (612 B.C.), the whole Middle East applauded. As the Bible put it: "Nineveh is in ruins—who will mourn for her?... Everyone who hears the news claps his hands at your fall, for who has not felt your endless cruelty?" (Nahum 3:7, 19).

The new capital was Babylon (50 miles south of modern Baghdad), ruled by King Nebuchadnezzar, who conquered Judea (586 B.C., the Bible's "Babylonian Captivity") and built a palace with the Hanging Gardens, one of the Seven Wonders of the World.

Over the succeeding centuries, Babylon/Baghdad fell to Persians (539 B.C.), Greeks (Alexander the Great, 331 B.C.), Persians again (second century B.C.), Arab Muslims (A.D. 634), Mongol hordes (Genghis Khan's grandson, 1258), Iranians (1502), Ottoman Turks (1535), British-controlled kings (1921), and military regimes (1958), the most recent headed by Saddam Hussein (1979).

After toppling Saddam Hussein in 2003, George W. Bush declared, "Mission accomplished!" Five thousand years of invasions, violence, and regime change, as well as current events, suggest otherwise.

LOUVRE

ORSAY
MUSEUM TOUR

Musée d'Orsay

The Musée d'Orsay (mew-zay dor-say) houses French art of the 1800s and early 1900s (specifically, 1848-1914), picking up where the Louvre's art collection leaves off. For us, that means Impressionism, the art of sun-dappled fields, bright colors, and crowded Parisian cafés. The Orsay houses the best general collection anywhere of Manet, Monet, Renoir, Degas, Van Gogh, Cézanne, and Gauguin. If you like Impressionism, visit this museum. If you don't like Impressionism, visit this museum. I find it a more enjoyable and rewarding place than the Louvre. Sure, ya gotta see the *Mona Lisa* and *Venus de Milo,* but after you get your gottas out of the way, enjoy the Orsay.

Keep in mind that the collection is always on the move—paintings on loan, in restoration, or displayed in different rooms. But with a little flexibility, you should be able to see most of the Orsay's masterpieces.

Orientation

Cost: €11, €8.50 Tue-Wed and Fri-Sun after 16:30 and Thu after 18:00, free on first Sun of month and often near closing time (explained below), covered by Museum Pass. Combo-tickets are available with the Orangerie (€16) or Rodin Museum (€18).

Hours: Tue-Sun 9:30-18:00, Thu until 21:45, closed Mon, last entry one hour before closing (45 minutes before on Thu). The top-floor Impressionist galleries begin closing 45 minutes early, frustrating unwary visitors.

Free Entry near Closing Time: Right when the ticket booth stops selling tickets, visitors can often (but not always) scoot in free of charge (Tue-Wed and Fri-Sun at 17:00, Thu at 21:00; they won't let you in much after that, however). Make a beeline for the Impressionist galleries, which start shutting down first.

When to Go: For shorter lines and fewer crowds, visit on Wed, Fri, or Thu evening (when the museum is open late). You'll battle the biggest hordes on Sun, as well as on Tue, when the Louvre is closed.

Avoiding Lines: You can skip long ticket-buying lines by using a Museum Pass or purchasing tickets in advance (available online—see the Orsay website for details); both entitle you to use a separate entrance.

You can also buy tickets and Museum Passes (no mark-up; tickets valid 3 months) at the newspaper kiosk just outside the Orsay entrance (along Rue de la Légion d'Honneur). If you're planning to get a combo-ticket with either the Orangerie or the Rodin Museum, consider starting at one of those museums instead, as they have shorter lines.

Getting There: The museum sits above the RER-C stop called Musée d'Orsay. The Solférino Métro stop is three blocks southeast of the Orsay. Bus #69 from the Marais neighborhood stops at the museum on the river side (Quai Anatole France); from the Rue Cler area, it stops behind the museum on Rue du Bac. From the Louvre, catch bus #69 along Rue de Rivoli. Or it's a lovely 15-minute walk through the Tuileries Garden and across the river on the pedestrian bridge from the Louvre or Orangerie museums. The museum is at 1 Rue de la Légion d'Honneur. A taxi stand is in front of the entry on Quai Anatole France. The Batobus boat stops here (see page 42).

Getting In: As you face the entrance, passholders and ticket holders enter on the right (Entrance C). Ticket purchasers enter on the left (Entrance A). Security checks slow down all entrances.

Information: The museum updates its website daily with the latest layout (click on "Interactive plan of the museum" at bottom of home page). The booth inside the entrance provides free floor plans that can help you navigate the ever-changing museum. Tel. 01 40 49 48 14, www.musee-orsay.fr.

Tours: Audioguides cost €5. English **guided tours** usually run daily at 11:30 (€6/1.5 hours, none on Sun, tours may also run at 14:30—inquire when you arrive).

🎧 Download my free Orsay Museum **audio tour.**

Length of This Tour: Allow two hours. With less time, focus on the Impressionists on the top floor, and Van Gogh and company on level 2.

Cloakroom *(Vestiaire):* Checking bags or coats is free. Day bags (but nothing bigger) are allowed in the museum. No valuables can be stored in checked bags (the clerk might ask

The Orsay's "19th Century" (1848-1914)

Einstein and Geronimo. Abraham Lincoln and Karl Marx. The train, the bicycle, the horse and buggy, the automobile, and the balloon. Freud and Dickens. Darwin's *Origin of Species* and the Church's Immaculate Conception. Louis Pasteur and Billy the Kid. Ty Cobb and V. I. Lenin.

The 19th century was a mix of old and new, side by side. Europe was entering the modern Industrial Age, with cities, factories, rapid transit, instant communication, and global networks. At the same time, it clung to the past with traditional, rural—almost medieval—attitudes and morals.

According to the Orsay, the "19th century" began in 1848 with the socialist and democratic revolutions (Marx's *Communist Manifesto*). It ended in 1914 with the pull of an assassin's trigger, which ignited World War I and ushered in the modern world. The museum shows art that is also both old and new, conservative and revolutionary.

you in French not to check cameras, passports, or anything particularly precious).

Photography: Photography without flash is allowed.

Cuisine Art: The snazzy **$$ Le Restaurant** is on the second floor, with affordable tea and coffee served daily except Thursday from 14:45 (Tue-Sun 11:45-17:30, Thu 11:45-14:45 & 19:00-21:00). A simple sandwich-and-salad **$ café** is on the main floor (far end), and a convenient-if-pricier one is on the fifth floor beyond the Impressionist galleries. Outside, behind the museum, a number of classy eateries line Rue du Bac.

Starring: Manet, Monet, Renoir, Degas, Van Gogh, Cézanne, and Gauguin.

ORSAY

The Tour Begins

• *Pick up a free map and belly up to the stone balustrade overlooking the main floor.*

Trains used to run right under our feet down the center of the gallery. This former train station, the Gare d'Orsay, barely escaped the wrecking ball in the 1970s, when the French realized it'd be a great place to house the enormous collections of 19th-century art scattered throughout the city. The ground floor (level 0) houses early-19th-century art, mainly conservative art of the Academy and Salon, plus Realism. On the top floor (not visible from here) is the core of the collection—the Impressionist rooms.

If you're pressed for time, go directly there (see directions on page 176). We'll start with conservatives and early rebels on the ground floor, then head upstairs to see how a few visionary young artists bucked the system and revolutionized the art world, paving the way for the 20th century. Clear as Seine water? *Bien.*

Remember that the museum rotates its large collection often, so find the latest arrangement on your current Orsay map, and be ready to go with the flow.

• *Walk down the steps to the main floor, a gallery filled with statues.*

CONSERVATIVE ART
Main Gallery Statues

No, this isn't ancient Greece. These statues are from the same era as the Theory of Relativity. It's the conservative art of the French schools, and it was very popular throughout the 19th century. It was well-liked for its beauty and refined emotion. The balanced poses, perfect anatomy, sweet faces, curving lines, and gleaming white stone—all of this is very appealing. (I'll bad-mouth it later, but for now appreciate the exquisite craftsmanship of this "perfect" art.)

• *Take your first right into the small Room 1, marked* Ingres, Delacroix, Chassériau. *Look for a nude woman with a pitcher of water.*

Ingres, *The Source (La Source),* 1856

Let's start where the Louvre left off. Jean-Auguste-Dominique Ingres (ang-gruh), who helped cap the Louvre collection, championed a Neoclassical style. *The Source*

is virtually a Greek statue on canvas. Like *Venus de Milo,* she's a balance of opposite motions—her hips tilt one way, her breasts the other; one arm goes up, the other down; the water falling from the pitcher matches the fluid curve of her body. Her skin is porcelain-smooth, painted with seamless brushstrokes.

Ingres worked on this painting over the course of 35 years and considered it his "image of perfection." Famous in its day, *The Source* influenced many artists whose classical statues and paintings are in this museum.

In the Orsay's first few rooms, you're surrounded by visions of idealized beauty—nude women in languid poses, Greek mythological figures, and anatomically perfect statues. This was the art adored by French academics and the middle-class *(bourgeois)* public. The 19th-century art world was dominated by two conservative institutions: the Academy (the state-funded art school) and the Salon, where

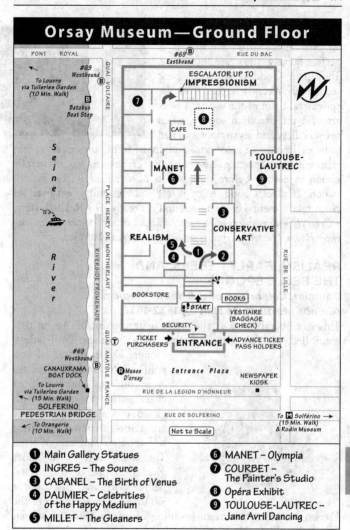

Orsay Museum—Ground Floor

PONT ROYAL · #69 Eastbound · RUE DU BAC

#69 Westbound
To Louvre via Tuileries Garden (10 Min. Walk)

Batobus Boat Stop

QUAI VOLTAIRE

PLACE HENRY DE MONTHERLANT

RIVERSIDE PROMENADE

QUAI ANATOLE FRANCE

Seine River

ESCALATOR UP TO **IMPRESSIONISM**

❼

CAFE

❽

MANET ❻

TOULOUSE-LAUTREC ❾

❸

REALISM ❺ ❹ ❶ ❷ **CONSERVATIVE ART**

RUE DE LILLE

BOOKSTORE

BOOKS

START

VESTIAIRE (BAGGAGE CHECK)

SECURITY

TICKET PURCHASERS

ENTRANCE

ADVANCE TICKET PASS HOLDERS

#69 Westbound

CANAUXRAMA BOAT DOCK
To Louvre via Tuileries Garden (15 Min. Walk)

SOLFERINO PEDESTRIAN BRIDGE

To Orangerie (10 Min. Walk)

Ⓡ Musee D'orsay

Entrance Plaza

NEWSPAPER KIOSK

RUE DE LA LEGION D'HONNEUR

RUE DE SOLFERINO

To Ⓜ Solférino (15 Min. Walk) & Rodin Museum

Not to Scale

❶ Main Gallery Statues
❷ INGRES – The Source
❸ CABANEL – The Birth of Venus
❹ DAUMIER – Celebrities of the Happy Medium
❺ MILLET – The Gleaners
❻ MANET – Olympia
❼ COURBET – The Painter's Studio
❽ Opéra Exhibit
❾ TOULOUSE-LAUTREC – Jane Avril Dancing

ORSAY

works were exhibited to the buying public. The art they produced was technically perfect, refined, uplifting, and heroic. Some might even say...boring.

• *Continue to Room 3 to find a pastel blue-green painting of a swooning Venus.*

Cabanel, *The Birth of Venus*
(La Naissance de Vénus), 1863

This painting and others nearby were popular items at the art market called the Salon. The public loved Alexandre Cabanel's *Venus.* Emperor Napoleon III purchased it.

Cabanel lays Ingres' *The Source* on her back. This goddess is a perfect fantasy, an orgasm of beauty. The Love Goddess stretches back seductively, recently birthed from the ephemeral foam of the waves. This is art of a pre-Freudian society, when sex was dirty and mysterious and had

to be exalted into a more pure and divine form. The sex drive was channeled into an acute sense of beauty. French folk would literally swoon in ecstasy before these works of art. Like it? Go ahead, swoon. If it feels good, enjoy it. (If you feel guilty, get over it.) Now, take a mental cold shower, and get ready for a Realist's view.
• *Cross the main gallery of statues, backtrack toward the entrance, and enter Room 4 (directly across from Ingres), marked* Daumier.

REALISM, EARLY REBELS, AND THE BELLE EPOQUE
Daumier, *Celebrities of the Happy Medium (Célébrités du Juste Milieu),* 1832-1835
This is a liberal's look at the stuffy bourgeois establishment that controlled the Academy and the Salon. In these 36 bustlets,

Honoré Daumier, trained as a political cartoonist, exaggerates each subject's most distinct characteristic to capture with vicious precision the pomposity and self-righteousness of these self-appointed arbiters of taste. The labels next to the busts give the name of the person being caricatured, his title or job (most were members of the French parliament), and an insulting nickname (like "gross, fat, and satisfied" or Monsieur "Platehead"). Give a few nicknames yourself. Can you find Reagan, Clinton, Kerry, Sarkozy, Al Sharpton, Gingrich, Trump, and Paul Ryan with sideburns? How about Margaret Thatcher...or is that a dude?

These people hated the art you're about to see. Their prudish faces tightened as their fantasy world was shattered by the Realists.
• *Nearby, find Millet's* Gleaners. *(Reminder: Paintings often move around, so you may need to use your Orsay map to find specific works.)*

Millet, *The Gleaners (Les Glaneuses),* 1867
Jean-François Millet (mee-yay) shows us three gleaners, the poor women who pick up the meager leftovers after a field has already

been harvested for the wealthy. Millet grew up on a humble farm. He didn't attend the Academy and despised the uppity Paris art scene. Instead of idealized gods, goddesses, nymphs, and winged babies, he painted simple rural scenes. He was strongly affected by the socialist revolution of 1848, with its affirmation of the working class. Here he captures the innate dignity of these stocky, tanned women who bend their backs quietly in a large field for their small reward.

This is "Realism" in two senses. It's painted "realistically," not prettified. And it's the "real" world—not the fantasy world of Greek myth, but the harsh life of the working poor.

• *For a Realist's take on the traditional Venus, find Manet's* Olympia *in Room 14.*

Manet, *Olympia,* 1863

"This brunette is thoroughly ugly. Her face is stupid, her skin cadaverous. All this clash of colors is stupefying." So wrote a critic when Edouard Manet's nude hung in the Salon. The public hated it, attacking Manet (man-ay) in print and literally attacking the canvas.

Compare this uncompromising nude with Cabanel's idealized, pastel, Vaseline-on-the-lens beauty in *The Birth of Venus.* Cabanel's depiction was basically soft-core pornography, the kind you see today selling lingerie and perfume.

Manet's nude doesn't gloss over anything. The pose is classic, used by Titian, Goya, and countless others. But the traditional pose is challenged by the model's jarring frankness. The sharp outlines and harsh, contrasting colors are new and shocking. The woman is Manet's favorite model, a sometime painter and free spirit who also appears in his *Déjeuner* (described later). Her hand is a clamp, and her stare is shockingly defiant, with not a hint of the seductive, hey-sailor look of most nudes. This prostitute, ignoring the flowers sent by her last customer, looks out as if to say, "Next." Manet replaced soft-core porn with hard-core art.

• *Make your way to the far left corner of level 0, to a room dominated by huge dark canvases, including...*

Courbet, *The Painter's Studio (L'Atelier du Peintre),* 1855

The Salon of 1855 rejected this dark-colored, sprawling, monumental painting that perplexed casual viewers. (It may be undergoing restoration in situ when

you visit.) In an age when "Realist painter" was equated with "bomb-throwing Socialist," it took courage to buck the system. Dismissed by the so-called experts, Gustave Courbet (coor-bay) held his own one-man exhibit. He built a shed in the middle of Paris, defiantly hung his art out, and basically mooned the shocked public.

Courbet's painting takes us backstage, showing us the gritty reality behind the creation of pretty pictures. We see Courbet himself in his studio, working diligently on a Realistic landscape, oblivious to the confusion around him. Milling around are ordinary citizens, not Greek heroes. The woman who looks on is not a nude Venus but a naked artist's model. And the little boy with an adoring look on his face? Perhaps it's Courbet's inner child, admiring the artist who sticks to his guns, whether it's popular or not.

• *At the far end of the gallery, you'll walk on a glass floor over a model of Paris.*

Opéra Exhibit

Expand to 100 times your size and hover over this scale-model section of the city. In the center sits the 19th-century Opéra Garnier, with its green-domed roof.

Nearby, you'll also see a cross-section model of the Opéra. You'd enter from the right end, buy your ticket in the foyer, then

move into the entrance hall with its grand staircase, where you could see and be seen by *tout* Paris. At curtain time, you'd find your seat in the red-and-gold auditorium, topped by a glorious painted ceiling. Notice that the stage, with elaborate riggings to raise and lower scenery, is as big as the seating area. Nearby are models of set designs from some famous productions. These days, Parisians enjoy their Verdi and Gounod at the modern opera house at Place de la Bastille.

The Opéra Garnier—opened in 1875—was the symbol of the belle époque, or "beautiful age." Paris was a global center of prosperity, new technology, opera, ballet, painting, and joie de vivre. But behind Paris' gilded and gas-lit exterior, a counterculture simmered. Revolutionaries battled to allow labor unions and give everyone the right to vote. Realist painters captured scenes of a grittier Paris, and Impressionists chafed against middle-class tastes, rejecting the careers mapped out for them to follow their artistic dreams.

• *For a taste of Parisian life during this golden age, find the Toulouse-Lautrec paintings tucked away in Room 10, to the right of the Opéra exhibit. They rightly belong with the Post-Impressionist works on level 2, but since you're already here, enjoy these paintings incarnating the artist's love of nightlife and show business...*

Henri de Toulouse-Lautrec (1864-1901)

Henri de Toulouse-Lautrec was the black sheep of a noble family. At age 14 he broke both legs, which left him with a normal-size torso but dwarf-size limbs. Shunned by his family, a freak to society, he felt more at home in the underworld of other outcasts—prostitutes, drunks, thieves, dancers, and actors. He settled in Montmartre, where he painted the life he lived, sketching the lowlife in the bars, cafés, dance halls, and brothels he frequented. He drank absinthe and hung out with Van Gogh. He carried a hollow cane filled with booze. When the Moulin Rouge nightclub opened, Henri was hired to do its posters. (See his poster of the singer Aristide Bruant on page 379.) Every night, the artist put on his bowler hat and visited the Moulin Rouge to draw the crowds, the can-can dancers, and the backstage action. Toulouse-Lautrec died at age 36 of syphilis and alcoholism.

Toulouse-Lautrec's painting style captures Realist scenes with strong, curvaceous outlines. He worked quickly, creating sketches in paint that serve as snapshots of a golden era.

In *Jane Avril Dancing* (*Jane Avril Dansant*, 1891), he depicts the slim, graceful, elegant, and melancholy dancer, who stood out above the rabble. Her legs keep dancing while her mind is far away. Toulouse-Lautrec, the "artistocrat," might have identified with her noble face—sad and weary of the nightlife, but immersed in it.

• *Next up—the Orsay's Impressionist collection. Consider reading ahead on Impressionism while you're still on the ground floor, as the Impressionist rooms can be very crowded. Then take the escalator up to the top floor. Pause to take in a commanding view of the Orsay, pass through the*

bookstore, glance at the backward clock, and enter the Impressionist rooms.

The Impressionist collection is scattered randomly through Rooms 29-36. You'll see Monet hanging next to Renoir, Manet sprinkled among Pissarro, and a few Degas here and a few Degas there. Shadows dance and the displays mingle. Where they're hung is a lot like their brushwork...delightfully sloppy. If you don't see a described painting, just move on.

IMPRESSIONISM

Light! Color! Vibrations! You don't hang an Impressionist canvas—you tether it. Impressionism features bright colors, easygoing open-air scenes, spontaneity, broad brushstrokes, and the play of light.

The Impressionists made their canvases shimmer by using a simple but revolutionary technique. Let's say you mix red, yellow, and green together—you'll get brown, right? But Impressionists didn't bother to mix them. They'd slap a thick brushstroke of yellow down, then a stroke of green next to it, then red next to that. Up close, all you see are the three messy strokes, but as you back up...*voilà!* Brown! The colors blend in the eye, at a distance. But while your eye is saying "bland old brown," your subconscious is shouting, "Red! Yellow! Green! Yes!"

There are no lines in nature, yet someone in the classical tradition (Ingres, for example) would draw an outline of his subject, then fill it in with color. Instead the Impressionists built a figure with dabs of paint...a snowman of color.

Although this top floor displays the Impressionists, you'll find a wide variety of styles. What united these artists was their commitment to everyday subjects (cafés, street scenes, landscapes, workers), their disdain for the uptight Salon, their love of color, and a sense of artistic rebellion. These painters had a love-hate relationship with the "Impressionist" label. Later in their careers, they all went their own ways and developed their own individual styles.

The Impressionists all seemed to know each other. You may see a group portrait by Henri Fantin-Latour depicting the circle of Parisian artists and intellectuals. Manet first met Degas while copying the same painting at the Louvre. Monet and Renoir set up their canvases in the country and painted side by side. Renoir painted with Cézanne and employed the mother of Utrillo as a model. Toulouse-Lautrec lived two blocks from Van Gogh. Van Gogh painted in Arles with Gauguin (an episode that ended disastrously—see page 185). Van Gogh's work was some of the first bought by an admiring Rodin.

They all learned from each other and taught each other, and they all influenced the next generation's artists (Matisse and Picasso), who created Modern art.

Remember, the following tour is less a room-by-room itinerary than an introduction to the Orsay's ever-changing collection. Have fun exploring: Think of it as a sun-dappled treasure hunt.

• *Start with the Impressionists' mentor, Manet, whose work is usually found in Room 29.*

Edouard Manet (1832-1883)

Manet had an upper-class upbringing and some formal art training, and had been accepted by the Salon. He could have cranked out pretty nudes and been a successful painter, but instead he surrounded himself

Orsay— Impressionism

To **WC** & Escalator to Level 2

CAFE

CEZANNE

TERRACE

36
35
34
33
32
MONET
RENOIR
DEGAS
MANET
31
30
MANET & MONET
ROOM 29

VIEW THRU CLOCK

FROM ESCALATOR

Seine River

ORSAY

with a group of young artists experimenting with new techniques. His reputation and strong personality made them their master, but he also learned equally from them.

Manet's thumbnail bio is typical of almost all the Impressionists: They rejected a "normal" career (lawyer, banker, grocer) to become artists, got classical art training, exhibited in the Salon, became fascinated by Realist subjects, but grew tired of the Salon's dogmatism. They joined the Impressionist exhibition of 1874, experimented with bright colors and open-air scenes, and moved on to forge their unique styles in later years.

Manet's starting point was Realism. Rather than painting Madonnas, Greek gods, and academic warhorses, he hung out in

Painting "in the Open Air"

The camera threatened to make artists obsolete. Now a machine could capture a better likeness faster than you could say "Etch-a-Sketch."

But true art is more than just painting reality. It gives us reality from the artist's point of view, with the artist's personal impressions of the scene. Impressions are often fleeting, so working quickly is essential.

The Impressionist painters rejected camera-like detail for a quick style more suited to capturing the passing moment. Feeling stifled by the rigid rules and stuffy atmosphere of the Academy, the Impressionists took as their motto, "Out of the studio, into the open air." They grabbed their berets and scarves and went on excursions to the country, where they set up their easels (and newly invented tubes of premixed paint) on riverbanks and hillsides, or they sketched in cafés and dance halls. Gods, goddesses, nymphs, and fantasy scenes were out; common people and rural landscapes were in.

The quick style and everyday subjects were ridiculed and called childish by the "experts." Rejected by the Salon, the Impressionists staged their own exhibition in 1874. They brashly took their name from an insult thrown at them by a critic who laughed at one of Monet's "impressions" of a sunrise. During the next decade, they exhibited their own work independently. The public, opposed at first, was slowly won over by the simplicity, the color, and the vibrancy of Impressionist art.

cafés, sketchbook in hand, capturing the bustle of modern Paris. His painting style was a bit messy with its use of rough brushstrokes—a technique that drew the attention of budding painters like Monet and Renoir. Manet was never a full-on Impressionist. He tried but disliked open-air painting, preferring to sketch on the spot, then do his serious painting in the studio. And his colors remained dark, with plenty of brown and figures outlined in black. But when Manet's paintings were criticized by the art establishment, the Impressionists rallied to his defense, and Manet became the best-known champion of the new movement.

Manet's ***Luncheon on the Grass*** (*Le Déjeuner sur l'Herbe*, 1863) shocked Paris. The staid citizens looked at this and wondered: What are these scantily clad women doing with these men? Or rather, what will they be doing after the last baguette is eaten? It isn't the nudity, but the presence of the men in ordinary clothes that suddenly makes the nudes look naked. The public judged

the painting on moral rather than artistic terms. Here too the pose is classical (as seen in works by Titian), but it's presented as though it were happening in a Parisian park in 1863.

You can see that a new revolutionary movement was starting to bud—Impressionism. Notice the background: the messy brushwork of trees and leaves, the play of light on the pond, and the light that filters through the trees onto the woman who stoops in the haze. Also note the strong contrast of colors (white skin, black clothes, green grass).

Let the Impressionist revolution begin!

Edgar Degas (1834-1917)

Degas (day-gah) was a rich kid from a family of bankers, and he got the best classical-style art training. Adoring Ingres' pure lines and cool colors, Degas painted in the Academic style. His work was exhibited in the Salon, he gained success and a good reputation, and then...he met the Impressionists.

Degas blends classical lines and Realist subjects with Impressionist color, spontaneity, and everyday scenes from urban Paris. He loved the unposed "snapshot" effect, catching his models off guard. Dance students, women at work, and café scenes are approached from odd angles that aren't always ideal but make the scenes seem more real. He gives us the backstage view of life.

Degas participated in the Impressionist exhibitions, but he disdained open-air painting, preferring to perfect his meticulous paintings in the studio. He painted few Impressionist landscapes, focusing instead on people. And he created his figures not as a mosaic of colorful brushstrokes, but with a classic technique—outline filled in with color. His influence on Toulouse-Lautrec is clear.

Degas loved dance and the theater. The play of stage lights off his dancers, especially the halos of ballet skirts, is made to order for an Impressionist. A dance rehearsal let Degas capture a behind-the-scenes look at bored, tired, restless dancers (*The Dance Class*, *La Classe de Danse*, c. 1873-1875). Besides his oil paintings of dancers, you may also see his small statues of them—he first modeled the figures in wax, then cast them in bronze.

Degas hung out with low-life Impressionists, discussing art, love, and life in the cheap cafés and bars in Montmartre. In the painting *In a Café* (*Dans un Café*, 1875-1876), a weary lady of the evening meets morning with a last, lonely, nail-in-the-coffin drink in the glaring light of a four-in-the-morning café. The pale green

ORSAY

drink at the center of the composition is the toxic substance absinthe, which fueled many artists and burned out many more.

• *Scattered all around you are works by two Impressionist masters at their peak, Monet and Renoir. You're looking at the quintessence of Impressionism. The two were good friends, often working side by side, and their canvases sometimes hang side by side in these rooms.*

Claude Monet (1840-1926)

Monet (mo-nay) is the father of Impressionism. He fully explored the possibilities of open-air painting and tried to faithfully reproduce nature's colors with bright blobs of paint. Throughout his long career, more than any of his colleagues, Monet stuck to the Impressionist credo of creating objective studies in color and light.

In the 1860s, Monet (along with Renoir) began painting landscapes in the open air. Although Monet did the occasional urban scene, he was most at home in the countryside, painting farms, rivers, trees, and passing clouds. He studied optics and pigments to know just the right colors he needed to reproduce the shimmering quality of reflected light. The key was to work quickly—at that "golden hour" (to use a modern photographer's term), when the light was just right. Then he'd create a fleeting "impression" of the scene. In fact, that was the title of one of Monet's canvases (now hanging in the Marmottan—see page 271); it gave the movement its name.

Monet is known for his series of paintings on the same subject. For example, you may see several canvases of the cathedral in Rouen. In 1893, Monet went to Rouen, rented a room across

ORSAY

from the cathedral, set up his easel...and waited. He wanted to catch "a series of differing impressions" of the cathedral facade at various times of day and year. He often had several canvases going at once. In all, he did 30 paintings of the cathedral, and each is unique. The time-lapse series shows the sun passing

slowly across the sky, creating different-colored light and shadows.

The labels next to the art describe the conditions: in gray weather, in the morning, morning sun, full sunlight, and so on.

As Monet zeroed in on the play of colors and light, the physical subject—the cathedral—dissolved. It's only a rack upon which to hang the light and color. Later artists would boldly throw away the rack, leaving purely abstract modern art in its place.

One of Monet's favorite places to paint was the garden he landscaped at his home in Giverny, west of Paris (and worth a visit, provided you like Monet more than you hate crowds—see the Giverny and Auvers-sur-Oise chapter). The Japanese bridge and the water lilies floating in the pond were his two favorite subjects. As Monet aged and his eyesight failed, he made bigger canvases of smaller subjects. The final water lilies are monumental smudges of thick paint surrounded by paint-splotched clouds that are reflected on the surface of the pond.

Monet's most famous water lilies are in full bloom at the Orangerie Museum, across the river in the Tuileries Garden (📖 see the Orangerie Museum Tour chapter). You can see more Monet at the Marmottan Museum (📖 see the Marmottan Museum Tour chapter).

Pierre-Auguste Renoir (1841-1919)

Renoir (ren-wah) started out as a painter of landscapes, along with Monet, but later veered from the Impressionist's philosophy and painted images that were unabashedly "pretty." He populated his canvases with rosy-cheeked, middle-class girls performing happy domestic activities, rendered in a warm, inviting style. As Renoir himself said, "There are enough ugly things in life."

He did portraits of his friends (such as Monet) and his own kids, including his son Jean (who grew up to make the landmark film *Grand Illusion*). But his specialty was always women and girls, emphasizing their warm femininity.

Renoir's lighthearted work uses light colors—no brown or black. The paint is thin and translucent, and the outlines are soft, so the figures blend seamlessly with the background. He seems to be searching for an ideal, the sort of pure beauty we saw in paintings on the ground floor.

In his last years (when he was confined to a wheelchair with arthritis), Renoir turned to full-figured nudes—like those painted by Old Masters such as Rubens or Boucher. He introduced more and more red tones, as if trying for even greater warmth.

Renoir's best-known work is ***Dance at the Moulin de la Galette*** (*Bal du Moulin de la Galette*, 1876). On Sunday afternoons, work-

ing-class folk would dress up and head for the fields on Butte Montmartre (near Sacré-Cœur basilica) to dance, drink, and eat little crêpes (galettes) till dark. Renoir liked to go there to paint the common Parisians living and loving in the afternoon sun. The sunlight filtering through the trees creates a kaleidoscope of colors, like the 19th-century equivalent of a mirror ball throwing darts of light onto the dancers.

He captured the dappled light with quick blobs of yellow staining the ground, the men's jackets, and the sun-dappled straw hat (right of center). Smell the powder on the ladies' faces. The painting glows with bright colors. Even the shadows on the ground, which should be gray or black, are colored a warm blue. Like a photographer who uses a slow shutter speed to show motion, Renoir paints a waltzing blur.

Camille Pissarro, Alfred Sisley, and Others

The Orsay features some of the "lesser" pioneers of the Impressionist style. Browse around and discover your own favorites. Pissarro is one of mine. His grainy landscapes are more subtle and subdued than those of the flashy Monet and Renoir—but, as someone said, "He did for the earth what Monet did for the water."

Paul Cézanne (1839-1906)

Paul Cézanne (say-zahn) brought Impressionism into the 20th century.

After the color of Monet, the warmth of Renoir, and the passion of Van Gogh, Cézanne's rather impersonal canvases can be difficult to appreciate. Bowls of fruit, landscapes, and a few portraits were Cézanne's passion (see ***The Card Players***, *Les Joueurs de Cartes*, 1890-1895). Because of his style (not the content), he is often called the first modern painter.

Cézanne was virtually unknown and unappreciated in his lifetime. He worked alone, lived alone, and died alone, ignored by all but a few revolutionary young artists who understood his genius.

Unlike the Impressionists, who painted what they saw, Cézanne reworked reality. He simplified it into basic geometric forms—circular apples, rectangular boulders, cone-shaped trees, triangular groups of people. He might depict a scene from multiple angles—showing a tabletop from above but the bowl of fruit resting on it from the side. He laid paint with heavy brushstrokes, blending the background and foreground to obliterate traditional 3-D depth. He worked slowly, methodically, stroke by stroke—a single canvas could take months.

Where the Impressionists built a figure out of a mosaic of individual brushstrokes, Cézanne used blocks of paint to create a more solid, geometrical shape. These chunks are like little "cubes." It's no coincidence that his experiments in reducing forms to their geometric basics inspired the...Cubists.

• *Break time. Continue to the jazzy café, which serves small-plate fare with savoir faire. In good weather, venture out on the terrace for fresh air and great views. Browse the top floor's other exhibits (including interesting temporary ones), and then move on.*

You'll find the Post-Impressionists downstairs. To get there from the café, find the down escalators and descend to level 2. Go along the right side of the open-air mezzanine, where you'll find the entrance to Rooms 71-72, containing works by Van Gogh and Gauguin mixed together.

POST-IMPRESSIONISM

Post-Impressionism—the style that employs Impressionism's bright colors while branching out in new directions—is scattered all around the museum. We got a taste of the style with Paul Cézanne, and it continues here on level 2 with...

Vincent van Gogh (1853-1890)

Impressionists have been accused of being "light"-weights. The colorful style lends itself to bright country scenes, gardens, sunlight on the water, and happy crowds of simple people. It took a remarkable genius to add profound emotion to the Impressionist style.

Like Michelangelo, Beethoven, and a select handful of others, Vincent van Gogh (pronounced "van-go," or van-HOCK by the Dutch and the snooty) put so much of himself into his work that art and life became one. In the Orsay's collection of paintings, you'll see both Van Gogh's painting style and his life unfold.

Vincent was the son of a Dutch minister. He too felt a religious calling, and he spread the gospel among the poorest of the poor—peasants and miners in overcast Holland and Belgium. He painted these hardworking, dignified folks in a crude, dark style reflecting the oppressiveness of their lives...and his own loneliness as he roamed northern Europe in search of a calling.

Encouraged by his art-dealer brother, Van Gogh moved to Paris, and *voilà!* The color! He met Monet, drank with Gauguin

ORSAY

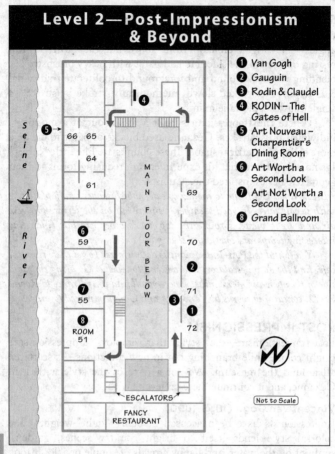

Level 2—Post-Impressionism & Beyond

1. Van Gogh
2. Gauguin
3. Rodin & Claudel
4. RODIN – The Gates of Hell
5. Art Nouveau – Charpentier's Dining Room
6. Art Worth a Second Look
7. Art Not Worth a Second Look
8. Grand Ballroom

Seine River

MAIN FLOOR BELOW

66 65
64
61
59
55
ROOM 51

69
70
71
72

ESCALATORS

FANCY RESTAURANT

Not to Scale

ORSAY

and Toulouse-Lautrec, and soaked up the Impressionist style. (For example, see how he might build a bristling brown beard using thick strokes of red, yellow, and green side by side.)

At first, he painted like the others, but soon he developed his own style. By using thick, swirling brushstrokes, he infused life into even inanimate objects. Van Gogh's brushstrokes curve and thrash like a garden hose pumped with wine.

The social life of Paris became too much for the solitary Van Gogh, and he moved to the south of France. At first, in the glow of the bright spring sunshine, he had a period of incredible creativity and happiness. He was overwhelmed by the bright colors, landscape vistas, and common

people. It was an Impressionist's dream (see **Midday**, *La Méridienne*, 1889-90).

But being alone in a strange country began to wear on him. An ugly man, he found it hard to get a date. A painting of his rented bedroom in Arles shows a cramped, bare-bones place (**Van Gogh's Room at Arles**, *La Chambre de Van Gogh à Arles*, 1889). He invited his friend Gauguin to join him, but after two months together arguing passionately about art, nerves got raw. Van Gogh threatened Gauguin with a razor, which

drove his friend back to Paris. In crazed despair, Van Gogh cut off a piece of his own ear.

The people of Arles realized they had a madman on their hands and convinced Vincent to seek help at a mental hospital. The paintings he finished in the peace of the hospital are more meditative—there are fewer bright landscapes and more closed-in scenes with deeper, almost surreal colors.

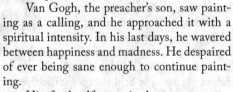

Van Gogh, the preacher's son, saw painting as a calling, and he approached it with a spiritual intensity. In his last days, he wavered between happiness and madness. He despaired of ever being sane enough to continue painting.

His final self-portrait shows a man engulfed in a confused background of brushstrokes that swirl and rave (**Self-Portrait**, *Portrait de l'Artiste*, 1889). But in the midst of this rippling sea of mystery floats a still, detached island of a face. Perhaps his troubled eyes know that in only a few months, he'll take a pistol and put a bullet through his chest.

• *Also in Rooms 71-72, look for...*

ORSAY

Paul Gauguin (1848-1903)

Gauguin (go-gan) got the travel bug early in childhood and grew up wanting to be a sailor. Instead, he became a stockbroker. In his spare time, he painted, and he was introduced to the Impressionist circle. He learned their bright clashing colors but diverged from their path about the time Van Gogh waved a knife in his face. At the age of 35, he got fed up with it all, quit his job, abandoned his wife (her stern portrait bust may be nearby) and family, and took refuge in his art.

Gauguin traveled to the South Seas in search of the exotic, finally settling on Tahiti. There he found his Garden of Eden. He simplified his life into a routine of eating, sleeping, and painting. He simplified his paintings still more, to flat images with heavy black outlines filled with bright, pure colors. The background and foreground colors are equally bright, producing a flat, stained-glass-like surface.

Gauguin also carved statuettes in the style of Polynesian pagan idols. His fascination with indigenous peoples and Primitive art had a great influence on later generations. Matisse and the Fauves (or "Wild Beasts") loved Gauguin's bright, clashing colors. Picasso used his tribal-mask faces for his groundbreaking early Cubist works.

Gauguin's best-known works capture an idyllic Tahitian landscape peopled by exotic women engaged in simple tasks and making music (***Arearea***, 1892). The native  girls lounge placidly in unselfconscious innocence (so different from Cabanel's seductive, melodramatic *Venus*). The style is intentionally "primitive," collapsing the three-dimensional landscape into a two-dimensional pattern of bright colors. Gauguin intended that this simple style carry a deep undercurrent of symbolic meaning. He wanted to communicate to his "civilized" colleagues back home that he'd found the paradise he'd always envisioned.

• *The open-air mezzanine of level 2 is lined with statues. Stroll the mezzanine from the near end (near Room 72) to the far end, enjoying the work of Rodin, Claudel, and other greats of…*

ORSAY

FRENCH SCULPTURE
Auguste Rodin (1840-1917)
Born of working-class roots and largely self-taught, Rodin (ro-dan) combined classical solidity with Impressionist surfaces to become the greatest sculptor since Michelangelo. He labored in obscurity for decades, making knickknacks and doorknobs for a construction company. By age 40, he started to gain recognition. He became romantically involved with a student, Camille Claudel, who became his model and muse.

Rodin's subject was always the human body, showing it in unusual poses that express inner emotion. The surface is alive, rippling with frosting-like gouges.

The style comes from Rodin's work process. Rodin paid models to run, squat, leap, and spin around his studio however they wanted. When he saw an interesting pose, he'd yell, "Freeze!" (or "statue maker") and get out his sketchpad. Rodin worked quickly, using his powerful thumbs to make a small statue in clay, which he would then reproduce as a life-size clay statue that in turn was used as a mold for casting a plaster or bronze copy. Authorized copies of Rodin's work are now included in museums all over the world.

Like his statue *The Walking Man* (*L'Homme Qui Marche*, c. 1900), Rodin had one foot in the past, while the other stepped into

the future. This muscular, forcefully striding man could be a symbol of Renaissance Man with his classical power. With no mouth or hands, he speaks with his body. But get close and look at the statue's surface. This rough, "unfinished" look reflects light in the same way the rough Impressionist brushwork does, making the statue come alive, never quite at rest in the viewer's eye. Rodin created this statue in a flash of inspiration. He took two unfinished statues—torso and legs—and plunked them together at the waist. You can still see the seam.

Camille Claudel (1864-1943)

Camille Claudel was Rodin's student and mistress. In *Maturity* (*L'Age Mur*, 1899-1903)—a small bronze statue group of three

figures—Claudel may have portrayed their doomed love affair. A young girl desperately reaches out to an older man, who is led away reluctantly by an older woman. The center of the composition is the empty space left when their hands separate. In real life, Rodin refused to leave his wife, and Claudel ended up in an insane asylum.

• *Continue along the mezzanine to the far end, where you'll find another well-known work by Rodin.*

Rodin, *The Gates of Hell (La Porte de l'Enfer)*, 1880-1917

Rodin worked for decades on these doors depicting Dante's hell, and they contain some of his greatest hits—small statues that he later executed in full size. Find *The Thinker* squatting above the doorway, contemplating Man's fate. *The Thinker* was meant to be Dante surveying the characters of Hell. But Rodin so identified with this pensive figure that he chose it to stand atop his own grave. This *Thinker* is only two feet high, but it was the model for the full-size work that has become one of the most famous statues in the world (you can see a full-size *Thinker* in the Rodin Museum garden).

ORSAY

The doors' 186 figures eventually inspired larger versions of *The Kiss*, the *Three Shades*, and more. (For more on *The Gates of Hell* and Rodin, 📖 see the Rodin Museum Tour.)

From this perch in the Orsay, look down to the main floor at all the classical statues between you and the big clock, and realize how far we've come—not in years, but in stylistic changes. Many of the statues below—beautiful, smooth, balanced, and idealized—were created at the same time as Rodin's powerful, haunting works. Rodin's sculptures capture the groundbreaking spirit of much of the art in the Orsay Museum. With a stable base of 19th-century stone, he launched art into the 20th century.

• *You've seen the essential Orsay and are permitted to cut out. But there's an "other" Orsay I think you'll find entertaining.*

THE "OTHER" ORSAY

The beauty of the Orsay is that it combines all the art from 1848 to 1914, both modern and classical, in one building. The classical art, so popular in its day, was maligned and largely forgotten in the later 20th century. It's time for a reassessment. Is it as gaudy and gawd-awful as we've been led to believe? From our 21st-century perspective, let's take a look at the opulent *fin de siècle* French high society and its luxurious art.

• *From the far end of level 2's open-air mezzanine (near Rodin's* Gates of Hell), *find the entry for Rooms 61-66. Browse through several galleries of curvaceous furniture.*

Art Nouveau

The Industrial Age brought factories, row houses, machines, train stations, geometrical precision—and ugliness. At the turn of the

20th century, some artists reacted against the unrelieved geometry of harsh, prag-matic, iron-and-steel Eiffel Tower art with a "new art"—Art Nouveau. (Hmm. I think I had a driver's ed teacher by that name.)

Stand amid a reconstructed wood-paneled dining room designed by Alexan-dre Charpentier *(Boiserie de la Salle à Man-gér)*. With its carved vines, leafy garlands, and tree-branch arches, it's one of the fin-est examples of Art Nouveau.

Like nature, which also abhors a straight line, Art Nouveau artists used the curves of flowers and vines as their pat-tern. They were convinced that "practical" didn't have to mean "ugly" as well. They turned everyday household objects into art. Another well-known example of Art Nouveau is the sinuous wrought-ironwork of some of Paris' early Métro entrances—which were commissioned by banker Adrien Bénard, the same man who ordered this dining room for his home.

• *Return to the open-air mezzanine and turn right. Enter Room 59.*

Art Worth a Second Look

We've seen some great art. Now let's see some not-so-great art—at least, that's what modern critics tell us. This is realistic art with a subconscious kick. Henri Martin's **Serenity** (*Sérénité*, 1899) is an idyll in the woods. Three nymphs with harps waft off to the right. These people are stoned on something. Jean Delville's **The School of Plato** (*L'Ecole de Platon,* 1898) could be subtitled "The Athens YMCA." A Christ-like Plato surrounded by adoring, half-naked nubile youths gives new meaning to the term "platonic relationship." Will the pendulum shift so that one day art like *The School of Plato* becomes the new, radical avant-garde style?

• *Continue down the mezzanine until you reach Room 55, labeled* Naturalism.

Art Not Worth a Second Look

A director of the Orsay once said, "Certainly, we have bad paintings. But we have only the greatest bad paintings." And here they are. Fernand Cormon's **Cain** (1880) depicts the world's first murderer, whose murder weapon is still in his belt as he's exiled with his family. Archaeologists had recently discovered a Neanderthal skull, so the artist makes Cain's family part of a prehistoric hunter-gatherer tribe. In Edouard Detaille's **The Dream** (*Le Rêve,* 1888), soldiers lie still, asleep without beds, while visions of Gatling guns dance in their heads. Léon Lhermitte, often called "the grandson of Courbet and Millet," depicts peasants getting their wages in his **Paying the Harvesters** (*La Paye des Moissonneurs,* 1882). The subtitle of the work could be, "Is this all there is to life?" (Or, "The Paycheck...After Deductions.")

• *Continue along the mezzanine. Near the escalators, turn right and find the palatial Room 51, with mirrors and chandeliers, marked* Salle des Fêtes *(Grand Ballroom).*

The Grand Ballroom (Salle des Fêtes)

This room was part of the hotel that once adjoined the Orsay train station. One of France's poshest nightspots, it was built in 1900, abandoned after 1939, condemned, and

then restored to the elegance you see today. You can easily imagine gowned debutantes and white-gloved dandies waltzing the night away to the music of a chamber orchestra. Take in the interior decoration: raspberry marble-ripple ice-cream columns, pastel ceiling painting, gold work, mirrors, and leafy garlands of chandeliers. Look around for the statue *(L'Aurore)* of the nymph with a canopy of hair, hide-and-seek face, and silver-dollar nipples, looking like a shampoo ad.

Is this stuff beautiful or merely gaudy? Divine or decadent? Whatever you decide, it was all part of the marvelous world of the Orsay's century of art.

• *A good place to ponder it all is Le Restaurant, located near the escalators on level 2. It's pricey, but there's an affordable coffee-and-tea happy hour (see page 169). After all this art, you deserve it. Or, for a good, fresh-air museum antidote, stroll the pedestrian-only riverside promenade (Les Berges du Seine), which starts below the Orsay and runs west to near the Eiffel Tower (see page 65).*

ORANGERIE MUSEUM TOUR

Musée de l'Orangerie

This Impressionist museum is as lovely as a water lily. Step out of the tree-lined, sun-dappled Impressionist painting that is the Tuileries Garden and into the Orangerie (oh-rahn-zhuh-ree), a little bijou of select works by Monet, Renoir, Matisse, Picasso, and others.

On the main floor you'll find the main attraction, Monet's *Water Lilies (Nymphéas)*, floating dreamily in oval rooms. The rooms

were designed in the 1920s to display this art, following the artist's exacting specifications. But in the 1960s the museum added a floor above the *Water Lilies,* cutting them off from the daylight that was, after all, their inspiration and subject matter. In 2006, after a renovation that took six years and $36 million, the upstairs collection was moved underground, and the upper floor was transformed into a tall skylight—drenching the *Water Lilies* in natural light.

In the underground gallery are select works from the personal collection of Paris' trend-spotting art dealer of the 1920s, Paul Guillaume. The museum is small enough to enjoy in a short visit, but complete enough to show the bridge from Impressionism to Modernism. And it's all beautiful.

Orientation

Cost: €9, €6.50 after 17:00 (though they start kicking people out at 17:45, there is ample time to saturate yourself in lilies), free for those under 18, €16 combo-ticket with Orsay Museum, covered by Museum Pass.

Hours: Wed-Mon 9:00-18:00, closed Tue.

Getting There: It's in the Tuileries Garden near Place de la Concorde (Mo: Concorde or scenic bus #24) and a lovely 15-minute stroll from the Orsay Museum through the Tuileries.

Getting In: A security checkpoint causes some lines, but it's seldom crowded inside. There's usually a shorter security line for Museum Pass holders.

Information: Tel. 01 44 77 80 07, www.musee-orangerie.fr.

Tours: €6 **guided tours** in English are usually offered Mon and Thu at 14:30 and Sat at 11:00. The €5 **audioguide** adds nothing beyond what's in this book on the *Water Lilies*, but it provides good detail about individual canvases in the Walter-Guillaume Collection.

Length of This Tour: Allow one hour. Temporary exhibitions often merit extra time. With less time, you could see (if not "experience") the two rooms of *Water Lilies* in a glance.

Starring: Claude Monet's *Water Lilies* and select works by the pioneers of modern painting.

The Tour Begins

MONET'S *WATER LILIES*

• *Monet's* Water Lilies *float serenely in two pond-shaped rooms, straight ahead past the ticket takers. Examine them up close to see Monet's technique; stand back to take in the whole picture.*

Salle I

Like Beethoven going deaf, a nearly blind Claude Monet (1840-1926) wrote his final symphonies on a monumental scale. Even

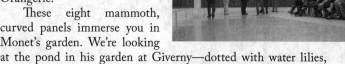

as he struggled with cataracts, he planned a series of huge six-foot-tall canvases of water lilies to hang in special rooms at the Orangerie.

These eight mammoth, curved panels immerse you in Monet's garden. We're looking at the pond in his garden at Giverny—dotted with water lilies, surrounded by foliage, and dappled by the reflections of the sky, clouds, and trees on the surface. The water lilies (*nymphéas* in French) range from plain green lily pads to flowers of red, white, yellow, lavender, and various combos.

The effect is intentionally disorienting; the different canvases feature different parts of the pond from different angles, at different times of day, with no obvious chronological order. Monet mingles the pond's many elements and lets us sort it out.

• *Start with the long wall on your right (as you enter) and work counterclockwise.*

It's *Morning* on the pond at Giverny. The blue pond is the center of the composition, framed by the green, foliage-covered banks at either end. Lilies float in the foreground, and the pond stretches into the distance.

The sheer scale of the Orangerie project was daunting for an artist in his twilight years. This vast painting is made from four

separate canvases stitched together and spans 6 feet 6 inches by 55 feet. Altogether, Monet painted 1,950 square feet of canvas to complete the *Water Lilies* series. Working at his home in Giverny, Monet built a special studio with skylights and wheeled easels to accommodate the canvases.

The panel at the far end, called *Green Reflections,* looks deep into the dark water. Green willow branches are reflected on the water in a vertical pattern; lily pads stretch horizontally.

Along the other long wall *(Clouds)*, green lilies float among lavender clouds reflected in blue water. Staring into Monet's pond, we see the intermingling of the four classical elements—earth (foliage), air (the sky), fire (sunlight), and water—the primordial soup of life.

The true subject of these works is the play of reflected light off the surface of the pond. Monet would work on several canvases at once, each dedicated to a different time of day. He'd move with

the sun from one canvas to the next. Pan slowly around this hall. Watch the pond turn from predawn darkness (far end) to clear morning light *(Morning)* to lavender late afternoon *(Clouds)* to glorious sunset— in the west, where the sun actually does set.

In *Sunset* (near end), the surface of the pond is stained

a bright yellow. Get close and see how Monet worked. Starting from the gray of the blank canvas (lower right), he'd lay down big, thick brushstrokes of a single color, weaving them in a (mostly) horizontal and vertical pattern to create a dense mesh of foliage. Over this, he'd add more color for the dramatic highlights, until (in the center of the yellow) he got a dense paste of piled-up paint. Up close, it's a mess—but back up, and the colors begin to resolve into a luminous scene. There are no clearly identifiable objects in this canvas—no lilies, no trees, no clouds, no actual sun—just pure reflected color.

• *Continue into Salle II, starting with the long wall on your right and working counterclockwise.*

Salle II

In this room, Monet frames the pond with pillar-like tree trunks and overhanging foliage. The compositions are a bit more symmetrical and the color schemes more muted, with blue and lavender and green-brown. Monet's paintings almost always deal with the foundation of life and unspoiled nature. This room begs you to stroll its banks, slowly ambling with the artist in a complete loop—perhaps while listening to Debussy.

In *Willows on a Clear Morning* (on the long wall to the right), we seem to be standing on the bank of the pond, looking out through overhanging trees at the water. The swirling branches and horizontal ripples on the pond suggest a gentle breeze.

The Two Willows (far end) frame a wide expanse of water dotted with lilies and the reflection of gray-pink clouds.

Stand close in front of *Morning Willows* (long left wall). Notice how a "brown" tree is a tangled Impressionist beard of purple, green, blue, and red. Each leaf is a long brushstroke, each lily pad a dozen smudges.

At the near end, *Reflections of Trees* is a dark mess of blue-purple paint brightened only by the lone rose lilies in the center. Each lily is made of many Impressionist brushstrokes—each brushstroke is itself a mix of red, white, and pink paints. Put a mental frame around a single lily, and it looks like an abstract canvas. Monet demonstrates both his mastery of color and his ability to render it with paint, applied generously and deftly. He wanted the vibrant colors to keep firing your synapses.

With this last canvas, darkness descends on the pond. The

Paul Guillaume (1891-1934)

For the first three decades of the 20th century, Paris was the center of the art world, and the center of Paris' art scene was Paul Guillaume. An art dealer, promoter of "modern" art, and friend of out-there artists, Guillaume rose from humble beginnings to become wealthy and famous.

In his early days, this self-made businessman struggled alongside struggling painters in Montmartre—Picasso, Modigliani, Derain, Laurencin, and many others. When the art market boomed in the 1920s (along with the stock market), he and his fellow bohemians became the toasts of high society. With his flamboyant wife, Domenica (also called Juliette), Guillaume hosted exotic parties featuring what we would now call "performance art" to shock and titillate the buying public.

Many of their artist friends honored Paul and Domenica by painting their portraits. In Modigliani's *Novo Pilota* (pictured above), young Paul strikes a pose as the dapper man-of-the-world he was soon to become. The title of the painting is Italian for "new helmsman," reflecting Paul's growing status as a champion of Modernism. Marie Laurencin's portrait captures the winsome beauty of Domenica, whose charm helped establish the nouveau riche couple in social circles. André Derain's and Kees van Dongen's portraits feature Paul and Domenica when they are older, more confident, and sophisticated.

The Orangerie displays Guillaume's personal collection of favorite paintings. After Paul's death, Domenica married Jean Walter and took her new husband's last name, which is why it's officially called the "Walter-Guillaume" collection.

room's large, moody canvases, painted by an 80-year-old man in the twilight of his life, invite meditation.

For 12 years (1914-1926), Monet worked on these paintings obsessively. A successful eye operation in 1923 gave him new energy. Monet completed all the planned canvases, but he didn't live to see them installed here. In 1927, the year after his death, these rooms were completed and the canvases put in place. Some call this the first "art installation"—art displayed in a space specially designed for it in order to enhance the viewer's experience.

Monet's final work was more "modern" than Impressionist. Each canvas is fully saturated with color, the distant objects as bright as the close ones. Monet's mosaic of brushstrokes forms a colorful design that's beautiful even if you just look "at" the canvas, like wallpaper. He wanted his paintings to be realistic and three-dimensional, but with a pleasant, two-dimensional pattern. As the subjects become fuzzier, the colors and patterns predominate.

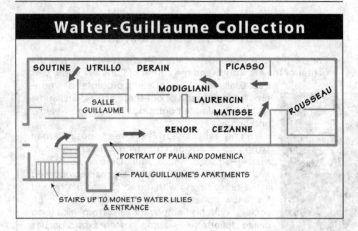

Walter-Guillaume Collection

SOUTINE   UTRILLO   DERAIN   PICASSO

MODIGLIANI

SALLE
GUILLAUME   LAURENCIN   ROUSSEAU

MATISSE

RENOIR   CEZANNE

◄— PORTRAIT OF PAUL AND DOMENICA

◄— PAUL GUILLAUME'S APARTMENTS

STAIRS UP TO MONET'S WATER LILIES
& ENTRANCE

Monet builds a bridge between Impressionism and modern, abstract art.

To see more of Monet's work, visit the Marmottan Museum (📖 see the Marmottan Museum Tour chapter), and to experience the place that inspired these water lilies, take a day trip to Giverny (see page 600).

• *Descend the stairs to the lower floor.*

WALTER-GUILLAUME COLLECTION

These paintings—Impressionist, Fauvist, and Cubist—were amassed by the art dealer Paul Guillaume and inherited by his wife, Domenica Guillaume Walter. (You might see portraits of them as you enter their collection in the basement.) This power couple's collection is a snapshot of what was hot in the world of art, circa 1920. The once-revolutionary Impressionists had become completely old-school, though their paintings—now classics—commanded a fortune. The bohemian Fauvists and Cubists, who invented modern art atop Butte Montmartre (c. 1900-1915), had suddenly become the darlings of the art world. But they refused to be categorized, and their work in the 1920s branched out in dozens of new directions. Use my map to browse the rooms and watch the various "isms" unfold.

• *At the bottom of the stairs, turn right and find a wall of Renoir canvases.*

Pierre-Auguste Renoir (1841-1919)

Renoir loved to paint *les femmes*—women and girls—nude and innocent, taking a bath or practicing the piano, all with rosy-red cheeks and a relaxed grace. We get a feel for the happy family life of middle-

ORANGERIE

class Parisians (including Renoir's own family) during the belle époque—the beautiful age of the late 19th century. Renoir's warm, sunny colors (mostly red) are Impressionist, but he adds a classical touch with his clearer lines and, in the later nudes, the voluptuousness of classical statues and paintings. He seems to enjoy capturing the bourgeoisie, soft and elegant, enjoying their leisure pursuits.

Paul Cézanne (1839-1906)

These small canvases of simple subjects pushed modern artists to reinvent the rules of painting.

The fruit of Cézanne's still lifes are "built" with an underlying geometry from patches of color. In the shapes of nature, Cézanne saw spheres, cylinders, and cones. He was fond of saying, "First you must learn to paint these simple shapes. Then you will be able to do whatever you want."

There's no traditional shading to create the illusion of three dimensions, but these fruit bulge out like cameos from the canvas. The fruit is clearly at eye level, yet it's also clearly placed on a table seen from above. Cézanne broke the rules, showing multiple perspectives at once. Picasso was fascinated with Cézanne's strange new world—which seems to give us a peek into the secret lives of fruits.

In his landscapes, Cézanne the Impressionist creates "brown" rocks out of red, orange, and purple, and "green" trees out of green, lime, and purple. Cézanne the proto-Cubist builds the rocks and trees with blocks of thick brushstrokes.

• *Turn the corner into a room featuring Picasso and Matisse—the 20th century's two great masters, their work displayed side by side.*

Pablo Picasso (1881-1973)

Picasso is a shopping mall of 20th-century artistic styles. In this room alone, he passes through his various periods: Blue (sad and tragic), Rose (red-toned nudes with timeless, masklike faces), Cubist (flat planes of interwoven perspectives), and Classical (massive, sculptural nudes—warm blow-up dolls with substance). If all roads lead to Paris, all art styles flowed through Picasso.

Henri Matisse (1869-1954)

After World War I, Matisse moved to the south of France. He abandoned his fierce Fauvist style and painted languid women in angular rooms with arabesque wallpaper. These paler tones evoke the sunny luxury of the Riviera. Traditional perspective is thrown out the occasional hotel window as the women and furnishings in the "foreground" blend with

the wallpaper "background" to become part of the decor.

Marie Laurencin (1883-1956)

As the girlfriend of the poet and art critic Guillaume Apollinaire, Laurencin was right at the heart of the Montmartre circle when modern art was born. Her work, featuring women and cuddly animals intertwined in pink, blue, and gray tones, spreads a pastel sheen over this tumultuous time.

André Derain (1880-1954)

Along with his friend Matisse, Derain helped invent Fauvism. Then, in Montmartre, along with his friend Picasso, he helped forge Cubism. In the 1920s, this former wild beast *(fauve)* tamed his colors. He and Picasso rode the rising wave of Classicism that surfaced after the chaos of the war years. With sharp outlines and studied realism, Derain's still lifes portray nudes, harlequins, portraits, and landscapes—all in odd, angular poses.

Amedeo Modigliani (1884-1920)

In his short, poverty-stricken, drug-addled life, Modigliani produced timeless-looking portraits of modern people. Born in Italy, Modigliani moved to Paris, where he hung around the fringes of the avant-garde crowd in the Montmartre. He gained a reputation for his alcoholic excesses and outrageous behavior.

Turning his back on the prevailing Fauvist/Cubist ambience of the times, Modigliani developed a unique style, influenced by primitive tribal masks. His canvases feature stylized heads, almond eyes, long necks, and puckered mouths. *Novo Pilota* (1915, pictured on page 195) portrays Paul Guillaume as a cool dandy, suavely cradling a cigarette. Modigliani died young, just as his work was gaining recognition.

• *The next artists may be featured in a different order, but in this small museum, they're not hard to find. Also, note that the "Salle Guillaume" often displays interesting exhibits on Paul and Domenica and their collection.*

Henri Rousseau (1844-1910)

Rousseau, a simple government worker, never traveled outside France. But in his artwork he created an exotic, dreamlike,

completely unique world. Here, a Parisian wedding is set amid tropical trees. Figures are placed in a 3-D world, but the lines of perspective recede so steeply into the distance that everyone is in danger of sliding down the canvas. Without any feet, the subjects seem barely tethered to the earth. The way Rousseau put familiar images in bizarre settings influenced the Surrealists. Enjoy France's biggest collection of Rousseaus.

Maurice Utrillo (1883-1955)

The hard-drinking, streetwise, bohemian artist is known for his postcard views of Montmartre—whitewashed buildings under perennially cloudy skies. For more on Utrillo, see page 380.

Chaim Soutine (1893-1943)

When his friend Modigliani died (and Modigliani's widow committed suicide), Soutine went into a tailspin of depression that

drove him to paint. The subjects are ordinary—landscapes, portraits, and a fine selection of your favorite cuts of meat—but the style is deformed and Expressionistic. It shows a warped world in a funhouse mirror, smeared onto the canvas with thick, lurid colors. The never-cheerful Soutine was known to destroy work that did not satisfy him. Stand and ponder why these made the cut.

Did I say that the Orangerie's collection was as beautiful as an Impressionist painting? Well, Soutine's misery is so complete, it's almost a thing of beauty.

ORANGERIE

RUE CLER WALK

The Art of Parisian Living

A stroll down this street introduces you to a thriving, traditional Parisian neighborhood and offers insights into the local culture. And although Rue Cler is a wealthy district, it retains an everyday charm still found in most neighborhoods throughout the city. This charming dimension of Paris is changing, however—with more and more affluence, mobility, and tourism, businesses that offer workaday practicalities are slowly morphing into trendy shops and cafés. But the Parisian love and appreciation of community persists, and it can be sampled even on touristy and affluent Rue Cler.

Shopping for groceries is the backbone of daily life here. Parisians shop nearly every day for three good reasons: Refrigerators are small (tiny kitchens), produce must be fresh, and it's an important social event. Shopping is a chance to hear about the butcher's vacation plans, see photos of the florist's new grandchild, relax over *un café*, and kiss the cheeks of friends (for proper kissing etiquette, see "Le French Kiss" sidebar on page 209).

Rue Cler—traffic-free since 1984—offers plenty of space for slender stores and their patrons to spill out onto the street. It's an ideal environment for this ritual to survive and for you to explore. The street is lined with the essential shops— wine, cheese, chocolate, bread—as well as a bank and a post office. And the shops of this community are run by people who've found their niche: boys who grew up on quiche and girls who know a good wine.

For those learning the fine art of living Parisian-style, Rue Cler provides an excellent classroom. And if you want to assemble the ultimate French picnic, there's no better place.

Rue Cler Walk

To Seine River ↑

CAFE ROUSSILLON **1**
"LATE-NIGHT" GROCERY
ⓑ#69

PETIT BATEAU **2**

RUE DE GRENELLE

3 FRANPRIX

TOP HALLES
GREENGROCER

To Eiffel Tower ←

To Army & Rodin Museums →

4 LE PETIT CLER CAFE

GRAND HOTEL LEVEQUE

TRAITEUR
ASIATIQUE

5 WINE BACCHUS

POISSONNERIE **7**

6 FROMAGERIE

HORSE MEAT SIGN **8**

RUE DUVIVIER

FLEURS

9 PHARMACY

CHARCUTERIE DAVOLI

10 OLDEST BUILDING &
CHARCUTERIE-TRAITEUR JEUSSELIN

CHOCOLATS

FROMAGERIE

WINE NICOLAS

RUE VALADON

CAFE DU MARCHE

LEADER PRICE
BULK SHOPPING

L'EPICERIE FINE **12** **11**

LOANER BIKES ←

RUE DU CHAMP DE MARS

13 ARTISAN
BOULANGERIE

To Eiffel Tower ←

REAL ESTATE
AGENCY

14 "A LA MERE DE FAMILLE"
CONFECTIONERY

15 MEPHISTO
SHOE STORE

CLER FLEURS **16**

RUE BOSQUET

☐ **Pedestrian area**
(approx. 200 meters in length)

RUE CLER

BUTCHER

BRASSERIE AUX PTT

PASSAGE DE LA VIERGE

To Army &
Rodin Museums →

CITY INFO
POST

17

18 TABAC
"LA CAVE A CIGARES"

To Ⓜ
Ecole Militaire ←

AVENUE DE LA MOTTE-PICQUET

Not to Scale

The Rue Cler Walk is the only tour in this guidebook you should start while hungry. Remember that your ability to enthusiastically embrace the local etiquette of greeting people in French as you enter each shop (see below) will raise the "happy quotient" of your Rue Cler experience way up.

Orientation

Length of This Walk: Allow an hour to browse and café-hop along this short walk of two or three blocks.

When to Go: Visit Rue Cler when its markets are open and lively (Tue-Sat 8:30-13:00 & 15:00-19:30, Sun 8:30-12:00, dead on Mon).

Getting There: Start your walk at the northern end of the pedestrian section of Rue Cler, at Rue de Grenelle (right by a bus #69 stop and a short walk from Mo: Ecole Militaire).

Shop Etiquette: Remember that these shops are busy serving regular customers; be careful not to get in the way. Be polite—say *"Bonjour, Madame* or *Monsieur"* as you enter and *"Au revoir, Madame* or *Monsieur"* when you leave. Get involved and buy something. Before making a purchase, watch the locals to see if self-service is allowed. Many shopkeepers prefer to serve you and don't want you to touch the goods. If you aren't sure of the protocol, ask, *"Je peux?"* (Can I?; zhuh puh). If you know what you want, point to your choice and say, *"S'il vous plaît"* (Please; see voo play). For extra credit, add, *"Je voudrais"* (I would like; zhuh voo-dray). And don't forget *"Merci beaucoup"* (Thank you very much; mehr-see boh-koo).

The Walk Begins

❶ Café Roussillon

This café is a neighborhood fixture. To the left of the door, you'll see the *Tarif des Consommations* sign required by French law, making the pricing clear: Drinks served at the bar *(comptoir)* are cheaper than drinks served at the tables *(salles)*. Notice that there is no café au lait listed. Parisians ask for *café crème* when they want coffee with steamed milk. Inside, the bar is always busy. The blackboard lists wines sold by the little, 7-centiliter glass (about 2.5 ounces), along with other drinks.

The small **late-night grocery** next door is one of many neighborhood shops nicknamed *dépanneurs* ("to help you out of difficulty"). Open nightly until midnight, these Parisian 7-Elevens are usually run by hardworking North Africans willing to keep long hours. Such shops are handy—not cheap. Locals happily pay the higher prices for the convenience *dépanneurs* provide.

• *If you're shopping for designer baby clothes, you'll find them across the street at...*

❷ Petit Bateau

The French spend at least as much on their babies as they do on their dogs—dolling them up with designer jammies. This store is one in a popular chain. Little children around here are really sophisticated. They speak French. And they just aren't comfortable unless they're making a fashion statement (such as underwear with sailor stripes).

In the last generation, an aging and shrinking population was a serious problem for Europe's wealthier nations. But France now has one of Europe's biggest baby populations—the fertile French average two children per family, compared to 1.6 for the rest of Europe. Babies are trendy today, and the government rewards parents with big tax incentives for their first two children—and then doubles the incentives after that. Since childcare is also subsidized and public school starts at age three, most new mothers get back into the workforce quickly.

Making babies is good business—and revered. Notice how locals give pregnant women the royal treatment: They get priority seating on subways and buses, and they go straight to the front of any line—no waiting on those swollen feet. And the French love to ogle babies. The community celebrates every new addition.

• *Cross Rue de Grenelle to find...*

❸ *Top Halles* Fruits and Vegetables

Each morning, fresh produce is trucked in from farmers' fields to Paris' huge Rungis market—Europe's largest, near Orly

Airport—and then dispatched to merchants with FedEx-like speed and precision. Good luck finding a shopping bag—locals bring their own two-wheeled carts or reusable bags. Also, notice how the earth-friendly French resist excessive packaging.

Parisians—who know they eat best by being tuned in to the seasons—shop with their noses. Try it. Smell the cheap foreign strawberries. One sniff of the torpedo-shaped French ones *(gariguettes)*, and you know which is better. Locals call those from Belgium "plastic strawberries"—red on the outside, white on the inside. Find the herbs in the back. Is today's delivery in? Look at the price of those melons. What's the country of origin? (It must be posted.) If they're out of season, they come from Guadeloupe. Many people buy only local products.

The **Franprix** across the street is a small outpost of a nationwide supermarket chain. Opposite Grand Hôtel Lévêque is a *traiteur asiatique.* Fast Asian food-to-go is popular in Paris. These shops—about as common as bakeries—have had an impact on traditional Parisian eating habits.

❹ Le Petit Cler

This small café, a fine choice for lunch or dinner, used to be a *tabac* (tobacco shop). It's a good example of how life is changing on Rue Cler. Not so long ago, Brasserie aux PTT, at the opposite end of the *rue,* was the only place with outdoor tables. Then others joined in, each displacing a more humble shop that addressed neighborhood needs. Now some locals regret that these shops are being lost to trendy café crowds.

• *Just past Grand Hôtel Lévêque is...*

❺ Wine Bacchus

Shoppers often visit the neighborhood wine shop last, after they've assembled their meal and are able to pick the appropriate wine. Wines are classified by region. Most "Parisians" (born elsewhere) have an affinity for the wines of their home region. You can travel throughout France by taking a spin tour of wines on the shelves. You'll notice a locker for the most expensive wines, one small section for foreign wines, and a shelf for craft beers (mostly Belgian, but more and more fine French brews). Notice the prices: Most are €20 or less, and several sell for under €6. You can get a fine bottle for €12. Wines of the month are stacked in the center and are usually great deals. The helpful clerk is a counselor who works with your menu and budget to help you select just the right wine. They can pop a bottle of white wine into "Le Chiller" and have it cooled for you in three minutes—and also equip you with plastic cups for a picnic (open until 20:30, except Sun).

• *Next door, smell the...*

❻ *Fromagerie*

A long, narrow, canopied cheese table brings the *fromagerie* into the street. Wedges, cylinders, balls, and miniature hockey pucks are all powdered white, gray, and burnt marshmallow—it's a festival of mold. The street cart and front window feature both cow *(vache)* and goat *(chèvre)* cheeses. Locals know the shape indicates the region of origin

(for example, a pyramid shape indicates a cheese from the Loire). And this is important. Regions create the *terroir* (physical and magical union of sun, soil, and generations of farmer love) that gives the production—whether wine or cheese—its personality. *Ooh la la* means you're impressed. If you like cheese, show greater excitement with more *la*s. *Ooh la la la la*. A Parisian friend once held the stinkiest glob close to her nose, took an orgasmic breath, and exhaled, "Yes, it smells like zee feet of angels." Go ahead... inhale.

Step inside and browse through more than 200 types of French cheese. A *fromagerie* is lab-coat-serious but friendly. Also known as a *crémerie* or a "BOF" (for *beurre, oeuf,* and *fromage*), this is where people shop for butter, eggs, and cheese. Just like wines, quality cheeses need to be aged in the cool, humid environment of a *cave* (cellar). Under the careful watch of an *affineur* (the "finisher"), some cheeses will rest a few weeks, others for months. Like produce, cheeses are seasonal, as the milk produced by cows or goats changes flavor according to the animal's varied diet. Ask what's in season.

In the back room, the shop keeps *les meules*—big, 170-pound wheels of cheese, made from 250 gallons of milk. The "hard" cheeses are cut from these. Don't eat the skin of these big ones... they're rolled on the floor. But the skin on most smaller cheeses— the Brie, the Camembert—is part of the taste. "It completes the package," says my local friend.

If buying soft cheese, tell the shop when you're planning to eat it—they'll squeeze the cheese to make sure it'll reach *la maturité parfaite* on the day you want to consume it. One of your authors' favorites is Epoisses, from Burgundy.

If you order a set menu at dinner tonight, you can take the cheese course just before or instead of dessert. On a good cheese plate you have a hard cheese (perhaps a Comté, similar to a white cheddar), a softer cheese (maybe Brie or Camembert), a bleu cheese, and a goat cheese—ideally from different regions. Because it's strongest, the goat cheese is usually eaten last.

• *Across the street, find the fish shop, known as the...*

❼ Poissonnerie

Fresh fish is brought into Paris daily from ports on the English Channel, 110 miles away. In fact, fish here is likely fresher than in many towns closer to the sea, because Paris is a commercial hub (from here, it's shipped to outlying towns). Anything wiggling? This *poissonnerie*, like all such shops, was upgraded to meet Europe-wide hygiene standards.

• *Next door at Crêperie Ulysée en Gaule (under the awning—get close to see) is a particularly tempting Rue Cler storefront.*

❽ No More Horse Meat

The stones and glass set over the doorway advertise horse meat: *Boucherie Chevaline*. While today this store serves souvlaki (the family is Greek) and crêpes, the classy old storefront survives from the previous occupant. Created in the 1930s and signed by the artist, it's a work of art fit for a museum—but it belongs right here, and that's where it will stay.

Notice that the door is decorated with lunch coupon decals (like *chèque déjeuner* or *ticket restaurant*) for local workers. In France, an employee lunch-subsidy program is an expected perk. Employers—responding to strong tax incentives designed to keep the café culture vital—issue voucher checks (worth about €8 each, half of which is paid for by the employee) for each day an employee works in a month. The lunchtime *plat du jour* is often €8 or under at local cafés. Sack lunches are rare, since a good lunch is sacred... and subsidized.

• *A few steps farther, across the street, is the...*

❾ Pharmacy

In France, as in much of Europe, pharmacists are the first point of contact for people who are ill. They make the first diagnosis and have the authority to prescribe certain drugs. If it's out of their league, they'll recommend a doctor. Pharmacies are also the only place to get many basic medical items, such as aspirin and simple reading glasses.

Inside, you'll notice locals handing over a green ID, the size of a credit card, with an embedded chip and a photo. This is the all-essential *Carte Vitale*, the French health insurance card. The national health-care system, *Sécurité Sociale*, pays about 75 percent of pharmacy, doctor, and hospital bills. Private employer-related insurance, a *Mutuelle*, covers a varying amount of the rest. Filling a prescription is often completely covered. The last time the World Health Organization ranked health-care systems by country, France came out on top. The French are deservedly proud of their nationalized health care. But budget shortfalls are forcing the government to cut back on parts of France's social safety net. If there's a strike during your trip, it likely has to do with the erosion of such benefits.

To the left of the pharmacy door, notice a condom-dispensing machine for practicing safe sex 24/7 in the City of Light. In France, sex is approached from a practical perspective. Back in the 1990s, when France's president, François Mitterrand, was the focus of a sex scandal (similar to the one that embroiled Bill Clinton), his infamous response to the prying press was simply, *"Et alors?"* (So what?). The French generally agreed. They like to say, "If he's good behind his desk, that's what matters."

⑩ Oldest Building and Charcuterie-Traiteur Jeusselin

Next to the pharmacy is Rue Cler's oldest building (with the two garret windows on the roof). It's from the early 1800s, when this street was part of a village near Paris and lined with structures like this. Over the years, Paris engulfed these surrounding villages—and now the street is a mishmash of architectural styles.

Occupying the ground floor of this house is Charcuterie-Traiteur Jeusselin. *Traiteurs* (one who "treats" food) sell mouthwatering deli food to go. Because Parisian kitchens are so small, these gourmet delis are handy, even for those who cook. It lets the hosts concentrate on creating the main course and then buy beautifully prepared side dishes to complete a fine dinner.

Charcuteries by definition are pork butchers, specializing in sausage, pâté, and ham. The charcuterie business is fiercely competitive in France, with countless cooking contests allowing owners to test their products and show off their skills. Jeusselin proudly displays its hard-won awards on the back wall. Even with such accolades, many charcuteries have had to add *traiteur* services to survive. They're now selling prepared dishes, pastries, and wines-to-go.

The photogenic Italian *charcuterie-traiteur* **Davoli** sits right across Rue Cler. Each day these two places go *tête à tête,* cooking up *plats du jour* (specials of the day). Note the system: Order, take your ticket to the cashier to pay, and return with the receipt to pick up your food.

Both of these charcuteries put out their best stuff just before lunch and dinner. If you want a roasted chicken off the spit, pick one up—cooked and hot—at 11:00 or at 17:00, when Parisians buy provisions for that day's meals.

• *A few doors down is...*

⑪ Café du Marché and More

Café du Marché, on the corner, is *the* place to sit and enjoy the action (described on page 422). It's Rue Cler's living room, where locals gather before heading home, many staying for a relaxed

and affordable dinner. The owner has priced his menu so that residents can afford to dine out on a regular basis, and it works—many patrons eat here five days a week. For a reasonable meal, grab a chair and check the chalk menu listing the *plat du jour.* Notice how the no-smoking-indoors laws have made outdoor seating and propane heaters a huge hit.

The sterile **Leader Price grocery store** (across the street) is a Parisian micro-Costco, selling items at discount prices. Because storage space is so limited in Parisian apartments, bulk purchases (à la Costco) are unlikely to become a big deal here. Walk in and notice how much shelf space is dedicated to bottled waters—the French take their water seriously. The latest shopping trend is to stock up on nonperishables online, pick up produce three times a week, and buy fresh bread daily. Compare this storefront with the elegance of the other shops on this street. Its *moderne* exterior suggests some corruption around the building permit. Normally, any proposed building modification on Rue Cler must undergo a rigorous design review in order for the owner to obtain the required permit.

City Hall has become enthusiastic about making the town bike-friendly. Notice the loaner bikes parked in the Vélib' rack. There are many of these self-service stands around town (for more on using this system, see the sidebar on page 37). The system is intended to let people take short one-way rides by bike. The city has now done the same thing with electric cars. Look for Autolib' cars plugged in at low-profile, curbside charging stations.

• *From Café du Marché, hook right and side-trip a couple of doors down Rue du Champ de Mars to visit...*

⑫ L'Epicerie Fine

A fine-foods boutique like this stands out because of its gentle owners, Pascal and Nathalie. Their mission in life is to explain to travelers, in fluent English, what the French fuss over food is all about. They'll tempt you with fine gourmet treats, Berthillon ice cream, and generous tastes of caramel, balsamic vinegar, and French and Italian olive oils. Their salted caramels from Normandy and small jars of mustards and jams make good souvenirs.

Across the street is a **real estate agency** advertising condos and apartments for rent or sale. The touch screen in the window gives the details: the arrondissement (neighborhood), whether it's an apartment or a condo, how many rooms (*pieces*—includes living and family rooms), square meters (25 square meters would be about 5 by 6 yards—the size of a spacious hotel room), and the monthly rent or sales price.

• *Return to Rue Cler. The neighborhood bakery on the corner is often marked by a line of people waiting to pick up their daily baguette.*

Le French Kiss *(Faire la Bise)*

You can't miss the cheek pecking in Paris. It's contagious—and it's how Parisians greet each other. Here's the skinny.

You won't see any American-style hugging in Paris; that's far too aggressive for the French. What you will see between acquaintances is a public display of proffered cheeks and puckered lips when saying hello and goodbye. Observe. The lips don't actually touch the cheek—only the cheeks touch, and a gentle kiss noise is made (except when parents kiss children). You usually start by going left (so the right cheeks almost touch), then alternate to the right. The number of times varies with the region or circumstances—two, three, or four kisses. Different regions kiss a different number of times. Parisians *faire la bise* in social settings but rarely in the workplace. When being introduced for the first time (at a dinner party, for example), women kiss women, men kiss women, but men shake hands with other men. If you haven't seen someone in a long while, Parisians often double the standard two kisses into four.

How many kisses are appropriate for an American? If it happens to you, my recommendation is to go for two with confidence, and then—hover and wait.

⓭ Artisan Boulangerie

Since the French Revolution, the government has regulated the cost of a basic baguette (meaning "wand" or "stick" of bread). By law, it must weigh 250 grams and consist of only four ingredients: flour, yeast, salt, and water. Parisians specify their preferences when they place a *boulangerie* order—some like their baguette well done, and others prefer it more doughy. More than one trip a day to the bakery is *normale* in Paris, as a good baguette can become stale in a matter of hours. To keep it fresh, wrap it in a cloth, never a plastic bag.

Locals debate the merits of Paris' many *boulangeries*, often remaining loyal to their local bread-baker. *Boulangeries* must make their bread on the premises (otherwise, they can't be called a *boulangerie*). I know of hotels that won't serve breakfast until the corner bakery opens, to avoid having to set out yesterday's bread and croissants for their guests. Each spring, the city hosts a competition for the Best Baguette of Paris. The top prize? A cash award of €4,000 and the honor of providing the French president with baguettes for the coming year. This annual contest is the equivalent of Michelin's star system for bakeries.

It's said that a baker cannot be good both at bread and at pastry—at cooking school, they major generally in one or the other. A *Boulangerie* diploma covers bread and *viennoiserie*, which includes all the breakfast items (croissants, *pain au chocolat*, and so on), and these bakers usually do *tartes* and anything with *choux* pastry (éclairs, for example). If you get a *Pâtisserie* diploma, your forte is pastries like *macarons* and fancy creamy cakes and chocolate creations. You can usually tell whether a *boulanger* or *pâtissier* runs a place by what a shop has more of—and what's selling best.

At Artisan Boulangerie, the baker bucks the trend and seems equally skilled in the two specialties. Rue Cler regulars agree that this man makes both good bread and delicious pastries.

• *A bit farther along is...*

⓮ A la Mère de Famille Confectionery

This shop has been in the neighborhood for 30 years. The owner sells modern treats but has always kept the traditional candies, too. "The old ladies, they want the same sweets that made them so happy 80 years ago," she says. You can buy "naked bonbons" right out of the jar and chocolate by the piece (about €0.75 each). You're welcome to assemble a small assortment.

Until a few years ago, the chocolate was dipped and decorated right on the premises. As was the tradition in Rue Cler shops, the merchants resided and produced in the back and sold in the front.

• *Next door, you'll find a...*

⓯ Mephisto Shoe Store

Shoe stores are almost as popular as bakeries in this city of footwear-loving fashionistas. (French-made Mephistos are cheaper here than in the US.) You may see the locals checking out your "foreign" shoes. In a city where many people don't have cars, good shoes matter. The average Parisian's daily life is active: walking to the Métro, to lunch, to the shops after work, and then home (probably up several flights of stairs). No need for the gym with this routine. (Hence, gyms here are rare, expensive, and not well-maintained.)

• *Across the street is...*

⓰ Cler Fleurs

Almost all Parisians who reside in the city center live in apartments or condos. Even the biggest, most luxury-laden city home shares walls with neighbors and has no yard. A lucky few may have access to a courtyard, but almost no one has a private garden. Parisians spend small fortunes bringing nature into their homes with plants and fresh flower arrangements. Notice the flower boxes on balconies—you work with what you have. When visiting friends in Paris, it's *de rigueur* to give a gift of flowers, and it's good form to have them delivered before you show up. Avoid chrysanthemums, as they are reserved for funerals.

Pop into the **butcher shop** a few doors down for a graphic peek at how far Parisians like to venture from beef when it comes to meat. You'll find everything here that'll be listed on your menu tonight (rabbit, lamb, duck, veal, and pigeon) and maybe even more (pig's ears, liver, brain, and tripe—very photogenic).

• *Walk on to the end of Rue Cler, where it hits a bigger street flooded with cars and buses.*

⓱ City Info Post

An electronic signpost (10 feet up) directs residents to websites for local information—transportation changes, surveys, employment opportunities, community events, and so on. Notice the big glass recycling bin nearby and the see-through garbage sacks. In the 1990s, Paris suffered a rash of trash-can bombings. Bad guys hid rigged camp-stove canisters in metal garbage cans, which shredded into deadly "shrapnel" when they exploded. City authorities solved this by replacing metal cans with translucent bags.

• *Across the busy Avenue de la Motte-Picquet is a tabac.*

⓲ Tabac La Cave à Cigares

Just as the US has liquor stores licensed to sell booze, the only place for people over 16 to buy tobacco legally in France is at a *tabac* (tah-bah) counter. Tobacco counters like this one are a much-appreciated fixture of each neighborhood, offering lots of services (and an insight into the local culture). Even nonsmokers enjoy perusing the wares at a *tabac*. Notice how European laws require a bold warning sign on cigarettes—about half the size of the package—that says, bluntly, *fumer tue* (smoking kills).

Tabacs serve their neighborhoods as a kind of government cash desk. All sell stamps and some sell public-transit tickets. This *tabac* also sells the Paris Museum Pass at no added charge—*très* handy. Locals pay for parking meters in *tabacs* by buying a card...or pay fines if they don't. Like back home, the LOTO is a big deal—and a lucrative way for the government to tax poor and less-educated people.

American smokers may not be able to resist the temptation to pick up a *petit* Corona—your chance to buy a fine Cuban cigar.

• *Your walk is done. I'm headed back to the bakery. But if you're ready to move on, the Ecole Militaire Métro stop is just down Avenue de la Motte-Picquet to the right. If you bought a picnic along this walk, here are two good places to enjoy it: Leaving Rue Cler, turn left on Avenue de la Motte-Picquet for the Army Museum (find the small park after crossing Boulevard de la Tour Maubourg). Or, turn right to reach the Champ de Mars park (and the Eiffel Tower).*

RUE CLER

EIFFEL TOWER TOUR

La Tour Eiffel

It's crowded, expensive, and there are probably better views in Paris, but visiting this 1,000-foot-tall ornament is worth the trouble. Visitors to Paris may find *Mona Lisa* to be less than expected, but the Eiffel Tower rarely disappoints, even in an era of skyscrapers. This is a once-in-a-lifetime, I've-been-there experience. Making the eye-popping ascent and ear-popping descent gives you membership in the exclusive society of the quarter of a billion other humans who have made the Eiffel Tower the most visited monument in the modern world.

Orientation

Cost: €17 to ride two elevators all the way to the top third level, €11.50 if you're only going up to the two lower levels, €5 to climb the stairs to the first or second level, a few euros less if you're under 25, not covered by Museum Pass.

Hours: Daily mid-June-Aug 9:00-00:45, last ascent to top at 23:00 and to lower levels at 24:00 (elevator or stairs); Sept-mid-June 9:30-23:45, last ascent to top at 22:30 and to lower levels at 23:00 (elevator) or at 18:00 (stairs). The top level can close temporarily in windy weather or when it reaches capacity.

Buying Tickets in Advance: Frankly, you'd be crazy to show up without a reservation. At www.toureiffel.paris, you can book an entry time (for example, June 12 at 16:30) and skip the initial entry line (the longest)—at no extra cost.

Time slots fill up months in advance

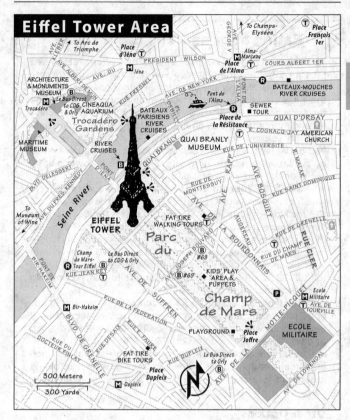

(especially from April through September). Online ticket sales open up about three months before any given date (at 8:30 Paris time)—and can sell out for that day within hours. Be sure of your date, as reservations are nonrefundable. If no reservation slots are available, try buying a "Lift entrance ticket with access to 2nd floor" only—you can upgrade once inside. Or, try the website again about a week before your visit—last-minute spots occasionally open up.

The website is easy to use, but here are a few tips: When you "Choose a ticket," make sure you select "Lift entrance ticket with access to the summit" if you'd like to go all the way to the top. Then select your date, the number of people in your party, and the time slot (available times show up in green). You must create an account, with your 10-digit mobile phone number as your log-in.

After paying with a credit card, print your tickets, following the printing specifications carefully (white paper, blank on

Eating at or near the Eiffel Tower

The tower has two classy restaurants that offer great views: 58 Tour Eiffel (on the first level) and Le Jules Verne (on the second level). Making a reservation at either one lets you skip the initial elevator line—your reservation includes a ride to the restaurant level. But you can't skip every line and you can't ascend more than 15-30 minutes prior to your reservation time (though you can linger afterward). Get details online when you book. Last-minute reservations for both restaurants may be available from their information kiosk at the tower's base, between the north and east pillars.

$$$$ **58 Tour Eiffel** serves a *picque-nique-chic* lunch, which comes to your table packaged in a little basket (€42, €19 for kids, daily 11:30-16:30, best to reserve ahead). Dinner here is pricey, as you must order a complete *menu* (€85-185, more expensive *menus* give you better view seating and more courses). Dinner seatings are at 18:30 and 21:00; reserve long in advance, especially if you want a view (tel. 01 72 76 18 46, toll tel. 08 25 56 66 62, www.restaurants-toureiffel.com). No jeans or tennis shoes, please, at dinner.

The more expensive $$$$ **Le Jules Verne** restaurant has one Michelin star and a higher viewpoint from its second-level perch (€105 weekday lunch *menu,* €190-230 weekend lunch or daily dinner *menus,* daily 12:15-13:30 & 19:00-21:30). In summer, reserve weeks in advance for dinner; off-season or lunch any time is easier. This is a dressy place—no shorts or overly casual sportswear (tel. 01 45 55 61 44, www.lejulesverne-paris.com).

Other Options

The tower's base offers not much more than sandwich stands. The first and second levels have small sandwich-and-pizza cafés. The first floor occasionally has temporary "pop-up" restaurants—open only for a season—that enliven the cuisine scene. At the very top of the tower, a champagne bar serves glasses of bubbly.

Rue Cler, with many options, is a 20-minute walk away (see page 201). Avenue de la Bourdonnais, a block east of the tower, has a few eateries and sandwich shops. The nearby $$ **Quai Branly Museum garden café** is a good but relatively pricey choice (see page 62).

Your tastiest option may be to assemble a picnic beforehand from any of several handy shops near Métro stop Ecole Militaire and picnic in the Champ de Mars park (on the side grassy areas or on benches along the central grass; the middle stretch is off-limits).

both sides, etc.). If you're on the road, ask your hotel reception-ist for help.

Alternatively, you can have the ticket text-messaged to your mobile phone—click on a link to download and save the ticket bar code to be scanned when you enter. Note that email or text confirmation notices will not get you in; you must have a ticket showing the bar code (print-out or phone version).

Buying Tickets On-Site: Crowds overwhelm this place much of the year, with one- to two-hour waits to get in (unless it's rainy, when lines can evaporate). Weekends and holidays are worst, but prepare for ridiculous crowds almost any time.

If you don't have a reservation, get in line 30 minutes before the tower opens. Going later is the next-best bet (after 19:00 May-Aug, after 17:00 off-season, after 16:00 in winter as it gets dark by 17:00). If you're in line to buy tickets, estimate about 20 minutes for every 100 yards, plus 30 minutes more after you reach the security check near the ticket booths.

The line to climb the stairs (to the first and second levels) is generally shorter. Once on the second level, you can buy a supplemental ticket (€6) to ride the elevator to the summit.

Other Tips for Avoiding Lines: You can bypass some (but not all) lines if you have a reservation at either of the tower's view restaurants. Or you can buy a reservation time (almost right up to the last minute) for €40 (or a €59 guided tour) through Fat Tire Tours (see page 43).

When to Go: For the best of all worlds, arrive with enough light to see the views, then stay as it gets dark to see the lights. The views are grand whether you ascend or not. At the top of the hour, a five-minute display features thousands of sparkling lights (best viewed from Place du Trocadéro or the grassy park below).

Getting There: The tower is about a 10-minute walk from the Métro (Bir-Hakeim or Trocadéro stops) or train (Champ de Mars-Tour Eiffel RER stop). The Ecole Militaire Métro stop in the Rue Cler area is 20 minutes away. Buses #42, #69, and #87 stop nearby on Avenue Joseph Bouvard in the Champ de Mars park.

Getting In: You may encounter a security checkpoint at the base of the tower. Those with reservations may have a special entry. Once past security, find the various entrances at the base of the tower's four *piliers* (pillars), named for their compass points: *nord* (north), *sud* (south), *est* (east), and *ouest* (west). The ticket offices move around from time to time, so make sure you get in the right line. If you have a reservation, arrive at the tower 10 minutes before your entry time and look for either of the two entrances marked *Visiteurs avec Reservation* (Visitors with

Reservation), where attendants scan your ticket and put you on the first available elevator. Even with a reservation, when you want to get from the second level to the summit, you'll still have to wait in line like everybody else (and show your ticket again).

If you don't have a reservation, follow signs for *Individuels* or *Visiteurs sans Tickets* (avoid lines selling tickets only for *Groupes*). If two entrances are marked *Visiteurs sans Tickets*, pick the shortest line. The stairs entrance (usually a shorter line) is at the south pillar (next to Le Jules Verne restaurant entrance). When you buy tickets on-site, all members of your party must be with you. To get reduced fares for kids, bring ID.

Information: Eiffel Tower information offices are between the north and east pillars and at the west pillar, next to the Group Desk. Recorded information tel. 08 92 70 12 39, www.toureiffel.paris.

Length of This Tour: Budget three to four hours to wait in line, get to the top, and sightsee your way back down. With online reservations and few crowds, the quickest you could get to the top and back (with minimal sightseeing) would be 90 minutes. With limited time, do the first level only (the views are fine).

Pickpockets: Beware. Street thieves plunder awestruck visitors gawking below the tower. And tourists in crowded elevators are like fish in a barrel for predatory pickpockets. *En garde.* A police station is at the Jules Verne pillar.

Security Check: Bags larger than 19" × 8" × 12" are not allowed, but there is no baggage check. All bags are subject to a security search. No knives, glass bottles, or cans are permitted.

Services: Free WCs are at the base of the tower, behind the east pillar. Inside the tower itself, WCs are on all levels, but they're small, with long lines.

Photography: All photos and videos are allowed.

Best Views of the Tower: The best place to view the tower is from Place du Trocadéro to the north. It's a 10-minute walk across the river, a happening scene at night, and especially fun for kids. Consider arriving at the Trocadéro Métro stop for the view, then walking toward the tower. Another delightful viewpoint is from the Champ de Mars park to the south.

Starring: All of Paris...and beyond.

OVERVIEW

There are three observation platforms, at roughly 200, 400, and 900 feet. Although being on the windy top of the Eiffel Tower is a thrill you'll never forget, the view is better from the second level, where you can actually see Paris' monuments. The first level also has nice views and more tourist-oriented sights. All three levels have some displays, WCs, souvenir stores, and a few other services.

For the hardy, stairs lead from the ground level up to the first and second levels—and rarely have a long line. It's 360 stairs to the first level and another 360 to the second. The staircase is enclosed with a wire cage, so you can't fall, but those with vertigo issues may still find them dizzying.

If you want to see the entire tower, from top to bottom, then

see it...from top to bottom. There isn't a single elevator straight to the top *(le sommet)*. To get there, you'll first ride an elevator to the second level. (Some elevators stop on the first level, but don't get off—it's more efficient to see the first level on the way down). Once on the second level, immediately line up for the next elevator, to the top. (Look for the shortest line; there are several elevators and feeder queues.) Enjoy the views, then ride back down to the second level. Frolic there for a while, and when you're ready, head to the first level via the stairs (no line and can take as little as five minutes) or take the elevator down (ask if it will stop on the first level—some don't). Explore the shops and exhibits on the first level and have a snack. To leave, you can line up for the elevator, but it's quickest and most memorable to take the stairs back down to earth.

The Tour Begins

Gaze up at the tower towering above you, and don't even think about what would happen if someone dropped a coin from the top.

Exterior

Delicate and graceful when seen from afar, the Eiffel Tower is massive—even a bit scary—close up. You don't appreciate its size until you walk toward it; like a mountain, it seems so close but takes forever to reach.

The tower, including its antenna, stands 1,063 feet tall, or slightly higher than the 77-story Chrysler Building in New York. Its four support pillars straddle an area of 3.5 acres. Despite the tower's 7,300 tons of metal and 60 tons of paint, it is so well-engineered that it weighs no more per square inch at its base than a linebacker on tiptoes.

Once the world's tallest structure, it's now eclipsed by a number

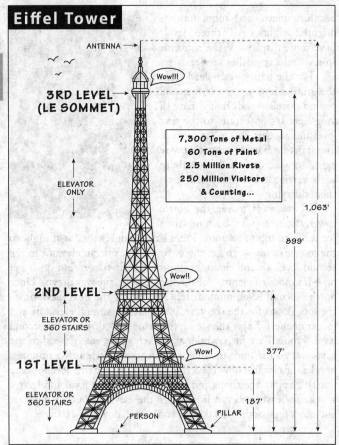

Eiffel Tower

ANTENNA →

Wow!!!

3RD LEVEL →
(LE SOMMET)

7,300 Tons of Metal
60 Tons of Paint
2.5 Million Rivets
250 Million Visitors
& Counting...

ELEVATOR
ONLY

1,063'

899'

2ND LEVEL →

Wow!!

ELEVATOR OR
360 STAIRS

Wow!

1ST LEVEL →

377'

ELEVATOR OR
360 STAIRS

187'

PERSON   PILLAR

of towers (Tokyo Skytree, 2,080 feet, for one), radio antennae (KVLY-TV mast, North Dakota, 2,063 feet), and skyscrapers (Burj Khalifa in Dubai, UAE, 2,717 feet). France's sleek Le Viaduc de Millau, a 1.5-mile-long suspension bridge completed in late 2004, also has a taller tower (1,125 feet). The consortium that built the bridge included the same company that erected the Eiffel Tower.

The long green lawn stretching south of the tower is the Champ de Mars, originally the training ground for troops and students of the nearby military school (Ecole Militaire) and now a park. On the north side, across the Seine, is the curved palace colonnade framing a square called the Trocadéro.

History

The first visitor to the Paris World's Fair in 1889 walked beneath the "arch" formed by the newly built Eiffel Tower and entered the fairgrounds. This event celebrated both the centennial of the French Revolution and France's position as a global superpower. Bridge builder Gustave Eiffel (1832-1923) won the contest to build the fair's centerpiece by beating out rival proposals such as a giant guillotine.

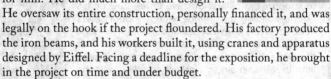

Eiffel deserved to have the tower named for him. He did much more than design it. He oversaw its entire construction, personally financed it, and was legally on the hook if the project floundered. His factory produced the iron beams, and his workers built it, using cranes and apparatus designed by Eiffel. Facing a deadline for the exposition, he brought in the project on time and under budget.

The tower was nothing but a showpiece, with no functional purpose except to demonstrate to the world that France had the wealth, knowledge, and can-do spirit to erect a structure far taller than anything the world had ever seen. The original plan was to dismantle the tower as quickly as it was built after the celebration ended, but it was kept by popular demand.

To a generation hooked on technology, the tower was the marvel of the age, a symbol of progress and human ingenuity. Not all were so impressed, however; many found it a monstrosity. The writer Guy de Maupassant (1850-1893) routinely ate lunch in the tower just so he wouldn't have to look at it.

In subsequent years, the tower has come to serve many functions: as a radio transmitter (1909-present), a cosmic-ray observatory (1910), a billboard (spelling "Citroën" in lights, 1925-1934), a broadcaster of Nazi TV programs (1940-1944), a fireworks launch pad (numerous times), and as a framework for dazzling lighting displays, including the current arrangement, designed in 2000 for the celebration of the millennium.

• *To reach the top, ride the elevator or walk (720 stairs) to the second level. From there, get in line for the next elevator and continue to the top. Pop out 900 feet above the ground.*

Third Level *(Le Sommet)*

You'll find wind and grand, sweeping views on the tiny top level. The city lies before you (pick out sights with the help of the

Building the Tower

As you ascend through the metal beams, imagine being a worker, perched high above nothing, riveting this thing together. It was a massive project, and it took all the ingenuity of the Industrial Age—including mass production, cutting-edge technology, and capitalist funding.

The foundation was the biggest obstacle. The soil, especially along the river, was too muddy to support big pillars. Gustave Eiffel drew on his bridge-building experience, where support piers needed to be constructed underwater. He sank heavy, bottomless compartments (caissons) into the wet soil. These were watertight and injected with breathable air, so workers could dig out the mud beneath them, allowing the caisson to sink farther. When the workers were done, the hole was filled in with cement 20 feet thick and capped with stone. The massive iron pillars were sunk into the ground at an angle, anchored in the subterranean stone.

The tower went up like an 18,000-piece erector set, made of 15-foot iron beams held together with 2.5 million rivets. The pieces were mass-produced in factories in the suburbs and brought in on wagons. For two years, 300 workers assembled the pieces, the tower rising as they went. First, they used wooden scaffolding to

panoramic maps). On a good day, you can see for 40 miles. Do a 360-degree tour of Paris.

Looking west *(ouest):* The Seine runs east to west (though at this point it's flowing more southwest). At the far end of the skinny "island" in the river, find the tiny copy of the Statue of Liberty, looking 3,633 miles away to her big sister in New York. Gustave Eiffel, a man of many talents, also designed the internal supports of New York's Statue of Liberty, which was cast in copper by fellow Frenchman Frederic Bartholdi (1886).

Looking north *(nord):* At your feet is the curved arcade of

the Trocadéro, itself the site of a World's Fair in 1878. Beyond that is the vast, forested expanse of the Bois de Boulogne, the three-square-mile park that hosts joggers and *boules* players by day and prostitutes by night. The track with bleachers

support the lower (angled) sections, until the pillars came together and the tower could support itself. Then the iron beams were lifted up with steam-powered cranes, including some on tracks (creeper cranes) that inched up the pillars as the tower progressed. There, daring workers dangled from rope ladders, balanced on beams, and tight-rope-walked their way across them as they put the pieces in place. The workers then hammered in red-hot rivets made on-site by blacksmiths. As the rivets cooled, they solidified the structure.

After a mere year and a half, the tower surpassed what had been the tallest structure in the world—the Washington Monument (555 feet)—which had taken 36 years to build.

The tower was painted a rusty red. Since then, it's sported several colors, including mustard and the current brown-gray. It is repainted every seven years, and will likely be receiving a new coat during your visit (it takes 25 full-time painters 18 months to apply 60 tons of paint by hand—no spraying allowed).

Two years, two months, and five days after construction began, the tower was done. On May 15, 1889, a red, white, and blue beacon was lit on the top, the World's Fair began, and the tower carried its first astounded visitor to the top.

is Paris' horseracing track, the Hippodrome de Longchamp. In the far distance are the skyscrapers of La Défense. Find the Arc de Triomphe to the right of the Trocadéro. The lone skyscraper between the Arc and the Trocadéro is the Palais des Congrès, a complex that hosts international conferences, trade shows, and major concerts.

Looking east *(est):* At your feet are the Seine and its many bridges, including the Pont Alexandre, with its four golden statues. Looking farther upstream, find the Orsay Museum, the Louvre, Pont Neuf, and the twin towers of Notre-Dame. On the Right Bank (which is to your left), find the Grand Palais, next to the

Pont Alexandre. Beyond the glass-roofed Grand Palais is the bullet-shaped dome of Sacré-Cœur, atop Butte Montmartre.

Looking south *(sud):* In a line, find the Champ de Mars, the Ecole Militaire, the Y-shaped UNESCO building, and the 689-foot Montparnasse

Up and Down

The tower—which was designed from the start to accommodate hordes of visitors—has always had elevators. Today's elevators are modern replacements. Back in the late 19th century, elevator technology was so new that this was the one job that Gustave Eiffel subcontracted to other experts (including an American company). They needed a special design to accommodate the angle of the tower's pillars. Today's elevators make about 100 round-trip journeys a day.

There are 1,665 stairs to the top level, though tourists can only climb 720 of them, up as far as the second level. During a race in 1905, a gentleman climbed from the ground to the second level—elevation gain nearly 400 feet—in 3 minutes, 12 seconds.

Tower skyscraper. To the left is the golden dome of Les Invalides, and beyond that, the state capitol-shaped dome of the Panthéon.

The tippy top: Ascend another short staircase to the open-air top. Look up at all the satellite dishes and communications equipment (and around to find the tiny WC). You'll see the small apartment given to Gustave Eiffel, who's now represented by a mannequin (he's the one with the beard).

The mannequins re-create the moment during the 1889 World's Fair when the American Thomas Edison paid a visit to his fellow techie, Gustave (and Gustave's daughter Claire), presenting them with his new invention, a phonograph. (Then they cranked it up and blasted The Who's "I Can See for Miles.") Feeling proud you made it this high? You can celebrate your accomplishment with a glass of champagne from the bar.

• *Ride the elevator down to the...*

Second Level

The second level (400 feet) has the best views because you're closer to the sights, and the monuments are more recognizable. (Refer to the descriptions given earlier, under "Third Level.") The second level has souvenir shops, WCs, and a small stand-up café.

The world-class Le Jules Verne restaurant is on this level, but you won't see it; access is by a private elevator. The head chef is currently Alain Ducasse, who operates restaurants around the world. One would hope his brand of haute cuisine matches the 400-foot haute of the restaurant.

• *Catch the elevator (after confirming it'll stop at the first level) or take the 360 stairs down to the...*

First Level

The first level (200 feet) has more great views, all well-described by the tower's panoramic displays. After a $38 million renovation, this

level is decked out with new shops, eateries, and displays. Pop-up restaurants and kiosks appear with every season—even a little playground for kids. In winter, part of the first level is often set up to host an ice-skating rink.

The highlight is the breathtaking, vertigo-inducing, selfie-inspiring **glass floor.** Venture onto it and experience what it's like to stand atop an 18-story building and look straight down. Then look up at the massive structure around you. Check out your fellow visitors—the crowds may make the place a total zoo, but everyone's still thrilled.

The 58 Tour Eiffel restaurant is on this level (also run by chef Alain Ducasse, with more accessible prices than its upstairs sibling). The Salon Gustave Eiffel is a private reception hall not open to the public.

Watch the original hydraulic pump (1889) at work. It once pumped water from here to the second level to feed the machin-

ery powering the upper elevator. Then look at the big wheels that wind and unwind heavy cables to lift the elevators. As part of the renovation, much of this level's energy needs are now green-powered—with the installation of wind turbines, solar panels, and a rainwater catchment system.

Explore the various exhibits (which change often). A continuously running film (in the glass-walled Ferrié Pavilion) shows a montage of the tower's construction, paint job, place in pop culture, and guts and glory. As you wander the first floor, you may find exhibits on the tower's past, jobs there, other creations by Monsieur Eiffel, or the tower's famous visitors—from Adolph Hitler to Katy Perry. You might learn how the sun warms the tower's metal, causing the top to expand and lean about five inches away from the sun, or how the tower oscillates slightly in the wind. Because of its lacy design, even the strongest of winds can't blow the tower down, but only cause it to sway a few inches. In fact, Eiffel designed the tower primarily with wind resistance in mind, wanting a structure seemingly "molded by the action of the wind itself."

• *Consider a drink or a sandwich while overlooking all of Paris, then take the elevator or stairs (five minutes, 360 steps) to the ground.*

Back on the Ground

Welcome back to earth. After you've climbed the tower, you come to appreciate it even more from a distance. For a final look, stroll

across the river to Place du Trocadéro or to the end of the Champ de Mars and look back for great views. However impressive it may be by day, the tower is an awesome thing to see at twilight, when it becomes engorged with light, and virile Paris lies back and lets night be on top. When darkness fully envelops the city, the tower seems to climax with a spectacular light show at the top of each hour... for five minutes.

• *Nearby, you can catch the Bateaux Parisiens boat for a Seine cruise (see page 39) or hop on bus #69 for a tour of the city (*📖 *see the Bus #69 Sightseeing Tour). The Trocadero viewpoint, which looks "right there," is a 20-minute walk away. Also nearby are the Quai Branly Museum (page 62), Rue Cler area (page 202), Army Museum and Napoleon's Tomb (page 236), and Rodin Museum (next chapter).*

RODIN MUSEUM TOUR

Musée Rodin

Auguste Rodin (1840-1917) was a modern Michelangelo, sculpting human figures on an epic scale, revealing through their bodies his deepest thoughts and feelings. Like many of Michelangelo's unfinished works, Rodin's statues rise from the raw stone around them, driven by the life force. With missing limbs and scarred skin, these are prefab classics, making ugliness noble. Rodin's people are always moving restlessly. Even the famous *Thinker* is moving; while he's plopped down solidly, his mind is a million miles away. The museum presents a full range of Rodin's work, housed in a historic mansion where the artist once lived and worked.

The museum's interior has been completely gutted and redone as part of a major years-long renovation. Until the layout of the collection settles down for good, it's best to use this chapter to get an overview of Rodin's life and work, then just enjoy what's currently on display.

Orientation

Cost: €10, free for those under 18, free on the first Sun of the month (Oct-March), €4 for garden only, €18 combo-ticket with Orsay Museum, both museum and garden covered by Museum Pass. Your ticket or Museum Pass also covers any special exhibits.

If you have a Museum Pass or a ticket purchased online (www.musee-rodin.fr, €2 booking fee), you can bypass both the line for buying tickets and the one for entering the museum building itself (lines usually only a problem on spring/summer weekends).

Hours: Tue-Sun 10:00-17:45, closed Mon; gardens close at 18:00, Oct-March at 17:00.

RODIN

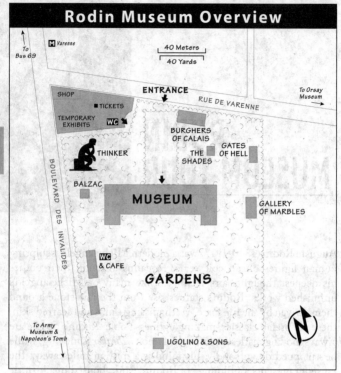

Rodin Museum Overview

To Bus 69

M Varenne

40 Meters
40 Yards

ENTRANCE

RUE DE VARENNE

To Orsay Museum

SHOP

TICKETS

TEMPORARY EXHIBITS WC

THINKER

BALZAC

BOULEVARD DES INVALIDES

BURGHERS OF CALAIS

THE SHADES

GATES OF HELL

MUSEUM

GALLERY OF MARBLES

WC & CAFE

GARDENS

To Army Museum & Napoleon's Tomb

UGOLINO & SONS

N

When to Go: The museum is busiest on weekends and on rainy days (when the building is packed and the gardens are unpleasant).

Getting There: It's at 77 Rue de Varenne, near the Army Museum and Napoleon's Tomb (Mo: Varenne). Bus #69 stops two blocks away at the intersection of Rue Grenelle and Rue Bellechasse. Bus #87 also stops nearby, a long block south on Rue de Babylone.

Information: Tel. 01 44 18 61 10, www.musee-rodin.fr.

Tours: A €6 audioguide covers the museum and gardens.

Length of This Tour: Allow one hour.

Baggage Check: Even a fairly small bag must be checked, unless you tuck it under your arm like a purse.

Photography: You can take photos without a flash.

Cuisine Art: A peaceful **$ self-service cafeteria** is in the gardens behind the museum. Picnics are not allowed in the gardens. For better options, you'll find many recommended cafés and restaurants in the **Rue Cler area** (a 15-minute walk; see page 422).

The Tour Begins

• *Enter and buy tickets in the modern entrance hall. There's a bookstore, a gallery for temporary exhibits, and WCs. Pick up the museum map (and audioguide, if interested).*

Exit the ticket hall, walk across the courtyard of the gardens, and enter the mansion (where you'll check your bag). Now enter Room 1, which generally displays...

Early Work

Rodin's early works match the belle époque style of the time—noble busts of bourgeois citizens, pretty portraits of their daughters, and classical themes. Born of working-class roots, Rodin taught himself art by sketching statues at the Louvre and then sculpting copies.

The Man with the Broken Nose (L'Homme au Nez Cassé, 1865)—a deliberately ugly work—was 23-year-old Rodin's first break from the norm. He meticulously sculpted this deformed man (one of the few models the struggling sculptor could afford), but then the clay statue froze in his unheated studio, and the back of the head fell off. Rodin loved it! Art critics hated it. Rodin persevered. (Note: The museum rotates the display of two different versions—the broken-headed one and a repaired version that Rodin made later and critics accepted.)

You may also see portraits of Rodin's future wife, Rose Beuret, the woman who would suffer with him through obscurity and celebrity.

To feed his family, Rodin cranked out small-scale works—portraits, ornamental vases, nymphs, and knickknacks to decorate buildings—with his boss' name on them (the more established sculptor Albert Carrier-Belleuse). Still, the series of mother-and-childs he was hired to do (perhaps depicting Rose and baby Auguste?) allowed him to experiment on a small scale with the intertwined twosomes he'd perfect later in his career.

Rodin's work brought in enough money for him to visit Italy, where he was inspired by the boldness, monumental scale, restless figures, and "unfinished" look of Michelangelo's sculptures. Rapidly approaching middle age, Rodin was ready to rock.

First Success

Rodin moved to Brussels, where his first major work, *The Age of Bronze* (*L'Âge d'Airain*, 1877), brought controversy and the fame

that surrounds it. This nude youth, perhaps inspired by Michelangelo's *Dying Slave* (in the Louvre—see page 158), awakens to a new world. It was so lifelike that Rodin was accused of not sculpting it himself but simply casting it directly from a live body. The boy's raised left arm looks like it should be leaning on a spear, but it's just that missing element that makes the pose more tenuous and interesting.

The art establishment still snubbed Rodin as an outsider, and no wonder. *Saint John the Baptist* (1880)—though now acknowledged as a classic—was savaged by the critics for its awkward, flat-footed pose. His ultra-intense *The Call of Arms* (*La Défense*, 1912-1918) screams, "Off with their heads!" at the top of her lungs. Rodin loved twisted poses, fragmented figures, and weird juxtapositions. He was forging a style that was unique. He was a slave to his muses, and some of them inspired monsters.

Little by little, Rodin gathered an entourage around him of like-minded souls: wealthy patrons, fellow artists who understood his vision, and students who adored him...including one he'd later become involved with, Camille Claudel.

Major Works

Rodin and his stable of talented artists began cranking out works that have become classics. As you'll see throughout the museum,

Rodin often started with small-scale versions of works that were later executed on a grand scale. He tinkered with *The Thinker* for years before creating the massive bronze version in the gardens (which we'll see later). *The Three Shades* (*Les Trois Ombres*, before 1886)—whose heads and hands join in the solidarity of the damned—would appear later on his epic *Gates of Hell* (which we'll also see in the gardens).

In *The Kiss* (*Le Baiser*, 1888-1889), a passionate woman twines around a solid man for their first, spontaneous kiss. Looking

Rodin's Creative Process

The beauty of the Rodin Museum is that it shows so many works in progress. Rodin loved the creative process and the unfinished look.

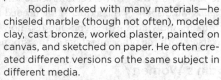

Rodin worked with many materials—he chiseled marble (though not often), modeled clay, cast bronze, worked plaster, painted on canvas, and sketched on paper. He often created different versions of the same subject in different media.

The first flash of inspiration for a huge statue might be a single line sketched on notepaper. Rodin wanted nude models in his studio at all times—walking, dancing, and squatting—in case they struck some new and interesting pose. Rodin thought of sculpture as simply "drawing in all dimensions."

Next, he might re-create a figure as a small-scale statue in plaster. The museum displays a number of these plaster "sketches," which you can compare with the final large-scale versions. Rodin employed and mentored many artists who executed these designs on a larger scale. Rodin rarely worked on the marble statues (though the museum often displays newsreel footage of him doing exactly that). For that robust work, he hired others.

Rodin's figures struggle to come into existence. They are dancers stretching, posing, and leaping. Legendary lovers kiss, embrace, and intertwine in yin-yang bliss. His embracing couples seem to emerge from the stone just long enough to love.

Rodin was fascinated by the theory of evolution—not Darwin's version of the survival of the fittest, but the ideas of Frenchman Jean-Baptiste Lamarck. Rodin's figures survive not by the good fortune of random mutation (Darwin) but by virtue of their own striving (Lamarck). They are driven by the life force, a restless energy that animates and shapes dead matter. Rodin must have felt that force even as a child, when he first squeezed soft clay and saw a worm emerge.

Rodin left many works "unfinished," reminding us that all creation is a difficult process of dragging a form out of chaos.

RODIN

at their bodies, we can almost read the thoughts, words, and movements that led up to this meeting of lips. *The Kiss* was the first Rodin work the public loved. Rodin came to despise it, thinking it simple and sentimental.

The Hand of God (*La Main de Dieu*, 1896) shapes Adam and Eve from the mud of the earth to which they will return. Rodin himself worked in "mud," using his hands to model clay figures, which were then reproduced in marble or bronze, usually by his assistants. Inspect this masterpiece from every angle. Rodin first worked on the front view, then checked the back and side profiles, then filled in the in-between.

Rodin excelled in creating ensembles. As he worked on small-scale studies for the grim execution scene known as *The Burghers of Calais* (on display in the gardens), he needed not only to capture each man's individual expression but also how his body language conversed with the other members of the group.

Rodin's Women

What did Rodin think of women? There are many different images from which you can draw your own conclusions.

He loved sculpting women, either alone or as part of an intertwined couple. *Danaïd* (1889) buries her head in the marble over her meaningless fate. *Eve* (1881) buries her head in shame, hiding her nakedness. But she can't hide the consequences—she's pregnant.

As Rodin became famous, wealthy, and respected, society ladies all wanted him to do their portraits. You may see a sculpture of his last mistress *(La Duchesse de Choiseul)*, an American who lived with him here in this mansion. Rodin purposely left in the metal base points (used in the sculpting process), placing them suggestively.

Throughout the museum are studies of the female body in its different forms—crouching, soaring, dying, open, closed, wrinkled, intertwined.

Rodin's Friends

Rodin started hanging out with Paris' intellectuals, artists, and glitterati, as one of their own. You may see statues and portrait busts of celebrities he knew personally. Remember, Rodin lived and worked in this mansion, renting rooms alongside Henri Matisse, the poet Rainer Maria Rilke (Rodin's secretary), and the dancer Isadora Duncan.

Rodin was especially fascinated with trying to capture the perfect portraits of his two famous writer friends, Victor Hugo and the controversial French novelist Honoré de Balzac. With Balzac, Rodin's feverish attempts ranged from a pot-bellied Bacchus to a headless nude cradling an erection (the display changes). In a moment of inspiration, Rodin threw a plaster-soaked robe over a nude form and watched it dry. This became the inspiration for the definitive version—proud and turning his nose up at his critics. (This version is displayed in the gardens, near *The Thinker;* other casts stand in the Orsay Museum and on a street median in Montparnasse.) When the Balzac statue was unveiled, the crowd booed, a

The Bronze Casting Process

Rodin made his bronze statues not by hammering sheets of metal but by using the classic "lost wax" technique. He'd start by shaping the figure from wet plaster. This sculptural model was covered with a form-fitting mold. By pouring molten bronze into the narrow space between the model and the mold around it, letting it cool, and removing the mold—*voilà!*—Rodin had a hollow bronze statue ready to be polished and varnished.

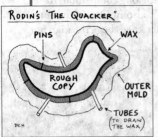

RODIN'S "THE QUACKER"

PINS   WAX

ROUGH COPY

OUTER MOLD

TUBES (TO DRAIN THE WAX)

DCH

There were actually a number of additional steps (involving two different molds) before the bronze was poured. Rodin was intimately involved in every step—sanding down the clay model, coating it with wax, and touching up the waxy skin to add crucial surface details. Once the final mold was ready, Rodin's employees fitted it with ventilation tubes and poured in the molten bronze. The wax melted away—the "lost wax" technique—and the bronze cooled and hardened in its place, thus forming the final bronze statue.

Using a mold, Rodin could produce multiple copies, which is why there are many authorized bronze versions of Rodin's masterpieces all over the world.

fitting tribute to both the defiant novelist and the bold man who sculpted him.

There are often paintings by fellow artists Rodin either knew or admired, such as Vincent van Gogh, Claude Monet, and Pierre-Auguste Renoir. Rodin enjoyed discussions with Monet and other artists and incorporated their ideas into his work. Rodin is often considered an Impressionist because he captured spontaneous "impressions" of figures and created rough surfaces that catch reflected light.

Camille Claudel

You'll find several works by Camille Claudel, mostly in the style of her master. The 44-year-old Rodin, inspired by 18-year-old Camille's beauty and spirit, took her as his pupil, muse, colleague, and lover, and often used her as a model. (See several versions of her head.) We can follow the arc of their relationship in the exhibits.

As his student, "Mademoiselle C" learned from Rodin, doing portrait busts in his lumpy, molded-clay style. Her bronze bust of Rodin shows the steely-eyed sculptor with strong frontal and side profiles, barely emerging from the materials they both worked with. Soon they were lovers. *The Waltz* (*La Valse*, 1892) captures the spinning exuberance the two must have felt as they embarked together on a new life. The couple twirls—hands so close but not touching—in a delicate balance.

But Rodin was devoted as well to his lifelong companion, Rose. Claudel's *Maturity* (*L'Âge Mûr*, 1895-1907, also in Orsay Museum) shows the breakup. A young woman on her knees begs the man not to leave her, as he's reluctantly led away by an older woman. The statue may literally depict a scene from real life, in which a naked, fragile Claudel begged Rodin not to return to his wife. In the larger sense, it may also be a metaphor for the cruel passage of time, as Youth tries to save Maturity from the clutches of Old Age.

Rodin did leave Claudel. Talented in her own right but tormented by grief and jealousy, she became increasingly unstable and spent her final years in an institution. Claudel's *The Wave* (*La Vague*, 1900), carved in green onyx in a very un-Rodin style, shows tiny, helpless women huddling together as a tsunami is about to engulf them.

Final Years: Looking Back, Looking Forward

By the end of Rodin's long and productive life, he had become as famous as his works. He was viewed as a modern master of the most classic of art forms—sculpture, a tradition that stretched back to ancient times. At the same time, he was always looking ahead, restlessly forging new forms of expression.

Rodin took classical Greek motifs—myths and nymphs— and used them to create something completely new. He loved the broken look of Greek ruins and created his own ready-made fragments. He expanded the age-old repertoire of "acceptable" poses by studying the fluid movements of dancers. He loved the off-balance, unposed pose (which the invention of the camera also helped to capture).

The tall bronze *Walking Man* (*L'Homme Qui Marche*, 1900-1907) depicts the bold spirit of the turn-of-the-century era. Armless and headless, he plants his back foot forcefully, as though he's about to stride, while his front foot has already stepped. Rodin captures two poses at once—of a man who has one foot in the classical past, one in the modernist future.

• *The visit continues outside in the gardens. There*

you can see the finished, large-scale versions of many small-scale "studies" you may have seen inside the museum.

THE GARDENS

Rodin loved the overgrown gardens that surrounded his home, and he loved placing his creations amid the flourishing greenery. These, his greatest works, show Rodin at his most expansive. The epic human figures are enhanced, not dwarfed, by the nature surrounding them.

• *Leaving the house, you've got four more stops: one to the left and three on the right. Beyond these stops is a big, breezy garden ornamented with many more statues, a cafeteria, and a WC.*

The Thinker (Le Penseur), 1906

Leaning slightly forward, tense and compact, every muscle working toward producing that one great thought, Man contemplates his fate. No constipation jokes, please.

This is not an intellectual but a linebacker who's realizing there's more to life than frat parties. It's the first man evolving beyond his animal nature to think the first thought. It's anyone who's ever worked hard to reinvent himself or to make something new or better. Said Rodin: "It is a statue of myself."

There are 29 other authorized copies of this statue, one of the most famous in the world. *The Thinker* was to have been the centerpiece of a massive project that Rodin wrestled with for decades—a doorway encrusted with characters from Dante's *Inferno*. It's our next stop, *The Gates of Hell*.

• *Follow* The Thinker's *gaze across the gardens. Standing before a tall, white backdrop is a big, dark door...*

The Gates of Hell (La Porte de l'Enfer), 1880-1917

These doors (never meant to actually open) were never finished for a museum that was never built. But the vision of Dante's trip into hell gave Rodin a chance to explore the dark side of human experience. "Abandon all hope ye who enter here," was hell's motto. The three Shades at the top of the door point down—that's where we're going. Beneath the Shades, pondering the whole scene from above, is Dante as the Thinker. Below him, the figures emerge from the darkness just long enough to

tell their sad tale of depravity. There are Paolo and Francesca (in the center of the right door), who were driven into the illicit love affair that brought them here. Ugolino (left door, just below center) crouches in prison over his kids. This poor soul was so driven by hunger that he ate the corpses of his own children. On all fours like an animal, he is the dark side of natural selection. Finally, find what some say is Rodin himself (at the very bottom, inside the right doorjamb, where it just starts to jut out), crouching humbly.

You'll find some of these figures writ large in the garden. *The Thinker* and *The Shades* (c. 1889) are behind you, and *Ugolino* (1901-1904) dines in the fountain at the far end.

It's appropriate that *The Gates*—Rodin's "cathedral"—remained unfinished. He was always a restless artist for whom the process of discovery was as important as the finished product. Studies for *The Gates* are scattered throughout the museum, and they constitute some of Rodin's masterpieces.

• *To the left of* The Gates of Hell, *along the street near where you entered, are...*

The Burghers of Calais (Bourgeois de Calais), 1889

The six city fathers trudge to their execution, and we can read in their faces and poses what their last thoughts are. They mill about, dazed, as each one deals with the decision he's made to sacrifice himself for his city.

Rodin depicts the actual event from 1347, when, in order to save their people, Calais' city fathers surrendered the keys of the city—and their lives—to the king of England. Rodin portrays them not in some glorious pose drenched in pomp and allegory, but as a simple example of men sacrificing their lives together. As the men head to the gallows, with ropes already around their necks, each body shows a distinct emotion, ranging from courage to despair.

Circle the work counterclockwise. The man carrying the key to the city tightens his lips in determination. The bearded man is weighed down with grief. Another buries his head in his hands. One turns, seeking reassurance from his friend, who turns away and gestures helplessly. The final key-bearer (in back) raises his hand to his head.

Each is alone in his thoughts, but they're united by their mutual sacrifice, by the base they stand on, and by their weighty robes—gravity is already dragging them down to their graves.

Pity the poor souls; view the statue from various angles (you can't ever see all the faces at once); then thank King Edward III, who, at the last second, pardoned them.

• *To the right of* The Gates of Hell *is a glassed-in building, the...*

Gallery of Marbles

Unfinished, these statues show human features emerging from the rough stone. Imagine Rodin in his studio, working to give them life.

Victor Hugo (at the far end of the gallery), the great champion of progress and author of *Les Misérables* and *The Hunchback of Notre-Dame,* leans back like Michelangelo's nude *Adam,* waiting for the spark of creation. He tenses his face and cups his ear, straining to hear the call from the blurry Muse above him. Once inspired, he can bring the idea to life (just as Rodin did) with the strength of his powerful arms. It's been said that all of Rodin's work shows the struggle of mind over matter, of brute creatures emerging from the mud and evolving into a species of thinkers.

ARMY MUSEUM AND NAPOLEON'S TOMB TOUR

Musée de l'Armée

If you're ever considering trying to conquer Europe to become its absolute dictator, come here before gathering your army. Hitler did, but still went out and made the same mistakes as his role model. (Hint: Don't invade Russia.) Napoleon's tomb rests beneath the golden dome of Les Invalides church.

In addition to the tomb, the complex of Les Invalides—a former veterans' hospital built by Louis XIV—has various military collections, collectively called the Army Museum. See medieval armor, Napoleon's horse stuffed and mounted, Louis XIV-era uniforms and weapons, and much more. The best part is the section dedicated to the two world wars, especially World War II. Visiting the different sections, you can watch the art of war unfold from stone axes to Axis powers.

Orientation

Cost: €11, €9 after 17:00 (16:00 in Nov-March), covered by Museum Pass (show it at the entrance to each sight or exhibit), admission includes Napoleon's Tomb and all museum collections within the Invalides complex. Special exhibits are extra. Children are free, but you must line up to get them a ticket. The sight is also free for military personnel in uniform.

Hours: Daily 10:00-18:00, Nov-March until 17:00; tomb also open July-Aug until 19:00 and April-Sept Tue until 21:00; museum (except for tomb) closed first Mon of month Oct-June; Charles de Gaulle exhibit closed Mon year-round.

Getting There: The museum and tomb are at Hôtel des Invalides, with its hard-to-miss golden dome (129 Rue de Grenelle). You can ride the **Métro** (Mo: La Tour Maubourg, Varenne, or Invalides), or you can take a **bus:** #69 from the Marais and Rue

Cler area, bus #87 from the Rue Cler and the Luxembourg Garden area, or #63 from the St. Germain-des-Prés area. The museum is a 10-minute **walk** from Rue Cler. There are two entrances: one from the Grand Esplanade des Invalides, and the other from behind the gold dome on Avenue de Tourville.

Information: A helpful, free map/guide is available at the ticket office. Tel. 08 10 11 33 99, www.musee-armee.fr.

Tours: The fine €6 videoguide covers the whole complex.

Length of This Tour: Women—two hours, men—three hours.

Photography: Allowed without flash.

Concerts: The museum hosts classical music concerts throughout the year. For schedules (in French only) see www.musee-armee.fr/programmation.

Eating: The cafeteria is reasonable, and the rear gardens are picnic-perfect. Rue Cler is a 10-minute walk away (see page 422), as is the riverside promenade (Les Berges du Seine; see page 65), with many eating options.

Nearby: You'll likely see the French playing *boules* on the esplanade (as you face Les Invalides from the riverside, look for the dirt area to the upper right; for the rules of *boules*, see page 389).

Starring: Napoleon's Tomb, exhibits on World War II, memorabilia of Napoleon (including his stuffed horse).

OVERVIEW

The Army Museum and Napoleon's Tomb are in the Invalides complex (or should I say "Napoleon complex"?). Various exhibits are scattered around the large complex. Consult your free Army Museum map for the whole list and their locations. Your ticket covers them all—just flash your ticket or Museum Pass at each entrance.

Pick your favorite war. With limited time, visit only ▲▲▲ **Napoleon's Tomb** and the excellent ▲▲▲ **World War I and World War II** exhibits. Next on my list would be the exhibit ▲▲ **From Louis XIV to Napoleon I (1643-1814)**, featuring swords and muskets, key battles of the Revolution, and memorabilia of Napoleon. If you still have energy, browse the ▲ **Charles de Gaulle Exhibit,** which honors France's WWII hero, or **Arms and Armor,** a vast collection of medieval suits of armor, pikes, swords, and cannons. Though there are other exhibits to see here, this chapter covers only the top sights in order of importance.

The Tour Begins

• *You can enter the Invalides complex from either the north or south side (ticket offices are at both entrances). Start at Napoleon's Tomb—underneath the golden dome, with its entrance on the south side (farthest from the Seine).*

NAPOLEON'S TOMB
Church and Tomb

Enter the church, gaze up at the dome, then lean over the railing and bow to the emperor lying inside the scrolled, red porphyry **tomb** (see photo on page 236). If the lid were opened, you'd find an oak coffin inside, holding another ebony coffin, housing two lead ones, then mahogany, then tinplate...until finally, you'd find Napoleon himself, staring up, with his head closest to the door. When his body was exhumed from the original grave and transported here (1840), it was still perfectly preserved, even after 19 years in the ground.

Born of humble Italian heritage on the French-owned isle of Corsica, Napoleon Bonaparte (1769-1821) went to school at Paris' Ecole Militaire, quickly rising through the ranks amid the chaos of the Revolution. The charismatic "Little Corporal" won fans by fighting for democracy at home and abroad. In 1799, he assumed power and, within five short years, conquered most of Europe. The great champion of the Revolution had become a dictator, declaring himself emperor of a new Rome.

Napoleon's red tomb on its green base stands 15 feet high in the center of a marble floor, circled by a mosaic crown of laurels and exalted by a glorious dome above.

Now, panning around the **chapel,** you'll find tombs of Napoleon's family. After conquering Europe, he installed his big brother, Joseph, as king of Spain (turn around to see Joseph's black-and-white marble tomb in the alcove to the left of the door); his little brother, Jerome, became king of the German kingdom of Westphalia (tucked into the chapel to the right of the door); and his baby boy, Napoleon II (downstairs), sat in diapers on the throne of Rome.

In other **alcoves,** you'll find more dead war heroes, including Marshal Ferdinand Foch, the commander in chief of the multinational Allied forces in World War I, his tomb lit with otherworldly blue light. To the right of Foch lies Maréchal Vauban, Louis XIV's great military engineer, who designed the fortifications of more than 100 French cities. Vauban's sarcophagus shows him

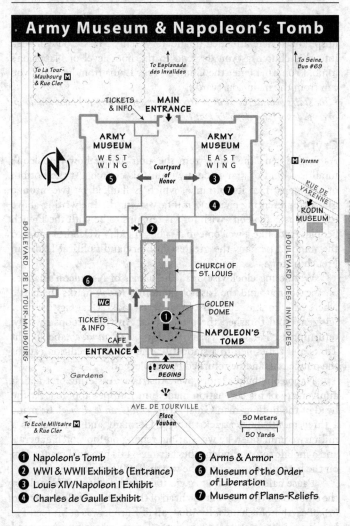

Army Museum & Napoleon's Tomb

❶ Napoleon's Tomb
❷ WWI & WWII Exhibits (Entrance)
❸ Louis XIV/Napoleon I Exhibit
❹ Charles de Gaulle Exhibit
❺ Arms & Armor
❻ Museum of the Order of Liberation
❼ Museum of Plans-Reliefs

reflecting on his work with his engineer's tools, flanked by figures of war and science. These heroes, plus many painted saints, make this the French Valhalla in the Versailles of churches.

Before moving on, consider the design of the church itself. It's actually a double church—one for the king and one for his soldiers—built under Louis XIV in the 17th century. You're standing in the **"dome chapel,"** decorated to the glory of Louis XIV and intended for royalty before it became the tomb of Napoleon. The original altar was destroyed in the Revolution. What you see today dates from the mid-1800s, and was inspired by the altar and canopy at St. Peter's Basilica in Rome.

Behind the altar is the **Church of St. Louis,** where the veterans hospitalized here attended (mandatory) daily Mass. You can peek into this church as you descend to the floor level of Napoleon's tomb. (You can't enter the Church of St. Louis from here, but you can from the main courtyard.)

• *The stairs behind the altar (with the corkscrew columns) take you down to crypt level for a closer look at the tomb.*

Crypt

As you descend the stairs from the altar, notice how Napoleon's tomb is a kind of grand room within this church. At the bottom of the steps, face its entrance, which is flanked by two **bronze giants** representing civic and military strength. The writing above the door is Napoleon's wish for his remains to be with the French people. And, like a welcome mat, a big inlaid *N* welcomes you into the tomb of perhaps the greatest military and political leader in French history.

Wandering clockwise, read the names of **Napoleon's battles** on the floor around the base of the tomb. *Rivoli* marks the battle where the rookie 26-year-old general took a ragtag band of "citizens" and thrashed the professional Austrian troops in Italy, returning to Paris a celebrity. In Egypt *(Pyramides),* he fought Turks and tribesmen to a standstill. The exotic expedition caught the public eye, and he returned home a legend.

Napoleon's huge victory over Austria at Austerlitz on the first anniversary of his coronation made him Europe's top dog. At the head of the million-man Great Army *(La Grande Armée),* he made a three-month blitz attack through Germany and Austria. As a military commander, he was daring, relying on top-notch generals and a mobile force of independent armies. His personal magnetism on the battlefield was said to be worth 10,000 additional men.

Pause halfway around to gaze at the grand **statue of Napoleon** the emperor in the alcove at the head of the tomb—royal scepter and orb of earth in his hands. By 1804, all of Europe was at his feet. He held an elaborate ceremony in Notre-Dame, where he proclaimed his wife, Josephine, empress, and himself—the 35-year-old son of humble immigrants—emperor. The laurel wreath, the robes, and the Roman eagles proclaim him the equal of the Caesars. The floor at the statue's feet marks the grave of his son, Napoleon II (*Roi de Rome,* 1811-1832).

Around the crypt are **relief panels** showing Napoleon's constructive side. Dressed in toga

Napoleon Bonaparte (1769-1821)

Born to Italian parents on the French-ruled isle of Corsica, Napoleon attended French schools, although he spoke the language with an Italian accent to the end of his days. He graduated from Paris' Ecole Militaire, where he trained in the latest high-tech artillery. His military career took an unexpected turn when the Revolution erupted (1789), and he chose to return to Corsica to fight royalist oppression.

In 1793, as commander of artillery, Napoleon besieged Toulon, forcing the royalists to surrender and earning his first great victory. He later defended the Revolutionary government from royalist mobs in Paris by firing a "whiff of grapeshot" into the crowd (1795). Such daring military exploits and personal charisma earned him promotions and the nickname the "Little Corporal"—not for his height (he was an average 5'7") but as a term of endearment from the rank and file. When he married the classy socialite Joṣéphine Beauharnais, Napoleon became a true celebrity. In 1798, having conquered Italy, Austria, and Egypt, Napoleon returned to Paris, where the weak government declared him First Consul—ostensibly as the champion of democracy, but, in fact, he was a virtual dictator over much of Europe. He was 29 years old.

During the next 15 years, Napoleon solidified his reign with military victories over Europe's kings—now allied against France. Under his rule, France sealed the Louisiana Purchase with America, and legal scholars drew up the Code of Napoleon, a system of laws still used by many European governments today. In 1804, his power peaked when he crowned himself emperor in a ceremony in Notre-Dame blessed by the pope. The Revolutionary general was now, paradoxically, part of Europe's royalty. Needing an heir to the throne, he divorced barren Josephine and married an Austrian duchess, Marie Louise, who bore him the boy known to historians as the "King of Rome."

In 1812, Napoleon decided to invade Russia, and the horrendous losses from that failed venture drained his power. Many of Europe's conquered nations saw their chance to pig-pile on France, toppling Napoleon and sending him to exile on the isle of Elba (1814). Napoleon escaped long enough to raise an army for a final hundred-day campaign before finally being defeated by British and Prussian forces at the Battle of Waterloo (1815). Guilty of war crimes, he was sentenced to exile on the remote South Atlantic island of St. Helena, where he talked to his dog, studied a little English, penned his memoirs, spoke his final word—"Josephine"—and died.

and laurel leaves, he dispenses justice, charity, and pork-barrel projects to an awed populace.

• *In the first panel to the right of the statue...*

He establishes an **Imperial University** to educate naked boys throughout *"tout l'empire."* The roll of great scholars links modern France with those of the past: Plutarch, Homer, Plato, and Aristotle. Three panels later, his various building projects (canals, roads, and so on) are celebrated with a list and his quotation, "Everywhere he passed, he left durable benefits" *("Partout où mon regne à passé...").*

Hail Napoleon. Then, at his peak, came his most tragic errors.

• *Turn around and look down to* **Moscowa** *(the Battle of Moscow— marked beneath his tomb).*

Napoleon invaded Russia with 600,000 men and returned to Paris with 60,000 frostbitten survivors. Two years later, the Russians marched into Paris, and Napoleon's days were numbered. After a brief **exile** on the isle of Elba, he skipped parole, sailed to France, bared his breast, and said, "Strike me down or follow me!" For 100 days, they followed him, finally into Belgium, where the British hammered the French at the Battle of Waterloo (conspicuously absent on the floor's décor—for more on this battle, see page 258). Exiled again by a war tribunal, he spent his last years in a crude shack on the small South Atlantic island of St. Helena. When Napoleon died, he was initially buried in a simple grave. The epitaph was never finished because the French and British wrangled over what to call the hero/tyrant. The stone simply read, "Here lies..."

• *To get to the Courtyard of Honor and the various military collections, exit the same way you entered, make a U-turn right, and march past the cafeteria and ticket hall. Continue to the end of the hallway, where you'll find the entrance to the World War I and World War II exhibits. Go upstairs, following blue banners reading* Les Deux Guerres Mondiales, 1871-1945. *The museum is laid out so you first see the coverage of World War I, though some may choose to skip ahead to the more substantial WWII section.*

WORLD WAR I

World War I (1914-1918) introduced modern technology to the age-old business of war. Tanks, chemical weapons, monstrous cannons, rapid communication, and airplanes made their debut, conspiring to kill nearly 10 million people in just four years. In addition, the war ultimately seemed senseless: It started with little provocation, raged on with few decisive battles, and ended with nothing resolved, a situation that sowed the seeds of World War II.

A quick walk-through of this 20-room exhibit leads you chronologically through World War I's causes, battles, and outcome, giving you the essential background for the next world war. Good English information is posted on the walls in most rooms, and video displays have English versions, but the displays are lackluster and low-tech: Move along quickly and don't burn out before getting to the World War II wing. Be prepared to hunt for some (not always prominent) room numbers.

The War Begins

Room 1: The first room bears a thought-provoking name: "Honour to the Unfortunate Bravery." **Paintings** of dead and wounded soldiers from the Franco-Prussian War make it clear that World War I actually "began" in 1871, when Germany thrashed France.

Suddenly, a recently united Germany was the new bully in Europe.

Rooms 2-3, France Rebounds: Snapping back from its loss, France began rearming itself, with spiffy new uniforms and weapons like the American-invented Gatling gun (early machine gun).

The French replaced the humiliation of defeat with a proud and extreme nationalism. Fanatical patriots hounded a (Jewish) officer named Alfred Dreyfus (**display** at the far end) on trumped-up treason charges (1890s).

Rooms 4-6, Tensions Rise: Europe's nations were in a race for wealth and power, jostling to acquire lucrative colonies in Africa and Asia (**exotic uniforms**). In a climate of mutual distrust, nations allied with their neighbors, vowing to protect each other if war ever erupted. In Room 6, a **map of Europe** in 1914 shows the division: France, Britain, and Russia (the Allies) teamed up against Germany, Austria-Hungary, and Italy (the Central Powers). Europe was ready to explode, but the spark that would set it off had nothing to do with Germany or France.

Room 7, Assassination and War Begins: Bang. On June 28, 1914, an Austrian archduke was shot to death (see **video**). One by one, Europe's nations were dragged into the regional dispute by their webs of alliances. The Great War had begun.

Room 8, The Battle of the Marne: German forces swarmed

into France, hoping for a quick knockout blow. Germany brought its big guns (photo and miniature model of **Big Bertha**). The **projection map** shows how the armies tried to outflank each other along a 200-mile battlefront. As the Germans (purple arrows) zeroed in on Paris, the French (blue arrows) and British ("BEF") scrambled

to send 6,000 crucial reinforcements, shuttled to the front lines in 670 Parisian taxis (one is displayed nearby). The German tide was stemmed, and the two sides faced off, expecting to duke it out and get this war over quickly. It didn't work out that way.

• *The war continues upstairs.*

ARMY MUSEUM

World at War

Rooms 9-10, The War in the Trenches: By 1915, the two sides reached a stalemate, and they settled in to a long war of attrition—French and Britons on one side, Germans on the other. The battle line, known as the Western Front, snaked 450 miles across Europe from the North Sea to the Alps. For protection against flying bullets, the soldiers dug **trenches** *(tranchées)*, which soon became home—24 hours a day, 7 days a week—for millions of men.

La guerre des tranchées

Life in the trenches was awful—cold, rainy, muddy, disease-ridden—and, most of all, boring. Every so often, generals waved their swords and ordered their men "over the top" and into "no man's land." Armed with rifles and bayonets, they advanced into a hail of machine gun fire. In a number of battles, France lost 70,000 men in a single day. The "victorious" side often won only a few hundred yards of meaningless territory that was lost the next day after still more deaths.

The war pitted 19th-century values of honor, bravery, and chivalry against **20th-century weapons:** grenades, machine guns, tanks, and poison gas. To shoot over the tops of trenches while staying hidden, they even invented crooked and periscope-style guns.

Rooms 11-13, "World" War: Besides the Western Front, the war extended elsewhere, including the colonies, where many natives (see their **exotic uniforms**) joined the armies of their "mother" countries. On the Eastern Front, Russia and Germany wore each other down. (Finally, the Russian people had enough; they overthrew their czar, brought the troops home, and fomented a revolution that put communists in power.)

• *Down a short hallway, enter Room 14.*

War Ends

Room 14, The Allies: By 1917, the Allied forces were beginning to outstrip the Central Powers, thanks to help from around the world. When Uncle Sam said, "I Want You," five million Americans answered the call to go "Over There" (in the words of a popular song) and fight the Germans. The Yanks were not an enormous military factor, but their very presence signaled that the Allies seemed destined to prevail.

Room 15, Armistice: Under the command of French Marshal Ferdinand Foch, the Allies undertook a series of offensives that, by 1918, would prove decisive. At the 11th hour of the 11th day of the 11th month (November 11, 1918), the guns fell silent. Allied Europeans celebrated the Armistice with victory parades...and then began assessing the damage.

Room 16, Costly Victory: Weary soldiers returned home to be honored (look for a painting of the **Arc de Triomphe parade**). After four years of battle, the war had left 9.5 million dead and 21 million wounded (see plaster casts of disfigured faces). Three out of every four French soldiers had been either killed or wounded. A generation was lost.

Rooms 17-19, From 1918 to 1938: The Treaty of Versailles (1919), signed in the Hall of Mirrors, officially ended the war. A map shows how it radically redrew **Europe's borders.** Germany was punished severely, leaving it crushed, humiliated, stripped of crucial land, and saddled with demoralizing war debts. Marshal Foch prophetically said of the Treaty: "This is not a peace. It is an armistice for 20 years."

France, one of the "victors," was drained, trying to hang on to its prosperity and its colonial empire. By the 1930s—swamped by the Great Depression and a stagnant military **(dummy on horseback)**—France was reeling, unprepared for the onslaught of a retooled Germany seeking revenge.

A **photo of Adolf Hitler** presages the awful events that came next.

• *World War II is covered directly across the hall, in the rooms marked 1939-1942.*

WORLD WAR II

World War II was the most destructive of earth's struggles. In this exhibit, the war unfolds in photos, displays, and newsreels, with special emphasis on the French contribution. (You may not have realized that it was Charles de Gaulle who won the war for us.) The museum takes you from Germany's quick domination (third floor), to the Allies turning the tide (second floor), to the final surrender (first floor). There are fine English descriptions throughout. Be ready—rooms come in rapid succession and flow into each other without obvious walls or dividers. Find your way with the room labels. Ideally, read this tour before your visit as an overview of the vast, complex, and horrific global spectacle known as World War II.

Third Floor: Axis Aggression, 1939-1941
The Phony War (La Drôle de Guerre) and the Defeat of 1940 (Le Defaite de 1940)

On September 1, 1939, Germany, under Adolf Hitler, invaded Poland, starting World War II. But in a sense the war had really begun in 1918, when the "war to end all wars" ground to a halt, leaving 9.5 million dead, Germany defeated, and France devastated (if victorious). For the next two decades, Hitler fed off German resentment over the Treaty of Versailles, which humiliated and ruined Germany.

After Hitler's move into Poland, France and Britain mobilized. For the next six months, the two sides faced off, with neither actually doing battle—a tense time known to historians as the "Phony War" *(Drôle de Guerre).*

Then, in spring of 1940, came the Blitzkrieg ("lightning war"), and Germany's better-trained and better-equipped soldiers and tanks (see **turret**) swept west through Belgium. France was immediately overwhelmed, and British troops barely escaped across the English Channel from Dunkirk. Within a month, Nazis were goose-stepping down the Champs-Elysées.

• *A few paces farther along you reach a room dedicated to...*

Charles de Gaulle (L'Appel du 18 Juin)

Just like that, virtually all of Europe was dominated by fascists. During those darkest days, as France fell and Nazism spread  across the Continent, one Frenchman—an obscure military man named Charles de Gaulle—refused to admit defeat. This 20th-century John of Arc had an unshakable belief in his mission to save France. De Gaulle (1890-1970) was born into a literate, upper-class family, raised in military academies, and became a WWI hero and POW. But when World War II broke out, he was still only a minor officer with limited political experience, who was virtually unknown to the French public.

After the invasion, de Gaulle escaped to London. From there he made inspiring speeches over the radio, beginning with a famous address broadcast on June 18, 1940. He slowly convinced a small audience of French expatriates that victory was still possible.

France After the Armistice (La France Apres l'Armistice)

After France's surrender, Germany ruled northern France, including Paris—see the **photo of Hitler as a tourist** at the Eiffel Tower. Hitler made a three-hour blitz tour of the city, including a stop at Napoleon's Tomb. Afterward he said, "It was the dream of my life to be permitted to see Paris. I cannot say how happy I am to have that dream fulfilled today."

The Nazis allowed the French to administer the south and the colonies (North Africa). This puppet government, centered in the city of Vichy, was right-wing and traditional, bowing to Hitler's demands as he looted France's raw materials and manpower for the war machine. (The movie *Casablanca*, set in Vichy-controlled Morocco, shows French officials following Nazi orders while French citizens defiantly sing "The Marseillaise.")

The Battle of Britain (La Solitude et la Bataille d'Angleterre)

Facing a "New Dark Age" in Europe, British Prime Minister Winston Churchill pledged, "We will fight on the beaches...We will fight in the hills. We will never surrender."

In June 1940, Germany mobilized to invade Britain across the English Channel. From June to September, they paved the way, sending bombers—up to 1,500 planes a day—to destroy military and industrial sites. When Britain wouldn't budge, Hitler concentrated on London and civilian targets. This was "The Blitz" of the winter of 1940, which killed 30,000 and left London in ruins. But

Britain hung on, armed with newfangled radar, speedy Spitfires, and an iron will.

They also had the Germans' secret "Enigma" code. The **Enigma machine** (in display case), with its set of revolving drums,

allowed German commanders to scramble orders in a complex code that could be broadcast securely to their troops. The British (with crucial help from Poland) captured a machine, broke the code, then monitored German airwaves. (An Enigma machine co-starred with actor Benedict Cumberbatch, who played code-breaking mathematician Alan Turing, in the 2014 movie *The Imitation Game*.) For the rest of the war, Britain had advance knowledge of many top-secret plans, but occasionally let Germany's plans succeed—sacrificing its own people—to avoid suspicion.

By spring of 1941, Hitler had given up any hope of invading the Isle of Britain. Churchill said of his people: "This was their finest hour."

Germany Invades the Soviet Union
(L'Allemagne Envoyer l'Union Soviet)
Perhaps hoping to one-up Napoleon, Hitler sent his state-of-the-art tanks speeding toward Moscow in June 1941 (betraying his

former ally Joseph Stalin). By winter, the advance had stalled at the gates of Moscow and was bogged down by bad weather and Soviet stubbornness. The Third Reich had reached its peak. From now on, Hitler would have to fight a two-front war. The French Renault **tank** (displayed) was downright puny compared with the big, fast, high-caliber German

Panzers. This war was often a battle of factories, to see who could produce the latest technology fastest and in the greatest numbers. And what nation might have those factories...?

• *In the corner is a glass case with a model of an aircraft carrier, announcing that...*

The United States Joins the War
(Les Etats-Unis Dans la Guerre)
On December 7, 1941, "a date which will live in infamy" (as US President Franklin D. Roosevelt put it), Japanese planes made

ARMY MUSEUM

a sneak attack on the US base at **Pearl Harbor,** Hawaii, and destroyed the pride of the Pacific fleet in two hours.

The US quickly entered the fray against Japan and her ally, Germany. In two short years, America had gone from isolationist observer to supplier of Britain's arms to full-blown war ally against fascism. The US now faced a two-front war—in Europe against Hitler, and in Asia against Japan's imperialist conquest of China, Southeast Asia, and the South Pacific.

America's first victory came when Japan tried a sneak attack on the US base at Midway Island (June 3, 1942). This time—thanks to the Allies who had cracked the Enigma code—America had the aircraft carrier **USS *Enterprise*** (see model) and two of her buddies lying in wait. In five minutes, three of Japan's carriers (with valuable planes) were mortally wounded, their major attack force was sunk, and Japan and the US were dead even, settling in for a long war of attrition.

Though slow to start, the US eventually had an army of 16 million strong, 80,000 planes, the latest technology, $250 million a day, unlimited raw materials, and a population of Rosie the Riveters fighting for freedom to a boogie-woogie beat.

• *Continue downstairs to the second floor.*

Second Floor: The Tide Turns, 1942-1944

In 1942, the Continent was black with fascism, and Japan was secure on a distant island. The Allies had to chip away on the fringes.

Battle of the Atlantic (La Bataille de l'Atlantique)

German U-boats (short for *Unterseeboot,* meaning submarine) and battleships such as the *Bismarck* patrolled Europe's perimeter, where they laid spiky mines to try to keep America from aiding Britain. (Until long-range transport planes were produced near war's end, virtually all military transport was by ship.) The Allies traveled in convoys with air cover, used sonar and radar, and dropped depth charges, but for years they endured the loss of up to 60 ships per month.

• *Don't bypass Room 14, tucked in the corner.*

Guadalcanal, El-Alamein, and Stalingrad

Three crucial battles in the autumn of 1942 put the first chink in the fascist armor. Off the east coast of Australia, 10,000 US Marines (see **kneeling soldier** in glass case 14D) took an airstrip on Guadalcanal, while 30,000 Japanese held the rest of the tiny, isolated island. For the next six months, the two armies were marooned together, duking it out in thick jungles and malaria-infested swamps while their countries struggled to reinforce or rescue them. By February 1943, America had won and gained a crucial launch pad for bombing raids.

A world away, German tanks under General Erwin Rommel rolled across the vast deserts of North Africa. In October 1942, a well-equipped, well-planned offensive by British General Bernard ("Monty") Montgomery attacked at El-Alamein, Egypt with 300 tanks. (See **British tank soldier** with headphones.) Monty drove "the Desert Fox" west into Tunisia for the first real Allied victory against the Nazi *Wehrmacht* war machine.

In 1942, the Allies began long-range bombing of German-held territory, including saturation bombing of civilians. It was global war and total war.

Then came Stalingrad. (See kneeling **Soviet soldier** in heavy coat.) In August 1942, Germany attacked the Soviet city,

an industrial center and gateway to the Caucasus oil fields. By October, the Germans had battled their way into the city center and were fighting house-to-house, but their supplies were running low, the Soviets wouldn't give up, and winter was coming. The snow fell, their tanks had no fuel, and relief efforts failed. Hitler ordered them to fight on through the bitter cold. On the worst days, 50,000 men died. (By comparison, the US lost a total of 58,000 in Vietnam.) Finally, on January 31, 1943, the Germans surrendered, against Hitler's orders. The six-month totals? Eight hundred thousand German and other Axis soldiers dead, 1.1 million Soviets dead. The Russian campaign put hard miles on the German war machine.

The Campaign in Tunisia (La Campagne in Tunis)

Winston Churchill and US President **Franklin D. Roosevelt** (see photo with de Gaulle), two of the 20th century's most dynamic and strong-willed statesmen, decided to attack Hitler indirectly by invading Vichy-controlled Morocco and Algeria. On November 8, 1942, 100,000 Americans and British— under the joint command of an unknown, low-key problem-solver named General Dwight ("Ike") Eisenhower—landed on three separate beaches (including Casablanca). More than 120,000

Vichy French soldiers, ordered by their superiors to defend the fascist cause, confronted the Allies and...gave up. (See display of some standard-issue **weapons:** Springfield rifle, Colt 45 pistol, Thompson submachine gun, hand grenade.)

The Allies moved east, but bad weather, inexperience, and the powerful Afrika Korps under Rommel stopped them in Tunisia. But with flamboyant General George S. ("Old Blood-and-Guts") Patton punching from the west, and Monty pushing from the south, they captured the port town of Tunis on May 7, 1943. The Allies now had a base from which to retake Europe.

The French Resistance (L'Unification de la Résistance)

Inside occupied France, other ordinary heroes fought the Nazis—the underground Resistance. Bakers hid radios within loaves of bread to secretly contact London. Barmaids passed along tips from tipsy Nazis. Communists in black berets cut telephone lines. Farmers hid downed airmen in haystacks. Housewives spread news from the front with their gossip. Printers countered Nazi propaganda with pamphlets.

Jean Moulin (see photo in exhibit), de Gaulle's assistant, secretly parachuted into France and organized these scattered heroes into a unified effort. In 1943, Moulin was arrested by the Gestapo (Nazi secret police), imprisoned, tortured, and sent to Germany, where he died in transit. Still, Free France now had a (secret) government again, rallied around de Gaulle, and was ready to take over when liberation came.

• *Meanwhile, on the Eastern Front...*

The Red Army (L'Armée Rouge)

Monty, Patton, and Ike certainly were heroes, but the war was won on the Eastern Front by Soviet grunts, who slowly bled Germany dry. Maps show the shifting border of the Eastern Front.

• *Bypass a couple of rooms, to...*

The Italian Campaign (La Campagne d'Italie)

On July 10, 1943, the assault on Hitler's European fortress began. More than 150,000 Americans and British sailed from Tunis and landed on the south shore of Sicily. (See **maps** and **video clips** of the campaigns.) Speedy Patton and methodical Monty began a "horse race" to take the city of Messina (the US won the friendly competition by a few hours). They met little resistance from 300,000 Italian soldiers, and were actually cheered as liberators. Mussolini was arrested by his own people, and Italy surrendered. Hitler quickly poured 50,000 German troops into Italy, reinstalled Mussolini, and ordered Italy to fight on.

In early September, the Allies launched a two-pronged landing onto the beaches of southern Italy. Finally, after four long years of war, free men set foot on the European continent. Lieutenant

General Mark Clark led the slow, bloody push north to liberate Rome—an offensive fought on the ground by foot soldiers and costing many lives for just a few miles.

In January 1944, the Germans dug in between Rome and Naples at Monte Cassino, a rocky hill topped by the monastery of St. Benedict. Thousands died as the Allies tried inching up the hillside. In frustration, the Allies air-bombed the historic **Monte Cassino monastery** to smithereens, killing many noncombatants... but no Germans, who dug in deeper. Finally, after four months of vicious, sometimes hand-to-hand combat by the Allies (Americans, Brits, Free French, Poles, Italian partisans, Indians, etc.), a band of Poles stormed the monastery, and the German back was broken.

Meanwhile, 50,000 Allies had landed near Rome at Anzio and held the narrow beachhead for months against massive German attacks. Finally the Allied troops broke out and joined the assault on the capital. Without a single bomb threatening its historic treasures, Rome fell on June 4, 1944.

• *Room 23 (with benches) shows a film on...*

D-Day

Three million Allies and six million tons of materiel were massed in England in preparation for the biggest fleet-led invasion in history—across the Channel to France, then eastward to Berlin. The Germans, hunkered down in northern France, knew an invasion was imminent, but the Allies kept the details top secret. On the night of June 5, 150,000 soldiers boarded ships and planes without knowing where they were headed until they were under way. Each one carried a note from General Eisenhower: "The tide has turned. The free men of the world are marching together to victory."

At 6:30 a.m. on June 6, 1944, Americans spilled out of troop transports into the cold waters off a beach in Normandy, code-named Omaha. The weather was bad, seas were rough, and the prep bombing had failed. The soldiers, many seeing their first action, were dazed and confused. Nazi machine guns pinned them against the sea. Slowly, they crawled up the beach on their stomachs. A thousand died. The survivors held on until the next wave of transports arrived.

All day long, Allied confusion did battle with German indecision; the Nazis never really counterattacked, thinking D-Day was just a ruse, instead of the main invasion. By day's end, the Allies had taken several beaches along the Normandy coast and began building artificial harbors, providing a tiny port-of-entry for the reconquest of Europe. The stage was set for a quick and easy end to the war. Right.

• *Go downstairs to the...*

First Floor: The War Ends, 1944-1945
Battle of Normandy and Landing in Provence
(Le Débarquement de Provence)
Through June, the Allies (mostly Americans) secured Normandy by taking bigger ports (Cherbourg and Caen) and amassing troops and supplies for the assault on Germany. In July they broke out and sped eastward across France, with Patton's tanks covering up to 40 miles a day. They had "Jerry" on the run.

On France's Mediterranean coast, American troops under General Alexander Patch landed near Cannes (see **parachute** photo), took Marseilles, and headed north to meet with Patton.

Les Maquis
French Resistance guerrilla fighters helped reconquer France from behind the lines. (Don't miss the **folding motorcycle** in its parachute case.) The liberation of Paris was started by a Resistance attack on a German garrison.

Liberation of Paris (La Libération de Paris)
As the Allies marched on Paris, Hitler ordered his officers to torch the city—but they sanely disobeyed and prepared to surrender. On August 26, 1944, General Charles de Gaulle walked ramrod-straight down the Champs-Elysées, followed by Free French troops and US GIs passing out chocolate and Camels. Two million Parisians went crazy.

Toward Berlin (Vers Berlin)
The quick advance from the west through France, Belgium, and Luxembourg bogged down at the German border in autumn of 1944. Patton outstripped his supply lines, an airborne and ground invasion of Holland (the Battle of Arnhem) was disastrous, and bad weather grounded planes and slowed tanks.

On December 16, the Allies met a deadly surprise. An enormous, well-equipped, energetic German army appeared from nowhere, punched a "bulge" deep into Allied territory through Belgium and Luxembourg, and demanded surrender. General Anthony McAuliffe sent a one-word response—"Nuts!"—and the momentum shifted. The Battle of the Bulge was Germany's last great offensive.

The Germans retreated across the Rhine River, blowing up bridges behind them. But one bridge, at Remagen, was captured by the Americans and stood just long enough for GIs to cross and establish themselves on the east shore of the Rhine. Soon US tanks were speeding down the autobahns and Patton could wire the good news back to Ike: "General, I have just pissed in the Rhine."

Soviet soldiers did the dirty work of taking fortified Berlin by launching a final offensive in January 1945, and surrounding the city in April. German citizens fled west to surrender to the more-benevolent Americans and Brits. Hitler, defiant to the end, hunkered in his underground bunker. (See photo of **ruined Berlin.**)

On April 28, 1945, Mussolini and his girlfriend were killed and hung by their heels in Milan. Two days later, Adolf Hitler and his new bride, Eva Braun, avoided similar humiliation by committing suicide (pistol in mouth and poison), and having their bodies burned beyond recognition. Germany formally surrendered on May 8, 1945.

• *To the left, don't miss the exhibits on...*

Concentration Camps (Les Camps de Concentration)

Lest anyone mourn Hitler or doubt this war's purpose, gaze at photos from Germany's concentration camps. Some camps held political enemies and prisoners of war, including two million French. Others were expressly built to exterminate peoples considered "genetically inferior" to the "Aryan master race"— particularly Jews, Gypsies, homosexuals, and the mentally ill.

War of the Pacific (Les Batailles du Pacific)

Often treated as an afterthought, the final campaign against Japan was a massive American effort, costing many lives, but saving millions of others from Japanese domination.

Japan was an island bunker surrounded by a vast ring of fortified Pacific islands. America's strategy was to take one island at a time, "island-hopping" until close enough for B-29 Superfortress bombers to attack Japan itself. The battlefield spread across thousands of miles. In a new form of warfare, ships carrying planes led the attack and prepared tiny islands (such as Iwo Jima) for troops to land on and build airfields. While General Douglas MacArthur island-hopped south to retake the Philippines ("I have returned!"), others pushed north toward Japan.

On March 9, Tokyo was firebombed, and 90,000 were killed. Japan was losing, but a land invasion would cost hundreds of thousands of lives. The Japanese had a reputation for choosing death over the shame of surrender—they even sent bomb-laden "kamikaze" planes on suicide missions.

America unleashed its secret weapon, an atomic bomb (originally suggested by German-turned-American Albert Einstein). On August 6, a B-29 dropped one (named **"Little Boy,"** see the replica dangling overhead) on the city of Hiroshima and instantly vaporized 100,000 people and four square miles. Three days later, a second bomb fell on Nagasaki. The next day, Emperor Hirohito unofficially surrendered. The long war was over, and US sailors returned home to kiss their girlfriends in public places.

The Closing Chapter (Actes de Conclusion)
The death toll for World War II, tallied from September 1939 to August 1945, totaled 80 million soldiers and civilians. The Soviet Union lost 26 million, China 13 million, France 580,000, and the US 340,000. The Nazi criminals who started the war and perpetrated war crimes were tried and sentenced in an international court—the first of its kind—held in Nuremburg, Germany.

World War II changed the world, with the US emerging as the dominant political, military, and economic superpower. Europe was split in two. The western half recovered, with American aid. The eastern half remained under Soviet occupation. For 45 years, the US and the Soviet Union would compete—without ever actually doing battle—in a "Cold War" of espionage, propaganda, and weapons production that stretched from Korea to Cuba, from Vietnam to the moon.

• *The next exhibit is located on the east side of the large Courtyard of Honor (where Napoleon honored his troops, Dreyfus had his sword broken, and de Gaulle once kissed Churchill). Start upstairs on the second floor.*

FROM LOUIS XIV TO NAPOLEON I, 1643-1814
This display traces the evolution of uniforms and weapons through France's glory days, with the emphasis on Napoleon Bonaparte. As you circle the second floor, the exhibit unfolds chronologically in four parts: the Ancien Régime (Louis XIV, XV, and XVI), the Revolution, the First Empire (Napoleon), and the post-Waterloo world. Many (but not all) exhibits have some English information.

This museum is best for browsing, but I've highlighted a handful of the (many) exhibits to get you started.

Hall 1: Ancien Régime (Louis XIV, XV, and XVI)
Louis XIV unified the army as he unified the country, creating the first modern nation-state with a military force. You'll see many glass cases of ❶ **weapons.** Gunpowder was quickly turning swords, pikes, and lances to pistols, muskets, and bayonets. Uniforms became more uniform, and everyone got a standard-issue flintlock.

At the end of the hall, a display case has some amazingly big and ❷ **odd-shaped rifles.** Nearby, a projection screen (with English commentary) shows a re-enactment of the ❸ **Battle of Fontenoy** (in present-day Belgium) in 1745. Watch how, at the turning point in the battle, the British troops (in red) cluster into a dense, square column and penetrate the French line of defenses.

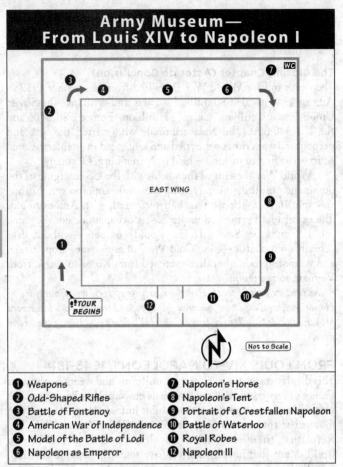

Army Museum—
From Louis XIV to Napoleon I

EAST WING

TOUR BEGINS

Not to Scale

1. Weapons
2. Odd-Shaped Rifles
3. Battle of Fontenoy
4. American War of Independence
5. Model of the Battle of Lodi
6. Napoleon as Emperor
7. Napoleon's Horse
8. Napoleon's Tent
9. Portrait of a Crestfallen Napoleon
10. Battle of Waterloo
11. Royal Robes
12. Napoleon III

But the French swarm around them on three sides, then drive them back, affirming French superiority on the Continent.

• *Turn the corner and enter...*

Hall 2: Révolution

Room 13 features the **❹ American War of Independence.** You'll see the sword *(épée)* of the French aristocrat Marquis de La Fayette, who—full of revolutionary fervor—sailed to America, where he took a bullet in the leg and fought alongside George Washington.

After France underwent its own Revolution, the king's Royal Army became the people's National Guard, protecting their fledgling democracy from Europe's monarchies while spreading revolutionary ideas by conquest.

Midway down Hall 2, find the large **❺ model of the Battle**

of Lodi in 1796. The French and Austrians faced off on opposite sides of a northern Italian river, each trying to capture a crucial bridge. The model shows the dramatic moment when the French cavalry charged across the bridge, overpowering the exhausted Austrians. They were led by a young, relatively obscure officer who had distinguished himself on the battlefield and quickly risen through the ranks—Napoleon Bonaparte. Stories spread that it was the brash General Bonaparte himself who personally sighted the French cannons on the enemy—normally the job of a lesser officer.

It turned the tide of battle and earned him a reputation and a nickname, "The Little Corporal."

Rooms 19-21 chronicle the era of ❻ **Napoleon as emperor.** While pledging allegiance to Revolutionary ideals of democracy, Napoleon staged a coup and soon ruled France as a virtual dictator. The museum displays General Bonaparte's hat, sword, and medals. In 1804, Napoleon donned royal robes and was crowned Emperor. The famous portrait by J. A. D. Ingres shows him at the peak of his power, stretching his right arm to supernatural lengths. The ceremonial collar and medal he wears in the painting are displayed nearby, as are an eagle standard and Napoleon's elaborate saddle.

Continue to the end of Hall 2 to find ❼ **Napoleon's beloved Arabian horse.** Le Vizir weathered many a campaign with Napoleon, grew old with him in exile, and now stands stuffed and proud.

Hall 3: The Reign of Napoleon

Ambitious Napoleon plunged France into draining wars against all of Europe. In Room 29 (midway down the hall), you'll find ❽ **Napoleon's tent** and bivouac equipment: a bed with mosquito netting, a director's chair, his overcoat and pistols, and a table that you can imagine his generals hunched over as they made battle plans.

Napoleon's plans to dominate Europe ended with disastrous losses when he attempted to invade Russia. The rest of Europe ganged up on France, and in 1814 Napoleon was forced to abdicate. At the end of the hall, find Room 35 with a ❾ **portrait of a crestfallen Napoleon,** now replaced by King Louis XVIII (whose bust stands opposite). Napoleon spent a year in exile on the isle of Elba. In March of 1815, he escaped, returned to France, rallied the army, and prepared for one last hurrah.

• *Turning the corner into Hall 4, you run right into what Napoleon did—Waterloo.*

Hall 4: Waterloo and the First Restoration

Study the projection screen that maps the course of the history-changing ❿ **Battle of Waterloo,** fought on the outskirts of Brussels, June 15-19, 1815.

On June 18, 72,000 French (the blue squares) faced off against the allied armies of 68,000 British-Dutch under Wellington (red and yellow) and 45,000 Prussians under Blücher (purple). Napoleon's only hope was to split the two armies and defeat them individually.

First, Napoleon's Marshal Ney advances on the British-Dutch, commanded by the Prince of Orange. Then the French attack the Prussians on the right. They rout the Prussians, driving them north. Napoleon's strategy is working. Now he prepares to finish Wellington off.

On the morning of June 18, Wellington hunkers down atop a ridge at Waterloo. Napoleon advances, and they face off. Nothing happens. Napoleon decides to wait two hours to attack, to let the field dry—some say it was his fatal mistake. Finally, Napoleon attacks from the left flank. Next he punches hard on the right. Wellington pushes them back. Meanwhile, the Prussians are advancing from the right, so Napoleon sends General Mouton to check it out. Napoleon realizes he must act quickly or have to fight both armies at once. He sends General Ney into the thick of Wellington's forces. Fierce fighting ensues. Ney is forced to retreat. The Prussians advance from the right. It's a two-front war. Caught in a pincer, Napoleon has no choice but to send in his elite troops, the Imperial Guard, who have never been defeated. The British surprise the Guard in a cornfield, and Wellington swoops down from the ridge, routing the French. By nightfall, the British and Prussian armies have come together, 12,000 men have died, and Napoleon's reign of glory is over.

Napoleon was sent into exile on St. Helena. Once the most powerful man in the world, Napoleon spent his final years as a lonely outcast suffering from ulcers, dressed in his nightcap and slippers, and playing chess, not war.

The French monarchy was restored, and King Louis XVIII donned the ⓫ **royal robes.**

• *Continuing on and crossing a hall, you run right into a portrait of* ⓬ *Napoleon III, the emperor of France in the 1850s and the nephew of the great Napoleon Bonaparte...but that's a whole other story. Our tour here is done.*

THE REST OF THE ARMY MUSEUM
• *Your ticket is good for all the exhibits and museums in the complex (consult your free museum map). In the east wing, follow signs to find the...*

Charles de Gaulle Exhibit
This engaging memorial, the "Historial Charles de Gaulle," brings France's history of war into the modern age. The exhibit leads you through the life of the greatest figure in 20th-century French history. You can use the free audioguide, or just circle counterclockwise and let the big photos and video images tell de Gaulle's life story. After helping to defeat Hitler, de Gaulle went on to lead the nation for two decades as its president. The multimedia displays lead you from de Gaulle's youth, through two world wars, to the rebuilding of France during his presidency, and the social unrest of the 1960s that toppled him.

• *On the west side of the Courtyard of Honor is the exhibit called...*

Arms and Armor
The collection starts with the suit of armor of France's great Renaissance king, Francois I, decorated with *fleur-de-lis*. He sits astride his horse, fitted out in matching armor. Connoisseurs of armor, cannons, swords, crossbows, and early guns will love this collection of weapons from the 13th to 17th centuries; others can browse a few rooms and move on.

More Sights
If you still haven't had enough of dummies in uniforms and endless glass cases of muskets, there's more. The **Museum of the Order of Liberation** honors heroes of the WWII Resistance. The **Museum of Plans-Reliefs** (on the top floor of the east wing) exhibits the 18th-century models of France's cities (1:1600 scale) that strategists used to thwart enemy attacks. Survey Antibes and ponder which hillside you'd use to launch an attack. Finally, you can end your visit in the pristine **Church of St. Louis**—the perfect place to remember all the fallen soldiers.

ARMY MUSEUM

BUS #69 SIGHTSEEING TOUR

From the Eiffel Tower to Père Lachaise Cemetery

Why pay €25 for a tour company to give you an overview of Paris when city bus #69 can do it for the cost of a Métro ticket? Get on the bus and settle in for a ride through some of the city's most interesting neighborhoods. Or use this tour as a handy way to lace together many of Paris' most important sightseeing districts. On this ride from the Eiffel Tower to Père Lachaise Cemetery,

you'll learn how great Paris' bus system is—and you'll wonder why you've been tunneling by Métro under this gorgeous city. And if you're staying in the Marais or Rue Cler neighborhoods, line #69 is a useful route for just getting around town.

At times the bus goes faster than you can read. It's best to look through this chapter and peruse the map (see page 262) ahead of time, then ride with an eye out for the various sights described here.

Orientation

Length of This Tour: Allow one hour. With limited time, get off at Bastille, with good Métro connections.

Cost: One Métro ticket per one-way ride.

When to Go: You can board daily until 22:30 (last departure from Eiffel Tower stop). It's best to avoid weekday rush hours (8:00-9:30 & 17:30-19:30) and hot days (no air-conditioning). Sundays are quietest, and it's easy to get a window seat. Evening bus rides are pretty from fall through spring (roughly Sept-April), when it gets dark early enough to see the floodlit monuments before the bus stops running—though some of the finer points are harder to see in the dark.

Getting There: Eastbound line #69 leaves from the Eiffel Tower on Avenue Joseph Bouvard (the street that becomes Rue St. Dominique as it crosses the Champ de Mars, two blocks from the tower through the park (see the map on page 390). Board at one of the first few stops to secure a view seat. The first stop is at the southwestern end of the avenue; the second stop is at the eastern end (just before Avenue de la Bourdonnais). Stops are located about every three blocks along the route. At whatever stop you plan to catch the bus, check if "69" is posted at the stop to make sure you're on the right route. To see all the stop names, check the official *Plan de Lignes* at www. ratp.fr (under "Services," click "Plan"—or "Map" if viewing in English—then "Bus"; type "69" in the box labeled *"Afficher un plan de ligne de bus"*). The map on page 31 shows part of the bus #69 route.

Bus Tips: Use a ticket from your *carnet*. If you hop off to see a sight, you'll need a new ticket to hop back on. Métro tickets work on buses, but you can't use the same ticket to transfer between the bus and Métro. Board through the front door, then validate your ticket in the machine behind the driver. If it's hot, you can usually open the upper part of the window. To let the driver know you'd like to get off at the next stop, push a red button. Exit through the rear door. Buses run every 10-15 minutes except in the late evening.

Some eastbound buses terminate a few stops after the Orsay; if so, just get off and wait for the next #69.

Tours: If you do get out and explore, note that some sights along this route have corresponding chapters and audio tours. ⬜ See the Eiffel Tower Tour, Orsay Museum Tour, Louvre Museum Tour, Left Bank Walk, Historic Paris Walk, Marais Walk, and Père Lachaise Cemetery Tour chapters. You can also 🎧 download my free Historic Paris Walk, Orsay Museum, and Louvre Museum audio tours.

BUS #69

OVERVIEW

Handy line #69 crosses the city east-west, running between the Eiffel Tower and Père Lachaise Cemetery. In between, it passes these great monuments and neighborhoods: Ecole Militaire, Rue Cler, Les Invalides (Army Museum and Napoleon's Tomb),

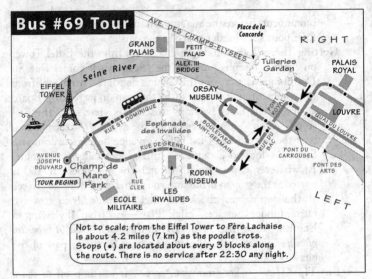

Bus #69 Tour

Not to scale; from the Eiffel Tower to Père Lachaise is about 4.2 miles (7 km) as the poodle trots. Stops (•) are located about every 3 blocks along the route. There is no service after 22:30 any night.

the Louvre, Ile de la Cité, Ile St. Louis, Hôtel de Ville, Pompidou Center, Marais, and Bastille.

This tour is best done in the direction it's written (east from the Eiffel Tower to Père Lachaise Cemetery)—in the other direction, one-way streets change the route. It's still a scenic ride if going westbound—and after dark, westbound riders get to pass through the Louvre courtyard, with its glowing pyramid.

Grab a window seat—either side toward the back is good (rear seats are higher). If you get on at one of the first stops, you're likely to secure a good seat. As you go, you can follow your progress by reading the names of the stops on the bus shelters you pass.

Many find the Bastille a good ending point (where you can begin my walking tour of the Marais). This ride also ties in well after a visit to the Eiffel Tower or on your way to visiting Père Lachaise Cemetery. Think of this as an overview. The sights you'll survey are written up in more depth elsewhere in the book. OK—let's roll.

The Tour Begins

Champ de Mars and the Eiffel Tower

Your tour begins below this 1,000-foot, reddish-brown hood ornament. The park surrounding you is called the Champ de Mars (named for the god of war). It served as a parade ground for the military school, Ecole Militaire, which seals the park at the right end. Napoleon Bonaparte is the school's most famous graduate.

In 1889, the Champ de Mars was covered with a massive temporary structure to house exhibitions of all sorts; it was a

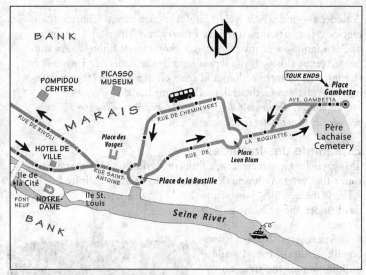

celebration of the Centennial World's Fair (the 100th anniversary of the French Revolution), the same event for which the Eiffel Tower was built. The apartments surrounding the park are among the most exclusive in Paris.

The grass that runs down the center of the park becomes a playground at night, when much of Paris seems to descend on it. Picnics at that time are a delight, and warm evenings reveal Paris' multicultural population. Dogs and kids romp as soccer balls fly past, all within the glow of the Eiffel Tower.

• *Leaving the Champ de Mars, the bus slices through the 7th arrondissement along its primary shopping street. As you head onto Rue St. Dominique, notice how well your driver navigates past delivery trucks and illegally parked cars.*

Rue St. Dominique

Paris functions as a city of hundreds of small neighborhoods. This area, which was once the village of Grenelle (before it was consumed by Paris), is a good example. Shops and cafés line the streets, topped by several floors of apartments, giving the district a lived-in feel not found in less-vibrant commercial districts. You can shop for anything you need on Rue St. Dominique (but not at any hour). Many locals feel no need to leave the area, and neighbors trust each other. The dry cleaner knows that if his customer forgets to bring her wallet, she'll return to pay him another time. If the plumber can only come during work hours, locals can leave their apartment keys with the nearest shop owner, who will make sure the plumber gets them.

This neighborhood has long been an attraction for

Americans—it's where you'll find the American Church (two blocks to the left), the American Library, the American University of Paris, and lots of my readers (in recommended hotels). As you cross Avenue Bosquet, you'll pass right by the American University (far left side of intersection) and see a church spire to the far left; it's the American Cathedral, on the Right Bank.

• *After crossing Boulevard de la Tour Maubourg, you'll enter the open world of Esplanade des Invalides.*

Esplanade des Invalides

This sprawling green esplanade links the **river** (to the left) and Europe's first veteran's hospital, **Les Invalides** (right), built by Louis XIV. Napoleon lies powerfully dead under the brilliant golden dome.

Afternoon *boules* (lawn bowling), near the Invalides building under the trees on the far right, is an engaging spectator sport. I spend more time watching the players' mannerisms than the game itself (see "The Rules of *Boules*" on page 389).

Look left and see the **Pont Alexandre III (Alexander III Bridge)** crossing the Seine. Spiked with golden statues and ironwork lamps, the bridge was built to celebrate a turn-of-the-20th-century treaty between France and Russia. Just across the bridge are the glass-and-steel-domed **Grand** and **Petit Palais** exhibition halls, built for the 1900 World's Fair. Like the bridge, they are fine examples of belle époque architecture. Impressive temporary exhibits fill the huge Grand Palais, and the smaller Petit Palais houses a permanent collection of 19th-century paintings, starring works by Courbet and Monet (among others).

• *Leaving Les Invalides, you'll reenter narrow streets lined with...*

Government Buildings

Many of France's most important ministries occupy these golden-hued buildings (look for police guarding doorways, heavily barred windows, and people in suits speaking in hushed tones). Opposite the frilly **Gothic church** (on your right at the Bourgogne bus stop) sprawls the **Ministry of Defense,** originally the mansion of Napoleon's mother.

• *You'll emerge from the government area onto the stylish and leafy...*

Boulevard St. Germain

Along this short stretch, colorful furniture stores tempt the neighborhood's upper-crust residents. Notice the fine Haussmann-era architecture. Several blocks farther down are the boulevard's famous cafés, once frequented by existentialists Albert Camus and Jean-Paul Sartre. But we turn left onto **Rue du Bac** and cross streets (to the right) filled with antiques, art galleries, and smart hotels. The **Orsay Museum** is a few blocks to the left (the best stop for this museum is Pont Royal, just before the river).

• *Next, you'll cross the river (see the Orsay Museum behind on the left) and enter the Right Bank.*

Tuileries Garden and Louvre Museum

The Tuileries Garden (Jardin des Tuileries) lies ahead and to the left as you cross the Seine. This was the royal garden of the Lou-

vre palace and is a wonderful place to clear your mind after touring the Louvre. Scattered among these pretty gardens are several cafés, ponds with toy boats for rent, and trampolines for jumping. After turning right along the river, you'll follow the immense Grand Gallery of the **Louvre,** dominating the left side of the street. Notice the bus lane you're in, separated from the traffic by a low curb. Bicyclists have the right to use these lanes as well, making vast parts of Paris bike-friendly.

The U-shaped Louvre, once the biggest building in the world, now houses 12 miles of galleries wallpapered with thousands of the world's greatest paintings. Various kings added new wings, marking their contributions with their initials and medallions carved into the decor. The statues put on a stony toga fashion show as you roll by.

Just before the end of the Louvre building on the right is the view-perfect pedestrian bridge **Pont des Arts.** That curved **building with a dome** on the other side is where the Académie Française has met since the 1600s to defend the French language from corrupting influences (like English) and to compose the official French dictionary. Notice the inviting **café-boats** across the river. There are about 2,000 barges docked on the Seine in Paris.

• *Next on the right is the island where Paris was founded. As you roll past the end of the long Louvre building, get ready for quick right–left–right head movements.*

Ile de la Cité

The river splits around this island where Paris began more than

2,000 years ago. The first bridge you see dates from about 1600. While it's called **Pont Neuf,** meaning "new bridge," it's now Paris' oldest. Pont Neuf leads to an equestrian statue of King Henry IV, who ignores the tiny and romantic tip-of-the-island park from which Seine tour boats depart (see listing for Vedettes du Pont Neuf on page 39). Those green boxes mounted on the wall to your right keep *bouquinistes'* books and souvenirs dry; see page 119.

A block to your left is Paris' primary **department-store shopping district** (centered on Rue de Rivoli). Next along this street are sidewalk **plant shops and pet stalls**—a hit with local children who dream of taking home a turtle, canary, or rabbit. Back across the river, find the squat and round medieval towers (wearing pointy black cone hats) of the **Conciergerie,** named for the concierge (caretaker) who ran these offices when the king moved to the Louvre. The towers guard Ile de la Cité's law courts, the Palais de Justice, the prison famous as the last stop for those about to be guillotined. That intricate needle—the **spire of Sainte-Chapelle**—marks the most beautiful Gothic interior in Paris. You'll see the tops of the twin towers and thin spire of **Notre-Dame Cathedral** soon after the Conciergerie. Back to the left, the grand **Hôtel de Ville** (Paris' City Hall) stands proudly behind playful fountains, energizing its lively big front yard. Each of the 20 arrondissements (governmental areas) in Paris has its own City Hall, and this one is the big daddy of them all. In the summer, the square in front of Hôtel de Ville hosts sand volleyball courts and, at Christmastime, a big ice-skating rink. It's beautifully lit after dark all year.

In summer, the street out of sight below you, running along the riverbank, is "paved" with sand and turned into a one-mile-long beach party (see "Paris *Plages*," page 57). Even though this is a major artery through the city, officials can close it because Parisians take their summer vacations en masse, leaving the city relatively free of traffic. Because of the success of these *plages,* the city is planning to make this riverbank section off-limits to cars year-round in 2017. As the bus curves away from the river, take a quick look through the trees back across the river to see the gray, steel **modern pedestrian bridge** that connects Paris' two islands.

• *The bus angles through the Marais neighborhood.*

Le Marais

This is jumbled, medieval Paris at its finest. It's been a swamp, an aristocratic district, and a bohemian hangout. Today, classy stone mansions sit alongside trendy bars, keeping the antique shops and fashion-conscious boutiques company. The Picasso Museum, Carnavalet Museum, Victor Hugo's House, Jewish Art and History

Museum, and Pompidou Center all have Marais addresses. On your left, two blocks past the Eglise St. Gervais bus stop, you'll see the **oldest houses** in Paris—tall, skinny, and half-timbered— clustered around #13.

The narrow street soon merges into **Rue St. Antoine,** the main street through the Marais and the main street of Paris in medieval times. The small-but-grand **Church of St. Paul and St. Louis** (on the right at #103, with classical columns) is the only Jesuit church in Paris. It was the neighborhood church of Victor Hugo. You may want to return to this charming district to browse and window shop later.

• *Rue St. Antoine leads straight into Place de la Bastille, marked with a giant pillar in the center. If you want to cut this bus tour short, get off at the Bastille - Rue St. Antoine stop (after the Birague stop and before Place de la Bastille). Options if you get off: my Marais Walk (* 🕮 *see the Marais Walk chapter), Promenade Plantée Park (see page 99), and Marais eateries (see the Eating in Paris chapter).*

Place de la Bastille

The namesake of this square, a fortress-turned-prison that symbolized royal tyranny, is long gone. But for centuries, the fortress that stood here was used to defend the city, mostly from its own people. On July 14, 1789, angry Parisians swarmed the Bastille, released its prisoners, and kicked off the French Revolution. Since then, the French have celebrated Bastille Day every July 14 as enthusiastically as Americans commemorate July 4.

In the middle of the square, you'll cross over **Canal St. Martin** (look to the right), which runs from the Seine underneath the tree-lined Boulevard Richard Lenoir (on the left) to northern Paris (see page 42 for a boat cruise on this canal). You'll then curve in front of the reflecting-glass **Opéra Bastille.**

• *Leaving Place de la Bastille, the bus angles left up Rue de la Roquette all the way to Père Lachaise.*

Rue de la Roquette

This street begins at the Bastille in a hip, less-touristy neighborhood. Here you'll find an intriguing mix of galleries, wholesale clothing shops, seedy bars, and trendy, cheap eateries. The first street to the right is **Rue de Lappe,** one of the wildest nightspots in Paris; it's filled with a dizzying array of wacky bistros, bars, and dance halls.

• *The bus eventually turns left onto Boulevard de Ménilmontant (which locals happily associate with a famous Maurice Chevalier tune) and rumbles past the Père Lachaise Cemetery. Although the bus stops at the front gate of the vast cemetery, stay on to the last stop, then hop off at Place Gambetta (a better starting point for visiting the cemetery; see map on page 357). Place Gambetta's centerpiece is another grandiose City*

Hall (this one for the 20th arrondissement). From here, follow Avenue du Père Lachaise for 100 yards, past inviting cafés and flower shops selling cyclamen, heather, and chrysanthemums—the standard flowers for funerals and memorials—to the gate of the cemetery. Take a short stroll through the evocative home of so many permanent Parisians.

Père Lachaise Cemetery

Navigating the labyrinthine rows is a challenge, but maps and my walking tour (◻ see the Père Lachaise Cemetery Tour chapter) will help you find the graves of greats such as Frédéric Chopin, Oscar Wilde, Gertrude Stein, and Jim Morrison. The tour is over. What better place for your final stop?

MARMOTTAN MUSEUM TOUR

Musée Marmottan Monet

The Marmottan has the best collection of works by the master Impressionist Claude Monet. In this mansion on the southwest fringe of urban Paris, you can walk through Monet's life, from black-and-white sketches to colorful open-air paintings to the canvas that gave Impressionism its name. The museum's highlights are scenes of his garden at Giverny, including larger-than-life water lilies. In addition, the Marmottan features a world-class collection of works by Impressionist painter Berthe Morisot.

Paul Marmottan (1856-1932) lived here amid his collection of exquisite 19th-century furniture and paintings. He donated his home and possessions to a private trust (which is why your Museum Pass isn't valid here). After Marmottan's death, the more daring art of Monet and others was added. The combination of the mansion, the furnishings, the Impressionist and Empire paintings, and the many Monet masterpieces makes the Marmottan an aesthetic pleasure.

Orientation

Cost: €11, not covered by Museum Pass; €18.50 combo-ticket with Claude Monet's home and garden at Giverny gives you line-skipping privileges at Giverny (see page 604).

Hours: Tue-Sun 10:00-18:00, Thu until 21:00, closed Mon.

Getting There: It's on Paris' west end at 2 Rue Louis-Boilly.

> **By Métro:** Take Métro line 9 to La Muette. Cross the street to the brown *Marmottan* sign, then follow signs down Chaussée de la Muette (turns into Avenue Ranelagh) through the delightful park, with its old-time kiddie carousel, to the museum (six blocks, 10 minutes). Make the most of the long trip here and combine a visit to the Marmottan with

Trocadéro-area sights, a short Métro ride away (see page 494).

By RER (handy from Rue Cler): Catch the RER-C from Austerlitz, St-Michel, Orsay, Invalides, or Pont de l'Alma (board any train called NORA or GOTA), get off at the Boulainvilliers stop, and follow signs to *sortie Rue des Vignes*. Turn right up Rue Boulainvilliers, then turn left down Chaussée de la Muette to reach the museum. When returning to your hotel on the RER, make sure your stop is listed on the monitor: You don't want to end up in Versailles.

By Bus: Handy east-west bus #63 (see page 32) gets you close, but it requires a walk of about 600 yards. Get off at the Octave Feuillet stop on Avenue Henri Martin, cross Avenue Henri Martin, and follow the tree-lined street to the right that curves around to the museum.

Information: Tel. 01 44 96 50 33, www.marmottan.fr.

Tours: An audioguide is available for €3.

Length of This Tour: Allow one hour.

Photography: Not allowed.

Cuisine Art: Cafés, *boulangeries,* and bistros are 10 minutes away around the La Muette Métro stop (Rue Mozart has good choices).

Family Tip: The park in front of the museum is terrific for families with small kids. Parents can take turns: While one visits the museum, the other can stay outside with the children.

Starring: Claude Monet, including *Impression: Sunrise* (shown at the top of this chapter); paintings of Rouen Cathedral, Gare St. Lazare, and Houses of Parliament; scenes from Giverny; and water lilies.

OVERVIEW

The Marmottan mansion has three pleasant, manageable floors, all worth perusing. (You might be free to see them in any order or, depending on crowd flow, be directed along a specific route.) The ground floor has several rooms of Paul Marmottan's period furnishings and paintings. Upstairs is the permanent collection, featuring illuminated manuscripts and works by Monet's fellow Impressionists—Edgar Degas, Camille Pissarro, Paul Gauguin, Pierre-Auguste Renoir, and especially Berthe Morisot. Monet's works—the core of the collection—are in the basement.

Because the museum rotates its large collection of paintings, this chapter is not designed as a room-by-room tour. Use it as a general background on Monet's life and some of the paintings you're likely to encounter. Read it once before you go, then let the museum surprise you.

The Tour Begins

• *You'll enter the museum on the ground floor. Descending the stairs to the basement, you're immediately plunged into the colorful and messy world of Claude Monet. You may be greeted by paintings from his beloved home at Giverny, and portraits of the man himself.*

In this one long room, you'll find some 50 paintings by Monet spanning his lifetime. They're generally (and very roughly) arranged in chronological order—from Monet's youthful discovery of Impressionism, to his mature "series" paintings, to his last great water lilies from Giverny.

CLAUDE MONET (1840-1926)

Claude Monet was the leading light of the Impressionist movement that revolutionized painting in the 1870s. Fiercely independent and dedicated to his craft, Monet gave courage to Renoir and other like-minded artists, who were facing harsh criticism.

You may see a **timeline** that lets you survey Monet's long life:

Born in Paris in 1840, Monet grew up in seaside Le Havre as the son of a grocer and began his art career sketching caricatures

of townspeople. He realized he had a gift for quickly capturing an overall impression with a few simple strokes. Monet defied his family, insisted he was an artist, and sketched the world around him—beaches, boats, and small-town life. Fellow artist Eugène Boudin encouraged Monet to don a scarf, set up his easel outdoors, and paint the scene exactly as he saw it. Today, we say, "Well, duh!" But "open-air" painting was unorthodox for artists of the day, who were trained to study their subjects thoroughly in the perfect lighting of a controlled studio setting.

At 19, Monet went to Paris but refused to enroll in the official art schools. His letters to friends make it clear he was broke and paying the price for his bohemian lifestyle.

In 1867—the same year the Salon rejected his work—his first child, Jean, was born to Monet and his partner Camille. They moved to the countryside of Argenteuil, where he developed his open-air,

Impressionist style. *Impression: Sunrise* was his landmark work at the breakthrough 1874 Impressionist Exhibition. He went on to paint several series of scenes, such as *Gare Saint-Lazare,* at different times of day. His career was gaining steam.

Monet's Family

You'll likely see portraits of Monet's wife and children. Monet's first wife, Camille, died in 1879, leaving Monet to raise 12-year-old Jean and babe-in-arms Michel. (Michel would grow up to inherit the family home and many of the paintings that ended up here.) But Monet was also involved with Alice Hoschede, who had recently been abandoned by her husband. Alice moved in with her six kids and took care of the dying Camille, and the two families made a Brady Bunch-style merger. Baby Michel became bosom buddies with Alice's baby, Jean-Pierre, while teenage Jean Monet and stepsister Blanche fell in love and later married.

After the birth of their second son, Michel, Camille's health declined, and she later died. Monet traveled a lot, painting landscapes *(Bordighera)*, people *(Portrait de Poly)*, and more series, including the famous Cathedral of Rouen. In 1890, he settled down at his farmhouse in Giverny and married Alice Hoschede. He traveled less, but visited London to paint the Halls of Parliament. Mostly, he painted his own water lilies and flowers in an increasingly messy style. He died in 1926 a famous man.

THE 1870s: PURE IMPRESSIONISM

While living at Argenteuil, Monet and Camille played host to Renoir, Edouard Manet, Alfred Sisley, and other painters. Monet led them on open-air painting sa-faris to the countryside. Inspired by the realism of Manet, they painted everyday things—landscapes, sea-scapes, street scenes, ladies with parasols, family picnics—in bright, basic colors.

They began perfecting the distinct Impressionist style—painting nature as a mosaic of short brushstrokes of different colors placed side by side, suggesting shimmering light.

First, Monet simplified. In *On the Beach at Trouville (Sur la Plage à Trouville*, 1870-1871), a lady's dress is a few thick strokes of paint. Monet gradually broke things down into smaller dots of different shades. If you back up from a Monet canvas, the pig-ments blend into one (for example, red plus green plus yellow equals a brown boat). Still, they never fully resolve, creating the effect of shimmering light. Monet limited his palette to a few bright basics—cobalt blue, white, yellow, two shades of red, and emerald green abound. But no black—even shadows are a combination of bright colors.

Monet's constant quest was to faithfully reproduce nature in blobs of paint. His eye was a camera lens set at a very slow shutter speed to admit maximum light. Then he "developed" the impression made on his retina with an oil-based solution.

In search of new light and new scenes, Monet traveled throughout France and Europe, painting landscapes in all kinds of weather. Picture Monet at work, hiking to a remote spot—carrying an easel, several canvases, brushes (large-size), a palette, tubes of paint (an invention that made open-air painting practical), food and drink, a folding chair, and an umbrella—and wearing his trademark hat, with a cigarette on his lip. He weathered the elements, occasionally putting himself in danger by clambering on cliffs to get the scenes he wanted.

The key was to work fast, before the weather changed and the light shifted, completely changing the colors. Monet worked "wet-in-wet," applying new paint before the first layer dried, mixing colors on the canvas, and piling them up into a thick paste.

• *Monet's most famous "impression" was the one that gave the movement its name.*

Impression: *Sunrise (Impression Soleil Levant)*, 1873

This is the painting that started the revolution—a simple, serene view of boats bobbing under an orange sun (see the photo that opens this chapter). At the first public showing by Monet, Renoir, Degas, and others in Paris in 1874, critics howled at this work and ridiculed the title. "Wallpaper," one called it. The sloppy brushstrokes and ordinary subject looked like a study, not a finished work. The style was dubbed "Impressionist"—an accurate name.

The misty harbor scene obviously made an "impression" on Monet, who faithfully rendered the fleeting moment in quick strokes of paint. The waves are simple horizontal brushstrokes. The sun's reflection on the water is a few thick, bold strokes of orange tipped with white. They zigzag down the canvas the way a reflection shifts on moving water.

THE 1890s: SERIES

Monet's claim to fame became a series of paintings of a single scene, captured at different times of day under different light. He first explored the idea with one of Paris' train stations, Gare St. Lazare, in the 1870s. Soon, he conceived paintings to be shown as a group, giving a time-lapse view of a single subject.

MARMOTTAN

In Rouen, he rented several rooms offering different angles overlooking the Rouen Cathedral. He worked on up to 14 different canvases at a time, shuffling the right one onto the easel as the sun moved across the sky. The cathedral is made of brown stone, but at sunset it becomes gold and pink with blue shadows, softened by thick smudges of paint. The true subject is not the cathedral but the full spectrum of light that bounces off it.

He did another series in London. Turning his hotel room into a studio, Monet—working on nearly a hundred canvases simul-

taneously—painted the changing light on the River Thames. He caught the reflection of the Houses of Parliament on the river's sur-face, stretching and bending with the current. London's famous fog epitomized Monet's favorite sub-ject—the atmosphere that distorts distant objects. That filtering haze gives even different-colored objects a similar tone, resulting in a more harmonious picture. When the light was just right and the atmosphere glowed, the moment of "in-stantaneity" had arrived, and Monet worked like a madman.

Monet started many of his canvases in the open air and then painstakingly perfected them later in the studio. He composed his scenes with great care—clear horizon lines give a strong horizon-tal axis, while diagonal lines (of trees or shorelines) create solid triangles.

These series—of London, the cathedral, haystacks, poplars, and mornings on the Seine—were very popular. Monet, poverty-stricken until his mid-40s, was slowly becoming famous, first in America, then London, and finally in France. He soon took up res-idence in what would be his home for the rest of his life, Giverny.

PAINTINGS OF GIVERNY (1883-1926)
Rose Trellises (L'Allée des Rosiers) and The Japanese Bridge (Le Pont Japonais)

In 1883, Monet's brood settled into a farmhouse in Giverny (50 miles west of Paris, see page 600). Financially stable and domesti-cally blissful, he turned Giverny into a garden paradise and painted nature without the long commute.

In 1890, Monet started work on his Japanese garden, inspired by tranquil scenes from the Japanese prints he collected. He di-verted a river to form a pond, planted willows and bamboo on the shores, filled the pond with water lilies, then crossed it with this wooden footbridge. As years passed, the bridge became overgrown with wisteria. Compare several versions. He painted the bridge at

different times of day and year, exploring different color schemes.

Monet uses the bridge as the symmetrical center of simple, pleasing designs. The water is drawn with horizontal brushstrokes that get shorter as you move up the canvas (farther away), creating the illusion of distance. The horizontal water contrasts with the vertical willows, while the bridge "bridges" the sides of the square canvas and laces the scene together.

In 1912, Monet began to go blind. Cataracts distorted his perception of depth and color and sent him into a tailspin of despair. The (angry?) red paintings date from this period.

Early Water Lilies, *Nymphéas,* c. 1900

As his vision slowly failed, Monet concentrated on painting close-ups of the surface of the pond and its water lilies—red, white, yellow, and lavender. Some lilies are just a few broad strokes on a bare canvas (a study); others are piles of paint formed with overlapping colors.

But more than the lilies, the paintings focus on the changing reflections on the surface of the pond. Pan slowly around the room and watch the pond go from predawn to bright sunlight to twilight.

Early lily paintings show the shoreline as a reference point. But increasingly, Monet crops the scene ever closer, until there is no shoreline, no horizon, no sense of what's up or down. Stepping back from the canvas, you see the lilies just hang there on the museum wall, suspended in space. The surface of the pond and the surface of the canvas are one. Modern abstract art—a colored design on a flat surface—is just around the corner.

• *The climax of the visit is a round room (with benches), where you can immerse yourself in the...*

NYMPHEAS AND LARGE-SCALE CANVASES
Big Weeping Willow, *Le Saule Pleureur,* 1918-1919

Get close—Monet did—and analyze the trunk. Rough "brown" bark is made of thick strokes (an inch wide and four inches long)

MARMOTTAN

of pink, purple, orange, and green. Impressionism lives. But to get these colors to resolve in your eye, you'd have to back up all the way to Giverny.

Later Water Lilies, *Nymphéas,* 1915-1926

In the midst of the chaos of World War I, Monet began a series of large-scale paintings of water lilies. They were installed at the Orangerie (for information, see the 📖 Orangerie Museum Tour chapter). Here at the Marmottan are smaller-scale studies for that series.

Some lilies are patches of thick paint circled by a squiggly "caricature" of a lily pad. Monet simplifies in a way that Henri

Matisse and Pablo Picasso would envy. But getting close, you can see that the simple smudge of paint that composes the flower is actually a complex mix of different colors. The sheer size of these studies (and his Orangerie canvases) is impressive.

When Monet died in 1926, he was a celebrity. Starting with meticulous line drawings, he had evolved into an open-air realist, then Impressionist color analyst, then serial painter, and finally master of reflections. In the latter half of his life, Monet's world shrank—from the broad vistas of the world traveler to the tranquility of his home, family, and garden. But his artistic vision expanded as he painted smaller details on bigger canvases and helped invent modern abstract art.

• *After seeing Monet, visit the rest of the Marmottan; it's worth browsing.*

THE REST OF THE MUSEUM

The ground floor and permanent collection upstairs show off Paul Marmottan's eclectic tastes. On the **ground floor** are his furnishings, which tended toward the Empire style: high-polished mahogany with upholstery featuring classical motifs like laurel wreaths and torches and brass highlights. Chairs have arched backs, armrests, and tapered legs. The paintings are also from this period, when the French bourgeoisie reigned supreme. You'll see portraits of ladies wearing tiaras and gentlemen in high-collared suits. They were painted in the seamless-brushstroke style that Monet rebelled against.

Upstairs, in the **permanent collection,** look for Napoleon's bed and a portrait of him at 30, having just been appointed consul. You'll see works that look famous—statues by Canova and scenes of Venice by Canaletto—but most are by their students. A darkened room displays the Marmottan's excellent medieval

Berthe Morisot (1841-1895)

The Marmottan's large collection of Berthe Morisot's work cements her reputation as one of Impressionism's Founding Mothers. Born into a cultured, supportive family, she found early success painting landscapes (in the open air) in the proto-Impressionist style of her mentor, Camille Corot. Still in her 20s, Morisot exhibited to good reviews at the official Salon for seven straight years.

Meanwhile, she'd met Edouard Manet, married his big brother, and experimented with the Impressionist style. She threw away her black paint and replaced it with a brighter palette. In 1874, she joined the Impressionist gang, exhibiting her work at the same "Salon des Refusés" where Monet's *Impression: Sunrise* had caused a minor revolution.

Her paintings focus mainly on women, either in gardens or in peaceful, domestic situations. Her subjects were landscapes, friends (such as Manet), and family (her daughter, Julie). She had a keen eye for ladies' fashions (*At the Ball*, 1875). Like Manet's, Morisot's brand of Impressionism was always naturalistic and understated. She avoided the gritty urban scenes of Degas, the pointillistic color theory of Seurat, and the proto-abstract work of Monet. But like Renoir, she loved painting small-scale domestic scenes of her rosy-cheeked daughter and niece picking cherries or frolicking in the gardens. The tranquil Marmottan mansion is the perfect setting for the peaceful world of Morisot.

MARMOTTAN

collection: illuminated manuscripts (that is, colorfully illustrated books), musical scores, stained glass, and miniature paintings of saints and Bible scenes.

The highlight of the permanent collection is an ever-changing display of works by Monet's fellow Impressionists—Degas, Pissarro, Gauguin, Renoir—who were also his colleagues and friends. Special attention is often given to Berthe Morisot (see the sidebar).

• *You've reached the end of the tour. From here, if you need a taxi, you'll find a stand at the La Muette Métro stop. Or, if you're up for a post-museum stroll, it's a pleasant one-hour walk (without stops) from here to the Eiffel Tower along Rue de Passy, one of Paris' most pleasant (and upscale) shopping streets. To reach Rue de Passy, head east up Chaussée de la Muette, past the La Muette Métro stop—follow that tower. After Rue de Passy ends, you could continue straight—on Boulevard Delessert—all the way to the Eiffel Tower.*

LEFT BANK WALK

From the Seine to Luxembourg Garden

The Left Bank is as much an attitude as it is an actual neighborhood. But this walk—from the Seine to St. Germain-des-Prés to Luxembourg Garden—captures some of the artistic, intellectual, and countercultural spirit long associated with the south side of the river. We'll pass through an upscale area of art galleries, home-furnishing boutiques, antique dealers, bookstores, small restaurants, classic cafés, evening hot spots, and the former homes of writers, painters, and composers. Though trendy now, the area still has the offbeat funkiness that has always defined the Rive Gauche. (*Gauche*, meaning "left," has come to imply social incorrectness, like giving a handshake with the wrong—left—hand.)

Use this walk as a series of historical markers as you explore the Left Bank of today. Frankly, the buildings where famous

people once lived can be pretty boring to look at, but this walk leads you through a fascinating neighborhood and dovetails perfectly with a shopping stroll (see "Sèvres-Babylone to St. Sulpice" on page 475) or downtime at Luxembourg Garden (where this walk ends). It also works well after a visit to the Louvre or after the Historic Paris Walk, and it's ideal for connoisseurs of contemporary art.

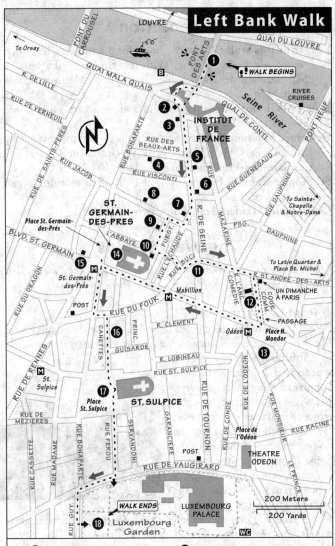

Left Bank Walk

1 Pont des Arts
2 Statue of Voltaire
3 Roger-Viollet Shop
4 Oscar Wilde's Hotel
5 George Sand's House
6 Café la Palette
7 Toy Store
8 Richard Wagner's House
9 Delacroix Museum
10 Abbey Mansion

11 Heart of the Left Bank
12 Café le Procope
13 Odéon Cinemas
14 St. Germain-des-Prés
15 Les Deux Magots Café & Le Café de Flore
16 Rue des Canettes
17 St. Sulpice
18 Luxembourg Garden
19 To Rue Vavin Cafés La Coupole & Le Select

LEFT BANK

Orientation

Length of This Walk: Allow two hours for the whole walk, which covers a little over a mile. With less time, end the walk at St. Germain-des-Prés, which has good Métro and bus connections.

When to Go: Evenings are pleasant, and many art galleries are open until 19:00.

Delacroix Museum: €7, free on first Sun of month, covered by Museum Pass, Wed-Mon 9:30-17:30, closed Tue.

St. Germain-des-Prés Church: Free, daily 8:00-20:00.

St. Sulpice Church: Free, daily 7:30-19:30, Sun morning organ recitals (see page 72).

Luxembourg Garden: Free, daily dawn until dusk.

The Walk Begins

• *Start on the pedestrian-only bridge across the Seine, the Pont des Arts (next to Louvre, Mo: Pont Neuf or Louvre-Rivoli).*

❶ Pont des Arts

Before dozens of bridges crossed the Seine, the two riverbanks were like different cities—royalty on the right, commoners on the left.

This bridge has always been a pedestrian bridge...and long a popular meeting point for lovers. For years, romantic couples wrote their names on a padlock, "locked" their love forever to the bridge, and tossed the key in the Seine. Unromantic city engineers became worried that the heavy locks were jeopardizing the bridge's structural integrity (a whole panel fell into the Seine in 2015), and newly installed glass panels now make this show of devotion impossible. The city is advising disappointed lovers to take selfies kissing in front of the bridge's railings instead.

The Pont des Arts leads to the domed Institut de France building, where 40 linguists meet periodically to decide whether it's acceptable to call email *"le mail"* (as the French commonly do), or whether it should be the French word *courriel* (which linguists prefer). The Académie Française, dedicated to halting the erosion of French culture, is wary of new French terms with strangely foreign sounds—like *le week-end, le marketing, le fast-food,* and *c'est cool.*

Besides the Académie Française, the Institut houses several

other Académies, such as the Académie des Beaux-Arts, which is dedicated to subjects appropriate for the Left Bank, such as music and painting.

• *Leave the bridge. Circle around the right side of the Institut de France building to the head of Rue de Seine. Or—if it's open—use the passageway to the right of the Institut's entrance, near #27. Once on the other side of the Institut, you're immediately met by a statue in a street-corner garden.*

❷ Statue of Voltaire

"Jesus committed suicide." The mischievous philosopher Voltaire could scandalize a party with a wicked comment like that, delivered with an enigmatic smile and a twinkle in his eye (meaning if Christ is truly God, he could have prevented his crucifixion). Voltaire—a commoner more sophisticated than the royalty who lived across the river—introduces us to the Left Bank.

Born François-Marie Arouet (1694-1778), he took up "Voltaire" as his one-word pen name. Although Voltaire mingled with aristocrats, he was constantly in trouble for questioning the ruling class and for fueling ideas that would soon spark a revolution. He did 11 months in the Bastille prison, then spent 40 years in virtual exile from his beloved Paris. Returning as an old man, he got a hero's welcome so surprising it killed him.

• *From here we'll head south down Rue de Seine to Boulevard St. Germain, making a few detours along the way. The first stop is a blue storefront at 6 Rue de Seine.*

❸ Roger-Viollet

Look in the windows at black-and-white photos of Paris' storied past. The display changes often, but you might see a half-built Eiffel Tower, glitterati of yesteryear (Colette, Simone de Beauvoir, Jean Cocteau), Hitler in Paris, and so on. Many more photos are tucked away inside the binders lining the walls, labeled alphabetically. This humble shop is the funky origin of a worldwide press agency (similar to Getty Images) dealing in historic photographs. The family of photographer Henri Roger expanded his photographs into an archive of millions of photos, chronicling Paris' changes through the years. (If you want a print of a photo you see, don't disturb the staff—order it at www.parisenimages.fr.)

• *Continue down Rue de Seine, which cuts through a neighborhood of art galleries and upscale shops selling lamps, sconces, vases, bowls, and statues for people who turn their living rooms into art.*

Wilde in the Left Bank

Oscar Wilde (1854-1900), the Irish playwright with the flamboyant clothes and outrageous wit, died in a Left Bank hotel on November 30, 1900 (don't blame the current owners).

Just five years earlier, he'd been at his peak. He had several plays running simultaneously in London's West End and had returned to London triumphant from a lecture tour through America. Then, news of his love affair with a lord leaked out, causing a scandal, and he was sentenced to two years in prison for "gross indecency." Wilde's wife abandoned him, refusing to let him see their children again.

After his prison term, a poor and broken Wilde was exiled to Paris, where he succumbed to an ear infection and died in a (then) shabby hotel room. Among his last words in the run-down place were: "Either this wallpaper goes, or I do."

Wilde is buried in Paris (🕮 see the Père Lachaise Cemetery Tour).

At the first intersection, a half-block detour to the right leads to ❹ *Oscar Wilde's hotel, where he died in 1900. The sight itself is hardly worth the walk there, but the story of how Wilde ended up here is fascinating (see the sidebar).*

Continuing along Rue de Seine, a plaque at #31 marks...

❺ George Sand's House

George Sand (1804-1876) divorced her husband, left her children behind, and moved into this apartment, determined to become a writer. In the year she lived here (1831), she wrote articles for *Le Figaro* while turning her real-life experiences with men into a sensational novel, *Indiana*. It made her a celebrity and allowed her to afford a better apartment.

George Sand is known for her novels, her cross-dressing (men's suits, slicked-down hair, cigars—and trading in her given name, Amantine, for a man's name), and for her complex love affair with a sensitive pianist from Poland, Frédéric Chopin.

• *At 43 Rue de Seine is...*

❻ Café la Palette

Though less famous than more historic cafés, this is a "real" one, where a *café crème*, beer, or glass of wine at an outdoor table is not outrageous. Inside, the 100-year-old, tobacco-stained wood paneling and faded Art Nouveau decor exudes Left Bank chic. Toulouse-Lautrec would have liked it here. Have something to drink at the bar, and examine your surroundings—notice the artist palettes above the bar. Nothing seems to have changed since it was built in 1903, except the modern espresso machine (open daily, tel. 01 43 26 68 15).

• *At the fork, veer right down small Rue de l'Echaudé. Four doors up, at 6 Rue de l'Echaudé, is a...*

❼ Toy Store

French and American kids share many of the same toys and storybook characters: Babar the Elephant, Maisy Mouse, Tintin, the Smurfs, Madeline, Asterix, and the Little Prince. This store features figurines of these and other whimsical folk.

In *The Little Prince* (1943), written by Antoine de Saint-Exupéry, a pilot crashes in the Sahara, where a mysterious little prince takes him to various planets, teaching him about life from a child's wise perspective.

In his actual life, "Saint-Ex" (1900-1944) was indeed a daring aviator who had survived wrecks in the Sahara. After France fell to the Nazis, he fled to America, where he wrote and published *The Little Prince*. He returned to Europe, then disappeared while flying a spy mission for the Allies. Lost for six decades, his plane was finally found off the coast of Marseille. The cause of the crash remains a mystery, part of a legend enduring in France as Amelia Earhart's is in the US.

• *At the intersection with Rue Jacob, a half-block detour to the right leads to #14.*

❽ Richard Wagner's House

Having survived a storm at sea on the way here, the young German composer (1813-1883) spent the gray winter of 1841-1842 in Paris in this building writing *The Flying Dutchman,* an opera about a ghost ship. It was the restless young man's lowest point of poverty. Six months later, a German company staged his first opera *(Rienzi),* plucking him from obscurity and leading to a production of *The Flying Dutchman* that launched his career.

Now the premises are occupied by an eccentric bar.

• *Backtrack a few steps along Rue Jacob, then turn right and continue south on Rue de Furstenberg to a tiny, pleasant, tree-bordered square. At #6 is the...*

❾ Delacroix Museum

The painter Eugène Delacroix (1798-1863) lived here on this peaceful square. Today, his home is a bite-sized museum with paintings and memorabilia. It's a delightful detour for his fans, skippable for most, and free with the Museum Pass (see the listing on page 73).

Delacroix lived a full and successful life. An ambassador's son, he studied at the Beaux-Arts (which we saw earlier) and exhibited

Art Galleries

You'll see many arts-oriented shops in this vibrant neighborhood. There are fine-art galleries selling paintings and statues, art supplies stores, antique dealers, and chic boutiques for the latest in interior design.

Paris' art scene thrives. In the 20th century, the city attracted many of the foreigners (Picasso, Chagall, Modigliani) who pioneered modern art. Artists here still get respect not always given to artists in the States ("So you're an artist, huh? And what's your real job?"). Paris remains a clearinghouse of creative ideas...and fine art is big business, too. Lots of money passes through this city. Oil-rich sultans come here looking for trendy new works to hang over their sofas back home. Museum curators from America troll these Left Bank streets, taking notes on what's hot. In general, people with money come to Paris on vacation to enjoy the finer things in life. If they come across something they love, they pull out their plastic and make it their own. An impulse buy can gladden the hearts of these gallery owners. Paris is the one city in the world where art supply does not necessarily outstrip art demand.

You're welcome to window shop or enter the galleries. Remember the niceties of shopping in Paris. Always say, *"Bonjour, Madame"* (or *Mademoiselle* or *Monsieur*) when entering, and *"Au revoir, Madame"* (or *Mademoiselle* or *Monsieur*) when leaving. *"Je regarde"* means "I'm just looking." *"Je voudrais acheter"* means "I would like to buy." The reality is that most clerks speak English and are happy to help or to let you browse. If you stroll neighborhoods in the evening, you're likely to pass what looks like a cocktail party spilling out of an art gallery. These "art openings," called *vernissages,* are sometimes private, though usually open to the public (even Americans). Be bold and join the party if you come across one.

at the Salon. His *Liberty Leading the People* (1831, in the Louvre, see page 157) was an instant classic, a symbol of French democracy. Trips to North Africa added exotic Muslim elements to his palette. He hobnobbed with aristocrats and bohemians like George Sand and Frédéric Chopin (whom he painted). He painted large-scale murals for the Louvre, Hôtel de Ville, and Luxembourg Palace. In 1857, nearing 60 and in failing health, Delacroix moved in here. He was seeking a quiet home/studio where he could concentrate on his final great works for the Church of St. Sulpice (which we'll see later).

• *Continue uphill as Rue de Furstenberg runs directly into* ❿ *Abbey Mansion. This building (1586) was the administrative center for the vast complex of monks gathered around the nearby church of St. Germain-des-Prés. Today, it's a Catholic school.*

Facing the Abbey Mansion, turn left on Rue de l'Abbaye and start working your way east. Along the way is a wine shop, at 6 Rue de Bourbon-Le-Château, called La Dernière Goutte—"The Last Drop." They welcome both connoisseurs and yokels for an unsnooty look at France's viniculture. At the T-intersection with Rue de Buci, turn left. You've arrived at what is, arguably, the geographical (if not spiritual)...

⓫ Heart of the Left Bank

Explore. Rue de Buci hosts *pâtisseries* and a produce market by day and bars by night. Mixing earthiness and elegance, it's a

quintessential Left Bank scene.

• *Continue east through the café cauldron of Rue de Buci, which crosses a busy five-corner intersection and becomes Rue St. André-des-Arts. At 61 Rue St. André-des-Arts, turn right into the covered passageway called Cour du Commerce St. André. Stroll a half-block down this colorful alleyway, past shops and enticing eateries. On your right, you'll pass the back door of...*

⓬ Café le Procope

Founded in 1686, Le Procope is one of the world's oldest continuously operating restaurants, and was one of Europe's first places to sample an exotic new stimulant—coffee—recently imported from the Muslim culture.

In the 1700s, Le Procope caffeinated the Revolution. Voltaire reportedly drank 30 cups a day, fueling his intellectual passion. Benjamin Franklin recounted old war stories about America's Revolution. Robespierre, Danton, and Marat plotted coups over cups of double-short, soy mochaccinos. And a young lieutenant named Napoleon Bonaparte ran up a tab he never paid.

Located midway between university students, royalty, and the counterculture Comédie Française, Le Procope attracted literary types who loved the free newspapers, writing paper, and quill pens. Today, the one-time coffeehouse is a full-service restaurant (affordable if mediocre *menus*, open daily). If you're interested in a meal surrounded by memorabilia-plastered walls (and tourists), enter through the main entrance at 13 Rue de l'Ancienne Comédie.

Across the lane, at #6, is Un Dimanche à Paris, with its open kitchen and gourmet chocolate creations too beautiful to eat.

• *Continue down the cobbled lane until it spills out onto Boulevard St. Germain at an intersection (and Métro stop) called Odéon.*

⑬ Odéon Cinemas

When night falls, the neon signs buzz to life, and Paris' many lovers of film converge here for the latest releases at several multiplexes in the area. Looking south up Rue de l'Odéon, you can see the classical columns of the front of the Théâtre de l'Odéon, the descendant of the original Comédie Française (now housed in the Palais Royal).

• *Walk to the right (west) along busy Boulevard St. Germain for six blocks, passing Café Vagenande (famous for its plush Art Nouveau interior) and other fashionable, noisy cafés with outdoor terraces. You'll reach the large stone church and square of...*

⑭ St. Germain-des-Prés

Paris' oldest church, dating from the 11th century (the square bell tower is original), stands on a site where a Christian church has stood since the fall of Rome. (The first church was destroyed by Vikings in the 885-886 siege.)

The restored interior is still painted in the medieval manner, like Notre-Dame (and others). The church is Romanesque, with round—not pointed—arches over the aisles of the nave.

The square outside is one of Paris' great gathering spots on warm evenings. The church is often lit up and open late. The rich come to see and be seen. And the poor come for a night of free spectacle.

• *Note that Métro stop St. Germain-des-Prés is here, and the Mabillon stop is just a couple of blocks east. On Place St. Germain-des-Prés, you'll find two venerable cafes—once meccas of creative coffee drinking, today just filled with tourists and milking their fabled past.*

⑮ Les Deux Magots Café and Le Café de Flore

Since opening in 1885, "The Two Chinamen Café" (wooden statues inside) has taken over from Le Procope as the café of ideas. From Oscar Wilde's Aestheticism (1900) to Picasso's Cubism (1910s) to Hemingway's spare prose (1920s) to Sartre's Existentialism (with Simone de Beauvoir and Albert Camus, 1930s and '40s) to rock singer Jim Morrison (early 1970s), worldwide movements have been born in the simple atmosphere of these two cafés. Le Café de Flore, once frequented by Picasso, is more hip, but Deux Magots, next door, is more inviting for just coffee. Across the street is Brasserie Lipp, a classic brasserie where Hemingway wrote much of *A Farewell to Arms* (see also "Les Grands Cafés de Paris," on page 447).

• *From the Church of St. Germain-des-Prés, cross Boulevard St. Germain and head south on Rue Bonaparte (not Rue de Rennes, from which you can see the Montparnasse Tower skyscraper in the distance). Jog left on Rue du Four, then right on...*

⑯ Rue des Canettes

Small, mid-priced restaurants, boutique shops, and comfortable brewpubs make this neighborhood a pleasant nightspot. It's easy to find a *plat du jour* or a two-course *formule* for under €20 (see restaurant listings on page 440). Chez Georges (at #11) is the last outpost of funkiness (and how!) in an increasingly gentrified neighborhood.

• *Continue south on Rue des Canettes to the church of...*

⑰ St. Sulpice

The impressive Neoclassical arcaded facade, with two round, half-finished towers, is modeled on St. Paul's in London. It has

a remarkable organ and offers Sunday-morning concerts. The lone café on the square in front (Café de la Mairie) is always lively and perfectly located for a break.

Inside, circle the church counterclockwise, making a few stops. In the first chapel on the right, find **Delacroix's three murals** (on the chapel's ceiling and walls) of fighting angels, completed during his final years while he was fighting a lengthy illness. They sum up his long career, from Renaissance/Baroque roots to furious Romanticism to proto-Impressionism.

The most famous is the agitated *Jacob Wrestling the Angel*. The two grapple in a leafy wood that echoes the wrestlers' rippling energy. Jacob fights the angel to a standstill, bringing him a well-earned blessing for his ordeal. The shepherd Laban and his daughter Rachel (Jacob's future wife) hover in the background. Get close and notice the thick brushwork that influenced the next generation of Impressionists—each leaf is a single brushstroke, often smudging two different colors in a single stroke. The "black" pile of clothes in the foreground is built from rough strokes of purple, green, and white. (Too much glare? Take a couple of steps to the right to view it. Also, there are three light buttons nearby.)

On the opposite wall, *Heliodorus Chased from the Temple* has the smooth, seamless brushwork of Delacroix's prime. The Syrian Heliodorus has killed the king, launched a coup, and has now entered the sacred Jewish Temple in Jerusalem trying to steal the treasure. Angry angels launch themselves at him, sending him sprawling. The vibrant, clashing colors, swirling composition, and over-the-top subject are trademark Delacroix Romanticism. On the ceiling, *The Archangel Michael* drives demons from heaven.

Walking up the right side of the church, pause at the **fourth chapel,** with a statue of Joan of Arc and wall plaques listing hundreds upon hundreds of names. These are France's WWI dead—from this congregation alone.

In the chapel at the far end of the church, ponder the cryptic symbolism of Mary and Child lit by a sunburst, standing on an orb, and trampling a snake, while a stone cloud tumbles down to a sacrificial lamb.

Continue around the church. On the wall of the north transept is an Egyptian-style obelisk used as a **gnomon,** or part of a sundial. At Christmas Mass, the sun shines into the church through a tiny hole—it's opposite the obelisk, high up on the south wall (in the upper-right window pane). The sunbeam strikes a mark on the obelisk that indicates the winter solstice. Then, week by week, the sunbeam moves down the obelisk and across the bronze rod in the floor, until, at midsummer, the sun lights up the area near the altar. (For a while, this corner of the church was busy with fans of *The Da Vinci Code*.)

In the final chapel before the exit, you may see on display a copy of the **Shroud of Turin** (the original is in Turin, Italy). This famed burial cloth is purported to have wrapped the body of Christ, who left it with a mysterious, holy stain of his image.

• *Back out on Place St. Sulpice, take note that several interesting shopping streets branch off from here. (See the "Sèvres-Babylone to St. Sulpice" boutique stroll on page 475.)*

*To complete this walk, turn left out of the church and continue south on Rue Henry de Jouvenel (soon turning into Rue Férou), which leads directly to Luxembourg Garden. On Rue Férou, you'll pass a **wall inscribed with a quotation** from one of France's most famous poems, "Le Bateau Ivre," by Arthur Rimbaud (1854–1891). He describes the feeling of drifting along aimlessly, like a drunken boat: "Comme je descendais...As I floated down calm rivers, I could no longer feel the control of my handlers..."*

Drift along to Luxembourg Garden. If the gate ahead of you is closed, circle to the right around the fence until you find an open entrance.

⑱ Luxembourg Garden

Paris' most beautiful, interesting, and enjoyable garden/park/recreational area, le Jardin du Luxembourg is a great place to watch Parisians at rest and play. This 60-acre garden, dotted with fountains and statues, is the property of the French Senate, which meets here in the Luxembourg

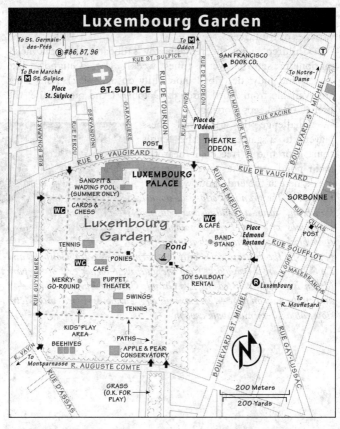

Luxembourg Garden

To St. Germain-des-Prés
B #86, 87, 96
To M Odéon
To M
SAN FRANCISCO BOOK CO.
To Notre-Dame
RUE ST. SULPICE
To Bon Marché & M St. Sulpice
Place St. Sulpice
ST. SULPICE
RUE DE L'ODÉON
RUE DE CONDÉ
RUE MONSIEUR LE PRINCE
RUE RACINE
BOULEVARD ST. MICHEL
RUE BONAPARTE
RUE FÉROU
SERVANDONI
GARANCIÈRE
RUE DE TOURNON
Place de l'Odéon
THEATRE ODEON
POST
RUE DE VAUGIRARD
RUE DE VAUGIRARD
SORBONNE
LUXEMBOURG PALACE
RUE DE MÉDICIS
RUE
CUJAS
SANDPIT & WADING POOL (SUMMER ONLY)
WC CARDS & CHESS
Luxembourg Garden
WC & CAFÉ
Place Edmond Rostand
POST
TENNIS
Pond
BAND-STAND
RUE SOUFFLOT
WC CAFÉ
PONIES
RUE LE GOFF
MALEBRANCHE
MERRY-GO-ROUND
PUPPET THEATER
TOY SAILBOAT RENTAL
R Luxembourg
RUE GUYNEMER
SWINGS
To R. Mouffetard
TENNIS
KIDS' PLAY AREA
PATHS
BEEHIVES
BOULEVARD ST. MICHEL
RUE GAY-LUSSAC
R. VAVIN
To Montparnasse
APPLE & PEAR CONSERVATORY
R. AUGUSTE COMTE
N
RUE D'ASSAS
GRASS (O.K. FOR PLAY)
200 Meters
200 Yards

Palace. Although it seems like something out of a movie, it's a fact that France's secret service *(Générale de la Sécurité Extérieure)* is "secretly" headquartered beneath Luxembourg Garden. (Don't tell anyone.)

The palace was created in 1615 by Marie de Médici. Recently widowed (by Henry IV) and homesick for Florence, she built the palace as a re-creation of her girlhood home, the Pitti Palace. When her son grew to be Louis XIII, he drove his mother from the palace, exiling her to Germany.

Luxembourg Garden has special rules governing its use (for example, where cards can be played, where dogs can be walked, where joggers can run, and when and where music can be played). The brilliant flower beds are completely changed three times a year, and the boxed trees are brought out of the *orangerie* in May. In the southwest corner of the gardens, you can see beehives that have been here since 1872. Honey is made here for the *orangerie*. Close by, check out the apple and pear conservatory, with more than 600 varieties of fruit trees.

Children enjoy the rentable toy sailboats. The park hosts marionette shows several times weekly (Les Guignols, like Punch and Judy; described more fully on page 457). Pony rides are available from April through October. (And meanwhile, the French CIA keeps plotting.)

Challenge the card and chess players to a game (near the tennis courts), or find a free chair near the main pond and take a well-deserved break, here at the end of our walk.

• *Nearby: The grand Neoclassical-domed Panthéon, now a mausoleum housing the tombs of great French notables, is three blocks away and worth touring (see page 75). The historic cafés of Montparnasse—⓳ La Coupole and Le Select—are a few blocks from the southwest-corner exit of the park (down Rue Vavin, listed in "Les Grands Cafés de Paris" on page 449 and on the map on page 442). Luxembourg Garden is ringed with Métro stops (all a 10-minute walk away).*

CLUNY
MUSEUM TOUR

Musée National du Moyen Age

The National Museum of the Middle Ages doesn't sound quite so boring as I sink deeper into middle age myself. Aside from the solemn religious art, there's some surprisingly lively stuff here.

Paris emerged on the world stage in the Middle Ages, the time between ancient Rome and the Renaissance. Europe was awakening from a thousand-year slumber. Trade was booming, people actually owned chairs, and the Renaissance was moving in like a warm front from Italy.

Orientation

Cost: €8, free on first Sun of the month, covered by Museum Pass.

Hours: Wed-Mon 9:15-17:45, closed Tue.

Getting There: The museum, a five-minute walk from Ile de la Cité, is a block above the intersection of Boulevards St. Germain and St. Michel, at 6 Place Paul Painlevé (Mo: Cluny-La Sorbonne, St. Michel, or Odéon; bus #63 from Rue Cler or #86 from the Marais).

Information: Pick up the free, handy museum map. Tel. 01 53 73 78 16, www.musee-moyenage.fr.

Tours: The helpful audioguide is included with admission, though Museum Pass holders must pay €1 for it.

Length of This Tour: It takes about one hour for my self-guided tour of the museum's highlights, but allow browsing time for "The Rest of" the underrated Cluny. With less time, focus on the Roman Bath and the Lady and the Unicorn tapestries.

Baggage Check: Required for bags larger than a purse, and free.

Photography: OK without flash.

Cuisine Art: Just a few blocks away, the charming Place de la Sorbonne has several good cafés (see page 444; walk up Boulevard St. Michel toward the Panthéon).

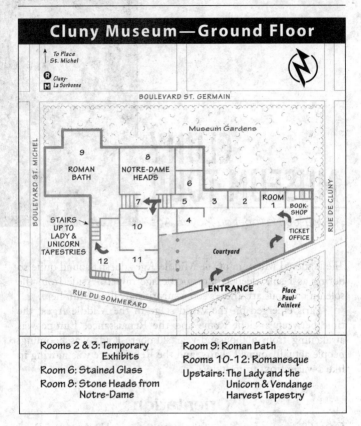

Cluny Museum—Ground Floor

To Place
St. Michel

Ⓡ Cluny-
Ⓜ La Sorbonne

BOULEVARD ST. GERMAIN

BOULEVARD ST. MICHEL

Museum Gardens

9 ROMAN BATH

8 NOTRE-DAME HEADS

6

7 5 3 2 ROOM 1 BOOK-SHOP

STAIRS UP TO LADY & UNICORN TAPESTRIES

10 4

TICKET OFFICE

Courtyard

RUE DE CLUNY

12 11

RUE DU SOMMERARD

ENTRANCE

Place Paul-Painlevé

Rooms 2 & 3: Temporary Exhibits

Room 6: Stained Glass

Room 8: Stone Heads from Notre-Dame

Room 9: Roman Bath

Rooms 10-12: Romanesque

Upstairs: The Lady and the Unicorn & Vendange Harvest Tapestry

The Tour Begins

• *Our tour begins in Room 6, with medieval stained glass. But take a moment to enjoy the first few rooms, which are usually reserved for temporary exhibits related to the theme of medieval life.*

CLUNY

Rooms 2 and 3: Temporary Exhibits

The museum may surprise you with its lack of grim, gray crucifixions and other symbols associated with medieval times. The Cluny feels more like a celebration of life in the Middle Ages. Among the temporary displays you may find joyfully elegant tapestries, golden altarpieces, and statues with a budding realism. Mother Mary is de-

picted elegantly sway-hipped and smiling. Colorful woven fabrics were brought back to France by Crusaders, who went off to conquer barbarian infidels but returned with tales of enlightened peoples on the fringes of Europe.

Not every work of art in the later medieval period was centered on religious themes. Having survived their Y1K crisis, these people realized the world wasn't about to end, and they turned their attention to the beauty of their surroundings.

• *After the two rooms of temporary exhibits, you enter a small hall. Turn right into a little, dark room full of luminous stained glass.*

Room 6: Stained Glass

Enter the Dark Ages, when life was harsh and brutal, angels and demons made regular appearances, and the Church was your only refuge. This room offers a rare close-up look at stained glass, which gave poor people a glimpse of the glories of heaven. These panels (many from the basilica of light, Sainte-Chapelle) give us a window into the magical, supernatural, miraculous—and often violent—medieval mind.

Read clockwise around the room, all at eye level (the bottom): 1) The angel Gabriel blasts his horn on Resurrection morning, rousting the grateful dead from their coffins. Notice that Gabriel's royal robe is made up of several different pieces of glass—purples, whites, blues—held together with lead. 2) Naked Christ is baptized in the squiggly River Jordan. 3) A red-faced, horned, horny demon, accompanied by an equally lascivious wolf and henchman, carries off a frightened girl in red on a date from hell. 4) Blond, pious boy Joseph is sold into slavery to camel merchants by his plotting brothers.

Next wall: 5) Samson is about to pull down the temple... 6) Then he has his eyes gouged out by Philistines. 7) Slaughter on the battlefield. Men with bloodstained hands and faces hack at each other with golden swords. 8) Aaron, disobeying God and Moses, worships a golden calf. 9) A king on a throne closes his eyes to all this wickedness.

Next wall (with some panels from the first Gothic church, St. Denis): 10) Two monks with prayer books gaze up, as one of their brothers disappears into heaven. The Latin inscription *"hec est via"* means "This is the way." 11) Seated Jesus, in a royal purple robe, is consoled by two angels. 12) Theophilus ("Lover of God") has struck a Faustian deal—shaking hands with the red-faced devil, yet feeling buyer's remorse. 13) Sleeping St. Martin is visited by a heavenly vision. 14) Angels in Rock-and-Roll Heaven.

Last wall: Four apostles—John (Ioannes), James (with his scallop shell), Paul, and Peter (Petrus, with key).

• *Before leaving, open the display cover under the Angel Gabriel and run your fingers along the glass and lead to get a feel for the thickness of each. Now, turn around and take in all the narrative medieval glass.*

Room 8: Stone Heads from Notre-Dame

This room has occasional exhibits, as well as the permanent displays, so be prepared to search for the objects described.

The 21 stone heads (sculpted 1220-1230) of the biblical kings of Judah once decorated the front of Notre-Dame. In 1793, an angry mob of Revolutionaries mistook the kings of Judah for the kings of France and abused and decapitated the statues. (Today's heads on the Notre-Dame statues are reconstructions.) Someone gathered up the heads and buried them in his back-

yard near the present-day Opéra Garnier. There they slept for two centuries, unknown and noseless, until 1977, when some diggers accidentally unearthed them and brought them to an astounded world. Their stoic expressions accept what fate, time, and liberals have done to them.

The statue of Adam (nearby) is also from Notre-Dame. He's scrawny and flaccid by Renaissance standards. And it will be another 200 years before naked Adam can step out from behind that bush.

Room 9: Roman Bath

This echoing cavern was a Roman *frigidarium*. Pretty cool. The museum is located on the site of a Roman bathhouse, which was in the center of town during the Roman years. The sunken area you see in the alcove was exactly what it looks like: a swimming pool. After hot baths and exercise in adjoining rooms, ordinary Romans would take a cold dip there, then relax cheek to cheek with such notables as Emperor Julian the Apostate (see his statue), who lived next door. As the empire decayed in the fourth century,

CLUNY

Julian avoided the corrupt city of Rome and made Paris a northern power base.

The 40-foot-high ceiling is the largest Roman vault in France, and it took the French another 1,000 years to improve on that crisscross-arch technology. The sheer size of this room—constructed in A.D. 200, when Rome was at its peak—gives an idea of the epic scale on which the Romans built. It inspired Europeans to greatness during the less civilized Middle Ages.

Often displayed in the baths are four square column fragments *(Le Pilier des Nautes)*. These are the oldest man-made objects you'll see from Paris. These pillars once fit together to support a 20-foot-high altar to the king of the gods in the Temple of Jupiter, where Notre-Dame now stands. The fragment labeled *Bloc dit "de Jupiter"* shows Jupiter in his royal robes leaning on a spear, as well as the god Vulcan hammering in his fiery forge. The fragment labeled *Pierre de la dedicace* is inscribed "TIB. CAESARE," announcing that the altar was built under Emperor Tiberius (A.D. 14-37, who reigned during the time of Jesus Christ) and was paid for by the

Parisian boatmen's union (see them holding their shields). On the column labeled *Pierre aux quatre divinites,* find the horned Celtic god Cernunnos, who is also known as the Stag Lord and god of the hunt. The eclectic Romans allowed this local "druid" god to support the shrine of Jupiter, in league with their own Vulcan, who hammers, and Castor and Pollux, who pet their horses.

Rooms 10-12: Romanesque

Rome lived on after the fall of the empire, in the "Roman"-esque grandeur of Christian churches. The 12 column capitals from St. Germain-des-Prés are monumental, in the style of the ancient *Pilier des Nautes* in the previous room. In the central capital, Christ sits in robes on a throne, ruling the world like a Roman emperor. Another shows Samson vividly killing a lion, while others feature floral patterns common in those times. Like many ancient works, these capitals were originally painted.

Browse these rooms, seeing how artists used Roman style and techniques to create religious art: statues of a smiling, gracefully posed Mary, decorative flourishes from church buildings, and exquisitely carved mini altarpieces in ivory (in the glass cases).

• *Continue upstairs to...*

Room 13: The Lady and the Unicorn Tapestries

As Europeans emerged from the Dark Ages, they rediscovered the beauty of the world around them.

These six mysterious tapestries were designed by an unknown (but probably French) artist before A.D. 1500 and were woven in Belgium out of wool and silk. Loaded with symbols—some serious, some playful—they have been interpreted in many ways, but, in short, the series deals with each of the five senses (find more detail by picking up the handheld explanations from slots hanging on the wall).

In medieval lore, unicorns were enigmatic, solitary creatures, so wild that only virgins could entice and tame them. In secular society, they symbolized how a feral man was drawn to his lady

love. Religiously, the unicorn was a symbol of Christ—radiant, pure, and somewhat remote—who is made accessible to humankind by the Virgin Mary. These tapestries likely draw inspiration from all these traditions.

• *Moving clockwise around the room...*

Touch: This is the most basic and dangerous of the senses. The scene is set in the wild: monkeys, a leopard, and exotic birds. A blond lady "strokes the unicorn's horn"—if you know what I mean—and the lion gets the double entendre. Medieval Europeans were exploring the wonders of love and the pleasures of sex.

Taste: The lady takes candy from a servant's dish to feed it to her parakeet. A unicorn—a species extinct since the Age of Rea-

son—and a lion look on. At the lady's feet, a monkey also tastes something, while the little white dog behind her wishes he had some. This was the dawn of the Age of Discovery, when overseas explorers spiced up Europe's bland gruel with new fruits, herbs, and spices.

The lion (symbol of knighthood?) and unicorn (symbol of "bourgeois nobility," purity, or fertility?) wave flags with the coat of arms of the family that commissioned the tapestries—three silver crescents in a band of blue.

Smell: The lady picks flowers and weaves them into a sweet-smelling wreath. On a bench behind, the monkey apes her. The flowers, trees, and animals are exotic and varied. Each detail is exquisite alone, but if you step back they blend together into pleasing patterns.

Hearing: Wearing a stunning dress, the lady plays sweet music on an organ, which soothes the savage beasts around her. The pattern and folds of the tablecloth are lovely. Humans and their fellow creatures (cats, dogs, and rabbits) live in harmony in an enchanted blue garden filled with flowers, all set in a red background.

Sight: The unicorn cuddles up and looks at himself in the lady's mirror, pleased with what he sees. The lion turns away and snickers. As the Renaissance dawns, vanity is a less-than-deadly sin.

Admire the great artistic skill in some of the detail work, such as the necklace and the patterns in the lady's dress. This tapestry had quality control in all its stages: the drawing of the scene, its enlargement and transfer to a cartoon, and the weaving. Still, the design itself is crude by Renaissance 3-D standards. The fox and rabbits, supposedly in the distance, simply float overhead, as big as the animals at the lady's feet.

Tapestry #6: The most talked-about tapestry gets its name from the words on our lady's tent: *A Mon Seul Désir (To My Sole Desire)*. What is her only desire? Is it jewelry, as she grabs a necklace from the jewel box? Or is she putting the necklace away and renouncing material things in order to follow her only desire?

Our lady has tried all things sensual and is now prepared to follow the one true impulse. Is it God? Love? Her friends the unicorn and lion open the tent doors. Flickering flames cover the tent. Perhaps she's stepping out from the tent. Or is she going in to meet the object of her desire? Human sensuality is awakening, an old dark age is ending, and the Renaissance is emerging.

The Rest of the Cluny

There's much more to this fine museum here on the upper floor. From the unicorn tapestries, continue on. The final rooms display medallions, more tapestries, medieval altarpieces, old books, swords and guns, and much more. The audioguide lets you key in on more exhibits.

In Room 19, pay your respects to the **tusk of a narwhal** (in a tall glass case in the corner), which must have convinced superstitious folk to believe in unicorns. In the Middle Ages, narwhal tusks were sold as unicorn relics.

In Room 22, the large **Vendange Harvest Tapestry** shows grape-stomping peasants during the *vendange,* the annual autumn harvest and wine celebration. A peasant man treads grapes in a vat while his wife collects the juice. A wealthy man gives orders. Above that, a peasant with a big wart turns a newfangled mechanical press. On the right, you'll see the joy of picking—pawns, knights, and queens all working side by side. Ah, the simple joys of the Middle Ages.

• *When you're ready, leave the Middle Ages and return to your modern, fast-paced life...*

CHAMPS-ELYSEES WALK

From the Arc de Triomphe to Place de la Concorde

Don't leave Paris without a stroll along Avenue des Champs-Elysées (shahnz ay-lee-zay). This is Paris at its most Parisian: monumental sidewalks, stylish shops, elegant cafés, glimmering showrooms, and proud Parisians on parade. The whole world seems to gather here to strut along the boulevard. It's a great walk by day, and even better at night, allowing you to tap into the city's increasingly global scene.

Orientation

Length of This Walk: This two-mile walk takes three hours, including a one-hour visit to the Arc de Triomphe. Métro stops are located every few blocks along the Champs-Elysées. With less time, end the walk at Rond-Point (Mo: FDR).

Getting There: To reach the Arc de Triomphe at Place Charles de Gaulle, take the Métro to Charles de Gaulle-Etoile. Then follow the *Sortie #1, Champs-Elysées/Arc de Triomphe* signs. From Rue Cler and the Montparnasse area, bus #92 works best.

Arc de Triomphe: Free and always viewable; steps to rooftop—€9.50, free for those under age 18, free on first Sun of month Oct-March, covered by Museum Pass; daily 10:00-23:00, Oct-March until 22:30, last entry 45 minutes before closing. Bypass the slooow ticket line with your Museum Pass (though if you have kids, you'll need to line up to get their free tickets). Expect another line (that you can't skip) at the entrance to the stairway up the arch. The elevator is only for people with disabilities (and runs only to the museum level, not to the top, which requires a 40-step climb). Lines disappear after 17:00—come for sunset.

Eating near the Champs-Elysées

Good eating options on the Champs-Elysées are slim. Most sit-down restaurants have lazy service, mediocre food, and in-flated prices. Instead, try the lovely café at the **Petit Palais,** or one of these places:

$$ Comptoir de L'Arc, a block from the Arc toward the Eiffel Tower, is a bustling place dishing out good *plats du jour* to locals, with side-Arc views from its terrace tables just below the tourist flow (Mon-Fri 7:00-24:00, closed Sat-Sun, 73 Avenue Marceau, tel. 01 47 20 72 04).

$ La Brioche Dorée and **$ Boulangerie Paul** sit side by side smack on the Champs-Elysées, each offering great Champs-side tables and good sandwiches and salads. Both are located about halfway along this walk at #82. Dorée has WCs, air-conditioning, and extra seating upstairs, while Paul provides heaters at its outside tables in cool weather. A second Dorée is at #144, closer to the Arc de Triomphe.

Grand Palais: Major exhibitions usually €11-15, not covered by Museum Pass, generally open daily 10:00-20:00, Wed until 22:00, some parts of building closed Mon, other parts closed Tue, closed between exhibitions.

Petit Palais: Free, Tue-Sun 10:00-18:00, Fri until 21:00 for special exhibits (fee), closed Mon.

Services: A small WC is inside the Arc de Triomphe, near the top, but it's often crowded. WCs are also at the Arcades des Champs-Elysées, Petit Palais (no lines), and Tuileries Garden (at the end of the walk). Most restaurants (McDonald's, etc.) and bigger stores along the route have WCs as well.

Starring: Grand boulevards, grander shops, and grandiose monuments.

The Walk Begins

❶ Arc de Triomphe

• *Start with the Arc de Triomphe, at the top of the Champs-Elysées. View the Arc from the right side of the boulevard ("right" as you face the Arc).*

Exterior

Construction of the 165-foot-high arch began in 1809 to honor Napoleon's soldiers, who, despite being vastly outnumbered by the Austrians, scored a remarkable victory at the Battle of Austerlitz. Patterned after the

ceremonial arches of ancient Roman conquerors (but more than twice the size), it celebrates Napoleon as emperor of a "New Rome." On the arch's massive left pillar, a relief sculpture shows a toga-clad Napoleon posing confidently, while an awestruck Paris—crowned by her city walls—kneels at his imperial feet. Napoleon died before the Arc's completion, but it was finished in time for his

1840 funeral procession to pass underneath, carrying his remains (19 years dead) from exile in St. Helena to Paris.

On the right pillar is the Arc's most famous relief, *La Marseillaise* (*Le Départ des Volontaires de 1792*, by François Rude). Lady Liberty—looking like an ugly reincarnation of Joan of Arc—screams, "Freedom is this way!" and points the direction with a sword. The soldiers beneath her are tired, naked, and stumbling, but she rallies them to carry on the fight against oppression.

• *Now approach the Arc. Take the underground pedestrian walkway—don't try to cross the roundabout in all the traffic, as there are no crosswalks. It's worthwhile to get to the base of the arch even if you don't climb it. There's no cost to wander around. After crossing through the tunnel, take the first left up a few steps, where you'll find the ticket booth (with a Museum Pass, you can skip the booth and its lines altogether, unless you need free tickets for kids). Now walk up to the arch.*

Today, the Arc de Triomphe is dedicated to the glory of all French armies. Walk to its center and stand directly beneath it on the faded eagle. You're surrounded by the lists of French victories since the Revolution—19th century on the arch's taller columns, 20th century in the pavement. On the shorter columns you'll see lists of generals (with a line under the names of those who died in battle). Find the nearby Tomb of the Unknown Soldier (from World War I). Every day at 18:30 since just after World War I, the flame has been rekindled and new flowers set in place.

Like its Roman ancestors, this arch has served as a parade gateway for triumphal armies (French or foe) and important ceremonies. From 1940 to 1944, a large swastika flew from here as Nazis goose-stepped down the Champs-Elysées. In August 1944 General Charles de Gaulle led Allied troops under this arch as they celebrated liberation. Today, national parades start and end here with one minute of silence.

1. Arc de Triomphe
2. Champs-Elysées View
3. Rue de Tilsitt & Qatar Embassy
4. McDonald's
5. Peugeot, Petit Bateau, Mercedes-Benz, Lido
6. Louis Vuitton
7. Fouquet's & Ladurée
8. Thomas Jefferson Plaque
9. Arcades Mall, Sephora, Guerlain
10. Renault
11. Int'l Shops & Citroën
12. Rond-Point
13. De Gaulle Statue
14. Grand & Petit Palais
15. Place de la Concorde
16. Hôtel Crillon
17. Pont de la Concorde

Eateries

A. Comptoir de L'Arc
B. Boulangerie Paul & La Brioche Dorée
C. La Brioche Dorée

Inside the Arc and the View from the Top

Ascend the Arc via the 284 steps inside the north pillar. Catch your breath two-thirds of the way up in the small exhibition area (WC also on this mezzanine level). It hosts ho-hum exhibits about the arch (though the down-camera is cool) and its founder, Napoleon. And, of course, there's a gift shop a few steps higher.

From the top you have an eye-popping view of *tout Paris*. You're gazing at the home of 11 million people, all crammed into an area the size of an average city in the US (the city center has about 2.3 million residents and covers 40 square miles). Paris has the highest density of any city in Europe, about 20 times greater than that of New York City.

Looking East: Look down the Champs-Elysées to the

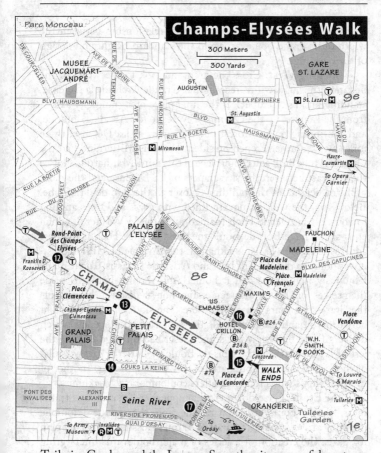

Champs-Elysées Walk

Tuileries Garden and the Louvre. Scan the cityscape of downtown Paris. That lonely hill to the left is Montmartre, topped by the dome of Sacré-Cœur; until 1860, this hill town was a separate city. Panning right, find the bulky Opéra Garnier's pitched roof rising above other buildings, the blue top of the modern Pompidou Center, and the Louvre and Tuileries Garden capping the east end of the Champs-Elysées. Let your eyes cross the river to see the distant twin towers of Notre-Dame, the dome of the Panthéon breaking the horizon, a block of small skyscrapers on a hill (the Quartier d'Italie), and the golden dome of Les Invalides. Near Les Invalides, find the lonely-looking Montparnasse Tower, standing like the box the Eiffel Tower came in; in the early 1970s, it served as a wake-up call to city planners that they needed to preserve building height restrictions and strengthen urban design standards. Aside from the Montparnasse Tower, notice the symmetry. Each corner building surrounding the arch is part of an elegant grand scheme. The beauty of Paris—basically a flat basin with a river running through it—is man-made. There's a harmonious relationship between the width of its grand boulevards and the standard height and design of the buildings.

Looking West: Cross the arch and look to the west. In the distance, the huge, white, rectangular Grande Arche de la Défense, standing amid skyscrapers, is the final piece of a grand city axis—from the Louvre, up the Champs-Elysées to the Arc de Triomphe, and continuing on to a forest of skyscrapers at La Défense, three miles away. Former French president François Mitterrand had the Grande Arche built as a centerpiece of this mini-Manhattan. Notice the contrast between the skyscrapers of La Défense and the more uniform heights of the buildings closer to the Arc de Triomphe. Below you, the wide boulevard lined with grass and trees angling to your left is Avenue Foch (named after the WWI hero), which ends at the huge Bois de Boulogne park. Avenue Foch is the best address to have in Paris. Nicknamed the "Avenue of Millionaires," it was home to the Shah of Iran and Aristotle Onassis. Today many fabulously rich Arabs call it home. And though Parisians pride themselves on being discreet, some not-so-discreet Homes-of-the-Stars-type tours are offered here. The skyscraper to the right between you and La Défense is the Hôtel Hyatt Regency, which delivers Paris' best view bar scene (described on page 84). To the left of La Défense (in the Bois de Boulogne) are the glassy "sails" of the Louis Vuitton Foundation. This wavy building, another of Frank Gehry's wild creations, offers contemporary art exhibits.

The Etoile: Gaze down at what appears to be a chaotic traffic mess. The 12 boulevards that radiate from the Arc de Triomphe (forming an *étoile,* star) were part of Baron Haussmann's master plan for Paris: the creation of a series of major boulevards intersecting at diagonals, with monuments (such as the Arc de Triomphe) as centerpieces of those intersections (see sidebar on page 89). Haussmann's plan did not anticipate the automobile—obvious when you watch the traffic scene below. But see how smoothly it functions. Cars entering the circle have the right of way (the only roundabout in France with this rule); those in the circle must yield. Still, there are plenty of accidents, many caused by tourists oblivious to the rules. Tired of disputes, insurance companies split the fault and damages of any Arc de Triomphe accident 50/50. The trick is to make a parabola—get to the center ASAP, and then begin working your way out two avenues before you want to exit.

• *We'll start our stroll down the Champs-Elysées at the Charles de Gaulle-Etoile Métro stop, on the north (sunnier) side of the street where the tunnel deposits you. Look straight down the Champs-Elysées to the Tuileries Garden at the far end.*

❷ Champs-Elysées

You're at the top of one of the world's grandest and most celebrated streets, home to big business, celebrity cafés, glitzy nightclubs,

high-fashion shopping, and international people-watching. People gather here to celebrate Bastille Day (July 14), World Cup triumphs, the finale of the Tour de France (see sidebar later in the chapter), and the ends of wars.

In 1667, Louis XIV opened the first section of the street as a short extension of the Tuileries Garden. This year is considered the birth of Paris as a grand city. The Champs-Elysées soon became *the* place to cruise in

your carriage. (It still is today; traffic can be gridlocked even at midnight.) One hundred years later, the café scene arrived. From the 1920s until the 1960s, this boulevard was pure elegance; Parisians actually dressed up to come here. It was mainly residences, rich hotels, and cafés. Then, in 1963, the government pumped up the neighborhood's commercial metabolism by bringing in the RER (commuter train). Suburbanites had easy access, and *pfft*—there went the neighborhood.

• *Start your descent, pausing at the first tiny street you cross, Rue de Tilsitt. This street is part of a shadow ring road—an option for drivers who'd like to avoid the chaos of the Arc—complete with stoplights.*

❸ Rue de Tilsitt and Qatar Embassy

A few steps down Rue de Tilsitt is a building housing the Qatar Embassy. It's one of the few survivors of a dozen uniformly U-shaped buildings from Haussmann's original 1853 grand design.

Back on the main drag, look across to the other side of the Champs-Elysées at the big, gray, concrete-and-glass "Publicis" building. Ugh. In the 1960s, venerable old buildings (similar to the Qatar Embassy building) were leveled to make way for new commercial operations like Publicis. Then, in 1985, a law prohibited the demolition of the old building fronts that gave the boulevard a uniform grace. Today, many modern businesses hide behind preserved facades.

The *nouveau* Champs-Elysées, revitalized in 1994, has newer benches and lamps, broader sidewalks, all-underground parking, and a fleet of green-suited workers who drive motorized street cleaners. Blink away the modern elements, and it's not hard to imagine the boulevard pre-1963, with only the finest structures lining both sides all the way to the palace gardens.

❹ McDonald's

The arrival of McDonald's—a hundred yards farther down on the left at #140—was a shock to the boulevard...and to the country. At first it was allowed to have only white arches painted on the window. Today, dining *chez MacDo* has become typically Parisian. France has a thousand McDonald's, and the Champs-Elysées branch is considered the most profitable one in the world.

A Big Mac here buys an hour of people-watching. Notice how many of the happy clients are French. The popularity of *le fast-food* in Paris is a sign that life is changing, and that the era of two-hour lunches is over. The most commonly ordered dish in French restaurants is now—by far and away—the hamburger (both as fast food and as a trendy gourmet dish). The French must now compete in a global world, and if that means adopting a more American lifestyle, *c'est la vie.*

❺ Glitz: Peugeot, Mercedes-Benz, Lido

Fancy car dealerships include **Peugeot,** at #136 (showing off its futuristic concept cars, often alongside the classic models), and **Mercedes-Benz,** a block down at #118, where you can pick up a Mercedes bag and perfume to go with your new car. In the 19th century this was an area for horse stables; today, it's the district of garages, limo companies, and car dealerships. If you're serious about selling cars in France, you must have a showroom on the Champs-Elysées.

Next to Mercedes is the famous **Lido,** Paris' largest cabaret (and a multiplex cinema). You can walk all the way into the lobby, passing a video advertising the show. Paris still offers the kind of burlesque-type spectacles that have been performed here since the 19th century, combining music, comedy, and scantily clad women. Moviegoing on the Champs-Elysées provides another kind of fun, with theaters showing the very latest releases. Check to see if there are films you recognize, then look for the showings *(séances).* A "v.o." *(version originale)* next to the time indicates the film will be shown in its original language; a "v.f." stands for *version française.*

Two doors farther down is **Petit Bateau.** The store's presence on the Champs-Elysées is proof of the success of the government's efforts to encourage couples to have more babies. With generous financial rewards for each child, France's birthrate is well above the rest of Europe's.

• *Next, cross the boulevard from in front of the Mercedes showroom—but*

*pause at the center on your way across for the next green light so you'll
have time to enjoy the view and energy. Look up at the Arc de Triomphe,
its rooftop bristling with tourists. Notice the variety of architecture
along this street—old and elegant, new, and new-behind-old-facades.
Continue to #101.*

❻ Louis Vuitton

The flagship store of this famous producer of leather bags may be
the largest single-brand luxury store in the world. Step inside. The
store insists on providing enough salespeople to treat each customer
royally—if there's a line, it means shoppers have overwhelmed the
place. If you need clothing and shoes to put in your fancy new bag,
head upstairs.

• *Continue downhill. Cross Avenue Georges V and find Fouquet's, a
Paris institution. The white spire you see down Avenue Georges V is the
American Cathedral.*

❼ Café Culture: Fouquet's and Ladurée

Fouquet's café-restaurant (#99), under the red awning, is a popular
spot among French celebrities, serving the most expensive shot
of espresso I've found in downtown Paris (€10). Opened in 1899
as a coachman's bistro, Fouquet's gained fame as the hangout of
France's WWI biplane fighter pilots—those who weren't shot
down by Germany's infamous "Red Baron." It also served as James
Joyce's dining room.

Since the early 1900s, Fouquet's has been a favorite of French
celebrities. The golden plaques at the entrance honor winners of
France's Oscar-like film awards, the Césars (one is cut into the
ground at the end of the carpet). There are plaques for Gérard
Depardieu, Catherine Deneuve, Yves Montand, Roman Polanski,
Juliette Binoche, and several famous Americans (but not Jerry
Lewis). More recent winners are shown on the floor just inside.
Every February, after the Césars are handed out at a nearby theater,
France's biggest movie stars descend on Fouquet's. Here they
emerge from their limos for the night's grandest red-carpet event
as they make their way inside for the official gala dinner.

The hushed interior is at once classy and intimidating—and
also a grand experience...if you dare (to say "I'm just looking" in
French, say *"Je regarde"*—zhuh ruh-gard—though fluent English
is spoken). The outdoor setting is more relaxed, but everyone still
looks rich and famous to me.

Once threatened with foreign purchase and eventual
destruction, Fouquet's was spared that fate when the government
declared it a historic monument. The café has now become
something of a symbol of excess in a country polarized by a rich-
poor gap. Case in point: Flamboyant ex-President Nicolas Sarkozy

celebrated his election-night victory with a huge party at Fouquet's, attended by France's glitterati—including the "French Elvis," Johnny Hallyday. By contrast, current President François Hollande, a Socialist, spent his election night in his humble hometown and does not frequent Fouquet's.

Ladurée (two blocks downhill at #75) is a classic 19th-century tea salon/restaurant/*pâtisserie*. Nonpatrons can discreetly wander around the place, though photos are not allowed. A coffee here is *très élégant* (only €4; I prefer the tables upstairs). The bakery sells traditional *macarons*, cute little cakes, and gift-wrapped finger sandwiches to go (your choice of four mini-*macarons* for €10). The rear café-bar feels otherworldly bizarre.

• *Cross back to the lively (north) side of the street and find two good-value lunch options,* **Boulangerie Paul** *and* **La Brioche Dorée** *(described in the sidebar on page 300). At #92 (50 yards uphill), a wall plaque marks the* ❽ *place Thomas Jefferson lived while serving as minister to France (1785-1789). He replaced the popular Benjamin Franklin but quickly made his own mark, extolling the virtues of America's Revolution to a country approaching its own.*

❾ French Shopping: Arcades Mall, Sephora, Guerlain

Stroll into the **Arcades des Champs-Elysées** mall at #76. With its fancy lamps, mosaic floors, glass skylight, and classical columns (try to ignore the Starbucks), it captures faint echoes of the *années folles*—the "crazy years," as the Roaring '20s were called in France. Architecture buffs can observe how the flowery Art Nouveau of the 1910s became the simpler, more geometric Art Deco of the 1920s.

Down the street at #74, the Galerie du Claridge building sports an old facade. You'd never guess that its ironwork awning, balconies, *putti*, and sculpted fantasy faces disguise an otherwise new building. One of the current tenants is FNAC, a large French chain that sells electronics, CDs, rare vinyl, concert tickets, and skip-the-queue tickets for many Paris sights (see page 52).

For a noisy and fragrant commercial carnival of perfumes, and a chance to sense the French passion for cosmetics, take your nose sightseeing at #72 and glide down the ramp of the largest **Sephora** in France. Grab a disposable white strip from a lovely clerk, spritz it with a sample, and sniff. The entry hall is lined with new products. In the main showroom, women's perfumes line the right wall and men's line the left—organized alphabetically by company, from Armani to Versace.

While Sephora seems to be going all out to attract the general public, the venerable **Guerlain** perfume shop sits next door and shows off a dash of the Champs-Elysées' old gold-leaf elegance. Notice the 1914 details. Climb upstairs. It's *très* French. If Sephora is a mosh-pit for your nose, Guerlain is a harem.

At the intersection with Rue la Boëtie, the English-speaking **pharmacy** is open until midnight (entrance around the corner).

Car buffs should detour across the Champs and park themselves at the sleek café in the ❿ **Renault** store (open until midnight). The car exhibits change regularly, but the great tables looking down onto the Champs-Elysées are permanent.

⓫ International Shopping and Citroën

Back on earth, a half-block farther down on the north side, the Disney, Gap, Zara, Nike, and Banana Republic stores are reminders of global economics: The French may live in a world of their own, but they love these places as much as Americans do. For a classic French brand, check out the five floors of glassy glitz at the **Citroën** auto showroom at #42. This isn't your father's *deux chevaux*, though you'll see echoes of that simple-but-dependable "two-horsepower" car from the '50s and '60s. Across the street at #23, that massive gilded gate and green alley no longer lead to a private mansion, but to Abercrombie & Fitch.

⓬ Rond-Point

At the Rond-Point des Champs-Elysées, the shopping ends and the park begins. This round, leafy traffic circle is always colorful, lined with flowers or seasonal decorations (thousands of pumpkins at Halloween, hundreds of decorated trees at Christmas). Avenue Montaigne, jutting off to the right, is lined by the most exclusive shops in town—the kinds of places where you need to make an appointment to buy a dress.

• *If you're pooped, Rond-Point's Métro stop is a good place to cut this walk short. Otherwise, continue downhill on the left side. Arc around Rond-Point and stroll for about 200 yards farther downhill. At Avenue de Marigny, look to the other side of the Champs-Elysées to find a* ⓭ *statue of Charles de Gaulle—ramrod-straight and striding purposefully, as he did the day Paris was liberated in 1944.*

⓮ Grand and Petit Palais

From the statue of de Gaulle, a grand boulevard (Avenue Winston Churchill) passes through the site of the 1900 World's Fair, leading between the glass-and-steel-domed Grand and Petit Palais exhibition halls, and across the river over the ornate bridge called Pont Alexandre III. (You can view these sights from the statue, if you don't feel like walking down to the bridge.) Imagine pavilions like

Le Tour de France

On one day every July, the Champs-Elysées is the focus of the world's sports fans, when it serves as the finish line of the Tour de France cycle race.

For three weeks, French sporting life comes to a standstill as the Tour de France whizzes across the nation's landscape and TV screens, pushing the world's top cyclists to their physical extremes and fans to the edges of their seats. What began in 1903 as a six-day publicity stunt for a cycling newspaper—in the era of wood-framed bikes and wine-and-cigarette breaks—has since grown into the sport's most prestigious race: a grueling 21-day, 2,000-mile test of strength and stamina, fueled by cutting-edge equipment and training regimens.

The route changes each year, but always finishes on the Champs-Elysées. The riders cycle slowly into Paris from its outskirts, savoring the views. Then, as they approach the city center, the race begins in earnest. Up and down the Champs-Elysées they go, making several laps. Thousands of spectators line the street, cheering them on. Finally, the cyclists speed down the boulevard one last  time and cross the finish line, spilling into Place de la Concorde. The winner takes a slow victory lap, followed by the *peloton* (the pack), to acknowledge the crowd and then stops at a makeshift podium at the base of the street. There he's declared champion and raises his fists in salute, exalted by the dramatic backdrop of the Arc de Triomphe.

The long race is divided into daily stages, during which riders compete both as individuals and as members of their nine-man team. While the Tour produces only one overall winner, cycling is

the two you see today lining this street all the way to the golden dome of Les Invalides—examples of the "can-do" spirit that ran rampant in Europe at the dawn of the 20th century.

Today, the huge Grand Palais (on the right side) houses impressive temporary exhibits. Classical columns and giant, colorful mosaics running the length of the Palais' facade wowed fairgoers. The Petit Palais (left side) has a pleasing permanent collection of lesser paintings by Courbet, Monet, Pissarro, and other 19th-century masters. It's a breathtaking building with a peaceful café (worth a quick detour), and just as important, the Petit Palais is free to enter and has fine WCs with no lines. For more on both museums, see page 81.

very much a team sport, and each member is critical (the loss of any rider along the way generally dooms a team's chances).

Minimizing air resistance is key to strategy, and riders spend most of each stage "drafting" behind *domestiques* ("servants," usually young riders paying their dues), who take turns pedaling in front. The team's constant maneuvering is a matter of choreographed precision, aimed at minimizing fatigue...and the chance of a collision. At the end of each stage, fans breathlessly watch for that critical moment when the lead riders break away for the final sprint. Meanwhile, the team tries to jockey its way to the best position within the peloton while plotting how best to tap its members' varied talents over the course of the race.

Specialists ride not just to bolster their team, but they also compete for their own distinctions: Climbers, usually smaller racers, battle to wear the *maillot à pois rouges* (red-polka-dot jersey), awarded to the "King of the Mountains." Bigger riders are usually sprinters, who vie for the *maillot vert* (green jersey). Time trialists help lower the team's aggregate time by excelling at individual races, where they must maintain high speeds over a long distance. The team's star is its captain, usually a solid "all-rounder." He's going for the famous *maillot jaune* (yellow jersey), worn by whoever holds the overall lead in the "general classification" standings at the end of each stage. A complex point system helps determine who has the lowest cumulative time—and, ultimately, who gets the €1.5 million prize, and recognition as the world's greatest cyclist.

If you catch the Tour in person, you'll experience the excitement firsthand and hear the loud whoosh of passing cyclists—but they're gone in a blink (viewing is best—and most crowded—on uphill slopes; for dates and details, see www.letour.fr). Any time of year, you can at least picture the Tour's final stretch here on the nation's grandest avenue, where cheering crowds cram the sidewalks, their necks craned for a glimpse of the yellow jersey.

The exquisite Pont Alexandre III, spiked with golden statues and ironwork lamps, was built to celebrate a turn-of-the-20th-century treaty between France and Russia. The grand and gilded dome in the distance marks Les Invalides, built by Louis XIV as a veterans' hospital for his battle-weary troops (covered in the Army Museum and Napoleon's Tomb Tour). The esplanade leading up to Les Invalides—possibly the largest patch of accessible grass in the city—gives soccer balls and Frisbees a warm Paris welcome.

• *From the de Gaulle statue it's a straight shot down the rest of the Champs-Elysées to the finish line. (Speaking of finish lines, this stretch is where the Tour de France reaches its annual climax—see sidebar.) The plane trees that you'll see—a kind of sycamore with peeling bark—do well in big-city pollution. They're a legacy of Napoleon III—president/ emperor from 1849 to 1870—who had 600,000 trees planted to green up the city.*

Since there's little to see on this final stretch of the Champs-Elysées, consider the following alternate route to Place de la Concorde. From the statue, circle clockwise to the left up Avenue de Marigny to the well-secured Elysée Palace, France's version of the White House. It feels like London's #10 Downing Street but with French style. From there you'll walk five blocks along Rue du Faubourg Saint-Honoré—past the fortified backsides of the US and British embassies and glittering high-end shops—and then cut back down to Place de la Concorde.

Either way, your final destination is the 21-acre Place de la Concorde. View it from the obelisk in the center.

⓯ Place de la Concorde

During the Revolution, this was the Place de la Révolution. The guillotine sat on this square, and many of the 2,780 people who were beheaded during the Revolution lost their bodies here during the Reign of Terror. A bronze plaque in the ground in front of the obelisk memorializes the place where Louis XVI, Marie-Antoinette, Georges Danton, Charlotte Corday, and Maximilien de Robespierre, among about 1,200 others, were made "a foot shorter on top." Three people worked the guillotine: One managed the blade, one held the blood bucket, and one caught the head, raising it high to the roaring crowd. (In 1981, France abolished the death penalty—one of many preconditions for membership in today's European Union.)

The 3,300-year-old, 72-foot, 220-ton, red granite, hieroglyph-inscribed **obelisk of Luxor** now forms the centerpiece of Place de la Concorde. Here—on the spot where Louis XVI was beheaded—his brother (Charles X) erected this obelisk to honor those who'd been executed. (Charles became king when the monarchy was restored after Napoleon.) The obe-

lisk was carted here from Egypt in the 1830s. The gold pictures on the pedestal tell the story of the obelisk's incredible two-year journey: pulled down from the entrance to Ramses II's Temple of Amon in Luxor; encased in wood; loaded onto a boat built to navigate both shallow rivers and open seas; floated down the Nile, across the Mediterranean, along the Atlantic coast, and up the Seine; and unloaded here, where it was reerected in 1836. Its glittering gold-leaf cap is a recent addition (1998), replacing the original, which was stolen 2,500 years ago.

The obelisk also forms a center point along a line that locals call the "royal perspective." You can hang a lot of history along this straight line (Louvre-obelisk-Arc de Triomphe-Grande Arche de la Défense). The Louvre symbolizes the old regime (divine-right rule by kings and queens). The obelisk and Place de la Concorde symbolize the people's Revolution (cutting off the king's head). The Arc de Triomphe calls to mind the triumph of nationalism (victorious armies carrying national flags under the arch). And the huge modern arch in the distance, surrounded by the headquarters of multinational corporations, heralds a future in which business entities are more powerful than nations.

• *Our walk is over. From here the closest Métro stop is Concorde (entrance on the Tuileries Garden side of the square, away from the river); handy buses #24 and #73 (see page 32) stop in the square; and taxis congregate outside Hôtel Crillon. But if you're not quite ready to go, Paris has more to offer...*

Near Place de la Concorde

The beautiful Tuileries Garden (with a public WC just inside on the right) is just through the iron gates. Pull up a chair next to a pond or at one of the cafés in the garden. From the garden you can access the Orangerie Museum and, at the other end, the Louvre (this book includes tours of both museums).

On the north side of Place de la Concorde is **⑯ Hôtel Crillon,** one of Paris' most exclusive hotels (likely closed for renovation for at least part of 2017). Of the twin buildings that guard the entrance to Rue Royale (which leads to the Greek-style Church of the Madeleine), it's the one on the left. This hotel is so fancy that one

of its belle époque rooms is displayed in New York's Metropolitan Museum of Art. Eleven years before Louis XVI lost his head on Place de la Concorde, he met with Benjamin Franklin in this hotel to sign a treaty recognizing the US as an independent country. (Today's low-profile, heavily fortified **US Embassy and Consulate** are located next door.)

Nearby, those of a certain generation may want to seek out **Maxim's** restaurant (3 Rue Royale), once the world's most glamorous bistro (c. 1900-1970) and a nightspot frequented by everyone from British royalty to Jackie O. Today, its famed carved-wood, Art Nouveau exterior and high prices remain intact, but it's become a generic link in a chain franchise. Farther north up Rue Royale is a fancy shopping area near Place de la Madeleine (see the Shopping in Paris chapter).

South of Place de la Concorde is the ❼ **Pont de la Concorde,** the bridge that leads to the many-columned building where the **French National Assembly** (similar to the US Congress) meets. The Pont de la Concorde, built of stones from the Bastille prison (which was demolished by the Revolution in 1789), symbolizes the *concorde* (harmony) that can come from chaos—through good government. The bridge arcs over a freeway underpass that was converted to a pedestrian-only promenade in 2014 and is well worth a stroll.

Stand midbridge and gaze upriver (east). The Orangerie hides behind the trees at 10 o'clock, and the tall building with the skinny chimneys at 11 o'clock is the architectural caboose of the sprawling Louvre palace. The thin spire of Sainte-Chapelle is dead center at 12 o'clock, with the twin towers of Notre-Dame to its right. The Orsay Museum is closer on the right, connected with the Tuileries Garden by a sleek pedestrian bridge (the next bridge upriver) or by the riverside promenade on the Left Bank. Paris awaits.

MARAIS WALK

From Place Bastille to the Pompidou Center

This walk takes you through one of Paris' most intriguing quarters, the Marais, and finishes in the artsy Beaubourg district. Naturally, when in Paris you want to see the big sights—but to experience the city, you also need to visit a vital neighborhood. The Marais fits the bill, with hip boutiques, busy cafés, trendy art galleries, narrow streets, leafy squares, Jewish bakeries, aristocratic châteaux, nightlife, and real Parisians. It's the perfect setting to appreciate the flair of this great city.

The walk has a little history (the Bastille, Place des Vosges), but the main focus here is on the shops and daily life. Follow this suggested route for a start, then explore. If at any point you want to wander into a store or savor a *café crème*, by all means, you have permission to press pause.

Orientation

Length of This Walk: Allow about 2 hours for this 2.25-mile walk. Figure on an additional hour for each museum you visit along the way.

When to Go: The Marais is liveliest on a Sunday afternoon (when many other parts of Paris close for business). Monday morning is sleepy. On Saturdays, Jewish businesses may close, but the area still hops.

Victor Hugo's House: Free, fee for optional special exhibits, Tue-Sun 10:00-18:00, closed Mon, 6 Place des Vosges.

Carnavalet Museum: Closed for renovation in 2017 and beyond.

Picasso Museum: €11, covered by Museum Pass, free on first Sun of month and for those under 18 with ID; Tue-Fri 11:30-18:00 (until 21:00 on third Fri of month), Sat-Sun 9:30-18:00, closed Mon, last entry 45 minutes before closing, 5 Rue de Thorigny.

MARAIS

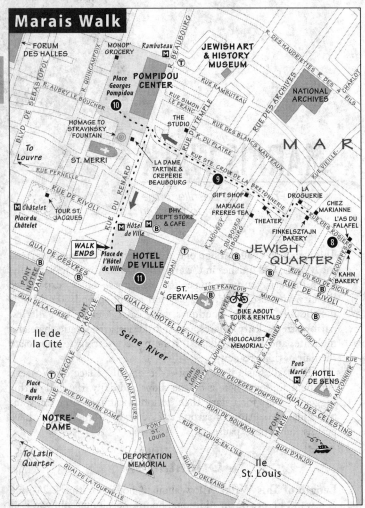

Marais Walk

- FORUM DES HALLES
- MONOP' GROCERY — Rambuteau
- **JEWISH ART & HISTORY MUSEUM**
- R. DES HAUDRIETTES — R. DES — R. DES 4 FILS — R. CHARLOT
- **NATIONAL ARCHIVES**
- Place Georges Pompidou — **POMPIDOU CENTER** ⑩
- RUE RAMBUTEAU
- R. BEAUBOURG
- RUE SIMON LE FRANC
- RUE DES ARCHIVES
- M A R
- HOMAGE TO STRAVINSKY FOUNTAIN
- THE STUDIO
- R. DU TEMPLE
- RUE DES BLANCS MANTEAUX
- RUE STE. CROIX DE LA BRETONNERIE
- RUE VIEILLE
- To Louvre
- ST. MERRI
- RUE PERNELLE
- LA DAME TARTINE & CRÊPERIE BEAUBOURG
- RUE DE RIVOLI
- ⑨
- GIFT SHOP
- LA DROGUERIE
- CHEZ MARIANNE
- L'AS DU FALAFEL ⑧
- MARIAGE FRERES TEA
- THEATER
- FINKELSZTAJN BAKERY
- Châtelet — Place du Châtelet
- TOUR ST. JACQUES
- R. DU RENARD
- R. MOUSSY
- R. DU BOURG TIBOURG
- R. DES ECOUFFES
- R. DES ROSIERS
- **JEWISH QUARTER**
- Hôtel de Ville
- BHV DEP'T STORE & CAFE
- QUAI DE GESVRES
- RUE DU ROI DE SICILE
- KAHN BAKERY
- **WALK ENDS** → Place de l'Hôtel de Ville
- **HOTEL DE VILLE** ⑪
- R. DE LOBAU
- RUE DE RIVOLI
- PONT NOTRE DAME
- QUAI DE LA CORSE
- PONT D'ARCOLE
- QUAI DE L'HÔTEL DE VILLE
- ST. GERVAIS
- RUE FRANÇOIS MIRON
- R. DES BARRES
- BIKE ABOUT TOUR & RENTALS
- R. DE JOUY
- Ile de la Cité
- Seine River
- R. LOUIS PHILIPPE
- HOLOCAUST MEMORIAL
- RUE G. L'ASNIER
- Pont Marie — **HOTEL DE SENS**
- QUAI DES CELESTINS
- RUE FALCONNIER
- Place du Parvis
- RUE DU NOTRE DAME
- QUAI AUX FLEURS
- **NOTRE-DAME**
- VOIE GEORGES POMPIDOU
- PONT LOUIS PHILIPPE
- QUAI DE BOURBON
- PONT MARIE
- QUAI D'ANJOU
- To Latin Quarter
- QUAI DE LA TOURNELLE
- DEPORTATION MEMORIAL
- PONT ST. LOUIS
- RUE ST. LOUIS-EN-L'ILE
- QUAI D'ORLEANS
- **Ile St. Louis**
- BLVD DE SEBASTOPOL
- R. AUBRY LE BOUCHER
- R. QUINCAMPOIX
- PONT D'ARCOLE

Jewish Art and History Museum: €9, covered by Museum Pass; Tue-Fri 11:00-18:00, Sat-Sun 10:00-18:00, open later during special exhibits—Wed until 21:00 and Sat-Sun until 19:00, closed Mon year-round, last entry 45 minutes before closing, 71 Rue du Temple.

Pompidou Center: €14, free on first Sun of month, €3 View of Paris ticket covers just the ride to the sixth floor view, Museum Pass covers permanent collection, sixth floor view, and occasional special exhibits; permanent collection open Wed-Mon 11:00-21:00, closed Tue, ticket counters close at 20:00; rest of the building open later—until 22:00 (Thu until 23:00).

MARAIS

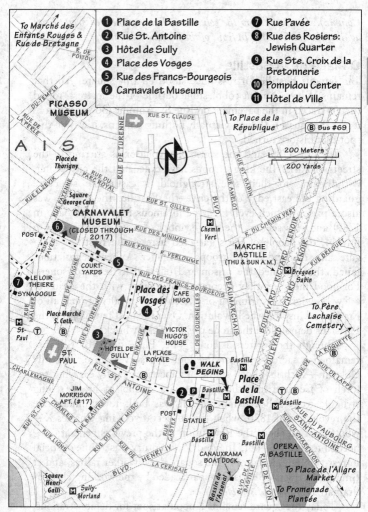

① Place de la Bastille
② Rue St. Antoine
③ Hôtel de Sully
④ Place des Vosges
⑤ Rue des Francs-Bourgeois
⑥ Carnavalet Museum
⑦ Rue Pavée
⑧ Rue des Rosiers: Jewish Quarter
⑨ Rue Ste. Croix de la Bretonnerie
⑩ Pompidou Center
⑪ Hôtel de Ville

Tours: Paris Walks offers excellent guided tours of this area (see page 42).

Services: There's free access to good WCs at Victor Hugo's House.

Starring: The grand Place des Vosges, the Jewish Quarter, several museums, and the boutiques and trendy lifestyle of today's Marais.

The Walk Begins

• *Start at the west end of Place de la Bastille. From the Bastille Métro, exit following signs to Place de la Bastille/Place des Vosges. Ascend onto a noisy traffic circle dominated by the bronze Colonne de Juillet (July*

Column). The figure atop the column is, like you, headed west. Lean against the black railing in front of the Banque de France.

❶ Place de la Bastille

The famous Bastille fortress once stood on this square. All that remains today is a faint cobblestone outline of the fortress' round turrets traced in the pavement on Rue St. Antoine (30 yards before it hits the square). Though virtually nothing remains, it was on this spot that history turned.

It's July 1789, and the spirit of revolution is stirring in the streets of Paris. The king's troops have evacuated the city center, withdrawing to their sole stronghold, a castle-like structure guarding the east edge of the city—the Bastille. The Bastille was also a prison (which even held the infamous Marquis de Sade in 1789) and was seen as the very symbol of royal oppression. On July 14, the people of Paris gathered here at the Bastille's main gate and demanded the troops surrender. When negotiations failed, they stormed the prison and released its seven prisoners. For good measure, they decorated their pikes with the heads of a few bigwigs. This triumph of citizens over royalty ignited all of France and inspired the Revolution. Over the next few months, the Parisians demolished the stone prison brick by brick.

Though the fortress is long gone, Place de la Bastille has remained a sacred spot for freedom lovers ever since. The July Column—with its gilded statue of Liberty elegantly carrying the torch of freedom into the future—is a symbol of France's long struggle to establish democracy. It was built to commemorate the revolution of 1830, when the conservative King Charles X—who forgot all about the Revolution of the previous generation—needed to be tossed out. The mid-19th century was a time of social unrest throughout Europe; the square drew worker rallies, and at times, the streets of Paris were barricaded by the working class, as dramatized in *Les Misérables*.

Today the square remains a popular spot for demonstrations, and the Bastille is remembered every July 14 on independence day—Bastille Day (see sidebar).

Across the square, the southeast corner is dominated (some say overwhelmed) by the flashy, curved, glassy gray facade of the Opéra Bastille. In a symbolic attempt to bring high culture to the masses, former French president François Mitterrand chose this location
for the building that would become Paris' main opera venue,

Bastille Day in France

Bastille Day—July 14, the symbolic kickoff date of the French Revolution—became the French national holiday in 1880. Traditionally, Parisians celebrate at Place de la Bastille starting at 20:00 on July 13, but the best parties are on the numerous smaller squares, where firefighter units sponsor dances. At 10:00 on the morning of the 14th, a grand military parade fills the Champs-Elysées. Then, at 22:30, there's a fireworks display at the Eiffel Tower (arrive at Champ de Mars park by 20:00 to get a seat on the grass). *Vive la France!*

---

edging out Paris' earlier "palace of the rich," the Garnier-designed opera house (see page 88). Designed by Canadian architect Carlos Ott, this grand Parisian project—one of the largest theaters in the world, with nine stages—was opened with fanfare by Mitterrand on the 200th Bastille Day, July 14, 1989. Tickets are heavily subsidized to encourage the unwashed masses to attend, though how much high culture they have actually enjoyed here is a subject of debate. (For opera ticket information, see page 492.)

• *Now turn your back on Place de la Bastille and head west down Rue St. Antoine about four blocks into the Marais.*

❷ Rue St. Antoine

From Paris' earliest days, this has been one of its grandest boulevards, part of the east-west axis from Place de la Concorde to the eastern gate, Porte St. Antoine. The street was broadened in the mid-1800s as part of the civic renovation plan by Baron Georges-Eugène Haussmann (see sidebar on page 89). Today, it's an ordinary street with a typical mix of workaday shops: banks, clothing stores, produce stands, restaurants.

Just past the first block, a **statue of Beaumarchais** (1732-1799) introduces you to the aristocratic-but-bohemian spirit of the Marais. Beaumarchais, who lived near here, made watches for Louis XV, wrote the bawdy *Marriage of Figaro* (which Mozart turned into an opera), and smuggled guns to freedom fighters in both the American and French Revolutions.

On the next block, pause at the **gas station/parking garage.** Notice how minimal the curbside gas pumps are, and ponder how much space most gas stations take up in the US. (Prices posted are for liters—about four liters per gallon.) This station is part of a full-service garage with precious in-city parking (€45/day!) and *"lavage traditionnel à la main"* (car wash by hand).

Across the street is a stately pre-Revolutionary mansion with its fine red carriage gate. It became a school after the Revolution.

Look ahead, along the roofline of this street of 19th-century facades with stout walls holding ranks of chimneys—one chimney for each fireplace, because back then any room that had heat had its own hearth.

Continuing on, at the intersection with Rue de Birague, hippies may wish to make a 100-yard detour to the left, down Rue Beautreillis to #17, the nondescript apartment **where rock star Jim Morrison died.** (For more on Morrison, see page 360.)

• *Otherwise, continue down Rue St. Antoine to #62 and enter the grand courtyard of Hôtel de Sully (daily 10:00-19:00). If the building is closed, you'll need to backtrack one block to Rue de Birague to reach the next stop, Place des Vosges.*

❸ Hôtel de Sully

During the reign of Henry IV (r. 1589-1610), this area—originally a swamp *(marais)*—became the hometown of the French aristocracy.

Big shots built their private mansions *(hôtels),* like this one, close to Henry's stylish Place des Vosges. *Hôtels* that survived the Revolution now house museums, libraries, and national institutions.

Nobles entered the courtyard by horse-drawn carriage, then parked under the four arches to the right. The elegant courtyard separated the mansion from the noisy and very public street. Look up at statues of Autumn (carrying grapes from the harvest), Winter (a feeble old man), and the four elements.

Enter the building between the sphinxes into a passageway. Continue into the back courtyard, where noisy Paris takes a back seat. Enjoy the oak tree, manicured hedges, vine-covered walls, birdsong, and the back side of the mansion with its warm stone and statues. Use the bit of Gothic window tracery (on the right) for a fun framed photo of your travel partner as a haloed Madonna. At the far end, the French doors are part of a former *orangerie,* or greenhouse, for homegrown fruits and vegetables throughout winter; these days it warms office workers. Ostentatious as a mansion like this might seem, it was typically just the city residence of a fabulously wealthy noble. The owner of such a mansion was a member of pre-Revolutionary France's one percent, whose primary residences were much grander chateaux in the countryside.

• *Continue through the small door at the far-right corner of the back courtyard, and pop out into one of Paris' finest squares.*

❹ Place des Vosges

Walk to the center, where Louis XIII, on horseback, gestures, "Look at this wonderful square my dad built." He's surrounded by locals

enjoying their community park. You'll see children frolicking in the sandbox, lovers warming benches, and pigeons guarding their fountains while trees shade this escape from the glare of the big city (you can refill your water bottle in the center of the square, behind Louis).

Study the architecture: nine pavilions (houses) per side. The two highest—at the front and back—were for the king and queen (but were never used). Warm red brickwork—some real, some fake—is topped with sloped slate roofs, chimneys, and another quaint relic of a bygone era: TV antennas. Beneath the arcades are cafés, art galleries, and restaurants—it's a romantic place for dinner (for recommendations, see page 430).

Henry IV built this centerpiece of the Marais in 1605 and called it "Place Royale." As he'd hoped, it turned the Marais into Paris' most exclusive neighborhood. Just like Versailles 80 years later, this was a magnet for the rich and powerful of France. The square served as a model for civic planners across Europe. With the Revolution, the aristocratic splendor of this quarter passed. To encourage the country to pay its taxes, Napoleon promised naming rights to the district that paid first—the Vosges region (near Germany).

The insightful writer **Victor Hugo** lived at #6 from 1832 to 1848. (It's at the southeast corner of the square, marked by the

French flag.) This was when he wrote much of his most important work, including his biggest hit, *Les Misérables*. Inside this free museum you'll wander through eight plush rooms, enjoy a fine view of the square, and find good WCs (see listing on page 100).

Sample the razzle-dazzle art galleries ringing the square (the best ones are behind Louis). Ponder a daring new piece for that blank wall at home. Or consider a pleasant break at one of the recommended eateries on the square.

• *Exit the square at the northwest (far left) corner. Head west on...*

❺ Rue des Francs-Bourgeois

From the Marais of yesteryear, immediately enter the lively neighborhood of today. Stroll down a block full of cafés and eclectic clothing boutiques with the latest fashions. A few doorways (including #8 and #13) lead into courtyards with more shops. Even this "main" street through the neighborhood is narrow and more fit for pedestrians than cars.

In the 19th century, the aristocrats moved elsewhere. The Marais became a working-class quarter, filled with gritty shops, artisans, immigrants, and a Jewish community. Haussmann's modernization plan put the Marais in line for the wrecking ball. But then the march of "progress" was halted by one tiny little event—World War I—and the Marais was spared. It limped along as a dirty, working-class zone until the 1960s, when it was transformed and gentrified.

Across the street from the Carnavalet Museum (described next), on the corner, is the storefront of a long-gone *boulangerie-pâtisserie*. Its facade is protected and so it survives, even though today's shop sells designer fashions.

• *Continue west along Rue des Francs-Bourgeois and find the entrance (at #16) of the museum.*

❻ Carnavalet Museum

Housed inside a Marais mansion, this museum (closed for renovation through 2017 and beyond) features the history of Paris, particularly the Revolution years. The bloody events of July 14, 1789, come to life in paintings and displays, including a model of the Bastille carved out of one of its bricks. The mansion itself provides the best possible look at the elegance of the neighborhood back when Place des Vosges was Place Royale.

• *From the Carnavalet continue west a half-block down Rue des Francs-Bourgeois to the post office. Modern-art fans can check out the nearby **Picasso Museum**, which features the whole range of styles and media from the artist's long life (*□□ *see the Picasso Museum Tour chapter). Turn left onto...*

❼ Rue Pavée

In a few steps, at #24, you'll pass the 16th-century Paris Historical Library (Bibliothèque Historique de la Ville de Paris). Step into the courtyard of this rare Renaissance mansion to see its unstained-glass windows and clean classical motifs. From the street, notice the corner tower—designed so guards could see from which direction angry peasants were coming.

Continue down Rue Pavée, keeping to the right, until you come to the intersection with Rue des Rosiers. Before we turn right on Rue des Rosiers, consider two little side-trips: A half-block straight ahead leads to the Agoudas Hakehilos synagogue (at #10) with its fine Art Nouveau facade (c. 1913, closed to public). It was designed by Hector Guimard, the same architect who designed Paris' Art Nouveau Métro stations. A half-block to the left, along Rue des Rosiers, is Le Loir dans la Théière (at #3). With tasty baked goods and hot drinks, this place provides the perfect excuse for a break (see description on page 436).

• *From Rue Pavée, turn right onto Rue des Rosiers, which runs straight for three blocks through Paris' Jewish Quarter.*

❽ Rue des Rosiers: Jewish Quarter

This street—the heart of the Jewish Quarter (and named for the roses that once lined the city wall)—has become the epicenter of Marais hipness and fashion.

Once the largest in Western Europe, Paris' Jewish Quarter is much smaller today but is still colorful. Notice the sign above #4,

which says *Hamam* (Turkish bath). Although still bearing the sign of an old public bath, it now showcases steamy women's clothing. Next door, at #4 bis, the Ecole de Travail (trade school) has a plaque on the wall (left of the door) remembering the headmaster, staff, and students who were arrested here during World War II and killed at Auschwitz.

The size of the Jewish population here has fluctuated. It expanded in the 19th century when Jews arrived from Eastern Europe, escaping pogroms (surprise attacks on villages). The numbers swelled during the 1930s as Jews fled Nazi Germany. Then, during World War II, 75 percent of the Jews here were taken to concentration camps (for more information, visit the nearby Holocaust Memorial—see page 98). And, most recently, Algerian exiles, both Jewish and Muslim, have settled in—living together peacefully here in Paris. (Nevertheless, much of the street has granite blocks on the sidewalk—an attempt to keep out any terrorists' cars.)

Currently the district's traditional population is being squeezed out by the trendy boutiques of modern Paris. Case in point—the

Eateries Along the Walk

Bring your appetite along, because I've peppered this walk with pleasant places to stop for a break. Some are best for a sit-down meal, and others for a quick coffee, crêpe, or snack. Find these spots on the map on page 316. For still more options in the Marais, see the Eating in Paris chapter.

$$$ La Place Royale: Traditional, well-priced cuisine on Place des Vosges, with outdoor seating under the arcade (daily, 2 bis Place des Vosges, tel. 01 42 78 58 16, see page 430).

$$ Café Hugo: Great for drinks (or standard café fare) on Place des Vosges (daily, 22 Place des Vosges, tel. 01 42 72 64 04, see page 430).

$$ Le Loir dans la Théière: A cozy, mellow teahouse for lunch or dessert, offering a welcoming ambience for tired travelers (daily 9:00-19:00, 3 Rue des Rosiers, tel. 01 42 72 90 61, see page 436).

$ L'As du Falafel: The "Ace" of the falafel scene in the Jewish quarter. Bustling setting, fast service, and inexpensive meals to eat in or take away (long hours most days except closed Fri evening and all day Sat, 34 Rue des Rosiers, tel. 01 48 87 63 60, see page 436).

$ Florence Kahn Yiddish bakery: Tiny takeaway shop for boutique baked goods and sandwiches (Wed-Sun 10:00-19:00, closed Mon-Tue, 24 Rue des Ecouffes, tel. 01 48 87 92 85).

snappy clothing boutique at the intersection of Rue des Rosiers and Rue Ferdinand Duval was once the venerable Jewish deli Jo Goldenberg. Note the classic facade and a red banner bearing its name still hanging. A plaque marks a 1982 terrorist bombing.

The intersection of Rue des Rosiers and Rue des Ecouffes marks the heart of the small neighborhood that Jews call the Pletzl ("little square"). Lively Rue des Ecouffes, named for a bird of prey, is a derogatory nod to the moneychangers' shops that once lined this lane. The next two blocks along Rue des Rosiers feature kosher *(cascher)* restaurants and fast-food places selling falafel, *shawarma*, *kefta*, and other Mediterranean dishes.  Bakeries specialize in braided challah, bagels, and strudels. Delis offer gefilte fish, piroshkis, and blintzes. Art galleries exhibit Jewish-themed works, and store windows post flyers for community events. Need a menorah? You'll find one here. You'll likely see Jewish men in yarmulkes, a few bearded Orthodox Jews, and Hasidic Jews with black coat and hat, beard, and earlocks.

Lunch Break: This is a good place to

$ Sacha Finkelsztajn: Another Yiddish bakery/deli with Polish and Russian cuisine, same price to sit or take away (Wed-Mon 10:00-19:00, closed Tue, 27 Rue des Rosiers, tel. 01 42 72 78 91).

$$ Chez Marianne: Neighborhood fixture for inexpensive Jewish cuisine (good vegetarian options) in a wonderful atmosphere. Sit inside (deli ambience) or out, or take it away (long hours daily, corner of Rue des Rosiers and Rue des Hospitalières-St.-Gervais, tel. 01 42 72 18 86, see page 436).

$ La Droguerie: Cheap takeaway crêpe stand (daily 12:00-22:00, 56 Rue des Rosiers, see page 436).

$$$ Mariage Frères: Luxurious tea extravaganza just off Rue Ste. Croix de la Bretonnerie (daily 10:30-19:30, serving tea from 12:00, 30 Rue du Bourg Tibourg).

$ La Dame Tartine and **$ Crêperie Beaubourg:** Two casual, inexpensive joints for salads, toasted sandwiches, and crêpes alongside Pompidou Center's Stravinsky fountain. Beaubourg offers a good €10 lunch special (Tartine daily 9:00-23:30, tel. 01 42 77 32 22; Beaubourg daily 11:30-23:00, tel. 01 42 77 63 62).

$ BHV Department Store fifth-floor cafeteria: Nice views, good-value cafeteria food with a salad bar, by Hôtel de Ville (Mon-Sat 11:30-18:00, open later Wed, closed Sun, corner of Rue du Temple and Rue de la Verrerie, see page 437).

stop. You'll be tempted by kosher pizza and plenty of cheap fast-food joints selling falafel "to go" *(emporter)*. Choose from L'As du Falafel (#34), with its bustling New York deli atmosphere, the Sacha Finkelsztajn Yiddish bakery at #27, or Chez Marianne for traditional Jewish meals. (For more options, see the sidebar on page 324.) For a breath of fresh air, step into the very Parisian Jardin des Rosiers, a half-block before L'As du Falafel, at 10 Rue des Rosiers (or backtrack and head behind the Carnavalet Museum to Square George Caïn on Rue Payenne).

• *Rue des Rosiers dead-ends at Rue Vieille du Temple. Turn left on Rue Vieille du Temple, then take your first right onto Rue Ste. Croix de la Bretonnerie and prepare for a little cultural whiplash (from Jewish culture to gay culture).*

   Side-Trip to the Holocaust Memorial: *Consider a five-block detour to see the memorial (for details on visiting the memorial, see the listing on page 98). To get there, head south on Rue Vieille du Temple, cross Rue de Rivoli, and make your second left onto the traffic-free passageway named Allée des Justes. It's at 17 Rue Geoffroy l'Asnier.*

MARAIS

❾ Rue Ste. Croix de la Bretonnerie

Gay Paree's openly gay main drag is lined with cafés, lively shops, and crowded bars at night. Check the posters at #7, Le Point Virgule theater (means "The Semicolon"), to see what form of edgy musical comedy is showing tonight (most productions of up-and-coming humorists are in French). A short detour left on Rue du Bourg Tibourg leads to the luxurious tea extravaganza of Mariage Frères (#30). Continue along Rue Ste. Croix de la Bretonnerie to #38 (on the right) and peruse real estate prices in the area—€500,000 for a one-bedroom flat?! Parisians willingly pay that for the neighborhood's high quality of life.

Farther ahead at Rue du Temple, consider detouring a few blocks to the right to the Jewish Art and History Museum (if visiting, see listing on page 95). On the way, you'll pass The Studio (41 Rue du Temple), a dance school wonderfully situated in a 17th-century courtyard.

• *Continue west on Rue Ste. Croix (which turns into Rue St. Merri). Up ahead you'll see the colorful pipes of the Pompidou Center. Cross Rue du Renard and enter the Pompidou's colorful world of fountains, restaurants, and street performers.*

❿ Pompidou Center

Survey this popular spot from the top of the sloping square. Tubular escalators lead to the museum and a great view.

The Pompidou Center subscribes with gusto to the 20th-century architectural axiom "form follows function." To get a more spacious and functional interior, the guts of this exoskeletal building are draped on the outside and color-coded: vibrant red for people lifts, cool blue for air ducts, eco-green for plumbing, don't-touch-it yellow for electrical stuff, and white for the structure's bones. (Compare the Pompidou Center to another exoskeletal building, Notre-Dame.) For details on visiting the museum, 📖 see the Pompidou Center Tour chapter.

Enjoy the adjacent fountain, an homage to Igor Stravinsky. Jean Tinguely and Niki de Saint-Phalle designed it as a tribute to the composer: Every sculpture within the fountain represents one of his hard-to-hum scores. For low-stress meals or an atmospheric spot for a drink, try the lighthearted Dame Tartine (or

the *crêperie* next door), which overlooks the fountains and serves good, inexpensive food.

• *Double back to Rue du Renard, turn right, and stroll past Paris' ugliest (modern) building on the left. Walk toward the river until you find...*

⓫ Hôtel de Ville

Looking more like a grand château than a public building, Paris' City Hall stands proud. This spot has been the center of city government since 1357. Each of Paris' 20 arrondissements has its own city hall and mayor, but this one is the big daddy of them all.

The Renaissance-style building (built 1533-1628 and reconstructed after a 19th-century fire) displays hundreds of statues of famous Parisians on its facade. Peek from behind the iron fences through the doorways to see elaborate spiral stairways, which are reminiscent of Château de Chambord in the Loire. Playful fountains energize the big, lively square in front.

This spacious stage has seen much of Paris' history. On July 14, 1789, Revolutionaries rallied here on their way to the Bastille. In 1870, it was home to the radical Paris Commune. During World War II, General Charles de Gaulle appeared at the windows to proclaim Paris' liberation from the Nazis. And in 1950, Robert Doisneau snapped a famous black-and-white photo of a kissing couple, with Hôtel de Ville as a romantic backdrop.

Today, it's the seat of the mayor of Paris, who has one of the most powerful positions in France. In the 1990s, Jacques Chirac used the mayorship as a stepping stone to another powerful position—president of France.

The square in front is a gathering place for Parisians. Demonstrators assemble here to speak their minds. Crowds cheer during big soccer games shown on huge TV screens. In summer, the square hosts sand volleyball courts; in winter, a big ice-skating rink. There's often a children's carousel, or *manège*. Now a Paris institution, carousels were first introduced by Henri IV in 1605—the same year Place des Vosges was built. Year-round, the place is always beautifully lit after dark.

After our walk through the Marais, one of the city's oldest neighborhoods, it's appropriate to end up here, at the governmental heart of Paris.

• *The tour's over. The Hôtel de Ville Métro stop is right here, and the towers of Notre-Dame poke above the rooftops to the south.*

PICASSO MUSEUM TOUR

Musée Picasso

The 20th century's most famous and—OK, I'll say it—greatest artist was the master of many styles (Cubism, Surrealism, Expressionism, etc.) and of many media (painting, sculpture, prints, ceramics, and assemblages). Still, he could make anything he touched look unmistakably like "a Picasso."

The Picasso Museum has over 400 of his works, showing the whole range of the artist's long life and many styles. The women he loved and the global events he lived through appear in his canvases, filtered through his own emotional lens. You don't have to admire Picasso's lifestyle or like his modern painting style. But a visit here might make you appreciate the sheer vitality and creativity of this hardworking and unique man.

The core of the museum is organized chronologically—and so is this chapter. Since the collection changes frequently, this is not a painting-by-painting tour. Rather, use the chapter to get an overview of Picasso's life and some of the themes in his work.

Orientation

Cost: €11, covered by Museum Pass, free on first Sun of month and for those under age 18 with ID.

Hours: Tue-Fri 11:30-18:00 (until 21:00 on third Fri of month), Sat-Sun 9:30-18:00, closed Mon, last entry 45 minutes before closing.

Avoiding Lines: You can skip the (usually short) ticket-buying lines by using a Museum Pass or by making a timed-entry reservation at www.musee-picasso.fr.

Getting There: The museum is at 5 Rue de Thorigny, Mo: St. Sébastien-Froissart, St. Paul, or Chemin Vert (see "Marais Walk" map on page 316).

Information: The museum has excellent posted information and a videoguide (€4). Tel. 01 42 71 25 21, www.musee-picasso.fr.
Length of This Tour: Allow one hour.
Photography: Permitted.

PABLO PICASSO (1881-1973)

Born in Spain, Picasso was the son of an art teacher. As a teenager he quickly advanced beyond his teachers. He mastered camera-eye realism but also showed an empathy for the people he painted that was insightful beyond his years. (Unfortunately, the museum has few early works. Many doubters of Picasso's genius warm to him somewhat after seeing his excellent draftsmanship and facility with oils from his youth.) As a teenager in Barcelona, he fell in with a bohemian crowd that mixed wine, women, and art.

In 1900, Picasso set out to make his mark in Paris, the undisputed world capital of culture. He rejected the surname his father had given him (Ruíz) and chose his mother's instead, making it his distinctive one-word brand: Picasso.

The Tour Begins

As you enter the museum courtyard, find the correct line: for ticket buyers (the longest line), for Paris Museum Pass holders, or for timed-entry reservations. After passing through security, you'll see the ticket-buying and videoguide counters.

The museum has five floors. This chapter covers floors 0 to 2, what the museum calls the "Picasso Grand Tour."

• *Show your ticket and enter the first room on floor 0 (labeled "0.1").*

Rooms 0.1-0.3: Early Years

The brash Spaniard quickly became a poor, homesick foreigner, absorbing the styles of many painters (especially Henri de Toulouse-Lautrec) while searching for his own artist's voice. He found companionship among fellow freaks and outcasts on Butte Montmartre, painting jesters, circus performers, and garish cabarets. When his best friend committed suicide (look for the painting *Death of Casagemas*, 1901), Picasso plunged into a **Blue Period**, painting emaciated beggars, hard-eyed pimps, and himself, bundled up against the cold, with eyes all cried out (*Autoportrait*, 1901; see photo at the beginning of the chapter).

In 1904, Picasso moved into his Bateau-Lavoir home/studio on Montmartre, got a steady girlfriend, and suddenly saw the world through rose-colored glasses (the **Rose Period,** though the museum has very few works from this time).

Rooms 0.4 and 0.5: Primitive Masks and Cubist Experiments

Only 25 years old, Picasso reinvented painting. Fascinated by the primitive power of African and Iberian tribal masks, he sketched human faces with simple outlines and almond eyes (*Autoportrait*, 1906). Intrigued by the body of his girlfriend, Fernande Olivier, he sketched it from every angle (the museum has a few nude studies), then experimented with showing several different views on the same canvas.

A hundred paintings and nine months later, Picasso gave birth to a monstrous canvas of five nude, fragmented prostitutes with masklike faces—*Les Demoiselles d'Avignon* (1907). The painting hangs in New York's Museum of Modern Art, but the Picasso Museum has some similar-looking primitive nudes. His friends were speechless over the bold new style, his enemies reviled it, and almost overnight, Picasso was famous.

Picasso went to the Louvre for a special exhibit on Cézanne, then returned to the Bateau-Lavoir to expand on Cézanne's chunky style and geometric simplicity—oval-shaped heads, circular breasts, and diamond thighs. Picasso rejected traditional 3-D. Instead of painting, say, a distant hillside in dimmer tones than the trees in the bright foreground, Picasso did it all bright, making the foreground blend into the background and turning a scene into an abstract design. Modern art was being born.

Room 0.6: Early Cubism

With his next-door neighbor, Georges Braque, Picasso invented Cubism, a fragmented, "cube"-shaped style. He'd fracture a figure (such as the musician in *Man with a Mandolin*, 1911) into a barely recognizable jumble of facets, and facets within facets. Even empty space is composed of these "cubes," all of them the same basic color, that weave together the background and foreground. Picasso sketches reality from every angle, then pastes it all together, a composite of different views. The monochrome color (mostly gray or brown) is less important than the experiments with putting the 3-D world on a 2-D canvas in a modern way. (For more on Cubism, see page 342 of the Pompidou Center Tour.)

• *Head upstairs to floor 1.*

Room 1.1: More Cubist Experiments

Picasso didn't stop there. His first stage had been so-called Analytic Cubism (1910-1913): breaking the world down into small facets, to "analyze" the subject from every angle. Now it was time to "synthesize" it back together with the real world (Synthetic Cubism). He created "constructions" that were essentially still-life paintings (a 2-D illusion) augmented with glued-on, real-life materials—wood, paper, rope, or chair caning (the real 3-D world). The contrast between real objects and painted objects makes it clear that while traditional painting is a mere illusion, art can be more substantial.

In a few short years, Picasso had turned painting in the direction it would go for the next 50 years.

Rooms 1.2-1.6: Family Life, Classicism

Personally, Picasso's life had fragmented into a series of relationships with women. In 1917 he met and married a graceful Russian dancer with the Ballet Russes, Olga Khokhlova (*Portrait of Olga in an Armchair*, 1917).

Soon he was a financially secure husband and father (see the portrait of his three-year-old son, *Paul en Harlequin*, 1924). After the disastrous Great War, Picasso took his family for summer vacations on the Riviera, where he painted peaceful scenes of women and children at the beach. He also moved from Montmartre to the Montparnasse neighborhood. (Over the years, Picasso had 13 different studios in Paris, mainly in Montmartre or Montparnasse.)

A trip to Rome inspired him to emulate the bulky mass of ancient statues, transforming them into plump but graceful

women, with Olga's round features. Picasso could create the illusion of a face or body bulging out from the canvas, like a cameo or classical bas-relief. Watching kids drawing in the sand with a stick, he tried drawing a figure without lifting the brush from the canvas.

In 1927, a middle-aged Picasso stopped a 17-year-old girl outside the Galeries Lafayette department store

Picasso's Women

Women were Picasso's main subject. As an artist, Picasso used women both as models and as muses. Having sex with his model allowed him to paint not just the woman's physical features but also the emotional associations of their relationship. At least, that's what he told his wife.

In today's psychobabble, Picasso was an egotistical and abusive male, a sex addict fueled by his own insecurities and inability to connect intimately with women.

In the lingo of Picasso's crowd—steeped in the psychoanalysis of Freud and Jung—relations with women allowed him to express primal urges, recover repressed memories, confront his relationship with his mother, discover hidden truths, connect with his anima (female side), and re-create the archetypal experiences lived since the beginning of time.

Borrowing from the Surrealist style, Picasso let the id speak in his paintings. His women—a jumble of clashing colors and twisted limbs—open their toothy mouths and scream their frustration (*Large Nude on a Red Armchair,* 1929). The artist and his model often became hopelessly entangled. Picasso needed a big ego to keep his big id out of trouble.

After about 1910, Picasso almost never painted (only sketched) from a posed model. His "portraits" of women were often composites of several different women from his large catalog of memories, filtered through emotional associations.

Throughout the museum, you'll likely see somewhat-recognizable portraits of some of Picasso's models/mistresses/muses:

María Picasso y López—his mom—wrote him a letter almost every day until her death. In childhood, Picasso was raised as a

lone boy among the many women of his extended family.

Dark-haired **Fernande Olivier,** an artist's model who'd lived a wild life, was Picasso's first real love. They lived together (1904-1909) in Montmartre (with a dog and a 10-year-old street urchin they'd taken in) when Picasso was inventing Cubism, and her features are seen in *Les Demoiselles d'Avignon.* Fernande claimed that Picasso locked her in or hid her shoes so she couldn't go out while he was gone.

In May 1913, Fernande left him for good, his father died, and **Eva Gouel** moved in. Picasso launched into Synthetic Cubism. Eva died two years later of tuberculosis.

Elegant **Olga Khokhlova** (1896-1955, see image at bottom left) gave Picasso a son (Pablo Jr.) and 10 years of stability. They lived high class, hobnobbing with the international set surrounding the Ballet Russes.

Blond, athletic **Marie-Thérèse Walter** (1910-1977) knew nothing of art and never mixed with Picasso's sophisticated crowd. But

even as she put on weight, Picasso found her figure worthy of painting. Marie-Thérèse had a classic profile—big chin and long nose with a straight bridge. Picasso would never tire of portraying her prominent features, often seen in paintings and sculpture simply titled *Head of a Woman.* They had a daughter together named Maya (b. 1935).

Sparkly-eyed **Dora Maar** (1909-1998) was the anti-Marie-Thérèse—an artsy, sophisticated woman who could converse with Picasso about his art. He met the photographer over coffee at Les Deux Magots in 1936. She photographed him in his studio working on *Guernica,* and they became romantically involved. Picasso still kept ties with Marie-Thérèse while also working out a complicated divorce from Olga.

In portraits, dark-haired Dora is slender, with long red nails and sparkling, intelligent eyes. She's often pictured crying. Go figure. She's attached to a physically abusive married man who refuses to leave his other mistress.

Françoise Gilot (b. 1921), a painter herself, is often depicted with a flower, perhaps symbolizing the new life (and two children) she gave to an aging Picasso. She stubbornly forced Picasso to sever ties with Dora Maar before she'd settle in. When he dumped her for his next conquest (1954), she went on to write a scathing tell-all book. Their children, Claude and Paloma, grew up amid lawsuits over whether they could use their father's famous last name.

Jacqueline Roque (1927-1986) married the god of painting when he was 80 and she was 33. She outlived him, but later took her own life.

So, I guess Picasso's ideal model would be a composite—a brainy but tubercular dancer with a curvaceous figure, as well as a youthful flower-child who could pose like a prostitute but remind him of his mother.

(by the Opéra Garnier) and said, "Mademoiselle, you have an interesting face. Can I paint it? I am Picasso." She said, "Who?"

The two had little in common, but the unsophisticated Marie-Thérèse Walter and the short, balding artist developed a strange attraction for each other. Soon, Marie-Thérèse moved into the house next door to Picasso and his wife, and they began an awkward three-wheeled relationship. Worldly Olga was jealous, young Marie-Thérèse was insecure and clingy, and Picasso was a workaholic artist who faithfully chronicled the erotic/neurotic experience in canvases of twisted, screaming nudes.

Rooms 1.7 and 1.8: *Guernica*
Europe was gearing up for war. From Paris, Picasso watched as his homeland of Spain erupted in a brutal civil war (1936-1939), in which a half-million of his countrymen died. Many canvases from this period are gray and gloomy. The most famous of Picasso's gray-colored war paintings—*Guernica* (1937)—captured the chaos of a Spanish village caught in an air raid. The Picasso Museum has some of the many studies he did for this monumental canvas (which hangs in Madrid's Reina Sofía museum), employing typical Spanish imagery—bulls, screaming horses, a Madonna. The work summed up the heartache of Spain and foreshadowed the onslaught of World War II. After 1936, Picasso vowed to never again set foot in fascist-controlled Spain, and he never did.
• *Go upstairs to floor 2.*

Room 2.1: Picasso and Spain
The Spaniard lived almost all of his adult life in France, but he remained a Spaniard at heart, incorporating Spanish motifs into his work.

Unrepentantly macho, he loved bullfights, seeing them as a metaphor for the timeless human interaction between the genders. Me bull, you horse, I gore you.

The Minotaur (a bull-headed man) symbolized man's warring halves: half rational human (Freud's superego) and half raging beast (the id). Picasso could be both tender and violent with women, thus playing out both sides of this love/war duality.

Rooms 2.2-2.5: World War II
In 1940, Nazi tanks rolled into Paris. Picasso decided to stay for the duration and live under gray skies and gray uniforms—painting many gray canvases. Not only did he suffer from wartime shortages, condescending Nazis, and the grief of having comrades killed or deported, he had girl trouble. "The worst time of my life," he said. His beloved mother had died, and he endured the endless, bitter

divorce from Olga, all the while juggling his two longtime, feuding mistresses—as well as the occasional fling.

After the pain of the war years, it was time for a change.

Room 2.6: The South of France
Sun! Color! Water! Spacious skies! Freedom!

At war's end, Picasso left Paris and all that emotional baggage behind, finding fun in the sun in the south of France. Sixty-five-year-old Pablo Picasso was reborn, enjoying worldwide fame and the love of a beautiful 23-year-old painter named Françoise Gilot. She soon offered him a fresh start at fatherhood, giving birth to son Claude and daughter Paloma.

Picasso spent mornings swimming in the Mediterranean, days painting, evenings partying with friends, and late nights painting again, like a madman. Dressed in rolled-up white pants and a striped sailor's shirt, bursting with pent-up creativity, he often cranked out more than a painting a day. Ever-restless Picasso had finally found his Garden of Eden and rediscovered his joie de vivre.

He palled around with Henri Matisse, his rival for the title of Century's Greatest Painter. Occasionally they traded masterpieces, letting the other pick out his favorite for his own collection.

Picasso's Riviera works set the tone for the rest of his life—sunny, light-hearted, childlike, experimenting in new media, and using motifs of the sea, Greek mythology (fauns, centaurs), and animals (birds, goats, and pregnant baboons). His childlike doves became an international symbol of peace. These joyous themes announce Picasso's newfound freedom in a newly liberated France.

Rooms 2.7 and 2.8: The Last Years
Picasso was fertile to the end, still painting with bright thick colors at age 91. With no living peers in the world of art, the great Picasso dialogued with dead masters, reworking paintings by Edouard Manet, Diego de Velázquez, and others. Oh yes, also in this period he met mistress number...um, whatever: 27-year-old Jacqueline Roque, whom he later married.

Throughout his long life, Picasso was intrigued by portraying people—always people, ignoring the background—conveying their features with a single curved line and their moods with colors. These last works have the humor and playfulness of someone much younger. It has been said of Picasso, "When he was a child, he painted like a man. When he was old, he painted like a child."

The Rest of the Museum
There's plenty more Picasso on the other two floors. The paintings

Picasso—Master of Many Media

Picasso had an encyclopedic knowledge of art history and a caricaturist's ability to easily "quote" another artist's style, which he would adapt to his own uses. Clever students of art can spot some of Picasso's sources, from Pierre-Auguste Renoir's plump women to Paul Cézanne's chunky surfaces to the simple outlines and bright, Fauvist colors of Henri Matisse.

He was one of the first great artists to branch out from oils on canvas to explore all kinds of new materials. It's so common in the 21st century for artists to work in multimedia that we forget how revolutionary it was when Picasso pioneered it. Ceramics, papier-mâché, statuettes, metalworking, mobiles—Picasso tried his hand at all of these.

Ceramics: The minute Picasso discovered ceramics (1947), the passion consumed him. Working in a small, family-owned ceramics factory in the south of France, he shaped wet clay, painted it, and fired up a dozen or more pieces a day—2,000 in a single year. He created plates with faces, bird-shaped vases, woman-shaped bottles, bull-shaped statues, and colorful tiles. Working in this timeless medium, he gives a Modernist's take on classic motifs: red-and-black Greek vases, fauns, primitive goddesses, Roman amphorae, and so on.

Sculpture: Picture Picasso with goggles and a blowtorch, creating 3-D Cubist statues out of scrap metal and other industrial junk. A true scavenger, Picasso took what he found, played with it, and transformed it into something interesting. Among the statues, find the distinctive features of Marie-Thérèse.

Assemblages: One of Picasso's most famous creations was a bicycle seat with handlebar horns that becomes the *Head of a Bull* (1942). This is quintessential Picasso—a timeless motif (the Minotaur) made of 20th-century materials and done with a twinkle in his eye.

are just as good as what we've seen, but they're organized differently.

The **third floor** has Picasso's private collection of works by painters he admired—Cézanne, his compatriot Braque, and more. Curators have cleverly interspersed these with Picasso's own works, showing how he was inspired by them.

Level -1 is called "The Studios." Each room on this

level has works created in the studios where Picasso worked on Montmartre, in Montparnasse, and elsewhere in Paris, along with photos of the studios. The most famous of the studios were Le Bateau-Lavoir (Room -1.1; see page 381 of the Montmartre Walk chapter) and the Left Bank space where he created *Guernica* (Room -1.3), chronicled here with photographs by Dora Maar.

POMPIDOU CENTER TOUR

Centre Pompidiou

Some people hate modern art. But the Pompidou Center contains what is possibly Europe's best collection of 20th-century art. After the super-serious Louvre and Orsay museums, finish things off with this artistic kick in the pants. You won't find classical beauty here—no dreamy Madonnas-and-children—just a stimulating, offbeat, and, if you like, instructive walk through nearly every art style of the wild-and-crazy last century.

The Pompidou's "permanent" collection...isn't. It changes so often that a painting-by-painting tour is impossible. So this chapter is more a general overview of the major trends of 20th-century art, with emphasis on artists you're likely to find in the Pompidou. Read this chapter ahead of time for background, or take it with you to the museum to look up specific painters as you stumble across their work. See the classics—Picasso, Matisse, etc.—but be sure to leave time to browse the thought-provoking and fun art of more recent artists.

Orientation

Cost: The €14 ticket gets you into all of the building's various exhibits—both the permanent collection (the Musée National d'Art Moderne) and the special exhibits that make this place so edgy. The €3 View of Paris ticket lets you ride to the sixth floor for the view but doesn't cover museum entry. The Museum Pass includes access to the permanent collection, the sixth floor view, and occasional special exhibits (but for special exhibits that are not covered, passholders can't buy a simple supplement to make up the difference).

Buy tickets on the ground floor. If lines are long, use the

red ticket machines (credit cards only). The museum is free on the first Sunday of the month.

Hours: Permanent collection open Wed-Mon 11:00-21:00, closed Tue, ticket counters close at 20:00; rest of the building open later—until 22:00 (Thu until 23:00). To avoid crowds (mainly for the special exhibits), arrive after 17:00.

Getting There: Take the Métro to Rambuteau or Hôtel de Ville. Bus #69 from the Marais and Rue Cler also stops a few blocks away at Hôtel de Ville. The wild, color-coded exterior of the museum makes it about as hard to locate as the Eiffel Tower.

Information: There's a helpful info desk in the lobby. The Espace de Médiation on the fifth floor is the museum's main information office. Note that Parisians call the complex the "Centre Beaubourg" (sahn-truh boh-boor), but official publications call it the "Centre Pompidou." The free "Centre Pompidou" app covers both the permanent collection and special exhibits. Tel. 01 44 78 12 33, www.centrepompidou.fr.

Length of This Tour: Allow one hour.

Services: Baggage check is free and required for bags bigger than a large purse. The terrific museum store on the main floor has zany gift ideas. There's also free Wi-Fi.

Photography: Allowed in the permanent collection, but no flash.

Cuisine Art: You'll find a sandwich-and-coffee café on the mezzanine (nice interior views, a bit pricey for its simple fare) and a gourmet view restaurant on the sixth floor (worth the splurge for a coffee-with-view, though I would not eat here). Outside the museum, the neighborhood abounds with cheap bistros and crêpe stands. My favorite places line the little square south of the museum (look for the playful fountain, an homage to composer Igor Stravinsky). Dame Tartine and Crêperie Beaubourg both have reasonable prices. The Monop' grocery store on the square across from the museum (#135) has all you need for a picnic.

View Art: The sixth floor has stunning views of the Paris cityscape. Your Pompidou ticket or Museum Pass gets you there, or you can buy the €3 View of Paris ticket (good for the sixth floor only; doesn't include museum entry).

Nearby: The studio of sculptor **Constantin Brancusi** (see page 345) is housed in the gray concrete bunker in front of the Pompidou and is free to visit. Brancusi (1876-1957) often hosted Paris' artistic glitterati in his humble studio, where he served home-cooked dishes of his native Romania. After Brancusi's death, the Pompidou Center had the studio reconstructed here. See the unique space and some of his revolutionary work (Wed-Mon 14:00-18:00, closed Tue, same contact info as Pompidou).

Just a few blocks west, the new glass-and-steel canopy covering part of the **Forum des Halles** shopping mall is the centerpiece of a €1 billion facelift that many locals view as a colossal waste of money (see page 485).

Starring: Matisse, Picasso, Chagall, Dalí, Warhol, and contemporary art.

OVERVIEW

That slight tremor you may feel comes from Italy, where Michelangelo has been spinning in his grave ever since 1977, when the Pompidou Center first disgusted Paris. Still, it's an appropriate modern temple for the controversial art it houses.

The building itself is "exoskeletal" (like Notre-Dame, or a crab), with its functional parts—the pipes, heating ducts, and escalator—on the outside and the meaty art inside. It's the epitome of modern architecture, where "form follows function."

This chapter covers the Musée National d'Art Moderne: Collection Permanente (labeled simply *Musée* on signs), which is on the fourth and fifth floors. But there's plenty more art scattered all over the building. Ask at the ground-floor information booth, or just wander. Generally, art from 1905 to 1980 is on the fifth floor (the core of this chapter), while the fourth floor contains more recent art. But 20th-century art resents being put in chronological order, and the Pompidou's collection is rarely in any neat-and-tidy arrangement. Use the museum's floor plans (posted on the wall) to find select artists. The museum is bigger than you think—and you're smart to focus on a limited number of artists. Don't hesitate to ask, *"Où est Kandinsky?"*

Remember, the following text is not a "tour" of the museum— it's a chronological overview of modern art.

The Tour Begins

• *Buy your ticket on the ground floor, then ride up the escalator (or run up the down escalator to get in the proper mood). When you see the view, your opinion of the Pompidou's exterior should improve a good 15 percent. Find the permanent collection—the entrance is either on the fourth or fifth floor (it varies). Enter and show your ticket.*

Start your tour on the fifth floor, make several spins, and click your heels. Toto, we're not in Kansas anymore.

FIFTH FLOOR: MODERN ART (1905-1980)

A.D. 1900: A new century dawns. War is a thing of the past. Science will wipe out poverty and disease. Rational Man is poised for a new era of peace and prosperity...

Right. This cozy Victorian dream was soon shattered by two world wars and rapid technological change. Nietzsche murdered God. Freud washed ashore on the beach of a vast new continent inside each of us. Einstein made everything merely "relative." Even the fundamental building blocks of the universe, atoms, were behaving erratically.

The 20th century—accelerated by technology and fragmented by war—was exciting and chaotic, and the art reflects the turbulence of that century of change.

Paris in the early 1900s was the cradle of modern art. For the previous 300 years (1600-1900), Paris had been the capital of the wealthiest, most civilized nation on earth. Europe's major artists—most of whom spoke French—flocked to Paris, knowing that if you could make it there, you'd make it anywhere.

The groundwork of modern art was first laid by the Impressionists and Post-Impressionists in the late 1800s. They pioneered the notion that the painted surface—of thick, colorful brushstrokes—was as inherently interesting as the subject itself. You can almost see the evolution: Monet's blurry *Water Lilies* canvases are patterns of color similar to a purely abstract canvas. Van Gogh would build a figure out of brushstrokes of different colors, Cezanne would turn those brushstrokes into patches of paint, then Picasso sharpened those patches into "cubes," which he would later shatter beyond recognition.

As you tour the Pompidou, remember that most of the artists, including foreigners, spent their formative years in Paris. In the 1910s, funky Montmartre was the mecca of Modernism—the era of Picasso, Braque, and Matisse. In the 1920s the center shifted to the grand cafés of Montparnasse, where painters mingled with American expats such as Ernest Hemingway and Gertrude Stein. During World War II, it was Jean-Paul Sartre's Existentialist scene around St. Germain-des-Prés. After World War II, the global art focus moved to New York, but by the late 20th century, Paris had reemerged as a cultural touchstone for the world of modern art.

Fauvism

The Fauves ("wild beasts") were artists inspired by African and Oceanic masks and voodoo dolls; they tried to inject a bit of the jungle into bored French society. The result? Modern art that looked primitive: long, masklike faces with almond eyes; bright, clashing colors; simple figures; and "flat," two-dimensional scenes.

POMPIDOU

Henri Matisse (1869-1954)

Matisse's colorful "wallpaper" works are not realistic. A man is a few black lines and blocks of paint. The colors are unnaturally bright. There's no illusion of the distance and 3-D that were so important to Renaissance Italians. The "distant" landscape is as bright as any close-up, and the slanted lines meant to suggest depth are crudely done.

Traditionally, the canvas was like a window you looked "through" to see a slice of the real world stretching off into the distance. Now, a camera could do that better. With Matisse, you look "at" the canvas, like wallpaper. Voilà! What was a crudely drawn scene now becomes a sophisticated and decorative pattern of colors and shapes.

Though fully "modern," Matisse built on 19th-century art—the bright colors of Vincent van Gogh, the primitive figures of Paul Gauguin, the colorful designs of Japanese prints, and the Impressionist patches of paint that blend together only at a distance.

Cubism and Beyond

I throw a rock at a glass statue, shatter it, pick up the pieces, and glue them onto a canvas. I'm a Cubist.

Pablo Picasso (1881-1973) and
Georges Braque (1882-1963)

Born in Spain, Picasso moved to Paris as a young man, settling into a studio (Le Bateau-Lavoir) in Montmartre (see page 381). He worked with next-door neighbor Georges Braque in poverty so dire they often didn't know where their next bottle of wine was coming from. They corrected each other's paintings (it's hard to tell whose is whose without the titles), and they shared ideas, meals, and girlfriends while inventing a whole new way to look at the world.

They show the world through a kaleidoscope of brown and gray. The subjects are somewhat recognizable (with the help of the titles), but they are broken into geometric shards (let's call them "cubes," though there are many different shapes), then pieced back together.

Cubism gives us several different angles of the subject at once—say, a woman seen from the front and side angles simultaneously, resulting in two eyes on the same side of the nose. This involves showing three dimensions, plus Einstein's new fourth dimension, the time it takes to walk around the subject to see other angles. Newfangled motion pictures could capture this moving 4-D world, but how to do it on a 2-D canvas? The Cubist "solution" is a kind of Mercator projection, where the round world is sliced up like an orange peel and then laid as flat as possible.

Notice how the "cubes" often overlap. A single cube might contain both an arm (in the foreground) and the window behind (in the background), both painted the same color. The foreground and the background are woven together, so that the subject dissolves into a pattern.

Picasso's Synthetic Cubism and Other Periods

If the Cubists were as smart as Einstein, why couldn't they draw a picture to save their lives? Picasso was one modern artist who could draw exceptionally well (see his partly finished *Harlequin*). But he constantly explored and adapted his style to new trends, and so became the most famous painter of the century. Scattered throughout the museum are works from the many periods of Picasso's life.

Picasso soon began to use more colorful "cubes" (1912-1915). Eventually, he used curved shapes to build the subject, rather than the straight-line shards of early Cubism.

Picasso married and had children. Works from this period (the 1920s) are more realistic, with full-bodied (and big-nosed) women and children. He tries to capture the solidity, serenity, and volume of classical statues.

As his relationships with women deteriorated, he vented his sexual demons by twisting the female body into grotesque balloon-animal shapes (1925-1931).

All through his life, Picasso explored new materials. He made collages, tried his hand at making "statues" out of wood, wire, or whatever, and even made statues out of everyday household objects. These multimedia works, so revolutionary at the time, have become stock-in-trade today.

📖 For more about Picasso, see the Picasso Museum chapter.

Marc Chagall (1887-1985)

At age 22, Marc Chagall arrived in Paris with the wide-eyed wonder of a country boy. Lovers are weightless with bliss. Animals smile and wink at us.

Musicians, poets, peasants, and dreamers ignore gravity, tumbling in slow-motion circles high above the rooftops. The colors are deep, dark, and earthy—a pool of mystery with figures bleeding through below the surface. (Chagall claimed his early poverty forced him to paint over used canvases, inspiring the overlapping images.)

Chagall's very personal style fuses many influences. He was raised in a small Belarus village, which explains his "naive" outlook and fiddler-on-the-roof motifs. His simple figures are like Russian Orthodox icons, and his Jewish roots produced Old Testament themes. Stylistically, he's thoroughly modern—Cubist shards, bright Fauve colors, and Primitive simplification. This otherworldly style was a natural for religious works, and so his murals and stained glass, which feature both Jewish and Christian motifs, decorate buildings around the world—including the ceiling of Paris' Opéra Garnier (see page 88).

Fernand Léger (1881-1955)

Fernand Léger's style has been called "Tubism"—breaking the world down into cylinders, rather than cubes. (He supposedly got his inspiration during World War I from the gleaming barrel of a cannon.) Léger captures the feel of the encroaching Age of Machines, with all the world looking like an internal-combustion engine.

Abstract Art

Abstract art simplifies. A man becomes a stick figure. A squiggle is a wave. A streak of red expresses anger. Arches make you want a cheeseburger. These are universal symbols that everyone from a caveman to a banker understands. Abstract artists capture the essence of reality in a few lines and colors, and they capture things even a camera can't— emotions, abstract concepts, musical rhythms, and spiritual states of mind. Again, with abstract art, you don't look *through* the canvas to see the visual world, but *at* it to read the symbolism of lines, shapes, and colors.

Wassily Kandinsky (1866-1944)

The bright colors, bent lines, and lack of symmetry tell us that Kandinsky's world was passionate and intense.

Notice titles like *Improvisation* and

Composition. Kandinsky was inspired by music, an art form that's also "abstract," though it still packs a punch. Like a jazz musician improvising a new pattern of notes from a set scale, Kandinsky plays with new patterns of related colors as he looks for just the right combination. Using lines and color, Kandinsky translates the unseen reality into a new medium...like lightning crackling over the radio. Go, man, go.

Piet Mondrian (1872-1944)

Like a blueprint for Modernism, Mondrian's T-square style boils painting down to its basic building blocks (black lines, white canvas)

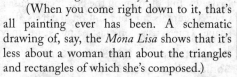

and the three primary colors (red, yellow, and blue), all arranged in orderly patterns.

(When you come right down to it, that's all painting ever has been. A schematic drawing of, say, the *Mona Lisa* shows that it's less about a woman than about the triangles and rectangles of which she's composed.)

Mondrian started out painting realistic landscapes of the orderly fields in his native Netherlands. Increasingly, he simplified them into horizontal and vertical patterns. For Mondrian, who was heavy into Eastern mysticism, "up vs. down" and "left vs. right" were the perfect metaphors for life's dualities: "good vs. evil," "body vs. spirit," "man vs. woman." The canvas is a bird's-eye view of Mondrian's personal landscape.

Constantin Brancusi (1876-1957)

Brancusi's curved, shiny statues reduce objects to their essence. A bird is a single stylized wing, the one feature that sets it apart from other animals. He rounds off to the closest geometrical form, so a woman's head becomes a perfect oval on a cubic pedestal.

Humans love symmetry (maybe because our own bodies are roughly symmetrical) and find geometric shapes restful, even worthy of meditation. Brancusi follows the instinct for order that has driven art from earliest times, from circular Stonehenge and Egyptian pyramids, to Greek columns and Roman arches, to Renaissance symmetry and the Native American "medicine wheel."

POMPIDOU

POMPIDOU

Paul Klee (1879-1940)

Paul Klee's small and playful canvases are deceptively simple, containing shapes so basic they can be read as universal symbols. Klee thought a wavy line, for example, would always suggest motion, whereas a stick figure would always mean a human—like the psychiatrist Carl Jung's universal dreams and symbols manifesting the "collective unconscious."

Klee saw these universals in the art of children, who express themselves without censoring or cluttering things up with learning. His art has a childlike playfulness and features simple figures painted in an uninhibited frame of mind.

Klee also turned to nature. The same forces that cause the wave to draw a line of foam on the beach can cause a meditative artist to draw a squiggly line of paint on a canvas. The result is a universal shape. True artists don't just paint nature, they become Nature.

Robert Delaunay (1885-1941) and
Sonia Delaunay (1885-1979)

This married couple both painted colorful, fragmented canvases (including a psychedelic Eiffel Tower) that prove the modern style doesn't have to be ugly or enigmatic.

Applied Arts: Gerrit Rietveld (1888-1964) and Alvar Aalto (1898-1976)

If you can't handle modern art, sit on it! (Actually, please don't.) The applied arts—chairs, tables, lamps, and vases—are as much a part of the art world as the fine arts. (Some say the first art object was the pot.) As machines became as talented as humans, artists embraced new technology and mass production to bring beauty to the masses.

World War I: The Death of Values

Ankle-deep in mud, a soldier shivers in a trench, waiting to be ordered "over the top." He'll have to run through barbed wire, over fallen comrades, and into a hail of machine-gun fire, only to capture a few hundred yards of meaningless territory that will be lost the next day. This soldier was not thinking about art.

World War I left nine million dead. (During the war, France lost more men in the Battle of Verdun than America lost in the entire Vietnam War.) The war also killed the optimism and faith in mankind that had guided Europe since the Renaissance. Now, rationality just meant schemes, technology meant machines of death, and morality meant giving your life for an empty cause.

Expressionism

Cynicism and decadence settled over postwar Europe, and artists such as Ernst Ludwig Kirchner, Max Beckmann, George Grosz, Chaïm Soutine, Otto Dix, and Oskar Kokoschka recorded it. They "expressed" their disgust by showing a distorted reality that emphasized the ugly. Using the lurid colors and simplified figures of the Fauves, they slapped paint on in thick brushstrokes and depicted a hypocritical, hard-edged, dog-eat-dog world that had

lost its bearings. The people have a haunted look in their eyes—the fixed stare of corpses and those who have to bury them.

Dada

When people could grieve no longer, they turned to grief's giddy twin: laughter. The war made all old values, including art, a

joke. The Dada movement, choosing a purposely childish name, made art that was intentionally outrageous: a moustache on the *Mona Lisa*, a shovel hung on a wall, or a modern version of a Renaissance "fountain"—a urinal (by either Marcel Duchamp, or I. P. Freeley, 1917). It was a dig at all the pompous prewar artistic theories based on the noble intellect of Rational Women and Men. While the

experts ranted on, Dadaists sat in the back of the class and made cultural fart noises.

Hey, I love this stuff. My mind says it's sophomoric, but my heart belongs to Dada.

Surrealism

Greek statues with sunglasses, a man as a spinning top, shoes becoming feet, and black ants as musical notes...Surrealism. The world was moving fast, and Surrealist artists such as Salvador Dalí, Max Ernst, and René Magritte caught the jumble of images. The artist scatters seemingly unrelated items on the canvas, which leaves us to trace the links in a kind of connect-the-dots without numbers. If it comes together, the synergy of unrelated things can be pretty startling. But even if the juxtaposed images don't ultimately connect, the artist has made you think, rerouting your thoughts through new neural paths. If you don't "get" it...you got it.

Complicating the modern world was Freud's discovery of the

"unconscious" mind that thinks dirty thoughts while we sleep. Many a Surrealist canvas is an uncensored, stream-of-consciousness "landscape" of these deep urges, revealed in the bizarre images of dreams.

In dreams, sometimes one object can be two things at once: "I dreamt that you walked in with a cat...no, wait, maybe you *were* the cat...no...." Surrealists paint opposites like these and let them speak for themselves.

Salvador Dalí (1904-1989)

Salvador Dalí could draw exceptionally well. He painted "unreal" scenes with photographic realism, thus making us believe they could

really happen. Seeing familiar objects in an unfamiliar setting—like a grand piano adorned with disembodied heads of Lenin—creates an air of mystery, the feeling that anything can happen. That's both exciting and unsettling. Dalí's images—crucifixes, political and religious figures, naked bodies—pack an emotional punch. Take one mixed bag of reality, jumble in a blender, and serve on a canvas...Surrealism.

Abstract Surrealists

Abstract artists such as Joan Miró, Alexander Calder, and Jean Arp described their subconscious urges using color and shapes alone, like Rorschach inkblots in reverse.

The thin-line scrawl of Joan Miró's work is like the doodling of a three-year-old. You'll recognize crudely drawn birds, stars, animals, and strange cell-like creatures with whiskers ("Biological Cubism"). Miró was trying to express the most basic of human emotions using the most basic of techniques.

Alexander Calder's mobiles hang like Mirós in the sky, waiting for a gust of wind to bring them to life.

And talk about a primal image! Jean Arp builds human beings out of amoeba-like shapes.

More Modernists

Georges Rouault (1871-1958)

Young Georges Rouault was apprenticed to a maker of stained-glass windows. Enough said?

His paintings have the same thick, glowing colors, heavy black outlines, simple subjects, and (mostly) religious themes. The style is modern, but the mood is medieval, solemn, and melancholy. Rouault captures the tragic spirit of those people—clowns, prostitutes, and sons of God—who have been made outcasts by society.

Decorative Art
Most 20th-century paintings are a mix of the real world ("representation") and the colorful patterns of "abstract" art. Artists purposely distort camera-eye reality to make the resulting canvas more decorative. So, Picasso flattens a woman into a pattern of colored shapes, Pierre Bonnard makes a man from a shimmer of golden paint, and Balthus turns a boudoir scene into colorful wallpaper.

Patterns and Textures
Increasingly, you'll have to focus your eyes to look *at* the canvases, not *through* them, especially in art by Jean Dubuffet, Lucio Fontana, and Karel Appel.

Enjoy the lines and colors, but also a new element: texture. Some works have very thick paint piled on—you can see the brushstroke clearly. Some have substances besides paint applied to the canvas, such as Dubuffet's brown, earthy rectangles of real dirt and organic waste. Fontana punctures the canvas so that the fabric itself (and the hole) becomes the subject. Artists show their skill by mastering new materials. The canvas is a tray, serving up a delightful array of different substances with interesting colors, patterns, shapes, and textures.

Alberto Giacometti (1901-1966)
Giacometti's skinny statues have the emaciated, haunted, and faceless look of concentration camp survivors. The simplicity of the figures may be "primitive," but these aren't stately, sturdy, Easter Island heads. Here, man is weak in the face of technology and the winds of history.

Abstract Expressionism
America emerged from World War II as the globe's superpower. With Europe in ruins, New York replaced Paris as the art capital of the world. The trend was toward bigger canvases, abstract designs, and experimentation with new materials and techniques. It was called "Abstract Expressionism"—expressing emotions and ideas using color and form alone.

Jackson Pollock (1912-1956)
"Jack the Dripper" attacks convention with a can of paint, dripping and splashing a dense web onto the canvas. Picture Pollock in his

studio, as he jives to the hi-fi, bounces off the walls, and throws paint in a moment of enlightenment. Of course, the artist loses some control this way—control over the paint flying in midair and over himself, now in an ecstatic trance. Painting becomes a whole-body activity, a "dance" between the artist and his materials.

The act of creating is what's important, not the final product. The canvas is only a record of that moment of ecstasy.

Barnett Newman (1905-1970) and
Robert Rauschenberg (1925-2008)

All those huge, sparse canvases with just a few lines or colors—what reality are they trying to show?

In the modern world, we find ourselves insignificant specks in a vast and indifferent universe. Every morning each of us must confront that big, blank, existentialist canvas and decide how we're going to make our mark on it. Like, wow.

Another influence was the simplicity of Japanese landscape painting. A Zen master studies and meditates for years to achieve the state of mind in which he can draw one pure line. These canvases, again, are only a record of that state of enlightenment. (What is the sound of one brush painting?)

On more familiar ground, postwar painters were following in the footsteps of artists such as Mondrian, Klee, and Kandinsky (whose work they must have considered "busy"). The geometrical forms here reflect the same search for order, but these artists painted to the 5/4 asymmetry of Dave Brubeck's jazz classic, "Take Five."

Pop Art

America's postwar wealth made the consumer king. Pop Art is created from the "pop"-ular objects of that throwaway society—a soup can, a car fender, mannequins, tacky plastic statues, movie icons, advertising posters.

Is this art? Are all these mass-produced objects beautiful? Or crap? If they're not art, why do we work so hard to acquire them? Pop Art, like Dada, questions our society's values.

Andy Warhol (1928-1987)

Warhol (who coined the idea of everyone having "15 minutes of fame" and became a pop star himself) concentrated on another mass-produced phenomenon: celebrities. He took publicity photos of famous people and repeated them. The repetition—like the constant bombardment we get from repeated images on television—cheapens even the most beautiful things.

Pop Art makes you reassess what

"beauty" really is. Take something out of Sears and hang it in a museum and you have to think about it in a wholly different way.

• *Head to the fourth floor for more contemporary art.*

FOURTH FLOOR: CONTEMPORARY ART FROM 1980 TO THE PRESENT

The "modern" world is history. Picasso and his ilk are now gathering dust and boring art students everywhere. Minimalist painting and abstract sculpture are old-school. Enter the "postmodern" world, as seen through the eyes of current artists.

You'll see fewer traditional canvases or sculptures. Artists have traded paintbrushes for blowtorches (Miró said he was out to "murder" painting), and blowtorches for computer mice. Mixed-media work is the norm, combining painting, sculpture, photography, video/film, digital graphics and computer programming, new resins, plastics, industrial techniques, and lighting and sound systems.

The Pompidou groups the work of these artists under somewhat arbitrary labels—the artist as documentarian, as an archivist of events, or as a producer of commercial goods. Don't worry about trying to understand these cryptic conceptual labels. Browse the floor and enjoy some of the following trends:

Installations: An entire room is given to an artist to prepare. Like entering an art funhouse, you walk in without quite knowing what to expect. (I'm always thinking, "Is this safe?") Using the latest technology, the artist engages all your senses by controlling the lights, sounds, and sometimes even the smells.

Digital Media: Holograms replace material objects, and elaborate computer programming creates a fantastic multimedia display.

Assemblages: Artists raid Dumpsters, recycling junk into the building blocks for larger "assemblages." Each piece is intended to be interesting and tell its own story, and so is the whole sculpture. Weird, useless Rube Goldberg machines make fun of technology.

Natural Objects: A rock in an urban setting is inherently interesting.

The Occasional Canvas: This comes as a familiar relief. Artists of the New Realism labor over painstaking, hyper-realistic canvases to re-create the glossy look of a photo or video image.

Interaction: Some exhibits require your participation, whether you push a button to get the contraption going, touch something, or just walk around the room. In some cases the viewer "does" art, rather than just staring at it. If art is really meant to change, it has to move you—literally.

Deconstruction: Late-20th-century artists critiqued (or "deconstructed") society by examining our underlying assumptions.

One way to do it is to take a familiar object (say, a crucifix) out of its normal context (a church), and place it in a new setting (a jar of urine). Video and film can deconstruct something by playing it over and over, ad nauseam. Ad copy painted on canvas deconstructs itself.

Conceptual Art: The *concept* of which object to pair with another to produce maximum effect is the key. (Crucifix + urine = million-dollar masterpiece.)

Postmodernism: Artists shamelessly recycled older styles and motifs to create new combinations: Greek columns paired with Gothic arches, Christmas lights, and a hip-hop soundtrack.

Performance Art: This is a kind of mixed media of live performance. Many artists—who in another day would have painted canvases—have turned to music, dance, theater, and performance art. This art form is often interactive, by dropping the illusion of a performance and encouraging audience participation. When you finish with the Pompidou Center, go outside for some of the street theater.

Playful Art: Children love the art being produced today. If it doesn't put a smile on your face, well, then you must be a jaded grump like me, who's seen the same repetitious s#%t passed off as "daring" since Warhol stole it from Duchamp. I mean, it's *so* 20th century.

PERE LACHAISE CEMETERY TOUR

Cimetière du Père Lachaise

Enclosed by a massive wall and lined with 5,000 trees, the peaceful, car-free lanes and dirt paths of Père Lachaise cemetery encourage parklike meandering. Named for Father *(Père)* La Chaise, whose job was listening to Louis XIV's sins, the cemetery is relatively new, having opened in 1804 to accommodate Paris' expansion. Today, this city of the dead (pop. 70,000) still accepts new residents, but real estate prices are sky high (a 21-square-foot plot costs more than €11,000).

The 100-acre cemetery is big and confusing, with thousands of graves and tombs crammed every which way, and only a few pedestrian pathways to help you navigate. The maps available from a nearby florist or from street vendors can help guide your way (see below), but you're better off taking my tour as you play grave-hunt with the cemetery's other visitors. This walk takes you on a one-way tour between two convenient Métro/bus stops (Gambetta and Père Lachaise), connecting a handful of graves from some of this necropolis' best-known residents.

Orientation

Cost: Free.

Hours: Mon-Fri 8:00-18:00, Sat 8:30-18:00, Sun 9:00-18:00, until 17:30 in winter.

Getting There: Take bus #69 eastbound to the end of the line at Place Gambetta (see the Bus #69 Sightseeing Tour chapter), or ride the Métro to the Gambetta stop (not to the Père Lachaise stop), exit at Gambetta Métro, and take *sortie* #3 (Père Lachaise exit). From Place Gambetta, it's a two-block walk past McDonald's and up Avenue du Père Lachaise to the cemetery.

Information: Maps are sold at J Poulain & Fils, a florist across from the Porte Gambetta entrance (about €2), or from wandering street vendors for a little more. An unofficial website, www. pere-lachaise.com, has a searchable map. Tel. 01 55 25 82 10.

Length of This Tour: Allow 1.5 hours for this walk and another 30 minutes for your own detours. Bring good walking shoes for the rough, cobbled streets.

Services: WCs are at the start of this tour, just inside the Porte Gambetta entrance (up to the right), and at the end of this tour, to the right just before you exit Porte Principale.

Eating: You'll pass several cafés and a small grocery shop between Place Gambetta and the cemetery. After the tour, you can walk downhill from the cemetery on Rue de la Roquette to a gaggle of lively, affordable cafés on the right side of the street, near the return stop for bus #69.

Starring: Oscar Wilde, Edith Piaf, Gertrude Stein, Molière, Jim Morrison, Frédéric Chopin, Héloïse and Abélard, Colette, and Rossini.

OVERVIEW

From the Porte Gambetta entrance, we'll walk roughly southwest (mostly downhill) through the cemetery. At the end of the tour, we'll exit Porte Principale onto Boulevard de Ménilmontant, near the Père Lachaise Métro entrance and another bus #69 stop. (You could follow the tour heading the other direction, but it's not recommended—it's confusing, and almost completely uphill.)

Be sure to keep referring to the map on page 357, and follow street signs posted at intersections. The layout of the cemetery makes an easy-to-follow tour impossible. It's a little easier if you buy a more detailed map to use along with our rather general one. Be patient, make a few discoveries of your own, and ask passersby for graves you can't locate.

The Tour Begins

• *Entering the cemetery at the Porte Gambetta entrance, walk straight up Avenue des Combattants Etrangers past world war memorials, cross Avenue Transversale No. 3, pass the first building, and look left to the...*

❶ Columbarium/Crematorium

Marked by a dome with a gilded flame and working chimneys

on top, the columbarium sits in a courtyard surrounded by about 1,300 niches, small cubicles for cremated remains, often decorated with real or artificial flowers.

Beneath the courtyard (steps leading underground) are about 12,000 smaller niches, including one for Maria Callas (1923-1977), an American-born opera diva known for her versatility, flair for drama, and affair with Aristotle Onassis (niche #16258, down aisle J).

• *Turn around and walk back to the intersection with Avenue Transversale No. 3. Turn right, heading southeast on the avenue, turn left on Avenue Carette, and walk half a block to the block-of-stone tomb (on the left) with heavy-winged angels trying to fly.*

❷ Oscar Wilde (1854-1900)

The writer and martyr to homosexuality is mourned by "outcast men" (as the inscription says) and by wearers of heavy lipstick, who used to cover the tomb and the angels' emasculated privates with kisses. (Now the tomb is behind glass, which has not stopped committed kissers.) Despite Wilde's notoriety, an inscription says, "He died fortified by the Sacraments of the Church." There's a short résumé scratched (in English) into the back side of the tomb. For more on Wilde and his death in Paris, see the sidebar on page 282.

> *"Alas, I am dying beyond my means."*
>
> —Oscar Wilde

• *Continue along Avenue Carette and turn right (southeast) down Avenue Circulaire. Almost two blocks down, you'll reach Gertrude Stein's unadorned, easy-to-miss grave (on the right, just before a beige-yellow stone structure—if you reach Avenue Pacthod, you've passed it by about 30 yards).*

❸ Gertrude Stein (1874-1946)

While traveling through Europe, the twentysomething American dropped out of med school and moved to Paris, her home for the rest of her life. She shared an apartment at 27 Rue de Fleurus (a couple of blocks west of Luxembourg Garden) with her brother Leo and, later, with her life partner, Alice B. Toklas (who's also buried here, see gravestone's flipside). Every Saturday night, Paris' brightest artistic lights converged *chez vingt-sept* (at 27) for dinner and intellectual stimulation. Picasso painted her portrait,

PÈRE LACHAISE

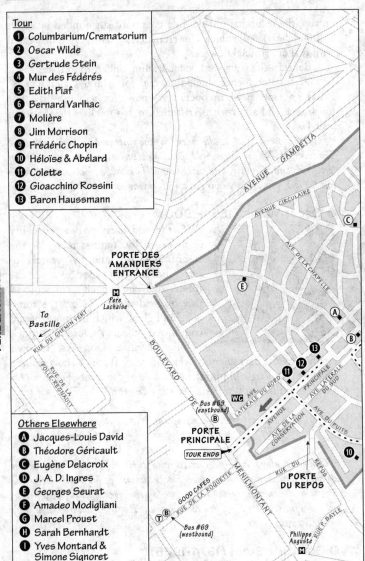

Tour
1. Columbarium/Crematorium
2. Oscar Wilde
3. Gertrude Stein
4. Mur des Fédérés
5. Edith Piaf
6. Bernard Varlhac
7. Molière
8. Jim Morrison
9. Frédéric Chopin
10. Héloïse & Abélard
11. Colette
12. Gioacchino Rossini
13. Baron Haussmann

Others Elsewhere
A. Jacques-Louis David
B. Théodore Géricault
C. Eugène Delacroix
D. J. A. D. Ingres
E. Georges Seurat
F. Amadeo Modigliani
G. Marcel Proust
H. Sarah Bernhardt
I. Yves Montand & Simone Signoret

Hemingway sought her approval, and Virgil Thompson set her words to music.

America discovered "Gerty" in 1933 when her memoirs, the slyly titled *Autobiography of Alice B. Toklas*, hit the best-seller list. After 30 years away, she returned to the United States for a triumphant lecture tour. Her writing is less well known than her persona, except for the oft-quoted, "A rose is a rose is a rose."

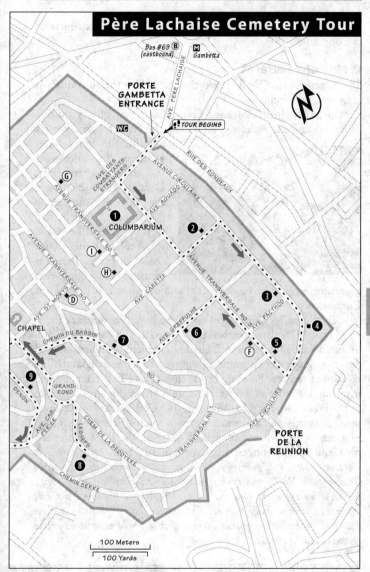

Père Lachaise Cemetery Tour

Stein's last words: When asked, "What is the answer?" she replied, "What is the question?"

• *Ponder Stein's tomb again and again and again, and continue southeast on Avenue Circulaire to where it curves to the right. Emaciated statues remember victims of the concentration camps and Nazi resistance heroes. Pebbles on the tombstones represent Jewish prayers. About 50 yards past Avenue Pacthod, veer left off the road where you see the green*

Avenue Circulaire street sign to find the wall marked Aux Morts de la Commune.

❹ Mur des Fédérés

The "Communards' Wall" marks the place where the quixotic Paris Commune came to a violent end.

In 1870, Prussia invaded France, and the country quickly collapsed and surrendered—all except the city of Paris. For six

months, through a bitter winter, the Prussians laid siege to the city. Defiant Paris held out, even opposing the French government, which had fled to Versailles and was collaborating with the Germans. Parisians formed an opposition government that was revolutionary and socialist, called the Paris Commune.

The Versailles government sent French soldiers to retake Paris. In May of 1871, they breached the west walls and swept eastward. French soldiers fought French citizens, and tens of thousands died during a bloody week of street fighting (La Semaine Sanglante). The remaining resisters holed up inside the walls of Père Lachaise and made an Alamo-type last stand before they were finally overcome.

At dawn on May 28, 1871, the 147 Communards were lined up against this wall and shot by French soldiers. They were buried in a mass grave where they fell. With them the Paris Commune died, and the city entered five years of martial law.

• *Return to the road, continue to the next (unmarked) street, Avenue Transversale No. 3, and turn right. A half-block uphill, Edith Piaf's grave is on the right. It's one grave off the street, behind a white tombstone with a small gray cross (Salvador family). Edith Gassion-Piaf rests among many graves. Hers is often adorned with photos, fresh flowers, and love notes.*

❺ Edith Piaf (1915-1963)

A child of the Parisian streets, Piaf was raised in her grandma's bordello and her father's traveling circus troupe. The teenager sang for spare change in Paris' streets, where a nightclub owner discovered her. Waif-like and dressed in black, she sang in a warbling voice under the

name "La Môme Piaf" (The Little Sparrow). She became the toast of pre-WWII Paris society.

Her offstage love life was busy and often messy, including a teenage pregnancy (her daughter is buried along with her, in a grave marked *Marcelle Dupont, 1933-1935*), a murdered husband, and a heartbreaking affair with costar Yves Montand.

With her strong but trembling voice, she buoyed French spirits under the German occupation, and her most famous song, "La Vie en Rose" (The Rosy Life) captured the joy of postwar Paris. In her personal life she struggled with alcohol, painkillers, and poor health, while onstage she sang, *"Non, je ne regrette rien"* ("No, I don't regret anything").

• *From Edith Piaf's grave, continue uphill, cross Avenue Pacthod, and turn left on the next street, Avenue Greffulhe. Follow Greffulhe straight for roughly 80 yards until you reach a shiny black grave on the left, just beyond a grave with a huge cylindrical statue on it (before crossing Avenue Transversale No. 2).*

❻ Bernard Verlhac (pseudonym Tignous, 1957-2015)

A cartoonist for the French satirical magazine *Charlie Hebdo*, Tignous was one of 12 people assassinated by terrorists at the magazine's office in January 2015. *Charlie Hebdo* had long attracted controversy and episodes of violence due to its inflammatory cartoons of the Prophet Muhammad. The magazine's editor-in-chief, Stéphane Charbonnier, who also was killed in the attack, once said about their work: "We have to carry on until Islam has been rendered as banal as Catholicism."

Look for some of Tignous' old cartoons, as well as notes left for him, many bearing the slogan of solidarity expressed around the world: *"Je suis Charlie."*

• *Continue down Avenue Greffulhe (even when it narrows) until it dead-ends at Avenue Transversale No. 1. Cross the street and venture down a dirt section that veers slightly to the right, then make a hard right onto another dirt lane named Chemin Molière et La Fontaine. Molière lies 30 yards down, on the right side of the street, just beyond the highest point of this lane.*

❼ Molière (1622-1675)

In 1804, the great comic playwright was the first to be reburied in Père Lachaise, a publicity stunt that gave instant prestige to the new cemetery.

Born in Paris, Molière was not of noble blood, but as

the son of the king's furniture supervisor, he had connections. The 21-year-old Molière joined a troupe of strolling players who ranked very low on the social scale, touring the provinces. Twelve long years later, they returned to Paris to perform before Louis XIV. Molière, by now an accomplished comic actor, cracked the king up. He was instantly famous—writing, directing, and often starring in his own works. He satirized rich nobles, hypocritical priests, and quack doctors, creating enemies in high places.

On February 17, 1675, an aging Molière went on stage in the title role of his latest comedy, *The Imaginary Invalid*. Though sick, he insisted he had to go on, concerned for all the little people. His role was of a hypochondriac who coughs to get sympathy. The deathly ill Molière effectively faked coughing fits...which soon turned to real convulsions. The unaware crowd roared with laughter while his fellow players fretted in the wings.

In the final scene, Molière's character becomes a doctor himself in a mock swearing-in ceremony. The ultimate trouper, Molière finished his final line—*"Juro"* ("I accept")—and collapsed while coughing blood. The audience laughed hysterically. He died shortly thereafter.

Irony upon irony for the master of satire: Molière—a sick man whose doctors thought he was a hypochondriac—dies playing a well man who is a hypochondriac, succumbing onstage while the audience cheers.

Molière lies next to his friend and fellow writer, La Fontaine (1621-1695), who wrote a popular version of Aesop's Fables.

> *"We die only once, and for such a long time."*
>
> —Molière

• *Continue downhill on Chemin Molière et La Fontaine (which becomes the paved Chemin du Bassin), and turn left where it ends on Avenue de la Chapelle. Twenty steps down, find the ticket-littered grave of* **Gilbert Morard**, *father of the Paris Métro. Add your Métro ticket and continue to the Rond Point roundabout intersection.*

Cross Carrefour Rond Point and continue straight (opposite where you entered, on unmarked Chemin de la Bédoyère). Just a few steps along, turn right onto Chemin Lauriston. Keep to the left at the fork (now on Chemin de Lesseps), and look (immediately) for the temple on the right with three wreaths. Jim Morrison lies just behind, often watched over by a personal security guard. You can't miss the commotion.

❽ Jim Morrison (1943-1971)

Perhaps the most visited tomb in the cemetery belongs to this American rock star—lead singer for the popular band The Doors, named for the "Doors of Perception" they aimed to open. An

iconic, funky bust of the rocker was stolen by fans and replaced with a more toned-down headstone. Even so, Morrison's faithful still gather here at all hours. The headstone's Greek inscription reads: "To the spirit (or demon) within." Graffiti-ing nearby tombs, fans write: "You still Light My Fire" (referring to Jim's biggest hit), "Ring my bell at the Dead Rock Star Hotel," and "Mister Mojo Risin'" (referring to the legend that Jim faked his death and still lives today).

When Morrison arrived in Paris in the winter of 1971, he was famous, notorious for his erotic onstage antics, and a burned-out alcoholic. Paris was to be his chance to leave celebrity behind, get healthy, and get serious as a writer.

Living under an assumed name in a nondescript sublet apartment near Place de la Bastille, he spent his days as a carefree artist. He scribbled in notebooks at Le Café de Flore and Les Deux Magots (see page 286 of the Left Bank Walk chapter), watched the sun set from the steps of Sacré-Cœur, visited Baudelaire's house, and jammed with street musicians. He drank a lot, took other drugs, gained weight, and his health declined.

In the wee hours of July 3, he died in his bathtub at age 27, officially of a heart attack, but likely from an overdose. (Any police investigation was thwarted by Morrison's social circle of heroin users, leading to wild rumors surrounding his death.)

Jim's friends approached Père Lachaise Cemetery about burying the famous rock star there, in accordance with his wishes. The director refused to admit him, until they mentioned that Jim was a writer. "A writer?" he said, and he found a spot.

> *"This is the end, my only friend, the end."*
>
> —Jim Morrison

• *Return to Rond Point, cross it, and retrace your steps—sorry, but there are no straight lines connecting these dead geniuses. Retrace your steps up Avenue de la Chapelle. At the intersection with the small park and big chapels, turn left onto Avenue Laterale du Sud. Walk down two sets of stairs and turn left onto narrow Chemin Denon. "Fred" Chopin's grave—usually adorned with flowers, burning candles, and his fans—is about 80 yards down on the left.*

❾ Frédéric Chopin (1810-1849)

Fresh-cut flowers and geraniums on the gravestone speak of the emotional staying power of Chopin's music, which still connects souls across the centuries. A muse sorrows atop the tomb, and a carved relief of Chopin in profile captures the delicate features of this sensitive artist.

The 21-year-old Polish pianist arrived in Paris, fell in love with the city, and never returned to his homeland (which was occupied by an increasingly oppressive Russia). In Paris, he could finally shake off the "child prodigy" label and performance schedule he'd lived with since age seven. Cursed with stage fright ("I don't like concerts. The crowds scare me, their breath chokes me, I'm paralyzed by their stares...") and with too light a touch for big venues, Chopin preferred playing at private parties for Paris' elite. They were wowed by his technique; his ability to make a piano sing; and his melodic, soul-stirring compositions. Soon he was recognized as a pianist, composer, and teacher and even idolized as a brooding genius. He ran in aristocratic circles with fellow artists, such as pianist Franz Liszt, painter Delacroix, novelists Victor Hugo and Balzac, and composer Rossini. (All but Liszt and Hugo lie in Père Lachaise.)

Chopin composed nearly 200 pieces, almost all for piano, in many different styles—from lively Polish dances to the Bach-like counterpoint of his *Preludes* to the moody, romantic *Nocturnes*.

In 1837, the quiet, refined, dreamy-eyed genius met the scandalous, assertive, stormy novelist George Sand (see page 282 of the Left Bank Walk chapter). Sand was swept away by Chopin's music and artistic nature. She pursued him, and sparks flew. Though the romance faded quickly, they continued living together for nearly a decade in an increasingly bitter love-hate relationship. When Chopin developed tuberculosis, Sand nursed him for years (Chopin complained she was killing him). Sand finally left, Chopin was devastated, and he died two years later at age 39. At the funeral, they played perhaps Chopin's most famous piece, the *Funeral March* (it's that 11-note dirge that everyone knows). The grave contains Chopin's body, but his heart lies in Warsaw, embedded in a church column.

> *"The earth is suffocating. Swear to make them cut me open, so that I won't be buried alive."*
>
> —Chopin, on his deathbed

• *Continue walking down Chemin Denon as it curves down and to the right. Stay left at the Chemin du Coq sign and walk down to Avenue Casimir Perier. Turn right and walk downhill 30 yards, looking to the left, over the tops of the graves, for a tall monument that looks like a church with a cross perched on top. Under this stone canopy lie...*

⑩ Héloïse (c. 1101-1164) and Abélard (1079-1142)

Born nearly a millennium ago, these are the oldest residents in Père Lachaise, and their story is timeless.

In an age of faith and Church domination of all aspects of life, the independent scholar Peter Abélard dared to say, "By questioning, we learn truth." Brash, combative, and charismatic, Abélard shocked and titillated Paris with his secular knowledge and reasoned critique of Church doctrine. He set up a school on the Left Bank (near today's Sorbonne) that would become the University of Paris. Bright minds from all over Europe converged on Paris, including Héloïse, the brainy niece of the powerful canon of Notre-Dame.

Abélard was hired (c. 1118) to give private instruction to Héloïse. Their intense intellectual intercourse quickly flared into physical passion and a spiritual bond. They fled Paris and married in secret, fearing the damage to Abélard's career. After a year, Héloïse gave birth to a son (named Astrolabe), and the news got out, soon reaching Héloïse's uncle. The canon exploded, sending a volley of thugs in the middle of the night to Abélard's bedroom, where they castrated him.

Disgraced, Abélard retired to a monastery and Héloïse to a convent, never again to live as man and wife. But for the next two decades, the two remained intimately connected by the postal service, exchanging letters of love, devotion, and intellectual discourse that survive today. (The dog at Abélard's feet symbolizes their fidelity to each other.) Héloïse went on to become an influential

abbess, and Abélard bounced back with some of his most critical writings. (He was forced to burn his *Theologia* in 1121 and was on trial for heresy when he died.) Abélard used logic to analyze Church pronouncements—a practice that would flower into the "scholasticism" accepted by the Church a century later.

When they died, the two were buried together in Héloïse's convent and were later laid to rest here in Père Lachaise. The can-

Other Notable Residents

Though not along our walking tour, the following folks can be found on our map, as well as the maps for sale from vendors.

ⓐ Jacques-Louis David (1748-1825), Section 56

The Neoclassical painter David chronicled the heroic Revolution and the Napoleonic Era. See his *Coronation of Emperor Napoleon* in the Louvre (page 155).

ⓑ Théodore Géricault (1791-1824), Section 12

Géricault was the master of painting extreme situations (ship-wrecks, battles) and extreme emotions (noble sacrifice, courage, agony, insanity) with Romantic realism. See his *Raft of the Medusa* in the Louvre (page 156).

ⓒ Eugène Delacroix (1798-1863), Section 49

For more on this Romantic painter, see his *Liberty Leading the People* in the Louvre (page 157) or visit the Delacroix Museum (see page 73).

ⓓ Jean-August-Dominique Ingres (1780-1867), Section 23

Often considered the anti-Delacroix, Ingres was a painter of placid portraits and bathing nudes, using curved outlines and smooth-surfaced paint. Despite his deliberate distortions (see his beautifully deformed *La Grande Odalisque* in the Louvre, page 156), he was hailed as the champion of traditional Neoclassical balance against the furious Romantic style (see *The Source* in the Orsay, page 170).

ⓔ Georges Seurat (1859-1891), Section 66

Georges spent Sunday afternoons in the park with his easel, capturing shimmering light with tiny dots of different-colored paint.

ⓕ Amadeo Modigliani (1884-1920), Section 96, not far from Edith Piaf

Poor, tubercular, and strung out on drugs and alcohol in Paris, this young Italian painter forged a distinctive style. His portraits and nudes have African masklike faces and elongated necks and arms.

ⓖ Marcel Proust (1871-1922), Section 85

Some who make it through the seven volumes and 3,000 pages

opy tomb we see today (1817) is made out of stones from both Héloïse's convent and Abélard's monastery.

> *"Thou, O Lord, brought us together, and when it pleased Thee, Thou hast parted us."*
>
> —From a prayer of Héloïse and Abélard

• *Continue walking downhill along Avenue Casimir Perier, and keep straight as it merges into Avenue du Puits (passing the exit to the left). Stay the course until you cross Avenue Principale, the street at the ceme-*

of Proust's autobiographical novel, *Remembrance of Things Past,* close the book and cry, "Brilliant!" Others get lost in the meandering, stream-of-consciousness style, and forget that the whole "Remembrance" began with the taste of a *madeleine* (a type of cookie) that triggered a flashback to Proust's childhood, as relived over the last 10 years of his life, during which he labored alone in his apartment on Boulevard Haussmann—midway between the Arc de Triomphe and Gare de l'Est—penning his life story with reflections on Time (as we experience it, not as we measure it on the clock) and Memory...in long sentences.

⑩ Sarah Bernhardt (1844-1923), Section 44

The greatest actress of her generation, she conquered Paris and the world. Charismatic Sarah made a triumphant tour of America and Europe (1880-1881), starring in *La Dame aux Camélias.* No one could die onstage like Sarah, and in the final scene—when her character succumbs to tuberculosis—she had cowboys and railroad workers sniffling in the audience. Of her hundred-plus stage roles and many silent films, her most memorable one may have been playing...Hamlet (1899). Offstage, her numerous affairs and passionate, capricious personality set a standard for future divas to aspire to.

❶ Yves Montand (1921-1991) and
Simone Signoret (1921-1985), Section 44

Yves Montand was a film actor and nightclub singer with blue-collar roots, left-wing politics, and a social conscience. Montand's career was boosted by his lover, Edith Piaf, when they appeared together at the Moulin Rouge during World War II. Yves went on to stardom throughout the world (except in America, thanks partly to a 1960 flop film with Marilyn Monroe, *Let's Make Love*). In 1951, he married actress Simone Signoret, whose on-screen persona was the long-suffering lover. They remain together still, despite rumors of Yves' womanizing. After their deaths, their eternal love was tested in 1998, when Yves' body was exhumed to take a DNA sample for a paternity suit. (It wasn't him.)

tery's main entrance. Cross Principale to find Colette's grave (third grave from corner on right side).

⑪ Colette (1873-1954)

France's most honored female writer led an unconventional life—thrice married and often linked romantically with other women—and wrote about it in semi-autobiographical novels. Her first fame came from a series of novels about naughty teenage Claudine's misadventures. In her 30s, Colette went on to a career as a music hall performer, scandalizing Paris by pulling a Janet Jackson onstage. Her late novel, *Gigi* (1945)—about a teenage girl groomed to be a professional mistress, who blossoms into independence—became a musical film starring Leslie Caron and Maurice Chevalier (1958). Thank heaven for little girls!

> "The only misplaced curiosity is trying to find out here, on this side, what lies beyond the grave."
>
> —Colette

• *Take a few steps back to Avenue Principale and go uphill a half-block. On the left, find Rossini, with Haussmann a few graves up.*

⑫ Gioacchino Rossini (1792-1868)

Dut. Dutta-dut. Dutta dut dut dut dut dut dut dut, dut dut dut dut dut dut dut...

The composer of the *William Tell Overture* (a.k.a. the *Lone Ranger* theme) was Italian, but he moved to Paris (1823) to bring his popular comic operas to France. Extremely prolific, he could crank out a three-hour opera in weeks, including the highly successful *Barber of Seville* (based on a play by Pierre Beaumarchais, who is also buried in Père Lachaise). When *Guillaume Tell* debuted (1829), Rossini, age 37, was at the peak of his career as an opera composer.

Then he stopped. For the next four decades, he never again wrote an opera and scarcely composed anything else. He moved to Italy, went through a stretch of bad health, and then returned to Paris, where his health and spirits revived. He even wrote a little music in his old age. Rossini's impressive little sepulcher is empty, as his remains were moved to Florence.

• *Four graves uphill, find...*

⑬ Baron Georges-Eugène Haussmann (1809-1891)

(Look through the green door long enough for your eyes to dilate.) Love him or hate him, Baron Haussmann made the Paris we see today. In the 1860s, Paris was a construction zone, with civil servant Haussmann overseeing the city's modernization. Narrow medieval lanes were widened and straightened into broad, traffic-carrying boulevards. Historic buildings were torn down. Sewers, bridges, and water systems were repaired. Haussmann rammed the Boulevard St. Michel through the formerly quaint Latin Quarter (as part of Emperor Napoleon III's plan to prevent revolutionaries from barricading narrow streets). The Opéra Garnier, Bois de Boulogne park, and avenues radiating from the Arc de Triomphe were all part of Haussmann's grand scheme, which touched 60 percent of the city. How did he finance it all? That's what the next government wanted to know when they canned him.

Thank God You Can Leave

Have you seen enough dead people? To leave the cemetery, return downhill on Avenue Principale and exit onto Boulevard de Ménilmontant. The Père Lachaise Métro stop is one long block to the right. To find the return stop for bus #69 heading west to downtown, cross Boulevard de Ménilmontant and walk downhill on the right side of Rue de la Roquette; the stop is four blocks down, on the right-hand side.

MONTMARTRE WALK

From Sacré-Cœur to the Moulin Rouge

Stroll along the hilltop of Butte Montmartre amid traces of the many people who've lived here over the years—monks stomping grapes (1200s), farmers grinding grain in windmills (1600s), dust-coated gypsum miners (1700s), Parisian liberals (1800s), Modernist painters (1900s), and all the struggling artists, poets, dreamers, and drunkards who came here for cheap rent, untaxed booze, rustic landscapes, and cabaret nightlife. In the jazzy 1920s, the neighborhood became the haunt of American GIs and expat African Americans (who enjoyed less discrimination here than in the US at that time). Today it's a youthful neighborhood in transition—both slightly seedy and extremely trendy.

Many tourists make the almost obligatory trek to the top of Paris' Butte Montmartre, eat an overpriced crêpe, and marvel at the view—but most miss out on the neighborhood's charm and history. Both are uncovered in this stroll. We'll start near the gleaming Sacré-Cœur Basilica, wander through the hilltop village, browse affordable art, ogle the Moulin Rouge nightclub, and catch echoes of those who once partied to a bohemian rhapsody during the belle époque.

Orientation

Length of This Walk: Allow more than two hours for this two-mile uphill/downhill walk.

When to Go: To minimize crowds at Sacré-Cœur, come on a weekday or by 9:30 on a weekend. Sunny weekends are the busiest—especially on Sunday, when Montmartre becomes a pedestrian-only zone and most shops stay open. On Friday afternoon, Place d'Anvers hosts a small open-air food market (15:00-20:00, at far side of square). If crowds don't get you down, come for the sunset and stay for dinner. This walk is best under clear skies, when views are sensational. Regardless of when you go, prepare for more seediness—particularly near Place Pigalle and Place d'Anvers—than you're accustomed to in Paris.

Getting There: This walk begins at Métro stop Anvers. Other stops nearby include Abbesses and Pigalle. (Avoid the seedy Métro station Barbès.)

You have several options to avoid climbing the hill to Sacré-Cœur: Take the funicular (covered in our walk), which runs near the Anvers Métro and costs one Métro ticket. Alternatively, from Place Pigalle, you could catch the "Montmartrobus," a city bus that drops you right by Sacré-Cœur (at the Funiculaire stop, costs one Métro ticket, 4/hour). A taxi from the Seine or the Bastille to Sacré-Cœur costs about €15 (€20 at night).

Scam Alert: At Sacré-Cœur and in the areas around the Pigalle and Anvers Métro stations, beware of pickpockets, smartphone snatchings, the "found ring" scam, the shell game, and the "friendship bracelet" scam; see page 22.

Sacré-Cœur: Church—free, daily 6:00-22:30; dome—€6, not covered by Museum Pass, daily May-Sept 8:30-20:00, Oct-April 9:00-17:00.

Church of St. Pierre-de-Montmartre: Free, Sat-Thu 8:45-19:00, Fri 8:45-17:00.

Dalí Museum (L'Espace Dalí): €11.50, not covered by Museum Pass, daily 10:00-18:00, July-Aug until 20:00, audioguide-€3.50, 11 Rue Poulbot, tel. 01 42 64 40 10, www.daliparis.com.

Montmartre Museum: €9.50, includes good 45-minute audioguide, not covered by Museum Pass, daily 10:00-18:00, Aug-Sept until 19:00, last entry 45 minutes before closing, 12 Rue Cortot.

Services: As you face Sacré-Cœur, WCs are down the stairs to the right (free, 10:00-18:15). Others are in the Square Suzanne Buisson park (north of #16 on the tour), the Montmartre Museum, in an automated cabin at the base of the funicular

MONTMARTRE

(long lines), in the souvenir shop at the top of the funicular (pay), and any cafés you patronize.

Eating: You'll find peaceful, picnic-ready benches all along this walk as well as a patch of grass in the park on the backside of the basilica. Good sandwiches are available from the award-winning bakeries along Rue des Abbesses, which also features several picnic-friendly cheese, wine, and fruit stalls. See page 445 for restaurant recommendations, including L'Eté en Pente Douce and other eateries along Rue Lepic and Rue des Abbesses.

Starring: Cityscape views, Sacré-Cœur, postcard scenes brought to life, a charming market street, and boring buildings where interesting people once lived.

The Walk Begins

• *To reach Sacré-Cœur by Métro, get off at Métro stop Anvers. Surface through one of the original Art Nouveau "Métropolitain" Métro entrances.*

❶ Place d'Anvers

The **Elysées Montmartre** theater across the street—with its swirling circa 1900 facade—is the oldest cancan dance hall in

Paris. More recently, it's been used as a rowdy dance club and concert hall, signaling this area's transition. (The famous Chat Noir—or Black Cat—cabaret was nearby.) Historically, people have moved to this neighborhood for cheap rents—and though it still feels a little neglected, urban gentrification is well under way, as young professionals restore dilapidated apartments, hotels renovate for a more upscale clientele, and rents increase. The inviting park, with its laughter-filled playground, is a reminder

that many families live in tight quarters above these streets too. A TI kiosk is a few steps to your left (daily 10:00-18:00).

You're standing on Boulevard de Rochechouart, where a wall once separated Montmartre from Paris (*boulevard* literally means "road that replaced a wall"). Let's take a walk on the wild side.

• *Walk up Rue de Steinkerque (the street to the right of Elysées Montmartre), through a low-rent gauntlet of cheap clothing and souvenir stores. Many tour buses drop off their groups near here. As hordes of naïve tourists from all over the world hike up this street, you're likely to see surly shell-game teams working their scam. The scene is fun to watch, with the*

MONTMARTRE

fake winners they've planted thrilled with the easy money, scouts on each corner looking out for the cops…and tourists snapping photos.

After two blocks you'll reach a grassy park way below the white Sacré-Cœur church. The terraced hillside was once dotted with openings to gypsum mines, the source of the white "plaster of Paris" that plastered Paris' buildings for centuries.

Hike up to the church, or ride the funicular (station to your left, costs one Métro ticket, closes periodically for maintenance). At the top, find a good viewing spot at the steps of the church.

❼ Sacré-Cœur Basilica and View

From Paris' highest natural point (420 feet), the City of Light fans out at your feet. Pan from left to right. The long triangular roof on your left is the Gare du Nord train station. The blue-and-red Pompidou Center is straight ahead, and the skyscrapers in the distance define the southern limit of Paris. Next is the domed Panthéon,

atop Paris' other (and far smaller) butte. Then, standing solo to the right, comes the modern Montparnasse Tower, and finally (if you're in position to see this far to the right), the golden dome of Les Invalides.

Now face the church. The Sacré-Cœur (Sacred Heart) Basilica's exterior, with its onion domes and bleached-bone pallor, looks ancient, but it was finished only a century ago by Parisians humiliated by German invaders. Otto von Bismarck's Prussian army laid siege to Paris for more than four months in 1870. Things got so bad for residents that urban hunting for dinner (to cook up dogs, cats, and finally rats) became accepted behavior. Convinced they were being punished for the country's liberal sins, France's Catholics raised money to build the church as a "praise the Lord anyway" gesture. The church was a kind of penitence by the French: Many were disgusted that in 1871 their government actually shot its own citizens, the Communards, who held out here on Montmartre after the French leadership surrendered to the Prussians (the Communards' monument is in Père Lachaise Cemetery—see page 358).

The five-domed, Roman-Byzantine-looking basilica took 44 years to build (1875-1919). It stands on a foundation of 83 pillars sunk 130 feet deep, necessary because the ground beneath was honeycombed with gypsum mines. The exterior is laced with gypsum, which whitens with age.

• *Go inside.*

MONTMARTRE

MONTMARTRE

Montmartre Walk

Montmartre
Cemetery

Ⓑ MB **Montmartrobus Stops**

❶ Place d'Anvers
❷ Sacré-Cœur Basilica & View
❸ Sacré-Cœur Interior
❹ Church of St. Pierre,
  Bus & Taxi Stop
❺ Cabaret de Patachou
❻ Place du Tertre
❼ Rue Norvins
❽ Dalí Museum
❾ Montmartre Ground Zero
❿ Montmartre Museum
  & Satie's House
⓫ La Maison Rose Restaurant
⓬ Clos Montmartre Vineyard
⓭ Au Lapin Agile Cabaret
⓮ Le Bateau-Lavoir
  (Picasso's Studio)
⓯ Moulin de la Galette
⓰ Toulouse-Lautrec's House
  & Studio
⓱ Van Gogh's House
⓲ Café des Deux Moulins
⓳ Moulin Rouge
⓴ Pig Alley

❸ Sacré-Cœur Interior

Crowd flow permitting, pause near the entrance and take in the
nave.

  Ⓐ **View of the Nave:** In the impressive mosaic high above
the altar, a 60-foot-tall Christ exposes his sacred heart, burning
with love and compassion for humanity. Joining him are a dove
representing the Holy Spirit and God the Father high above.

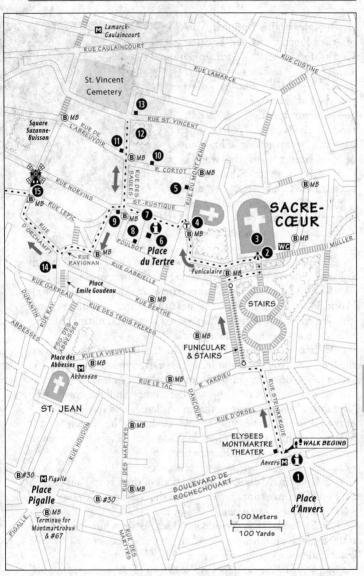

Christ is flanked by biblical figures on the left (including St. Peter, kneeling) and French figures on the right (a kneeling Joan of Arc in her trademark armor). As you get closer, you'll see other French figures: clergymen (who offer a model of this church to the Lord), government leaders (in business suits), and French saints (including St. Bernard, above, with his famous dog, and St. Louis, with the crown of thorns). Remember, the church was built by a French populace recently humbled by a devastating war. At the base of

the mosaic is the National Vow of the French people begging God's forgiveness: *"Sacritissimo Cordi Jesu Gallia poenitens et devota..."*—which means, "To the Sacred Heart of Jesus, we are penitent and devoted." Right now, in this church, at least one person is praying for Christ to be understanding of the world's sins—part of a tradition that's been carried out here, day and night, 24/7, since Sacré-Cœur's completion nearly a century ago.

• *Start shuffling clockwise around the church. Near the entrance, find the white...*

❶ Statue of St. Thérèse: Follow Thérèse's gaze to a pillar with a plaque *("L'an 1944...")*. The plaque's map shows where, on April 21, 1944, 13 bombs fell on Montmartre in an Allied air raid during World War II—all in a line, all near the church—killing no one. This fueled local devotion to the Sacred Heart and to this church.

• *Continue up the side aisles, and find a...*

❷ Scale Model of the Church: It shows the church from the long side (you'd enter at left). This early-version model doesn't accurately reflect the finished product, but it's close. You see its central dome surrounded by smaller domes and the tower. The "Byzantine" style is clear in the onion domes and in the arches—heavy horseshoe arches atop slender columns. The church is built of large rectangular blocks (just look around you), with no attempt to plaster over the cracks/lines in between.

• *Continue along, looking to the right at...*

❸ Colorful Mosaics of the Stations of the Cross: Pause to rub **St. Peter's bronze foot** and look up to the heavens.

• *Continue your circuit around the church.*

❹ Stained-Glass Windows: Because the church's original stained-glass windows were broken by the concussion of WWII bombs, all the glass you see is post-1945.

• *As you approach the entrance you'll walk straight toward three stained-glass windows dedicated to...*

❺ Joan of Arc (Jeanne d'Arc, 1412-1431): See the teenage girl as she hears the voice of the Archangel Michael (right panel, at bottom) and later (above on the same panel) as she takes up the Archangel's sword. Next, she kneels to take communion (central panel, bottom), then kneels before the bishop to tell him she's been sent by God to rally France's soldiers and save Orléans from English invaders (central panel, top). However, French forces allied

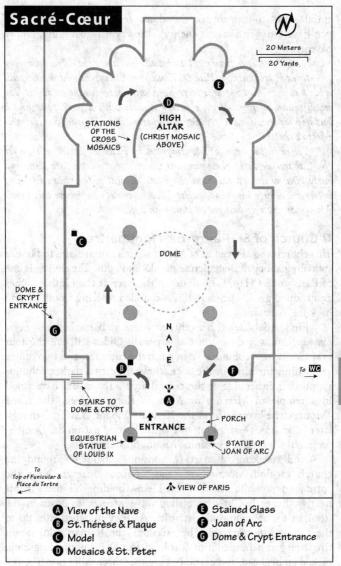

Sacré-Cœur

20 Meters
20 Yards

STATIONS
OF THE
CROSS
MOSAICS

D

**HIGH
ALTAR**
(CHRIST MOSAIC
ABOVE)

E

DOME

C

DOME &
CRYPT
ENTRANCE

G

N
A
V
E

To WC

B

F

STAIRS TO
DOME & CRYPT

A

ENTRANCE

PORCH

EQUESTRIAN
STATUE
OF LOUIS IX

STATUE OF
JOAN OF ARC

To
Top of Funicular &
Place du Tertre

VIEW OF PARIS

A View of the Nave
B St. Thérèse & Plaque
C Model
D Mosaics & St. Peter

E Stained Glass
F Joan of Arc
G Dome & Crypt Entrance

MONTMARTRE

with England arrest her, and she's burned at the stake as a heretic (left panel), dying with her eyes fixed on a crucifix and chanting, "Jesus, Jesus, Jesus..."

• Exit the church. A public WC is to your left, down 50 steps. To your right is the entrance to the church's...

G Dome and Crypt: For an unobstructed panoramic view of Paris, climb 260 feet (300 steps) up the tight and claustrophobic spiral stairs to the top of the dome (especially worthwhile if you have kids with excess energy). The crypt is just a big, empty basement.

• *Leaving the church, turn right and walk west along the ridge, following tree-lined Rue Azaïs. At Rue St. Eleuthère, turn right and walk uphill a block to the Church of St. Pierre-de-Montmartre (at top on right). The small square in front of the church has a convenient taxi stand and a bus stop for the Montmartrobus to and from Place Pigalle (bus costs one Métro ticket).*

You're in the heart of Montmartre, by Place du Tertre. A sign for the *Cabaret de la Bohème* reminds visitors that in the late 19th and early 20th centuries, this was the world capital of bohemian life. But before we plunge into that tourist-filled scene, let's see where this whole Montmartre thing first got its start—in a nearby church.

❹ Church of St. Pierre-de-Montmartre

This church was the center of Montmartre's initial claim to fame, a sprawling abbey of Benedictine monks and nuns. The church is one of Paris' oldest (1147). Look down the nave at the Gothic arches and stained glass. The church was founded by King Louis VI and his wife, Adelaide.

Find Adelaide's 12th-century white slab tombstone *(pierre tombale)* midway down on the left wall. Older still are the four gray Corinthian columns—two flank the entrance, and two others are behind the altar in the apse (they're the two darker columns supporting either side of the central arch). These may have stood in a temple of Mercury or Mars in Roman times. The name "Montmartre" comes from the Roman "Mount of Mars," though later generations—thinking of their beheaded patron St. Denis—preferred a less pagan version, "Mount of Martyrs."

And speaking of martyrs, continue clockwise around the church to find Montmartre's most famous martyr. Near the entrance is a white statue of St. Denis, holding his head in his hands. This early Christian bishop was sentenced to death by the Romans for spreading Christianity. As they marched him up to the top of Montmartre to be executed, the Roman soldiers got tired and just beheaded him near here. But Denis popped right up, picked up his head, and carried on another three miles north before he finally died.

Next to Denis, the statue of "Notre Dame de Montmartre" marks a modern miracle—how the Virgin spared the neighborhood from the WWII bombs of April 21, 1944.

Before leaving, rub St. Peter's toe (again), look up, and ask for *délivrance* from the tourist mobs outside.

• *Now step back outside. Before entering the crowded Place du Tertre, get a quick taste of the area by making a short detour to the right down Rue du Mont-Cenis. These days it's lined with cafés and shops. But back in the day, #13 Rue du Mont-Cenis was the...*

❺ Cabaret de Patachou

This building, now a pleasant art gallery (with serious art rather than touristy posters, run by friendly Julien Rousserd), is where singer Edith Piaf (1915-1963) once trilled "La Vie en Rose" to an intimate crowd of 80 diners. Piaf—a destitute teenager who sang for pocket change in the streets of pre-WWII Paris—was discovered by a nightclub owner and became a star. Her singing inspired the people of Nazi-occupied Paris. In the heady days after the war, she sang about the joyous, rosy life in the city. For more on this warbling-voiced singer, see page 358.

• Head back to the always-lively square, and stand on its cusp for the best perspective of...

❻ Place du Tertre: Bohemian Montmartre

Lined with cafés, shaded by acacia trees, and filled with artists, hucksters, and tourists, the scene mixes charm and kitsch in ever-changing proportions. The Place du Tertre has been the town square of the small village of Montmartre since medieval times. (*Tertre* means "stepped lanes" in French.)

In 1800, a wall separated Paris from this hilltop village. To enter Paris you had to pass tollbooths that taxed anything for sale. Montmartre was a mining community where the wine flowed cheap (tax-free) and easy. Life here was a working-class festival of cafés, bistros, and dance halls. Painters came here for the ruddy charm, the light, and the low rents. In 1860, Montmartre was annexed into the growing city of Paris. The "bohemian" ambience survived, and it attracted sophisticated Parisians ready to get down and dirty in the belle époque of cancan. The Restaurant Mère Catherine is often called the first bistro—this is where Russian soldiers first coined the word by saying, "I'm thirsty, bring my drink *bistro!*" (meaning "right away").

The square's artists, who at times outnumber the tourists, are the great-great-grandkids of the Renoirs, Van Goghs, and Picassos

who once roamed here—poor, carefree, seeking inspiration, and occasionally cursing a world too selfish to bankroll their dreams.

• Plunge headlong into the square. The Montmartre TI (Syndicat d'Initiative) across the square sells good maps and pots of honey from hives sprinkled around the hill (daily 10:00-18:00). Just south of

the square (in the far corner) is the quiet, tiny Place du Calvaire, with the recommended Chez Plumeau restaurant. But for now continue west along the main drag, called...

❼ Rue Norvins

Montmartre's oldest and main street is still the primary commercial artery, serving the current trade—tourism.

• *If you're a devotee of Dalí, a detour left on Rue Poulbot will lead you to the...*

❽ Dalí Museum (L'Espace Dalí)

This beautifully lit black gallery offers a walk through statues, etchings, and paintings by the master of Surrealism. The Spaniard found fame in Paris in the 1920s and '30s. He lived in Montmartre for a while, hung with the Surrealist crowd in Montparnasse, and shocked the world with his dreamscape paintings and experimental films. Don't miss the printed interview on the exit stairs.

• *Continue west down Rue Norvins a dozen steps to the picturesque intersection with Rue des Saules. You've arrived at...*

❾ Montmartre Ground Zero

Here you seem to leave the tourists and enter the residential part of Montmartre. Pause to survey the colorful jumble of classic

storefronts, cafés, and charm. The yellow café on the left—formerly a venerable old *boulangerie* (bakery)—dates from 1900. Its facade is one of the last surviving bits of the old-time scenery, made famous in a painting by the artist Maurice Utrillo (see sidebar on page 380). From the *boulangerie*, look back up Rue Norvins, then backpedal a few steps to catch the classic view up Rue St-Rustique to the dome of Sacré-Cœur rising above the rooftops. Forty yards up this lane is an art-supply shop (where, if inspired, you can pick up a small framed canvas and a few pastels—a €10 starter kit for a new career).

• *Let's lose the tourists. Follow Rue des Saules downhill (north) onto the back side of Montmartre. Enjoy the "Van Gogh in Paris" info panels along the way. A block downhill, turn right on Rue Cortot to reach the...*

❿ Montmartre Museum and Satie's House

In what is now the Montmartre Museum (at #12), Pierre-Auguste Renoir once lived while painting his best-known work, *Bal du Moulin de la Galette* (pictured on page 382). Every day he'd lug the four-foot-by-six-foot canvas from here to the other side of the butte to paint in the open air the famous windmill ballroom, which we'll see later.

A few years later, Utrillo lived and painted here with his mom, Suzanne Valadon. In 1893, she carried on a torrid six-month relationship with the lonely, eccentric man who lived two doors up at #6—composer Erik Satie, who wrote *Trois Gymnopédies* and who was eking out a living playing piano in Montmartre nightclubs.

The Montmartre Museum offers the best look at the artistic golden age of this neighborhood (1870-1910). The museum's  collection of paintings, posters, old photos, music, and memorabilia is split between two creaky 17th-century manor houses. You'll see artifacts from the butte's 2,000-year history: a headless St. Denis from the hill's religious origins and photos of the gypsum quarries and flour-grinding windmills of the Industrial Age. Learn how Sacré-Cœur's construction was an act of national penitence resulting from the Prussian invasion of 1870 (explained earlier in the chapter).

Montmartre's cabaret years are particularly well represented. There's the original *Lapin Agile* sign, the famous Chat Noir poster, and Toulouse-Lautrec's dashing portrait of red-scarved Aristide Bruant, the earthy cabaret singer and club owner. You'll see more Toulouse-Lautrec posters and displays on the biggest and most famous cabaret of all, the cancan-kickers of the Moulin Rouge.

An eight-minute video lets you rest while enjoying an introduction to the world of the bohemian artists—Renoir, Picasso, Edith Piaf, Toulouse-Lautrec, and more—who lived here. The museum's highlight (hiding on the top floor of the building with the café) is the apartment and painting studio of Maurice Utrillo. Rarely has so much artistic talent and creative energy been concentrated in one place at the same time.

Outside in the grounds, you have nice views over the hill's vineyard and can enjoy a coffee in a peaceful garden far from the throngs of tourists.

• *Return to Rue des Saules and walk downhill to...*

⓫ La Maison Rose Restaurant

The restaurant, made famous by an Utrillo painting, was once frequented by Utrillo,

MONTMARTRE

Maurice Utrillo (1883-1955)

Born to a free-spirited single mom and raised by his grand-mother, Utrillo had his first alcohol detox treatment at age 18. Encouraged by his mother and doctors, he started painting as occupational therapy. That, plus guidance from his mother (and, later, from his wife), allowed him to live productively into his 70s, becoming wealthy and famous, despite occasional relapses into drinking and mental problems.

Utrillo grew up on Montmartre's streets. He fought, broke street lamps, and haunted the cafés and bars, paying for drinks with masterpieces. A very free spirit, he's said to have exposed himself to strangers on the street, yelling, "I paint with this!"

His simple scenes of streets, squares, and cafés in a vaguely Impressionist style became popular with commoners and scholars alike. He honed his style during his "white period" (c. 1909-1914), painting a thick paste of predominantly white tints—perfect for capturing Sacré-Cœur. In later years, after he moved out of Montmartre, he still painted the world he knew in his youth, using postcards and photographs as models. Utrillo's mom, Suzanne Valadon, was a former trapeze performer and artist's model who posed for Toulouse-Lautrec, slept with Renoir, studied under Degas, and went on to become a notable painter in her own right.

Pablo Picasso, and Gertrude Stein. Today it serves lousy food to nostalgic tourists.

• *Just downhill from the restaurant is Paris' last remaining vineyard.*

⓬ Clos Montmartre Vineyard

What originally drew artists to Montmartre was country charm like this. Ever since the 12th century, the monks and nuns of the large abbey have produced wine here. With vineyards, wheat fields, windmills, animals, and a village tempo of life, it was the perfect escape from grimy Paris. In 1576, puritanical laws taxed wine in Paris, bringing budget-minded drinkers outside the Paris city gates to Montmartre. Today's vineyard is off-limits to tourists except during the annual grape-harvest fest (first Sat in Oct, www.fetedesvendangesdemontmartre.com), when a thousand costumed locals bring back the boisterous old days. The vineyard's annual production of 300 liters is auctioned off at the fest to support local charities. Bottles average €45 apiece and are considered mediocre at best.

• *Continue downhill to the intersection with Rue St. Vincent.*

⓭ Au Lapin Agile Cabaret

The poster above the door gives the place its name. A rabbit *(lapin)* makes an agile leap out of the pot while balancing the bottle of wine that he can now drink—rather than be cooked in. This was the village's hot spot. Picasso and other artists and writers (Renoir, Utrillo, Paul Verlaine, Aristide Bruant, Amedeo Modigliani, etc.) would gather for "performances" of serious poetry, dirty limericks, sing-alongs, parodies of the famous, or anarchist manifestos. Once,

to play a practical joke on the avant-garde art community, patrons tied a paintbrush to the tail of the owner's donkey and entered the resulting "abstract painting" in a show at the Salon. Called *Sunset over the Adriatic,* it won critical acclaim and sold for a nice price.

The old Parisian personality of this cabaret survives. Every night except Monday a series of performers takes a small, French-speaking audience on a wistful musical journey back to the good old days (for details, see page 490).

• *Backtrack uphill on Rue des Saules to "ground zero." Circle around the right side of the* boulangerie, *and go downhill. Don't curve right on car-filled Rue Lepic; instead, go straight, down the pedestrian-only Place J. B. Clement, hugging the buildings on the left. Directly ahead, above #49, is a north-facing artist's studio—designed to catch the indirect light. This was Picasso's first studio when he arrived here from Barcelona around 1900. To see the studio he moved to later, turn right on Rue Ravignan and follow it down to the leafy little square with the TIM Hôtel. Next to the hotel, at 13 Place Emile Goudeau, is...*

⑩ Le Bateau-Lavoir (Picasso's Studio)

A humble facade marks the place where modern art was born. Here, in a lowly artists' abode (destroyed by fire in 1970, rebuilt

a few years later), as many as 10 artists lived and worked. This former piano factory, converted to cheap housing, was nicknamed the "Laundry Boat" for its sprawling layout and crude facilities (sharing one water tap). It was "a weird, squalid place," wrote one resident, "filled with every kind

of noise: arguing, singing, bedpans clattering, slamming doors, and suggestive moans coming from studio doors."

In 1904, a poor, unknown Spanish émigré named Pablo Picasso (1881-1973) moved in. He met dark-haired Fernande Olivier, his first real girlfriend, in Place Emile-Goudeau, the romantic square outside. She soon moved in, lifting him out of his melancholy Blue

Period into his rosy Rose Period. *La belle Fernande* posed nude for him, inspiring a freer treatment of the female form.

In 1907, Picasso started on a major canvas. For nine months he produced hundreds of preparatory sketches, working long into the night. When he unveiled the work, even his friends were shocked. *Les Demoiselles d'Avignon* showed five nude women in a brothel (Fernande claimed they were all her), with primitive masklike faces and fragmented bodies. Picasso had invented Cubism.

For the next two years, he and his neighbors Georges Braque and Juan Gris revolutionized the art world. Sharing paints, ideas, and girlfriends, they made Montmartre "The Cubist Acropolis," attracting freethinking "Moderns" from all over the world to visit their studios—the artists Amedeo Modigliani, Marie Laurencin, and Henri Rousseau (see page 199); the poet Guillaume Apollinaire; and the American expatriate writer Gertrude Stein. By the time Picasso moved to better quarters (and dumped Fernande), he was famous. Still, Picasso would later say, "I know one day we'll return to Bateau-Lavoir. It was there that we were really happy—where they thought of us as painters, not strange animals."

Before continuing, step down to the railing of Place Emile-Goudeau and marvel at Paris. Just below is the Pâtisserie Gilles Marchal (selling top-end treats) and an inviting café with fine terrace seating.

• *Walk back half a block uphill and turn left on Rue d'Orchampt. Walk the length of this short street (ahead is a memorial to Dalida—a Madonna-like pop star Europeans still idolize) and right into a tiny alley that spits you out the other end at the intersection with Rue Lepic, where you're face-to-face with a wooden windmill.*

ⓕ Moulin de la Galette

Only two windmills *(moulins)* remain on a hill that was once dotted with 30 of them. Originally, they pressed monks' grapes and farmers' grain and crushed  gypsum rocks into powdery plaster of Paris. When the gypsum mines closed (c. 1850) and the vineyards sprouted apartments, the grounds around these windmills were turned into the ceremonial centerpiece of a popular outdoor dance hall. Renoir's *Bal du Moulin de la Galette* (in the Orsay, see page 181) shows it in its heyday—a sunny Sunday afternoon in the acacia-shaded gardens with working-class people dancing, laughing, drinking, and eating the house crêpes, called galettes. Some call Renoir's version the quintessential Impressionist work and the painting that best captures—on a large canvas in bright colors—the joy of the Montmartre lifestyle.

• *Follow Rue Lepic as it winds down the hill. The green-latticed building on the right side, with the windmill above through the trees, is the actual spot immortalized by Renoir. Rounding the bend, pause and look to the right when you reach Rue Tourlaque. The building one block down Rue Tourlaque was...*

⓰ Henri de Toulouse-Lautrec's House and Studio

Find the building on the southwest corner (across the intersection on the left) with the tall, brick-framed art-studio windows under the heavy mansard roof. Every night Toulouse-Lautrec (1864-1901, see page 175)—a nobleman turned painter, whose legs were deformed in a horse-riding accident during his teenage years—would dress up here and then journey down Rue Lepic to the Moulin Rouge. One of Henri's occasional drinking buddies and fellow artists lived nearby.

• *Continue down Rue Lepic and, at #54, find...*

⓱ Vincent van Gogh's House

Vincent van Gogh lived here with his brother from 1886 to 1888, enjoying a grand city view from his top-floor window. In those two short years, Van Gogh transformed from a gloomy Dutch painter of brown and gray peasant scenes into an inspired visionary with wild ideas and Impressionist colors.

• *Follow Rue Lepic downhill to where it makes a hard right at #36 and becomes a lively market street. At this point you have a choice: Continue with this walk to see the famous Moulin Rouge and Pig Alley, or head left on Rue des Abbesses to explore and enjoy some lively shopping and market-street action. Near Métro Pigalle, you'll come to the start of my* **Rue des Martyrs boutique stroll** *(see page 479).*

To continue with this walk, proceed downhill on Rue Lepic. Take in the small shops and neighborhood ambience. Two blocks down, on the corner to your right (at #15), you'll find the pink...

⓲ Café des Deux Moulins

This café has become a pilgrimage site for movie buffs worldwide, since it was featured in the quirky 2001 film *Amélie*. Today it's just another funky place with unassuming ambience and reasonably priced food and drinks, frequented by the next generation of real-life Amélies who ignore the movie poster on the back wall (long hours daily, 15 Rue Lepic, tel. 01 42 54 90 50).

• *Continue downhill on Rue Lepic to Place Blanche. On busy Place Blanche is the...*

MONTMARTRE

⓳ Moulin Rouge

Oh là là. The new Eiffel Tower at the 1889 World's Fair was nothing compared to the sight of pretty cancan girls kicking their legs at the newly opened "Red Windmill."

The nightclub seemed to sum up the belle époque—the age of elegance, opulence, sophistication, and worldliness. The big draw was amateur night, when working-class girls in risqué dresses danced "Le Quadrille" (dubbed "cancan" by a Brit). Wealthy Parisians slummed it by coming here.

On most nights you'd see a small man in a sleek black coat, checked pants, a green scarf, and a bowler hat peering through his pince-nez glasses at the dancers and making sketches of them—Henri de Toulouse-Lautrec. Perhaps he'd order an absinthe, the dense green liqueur (evil ancestor of today's *pastis*) that was the toxic muse for so many great (and so many forgotten) artists. Toulouse-Lautrec's sketches of dancer Jane Avril and comic La Goulue hang in the Orsay (see reproductions in the entryway).

After its initial splash, the Moulin Rouge survived as a venue for all kinds of entertainment. In 1906, the novelist Colette kissed her female lover onstage, and the authorities closed the "Dream of Egypt" down. Yves Montand opened for Edith Piaf (1944), and the two fell in love offstage. It has hosted such diverse acts as Ginger Rogers, Dalida, and the Village People—together on one bill (1979). Mikhail Baryshnikov leaped across its stage (1986). And the club celebrated its centennial (1989) with Ray Charles, Tony Curtis, Ella Fitzgerald, and...a French favorite, Jerry Lewis.

Tonight they're showing...well, find out yourself: Walk into the open-air entryway or step into the lobby to mull over the photos, show options, and prices. Their souvenir shop is back up Rue Lepic a few steps at #9.

• *Our tour is over. The Blanche Métro stop is here in Place Blanche. (Plaster of Paris from the gypsum found on this mount was loaded sloppily at Place Blanche...the white square.) The area east of here, down Boulevard de Clichy, was known as...*

⓴ Pig Alley

The stretch of the Boulevard de Clichy from Place Blanche to Place Pigalle is the den mother of all iniquities. Remember, this was once the border between Montmartre and Paris, where bistros had tax-free status, wine was cheap, and prostitutes roamed freely. Today, sex shops, peep shows, the Museum of Erotic Art, live sex shows, chatty pitchmen, and hot-dog stands line the busy boulevard. Dildos abound.

In the Roaring Twenties, this neighborhood at the base of the hill became a new center of cabaret nightlife. It was settled by African American jazz musicians and WWI veterans who didn't want to return to a segregated America. Black-owned nightclubs sprang up. There was Zelli's (located at 16 bis Rue Fontaine, a block southeast of the Moulin Rouge), where clarinetist-saxophonist Sidney Bechet played. A block away was the tiny Le Grand Duc (at Rue Fontaine and Rue Pigalle), where poet Langston Hughes bused tables. Next door was the most famous of all, Bricktop's (at #73 and then at 66 Rue Pigalle), owned by the vivacious faux-redhead who hosted Cole Porter, Duke Ellington, Picasso, the Prince of Wales, F. Scott Fitzgerald, Josephine Baker, and many more. The area was "Harlem East," where rich and poor, black and white, came for a good time.

By World War II, the good times were becoming increasingly raunchy, and GIs nicknamed the Pigalle neighborhood "Pig Alley." Although today's government is cracking down on prostitution, and the ladies of the night are being driven deeper into their red-velvet bars as the area is gradually being gentrified, very few think of the great French sculptor Pigalle when they hear the district's name. Bars lining the streets downhill from Place Pigalle (especially Rue Pigalle) are lively with working girls eager to share a drink with anyone passing by.

SLEEPING IN PARIS

Paris is a good hotel city. I've focused my recommendations on five safe, handy, and colorful neighborhoods: the village-like Rue Cler (near the Eiffel Tower); the artsy and trendy Marais (near Place de la Bastille); the historic island of Ile St. Louis (next door to Notre-Dame); the lively, Latin, and classy Luxembourg Garden neighborhood (on the Left Bank); and the less polished, less central, but less pricey Montmartre neighborhood. I recommend the best accommodations values in each, from €25 dorm beds to deluxe €500 doubles with all the comforts.

For each neighborhood I also list helpful hints and a selection of restaurants and cafés (see the Eating in Paris chapter). Before choosing a hotel, read the descriptions of the neighborhoods closely. Each offers different pros and cons: Your neighborhood is as important as your hotel for the success of your trip.

For lower rates or greater selection, look farther from the river (prices drop proportionally with distance from the Seine), but be prepared to spend more time on the Métro or the bus getting to sights. Those staying at least a week can save on meal costs (if not lodging) by renting an apartment. I also list a few bed-and-

Sleep Code

Hotels are classified based on the average price of a standard double room without breakfast in high season.

$$$$	**Splurge:** Most rooms over €200
$$$	**Pricier:** €150-200
$$	**Moderate:** €100-150
$	**Budget:** €50-100
¢	**Backpacker:** Under €50
RS%	**Rick Steves discount**
*	**French hotel rating system** (0-5 stars)

Unless otherwise noted, credit cards are accepted, hotel staff speak basic English, and free Wi-Fi is available. Most hotels have air-conditioning and an elevator; breakfast is usually extra. Comparison-shop by checking prices at several hotels (on each hotel's website, on a booking site, or by email). For the best deal, *book directly with the hotel.* Ask for a discount if paying in cash; if the listing includes **RS%,** request a Rick Steves discount.

breakfast agencies and give suggestions for sleeping near Paris' airports.

Book your accommodations well in advance if you'll be traveling during peak season or if your trip coincides with a major holiday (see page 677). For accommodations in Versailles, Chartres, Giverny, and Auvers-sur-Oise, see those chapters. For Fontainebleau, see page 574; for Disneyland Paris, see page 464. For information and tips on pricing, getting deals, making reservations, seasonal differences, and chain hotels in Paris, see page 632.

RUE CLER NEIGHBORHOOD
(7th arrond., Mo: Ecole Militaire, La Tour Maubourg, Invalides)

Rue Cler, lined with open-air produce stands and cafés, is a safe, tidy, pedestrian street. It's so French that when I step out of my hotel in the morning, I feel like I must have been a poodle in a previous life. How such coziness lodged itself between the high-powered government district, the Eiffel Tower, and Les Invalides, I'll never know. This is a neighborhood of wide, tree-lined boulevards, stately apartment buildings, and lots of Americans. The American Church and Franco-American Center, American Library, American University, and many of my readers call this area home. Hotels here are a fair value, considering the elegance of the neighborhood. And for sightseeing, you're within walking distance of the Eiffel Tower, Army Museum, Quai Branly Museum, Seine River, Champs-Elysées, and Orsay and Rodin museums.

Become a local at a Rue Cler café for breakfast, or join the afternoon crowd for *une bière pression* (a draft beer). On Rue Cler you can eat and browse your way through a street full of cafés, pastry shops, delis, cheese shops, and colorful outdoor produce stalls. Afternoon *boules* (outdoor bowling) on the Esplanade des Invalides is a relaxing spectator sport (look for the dirt area to the upper right as you face the front of Les Invalides; see "The Rules of *Boules*" sidebar on page 389. The manicured gardens behind the golden dome of the Army Museum are free, peaceful, and filled with flowers (at southwest corner of grounds, closes at about 19:00), and the riverfront promenade along the Seine (Les Berges du Seine) is a fine place to walk, run, bike, or just sit and watch the river of people stroll by.

Though hardly a happening nightlife spot, Rue Cler offers many low-impact after-dark activities. Take an evening stroll above or along the river through the parkway between Pont de l'Alma and Pont des Invalides. For an after-dinner cruise on the Seine, it's a 15-minute walk to the river and the Bateaux-Mouches (see page 39). For a post-dinner cruise on foot, saunter into the Champ de Mars park to admire the glowing Eiffel Tower. For more ideas on nightlife activities here, see page 429.

The American Church and Franco-American Center is the community center for Americans living in Paris. It hosts interdenominational worship services every Sunday (traditional services at 9:00 and 11:00; contemporary service at 13:30), and free Sunday concerts (generally Sept-June at 17:00—but not every week and not in Dec, 65 Quai d'Orsay, Mo: Invalides, tel. 01 40 62 05 00, www.acparis.org).

Breakfast on Rue Cler: For a great Rue Cler start to your day, drop by **Brasserie Aux PTT,** where Rick Steves readers are promised a *deux pour douze* breakfast special (two "American" breakfasts—juice, a big coffee, croissant, bread, ham, and eggs—for €12; closed Sun, opposite 54 Rue Cler, described in more detail on page 423).

Services: There's a large **post office** at the end of Rue Cler on Avenue de la Motte-Picquet and a handy **SNCF Boutique** at 80 Rue St. Dominique (Mon-Fri 9:00-18:00, Sat 10:00-13:00 & 14:00-18:00, closed Sun). You can buy your Paris Museum Pass at **Tabac La Cave à Cigares** on Avenue de la Motte-Picquet, across from where Rue Cler ends (see page 211 of my Rue Cler Walk), or at **Paris Webservices** on 12 Rue de l'Exposition (see "Travel Services," later).

Markets and Shopping: Cross the Champ de Mars park to mix it up with bargain hunters at the twice-weekly open-air market, **Marché Boulevard de Grenelle,** under the Métro, a few blocks southwest of the Champ de Mars park (Wed and Sun 7:00-12:30,

The Rules of *Boules*

The game of *boules*—also called *pétanque*—is the horseshoes of France. Invented here in the early 1900s, it's a social yet serious sport, and endlessly entertaining to watch—even more so if you understand the rules.

The game is played with heavy metal balls and a small wooden target ball called a *cochonnet* (piglet). Whoever gets his *boule* closest to the *cochonnet* is awarded points. Teams commonly have specialist players: a *pointeur* and a *tireur*. The *pointeur's* goal is to lob his balls as close to the target as he can. The *tireur's* job is to blast away opponents' *boules*.

In teams of two, each player gets three *boules*. The starting team traces a small circle in the dirt (in which players must stand when launching their *boules*), and tosses the *cochonnet* about 30 feet to establish the target. The *boule* must be thrown underhand, and can be rolled, launched sky-high, or rocketed at its target. The first *pointeur* shoots, then the opposing *pointeur* shoots until his *boule* gets closer. Once the second team lands a *boule* nearer the *cochonnet*, the first team goes again. If the other team's *boule* is very near the *cochonnet*, the *tireur* will likely attempt to knock it away.

Once all *boules* have been launched, the tally is taken. The team with a *boule* closest to the *cochonnet* wins the round, and they receive a point for each *boule* closer to the target than their opponents' nearest *boule*. The first team to get to 13 points wins. A regulation *boules* field is 10 feet by 43 feet, but the game is played everywhere—just scratch a throwing circle in the sand, toss the *cochonnet*, and you're off.

between Mo: Dupleix and Mo: La Motte-Picquet-Grenelle). **Rue St. Dominique** is the area's boutique-browsing street.

Two minuscule grocery stores, both on Rue de Grenelle, are open until midnight: **Epicerie de la Tour** (at #197) and **Alimentation** (at corner with Rue Cler).

Laundry: Launderettes are omnipresent; ask your hotel for the nearest. Here are three handy locations: on Rue Augereau, on Rue Amélie (both between Rue St. Dominique and Rue de Grenelle), and at the southeast corner of Rue Valadon and Rue de Grenelle.

Travel Services: Contact the helpful staff at **Paris Webservices** to book *"coupe-file"* tickets that allow you to skip the line at key sights, to buy the Paris Museum Pass, or for assistance with hotels,

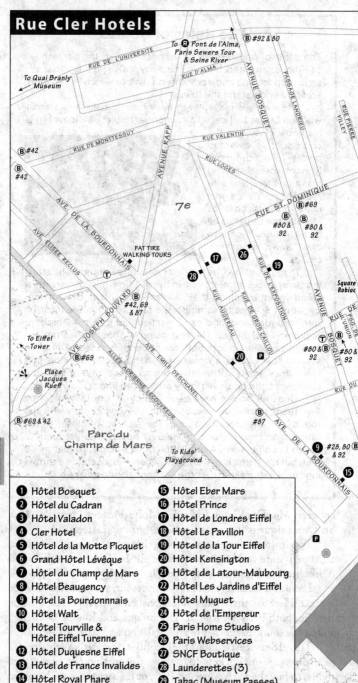

Rue Cler Hotels

1. Hôtel Bosquet
2. Hôtel du Cadran
3. Hôtel Valadon
4. Cler Hotel
5. Hôtel de la Motte Picquet
6. Grand Hôtel Lévêque
7. Hôtel du Champ de Mars
8. Hôtel Beaugency
9. Hôtel la Bourdonnnais
10. Hôtel Walt
11. Hôtel Tourville & Hôtel Eiffel Turenne
12. Hôtel Duquesne Eiffel
13. Hôtel de France Invalides
14. Hôtel Royal Phare
15. Hôtel Eber Mars
16. Hôtel Prince
17. Hôtel de Londres Eiffel
18. Hôtel Le Pavillon
19. Hôtel de la Tour Eiffel
20. Hôtel Kensington
21. Hôtel de Latour-Maubourg
22. Hôtel Les Jardins d'Eiffel
23. Hôtel Muguet
24. Hôtel de l'Empereur
25. Paris Home Studios
26. Paris Webservices
27. SNCF Boutique
28. Launderettes (3)
29. Tabac (Museum Passes)

SLEEPING

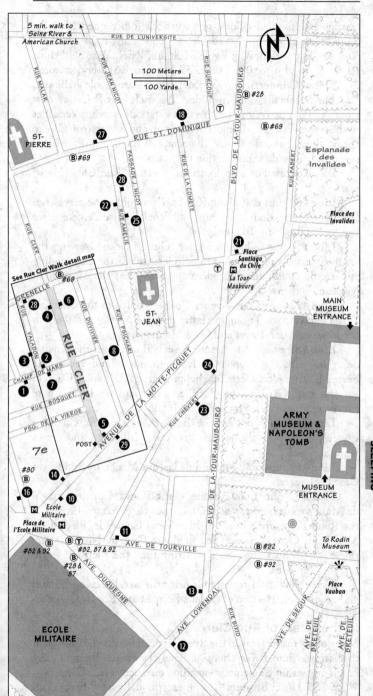

5 min. walk to
Seine River &
American Church

RUE DE L'UNIVERSITÉ

100 Meters
100 Yards

RUE MALAR

RUE JEAN NICOT

RUE SURCOUF

BLVD. DE LA-TOUR-MAUBOURG

Ⓑ #28

Ⓑ #69

18

Ⓣ

ST-
PIERRE

27

RUE ST. DOMINIQUE

Ⓑ #69

Esplanade
des
Invalides

RUE FABERT

RUE DE LA COMÈTE

PASSAGE J. NICOT

28

22

RUE AMÉLIE

25

RUE CLER

Place des
Invalides

21

Place
Santiago
du Chile

Ⓣ

La Tour-
Maubourg

MAIN
MUSEUM
ENTRANCE

See Rue Cler Walk detail map

Ⓑ #69

RUE GRENELLE

28

RUE VALADON

4

6

RUE DUVIVIER

RUE PSICHARI

ST-
JEAN

RUE CLER

3

2

CHAMP DE MARS

7

8

RUE DE LA MOTTE-PICQUET

1

RUE BOSQUET

24

ARMY
MUSEUM &
NAPOLEON'S
TOMB

RUE CHEVERT

23

PSG. DE LA VIERGE

5

MUSEUM
ENTRANCE

7e

POST

AVENUE DE LA MOTTE-PICQUET

29

To Rodin
Museum

#80
Ⓑ

14

16

10

M Ecole
Militaire

Place de
l'Ecole Militaire

M

Ⓑ Ⓣ

11

AVE. DE TOURVILLE

Ⓑ #92

BLVD. DE LA-TOUR-MAUBOURG

#82 & 92

#82, 87 & 92

Ⓑ #92

Ⓑ
#28 &
87

AVE. DUQUESNE

13

AVE. LOWENDAL

RUE BIXIO

Place
Vauban

AVE. DE SÉGUR

AVE. DE BRETEUIL

AVE. DE BRETEUIL

ECOLE
MILITAIRE

12

SLEEPING

transportation, local guides, or excursions (office open Mon-Sat 8:00-18:00, closed Sun; available by phone daily 6:00-22:00, 12 Rue de l'Exposition, Mo: Ecole Militaire, RER: Pont de l'Alma, tel. 01 45 56 91 67 or 09 52 06 02 59, www.pariswebservices.com).

Métro Connections: Key Métro stops are Ecole Militaire, La Tour Maubourg, and Invalides. The useful RER-C line runs from the Pont de l'Alma and Invalides stations, serving Versailles to the southwest; the Marmottan Museum and Auvers-sur-Oise to the northwest; and the Orsay Museum, Latin Quarter (St. Michel stop), and Austerlitz train station to the east.

Bus Routes: For stop locations, see the "Rue Cler Hotels" map.

Line #69 runs east along Rue St. Dominique and serves Les Invalides, Orsay, Louvre, Marais, and Père Lachaise Cemetery (see Bus #69 Sightseeing Tour chapter).

Line #63 runs along the river (Quai d'Orsay), serving the Latin Quarter along Boulevard St. Germain to the east (ending at Gare de Lyon), and Trocadéro and areas near the Marmottan Museum to the west.

Line #92 runs along Avenue Bosquet, north to the Champs-Elysées and Arc de Triomphe (faster than the Métro) and south to the Montparnasse Tower and Gare Montparnasse.

Line #87 runs from Avenue Joseph Bouvard in the Champ de Mars park up Avenue de la Bourdonnais and serves the Sèvres-Babylone/St. Germain shopping area, St. Sulpice Church, Luxembourg Garden, the Bastille, and Gare de Lyon (more convenient than Métro for these destinations).

Line #80 runs on Avenue Bosquet, crosses the Champs-Elysées, stops near the Jacquemart-André Museum, and serves Gare St. Lazare.

Line #28 runs on Boulevard de la Tour Maubourg and serves Gare St. Lazare.

Line #42 runs from Avenue Joseph Bouvard in the Champ de Mars park (same stop as #87), crosses the Champs-Elysées at the Rond-Point, then heads to Place de la Concorde, Place de la Madeleine, Opéra Garnier, and finally to Gare du Nord—a long ride to the train station but less tiring than the Métro if you're carrying suitcases.

Taxi: You'll find taxi stands just off Place L'Ecole Militaire and near the intersection of Avenue Bosquet and Rue de Grenelle.

In the Heart of Rue Cler

Many of my readers stay in the Rue Cler neighborhood. If you want to disappear into Paris, choose a hotel elsewhere. The following hotels are within Camembert-smelling distance of Rue Cler.

$$$$ Hôtel Bosquet*** is an exceptionally good hotel in an

Rue Cler Musts for Temporary Residents

- Stroll the riverside promenade running from Pont de l'Alma east all the way to the Orsay Museum.
- Relax in the flowery park at the southwest corner of Les Invalides, where Avenue de Tourville meets Boulevard de la Tour Maubourg.
- See the Eiffel Tower at night, from the park below, and from across the river on Place du Trocadéro (dinner picnics are best).
- See the golden dome of Les Invalides in all its glory—at night. Choose from two good viewpoints: from the Esplanade between the monument and the river, or from the south side of the complex, along the greenway in the middle of Avenue de Breteuil. I'd do both.
- Take a Bateaux-Mouches cruise after dark (see page 39).
- Linger at a Rue Cler café and observe daily life.

ideal location, with comfortable public spaces and well-configured rooms that are large by local standards and feature effective darkness blinds. The staff are politely formal (RS% but check their Facebook or Instagram pages for other discounts, good but pricey breakfast buffet with eggs and sausage, 19 Rue du Champ de Mars, tel. 01 47 05 25 45, www.hotel-paris-bosquet.com, hotel@relaisbosquet.com).

$$$$ Hôtel du Cadran,*** a well-located *boule* toss from Rue Cler, is over-the-top modern for my taste. I prefer their nearby annex, described next (RS% includes big breakfast—use code "RICK" on their website; 10 Rue du Champ de Mars, tel. 01 40 62 67 00, www.cadranhotel.com, resa@cadranhotel.com).

$$$$ Hôtel Valadon*** is an annex of Hôtel du Cadran, which is almost across the street (it's also where you'll check in and, if you want, have breakfast). The Valadon's 12 cute-and-quiet rooms are larger than those at the Cadran, with the same comfort, prices, and discounts (family rooms, 16 Rue Valadon, tel. 01 47 53 89 85, www.hotelvaladon.com, info@hotelvaladon.com).

$$$$ Cler Hotel*** is a smart boutique hotel with appealing decor, a small outdoor patio, and a great location right on Rue Cler (RS%, 24 bis Rue Cler, tel. 01 45 00 18 06, www.clerhotel.com, contact@clerhotel.com).

$$$ Hôtel de la Motte Picquet,*** at the corner of Rue Cler and Avenue de la Motte-Picquet, is an intimate and modest little place with 16 compact yet comfortable rooms. The terrific staff make staying here a pleasure (RS%—use code STEVE-SMITH, family rooms, good breakfast served in a miniscule breakfast room, 30 Avenue de la Motte-Picquet, tel. 01 47 05 09 57, www. hotelmottepicquetparis.com, book@hotelmottepicquetparis.com).

$$$ Grand Hôtel Lévêque,* ideally situated on Rue Cler, is all about location. It's a busy place with a sliver of an elevator and thin walls (noise can be an issue, especially in rooms facing the street). Though the rooms are sufficiently comfortable, the place feels in need of some TLC. Still, the location makes it a reasonable value (29 Rue Cler, tel. 01 47 05 49 15, www.hotel-leveque.com, info@hotel-leveque.com).

$$ Hôtel du Champ de Mars* is a top choice, brilliantly located barely 10 steps off Rue Cler. This plush little hotel has a small-town feel from top to bottom. The adorable rooms are snug but lovingly kept by hands-on owners Françoise and Stéphane, and single rooms can work as tiny doubles. It's popular, so book well ahead (no air-con, 30 yards off Rue Cler at 7 Rue du Champ de Mars, tel. 01 45 51 52 30, www.hotelduchampdemars.com, reservation@hotelduchampdemars.com).

$$ Hôtel Beaugency* has 30 smallish rooms and a lobby that you can stretch out in. It's a fair value on a quieter street a short block off Rue Cler (RS%, 21 Rue Duvivier, tel. 01 47 05 01 63, www.hotel-beaugency.com, infos@hotel-beaugency.com).

Near Ecole Militaire Métro Stop

These listings are a five-minute walk from Rue Cler, near the Ecole Militaire Métro stop or RER: Pont de l'Alma.

$$$$ Hôtel la Bourdonnais,** near the Champ de Mars park, is an upscale and tastefully designed place with comfy public spaces and rooms that blend modern and traditional accents. It's run well, with American-style service (elaborate breakfast—free for Rick Steves readers, 113 Avenue de la Bourdonnais, tel. 01 47 05 45 42, www.labourdonnais.com, labourdonnais@inwood-hotels.com). Two sister hotels in the neighborhood—owned by the same company as Hôtel la Bourdonnais—are worth considering, particularly if you can get a deal: **Hôtel Walt** (very modern) and **Hôtel Tourville** (more traditional). All three are top-quality, four-star places in terrific locations (www.inwood-hotels.com).

$$$$ Hôtel Duquesne Eiffel,* a few blocks farther from the action, is handsome and hospitable with a helpful staff. It features a welcoming lobby, comfortable rooms (some with terrific Eiffel Tower views), and connecting rooms that work well for families (RS%, big, hot breakfast—free for Rick Steves readers, 23 Avenue Duquesne, tel. 01 44 42 09 09, www.hde.fr, contact@hde.fr).

$$$ Hôtel de France Invalides is a fair midrange option run by a brother-sister team (Alain and Marie-Hélène). It has contemporary decor and 60 rooms, some with knockout views of Invalides' golden dome (but with some traffic noise). Rooms on the courtyard are quieter, smaller, and cheaper (RS%, connecting rooms possible, good breakfast—free for Rick Steves readers, no air-con, 102 Boulevard de la Tour Maubourg, tel. 01 47 05 40 49, www.hoteldefrance.com, contact@hoteldefrance.com).

$$$ Hôtel Royal Phare*** faces the busy Ecole Militaire Métro stop. It's a small place with sharp, well-configured rooms. Courtyard rooms are quieter, but those from the fifth floor up have peekaboo views of the Eiffel Tower (fridges in rooms, 40 Avenue de la Motte-Picquet, tel. 01 47 05 57 30, www.hotel-royalphare-paris. com, hotel-royalphare@wanadoo.fr, friendly manager Hocin).

$$$ Hôtel Eiffel Turenne*** is a reasonable bet with good rooms (20 Avenue de Tourville, tel. 01 47 05 99 92, www. hoteleiffelturenne.com, reservation@hoteleiffelturenne.com).

$$$ Hôtel Eber Mars,** a few steps from Champ de Mars park, has comfortable, bigger-than-average rooms, an I-try-harder owner (Monsieur Eber), and a very narrow elevator (free breakfast for Rick Steves readers who book directly, 117 Avenue de la Bourdonnais, tel. 01 47 05 42 30, www.hotelebermars.com, reservation@hotelebermars.com).

$$ Hôtel Prince,** across from the Ecole Militaire Métro stop, has a spartan lobby and drab halls, but offers good rooms for the price (66 Avenue Bosquet, tel. 01 47 05 40 90, www.hotel-paris-prince.com, paris@hotelprinceparis.com).

Closer to Rue St. Dominique (and the Seine)

$$$$ Hôtel de Londres Eiffel*** is my closest listing to the Eiffel Tower and the Champ de Mars park. Here you get immaculate, warmly decorated, but tight rooms (several are connecting for families), comfy public spaces, and a service-oriented staff. It's less convenient to the Métro (10-minute walk), but very handy to buses #69, #80, #87, and #92, and to RER-C: Pont de l'Alma (some Eiffel Tower view rooms, 1 Rue Augereau, tel. 01 45 51 63 02, www.hotel-paris-londres-eiffel.com, info@londres-eiffel.com, helpful Cédric and Arnaud). The owners also run a good two-star hotel with similar comfort in the cheaper Montparnasse area: **$$ Hôtel Apollon Montparnasse**** (look for Web deals, 91 Rue de l'Ouest, Mo: Pernety, tel. 01 43 95 62 00, www.paris-hotel-paris. net, info@apollon-montparnasse.com).

$$ Hôtel Le Pavillon*** attracts attention with its romantic setting away from the street. Rooms are gray-toned and a tad mod, the comfy breakfast room doubles as a lounge, and the small patio with outdoor tables offers a peaceful refuge (several loft triples, 54 Rue St. Dominique, tel. 01 45 51 42 87, www.hotel-lepavillon.com, lepavillon@green-spirit-hotels.com).

$$ Hôtel de la Tour Eiffel** is a terrific value on a quiet street near several of my favorite restaurants. The rooms are well-designed and comfortable with air-conditioning (but no breakfast). The six sets of connecting rooms are ideal for families (17 Rue de l'Exposition, tel. 01 47 05 14 75, www.hotel-toureiffel.com, hte7@ wanadoo.fr).

$$ Hôtel Kensington**** is a fair budget value close to the Eiffel Tower and run by formal Daniele. It's an unpretentious place offering classic two-star comfort (RS%, some partial Eiffel Tower views, no air-con but ceiling fans, 79 Avenue de la Bourdonnais, tel. 01 47 05 74 00, www.hotel-kensington.com, hk@hotel-kensington.com).

Near La Tour Maubourg Métro Stop

These listings are within three blocks of the intersection of Avenue de la Motte-Picquet and Boulevard de la Tour Maubourg.

$$$$ Hôtel de Latour-Maubourg***** boasts a peaceful manor-home setting with 17 plush, relatively large, and *très* traditional rooms (across from the Métro station at 160 Rue de Grenelle, tel. 01 47 05 16 16, www.latourmaubourg.com, info@latourmaubourg.com).

$$$$ Hôtel Les Jardins d'Eiffel***** is a big place on a quiet street, with professional service, a peaceful patio, and a lobby you can stretch out in. The 81 well-configured rooms—some with partial Eiffel Tower views, some with balconies—offer a bit more space and quiet than other hotels (RS%, parking garage, 8 Rue Amélie, tel. 01 47 05 46 21, www.hoteljardinseiffel.com, reservations@hoteljardinseiffel.com).

$$$ Hôtel Muguet***** is quiet, well-located, well-run, and reasonable, with tastefully appointed rooms (some view rooms, strict 7-day cancellation policy, 11 Rue Chevert, tel. 01 47 05 05 93, www.hotelparismuguet.com, contact@hotelparismuguet.com).

$$$ Hôtel de l'Empereur***** is stylish and delivers smashing views of Invalides from many of its fine rooms. All rooms have queen- or king-size beds, are tastefully designed with hints of the emperor, and are large by Paris standards (some view rooms, family rooms, strict 7-day cancellation policy, tel. 01 45 55 88 02, www.hotelempereurparis.com, contact@hotelempereur.com).

MARAIS

Those interested in a more central, diverse, and lively urban locale should make the Marais their Parisian home. Once a forgotten Parisian backwater, the Marais—which runs from the Pompidou Center east to the Bastille (a 15-minute walk)—is now one of Paris' most popular residential, tourist, and shopping areas. This is jumbled, medieval Paris at its finest, where classy stone mansions sit alongside trendy bars, antique shops, and fashion-conscious boutiques. The streets are an intriguing parade of artists, students, tourists, immigrants, and baguette-munching babies in strollers. The Marais is also known as a hub of the Parisian gay and lesbian scene. This area is *sans* doubt livelier and edgier than the Rue Cler area.

In the Marais you have these major sights close at hand: Carnavalet Museum (closed for renovation through 2017 and beyond), Victor Hugo's House, Jewish Art and History Museum, Pompidou Center, and Picasso Museum. You're also a manageable walk from Paris' two islands (Ile St. Louis and Ile de la Cité), home to Notre-Dame and Sainte-Chapelle. The Opéra Bastille, Promenade Plantée park, Place des Vosges (Paris' oldest square), the Jewish Quarter (Rue des Rosiers), the Latin Quarter, and nightlife-packed Rue de Lappe are also walkable. Strolling home (day or night) from Notre-Dame along Ile St. Louis is marvelous.

Most of my recommended hotels are located a few blocks north of the Marais' main east-west drag, Rue St. Antoine/Rue de Rivoli. For those who prefer a quieter home with fewer tourists, I list several hotels in the northern limits of the Marais, near Rue de Bretagne, the appealing commercial spine of this area.

Tourist Information: The nearest TI is at the Pyramides Métro station (daily May-Oct 9:00-19:00, Nov-April 10:00-19:00, 25 Rue des Pyramides).

Services: Most banks and other services are on Rue de Rivoli, which becomes Rue St. Antoine as it heads east. Marais **post offices** are on Rue Castex and at the corner of Rue Pavée and Rue des Francs-Bourgeois. A busy **SNCF Boutique** is just off Rue St. Antoine at 2 Rue de Turenne (Mon-Fri 8:00-20:30, Sat 10:00-20:30, closed Sun); a quieter SNCF Boutique is nearer to Gare de Lyon at 5 Rue de Lyon (Mon-Sat 8:30-18:00, closed Sun). An English-language **bookstore** called I Love My Blender is located at 36 Rue du Temple (closed Sun-Mon).

Markets and Shopping: The Marais has three good farmers markets. These include the sprawling **Marché de la Bastille,** along Boulevard Richard Lenoir, on the north side of Place de la Bastille (Thu and Sun until 14:30, Mo: Bastille); the **Marché d'Aligre** on Place d'Aligre (Tue-Sun 9:00-13:30, closed Mon, Mo: Ledru-Rollin); and Paris' oldest covered market, the **Marché des Enfants Rouges,** at 39 Rue de Bretagne, a 10-minute walk north of Rue de Rivoli (Mo: Filles du Calvaire or Temple). A **Monoprix** with a basement grocery is near the St-Paul Métro stop (Mon-Sat 9:00-21:00, closed Sun, 62 Rue St. Antoine). To shop at a Parisian Sears, find the **BHV** department store next to Hôtel de Ville.

Laundry: Launderettes are scattered throughout the Marais; ask your hotelier for the nearest. Here are two that you can count on: on Impasse Guéménée (north of Rue St. Antoine), and on Rue du Petit Musc (south of Rue St. Antoine).

SLEEPING

Marais Musts for Temporary Residents

- Have dinner or a drink on Place du Marché Ste. Catherine.
- Dine or enjoy a drink on Place des Vosges.
- Take a late-night art gallery stroll around Place des Vosges.
- Have lunch at Paris' oldest covered market (Marché des Enfants Rouges—see page 486).
- Find the remnants of the 12th-century wall built by Philippe Auguste (opposite the school at 14 Rue Charlemagne).
- Walk Ile St. Louis after dark and enjoy the floodlit view of Notre-Dame (see page 494).
- Cross Ile St. Louis on Pont de Sully and meander the riverside promenade on the Seine's Left Bank.
- Have tea and a pastry at Le Loir dans la Théière (3 Rue des Rosiers) and/or a glass of wine at La Belle Hortense wine bar/bookstore (31 Rue Vieille du Temple).

Métro Connections: Key Métro stops in the Marais are, from east to west: Bastille, St-Paul, and Hôtel de Ville (Sully-Morland, Pont Marie, and Rambuteau stops are also handy). Métro connections are excellent, with direct service to the Louvre, Champs-Elysées, Arc de Triomphe, and La Défense (all on line 1); the Rue Cler area, Place de la Madeleine (see "Boutique Strolls," page 470), and Opéra Garnier/Galeries Lafayette (line 8 from Bastille stop); and four major train stations: Gare de Lyon, Gare du Nord, Gare de l'Est, and Gare d'Austerlitz (all accessible from Bastille stop).

Bus Routes: For stop locations, see the "Marais Hotels" map.

Line #69 on Rue St. Antoine takes you eastbound to Père Lachaise Cemetery and westbound to the Louvre, Orsay, and Rodin museums, plus the Army Museum, ending at the Eiffel Tower (see the Bus #69 Sightseeing Tour chapter).

Line #87 runs down Boulevard Henri IV, crossing Ile St. Louis and serving the Latin Quarter along Boulevard St. Germain, before heading to St. Sulpice Church/Luxembourg Garden, the Eiffel Tower, and the Rue Cler neighborhood to the west. The same line, running in the opposite direction, brings you to Gare de Lyon.

Line #96 runs on Rues Turenne and Rivoli, serves Ile de la Cité and St. Sulpice Church (near Luxembourg Garden), and ends at Gare Montparnasse.

Line #65 runs from Gare de Lyon up Rue de Lyon, around Place de la Bastille, and then up Boulevard Beaumarchais to Gare de l'Est and Gare du Nord.

Line #67 runs from Place d'Italie to the Jardin des Plantes (just south of the Seine), across Ile St. Louis, and then along Rue de Rivoli, past the Louvre, and up to Montmartre.

Taxi: You'll find taxi stands on the north side of Rue St. Antoine (where Rue Castex crosses it), on Place de la Bastille (where Boulevard Richard Lenoir meets the square), on the south side of Rue St. Antoine (in front of St. Paul Church), and behind the Hôtel de Ville on Rue du Lobau (where it meets Rue de Rivoli).

Near Place des Vosges
(3rd and 4th arrond., Mo: Bastille, St-Paul, or Hôtel de Ville)
$$$$ Hôtel le Pavillon de la Reine,***** 15 steps off the beautiful Place des Vosges, merits its stars with top service and comfort and exquisite attention to detail, from its melt-in-your-couch lobby to its luxurious rooms (free access to spa and fitness room, loaner bikes, parking, 28 Place des Vosges, tel. 01 40 29 19 19, www.pavillon-de-la-reine.com, contact@pavillon-de-la-reine.com).

$$$$ Hôtel Bastille Spéria* is situated a short block off Place de la Bastille, offering business-type service and good comfort in a happening location. The 42 well-configured rooms are relatively spacious, simply appointed, and fairly priced (1 Rue de la Bastille, Mo: Bastille, tel. 01 42 72 04 01, www.hotelsperia.com, info@hotelsperia.com).

$$$$ Hôtel St. Louis Marais* is an intimate and sharp little hotel that sits on a quiet street a few blocks from the river. The handsome rooms have character...and spacious bathrooms (family rooms, 1 Rue Charles V, Mo: Sully-Morland, tel. 01 48 87 87 04, www.saintlouismarais.com, marais@saintlouis-hotels.com).

$$$$ Hôtel Jeanne d'Arc,* a lovely if pricey hotel with thoughtfully appointed rooms, is ideally located for connoisseurs of the Marais who don't need air-conditioning. Corner rooms are wonderfully bright in the City of Light. Rooms on the street can be noisy until the bars close (family rooms, some view rooms, 3 Rue de Jarente, Mo: St-Paul, tel. 01 48 87 62 11, www.hoteljeannedarc.com, information@hoteljeannedarc.com).

$$$ Hôtel Castex* is a well-located place—on a quiet street near Place de la Bastille—with narrow and tile-floored rooms. Their system of connecting rooms allows families total privacy between two rooms, each with its own bathroom (free buffet breakfast for Rick Steves readers, just off Place de la Bastille and Rue St. Antoine at 5 Rue Castex, Mo: Bastille, tel. 01 42 72 31 52, www.castexhotel.com, info@castexhotel.com).

$$$ Hôtel de Neuve* is a small, dignified place with classical music in the lobby and high tea in the afternoon. Rooms are plush, quiet, and a good value in this pricey area (behind the Monoprix at 14 Rue de Neuve, Mo: St-Paul, tel. 01 44 59 28 50, www.hoteldeneuveparis.com, reservation@hoteldeneuveparis.com.)

$$ Hôtel Pratic, just off the quiet and charming Place du

SLEEPING

Marais Hotels

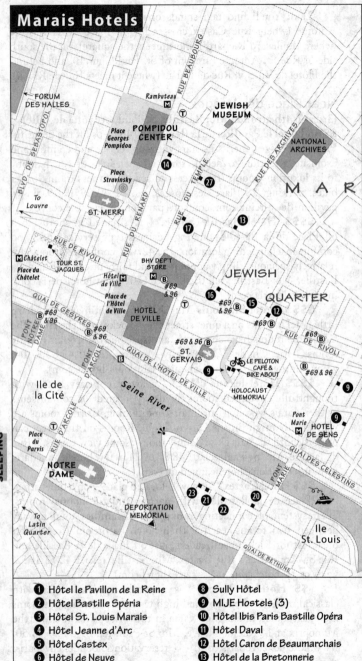

1. Hôtel le Pavillon de la Reine
2. Hôtel Bastille Spéria
3. Hôtel St. Louis Marais
4. Hôtel Jeanne d'Arc
5. Hôtel Castex
6. Hôtel de Neuve
7. Hôtel Pratic
8. Sully Hôtel
9. MIJE Hostels (3)
10. Hôtel Ibis Paris Bastille Opéra
11. Hôtel Daval
12. Hôtel Caron de Beaumarchais
13. Hôtel de la Bretonnerie
14. Hôtel Beaubourg

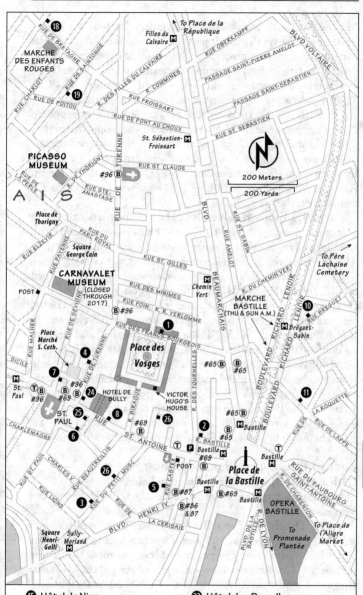

To Place de la
République

Filles du
Calvaire

MARCHE
DES ENFANTS
ROUGES

RUE DE BRETAGNE

RUE CHARLOT

RUE DE SAINTONGE

RUE DE POITOU

RUE DES FILLES DU CALVAIRE

R. COMMINES

RUE FROISSART

RUE DE PONT AU CHOUX

RUE OBERKAMPF

BLVD VOLTAIRE

PASSAGE SAINT-PIERRE AMELOT

PASSAGE SAINT-SEBASTIEN

RUE ST. SEBASTIEN

PICASSO
MUSEUM

A I S

RUE DE LA PERLE

R. DE THORIGNY

RUE STE-ANASTASE

St. Sébastien-
Froissart

RUE ST. CLAUDE

#96 B

200 Meters

200 Yards

Place de
Thorigny

RUE ELZEVIR

RUE PAYENNE

Square
George Cain

RUE DU
PARC ROYAL

RUE ST. GILLES

RUE ST. SABIN

To Père
Lachaise
Cemetery

CARNAVALET
MUSEUM
(CLOSED
THROUGH
2017)

POST

RUE MALHER

Place Marché
S. Cath.

SICILE

M
St.
Paul

RUE DES MINIMES

RUE FOIN

RUE R. VERLOMME

#96 B

RUE DES FRANCS-BOURGEOIS

RUE DE SEVIGNE

Chemin
Vert

BEAUMARCHAIS

BLVD

RUE AMELOT

R. DU CHEMIN VERT

MARCHE
BASTILLE
(THU & SUN A.M.)

RICHARD LENOIR

Bréguet-
Sabin

T

10

RUE BRÉGUET

RUE DE TURENNE

1

Place des
Vosges

#65 B

B
#65

B
#65

11

BOULEVARD

RUE DE LA ROQUETTE

T B
#96

B
#69

4

7

#96

24

HOTEL DE
SULLY

8

VICTOR
HUGO'S
HOUSE

RUE DES TOURNELLES

R. BIRAGUE

25

ST. PAUL

CHARLEMAGNE

6

#69

26

2

M Bastille

B
#65

RUE DE
RUE DE LAPPE

SLEEPING

RUE ST. PAUL

CHARLES V

RUE BEAUTREILLIS

RUE ST. ANTOINE

T

Bastille
#69

P

Bastille

POST

B

Bastille

T

RUE DU FAUBOURG
SAINT-ANTOINE

26

RUE LIONS

RUE DU PETIT MUSC

5

RUE CASTE

3

RUE DE

HENRI IV

LA CERISAIE

B#87

B
#65
#69

B #86
& 87

Place de
la Bastille

Bastille
M

M
B#69

OPERA
BASTILLE

To Place de
l'Aligre
Market

Square
Henri-
Galli

Sully-
Morland
M

BLVD.

BLVD. DE LA
BASTILLE

RUE DE LYON

To
Promenade
Plantée

---

15 Hôtel de Nice
16 Hôtel du Loiret
17 D'Win Hôtel
18 Hôtel du Vieux Saule
19 Hôtel Saintonge
20 Hôtel du Jeu de Paume
21 Hôtel de Lutèce

22 Hôtel des Deux-Iles
23 Hôtel Saint-Louis
24 SNCF Boutique
25 Monoprix (Grocery)
26 Launderettes (2)
27 I Love My Blender Book Store

Marché Ste. Catherine, works for budget travelers who don't mind squeezing sideways to make it past the bed into the bathroom. The half-timbered interior gives the lobby a trace of character, but also makes for dark hallways. Rooms are clean, but lack charm (some view rooms, no elevator, no air-con, 9 Rue d'Ormesson, tel. 01 48 87 80 47, www.pratichotelparis.com, pratic.hotel@wanadoo.fr).

$ Sully Hôtel, right on Rue St. Antoine, is a basic, cheap dive run by no-nonsense Monsieur Zeroual. The rooms are frumpy, dimly lit, and can smell of smoke, the entry is dark and narrow (need I say more?), but the price fits. Two can spring for a triple for more room (family rooms, no elevator, no air-con, 48 Rue St. Antoine, Mo: St-Paul, tel. 01 42 78 49 32, www.sullyhotelparis. com, sullyhotel@orange.fr).

¢ MIJE Youth Hostels: The Maison Internationale de la Jeunesse et des Etudiants (MIJE) runs three classy, old residences, ideal for budget travelers who are at least 18 years old or traveling with someone who is. Each is well-maintained, with simple, clean, single-sex (unless your group takes a whole room) one- to four-bed rooms. The hostels are **MIJE Fourcy** (biggest and loudest, dirt-cheap dinners available with a membership card, 6 Rue de Fourcy, just south of Rue de Rivoli), **MIJE Fauconnier** (no elevator, 11 Rue du Fauconnier), and **MIJE Maubisson** (smallest and quietest, no outdoor terrace, 12 Rue des Barres). None has double beds or air-conditioning, all have private showers in every room—but bring your own towel (includes breakfast, required membership card-€2.50 extra/person, Wi-Fi in common areas only, rooms locked 12:00-15:00). They all share the same contact information (tel. 01 42 74 23 45, www.mije.com, info@mije.com) and Métro stop (St-Paul). Show up by noon or call to confirm a later arrival time.

East of Boulevard Richard Lenoir
(11th arrond., Mo: Bastille or Bréguet–Sabin)

These cheaper hotels are located a 10-minute walk from Place des Vosges.

$$$ Hôtel Ibis Paris Bastille Opéra*** is well-run and massive, with 300 reasonably priced, modern, comfortable rooms and a lobby with guest computers and room to roam. Amenities include an economical restaurant and private parking (15 Rue Breguet, Mo: Bréguet–Sabin, tel. 01 49 29 20 20, www.ibishotel. com, H1399@accor.com).

$$ Hôtel Daval,** a simple place on the wild side of Place de la Bastille, is handy for night owls. The 23 rooms are small, modest, and clean, with bathrooms like ship cabins, but the rates are good for an air-conditioned place. Ask for a quieter room on the courtyard side (family rooms, 21 Rue Daval, Mo: Bastille, tel. 01 47 00 51 23, www.hoteldaval.com, hoteldaval@wanadoo.fr).

Near the Pompidou Center
(4th arrond., Mo: St-Paul, Hôtel de Ville, or Rambuteau)

These hotels are farther west, closer to the Pompidou Center than to Place de la Bastille.

$$$$ Hôtel Caron de Beaumarchais* ** transports you to the 18th century, with a small lobby that's cluttered with bits from an elegant old Marais house. If you want traditional French decor, stay here. Located on a busy street, it is well cared for and filled with character (12 Rue Vieille du Temple, tel. 01 42 72 34 12, www.carondebeaumarchais.com, hotel@carondebeaumarchais.com).

$$$ Hôtel de la Bretonnerie* ** makes a fine Marais home. Located three blocks from the Hôtel de Ville, it has a warm, welcoming lobby and helpful staff. Its 29 good-value rooms are on the larger side with an antique, open-beam warmth (family rooms, free breakfast for Rick Steves readers who book directly, no air-con, between Rue Vieille du Temple and Rue des Archives at 22 Rue Ste. Croix de la Bretonnerie, tel. 01 48 87 77 63, www.hotelparismaraisbretonnerie.com, hotel@bretonnerie.com).

$$$ Hôtel Beaubourg* ** is a terrific three-star value on a small street in the shadow of the Pompidou Center. The lounge is inviting, and the 28 plush and traditional rooms are well-appointed and quiet (bigger doubles are worth the extra cost, 11 Rue Simon Le Franc, Mo: Rambuteau, tel. 01 42 74 34 24, www.hotelbeaubourg.com, reservation@hotelbeaubourg.com).

$$ Hôtel de Nice,* ** on the Marais' busy main drag, features a turquoise-and-fuchsia "Marie-Antoinette-does-tie-dye" decor. This character-filled place is littered with paintings and layered with carpets, and its 23 Old World rooms have thoughtful touches. Rooms on the street come with some noise; bathrooms are tight (reception on second floor, 42 bis Rue de Rivoli, tel. 01 42 78 55 29, www.hoteldenice.com, contact@hoteldenice.com).

$$ Hôtel du Loiret* ** feels like the budget place it is when you walk in, but the rooms are surprisingly sharp—though bathrooms are small, and the service lacks a certain *je ne sais quoi* (no air-con, expect some noise, 8 Rue des Mauvais Garçons, tel. 01 48 87 77 00, www.hotel-du-loiret.fr, hotelduloiret@hotmail.com).

$$ D'Win Hôtel ** is a rare two-star value in the thick of the Marais, with 40 updated and relatively spacious rooms, no elevator, and red accents everywhere (family rooms, 20 Rue du Temple, tel. 01 44 54 05 05, www.dwinhotel.com, contact@dwinhotel.com).

Near Rue de Bretagne
(3rd arrond., Mo: Filles du Calvaire or Temple)

Called the Haute (upper) Marais, this part of town attracts those wanting easy access to the heart of the Marais and a quieter neighborhood with a more local vibe. Appealing Rue de Bretagne is the soul of this area, with broad sidewalks, a healthy dose of cafés and shops, plus the lively Marché des Enfants Rouges market area. Allow 15 minutes to walk from these hotels to the Marais' main drag, Rue St. Antoine. The hotels themselves are all within a short walk of Rue de Bretagne.

$$$ Hôtel du Vieux Saule,*** well located across from the Marché des Enfants Rouges, offers 26 simple rooms in a good location at fair rates (smoking allowed in rooms on third floor, small sauna free for guests, 6 Rue de Picardie, Mo: Filles du Calvaire or Temple, tel. 01 42 72 01 14, www.hotelvieuxsaule.com, reserv@hotelvieuxsaule.com).

$$$ Hôtel Saintonge*** is a tastefully decorated and well-maintained place with wooden beams and stone floors (16 Rue de Saintonge, Mo: Filles du Calvaire, tel. 01 42 77 91 13, www.saintlouissaintonge.com, saintonge@saintlouis-hotels.com).

ILE ST. LOUIS
(4th arrond., Mo: Pont Marie)

The peaceful, residential character of this river-wrapped island, with its brilliant location and homemade ice cream, has drawn Americans for decades. There are no budget deals here—all of the hotels are three-star or more—though prices are respectable considering the level of comfort and wonderful location. The island's village ambience and proximity to the Marais, Notre-Dame, and the Latin Quarter make this area well worth considering. All of the following hotels are on the island's main drag, Rue St. Louis-en-l'Ile, where I list several restaurants (see page 438 in the Eating in Paris chapter). For nearby services, see the Marais neighborhood section; for locations, see the "Marais Hotels" map on page 400. There are no Métro stops on Ile St. Louis; expect a 10-minute walk to the closest stations.

$$$$ Hôtel du Jeu de Paume**** occupies a 17th-century tennis center. Its magnificent lobby and cozy public spaces make it a fine splurge. Greet Lemon (luh-moe), *le chien*, then take a spin in the glass elevator for a half-timbered treehouse experience. The 30 rooms are carefully designed and tasteful, though not particularly spacious (you're paying for the location and public areas). Most rooms face a small garden courtyard; all are pin-drop peaceful (apartments for 4-6 people, 54 Rue St. Louis-en-l'Ile, tel. 01 43 26 14 18, www.jeudepaumehotel.com, info@jeudepaumehotel.com).

$$$$ Hôtel de Lutèce*** comes with a welcoming wood-paneled lobby and a real fireplace. Rooms are traditional and warm, and those on lower floors have high ceilings. Twin rooms are larger and the same price as doubles; most beds are doubles (no queens). Rooms with bathtubs are on the louder street-side, while those with showers are on the courtyard (65 Rue St. Louis-en-l'Ile, tel. 01 43 26 23 52, www.hoteldelutece.com, info@hoteldelutece.com).

$$$$ Hôtel des Deux-Iles*** has the same owners, comfort, and prices as the Lutèce (listed above)—but a tad less personality (single rooms available, 59 Rue St. Louis-en-l'Ile, tel. 01 43 26 13 35, www.hoteldesdeuxiles.com, info@hoteldesdeuxiles.com).

$$$ Hôtel Saint-Louis*** blends character with modern comforts. The sharp rooms come with cool stone floors and exposed beams. Rates are reasonable...for the location (some rooms with balcony, iPads available for guest use, 75 Rue St. Louis-en-l'Ile, tel. 01 46 34 04 80, www.hotelsaintlouis.com, isle@saintlouis-hotels. com).

LUXEMBOURG GARDEN AREA

This neighborhood revolves around Paris' loveliest park and offers quick access to the city's best shopping streets and grandest café-hopping. Hotels in this central area run the gamut from cheap sleeps to pricey boutique places. Sleeping in the Luxembourg area offers a true Left Bank experience without a hint of the low-end commotion of the nearby Latin Quarter tourist ghetto. The Luxembourg Garden, Boulevard St. Germain, Cluny Museum, and Latin Quarter are all at your doorstep, and Place St. Michel is a 15-minute walk away. Here you get the best of both worlds: youthful Left Bank energy and the classic trappings that surround the monumental Panthéon and St. Sulpice Church.

Having the Luxembourg Garden as your backyard allows strolls through meticulously cared-for flowers, a great kids' play area (see the Paris with Children chapter), and a purifying escape from city traffic. Place St. Sulpice presents an elegant, pedestrian-friendly square and quick access to some of Paris' best boutiques (see the Shopping in Paris chapter). You're near several movie theaters (at Métro stop: Odéon), as well as lively cafés on Boulevard St. Germain, Rue de Buci, Rue des Canettes, Place de la Sorbonne, and Place de la Contrescarpe, all of which buzz with action until late.

It takes only about 15 minutes to walk from one end of this neighborhood to the other. Most hotels are within a five-minute walk of the Luxembourg Garden.

Services: The nearest **TI** is across the river at the Pyramides Métro station (daily May-Oct 9:00-19:00, Nov-April 10:00-19:00, 25 Rue des Pyramides). There are two useful **SNCF Boutiques** nearby, at 79 Rue de Rennes (Mon-Sat 10:00-19:00, closed Sun)

Hotels near Luxembourg Garden

200 Meters
200 Yards

N

Rue du Bac

To Orsay

To Pont des Arts & Louvre

RUE DES BEAUX-ARTS

R. BONAPARTE

RUE VISCONTI

RUE MAZARINE

RUE JACOB

R. FÜRST

RUE DE SEINE

BOULEVARD ST. GERMAIN

RUE PRE AUX CLERCS

RUE DE GRENELLE

RUE DES STS.-PÈRES

RUE ST. BENOIT

RUE DU DRAGON

RUE DE L'ABBAYE

Place St. Germain-des-Prés

DELACROIX MUSEUM

St-Germain-des-Prés

ST. GERMAIN-DES-PRES

RUE DE BUCI

RUE LE GRANDE

BLVD. RASPAIL

RUE CHAIX

RUE DE SÈVRES

RUE REC.

RUE DE RENNES

CHERCHE-MIDI

#86 & 87

Mabillion

RUE DU FOUR

POST

RUE BONAPARTE

R. CANETTES

R. PRINC.

R. GUISARDE

#70

R. CHOMEL

R. DE BABYLONE

Sèvres-Babylone

RUE DE SÈVRES

St. Sulpice

#86, 87, 96

Place St. Sulpice

RUE ST.-SULPICE

RUE DE TOURNON

ST. SULPICE

RUE MEZIERES

GARANCIÈRE

POST

RUE MADAME

RUE CASSETTE

RUE BONAPARTE

RUE FEROU

RUE SERVANDONI

RUE DE VAUGIRARD

LUXEMBOURG PALACE

BLVD. RASPAIL

RUE DU REGARD

RUE SAINT-PLACIDE

Rennes

RUE D'ASSAS

RUE GUYNEMER

SANDPIT & WADING POOL (SUMMER ONLY)

CARDS & CHESS

WC

Luxembourg Garden

TENNIS

PONIES

Pond

St. Placide

WC

CAFE

MERRY-GO-ROUND

PUPPET THEATER

TOY SAILBOAT RENTAL

SWINGS

KIDS' PLAY AREA

TENNIS

Notre-Dame-des-Champs

RUE NOTRE-DAME-DES-CHAMPS

RUE YAVIN

RUE AUGUSTE COMTE

GRASS (OK FOR PLAY)

RUE DE MONTPARNASSE

To Montparnasse Tower

SLEEPING

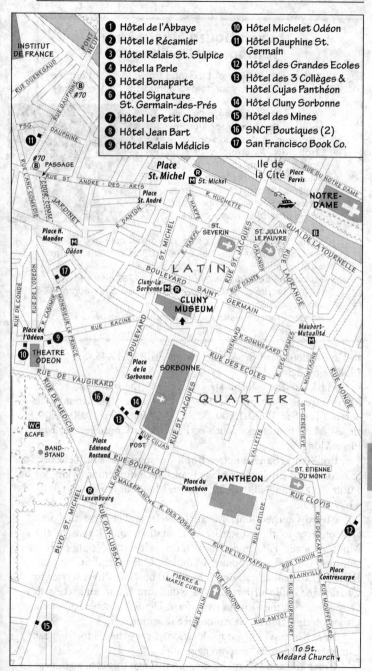

1 Hôtel de l'Abbaye
2 Hôtel le Récamier
3 Hôtel Relais St. Sulpice
4 Hôtel la Perle
5 Hôtel Bonaparte
6 Hôtel Signature St. Germain-des-Prés
7 Hôtel Le Petit Chomel
8 Hôtel Jean Bart
9 Hôtel Relais Médicis
10 Hôtel Michelet Odéon
11 Hôtel Dauphine St. Germain
12 Hôtel des Grandes Ecoles
13 Hôtel des 3 Collèges & Hôtel Cujas Panthéon
14 Hôtel Cluny Sorbonne
15 Hôtel des Mines
16 SNCF Boutiques (2)
17 San Francisco Book Co.

Luxembourg Musts for Temporary Residents

- Pass oodles of time at Luxembourg Garden, sitting in a green chair with your feet propped up on the pond's edge.
- Join the locals at the only café on Place St. Sulpice for a morning coffee or afternoon drink.
- Stroll Rue Mouffetard day or night, and stop for a drink on Place de la Contrescarpe.
- Window shop the boutiques between Sèvres-Babylone and St. Sulpice (described on page 475).
- Spend too much for a coffee at a grand café and watch the world go by (see "Les Grands Cafés de Paris," page 447).
- Follow my Left Bank Walk (see page 278) and find Voltaire's favorite café (Café le Procope, now a restaurant—see page 285).
- Ponder France's history in the Panthéon (see page 75).

and at 54 Boulevard St. Michel (Mon-Fri 8:15-19:45, Sat 10:00-18:00, closed Sun).

Markets: The colorful street market at the south end of Rue Mouffetard is a worthwhile 10- to 15-minute walk from these hotels (Tue-Sat 10:00-13:00 & 16:00-19:00, Sun 10:00-13:00, closed Mon, five blocks south of Place de la Contrescarpe, Mo: Place Monge).

Bookstore: San Francisco Book Company has a full selection of secondhand English-language books, including mine (Mon-Sat 11:00-21:00, Sun 14:00-19:30, 17 Rue Monsieur le Prince, tel. 01 43 29 15 70).

Métro Connections: Métro lines 10 and 4 serve this area (10 connects to the Austerlitz train station, and 4 runs to the Montparnasse, Est, and Nord train stations). Neighborhood stops are Cluny-La Sorbonne, Mabillon, Odéon, and St. Sulpice. RER-B (Luxembourg station is handiest) provides direct service to Charles de Gaulle airport and Gare du Nord trains, and access to Orly airport via the Orlybus (transfer at Denfert-Rochereau) or via Orlyval trains (transfer at Antony RER station).

Bus Routes: For stop locations, see the "Hotels near Luxembourg Garden" map on page 406.

Lines #86 and **#87** run eastbound through this area on or near Boulevard St. Germain, to the Marais (#87 continues to Gare de

Lyon). They run westbound along Rue des Écoles, stopping on Place St. Sulpice (#87 continues to the Rue Cler area).

Line #63 provides a direct connection along Boulevard St. Germain west to the Rue Cler area, serving the Orsay and Marmottan museums along the way, and east to Gare de Lyon.

Line #96 stops at Place St. Sulpice southbound en route to Gare Montparnasse and runs north along Rue de Rennes and Boulevard St. Germain into the Marais.

Line #70 runs along Rue de Sèvres, connecting Sèvres-Babylone and St. Sulpice with the Pompidou Center and the Hôtel de Ville.

Taxi: A taxi stand is near Place Pigalle, along Boulevard de Clichy.

Near St. Sulpice Church
(6th arrond., Mo: St. Sulpice, Rennes, Sèvres-Babylone, Mabillon, Odéon, or Saint-Germain-des-Prés; RER: Luxembourg)
These hotels are all within a block of St. Sulpice Church and two blocks from famous Boulevard St. Germain. This is nirvana for boutique-minded shoppers—and you'll pay extra for the location.

$$$$ Hôtel de l'Abbaye**** is a lovely refuge just west of Luxembourg Garden; it's a find for well-heeled connoisseurs of this area. The hotel's four-star luxury includes refined lounges inside and out, with 44 sumptuous rooms and every amenity (apartments, includes breakfast, 10 Rue Cassette, tel. 01 45 44 38 11, www.hotelabbayeparis.com, hotel.abbaye@wanadoo.fr).

$$$$ Hôtel le Récamier,**** romantically tucked in the corner of Place St. Sulpice, is a polished place with designer public spaces, elaborately appointed rooms, a courtyard tea salon serving guests complimentary tea and treats in the afternoon, and top-notch professional service (connecting family rooms, 3 bis Place St. Sulpice, tel. 01 43 26 04 89, www.hotelrecamier.com, contact@hotelrecamier.com).

$$$$ Hôtel Relais St. Sulpice,*** burrowed on the small street just behind St. Sulpice Church, is a high-priced boutique hotel with a cozy lounge and 26 stylish rooms, most surrounding a leafy glass atrium. Street-facing rooms get more light and are worth requesting (sauna free for guests, 3 Rue Garancière, tel. 01 46 33 99 00, www.relais-saint-sulpice.com, relaisstsulpice@wanadoo.fr).

$$$$ Hôtel la Perle*** is a spendy place in the thick of the lively Rue des Canettes, a block off Place St. Sulpice. This modern business-class hotel is built around a central bar and atrium but lacks character (luxury apartment, 14 Rue des Canettes, tel. 01 43 29 10 10, www.hotellaperle.com, booking@hotellaperle.com).

$$$ Hôtel Bonaparte*** is an unpretentious and welcoming

SLEEPING

place wedged between boutiques, a few steps from Place St. Sulpice. The simple, recently refurbished decor highlights the beauty of this traditional building (61 Rue Bonaparte, tel. 01 43 26 97 37, www. hotelbonaparte.fr, reservation@hotelbonaparte.fr; helpful Eric, Fréderic, and owner Olivier at reception).

West of Luxembourg Garden
(6th and 7th arrond., Mo: Sèvres-Babylone or St. Sulpice)
$$$$ Hôtel Signature St. Germain-des-Prés,*** on a quiet street just steps from the trendy Sèvres-Babylone shopping area, feels as chic as its neighboring boutiques. Young owner Delphine takes great care of her guests with 26 colorful and tastefully decorated rooms, several with balconies. There are good rooms for families and some wonderfully large "prestige" rooms (5 Rue Chomel, Mo: Sèvres-Babylone, tel. 01 45 48 35 53, www.signature-saintgermain. com, info@signature-saintgermain.com).

$$$$ Hôtel Le Petit Chomel*** sits a few doors down, offering the same great location and comfort, warm public spaces, and traditional country-French decor (15 Rue Chomel, tel. 01 45 48 55 52, www.lepetitchomel.com, info@lepetitchomel.com).

$$ Hôtel Jean Bart**** feels like it's from another era—prices included. Run by smiling Madame Lechopier and her family, it's a rare budget find in this neighborhood, one block from Luxembourg Garden. Beyond the dark lobby, you'll find 33 suitably comfortable rooms with creaking floors and tight bathrooms (includes breakfast, no air-con, 9 Rue Jean-Bart, tel. 01 45 48 29 13, www.hotel-jean-bart.fr, hotel.jean.bart@gmail.com).

Near the Odéon Theater
(6th arrond., Mo: Odéon, Cluny-La Sorbonne, or Mabillon; RER: Luxembourg)
The first hotel is between the Odéon Métro stop and Luxembourg Garden, and may have rooms when others don't. Hôtel Dauphine St. Germain is closer to the Seine.

$$$$ Hôtel Relais Médicis*** is ideal if you've always wanted to live in a Monet painting and can afford it. A glassy entry hides 17 rooms surrounding a fragrant little garden courtyard and fountain, giving you a countryside break fit for a Medici in the heart of Paris. This delightful refuge is tastefully decorated with floral Old World charm and permeated with thoughtfulness (family rooms, includes continental breakfast, faces the Odéon Theater at 5 Place de l'Odéon, tel. 01 43 26 00 60, www.relaismedicis.com, reservation@relaismedicis.com).

$$$ Hôtel Dauphine St. Germain*** delivers all the comforts you need in a killer location between the river and Boule-

SLEEPING

vard St. Germain (36 Rue Dauphine, tel. 01 43 26 74 34, www.
dauphine-st-germain.com, hotel@dauphine-st-germain.com).

$$ Hôtel Michelet Odéon** sits in a corner of Place de
l'Odéon with big windows overlooking the square. Rooms come
with stylish colors but no frills (family rooms, no air-con, 6 Place
de l'Odéon, tel. 01 53 10 05 60, www.hotelmicheletodeon.com,
hotel@micheletodeon.com).

Near the Panthéon and Rue Mouffetard
**(5th arrond., Mo: Cardinal Lemoine, Place Monge, Jussieu, or
Cluny-La Sorbonne; RER: Luxembourg)**
$$ Hôtel des Grandes Ecoles*** is idyllic. A private cobbled
lane leads to three buildings that protect a flower-filled garden
courtyard, preserving a sense of tranquility rare in this city. Its
51 rooms are French-countryside pretty, reasonably spacious,
and lovingly cared for by your host, Marie. This romantic spot is
deservedly popular; book ahead (no TVs or air-con but no street
noise, pricey pay parking, 75 Rue du Cardinal Lemoine, Mo:
Cardinal Lemoine, tel. 01 43 26 79 23, www.hotel-grandes-ecoles.
com, hotel.grandes.ecoles@free.fr).

$$ Hôtel des 3 Collèges** greets clients with a bright
lobby, narrow hallways, and plain rooms. Rates are fair, and the
smiling staff is eager to please (16 Rue Cujas, tel. 01 43 54 67 30,
www.3colleges.fr, hotel@3colleges.fr@3colleges.fr).

$$ Hôtel Cujas Panthéon** gives boring, standard two-star
comfort at affordable prices (Db-€130-155, 18 Rue Cujas, tel. 01 43
54 58 10, www.cujas-pantheon-paris-hotel.com, cujaspantheon@
gmail.com).

$ Hôtel Cluny Sorbonne** is a basic budget place located in
the thick of things across from the famous university and below the
Panthéon. Rooms are well-worn, with thin walls (no air-con, 8 Rue
Victor Cousin, tel. 01 43 54 66 66, www.hotel-cluny.fr, cluny@
club-internet.fr).

South of Luxembourg Garden
(5th arrond., RER: Luxembourg or Port-Royal)
$$$ Hôtel des Mines** is less central, but its good-size lobby and
50 well-maintained rooms make this a decent value. Avoid the
fifth- and sixth-floor rooms, which lack double-glazed windows
(family rooms, between Luxembourg and Port-Royal stations on
the RER-B line, a 10-minute walk from Panthéon, one block past
Luxembourg Garden at 125 Boulevard St. Michel, tel. 01 43 54
32 78, www.hoteldesminesparis.com, hotel@hoteldesminesparis.
com).

SLEEPING

Hotels & Restaurants near Rue Mouffetard

1. Port-Royal-Hôtel
2. Hôtel de L'Espérance
3. Young & Happy Hostel
4. Café Delmas
5. Cave de Bourgogne

At the Bottom of Rue Mouffetard
(5th arrond., Mo: Censier Daubenton or Les Gobelins)

These accommodations, away from the Seine and other tourists, lie in an appealing and unpretentious area and offer more room for your euro. Rue Mouffetard is the bohemian soul of this area. Two thousand years ago, it was the principal Roman road south to Italy. Today, this small, meandering street has a split personality. The lower half thrives in the daytime as a pedestrian shopping street. The upper half sleeps during the day but comes alive after dark with a fun collection of restaurants and bars. A lively Saturday market sprawls along Boulevard Port Royal, just east of the Port Royal Métro stop.

$ Port-Royal-Hôtel* has only one star, but don't let that fool you. Its 46 rooms are polished top to bottom and have been well-run by the same proud family for 80-plus years. You could eat off the floors of its spotless, comfy rooms...but you won't find air-conditioning or a TV. Ask for a room away from the street (cheaper rooms with pay shower down the hall, cash only or wire transfer, on busy Boulevard de Port-Royal at #8, Mo: Les Gobelins, tel. 01 43 31 70 06, www.hotelportroyal.fr, portroyalhotel@wanadoo.fr).

$ Hôtel de L'Espérance** is simply a terrific two-star value. It's quiet and cushy, with soft rooms, canopy beds, and a welcoming lobby with a small bar (15 Rue Pascal, Mo: Censier Daubenton, tel. 01 47 07 10 99, www.hoteldelesperance.fr, hotel.esperance@wanadoo.fr).

¢ Young & Happy Hostel is easygoing and English-speaking, with kitchen facilities and basic hostel conditions. It sits dead-center in the Rue Mouffetard action...which can be good or bad (private rooms available, includes breakfast, no air-con, key deposit, 11:00-16:00 lockout but reception stays open and you can stash your bags, no curfew, 80 Rue Mouffetard, Mo: Place Monge, tel. 01 47 07 47 07, www.youngandhappy.fr, smile@youngandhappy.fr).

MONTMARTRE

Those interested in a more SoHo/Greenwich Village-type locale should consider making Montmartre their Parisian home. While the top of Montmartre's hill is terribly touristy, just below lies an overlooked workaday neighborhood happily living in the shadow of Sacré-Cœur.

Montmartre is a mix of young families, artists, and spritely senior citizens, and it is fast becoming popular with the *bobo* crowd (*bourgeois bohemian*, French for "hipster"). Travelers staying here trade a central location and level terrain for good deals on hotel rooms and a lively atmosphere, especially in the evenings when the terraces are full and tiny bars spill crowds onto the narrow streets. Expect some ups and downs here on Paris' lone hill.

Most of the action is centered around Rue des Abbesses, starting at Place des Abbesses and stretching several blocks to Rue Lepic. Rue Lepic has good shops and services, but the lower you go the seedier it gets: Scammers and shady characters prowl the base of the hill after hours (along Boulevard Clichy and Boulevard Rochechouart, where you'll find what's left of Paris' red light district). For fun nightlife, stick to the narrow streets uphill from Rue des Abbesses around Rue Durantin and along Rue des Trois Frères. For restaurant suggestions, see page 445.

Tourist Information: TI kiosks are located at the Anvers Métro stop (daily 10:00-18:00, 72 Boulevard Rochechouart) and on the top of the hill on Place du Tertre (daily 10:00-18:00, 21 Place du Tertre).

Services: Several ATMs are located along Rue des Abbesses and on Rue Lepic. You'll find a **post office** on Place des Abbesses (to your left as you exit the Abbesses Métro stop).

Markets and Shopping: A Friday-evening farmers' market reflects this working-class neighborhood's shopping needs (15:00-20:00, Place d'Anvers). On Saturday mornings, one of Paris' only organic markets takes place within reasonable walking

Hotels & Restaurants in Montmartre

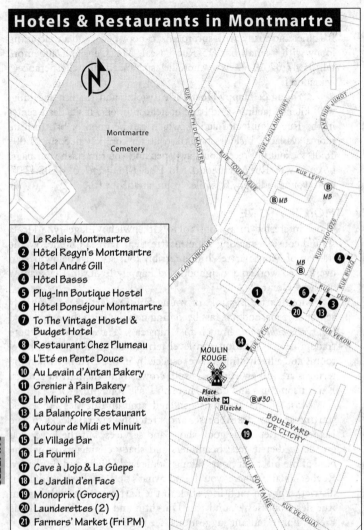

1 Le Relais Montmartre
2 Hôtel Regyn's Montmartre
3 Hôtel André Gill
4 Hôtel Basss
5 Plug-Inn Boutique Hostel
6 Hôtel Bonséjour Montmartre
7 To The Vintage Hostel & Budget Hotel
8 Restaurant Chez Plumeau
9 L'Eté en Pente Douce
10 Au Levain d'Antan Bakery
11 Grenier à Pain Bakery
12 Le Miroir Restaurant
13 La Balançoire Restaurant
14 Autour de Midi et Minuit
15 Le Village Bar
16 La Fourmi
17 Cave à Jojo & La Gûepe
18 Le Jardin d'en Face
19 Monoprix (Grocery)
20 Launderettes (2)
21 Farmers' Market (Fri PM)

SLEEPING

distance (Marché des Batignolles, 9:00-15:00, 34 Boulevard des Batignolles). A **Monoprix** store is near the Blanche Métro stop on Boulevard de Clichy. Both Rue Lepic and Rue des Abbesses are peppered with *épiceries,* cheese shops, wine shops, delis, butchers, and bakeries.

Laundry: Handy self-service launderettes are located at 92 Rue des Martyrs and 44 Rue Veron.

Métro Connections: Métro line 12 is the handiest (use the Abbesses stop and take the elevator, as it's a long climb to the exit). Line 2 uses the Blanche, Pigalle, or Anvers stops, but requires a

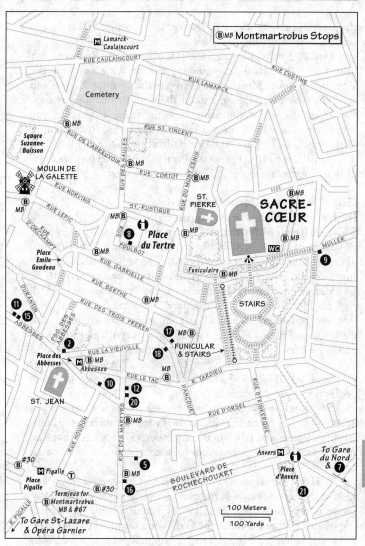

ⒷMB **Montmartrobus Stops**

four-block uphill walk to reach my recommended hotels. The Barbès Rochechouart Métro stop is also close by, but it should be avoided thanks to the number of young hooligans who hang out there.

Bus Routes: At the base of the hill are several good bus options, but there's only one bus line on the hill itself—the Montmartrobus electric bus—which connects Pigalle, Abbesses, and Place du Tertre in 10 minutes (4/hour). For stop locations, see the "Hotels & Restaurants in Montmartre" map.

Line #67 (catch it next to the Pigalle Métro station) goes to the Louvre, along the Seine by the Marais, across Ile St. Louis, and eventually to the Jardin des Plantes.

Line #30 picks up on the north side of Boulevard Rochechouart (direction: Trocadéro) and goes past Parc Monceau and the Jacquemart-André Museum, to the top of the Champs-Elysées and around the Arc de Triomphe roundabout, to its final destination, the Trocadéro, across the Seine from the Eiffel Tower. Or, you could catch line #30 on the south side of Boulevard Rochechouart (direction: Gare de l'Est) and ride it directly to Gare de l'Est.

Taxi: A taxi stand is near the Pigalle Métro stop on the corner of Rue Houdon and busy Boulevard Rochechouart.

Good Values in Montmartre
(18th arrond., Mo: Abbesses or Anvers)

$$$$ Le Relais Montmartre*** is a spotless hotel with cushy public spaces, pastel paint, and 26 cozy rooms sporting floral curtains. There are lots of guest-centered amenities, including a shared iPad, a fireplace, and a quiet central courtyard (6 Rue Constance, tel. 01 70 64 25 25, www.relaismontmartre.fr, contact@relaismontmartre.fr).

$$ Hôtel Regyn's Montmartre** is located on the lively Abbesses square, with 22 small but comfortable-enough rooms and mediocre bathrooms. Rooms in the front come with pleasant views and noise from the square. Guests in fourth- and fifth-floor rooms can see all the way to the Eiffel Tower (no air-con, 18 Place des Abbesses, tel. 01 42 54 45 21, www.hotel-regyns-paris.com, resa@hotel-regyns-montmartre.net).

$$ Hotel Basss offers snappy modern rooms with splashes of color and trendy furniture. Guests are invited to lounge in the lobby with free coffee and treats in the afternoon (57 Rue des Abbesses, tel. 01 42 51 50 00, www.hotel-basss.com, contact@hotel-basss.com).

$ Hôtel Bonséjour Montmartre, run by eager Michel and his family, was old and worn, but it's slowly modernizing. Most rooms now come with toilets, showers, and new beds; the remaining (cheaper) ones maintain the Old World tradition of shared facilities. Request an upgraded room, especially one with a balcony (RS%, includes breakfast, no air-con, 11 Rue Burq, tel. 01 42 54 22 53, www.hotel-bonsejour-montmartre.fr, hotel-bonsejour-montmartre@wanadoo.fr).

$ Hôtel André Gill** is a family affair. The hallways and elevator are alarmingly dark and narrow, but the rooms are bright and clean (some view rooms, 4 Rue André Gill, tel. 01 42 62 48 48, andregill@hotmail.fr).

¢ Plug-Inn Boutique Hostel is part hotel and part hostel, but with a hotel vibe. A half-block off Rue des Abbesses, it has a young, loud clientele and bathrooms in all 30 rooms. Early arrivals can leave their luggage and take a shower (private rooms available, includes breakfast, 24-hour front desk staff, no curfew, 7 Rue Aristide Bruant, tel. 01 42 58 42 58, www.plug-inn.fr, bonjour@plug-inn.fr).

¢ The **Vintage Hostel & Budget Hotel** sits halfway between the hill of Montmartre and Gare du Nord (both destinations are a 10-minute walk away). This hostel-hotel hybrid appeals to youngsters and oldsters alike. Private double rooms, many with balconies, are on the top two floors (includes breakfast, 73 Rue de Dunkerque, tel. 01 40 16 16 40, www.vintage-hostel.com, contact@vintage-hostel.com).

AT OR NEAR PARIS' AIRPORTS
At Charles de Gaulle Airport

These places are located a few minutes from the terminals, outside the T-3 RER stop, and have restaurants. For locations, see the map on page 510.

$$$ Novotel*** is a step up from cookie-cutter airport hotels (tel. 01 49 19 27 27, www.novotel.com, h1014@accor.com).

$$ Hôtel Ibis CDG Airport** is huge and offers standard airport accommodations (tel. 01 49 19 19 19, www.ibishotel.com, h1404@accor.com).

Near Charles de Gaulle Airport, in Roissy

The small village of Roissy-en-France (you'll see signs just before the airport as you come from Paris) has better-value chain hotels with free airport-shuttle service (4/hour, 15 minutes, look for *navettes hôtels* signs to reach these hotels, see www.hotels-roissy-tourisme.com/en). Hotels have reasonably priced restaurants with long hours, though it's more pleasant to walk into the town, where you'll find a bakery, pizzeria, cafés, and a few restaurants. Most Roissy hotels list specials on their websites.

The following hotels are within walking distance of the town. **$$ Hôtel Ibis CDG Paris Nord 2**** is usually cheaper than the Ibis right at the airport (335 Rue de la Belle Etoile, tel. 01 48 17 56 56, www.ibishotel.com, h3299@accor.com). **$$ Hôtel Campanile Roissy***** is a decent place to sleep, and you can have a good dinner next door at Hôtel Golden Tulip (Allée des Vergers, tel. 01 34 29 80 40, www.campanile-roissy.fr, roissy@campanile.fr). **$$$ Hôtel Golden Tulip Paris CDG***** has a fitness center, sauna, and good restaurant for the suburbs (11 Allée des Vergers, tel. 01 34 29 00 00, www.goldentulipcdgvillepinte.com, info@goldentulipcdgvillepinte.com). The cheapest option is **$ B&B Hôtel Roissy CDG***, where many flight attendants stay (17 Allée des Vergers, tel. 01 34 38 55 55, or 02 98 33 75 29, www.hotel-bb.com/roissy).

To avoid rush-hour traffic, drivers can consider sleeping north

SLEEPING

of Paris in either **Auvers-sur-Oise** (30 minutes west of airport; see recommendations on page 612) or in the pleasant medieval town of **Senlis** (15 minutes north of airport). **$$ Hôtel Ibis Senlis**** is a few minutes from town (Route Nationale A1, tel. 03 44 53 70 50, www.ibishotel.com, h0709@accor.com).

Near Orly Airport

Two chain hotels, owned by the same company and very close to the Sud terminal, are your best options near Orly. Both have free shuttles *(navettes)* to the terminal.

$$$ Hôtel Mercure Paris Orly*** provides high comfort for a high price (tel. 08 25 80 69 69, www.accorhotel.com, h1246@accor.com).

$$ Hôtel Ibis Orly Aéroport** is reasonable and basic (tel. 01 56 70 50 60, www.ibishotel.com, h1413@accor.com).

APARTMENT RENTALS

Consider this option if you're traveling as a family, in a group, or staying at least a few nights. Intrepid travelers around the world are accustomed to using Airbnb and VRBO when it comes to renting a vacation apartment. In Paris, you have many additional options among rental agencies, and I've found the following to be the most reliable. Their websites are good and essential to understanding your choices. Read the rental conditions very carefully.

Most of these agencies are middlemen, offering an ever-changing selection of private apartments for rent on a weekly basis (or longer). If staying a month or more, you may save money by renting directly from the apartment owners. Check the housing section in the ad-filled paper *France-USA Contacts* (available at the American Church and elsewhere in Paris), or check out www.fusac.fr. For more information on renting apartments, see page 637 in the Practicalities chapter.

Paris Perfect has offices in Paris with English-speaking staff who seek the "perfect apartment" for their clients and are selective about what they offer. Their service gets rave reviews. Many units have Eiffel Tower views, and most include free Wi-Fi, free local and international phone calls, satellite TV, air-conditioning, and washers and dryers (RS%, US toll-free tel. 888-520-2087, www.parisperfect.com, reservations@parisperfect.com).

Adrian Leeds Group offers apartments owned by North Americans and is ideal for travelers looking for all the comforts, conveniences, and amenities of home (tel. 877-880-0265, ext. 701, www.adrianleeds.com, apartments@adrianleeds.com).

France Homestyle is run by Claudette, a service-oriented French woman who now lives in Seattle and has hand-picked every apartment she lists (US tel. 206/325-0132, www.francehomestyle. com, info@francehomestyle.com).

Home Rental Service has been in business for 20-something years and offers a big selection of apartments throughout Paris with no agency fees (120 Champs-Elysées, tel. 01 42 25 65 40, www. homerental.fr, info@homerental.fr).

Haven in Paris offers exactly that—well-appointed, stylish havens for travelers looking for a place to temporarily call home. Their fun blog, *Hip Paris,* is also worth checking out (tel. 617/395-4243, www.haveninparis.com, info@haveninparis.com).

Paris Home is a small outfit, with only two little studios and a one-bedroom unit, located on Rue Amélie in the heart of the Rue Cler area (see map on page 390). Each has modern furnishings and laundry facilities. Friendly Slim, the owner, is the best part (no minimum stay, special rates for longer stays, credit cards accepted, free maid service, airport/train station transfers possible, mobile 06 19 03 17 55, www.parishome2000.com, parishome2000@yahoo.fr).

Cobblestone Paris Rentals is a small, North American-run outfit offering furnished rentals in central neighborhoods. All apartments have Wi-Fi, international phone calls, and cable TV for free. Apartments come stocked with English-language DVDs about Paris, coffee, tea, cooking spices, basic bathroom amenities, and an English-speaking greeter who will give you the lay of the land (two free river cruises for Rick Steves readers who book a stay of five nights or more, www.cobblestoneparis.com, reservations@cobblestoneparis.com).

Paris for Rent, a San Francisco-based group, has been renting top-end apartments in Paris for more than a decade (US tel. 866-4-FRANCE, www.parisforrent.com).

Cross-Pollinate is a reputable online booking agency representing B&Bs and apartments in a handful of European cities. Paris listings range from a small studio near the Bastille to a two-bedroom apartment in the Marais. Minimum stays vary from one to seven nights (US tel. 800-270-1190, France tel. 09 75 18 11 10, www.cross-pollinate.com, info@cross-pollinate.com).

BED-AND-BREAKFASTS

Several agencies can help you go local by staying in a private home in Paris. While prices and quality can range greatly, most rooms have a private bath and run from €85 to €150. Most owners won't take bookings for fewer than two nights. To limit stair-climbing, ask whether the building has an elevator. The agencies listed below have a good selection, but there's no good way to check the quality of the rooms as I do with hotels (agencies work with an ever-changing list of owners—each with a few rooms at most). You are at the mercy of whatever information you get from the agency and its website. Buyer beware.

Alcôve & Agapes is the most-used B&B resource in Paris, offering a broad selection of addresses throughout the city. Their useful website helps you sort through the options with prices, information about the owners, and helpful photos (tel. 07 64 08 42 77, www.bed-and-breakfast-in-paris.com).

Meeting the French offers several interesting services for travelers wanting to meet the French, including a list of locals who happily rent out their spare rooms to travelers. Most of the hosts are older Parisians with big apartments offered at fair rates (tel. 01 42 51 19 80, http://en.meetingthefrench.com).

Good Morning Paris is another source, listing more than 100 properties (tel. 01 47 07 28 29, www.goodmorningparis.fr).

EATING IN PARIS

The Parisian eating scene is kept at a rolling boil. Entire books (and lives) are dedicated to the subject. Paris is France's wine-and-cuisine melting pot. Though it lacks a style of its own (only French onion soup is truly Parisian; otherwise, there is no "Parisian cuisine" to speak of), it draws from the best of France. Paris could hold a gourmet Olympics and import nothing.

My restaurant recommendations are centered on the same great neighborhoods listed in the Sleeping in Paris chapter; you can come home exhausted after a busy day of sightseeing and find a good selection of eateries right around the corner. And evening is a fine time to explore any of these delightful neighborhoods, even if you're sleeping elsewhere. Serious eaters looking for even more suggestions should consult the always appetizing www.parisbymouth.com, an eating-and-drinking guide to Paris.

To save piles of euros, go to a bakery for takeout, or stop at a café for lunch. Cafés and brasseries are happy to serve a *plat du jour* (plate of the day, about €12-20) or a chef-like salad (about €10-14) day or night. To save even more, consider picnics (tasty takeout dishes available at charcuteries). Try eating your big meal at lunch, when many fine restaurants offer their dinnertime fixed-price *menus* at a reduced price.

Linger longer over dinner—restaurants expect you to enjoy a full meal. Most restaurants I've listed have set-price *menus* between €20 and €38. In most cases, the few extra euros you pay are well spent and open up a variety of better choices. Remember that a service charge is included in the prices (so little or no tipping is expected—see page 627 for detailed tipping advice).

Many restaurants close Sunday and/or Monday. They open for dinner around 19:00 (a few at 18:30), with last seating at about 22:00 or later. Eat early with tourists or late with locals—smaller restaurants that are popular with locals get crowded after 21:00. If a restaurant is open for lunch, the hours are generally 12:00-14:30 (last orders at 14:00). If you want to eat in the late afternoon, when restaurants are closed, pop in to a brasserie or café. At any eatery, before choosing a seat outside, remember that smokers love outdoor tables.

For details on dining in Paris' restaurants, cafés, and brasseries, getting takeout, and assembling a picnic—as well as a rundown of French cuisine—see the "Eating" section in the Practicalities chapter (page 640).

RUE CLER NEIGHBORHOOD

The Rue Cler neighborhood caters to its residents. Its eateries, while not destination places, have an intimate charm. I've provided a full range of choices—from cozy ma-and-pa diners to small and trendy boutique restaurants to classic, big, boisterous bistros.

On Rue Cler
(Mo: Ecole Militaire)

$ Café du Marché boasts the best seats on Rue Cler. The owner's philosophy: Brasserie on speed—crank out good enough food at great prices to appreciative locals and savvy tourists. It's high-energy, with young waiters who barely have time to smile...*très* Parisian. This place works well if you don't mind a limited selection and want to eat an inexpensive one-course meal among a commotion of people. The chalkboard lists your choices: good, hearty salads or more filling *plats du jour*. Arrive before 19:30 to avoid long waits (Mon-Sat 11:00-23:00, Sun 11:00-17:00, no reservations, at the corner of Rue Cler and Rue du Champ de Mars, 38 Rue Cler, tel. 01 47 05 51 27).

$$ Tribeca Restaurant, next door to Café du Marché, is less trendy and more family-friendly, serving more varied cuisine. Choose from kid-pleasing Italian dishes or try the roasted Camembert *à la crème* (pizzas, pastas, and salads; daily, tel. 01 45 55 12 01).

> # Restaurant Price Code
>
> I've assigned each eatery a price category, based on the aver-
> age cost of a typical main course. Drinks, desserts, and splurge
> items (steak and seafood) can raise the price considerably.
>
> **$$$$**   **Splurge:** Most main courses over €25
> **$$$**   **Pricier:** €20-25
> **$$**   **Moderate:** €15-20
> **$**   **Budget:** Under €15
>
> In France, a crêpe stand or other takeout spot is **$;** a sit-down
> brasserie, café, or bistro with affordable *plats du jour* is **$$;**
> a casual but more upscale restaurant is **$$$;** and a swanky
> splurge is **$$$$.**

$ Le Petit Cler is an adorable and popular little bistro with
long leather booths, a vintage interior, tight ranks of tiny outdoor
tables, and simple, tasty, inexpensive dishes such as €9 omelets and
€7 soup of the moment (delicious *pots de crème,* daily, opens early
for dinner, arrive early or call in advance, 29 Rue Cler, tel. 01 45
50 17 50).

$$ Café le Roussillon offers a younger, publike ambience
with good-value food. You'll find hearty salads, design-your-own
omelets, fajitas, and easygoing waiters (daily, indoor seating only,
corner of Rue de Grenelle and Rue Cler, tel. 01 45 51 47 53).

$ Crêperie Ulysée en Gaule offers cheap seats on Rue Cler
with crêpes to go. Readers of this book who buy a drink can enjoy
a crêpe at a table for takeaway prices. The family adores its Greek
dishes, but their crêpes are your least expensive hot meal on this
street (28 Rue Cler, tel. 01 47 05 61 82).

$ Brasserie Aux PTT, a simple traditional café delivering
fair-value fare, reminds Parisians of the old days on Rue Cler. Rick
Steves diners are promised a free *kir* with their dinner (cheap wine,
closed Sun, opposite 53 Rue Cler, tel. 01 45 51 94 96).

Close to Ecole Militaire
(Mo: Ecole Militaire)
$$$ Le Florimond is fun for a special occasion. The setting is
warm and welcoming. Locals come for classic French cuisine at fair
prices. Friendly Laurent, whose playful ties change daily, gracefully
serves one small room of tables and loves to give suggestions.
Pascale, his chef of more than 20 years, produces particularly tasty
stuffed cabbage, lobster ravioli, and *confit de canard.* The Château
Chênaie house wine is excellent (closed Sun and first and third
Sat of month, reservations encouraged, 19 Avenue de la Motte-
Picquet, tel. 01 45 55 40 38, www.leflorimond.com).

EATING

Rue Cler Restaurants

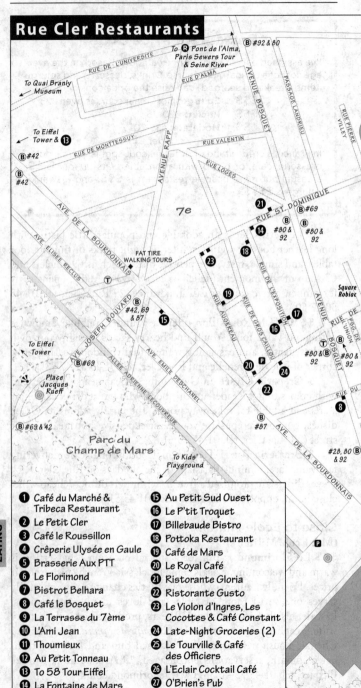

1. Café du Marché & Tribeca Restaurant
2. Le Petit Cler
3. Café le Roussillon
4. Crêperie Ulysée en Gaule
5. Brasserie Aux PTT
6. Le Florimond
7. Bistrot Belhara
8. Café le Bosquet
9. La Terrasse du 7ème
10. L'Ami Jean
11. Thoumieux
12. Au Petit Tonneau
13. To 58 Tour Eiffel
14. La Fontaine de Mars
15. Au Petit Sud Ouest
16. Le P'tit Troquet
17. Billebaude Bistro
18. Pottoka Restaurant
19. Café de Mars
20. Le Royal Café
21. Ristorante Gloria
22. Ristorante Gusto
23. Le Violon d'Ingres, Les Cocottes & Café Constant
24. Late-Night Groceries (2)
25. Le Tourville & Café des Officiers
26. L'Eclair Cocktail Café
27. O'Brien's Pub

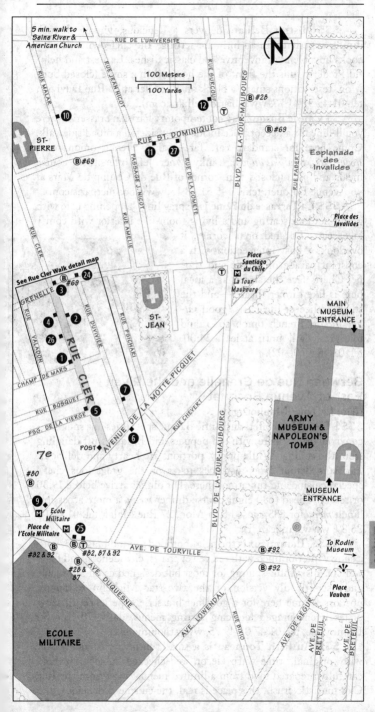

$$$ Bistrot Belhara delivers a delicious, vintage French dining experience in an intimate setting. The chef-owner Thierry cooks up a blend of inventive and classic dishes. Earnest and helpful Frédéric runs the front of the house with a smile (closed Sun-Mon, reservations smart, a block off Rue Cler at 23 Rue Duvivier, tel. 01 45 51 41 77, www.bistrotbelhara.com).

$$ Café le Bosquet is a contemporary Parisian brasserie where you'll dine for a decent price inside or outside on a broad sidewalk. Come here for standard café fare—salad, French onion soup, *steak-frites*, or a *plat du jour*. Lanky owner "Jeff" offers three-course meals and *plats* (closed Sun, corner of Rue du Champ de Mars at 46 Avenue Bosquet, tel. 01 45 51 38 13, www.bosquetparis.com).

$$$ La Terrasse du 7ème is a sprawling, happening café with grand outdoor seating and a living room-like interior with comfy love seats. Located on a corner, it overlooks a busy intersection with a constant parade of people and traffic. Chairs face the street, as a meal here is like dinner theater—and the show is slice-of-life Paris (good *salade niçoise*, French onion soup, and foie gras, daily until at least 24:00, tel. 01 45 55 00 02).

Between Rue de Grenelle and the River, East of Avenue Bosquet
(Mo: La Tour-Maubourg)

$$$$ L'Ami Jean offers authentic Basque specialties in a snug-but-convivial atmosphere with red peppers and Basque stuff dangling from the ceiling. While pricey, portions are hearty and delicious. Parisians detour long distances to savor the gregarious chef's special cuisine and fun atmosphere. For dinner arrive before 19:30 or reserve ahead (€80 eight-course dinner *menu*, a more accessible lunch *menu* for €35, closed Sun-Mon, 27 Rue Malar, tel. 01 47 05 86 89, www.lamijean.fr).

$$$$ Thoumieux is the neighborhood's grand brasserie, with a showy interior lined with red velvet chairs, chandeliers, and fussy waiters. It's a mini-splurge for most but designed as an affordable and user-friendly version of the two-star Michelin restaurant upstairs. Come here for a gourmet brasserie experience. Sharing plates is encouraged (enticing tasting menus, daily, 79 Rue St. Dominique, tel. 01 47 05 49 75, www.thoumieux.fr).

$$$ Au Petit Tonneau is a small, authentic French bistro with original, time-warp decor, red-checked tablecloths, and carefully prepared food from a limited menu. Away from the Rue Cler touristic crush, this place is real, the cuisine is delicious, and the experience is what you came to France for (good à la carte choices or three-course *menu* that changes with season, well-priced wines, closed Mon, 20 Rue Surcouf, tel. 01 47 05 09 01, charming owner Arlette at your service).

Between Rue de Grenelle and the River, West of Avenue Bosquet
(Mo: Ecole Militaire unless otherwise noted)
Some of these places line peaceful Rue de l'Exposition (a few blocks west of Rue Cler), allowing you to do a quick survey before sitting down.

$$$$ 58 Tour Eiffel, on the tower's first level, provides a feast for both your belly and your eyes, with incredible city views. Dinner here is pricey and requires a reservation (two seatings: 18:30 with €85-125 *menus,* and 21:00 with €100-185 *menus;* reserve long in advance, especially if you want a view, no jeans or tennis shoes at dinner). During the day they serve a €42 *picque-nique-chic* lunch, which is packaged in a little basket (€19 for kids, daily 11:30-16:30, reservations are a good idea, Mo: Bir-Hakeim or Trocadéro, RER: Champ de Mars-Tour Eiffel, tel. 01 72 76 18 46, toll tel. 08 25 56 66 62, www.restaurants-toureiffel.com). With a reservation, you ride up for free in the restaurant elevator.

$$$$ La Fontaine de Mars, a longtime favorite and neighborhood institution, is charmingly situated on a tiny, jumbled square with tables jammed together for the serious business of eating. Reserve in advance for a table on the ground floor or square, and pass on the upstairs room (superb foie gras and desserts, daily, 129 Rue St. Dominique, tel. 01 47 05 46 44, www.fontainedemars. com).

$$$ Au Petit Sud Ouest comes wrapped in stone walls and wood beams, making it a cozy place to sample cuisine from southwestern France. Duck, goose, foie gras, *cassoulet,* and truffles are all on *la carte.* Tables come with toasters to heat your bread—it enhances the flavors of the foie gras. Try the *salade* with foie gras or the *cassoulet* (closed Sun-Mon, 46 Avenue de la Bourdonnais, tel. 01 45 55 59 59, www.au-petit-sud-ouest.fr, managed by friendly Chantal).

$$$ Le P'tit Troquet is a petite eatery taking you back to the Paris of the 1920s. Marie serves and José cooks a delicious range of traditional choices prepared creatively. The homey charm and tasty food make this restaurant a favorite of connoisseurs (their €35 three-course *menu* is available for €25 at lunch, dinner service from 18:30, closed Sun, reservations smart, 28 Rue de l'Exposition, tel. 01 47 05 80 39).

$$$ Billebaude, run by patient Pascal, is a small bistro popular with locals and tourists. The focus is on what's fresh, including catch-of-the-day fish and meats from the hunt (available in fall and winter). Chef Sylvain, an avid hunter (as the decor suggests), is determined to deliver quality at a fair price. Skip this place if you're in a hurry (closed Sun-Mon, 29 Rue de l'Exposition, tel. 01 45 55 20 96).

$$$ Pottoka attracts locals willing to crowd into this shoebox for a chance to sample tasty Basque cuisine. Service is friendly, wines are reasonable, and the focus is on food rather than decor (daily, book ahead, 4 Rue de l'Exposition, tel. 01 45 51 88 38, www.pottoka.fr).

$$ Café de Mars is a relaxed place for a reasonably priced and well-prepared meal. It's also comfortable for single diners thanks to a convivial counter (closed Sun, 11 Rue Augereau, tel. 01 45 50 10 90, www.cafedemars.com).

$ Le Royal is a tiny neighborhood fixture offering the cheapest meals in the area. This humble time-warp place, with prices and decor from another era, comes from an age when cafés sold firewood and served food as an afterthought. Parisians dine here because "it's like eating at home." Gentle Guillaume is a fine host (daily, 212 Rue de Grenelle, tel. 01 47 53 92 90).

$$ Affordable Italian: You'll find two good choices for reasonably priced Italian cuisine in the neighborhood. **Ristorante Gloria** is almost elegant (108 Rue St. Dominique, tel. 01 45 56 00 98). **Ristorante Gusto** is more fun, tight, and characteristic (199 Rue de Grenelle, tel. 01 45 55 00 43).

The Constant Lineup
(Mo: Ecole Militaire or RER: Pont de l'Alma)

Ever since leaving the venerable Hôtel Crillon, famed chef Christian Constant has made a career of taking the "snoot" out of French cuisine—and making it accessible to people like us. Today you'll find three of his restaurants strung along one block of Rue St. Dominique between Rue Augereau and Rue de l'Exposition. Each is distinct, offering a different experience and price range. None is cheap, but they're all a good value, delivering top-quality cuisine.

$$$$ Le Violon d'Ingres, where Christian won his first Michelin star, makes for a good excuse to dress up and dine finely in Paris. Glass doors open onto a chic eating scene—hushed and elegant. Service is formal yet helpful; the cuisine is what made this restaurateur's reputation (order à la carte or consider their €110 seven-course tasting menu, cheaper weekday lunch *menu,* daily, reservations essential, 135 Rue St. Dominique, tel. 01 45 55 15 05, www.maisonconstant.com).

$$$ Les Cocottes attracts a crowd of trendy Parisians with its fun energy and creative dishes served in *cocottes*—small cast-iron pots (tasty soups, daily, dinner service from 18:30, go early as they don't take reservations, 135 Rue St. Dominique).

$$ Café Constant is a cool, two-level place that feels more like a small bistro-wine bar than a café. Delicious and well-priced dishes are served in a snug setting. Arrive early to get a table downstairs if you can—upstairs seating is less fun (daily, opens at 7:00 for breakfast, meals served nonstop 12:00-23:00, no reservations, corner of Rue Augereau and Rue St. Dominique, next to recommended Hôtel de Londres Eiffel, tel. 01 47 53 73 34).

Picnicking near Rue Cler

Picnics with floodlit views of the Eiffel Tower or along the riverside promenade are *très romantique,* and Rue Cler is a festival of food just waiting to be celebrated. For a magical picnic dinner, assemble it in no fewer than five shops on Rue Cler. For less character and more efficiency, there are fine supermarkets (long hours daily) next to the recommended Hôtel la Bourdonnais (Avenue de la Bourdonnais) and Hôtel Bosquet (Rue du Champ de Mars). If shops are closed, small, late-night groceries are at 197 Rue de Grenelle, as well as where Rues Cler and Grenelle cross.

Nightlife in Rue Cler

This sleepy neighborhood was not made for night owls, but there are a few notable exceptions. The focal point of before- and after-dinner posing occurs along the broad sidewalk at the intersection of Avenues de la Motte-Picquet and Tourville (Mo: Ecole Militaire). **Le Tourville** and **Café des Officiers** gather a sea of outward-facing seats for the important business of people-watching.

La Terrasse du 7ème, across the avenue, has a less pretentious clientele (see listing, earlier). On Rue Cler, **Café du Marché** (listed earlier) attracts a Franco-American café crowd until at least midnight, though the younger-in-spirit **L'Eclair** cocktail café (a few doors down at #32) rocks it until very late. **Café Roussillon** has a good French pubby atmosphere at the corner of Rue de Grenelle and Rue Cler. **O'Brien's Pub** is a relaxed Parisian rendition of an Irish pub/sports bar, with French men in suits tossing darts and drinking pints (77 Rue St. Dominique, Mo: La Tour Maubourg).

MARAIS

The trendy Marais is filled with diners enjoying good food in colorful and atmospheric eateries. The scene is competitive and changes all the time. I've listed an assortment of eateries—all handy to recommended hotels—that offer good food at decent prices, plus a memorable experience.

Good Picnic Spots

Paris is picnic-friendly. Almost any park will do. Many have benches or grassy areas, though some lawns are off-limits—obey the signs. Parks generally close at dusk, so plan your sunset picnics carefully. Here are some especially scenic areas located near major sights (for tips on assembling a picnic in Paris, see page 642):

Palais Royal: Escape to a peaceful courtyard full of relaxing locals across from the Louvre (Mo: Palais Royal-Musée du Louvre). The nearby Louvre courtyard surrounding the pyramid is less tranquil, but very handy.

Place des Vosges: Relax in an exquisite grassy courtyard in the Marais, surrounded by royal buildings (Mo: Bastille).

Square du Vert-Galant: For great river views, try this little triangular park on the west tip of Ile de la Cité. It's next to the statue of King Henry IV (Mo: Pont Neuf).

Pont des Arts: Munch from a bench on this pedestrian bridge over the Seine near the Louvre (Mo: Pont Neuf).

Along the Seine: A grassy parkway runs along the left bank of the Seine between Les Invalides and Pont de l'Alma (Mo: Invalides, near Rue Cler).

Tuileries Garden: Have an Impressionist "Luncheon on the Grass" nestled between the Orsay and Orangerie museums (Mo: Tuileries).

Luxembourg Garden: The classic Paris picnic spot is this expansive Left Bank park (Mo: Odéon).

Les Invalides: Take a break from the Army Museum and Napoleon's Tomb in the gardens behind the complex (Mo: Varenne).

Champ de Mars: The long, grassy strip beneath the Eiffel Tower has breathtaking views of this Paris icon, but I prefer the smaller, side park areas (Mo: Ecole Militaire).

Pompidou Center: There's no grass, but the people-watching is unbeatable; try the area by the *Stravinsky* fountain (Mo: Rambuteau or Hôtel de Ville).

EATING

On Romantic Place des Vosges
(Mo: St-Paul or Bastille)

This square offers Old World Marais elegance, a handful of eateries, and an ideal picnic site until dusk, when the park closes. Strolling around the arcade after dark is more important than dining here—fanciful art galleries alternate with restaurants and cafés. Choose a restaurant that best fits your mood and budget; most have arcade seating and provide big space heaters to make outdoor dining during colder months an option. Also consider just a drink on the square at Café Hugo.

$$$ **La Place Royale** offers a fine location on the square with

good seating inside or out. Expect patient waiters (owner Arnaud prides himself on service), and a family-friendly menu with salads, pizzas, and classic dishes. The cuisine is priced well and served nonstop all day, and the exceptional wine list is reasonable (try the Sancerre white). The €42 *menu* comes with three courses, a half-bottle of wine per person, and coffee (lunch specials, daily, reserve ahead to dine outside under the arcade, 2 bis Place des Vosges, tel. 01 42 78 58 16).

$$ Café Hugo, named for the square's most famous resident, serves salads and basic café fare with a fun energy. The food's good enough, but the setting's terrific, with good seating under the arches (daily, 22 Place des Vosges, tel. 01 42 72 64 04).

Near Place des Vosges
(Mo: Chemin Vert)
$$$ Chez Janou, a Provençal bistro, tumbles out of its corner building and fills its broad sidewalk with happy eaters. Don't let the trendy and youthful crowd intimidate you: It's relaxed and charming, with helpful and patient service. The curbside tables are inviting, but I'd sit inside (with very tight seating) to immerse myself in the happy commotion. The style is French Mediterranean, with an emphasis on vegetables (daily—book ahead or arrive when it opens, 2 blocks beyond Place des Vosges at 2 Rue Roger Verlomme, tel. 01 42 72 28 41, www.chezjanou.com). They serve 81 varieties of *pastis* (licorice-flavored liqueur, browse the list above the bar).

$$$ Le Petit Marché delivers a cozy and intimate bistro experience inside and out with friendly service and a delicious cuisine that blends French classics with a slight Asian influence (daily, 9 Rue du Béarn, tel. 01 42 72 06 67).

Near Place de la Bastille
(Mo: Bastille)
$$$ Brasserie Bofinger, an institution for over a century, is famous for seafood and traditional cuisine with Alsatian flair. You'll eat in a sprawling interior, surrounded by brisk, black-and-white-attired waiters. Come here for the one-of-a-kind ambience in the elaborately decorated ground-floor rooms, reminiscent of the Roaring Twenties. Reserve ahead to dine under the memorable, grand 1919 *coupole* (avoid eating upstairs). If you've always wanted one of those picturesque seafood platters, this is a good place (open daily for lunch and for dinner, fun kids' menu, fair-value *menus* and reasonably priced wines, 5 Rue de la Bastille, don't be confused by the lesser "Petite" Bofinger across the street, tel. 01 42 72 87 82, www.bofingerparis.com).

$$$ Au Temps des Cerises is a warm place with wads of character and tight inside seating (and a couple of outdoor tables).

Marais Restaurants

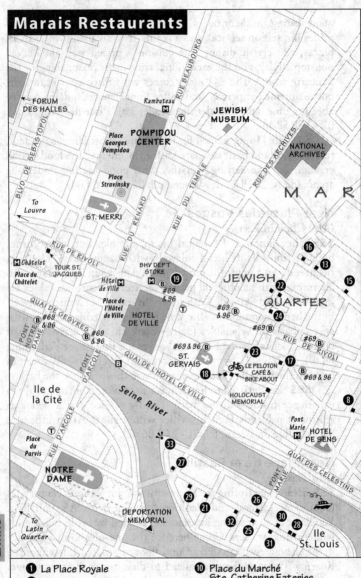

1 La Place Royale
2 Café Hugo
3 Chez Janou
4 Le Petit Marché
5 Brasserie Bofinger
6 Au Temps des Cerises
7 Vin des Pyrénées
8 Chez Mademoiselle
9 Breizh Café

10 Place du Marché
     Ste. Catherine Eateries
11 Les Bougresses
12 Rue St. Antoine Eateries
13 Chez Marianne
14 Le Loir dans la Théière
15 L'As du Falafel
16 La Droguerie Crêperie
17 Au Bourguignon du Marais

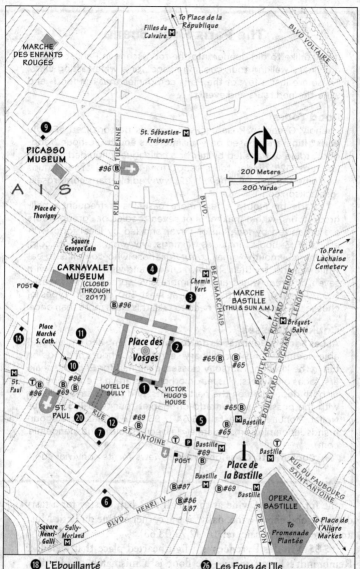

MARCHE DES ENFANTS ROUGES

To Place de la République

Filles du Calvaire Ⓜ

BLVD VOLTAIRE

❾

PICASSO MUSEUM

St. Sébastien-Froissart Ⓜ

RUE DE TURENNE

N

200 Meters

200 Yards

A I S

Place de Thorigny

Square George Cain

#96 Ⓑ

BLVD

BEAUMARCHAIS

CARNAVALET MUSEUM (CLOSED THROUGH 2017)

POST

❹

Chemin Vert Ⓜ

❸

Ⓑ #96

To Père Lachaise Cemetery

MARCHE BASTILLE (THU & SUN A.M.)

Bréguet-Sabin Ⓜ

BOULEVARD RICHARD LENOIR

BOULEVARD RICHARD LENOIR

Place Marché S. Cath.

⓮

⓫

❿

#96

Ⓑ Ⓑ

#96 #69

Place des Vosges

❷

#65 Ⓑ

Ⓜ St. Paul

Ⓣ

HOTEL DE SULLY

❶

VICTOR HUGO'S HOUSE

#65Ⓑ

ST. PAUL Ⓜ

⓴

⓬

RUE

#69

❺

Ⓜ Bastille

❼

ST. ANTOINE

Ⓣ

Ⓑ #69

#65Ⓑ

Ⓟ

Bastille Ⓜ

POST

Bastille Ⓣ

RUE DU FAUBOURG SAINT-ANTOINE

Place de la Bastille

Ⓑ #87 Ⓜ

Ⓑ #69 Bastille

❻

Ⓑ#86 & 87

OPERA BASTILLE

To Place de l'Aligre Market

Square Henri-Galli

Sully-Morland Ⓜ

BLVD. HENRI IV

R. DE LYON

To Promenade Plantée

EATING

⑱ L'Ebouillanté	㉖ Les Fous de l'Ile
⑲ BHV Cafeteria	㉗ La Brasserie de l'Ile St. Louis
⑳ Monoprix (Grocery)	㉘ L'Orangerie & Auberge de la Reine Blanche
㉑ Late-Night Grocery	㉙ Café Med
㉒ Au Petit Fer à Cheval & La Belle Hortense	㉚ Bakery & 38 Saint Louis Deli
㉓ La Perla Bar	㉛ Berthillon Ice Cream
㉔ Le Pick-Clops Bar Rest.	㉜ Amorino Gelati
㉕ Nos Ancêtres les Gaulois	㉝ Good Picnic Spot

The Paris Food Scene

If you'd like to dig deeper into the food scene in Paris, consider a culinary walking tour, cooking school, or a wine-tasting class. These are just a few of the Paris companies that run food- and wine-themed tours and events.

Food Tours

Friendly Canadian Rosa Jackson designs personalized **"Edible Paris"** itineraries based on your interests and three-hour "food-guru" tours of Paris led by her or a colleague (unguided itineraries from €125, guided tours—€300 for 1-2 people, larger groups welcome too, tel. 06 81 67 41 22, www.edible-paris.com, rosa@rosajackson.com).

Paris by Mouth offers more casual and frequent small-group tours, with a maximum of seven foodies per group. Tours are organized by location or flavor and led by local food writers (€95/3 hours, includes tastings, www.parisbymouth.com, tasteparisbymouth@gmail.com). For those who don't like to eat while walking, try their sit-down cheese and wine workshop with seven different wines and an impressive spread of 14 cheeses (€95/3 hours). Given that there at least 350 different types of cheese in France, you may need to take this class more than once.

Cooking Classes

At **Les Secrets Gourmands de Noémie,** charming and knowledgeable Noémie shares her culinary secrets in 2.5 hours of hands-on fun in the kitchen. Thursday classes, designed for English speakers, focus on sweets; classes on other days are in French, English, or both depending on the participants, and tackle savory dishes with the possibility of an add-on market tour (€75-105, 92 Rue Nollet, Mo: La Fourche, tel. 06 64 17 93 32, www.lessecretsgourmandsdenoemie.com, noemie@lessecretsgourmandsdenoemie.com).

Cook'n with Class gets rave reviews for its convivial cook-

Come for a glass of wine at the small zinc bar, or stay for a tasty dinner (good cheap wine, daily, at the corner of Rue du Petit Musc and Rue de la Cerisaie, tel. 01 42 72 08 63).

$$$ Vin des Pyrénées is a lighthearted place that feels like Rembrandt's living room—the floor is a mismatch of old tiles, knickknacks, and Old World decor. The chalkboard lists a mélange of authentic and nicely presented dishes (two-course lunch special, daily, 25 Rue Beautreillis, tel. 01 42 72 64 94).

In the Heart of the Marais
(Mo: St-Paul)

$$$ At **Chez Mademoiselle,** the country-elegant, candlelit decor recalls charming owner Alexia's previous career as a French

ing and wine and cheese classes with a maximum of six students; tasting courses offered as well (6 Rue Baudelique, Mo: Jules Joffrin or Simplon, tel. 06 31 73 62 77, www.cooknwithclass.com).

La Cuisine Paris has a great variety of classes in English, reasonable prices, and a beautiful space in central Paris (2- or 3-hour classes-€65-95, 4-hour class with market tour-€150, gourmet visit of Versailles—see website for details, 80 Quai de l'Hôtel de Ville, tel. 01 40 51 78 18, www.lacuisineparis.com).

Susan Herrmann Loomis, an acclaimed chef and author, offers cooking courses in Paris or at her home in Normandy. Your travel buddy can skip the class but should come for the meal at a reduced "guest eater" price (www.onruetatin.com).

If you're looking for a pricey demonstration course, you'll find it at **Le Cordon Bleu** (tel. 01 53 68 22 50, www.lcbparis.com) or **Ritz Escoffier Ecole de Gastronomie** (tel. 01 43 16 30 50, www.ritzparis.com).

Wine Tasting

Olivier Magny and his team of sommeliers teach wine-tasting classes at the Ô Château wine school/bar, in the 17th-century residence of Madame de Pompadour. Olivier's goal is to "take the snob out of wine." At these informal classes, you'll learn the basics of French wine regions, the techniques of tasting, and how to read a French wine label. Classes range from Introductory Tasting (€30, 1 hour) to wine-tasting dinners (€100, about 2 hours). Register online using code "RS2017" for a 10-percent discount (68 Rue Jean-Jacques Rousseau, Mo: Louvre-Rivoli or Etienne Marcel, tel. 01 44 73 97 80, www.o-chateau.com). The same team offers hands-on two-hour workshops in wine blending. You'll leave with a bottle of your very own blend (€75, near the Louvre at 52 Rue de l'Arbre Sec, Mo: Louvre-Rivoli, tel. 01 44 73 97 80, www.cavesdulouvre.com).

comédienne. Enjoy a French-paced dinner in a relaxing atmosphere inside or at a sidewalk table. Ingredients are fresh and prepared simply. The tender *château filet* is served all year, but most dishes follow the seasons (good wine list, daily, 16 Rue Charlemagne, tel. 01 42 72 14 16).

$$ Breizh Café is worth the hike for some of the best Breton crêpes in Paris ("Breizh" means Brittany). This simple joint serves organic crêpes—both sweet and savory—and small rolls made for dipping in rich sauces and salted butter. The crêpes run the gamut from traditional ham, cheese, and egg to Asian fusion. They also talk about cider like a sommelier would talk about wine. Try a sparkling cider, a Breton cola, or my favorite—*lait ribot,* a buttermilk-like drink (closed Mon-Tue, serves nonstop 11:30-late, reservations highly recommended, 109 Rue du Vieille du Temple, tel. 01 42 72 13 77, www.breizhcafe.com).

$$ On Place du Marché Ste. Catherine: This small, romantic square, just off Rue St. Antoine, is cloaked in extremely Parisian, leafy-square ambience. It feels like the Latin Quarter but classier. On a balmy evening, this is a neighborhood favorite, with a handful of restaurants offering mediocre cuisine (you're here for the setting). It's also family-friendly: Most places serve French hamburgers, and kids can dance around the square while parents breathe. Survey the square. You'll find three French bistros with similar features and menus: **Le Marché, Chez Joséphine,** and **Le Bistrot de la Place** (all open daily, cheaper for lunch, tight seating on flimsy chairs indoors and out, Chez Joséphine has best chairs). Just off the square, the fun-loving **Les Bougresses** offers less romance but far better food for the price (inside seating only, daily from 18:30, 6 Rue de Jarente, tel. 01 48 87 71 21).

$ On Rue St. Antoine: Several hardworking **Asian fast-food eateries,** great for an inexpensive meal, line this street.

In the Jewish Quarter, Rue des Rosiers
(Mo: St-Paul or Hôtel de Ville)

$$ Chez Marianne is a neighborhood fixture that serves tasty Jewish cuisine in a fun atmosphere with Parisian *élan*. Choose from several indoor zones with a cluttered wine shop/deli feeling, or sit outside. You'll select from two dozen *zakouskis* (hot and cold hor d'oeuvres) to assemble your *plat*. Vegetarians will find great options (takeaway falafel sandwiches, long hours daily, corner of Rue des Rosiers and Rue des Hospitalières-St-Gervais, tel. 01 42 72 18 86).

$$ Le Loir dans la Théière ("The Dormouse in the Teapot"— think Alice in Wonderland) is a cozy, mellow teahouse offering a welcoming ambience for tired travelers (laptops and smartphones are not welcome). It's ideal for lunch and popular on weekends. They offer a daily assortment of creatively filled quiches and bake up an impressive array of homemade desserts that are proudly displayed in the dining room (daily 9:00-19:00 but only dessert-type items offered after 15:00, 3 Rue des Rosiers, tel. 01 42 72 90 61).

$ L'As du Falafel rules the falafel scene in the Jewish quarter. Monsieur Isaac, the "Ace of Falafel" here since 1979, brags, "I've got the biggest pita on the street...and I fill it up." Your cheap meal comes on a plastic plate; the €8 "special falafel" is the big hit, but many enjoy the lighter chicken version *(poulet grillé)* or the tasty and massive *assiette de falafel*. Wash it down with a cold Maccabee beer. Their takeout service draws a constant crowd (long hours most days except closed Fri evening and all day Sat, air-con, 34 Rue des Rosiers, tel. 01 48 87 63 60).

$ La Droguerie, a hole-in-the-wall crêpe stand a few blocks farther down Rue des Rosiers, is a good budget option if falafels don't work for you but cheap does. Grab a stool, or get a crêpe to go (daily 12:00-22:00, 56 Rue des Rosiers).

Near Hôtel de Ville
(Mo: Hôtel de Ville)

$$$$ Au Bourguignon du Marais is a dressy wine bar/bistro for Burgundy lovers, where excellent wines (Burgundian only, available by the glass) blend with a good selection of well-designed dish-

es and efficient service. The *œufs en meurette* are mouthwatering, and the *bœuf bourguignon* could feed two (daily, pleasing indoor and outdoor seating on a perfect Marais corner, 52 Rue François Miron, tel. 01 48 87 15 40).

$$ L'Ebouillanté is a breezy café, romantically situated near the river on a broad, cobbled pedestrian lane behind a church. With great outdoor seating and an artsy, cozy interior, it's perfect for an inexpensive and relaxing tea, snack, or lunch—or for dinner on a warm evening. Their €15 *bricks*—paper-thin, Tunisian-inspired pancakes stuffed with what you would typically find in an omelet—come with a small salad (daily 12:00-21:30, closes earlier in winter, a block off the river at 6 Rue des Barres, tel. 01 42 74 70 57).

$ BHV Department Store's fifth-floor cafeteria provides nice views, good prices, and many main courses to choose from, with a salad bar, pizza by the slice, and pasta. It's family-easy (Mon-Sat 11:30-18:00, hot food served until 16:00, open later Wed, closed Sun, at intersection of Rue du Temple and Rue de la Verrerie, one block from Hôtel de Ville).

Picnicking in the Marais

Picnic at peaceful Place des Vosges (closes at dusk), Square George Caïn (near the Carnavalet Museum), or on the Ile St. Louis *quais*. Stretch your euros at the basement supermarket of the **Monoprix** department store (closed Sun, near Place des Vosges on Rue St. Antoine). You'll find a small **grocery** open until 23:00 on Ile St. Louis.

Nightlife in the Marais

Trendy cafés and bars—popular with gay men—cluster on Rue des Archives and Rue Ste. Croix de la Bretonnerie. There's also a line of bars and cafés providing front-row seats for the buff parade on Rue Vieille du Temple, a block north of Rue de Rivoli—the horseshoe-

EATING

shaped **Au Petit Fer à Cheval** bar (with tiny dining room in back) and the atmospheric **La Belle Hortense** bookstore/wine bar are the focal points of the action. Nearby, Rue des Rosiers bustles with youthful energy, but there are no cafés to observe from. **La Perla** dishes up imitation Tex-Mex and is stuffed with Parisian millennials in search of the perfect margarita (26 Rue François Myron, tel. 01 42 77 59 40).

$ Le Pick-Clops bar-restaurant is a happy peanuts-and-lots-of-cocktails diner with bright neon, loud colors, and a garish local crowd. It's perfect for immersing yourself in today's Marais world—a little boisterous, a little edgy, a little gay, fun-loving, easygoing...and *sans* tourists. Sit inside on old-fashioned diner stools or streetside to watch the constant Marais parade (daily 7:00-24:00, 16 Rue Vieille du Temple, tel. 01 40 29 02 18).

More Options: The best scene for hard-core clubbers is the dizzying array of wacky eateries, bars, and dance halls on **Rue de Lappe.** Just east of the stately Place de la Bastille, it's one of the wildest nightspots in Paris and not for everyone.

The most enjoyable peaceful evening may be simply mentally donning your floppy "three musketeers" hat and slowly strolling **Place des Vosges,** window shopping the art galleries.

ILE ST. LOUIS
(Mo: Pont Marie)
This romantic and peaceful neighborhood merits a trip for dinner even if your hotel is elsewhere. Cruise the island's main street for a variety of options, and after dinner, sample Paris' favorite ice cream (described below) before strolling across to Ile de la Cité to see a floodlit Notre-Dame. These recommended spots—ranging from rowdy to petite, rustic to elegant—line the island's main drag, Rue St. Louis-en-l'Ile (see map on page 432).

$$ Nos Ancêtres les Gaulois ("Our Ancestors the Gauls"), famous for its rowdy, medieval-cellar atmosphere, is made for hungry warriors and wenches who like to swill hearty wine. For dinner they serve up rustic, all-you-can-eat fare with straw baskets of raw veggies and bundles of *saucisson* (cut whatever you like with your dagger), plates of pâté, a meat course, cheese, a dessert, and all the wine you can stomach for €40. The food is perfectly edible; burping is encouraged. If you want to overeat, drink too much wine, be surrounded by tourists (mostly

French), and holler at your friends while receiving smart-aleck buccaneer service, you're home (daily, 39 Rue St. Louis-en-l'Ile, tel. 01 46 33 66 07).

$$ Les Fous de l'Ile is a lighthearted mash-up of a collector's haunt, art gallery, and bistro. It's a fun place to eat bistro fare with gourmet touches for a good price (daily, serves nonstop, 33 Rue des Deux Ponts, tel. 01 43 25 76 67).

$$ La Brasserie de l'Ile St. Louis offers purely Alsatian cui-
sine (hearty pork and kraut fare—
try the *choucroute garnie* or *coq au riesling* for €22), served in a vigor-
ous, hunting-lodge setting with no-
nonsense, slap-it-down service on wine-stained paper tablecloths. The front tables make a good, balmy-
evening perch for watching the the-
atrical street scene—often with live

music. If it's chilly, the interior is also fun for a memorable night out (closed Wed, no reservations, faces Ile de la Cité at 55 Quai de Bourbon, tel. 01 43 54 02 59).

$$$ L'Orangerie is an inviting, rustic-yet-elegant place with soft lighting and comfortable,
spacious seating. The cuisine is traditional with occasional modern touches (closed Mon, 28 Rue St. Louis-en-l'Ile, tel. 01 46 33 93 98).

$$ Auberge de la Reine Blanche—woodsy, cozy, and tight—welcomes diners will-
ing to rub elbows with their neighbors. Earnest owner Michel serves basic, traditional cuisine at reasonable prices (closed Wed, 30 Rue St. Louis-en-l'Ile, tel. 01 46 33 07 87).

$ Café Med, near the pedestrian bridge to Notre-Dame, is a tiny, cheery *crêperie* with good-value salads, crêpes, and *plats* (daily, 77 Rue St. Louis-en-l'Ile, tel. 01 43 29 73 17). Two similar *crêperies* are just across the street.

Riverside Picnic for Impoverished Romantics

On sunny lunchtimes and balmy evenings, the *quai* on the Left Bank side of Ile St. Louis is lined with locals who have more class than money, spreading out tablecloths and even lighting candles for elegant picnics. And tourists can enjoy the same budget meal. A handy grocery store at #67 on the main drag (closed Tue) has tabbouleh and other simple, cheap takeaway dishes for your picnicking pleasure. The bakery a few blocks down at #40 serves quiche and pizza (open until 20:00, closed Sun-Mon), and a gourmet deli and cheese shop—aptly named **38 Saint Louis**—can be found at #38.

Ice-Cream Dessert

Half the people strolling Ile St. Louis are licking an ice-cream cone because this is the home of *les glaces Berthillon* (now sold throughout Paris, though still made here on Ile St. Louis). The original **Berthillon** shop, at 31 Rue St. Louis-en-l'Ile, is marked by the line of salivating customers (closed Mon-Tue). For a less famous but satisfying treat, the Italian gelato a block away at **Amorino Gelati** is giving Berthillon competition (no line, bigger portions, easier to see what you want, and they offer little tastes—Berthillon doesn't need to, 47 Rue St. Louis-en-l'Ile, tel. 01 44 07 48 08). Having some of each is not a bad thing.

LUXEMBOURG GARDEN AREA

Sleeping in the Luxembourg neighborhood puts you near many appealing dining and after-hours options. Because my hotels cluster near St. Sulpice Church, the Panthéon, and Rue de Sèvres, I've focused my restaurant picks in the same areas. Restaurants around St. Sulpice tend to be boisterous; those near the Panthéon are calmer; it's a short walk from one area to the other.

Restaurant Row Streets near St. Sulpice Church
(Mo: St-Sulpice or St-Germain-des-Prés)

Rue des Canettes and Rue Guisarde teem with busy eateries offering a huge selection of cuisines at generally affordable prices. It's hard to recommend one over the next, but it's a fun neighborhood to browse. Consider **Boucherie Roulière** (for steaks, 24 Rue des Canettes), **Monte Verdi** (romantic Italian with piano nightly from 20:00, 5 Rue Guisarde), **Chez Georges** (dive bar with dank cellar for a drink before or after dinner, 11 Rue des Canettes), **Chez Fernand** (friendly French bistro fare, 13 Rue Guisarde), and a couple of crêperies (on Rue des Canettes).

A block north of Boulevard St. Germain (toward the river), **Rue de Buci** has a lineup of bars, cafés, and bistros targeted toward a young, trendy clientele. It's terrific theater for passersby from 18:00 until late. Consider **Café de Paris,** a classic brasserie with hearty and creative dinner salads (daily, 10 Rue de Buci).

Near the Odéon Theater
(Mo: Odéon)

$ Pasta Luna is a deli specializing in porky fare from the southernmost French island of Corsica. The proud owner lovingly and slowly makes €6 sandwiches to order. Try the sheep cheese with fig jam or the cured pork loin (served from 11:00 until the bread runs out—usually about 19:00, closed Sun, 15 Rue Mézières, tel. 01 45 44 32 02).

$$$ Brasserie Bouillon Racine takes you back to 1906 with an Art Nouveau carnival of carved wood, stained glass, and old-time lights reflected in beveled mirrors. The over-the-top decor and energetic waiters give it an inviting conviviality. Check upstairs before choosing a table. Their roast suckling pig (€20) is a favorite. There's Belgian beer on tap and a fascinating history on the menu (daily, serves nonstop, 3 Rue Racine, tel. 01 85 15 21 33, www.bouillon-racine.com).

$$$ La Méditerranée is all about seafood from the south served in a pastel and dressy setting...with similar clientele. The scene and the cuisine are sophisticated yet accessible, and the view of the Odéon is *formidable* (daily, reservations smart, facing the Odéon at 2 Place de l'Odéon, tel. 01 43 26 02 30, www.la-mediterranee.com).

$$ Café de l'Odéon, on a square with the venerable theater, is a place to savor a light meal with a stylish young crowd (but only in good weather, as it's all outdoors). The menu offers a limited selection of well-prepared dishes at fair prices—you'll feel like a winner eating so well in such a Parisian setting (good salads, reasonable *plats,* May-Oct daily 12:00-23:00, no reservations, Place de l'Odéon, tel. 01 44 85 41 30).

$$$$ Le Comptoir Restaurant is a trendy but relaxed splurge where trusting foodies book long in advance to enjoy gourmet dishes with a modern flair. In a lively, street-front setting, you'll eat what the chef cooks—the lone *menu* changes daily based on his inspiration, and there are no other choices (incredible five-course €60 *menu,* daily, book well ahead, 9 Carrefour de l'Odéon, tel. 01 44 27 07 97).

$$ L'Avant Comptoir, a stand-up-only hors d'oeuvres bar, serves a delightful array of French-Basque tapas on a sleek zinc counter. With illustrated menu cards hanging from the ceiling, this popular place is designed to make the cuisine from next door's pricey Le Comptoir more accessible. At the walk-up counter outside, you can get top quality sandwiches and crêpes to go (for less and with less commotion). But step inside for the foodie bar and it's another world (daily 12:00-23:00, 3 Carrefour de l'Odéon).

$ Restaurant Polidor is the Parisian equivalent of a beloved neighborhood diner. A fixture here since 1845, it's much loved for its unpretentious quality cooking, fun old-Paris atmosphere, and fair value. Noisy, happy diners sit tightly at shared tables, savoring classic bourgeois *plats* from every corner of France (daily 12:00-14:30 & 19:00-23:00, cash only, no reservations, 41 Rue Monsieur-le-Prince, tel. 01 43 26 95 34).

Restaurants near Luxembourg Garden

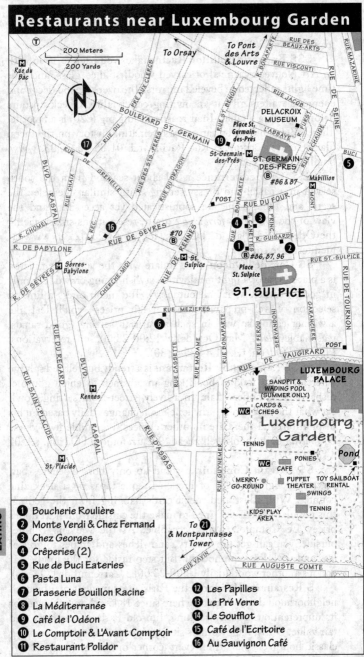

EATING

1. Boucherie Roulière
2. Monte Verdi & Chez Fernand
3. Chez Georges
4. Crêperies (2)
5. Rue de Buci Eateries
6. Pasta Luna
7. Brasserie Bouillon Racine
8. La Méditerranée
9. Café de l'Odéon
10. Le Comptoir & L'Avant Comptoir
11. Restaurant Polidor
12. Les Papilles
13. Le Pré Verre
14. Le Soufflot
15. Café de l'Ecritoire
16. Au Sauvignon Café

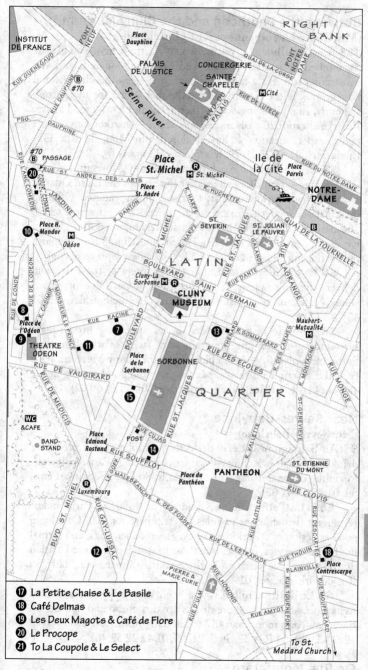

17 La Petite Chaise & Le Basile
18 Café Delmas
19 Les Deux Magots & Café de Flore
20 Le Procope
21 To La Coupole & Le Select

EATING

Between the Panthéon and the Cluny Museum
(Mo: Cluny-La Sorbonne or RER: Luxembourg)

$$$ **Les Papilles** is a warm, woody bistro where you'll dine surrounded by bottles of wine and eat what's offered...and you won't complain. It's a foodie's dream: one *menu*, no choices, and no regrets. Choose your wine from the shelf or ask for advice from the burly, rugby-playing owner, then relax and let the food arrive. Reserve ahead (€20 daily *marmite du marché*—market stew, bigger and cheaper selection at lunch, closed Sun-Mon, 30 Rue Gay Lussac, tel. 01 43 25 20 79, www.lespapillesparis.fr).

$$ **Le Pré Verre,** a block from the Cluny Museum, is a chic wine bistro—a refreshing alternative in a part of the Latin Quarter mostly known for low-quality, tourist-trapping eateries. Offering imaginative, modern cuisine at fair prices, the place is packed. The bargain lunch *menu* includes a starter, main course, glass of wine, and coffee (good wine list, closed Sun-Mon, 8 Rue Thénard, reservations necessary, tel. 01 43 54 59 47, www.lepreverre.com).

$$ **Le Soufflot,** named after the architect of the Panthéon, delivers dynamite views of the inspiring dome. Dine on good-enough café cuisine or just enjoy a drink (16 Rue Soufflot, tel. 01 43 26 57 56).

$$ **Café de l'Ecritoire** sits on an appealing little square surrounding a gurgling fountain and facing Paris' legendary Sorbonne University—just a block from the Cluny Museum. It's a typical brasserie with salads, *plats du jour,* and good seating inside and out (daily, 3 Place de la Sorbonne, tel. 01 43 54 60 02).

Near Sèvres-Babylone
(Mo: Sèvres-Babylone)

$$ **Au Sauvignon Café** is perfectly positioned for a predinner drink and people-watching. The interior is vintage Paris, with wall-to-ceiling decor and a fine zinc bar (daily, 80 Rue des Saints-Pères, tel. 01 45 48 49 02).

$$$ **La Petite Chaise,** founded in 1680, is Paris' oldest restaurant (which alone justifies the trip here for me). Offering a good selection of traditional dishes, generous servings, and formal but friendly service, it appeals to those in search of a classic Parisian dining experience (terrific €36 three-course dinner *menu,* daily, 36 Rue de Grenelle, tel. 01 42 22 13 35).

$$ **Le Basile** is full of young, loud, and happy eaters thrilled to have found a place where drinks are dirt cheap and nothing on the menu costs more than €17 (open daily from 7:00, food served 12:00-23:00, 34 Rue de Grenelle, tel. 01 42 22 59 46).

On Rue Mouffetard
(Mo: Censier Daubenton or Place Monge)

Several blocks behind the Panthéon, Rue Mouffetard is a conveyor belt of comparison-shopping eaters with wall-to-wall budget options (fondue, crêpes, Italian, falafel, and Greek). Come here to sift through the crowds and eat cheaply. This street stays up late and likes to party (particularly around Place de la Contrescarpe). The gauntlet begins on top, at thriving Place de la Contrescarpe, and ends below where Rue Mouffetard stops at St. Médard Church. Both ends offer fun cafés where you can watch the action. The upper stretch is pedestrian and touristy; the bottom stretch is purely Parisian. Anywhere between is no-man's land for consistent quality. Still, strolling with so many fun seekers is enjoyable, whether you eat or not. For locations, see map on page 412.

$$$ Café Delmas, at the top of Rue Mouffetard on picturesque Place de la Contrescarpe, is *the* place to see and be seen. Come here for an expensive before- or after-dinner drink on the terrace or typical but pricey café cuisine (open daily).

$$ Cave de Bourgogne, a local hangout, has reasonably priced, good café fare at the bottom of Rue Mouffetard. The outside has picture-perfect tables on a raised terrace; the interior is warm and lively (specials listed on chalkboards, daily, 144 Rue Mouffetard).

MONTMARTRE

Montmartre can be hit or miss; the top of the hill is extremely touristy, with mindless mobs following guides to cancan shows. But if you walk a few blocks away, you'll find a quieter, more authentic meal at one of the places I've listed below. For locations, see map on page 414.

Near Sacré-Cœur
(Mo: Abbesses or Anvers)

The steps in front of Sacré-Cœur are perfect for a picnic with a view, though the spot comes with lots of company. For a quieter setting, consider the park directly behind the church. Along the touristy main drag (near Place du Tertre and just off it), several fun piano bars serve mediocre crêpes and overpriced bistro fare but offer great people-watching. The options become less touristy and more tasty as you escape from the top of the hill.

$$$ Restaurant Chez Plumeau, just off jam-packed Place du Tertre, is touristy yet moderately priced, with formal service but great seating either in a characteristic dining room or on a tiny square under a wisteria arbor (elaborate salads, daily, 4 Place du Calvaire, Mo: Abbesses, tel. 01 46 06 26 29).

$$ L'Eté en Pente Douce is a good Montmartre choice, hiding under some trees just downhill from the crowds on a classic neighborhood corner. It features cheery indoor and outdoor seating, €10 *plats du jour* and salads, vegetarian options, and good wines (daily, many steps below Sacré-Cœur to the left as you leave, 23 Rue Muller, Mo: Anvers, tel. 01 42 64 02 67).

Near Place des Abbesses
(Mo: Abbesses unless otherwise noted)
At the bottom of Montmartre, residents pile into a long lineup of brasseries and cafés near Place des Abbesses, especially along Rue des Abbesses, Rue des Trois Frères, and Rue des Martyrs. Locals tend to gravitate to the cafés on the north side of Rue des Abbesses, leaving the sunnier and pricier cafés on the south side to visitors. Come here for a lively, less touristy scene. Rue des Abbesses is perfect for a picnic-gathering stroll with cheese shops, delis, wine stores, and bakeries. In fact, the bakers at **Grenier à Pain** (closed Tue-Wed, 38 Rue des Abbesses) and at **Au Levain d'Antan** (closed Sat-Sun, 6 Rue des Abbesses) have won the award for the best baguette in Paris.

$$$ Le Miroir's kitchen is run by a young and enthusiastic chef cooking up seasonal French fare. Go for the high-quality ingredients served to a locals-only crowd (good-value lunch special, closed Sun-Mon, 94 Rue des Martyrs, tel. 01 46 06 50 73, www. restaurantmiroir.com).

$$$ La Balançoire's rope swing, dangling from the ceiling, sets the tone for this playful spot serving French childhood favorites with a grown-up twist (closed Sun-Mon, 6 Rue Aristide Bruant, tel. 01 42 23 70 83).

$$$ Autour de Midi et Minuit is a classic French bistro sitting on top of a jazz cellar (see page 490 for concert details). Find hot food upstairs and cool jazz downstairs (closed Mon, 11 Rue Lepic, Mo: Blanche or Abbesses, tel. 01 55 79 16 48).

$$ Le Village is a dive bar turned trendy, serving tiny cups of espresso to garbage collectors in the morning and to mustached nonconformists in the afternoon. They have one or two warm *plats du jour* and several meat-and-cheese-plate combinations (daily 7:00-24:00, 36 Rue des Abbesses, tel. 01 42 54 99 59).

$ La Fourmi, sitting at the bottom of the hill, is a raucous café/bar with lovable rough edges. Open all day, they offer coffee, croissants, and simple, affordable lunches. In the evening, the place is taken over by hilltop hipsters who come for the inexpensive beer and generous cheese plates (daily, 74 Rue des Martyrs, Mo: Anvers or Pigalle, tel. 01 42 64 70 35, Eloise).

Rue des Trois Frères: This street, alive with bars and eateries, is a fun place to comparison shop. **Cave à Jojo** (#26) anchors the northern edge of the street, with generous cheese and charcuterie plates and an accordion-fueled ambience straight out of the 1950s (closed Sun, 18:00-late, accordion players on Sat nights, tel. 01 42

62 58 54). Across the way at **Le Jardin d'en Face** (#29), you'll find more vegetable-focused cooking and outdoor seating (daily, tel. 01 53 28 00 75). **La Gûepe** (#14), one of the liveliest spots on the street, serves cocktails and small plates that are fun to share (closed Mon, 18:00-late, tel. 01 42 64 98 32).

DINNER CRUISES

The following companies all offer **$$$$** dinner cruises (reservations required). Bateaux-Mouches and Bateaux Parisiens have the best reputations and the highest prices; Le Capitaine Fracasse is a tad more relaxed. All offer multicourse meals and music in aircraft-carrier-size dining rooms with glass tops and good views. Ask ahead about proper attire (no denim, shorts, or sport shoes); Bateaux-Mouches requires a jacket and tie for men.

Bateaux Parisiens, considered the best of the lot, features a lively atmosphere with a singer, band, and dance floor. Several departures leave daily from Port de la Bourdonnais, just east of the bridge under the Eiffel Tower. The early trip at 18:15 has *menus* from €69; later cruises are €99-205/person (price depends on seating and *menu* option; tel. 01 76 64 14 45, www.bateauxparisiens.com). On board, the middle level is best. Pay the extra euros to get seats next to the windows—it's more romantic and private, with sensational views.

Bateaux-Mouches, started in 1949 and hands-down the most famous, entertains with violin and piano music. You can't miss its sparkling port on the north side of the river at Pont de l'Alma (€69 for 18:00 cruise, €99-200/person for later trips, RER: Pont de l'Alma, tel. 01 42 25 96 10, www.bateaux-mouches.fr).

Le Capitaine Fracasse offers the budget option (€55-65/ person, €80-140 with wine or champagne; reserve ahead online or get there early to secure a table; boarding times vary by season and day of week, walk down stairs in the middle of Bir-Hakeim bridge near the Eiffel Tower to Iles aux Cygne, Mo: Bir-Hakeim or RER: Champ de Mars-Tour Eiffel, tel. 01 46 21 48 15, www. croisiere-paris.com).

LES GRANDS CAFES DE PARIS

Here's a short list of grand (expensive) Parisian cafés, worth the detour only if you've got the time and money for such touristy elegance. Think of these cafés as monuments to another time, and learn why they still matter (see sidebar). For tips on enjoying Parisian cafés, review the "Cafés and Brasseries" section on page 646; for locations, see the map on page 442. All are open daily.

History of Cafés in Paris

The first café in the Western world was in Paris—established in 1686 at Le Procope (still a restaurant today; see listing). The French had just discovered coffee, and their robust economy was growing a population of pleasure seekers and thinkers looking for places to be seen, to exchange ideas, and to plot revolutions—both political and philosophical. And with the advent of theaters such as La Comédie Française, the necessary artsy, coffee-sipping crowds were born. By 1700, more than 300 cafés had opened their doors; at the time of the Revolution (1789), there were more than 1,800 cafés in Paris. Revolutionaries from Jean-Paul Marat and Napoleon to Salvador Dalí enjoyed the freethinking café spirit.

Café society took off in the early 1900s. Life was changing rapidly, with new technology and wars on a global scale. Many retreated to Parisian cafés to try to make sense of the confusion. Vladimir Lenin, Leon Trotsky, Igor Stravinsky, Ernest Hemingway, F. Scott Fitzgerald, James Joyce, Albert Einstein, Jean-Paul Sartre, Simone de Beauvoir, Gene Openshaw, and Albert Camus were devoted members of café society. Some practically lived at their favorite café, where they kept their business calendars, entertained friends, and ate every meal. Parisian apartments were small, walls were thin (still often the case), and heating (particularly during war times) was minimal, making the warmth of cafés all the harder to leave.

There are more than 12,000 cafés in Paris today, though their numbers are shrinking. They're still used for business meetings, encounter sessions, political discussions, and romantic interludes. Most Parisians are loyal to their favorites and know their waiter's children's names.

On and near St. Germain-des-Prés
(Mo: St. Germain-des-Prés)

Where Boulevard St. Germain meets Rue Bonaparte (and nearby) you'll find several cafés.

$$$ Les Deux Magots offers prime outdoor seating and a warm interior. Once a favorite of Ernest Hemingway (in *The Sun Also Rises*, Jake met Brett here) and Jean-Paul Sartre (he and Simone de Beauvoir met here), today the café is filled with international tourists (6 Place St. Germain-des-Prés, tel. 01 45 48 55 25).

$$$ Café de Flore, in the next block, feels more literary—wear your black turtleneck. Pablo Picasso was a regular at the time he painted *Guernica* (172 Boulevard St. Germain-des-Prés, tel. 01 45 48 55 26).

$$ Le Procope, Paris' first and most famous café (1686), was a *café célèbre*, drawing notables such as Voltaire, Rousseau, Balzac, Zola, Robespierre, Victor Hugo, and two Americans, Benjamin

Franklin and Thomas Jefferson. The dining rooms are beautiful, but the cuisine is average (13 Rue de l'Ancienne Comédie, tel. 01 40 46 79 00).

Near Luxembourg Garden
(Mo: Vavin)

An eclectic assortment of historic cafés gathers along the busy Boulevard du Montparnasse near its intersection with Boulevard Raspail. Combine these historic cafés with a visit to Luxembourg Garden, which lies just a few blocks away, down Rue Vavin (next to Le Select).

$$$ La Coupole, built in the 1920s, was decorated by aspiring artists (Léger, Brancusi, and Chagall, among others) in return for free meals. It still supports artists with regular showings on its vast walls. This cavernous café feels like a classy train station, with acres of seating, brass decor, and tuxedoed waiters by the dozen. The food is basic and the service impersonal, but you come for the crazy social scene (food served from 12:00 until the wee hours, come early to get better service, 102 Boulevard du Montparnasse, tel. 01 43 20 14 20).

$$$ Le Select, more easygoing and traditional, was once popular with the more rebellious types—Leon Trotsky, Jean Cocteau, and Pablo Picasso loved it. It feels rather conformist today, with good outdoor seating and pleasant tables just inside the door—though the locals hang out at the bar farther inside (99 Boulevard du Montparnasse, across from La Coupole, tel. 01 45 48 38 24).

At Gare de Lyon

$$$$ Le Train Bleu is a grandiose restaurant with a low-slung, leather-couch café-bar area built right into the train station for the

Paris Exhibition of 1900 (which also saw the construction of the Pont Alexandre III and the Grand and Petit Palais). It's simply a grand-scale-everything experience, with over-the-top belle époque decor that speaks of another age, when going to dinner was an event—a chance to see and be seen. Forty-one massive paintings of scenes along the old rail lines tempt diners to consider a getaway. Reserve ahead for dinner, or drop in for a drink before your train leaves (up the stairs opposite track L, tel. 01 43 43 09 06, www.le-train-bleu.com).

EATING

PARIS WITH CHILDREN

Paris works well with children—smart parents enjoy the "fine art" of simply experiencing Paris' great neighborhoods, parks, and monuments while watching their kids revel in the City of Light. After enjoying the city's most family-friendly sights, your children may want to return to Paris before you do.

Trip Tips

PLAN AHEAD

Choose hotels in a kid-friendly area near a park. The Rue Cler and Luxembourg neighborhoods are both good. If you're staying more than a few days, think about renting an apartment (see page 418).

If traveling with infants, plan on bringing or buying a light stroller (*poussette*) for neighborhood walks and a child backpack (*porte bébé*) for riding the Métro. Strollers usually work fine on the bus (enter through buses' larger central doors, then park the stroller in the designated *poussette* area...if there's room), but they're tough in the Métro (miles of stairs). Many sights allow either strollers or backpacks, but usually not both (some museums that don't allow backpacks even provide strollers).

If traveling with older kids, you can help them keep in touch with friends at home with cheap texting plans. Readily available Wi-Fi (at hotels, some cafés, and all Starbucks and McDonald's) makes bringing a mobile device

Parenting French-Style

Famous for their topless tanning, French women are equally comfortable with public breastfeeding of their babies—no need for large scarves or "Hooter Hiders" here. Changing tables are nonexistent, so bring a roll-up changing mat and get comfortable changing your baby on your knees, on a bench, or wherever you find enough space.

French grandmothers take their role as community elders seriously and won't hesitate to recommend that you put more sunscreen on your child in the summer or add a layer of clothing if it's breezy.

For older kids, the drinking age is 16 for beer and wine and 18 for the hard stuff: Your waiter will assume that your teen will have wine with you at dinner. Teens are also welcome in most bars and lounges (there's no 21-and-older section).

Consider hiring a babysitter for a night or two—ask your hotelier or apartment rental agency for a babysitting recommendation, or look up babysitting agencies in Paris.

worthwhile. Most parents find it worth the peace of mind to buy a supplemental messaging plan for the whole family: Adults can stay connected to teenagers while allowing them maximum independence (see page 659).

EATING
Try these tips to keep your kids content throughout the day.

- Eat dinner early, before the sophisticated Parisian crowd dines (aim for sitting down at 19:00-19:30 at restaurants, earlier at cafés). Skip romantic places.
- Look for cafés (or fast-food restaurants) where kids can move around without bothering others.
- Kid-friendly foods that are commonly available and easy to order include crêpes (available at many takeout stands), *croque monsieurs* (grilled ham-and-cheese sandwiches), and *tartines* (open-faced sandwiches). Meaty choices include hamburgers (*à la française*, of course), *saucisse* (skinny grilled sausages), or *steak haché* (a burger without the bun or toppings). Plain pasta is available at many cafés and some bistros (ask for *pâtes au beurre*). For breakfast, try a *pain au chocolat* (chocolate-filled pastry) or dip your baguette in a *chocolat chaud* (hot chocolate). Fruit, cereals, and yogurt are usually available. Carry a baguette to snack on.
- If your kids love peanut butter, bring it from home (hard to find in France) for food emergencies...or let them acquire a taste for Nutella (chocolate and hazelnut spread), available everywhere.

Books and Films for Kids

Get your kids into the Parisian spirit with books and movies about France. (Also see "Recommended Books and Films," including some good choices for teenagers, on page 678.) Bring along plenty of kids' books; they're harder to find and more expensive in Paris. If you run out, visit one of the English-language bookstores listed on page 24.

Adèle and Simon (Barbara McClintock, 2006). Kids will enjoy this sweet, watercolored peek into early-20th-century Paris.

Anatole (Eve Titus, 1956). This Caldecott Honor Book introduces young readers to the great world of French food via a mouse who finds work in a cheese factory (foreshadowing the animated flick *Ratatouille* decades later).

Cathedral (David Macauley, 1973). Macauley re-creates the building of a French Gothic cathedral in detailed pen-and-ink sketches.

Discovering Great Artists: Hands-On Art for Children in the Styles of the Great Masters (MaryAnn Kohl, 1997). Get to know your favorite artists, from the Renaissance to the present day, by learning their techniques through various art activities.

Everybody Bonjours! (Leslie Kimmelman, Sarah McMenemy, 2008). A little girl and her family are at the heart of this fun introduction to the city and its language.

The History of Art for Young People (H.W. Janson, Anthony F. Janson, 1971). Older kids will appreciate this visually appealing reference guide to famous works of art.

How Would You Survive in the Middle Ages? (Fiona MacDonald, 1995). MacDonald makes history fun for kids and adults alike in this engaging guide to life in the Middle Ages.

- Picnics work well. *Boulangeries* are good places to grab off-hour snacks when restaurants aren't serving. (See page 642 for picnic tips.)

SIGHTSEEING

The key to a successful Paris family vacation is to slow down. Take extended breaks when needed.

- It's good to have a "what if" procedure in place in case something goes wrong. Give your kids your hotel's business card, your phone number (if you brought a mobile phone), and emergency taxi fare. Let them know to ask to use the phone at a hotel if they are lost. And if they have mobile phones, show them how to make calls in France (see page 659).
- Involve your children in the trip. Let them help choose daily activities, lead you through the Métro, and so on.

Hugo (2011). Paris in the 1930s is the setting of Scorsese's film about an orphan who lives in a train station and fixes clocks.

Kiki and Coco in Paris (Nina Gruener, Stephanie Rausser, 2011). The story of a friendship between a young girl and her doll unfolds in a series of photographs, documenting their journey to Paris.

Madeline (Ludwig Bemelmans, 1939). Kids love the *Madeline* series, where "in an old house in Paris that was covered with vines, lived twelve little girls in two straight lines." It's also a live-action film from 1998.

Mission Paris: A Scavenger Hunt Adventure (Catherine Aragon, 2014). Young explorers will have hands-on fun completing missions while discovering the city.

The Mona Lisa Caper (Rick Jacobson, Laura Fernandez, 2005). This Louvre-heist adventure will engage the under-10 set.

Paris: Great Cities Through the Ages (Renzo Rossi, 2003). Kid historians will devour this fun introduction to the city and its history, told mainly through illustrations.

Ratatouille (2007). A mouse becomes a chef at a fine Parisian restaurant in this Pixar film.

The Red Balloon (1956). In this classic film, a small boy chases his balloon through the streets of Paris, showing how beauty can be found even in the simplest toy.

This Is Paris (Miroslav Sasek, 1959). Kids of all ages will enjoy the whimsical impressions in Sasek's classic picture book.

A Walk in Paris (Salvatore Rubbino, 2014). The littlest travelers can prepare themselves for the City of Light by joining a girl and her grandfather on a stroll through Paris.

- For information on children's activities, including shows, museums, and park events, look in *Pariscope* magazine under "Enfants" (see page 22).
- Limit museum visits to 45 minutes—period! Kids will tolerate a little culture if it's short and focused, with plenty of breaks. At the Eiffel Tower, that first level may be plenty (rather than waiting in line for the top).
- Follow this book's crowd-beating tips. Kids despise long lines even more than you do.
- Since school lets out early on Wednesdays, expect parks and other children's sights to be busy on Wednesday afternoons, and expect more kid activities at those sights.
- Museum audioguides are great for older children. For younger children, hit the gift shop first so they can buy postcards and have a scavenger hunt to find the pictured artwork. When

boredom sets in, try "I spy" games or have them count how many babies or dogs they can spot in all the paintings in the room.

- Let kids pick out some toys and books. Large department stores, such as Bon Marché, tend to have a good selection of toys. Visit a bookstore to pick out books together (see page 24).

- Learn and play *boules,* a form of outdoor bowling (see the sidebar on page 389). The best thing we did on one trip was to buy our own set of *boules.* We'd play before dinner, side by side with real players at the neighborhood park. Buy your *boules de pétanque* at a Décathlon sports store (www.decathlon.fr). The *boules* make great (if weighty) souvenirs and also provide entertainment (and memories) once you're back home.

- Instead of hot daytime sightseeing, try a nighttime stroll among the street performers on Paris' pedestrian-friendly streets. See "Night Walks" on page 493 for ideas.

Top Kids' Activities and Sights

ATTRACTIONS

When it comes to sightseeing with kids, don't overdo it. Tackle one key sight each day (Louvre, Orsay, Versailles), and mix it with a healthy dose of lighter activities. To minimize unnecessary travel, try to match kid activities with areas where you'll be sightseeing (for example, the Louvre is near the kid-friendly Palais Royal's courtyards and Tuileries Garden). Kids prefer the Louvre after dark, when it's less busy (Wed and Fri only). Additional kid-friendly sights are located within Paris' parks; see "Parks and Gardens," later.

Note: At some sights (such as the Army Museum and Arc de Triomphe), Museum Pass holders must wait in line to pick up their free children's tickets.

Eiffel Tower and Nearby

You could fill an entire kid-centric day here. Come early and ride the elevator up the tower before crowds appear, or ride it above the lights at night (📖 see the Eiffel Tower Tour chapter). The **Champ de Mars** park stretches out from the tower's base, with picnic-perfect benches, sand pits, and other fun. Big toys are located at the nonriver end of the park (with your back to the tower, it's to the right). Pony rides, puppet shows, and pedal go-carts are in the center in

the park (usually after 11:00 Wed, Sat-Sun, and on all summer days; after 15:00 otherwise, Mo: Ecole Militaire, RER-C: Champ de Mars-Tour Eiffel, or bus #69).

All ages enjoy the view from **Place du Trocadéro,** across the river from the Eiffel Tower, especially after dark (Mo: Trocadéro). The terrific **National Maritime Museum** (Musée National de la Marine) is docked at Trocadéro, with all things nautical, including wonderful ship models (see listing on page 66). The **Cinéaqua** aquarium/cinema in the gardens below the Trocadéro boasts 10,000 fish in more than 40 tanks (some English explanations), along with regular shows (French only) and subtitled kids' movies, usually with a "sea creatures" theme (€13 for kids 12 and under, €16 for kids 13-17, €21 for adults, daily 10:00-19:00, 5 Avenue Albert de Mun, Mo: Trocadéro, tel. 01 40 69 23 23, www. cineaqua.com).

Notre-Dame

Paris' famous Gothic cathedral doesn't have to be old and boring. Replay Quasimodo's stunt and climb the tower (go early to avoid long lines). Kids love being on such a lofty perch with a face-to-face look at a gargoyle. The crypt on the square in front of Notre-Dame is quick and interesting (covered by Museum Pass). Kids can push buttons to highlight remains of Roman Paris and leave with a better understanding of how different civilizations build on top of each other. The small but beautiful park along the river outside Notre-Dame's south side has sandboxes, picnic benches, and space to run (Mo: Cité). My preteen son loved the traffic-free lanes of the Latin Quarter across the river.

◫ See the Historic Paris Walk chapter or ∩ download my free audio tour.

Arc de Triomphe and the Champs-Elysées

This area is popular with teenagers, day and night. Mine couldn't get enough of it. Watch the crazy traffic rush around the Arc de Triomphe for endless entertainment, then stroll Avenue des Champs-Elysées with its car dealerships (particularly Renault's razzle-dazzle café), Disney store, and the river of humanity that flows along its broad sidewalks. Take your teenager to see a movie on the Champs-Elysées ("v.o."  next to the showtime means it's shown in the original language).

◫ See the Champs-Elysées Walk chapter.

CHILDREN

Pompidou Center

Teens like the Pompidou Center for its crazy outdoor entertainers, throngs of young people, happening cafés, and fun fountains next door (but it's dead on Tue, when the museum is closed). Inside, the temporary exhibits and gift shop on the main floor are visually impressive. The escalator to the top is a good ride for all ages.

📖 See the Pompidou Center Tour chapter.

Paris Zoo
(Le Parc Zoologique de Paris)

The recently renovated Paris Zoo is spectacular, re-creating habitats from five continents for both beasts and visitors to enjoy. Visit the modern glass greenhouse and walk among colorful birds, jumping monkeys, and other furry tree dwellers. Combining time at the zoo with a picnic lunch (pick up elsewhere) in the Bois de Vincennes park (with paddleboats, pony rides, and chateau tours) is a delightful way to spend the day.

Cost and Hours: €14 for kids 3-11, €16.50 for ages 12-25, free for kids 2 and under, €22 for adults; Mon-Fri 10:00-18:00, Sat-Sun 9:30-19:30, shorter hours off-season; Mo: Porte Dorée or St. Mandé, then 15-minute walk—head toward the skyscraper-sized rock at edge of Bois de Vincennes; bus #46 or #86 brings you closer, tel. 08 11 22 41 22, www.parczoologiquedeparis.fr.

Musée en Herbe

For budding *artistes,* a trip here is a must. This small art museum near the Louvre, designed with the youngest of art lovers in mind, offers contemporary art exhibits, a colorful bookstore, and workshops where kids can make their own art. Workshops are offered only in French—but the smiling, paint-covered kids don't seem to mind.

Cost and Hours: €6, daily 10:00-19:00; €10-16 one-hour workshops offered daily July-Aug, Wed and Sat only during school year, for ages 2.5-5 parents must stay, for ages 5-12 parents must leave; call, email, or stop by to reserve; 21 Rue Hérold, Mo: Palais Royal, tel. 01 40 67 97 66, www.musee-en-herbe.com, resa.meh@gmail.com.

Versailles

This massive conglomeration of palaces, gardens, fountains, and forest can be brutal—or a good family getaway if well-planned. Avoid Sundays, Tuesdays, and Saturdays (in that order), when the place is packed from opening to closing. Strollers are allowed in the gardens, but not inside the palace (you'll have to check yours). Rent a bike and let the kids go wild on park paths (bikes of all sizes are available, even toddler bikes with training wheels). Or explore the gardens in a rented golf cart—while pricey, it's great fun and extremely easy. (For liability reasons, the staff wants only parents to do the driving, but once away from the palace...) Or you can row row row a boat on the Grand Canal or attend an equestrian performance at Versailles' stables. The Domaine de Marie-Antoinette (opens at noon) has trails for scampering on, and her Hamlet has barnyard animals up close and personal.

📖 See the Versailles chapter or 🎧 download my free audio tour.

PARKS AND GARDENS

Paris' public parks are perhaps your single best source of kid-friendly fun. Besides providing an outlet for high-energy kids (and a chance for the whole family to take a sightseeing breather), Parisian parks host a variety of activities, many of them with a quintessentially French flair.

Marionette shows, called *guignols* (geen-yohl), can be interesting for children patient enough to sit still. Shows are in French, but have fairly easy-to-follow plots and some internationally understood slapstick (look for them in bigger parks, such as Luxembourg Garden, and check *Pariscope* or *L'Officiel des Spectacles,* under "Marionettes," for times and places). The game of *boules* is played nearly everywhere (for rules, see page 389).

Temporary **amusement parks** come to life in public parks throughout the city; the Ferris wheel pops up in high season either on Place de la Concorde or in the Tuileries Garden, and the rides in the Tuileries are the best—my daughter preferred them to Disneyland Paris.

You can rent **toy boats** to sail on a park's pond, or rent real **rowboats** at bigger parks, such as in Versailles' gardens (along the Grand Canal) or in the huge Bois de Vincennes (Mo: Porte Dorée). Bigger parks can be perfect for a relaxing **bike ride. Pony rides** are offered on certain days in some parks, such as Luxembourg Garden, the Champ de Mars, and the Bois de Vincennes; to learn when and where the ponies are trotting, check www.animaponey. com or call 06 07 32 53 95.

Luxembourg Garden

This is my favorite place to mix kid business with pleasure. This perfectly Parisian park has it all—from tennis courts to cafés—as well as a big-toys play area with imaginative slides, swings, jungle gyms, rope towers, and chess games (see map on page 289). To find the big-toys play area, head to the southwest corner (small fee, entry good all day, many parents watch from chairs outside the play area, open daily, usually 10:00-19:00 in summer, until 16:00 in winter, pay WC nearby). Kids also like the speedy merry-go-round (small fee), the pony rides, and the toy sailboats for rent in the main pond (activities open daily in summer, otherwise only Wed and Sat-Sun). Near the main building is a toddler wading pool (summer only) and sand pit (both free). A puppet theater hosts *guignol* shows (in French), located in the southwest corner of the park near the children's play area (about €6; shows year-round Sat-Sun at 11:00 and also Sat-Sun and Wed at 15:30 or 16:00—times vary by season, 1-2 shows daily for most

of July-Aug, check schedule online; 45 minutes, no air-con, tel. 01 43 26 46 47, www.marionnettesduluxembourg.fr). The park has many shaded paths as well as big, open areas perfect for kicking a ball. Kids can even play in the grass opposite the palace (Mo: St. Sulpice, Odéon, or Notre-Dame-des-Champs).

Tuileries Garden

This central park, located between the Louvre and Place de la Concorde, across the river from the Musée d'Orsay, comes in handy for kid breaks. You'll find the usual children's activities on Wednesdays, Saturdays, and Sundays (toy sailboat rental in pond and pony rides) and fun trampolines in the northwest corner of the park near the Place de la Concorde Métro stop (about €3 for 5-10 minutes, 2-12-year-olds only, daily 11:00-19:00, see map on page 59 for specific location). Nearby is a play area with rope towers and slides, and an old-fashioned merry-go-round. The Tuileries Garden also hosts a summer fair with rides, games, and possibly a Ferris wheel.

Riverside Promenade (Les Berges du Seine)

This one-time expressway turned riverfront park—running from near the Eiffel Tower to the Orsay Museum—is a joy for families, with kid activities such as climbing walls and big chess sets, plus good eating options (for details, see page 65).

Jardin des Plantes

These colorful gardens are a must for gardeners and good for kids. Located on the Left Bank southeast of the Latin Quarter, the park is short on grass but long on kid activities, including several play areas and a few kid-friendly natural-science museums. There's also a zoo, but it has just a few animals in old cages. From the park entrance near the river on Place Valhubert, you'll find these museums lining the left side of the park (Mo: Gare d'Austerlitz or Jussieu).

Young kids enjoy the dinosaur exhibit at the **Galerie d'Anatomie Comparée et de Paléontologie;** there are no English explanations, but they're not really needed (€7 for adults, free for ages 25 and under, not covered by Museum Pass, Wed-Mon 10:00-17:00, until 18:00 on April-Sept weekends, closed Tue, busiest on weekends, entrance faces river next to McDonald's).

The **Grande Galerie de l'Evolution,** at the nonriver end of the park, is an Old World museum describing the evolution of animals. It features a giant whale skeleton, tons of dead bugs under glass, all sorts of taxidermied animals, and many other kid-cool exhibits. Pick up the map and look for the good English explanations inserted into wood benches throughout the gallery (free for ages 25 and under, €9 for adults, not covered by Museum Pass, Wed-Mon 10:00-18:00, closed Tue, busiest on weekends, gift shop may have some helpful books in English, tel. 01 40 79 30 00, www.mnhn.fr). You can pay extra to visit the **Galerie des Enfants du Muséum,** a cool series of exhibits within the Galerie de l'Evolution. It's stuffed with animal-centric interactive displays and activities designed for 6- to 12-year-olds, all in English. Visitors are admitted only at 15-minute intervals, and the gallery can fill up fast—consider booking a time slot online a few days ahead (€9 for ages 4-25, free for kids 3 and under, €11 for adults, Wed-Mon 10:00-18:00, closed Tue, last entry at 16:45, tel. 01 40 79 54 79, www.galeriedesenfants.fr).

The small zoo, **Ménagerie des Jardins des Plantes,** displays live animals as opposed to stuffed ones—although the population here is old and a bit sleepy (€10 for kids 4-16, free for kids 3 and under, €14 for adults, daily 9:00-18:00, tel. 01 40 79 37 94).

The **Galerie de Minéralogie** is made for fans of stuff that comes from the earth—your kids may dig the collection of rocks, crystals, and more (€4 for ages 25 and under, €6 for ages 26 and over, daily 10:00-18:00, shorter hours off-season, tel. 01 40 79 56 01).

Parc de la Villette

This vast area of parks and museums has outdoor concerts, outdoor movies, a playground that's great for summer visits, and grass you're allowed to run around on (a rare treat in Paris). Main attractions for kids are Europe's largest science museum (Cité des Sciences et de l'Industrie), an IMAX theater, a real French submarine, acres of parks, play areas, and a working canal (211 Avenue Jean Jaurès, Mo: Porte de la Villette, follow *Corentin-Cariou* or *Porte de Pantin* signs, tel. 01 40 03 75 75, www.villette.com).

Cité des Sciences et de l'Industrie: For families, the best part of this big science-museum complex is **Cité des Enfants,** a fun place that's perfect for simultaneously teaching and exhausting your children. Kids can climb inside a living ant farm, operate a crane (safety vest and hard hat provided), create whirlpools in the water exhibit, step into a tornado, film themselves driving down the highway in front of a green screen, and much more. Tickets are sold for a specific 1.5-hour time slot, and for one of two sections of the museum: the area designed for 2- to 7-year-olds, or the one designed for 5- to 12-year-olds (€7 for kids, €9 for adults; Tue-Fri starting at 10:00, 11:45, 13:30, or 15:15; Sat-Sun starting at 10:30, 12:30, 14:30, or 16:30—verify times on website; closed Mon, www. cite-sciences.fr). There is a good café with healthy options on the ground floor, an indoor picnic space, and a bookshop to keep you busy while you wait for your entrance time.

The science exhibit designed for adults, the **Expositions d'Explora,** is dense—likely to appeal only to hard-core science fans and teenagers on the honor roll (€7 for ages 6-26, free for kids 5 and under, €9 for adults, Tue-Sat 10:00-18:00, Sun 10:00-19:00, closed Mon, no specific entrance time required).

A midsized 1950s military **submarine** is permanently parked outside the Cité des Sciences. It comes with videos, buttons to press, a working periscope, and tight quarters—even on uncrowded days (€3, closes 30 minutes before rest of Cité des Sciences).

OTHER EXPERIENCES
Biking
Take your kids out for a bike ride (see page 68 for a suggested route). If the city's streets seem too intimidating, consider heading to one of the parks outside the city center—many of them are great for biking, and even offer rentals (such as the gardens of Versailles). **Bike About Tours** has good information and rentals (baby seats, tandem attachments, kids' bikes). They also offer private family tours of Paris that include fun activities like scavenger hunts (€200 for the first 2 people, €25/person after that, 15 percent discount for Rick Steves readers, 4 hours; for contact information, see page 36).

Rollerblading
Sunday afternoons are fun for rollerblading with locals at your own pace, starting at the south side of Place de la Bastille at 14:30 (see page 38, www.rollers-coquillages.org; skate-rental shop nearby).

Riverboat Rides
A variety of companies offer one-hour Seine cruises on huge glass-domed boats. Or hop on a Batobus, a river bus connecting eight stops along the river: Eiffel Tower, Orsay Museum, St. Germain-des-Prés, Notre-Dame, Jardin des

Plantes, Hôtel de Ville, the Louvre, and Pont Alexandre III—near the Champs-Elysées. Longer boat trips ply the tranquil waters of a peaceful canal between the Orsay and Bassin de la Villette (see page 42).

Bus and Car Tours

The hop-on, hop-off double-decker bus tours (see page 37) are a good way to begin your visit. Taking a nighttime tour in a convertible Deux Chevaux is a terrific way to end your trip (page 496).

Watery Fun

Paris has more than three dozen swimming pools. Ask your hotelier for the location of the nearest pool, or head for one of the places listed below. Note that boys and men are required to wear Speedo-style (tight) swimsuits at pools *(oh là là!);* and most public pools require everyone to wear a swim cap (bring one with you, or find them at a Monoprix or Décathlon sporting-goods store).

Aquaboulevard: Paris' best pool/waterslide/miniature golf complex is easy to reach and a complete escape from the museum scene. Indoor and outdoor pools with high-flying slides, waves, geysers, and whirlpool tubs draw kids of all ages. It's pricey (and steamy inside), but a good opportunity to see soaked Parisians at play (for 6 hours, it's €19 for kids 3-11, €29 for adults, much cheaper rates for more than one visit, no children under 3, daily 9:00-23:00, English-speaking staff, keep spare change for lockers, men's swimsuits and swim caps are affordable at the Décathlon store right there, tel. 01 40 60 10 00, www.aquaboulevard.fr). Ride the Métro to the end of line 8 (Balard stop), walk two blocks under the elevated freeway, veer left across the traffic circle, and find Aquaboulevard in a complex of theaters and shops.

Joséphine Baker Pool: Housed in a giant barge docked along the Seine, this state-of-the-art floating swimming pool (Piscine Joséphine Baker) boasts generous wood decks and views of the city that get even better (though the pool gets more crowded) on sunny days, when the retractable rooftop is opened up (€5 for first 2 hours, then €2.60/hour, less for kids and in winter, daily approximately 13:00-21:00, opens earlier in summer, cabana-type cafés next door, near Gare d'Austerlitz at 8 Quai François Mauriac, Mo: Quai de la Gare or François Mitterrand, tel. 01 56 61 96 50).

DISNEYLAND PARIS

Europe's Disneyland is a remake of California's, with most of the same rides and smiles. The main difference is that Mickey Mouse speaks French, and you can buy wine with your lunch. My kids went ducky for it.

The Disneyland Paris Resort is a sprawling complex housing two theme parks (Disneyland Paris and Walt Disney Studios), a few entertainment venues, and several hotels. Opened in 1992, it was the second Disney resort built outside the US (Tokyo was first). With upwards of 15 million visitors a year, it has quickly become Europe's single leading tourist destination.

Disneyland Paris: This park has cornered the fun market, with classic rides and Disney characters. You'll find familiar favorites wrapped in French packaging, like Space Mountain (a.k.a. *De la Terre à la Lune*) and Pirates of the Caribbean *(Pirates des Caraïbes)*.

Walt Disney Studios: This zone has a Hollywood focus geared for an older crowd, with animation, special effects, and movie magic "rides." The cinema-themed rides include CinéMagique (a slow-motion cruise through film history on a people mover, mixing film clips, audio-animatronic figures, and live actors); Studio Tram Tour: Behind the Magic (another slow-mo ride, this time mostly outdoors, through a "movie backlot"); and Moteurs... Action! Stunt Show Spectacular (an actual movie sequence is filmed with stunt drivers, audience bit players, and brash MTV-style hosts). The top thrill rides include the Rock 'n' Roller Coaster (which starts out by accelerating from a standstill to nearly 60 miles per hour in less than three seconds, all while Aerosmith tunes blast in your ears) and the Twilight Zone Tower of Terror (which drops passengers from a precarious 200-foot-high perch). Gentler attractions include a recreation of the parachute jump in *Toy Story* and a *Finding Nemo*-themed ride that whisks you through the ocean current.

Getting There

Disneyland is easy to get to, and may be worth a day—if Paris is handier than Florida or California.

By Bus or Train from Downtown Paris: The slick 45-minute RER trip is the best way to get to Disneyland from Paris. Take RER line A to Marne-la-Vallée-Chessy (check the signs over the platform to be sure Marne-la-Vallée-Chessy is served, because the line splits near the end). Catch it from one of these stations: Charles de Gaulle-Etoile, Auber, Châtelet-Les Halles, or Gare de Lyon (at least 3/hour, drops you 45 minutes later right in the park, about €8 each way). The last train back to Paris leaves shortly after midnight. When returning, remember to use the same RER ticket for your Métro connection in Paris.

The all-day Mobilis ticket is a smart purchase for some Disney day-trippers, as it covers your Paris Métro rides for the day and the round-trip train to Disneyland (€16.60 for zones 1-5 ticket). Buy it at any Métro station, fill in your name and date of travel on the ticket, and validate it the day you use it.

Disneyland Express runs buses to Disneyland from several stops in central Paris (including Opéra, Madeleine, Châtelet, and Gare du Nord). A single ticket combines transportation and entrance to Disneyland (€80 for kids 3-11, free for kids 2 and under, €90 for adults; several morning departures to choose from and one return time of 20:00, book tickets online, www.disneylandparis-express.com).

By Bus or Train from the Airport: Both of Paris' major airports (Charles de Gaulle and Orly) have direct shuttle buses to Disneyland Paris (€20; about hourly and takes 45 minutes, www.magicalshuttle.co.uk). Fast TGV trains run from Charles de Gaulle to Disneyland in 10 minutes, leaving hourly (shuttle bus ride required to get from train station to Disneyland).

By Car: Disneyland is about 40 minutes (20 miles) east of Paris on the A-4 autoroute (direction Nancy/Metz, exit #14). Parking is about €15/day at the park.

Orientation to Disneyland

Cost: A one-day pass to either park—Disneyland Paris or Walt Disney Studios—is about €62 for kids ages 3-11, free for kids 2 and under, €69 for adults. Multiday passes are available. Regular prices are discounted about 25 percent Nov-March, and promotions are offered occasionally (check www. disneylandparis.com).

Hours: Disneyland—daily 10:00-22:00, mid-May-Aug until 23:00, until 20:00 in winter, open later on weekends, hours fluctuate with the seasons—check website for precise times. Walt Disney Studios—daily 10:00-19:00.

Skipping Lines: The free Fastpass system is a worthwhile timesaver for the most popular rides (check map and legend for details; you may have only one Fastpass at a time, so choose wisely). At the ride, check the Fastpass sign to see when you can return and skip the line. Insert your park admission ticket into the Fastpass machine, which spits out a ticket printed with your return time. You'll also save time by buying park tickets in advance (at airport TIs, some Métro stations, or along the Champs-Elysées at the Disney Store).

Avoiding Crowds: Saturday, Sunday, Wednesday, public holidays, and any day in July and August are the most crowded. After dinner, crowds are gone.

Information: Disney brochures are in every Paris hotel. For more info and to make reservations, call 01 60 30 60 53, or try www. disneylandparis.com.

CHILDREN

Eating with Mickey: Food is fun and not outrageously priced. (Still, many smuggle in a picnic.) The Disneyland Hotel restaurant Inventions offers an expensive gourmet brunch on Sundays (roughly €60/person) and daily dinners where the most famous Disney characters visit with starstruck eaters.

Sleeping at Disneyland

Most are better off sleeping in the real world (i.e., Paris), though with direct buses and freeways to both airports, Disneyland makes a convenient first- or last-night stop. Seven different Disney-owned hotels offer accommodations at or near the park in all price ranges. Prices are impossible to pin down, as they vary by season and by the package deal you choose (deals that include park entry are usually a better value, with more in the $$$$ range). To reserve any Disneyland hotel, call 01 60 30 60 53, or check www.disneylandparis.com. The prices you'll be quoted include entry to the park. **Hotel Santa Fe**** offers a fair midrange value, with frequent shuttle service to the park. Another cheap option is **Davy Crockett's Ranch,** but you'll need a car to stay there. The most expensive is the **Disneyland Hotel,****** right at the park entry, about three times the price of the Santa Fe. The **Vienna House Dream Castle Hotel****** is another higher-end choice, with nearly 400 rooms done up to look like a lavish 17th-century palace (40 Avenue de la Fosse des Pressoirs, tel. 01 64 17 90 00, www.dreamcastle-hotel.com, info@dreamcastle-hotel.com).

SHOPPING IN PARIS

Shopping in chic Paris is altogether tempting—even reluctant shoppers can find good reasons to indulge. Wandering among elegant boutiques provides a break from the heavy halls of the Louvre, and, if you approach it right, a little cultural enlightenment.

If you need just souvenirs, visit a souvenir shop. A neighborhood supermarket is a good place to find that Parisian box of tea, jam, or cookies—perfect for tucking into your suitcase at the last minute. For more elaborate purchases, large department stores provide painless one-stop shopping in classy surroundings. Neighborhood boutiques offer the greatest reward at the highest risk. Clerks and prices can be intimidating, but the selection is more original and the experience is purely Parisian. Just be sure you don't leave your shopping for Sunday, when most stores are buttoned up tight.

Even if you don't intend to buy anything, budget some time for window shopping, or, as the French call it, *faire du lèche-vitrines* ("window licking").

TIPS ON SHOPPING

Before you enter a Parisian store, remember the following points:

- In small stores, always say, *"Bonjour, Madame* or *Mademoiselle* or *Monsieur"* when entering. And remember to say *"Au revoir, Madame* or *Mademoiselle* or *Monsieur"* when leaving.
- The customer is not always right. In fact, figure the clerk is doing you a favor by waiting on you.
- Except in department stores, it's not normal for the customer to handle clothing. Ask first before you pick up an item: *"Je peux?"* (zhuh puh), meaning, "Can I?"
- By law the price of items in a window display must be visible, often written on a slip of paper set on the floor or framed on

Key Shopping Phrases

English	French
Just looking.	*Je regarde.* (zhuh ruh-gard)
How much is it?	*Combien?* (kohn-bee-an)
Too big/small/ expensive.	*Trop grand/petit/cher.* (troh grahn/puh-tee/shehr)
May I try it on?	*Je peux l'essayer?* (zhuh puh lay-say-yay)
Can I see more?	*Je peux en voir d'autres?* (zhuh puh ahn vwahr doh-truh)
I'd like this.	*Je voudrais ça.* (zhuh voo-dray sah)
On sale	*Solde* (sohld)
Discounted price	*Prix réduit* (pree ray-dwee)
Big discounts	*Prix choc* (pree shohk)

the wall. This gives you an idea of how expensive or affordable the shop is before venturing inside.

- For clothing size comparisons between the US and France, see page 682 of the appendix.
- Forget returns (and don't count on exchanges).
- Observe French shoppers. Then imitate.
- Saturday afternoons are *très* busy and not for the faint of heart.
- Stores are generally closed on Sunday. Exceptions include the Carrousel du Louvre (underground shopping mall at the Louvre with a Printemps department store), and some shops near Sèvres-Babylone, along the Champs-Elysées, and in the Marais.
- Some small stores don't open until 14:00 on Mondays.
- Don't feel obliged to buy. If a shopkeeper offers assistance, just say, *"Je regarde, merci."*
- For information on VAT refunds and customs regulations, see page 628.

SOUVENIR SHOPS

Avoid souvenir carts in front of famous monuments and, instead, look for souvenir shops. You can find cheaper gifts around the Pompidou Center, on the streets of Montmartre, and in some department stores (see next). The riverfront stalls near Notre-Dame sell a variety of used books, old posters and postcards, magazines, refrigerator magnets, and other tourist paraphernalia in the most romantic setting; see page 119 in the Historic Paris Walk chapter. You'll find better deals at the souvenir shops that line Rue d'Arcole between Notre-Dame and Hôtel de Ville and on Rue de Rivoli, across from the Louvre.

DEPARTMENT STORES (LES GRANDS MAGASINS)

Like cafés, department stores were invented here (surprisingly, not in America). These popular stores are often crowded (every day here feels like Black Friday) and may seem overwhelming at first, but the ones listed here are accustomed to wide-eyed foreign shoppers and have English-speaking staff. These stores are not just beautiful monuments; they also offer insights into how Parisians live. It's instructive to see what's in style, check out Parisians' current taste in clothes and furniture, and compare the selection with stores back home.

Parisian department stores begin with their showy perfume sections, almost always central on the ground floor, and worth a visit to see how much space is devoted to pricey, smelly water. Helpful information desks are usually located at the main entrances near the perfume section (with floor plans in English). Stores generally have affordable restaurants (some with view terraces) and a good selection of fairly priced souvenirs and toys. Opening hours are customarily Monday through Saturday from 10:00 to 19:00. Some are open later on Thursdays, and all are jammed on Saturdays and closed on Sundays (except in December). The Printemps (prantahn) store in the Carrousel du Louvre is an exception—it's open daily, including Sundays.

You'll find both Galeries Lafayette and Printemps stores in several neighborhoods. The most convenient and most elegant sit side by side behind the Opéra Garnier, complementing that monument's similar, classy ambience (Mo: Chaussée d'Antin-La Fayette, Havre-Caumartin, or Opéra, see map on page 83). Both stores sprawl over multiple buildings and consume entire city blocks. The selection is huge, crowds can be huger (especially on summer Saturdays), and the prices are considered a tad high.

Galeries Lafayette is a must-see for its colorful ceiling, trad-chic ambience, and city views from the rooftop. To reach the store, circle around the right side of the Opéra Garnier to the main build-

ing (of three) located right at the Chaussée d'Antin Métro stop, at 40 Boulevard Haussmann. Enter and work your way to the heart of the store, where you can gaze up at the store's main attraction: a sensational, stained-glass belle époque dome hovering 150 feet overhead. Ride the escalator up. The first three floors up have

SHOPPING

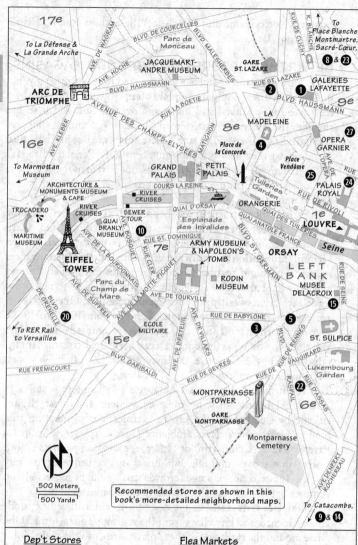

Recommended stores are shown in this book's more-detailed neighborhood maps.

500 Meters
500 Yards

To Catacombs, **9** & **14**

Dep't Stores
1 Galeries Lafayette
2 Printemps
3 Bon Marché

Boutique Strolls
4 Place de la Madeleine to Place de l'Opéra
5 Sèvres-Babylone to St. Sulpice
6 The Marais
7 Rue des Martyrs

Flea Markets
8 To Puces St. Ouen
9 To Puces de Vanves

Traffic-Free Shopping & Café Streets
10 Rue Cler
11 Rue Montorgueil
12 Forum des Halles
13 Rue Mouffetard
14 To Rue Daguerre
15 Rues de Seine & de Buci
16 Marché des Enfants Rouges

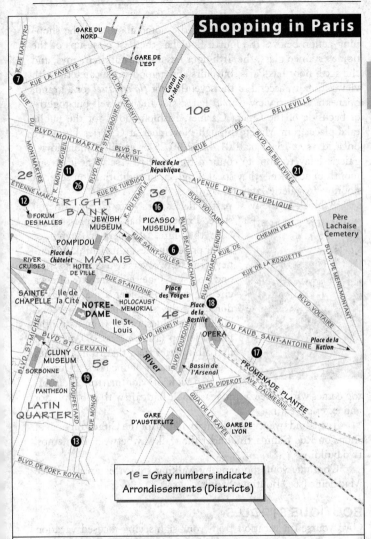

Shopping in Paris

GARE DU NORD

GARE DE L'EST

Canal St-Martin

RUE LA FAYETTE

BLVD. DE MAGENTA

BLVD. DE STRASBOURG

10e

BELLEVILLE

RUE DE

BLVD. DE BELLEVILLE

RUE DU

BLVD. MONTMARTRE

MONTMARTRE

BLVD. ST-MARTIN

Place de la République

AVENUE DE LA REPUBLIQUE

ÉTIENNE MARCEL

2e

R. MONTORGUEIL

RUE DE TURBIGO

R. DU TEMPLE

3e

BLVD. VOLTAIRE

11

26

RIGHT BANK

JEWISH MUSEUM

PICASSO MUSEUM

BLVD. BEAUMARCHAIS

21

12

FORUM DES HALLES

16

RUE SAINT-GILLES

6

CHEMIN VERT

Père Lachaise Cemetery

POMPIDOU

MARAIS

RUE RICHARD-LENOIR

RUE DE LA ROQUETTE

BLVD. DE MÉNILMONTANT

RIVER CRUISES

Place du Châtelet

HOTEL DE VILLE

RUE ST-ANTOINE

Place des Vosges

BLVD. VOLTAIRE

SAINTE-CHAPELLE

Ile de la Cité

NOTRE-DAME

HOLOCAUST MEMORIAL

Place de la Bastille

18

R. DU FAUB. SANT-ANTOINE

Place de la Nation

BLVD. ST-MICHEL

BLVD. ST-GERMAIN

Ile St-Louis

BLVD. HENRI IV

OPERA

17

CLUNY MUSEUM

5e

River

BLVD. BOURDON

Bassin de l'Arsenal

PROMENADE PLANTEE

AVE DAUMESNIL

SORBONNE

R. MONGE

PANTHEON

LATIN QUARTER

R. MOUFFETARD

19

BLVD. DIDEROT

QUAI DE LA RAPEE

QUAI DE LA RAPEE

GARE D'AUSTERLITZ

GARE DE LYON

13

BLVD. DE PORT-ROYAL

1e = Gray numbers indicate Arrondissements (Districts)

Open-Air Food Markets

17 Place d'Aligre

18 Bastille

19 Place Monge

20 Blvd. de Grenelle

21 Belleville

22 Raspail

23 To Batignolles

Arcades

24 Galerie Vivienne

25 Passages Choiseul & Ste. Anne

26 Passage du Grand Cerf

27 Passages Panoramas & Jouffroy

bars or cafés with great views of the dome above and the shopping action below. The fourth floor has the best close-ups of the dome's stained glass, the fifth floor has unique children's toys, and the sixth floor has Paris souvenirs and a good-value cafeteria with views. Finally, ascend to the seventh floor *(la terrasse)* for a grand, open-air rooftop view of *tout* Paris, starring the well-put-together backside of the Opéra Garnier. Fashion shows for the public take place from March through November at Galeries Lafayette on Fridays at 15:00 (call 01 42 82 30 25 or email fashionshow@galerieslafayette.com to confirm time and to reserve at least one month in advance—they speak English, in auditorium on seventh floor, www.galerieslafayette.com).

A block to the west past Galeries Lafayette *Hommes* (men's) store, **Printemps** has an impressive facade that lures shoppers in search of lower prices and less glitz (think JCPenney). The store covers two buildings. The one closest to Galeries Lafayette offers a circular cafeteria under a massive glass dome on the sixth floor. The second building provides a view from its ninth-floor rooftop (ask: *la terrasse?*), which I find a bit better than that from Galeries Lafayette because it includes an unobstructed view of Montmartre. The rooftop comes with a breezy and reasonable bar/café with good interior and exterior seating.

Teens and twentysomethings will flip for the **Citadium** mall of shops on Rue Caumartin, under the walkway between Printemps' two buildings.

Continue your shopping by walking from this area to Place Madeleine (see "Boutique Strolls," next).

BOUTIQUE STROLLS

Give yourself a vacation from your sightseeing-focused vacation by sifting through window displays, pausing at corner cafés, and feeling the rhythm of neighborhood life. (Or have you been playing hooky and doing this already?) Though smaller shops are more intimate, sales clerks are more formal—so mind your manners. Three very different areas to lick some windows are: Place de la Madeleine to Place de l'Opéra, Sèvres-Babylone to St. Sulpice, and along Rue des Martyrs.

Most shops are closed on Sunday, which is a good day to head for the **Marais,** where many shops are open on Sunday (and closed on Saturday). For eclectic, avant-garde boutiques in this neighborhood, peruse the artsy shops between Place des Vosges and the Pompidou Center (see map on page 316).

Place de la Madeleine to Place de l'Opéra

The ritzy streets connecting several high-priced squares—Place de la Madeleine, Place de la Concorde, Place Vendôme, and Place de l'Opéra—form a miracle mile of gourmet food shops, glittering jewelry stores, five-star hotels, exclusive clothing boutiques, and people who spend more on clothes in one day than I do in a year. This walk highlights the value Parisians place on outrageously priced products.

This walk takes about 1.5 hours (one hour if you skip the extension to Place Vendôme and Place de l'Opéra). Most stores are open Monday through Saturday from around 10:00 in the morning (or earlier) until 19:00 (or later) at night. Most places are closed on Sunday.

• Start at Place de la Madeleine, at the Métro stop Madeleine, in the northeast corner of the square. From here, work counterclockwise around the square.

❶ **Place de la Madeleine:** The Madeleine Church—looking like a Roman temple with fifty-two 65-foot Corinthian columns—dominates the center of the square. Yes, this is a shopping stroll and there's nothing on sale inside this church, but it's free and worth a quick look. Originally designed as a secular temple to honor Napoleon's great army, it was turned into a church in 1842 and today is still used as both a church and concert venue.

Step through the massive bronze doors and approach the altar featuring a striking marble Mary Magdalene with three angels. The ceiling fresco celebrates great French Christians—from Saint Louis (King Louis IX) to Jean d'Arc—in the company of Mary Magdalene and Christ in heaven above. During Chopin's funeral, in 1849, 3,000 mourners packed this church as musicians played the famous dirge of Chopin's *Funeral March* (free, daily 9:30-19:00).

The neighborhood surrounding the square was originally a suburb of medieval Paris, but by the time the church was completed in the mid-1800s, it had become Paris' most fashionable neighborhood. The glitzy belle époque of turn-of-the-century Paris revolved around this square and its surrounding streets. Today, the square is a gourmet's fantasy, lined with Paris' most historic and tasty food shops.

• OK, let's shop. Our first shop is perhaps the most famous of all. In the northeast corner at #24 is the black-and-white awning of...

❷ **Fauchon:** Founded on this location in 1886, this bastion of over-the-top edibles became famous around the world, catering to the refined tastes of the rich and famous. Its tea, caviar, foie gras, and pastries set the standard for nearly a century. In the late 20th

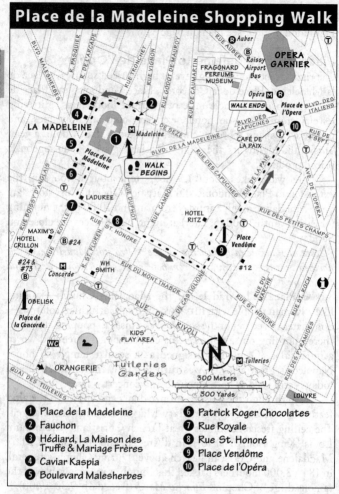

Place de la Madeleine Shopping Walk

1. Place de la Madeleine
2. Fauchon
3. Hédiard, La Maison des Truffe & Mariage Frères
4. Caviar Kaspia
5. Boulevard Malesherbes
6. Patrick Roger Chocolates
7. Rue Royale
8. Rue St. Honoré
9. Place Vendôme
10. Place de l'Opéra

century, it faded from its glory days, closing many franchises—but recently it's on the rebound.

There are two Fauchon storefronts here. The **Traiteur-Pâtisserie** at #24 is like a delicatessen, with meats, meals, breads, and pastries *(pâtisseries)*. These takeout items can cost more than many sit-down restaurant meals. Check out the various places you can buy something to eat-in: There's the tasting bar for caviar and champagne, sidewalk seating, plus more tables (and a WC) upstairs. Or grab a stool at the *boulangerie* and enjoy a sponge-cake cookie: a *madeleine* on Place de la Madeleine (though the names are only coincidental).

Just across the street at #30 is Fauchon's more impressive

shop, the **Cave, Chocolat, Epicerie.** This razzle-dazzle store is all about style, branding, and packaging. Tourists gobble up anything wrapped in pink and black with Fauchon's name emblazoned on it. Stroll downstairs to find the wine cellar, with €5,000 bottles of century-old Cognac—who buys this stuff? Up on the first floor is a fashionable café with view tables of La Madeleine.

• *Continue your counterclockwise tour around Place de la Madeleine.*

❸ **More Gourmet Shops:** Founded in 1854, **Hédiard** (#21, northwest corner of the square) is older than Fauchon, and it's

weathered the tourist mobs a bit better. Wafting the aroma of tea and coffee, it showcases handsomely displayed produce and wines. Hédiard's small red containers—of mustards, jams, coffee, candies, and tea—make great souvenirs. Anyone can enter the glass doors of the wine cellar, marked *Le Chais* (with €2,500 bottles of Petrus), but you need special permission to access *Les Vénérables* wines. Upstairs (take the glass elevator) is a smart café for coffee or a pricey lunch.

Return to the square, pass by Crab Royale, then step inside tiny **La Maison des Truffe** (#19) to get a whiff of the product—truffles, those prized, dank, and dirty cousins of mushrooms. Check out the tiny jars in the display case. Ponder how something so ugly, smelly, and deformed can cost so much. Choose from a selection that varies from run-of-the-mill black truffles (a bargain at €50 a pound) to rare white truffles from Italy—up to €3,000 a pound. At the counter they sell every possible food that can be made with truffles, including Armagnac brandy. The shop also houses a sharp little restaurant serving truffle dishes (e.g., truffle omelet for €40, or chocolate cake with truffle ice cream for €15).

The venerable **Mariage Frères** (#17) shop demonstrates how good tea can smell and how beautifully it can be displayed.

• *A few steps along, you'll find...*

❹ **Caviar Kaspia** (#16): Here you can add Iranian caviar, eel, and vodka to your truffle collection. Find the price list for these cured fish eggs. The sharper-tasting caviars run €100 for a small tin. The "finer" ones, from beluga sturgeon in the Caspian Sea, sell for up to €12,000 a kilo. The restaurant upstairs serves what you see downstairs—at equally exorbitant prices. Demand for fish eggs must be strong, because a competitor (Caviar Prunier) has opened next door.

• *Continue along, past Marquise de Sévigné chocolates (#11) to the intersection with...*

❺ **Boulevard Malesherbes:** Look to the right, down the

boulevard. This kind of vista—of a grand boulevard anchored by a domed church (dedicated to St. Augustine)—is vintage Haussmann. (For more on the man who shaped modern-day Paris, see the sidebar on page 89.) When the street officially opened in 1863, it ushered in the golden age of this neighborhood.

• *Cross the three crosswalks traversing Boulevard Malesherbes. Straight ahead is...*

❻ **Patrick Roger Chocolates** (#3): This place is famous for its chocolates, and even more so for M. Roger's huge, whimsical, 150-pound chocolate sculptures of animals and fanciful creatures.

• *Continue on, turning right down...*

❼ **Rue Royale:** Along this broad boulevard, we trade expensive food for expensive...stuff. There's Dior, Chanel, and Gucci. A half block down Rue Royale, dip into the classy Village Royale shopping courtyard with its restful Le Village Café.

If you went a few hundred yards farther down Rue Royale—which we won't on this walk—you'd reach the once-famous restaurant Maxim's (at #3), and then spill into Place de la Concorde, with the still-famous Hôtel Crillon (see page 313). The US Embassy is located nearby, and this area has long been the haunt of America's wealthy, cosmopolitan jet set.

• *At Rue St. Honoré, turn left and cross Rue Royale, pausing in the middle for a great view both ways. Check out **Ladurée** (#16) for an out-of-this-world pastry break in the busy 19th-century tea salon, or to just pick up some world-famous macarons.*

If you've had enough, you're a few blocks from the Place de la Concorde Métro stop, the Tuileries Garden, and the Orangerie Museum. If you have more shopping in you, continue east down...

❽ **Rue St. Honoré:** The street is a three-block parade of chic boutiques—L'Oréal cosmetics, Jimmy Choo shoes, Valentino, and so on. Looking for a €1,000 handbag? This is your spot. (Or, it's a good place to ponder the fact that about half of the seven billion people living on this planet are doing it on $2 a day.) The place has long been tied to fashion. Industry titans like Hermès, Givenchy, and Lancôme were launched a few blocks west of this stretch. You'll pass the domed Church of the Assumption, a former convent that now caters to Paris' Polish community.

• *Turn left on Rue de Castiglione to reach...*

❾ **Place Vendôme:** This octagonal square is *très* elegant—enclosed by symmetrical Mansart buildings around a 150-foot column. On the left side is the original Hôtel Ritz, opened in 1898. Since then, it's been one of the world's most fashionable hotels. It gives us our word "ritzy." Hemingway liberated its bar in World War II.

The square was created by Louis XIV during the 17th century as a setting for a statue of himself (then called Place Louis le

Grand). One hundred and fifty years later, Louis XIV was replaced by a towering monument to Napoleon capped by a statue of the emperor himself. That column, designed in the style of Trajan's Column in Rome, was raised by Napoleon to commemorate his victory at the Battle of Austerlitz. The encircling bronze reliefs were made from cannons won in this and other battles. Look for images of the emperor directing battle with his distinctive hat as you scroll up the column. Elsewhere on the square, Chopin died at #12.

The square is also known for its upper-crust jewelry and designer stores—Van Cleef & Arpels, Dior, Chanel, Cartier, and others (if you have to ask how much...).

• *Leave Place Vendôme by continuing straight, up* **Rue de la Paix**—*strolling by still more jewelry, high-priced watches, and crystal—and enter...*

❿ **Place de l'Opéra:** You're in the middle of Right Bank glamour. Here you'll find the Opéra Garnier and the Fragonard Perfume Museum (described on pages 88-93). If you're shopping 'til you're dropping, the Galeries Lafayette and Printemps department stores (both described earlier) are located a block or two north, up Rue Halévy. If you're exhausted from counting the zeroes on price tags, relax with a drink at venerable **Café de la Paix** across from the Opéra (daily, 12 Boulevard des Capucines). It's an appropriately elegant—and pricey—way to end this tour.

• *When you're ready to go, look for the convenient Opéra Métro stop.*

Sèvres-Babylone to St. Sulpice

This Left Bank shopping stroll runs from the Sèvres-Babylone Métro stop to St. Sulpice Church, near Luxembourg Garden and Boulevard St. Germain. You'll sample smart clothing boutiques and clever window displays while enjoying one of Paris' more attractive neighborhoods. This shopping walk ties in well with my Left Bank Walk. Some stores on this walk are open Sunday afternoons, though the walk is better on other days.

Start at the Sèvres-Babylone Métro stop (take the Métro or bus #87). You'll find the ❶ **Bon Marché** behind a small park. The Bon

Marché (means "inexpensive," but it's not) is Paris' oldest department store. It opened in 1852, when fascination with iron and steel construction led to larger structures (like train stations, exhibition halls, and Eiffel Towers). The Bon Marché was the first large-scale store to offer fixed prices (no bargaining)

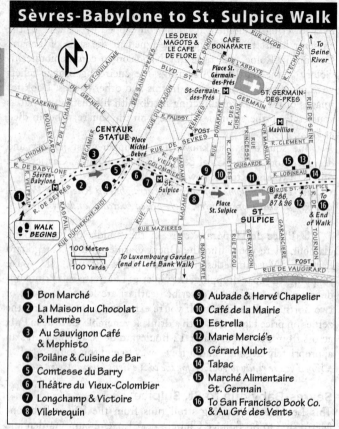

Sèvres-Babylone to St. Sulpice Walk

1. Bon Marché
2. La Maison du Chocolat & Hermès
3. Au Sauvignon Café & Mephisto
4. Poilâne & Cuisine de Bar
5. Comtesse du Barry
6. Théâtre du Vieux-Colombier
7. Longchamp & Victoire
8. Vilebrequin
9. Aubade & Hervé Chapelier
10. Café de la Mairie
11. Estrella
12. Marie Mercié's
13. Gérard Mulot
14. Tabac
15. Marché Alimentaire St. Germain
16. To San Francisco Book Co. & Au Gré des Vents

and a vast selection of items under one glass roof, arranged in various "departments." This rocked the commercial world and forever changed the future of shopping. High-volume sales allowed low prices and created loyal customers—can you say "Costco"? But what began as a bargain store has evolved into one of Paris' most elegant shopping destinations.

Start your tour in the center, under the atrium with a high glass ceiling and crisscross elevators. Browse the perfumes, then take the escalator up to higher floors for a better perspective. Notice the sales clerks seated behind desks rather than standing at counters (at these prices, they seem more like loan officers). Find the less glamorous escalators in the corners of the store to bring you to the very top floor, where you'll find a treasure trove of children's books, toys, and clothing. If you're hungry, there are trendy restaurants in the basement and an elegant tea salon on the third floor.

From the Bon Marché, walk through the small park, cross

Boulevard Raspail, and start heading down Rue de Sèvres (along the right side). The Hôtel Lutetia to your right was built for shoppers by the Bon Marché's owners and is now undergoing a floor-to-ceiling renovation. A few steps down Rue de Sèvres, you'll find ❷ **La Maison du Chocolat** at #19. Their mouthwatering window display will draw you helplessly inside. The shop sells handmade chocolates in exquisitely wrapped boxes and delicious ice-cream cones in season. Parisians commonly offer chocolates when invited over, and no gift box better impresses than one from this store.

Be sure to lick the chocolate off your fingers before entering **Hermès** (a few doors down, at #17), famous for pricey silk scarves—and for the former designer of its fashion house, Jean-Paul Gaultier. Don't let the doorman intimidate you: Everyone's welcome here. This store, opened in 2011, is housed in the original Art Deco swimming pool of Hôtel Lutetia, built in 1935. Take a spin through this ultra-trendy space, which covers more than 20,000 square feet.

Across the street sits the marvelously old-school ❸ **Au Sauvignon Café** (10 Rue de Sèvres, open daily). It's well situated for watching the conveyor belt of smartly coiffed shoppers glide by. Check in for a hot or cold drink, and check out the zinc bar and picture-crazy interior. If your feet hurt, relief is at hand—a **Mephisto** shoe store is almost next door.

Continue a block farther down Rue de Sèvres to Place Michel Debré, a six-way intersection. A wicked half-man, half-horse statue (ouch), the *Centaur*, stands guard. Designed by French sculptor César in 1985, it was originally intended for a more prominent square, but was installed here after many deemed it too provocative because of its metallic genitalia. The face is of the sculptor himself.

From Place Michel Debré, boutique-lined streets fan out like spokes on a wheel. Each street merits a detour if shopping matters to you.

Make a short detour up Rue du Cherche-Midi (follow the horse's fanny). This street offers an ever-changing but always chic selection of shoe, purse, and clothing stores. Find Paris' most celebrated bread—beautiful round loaves with designer crust—at the low-key ❹ **Poilâne** at #8 (Mon-Sat 7:15-20:15, closed Sun). Enter for a sample. Notice the care with which each loaf of bread is wrapped. Next door, the small **Cuisine de Bar** café is a *bar à pains* (bread bar) and serves open-faced sandwiches (tartines) and salads with Poilâne bread (closed Mon).

Return to the *Centaur* in Place Michel Debré. Check out the ❺ **Comtesse du Barry** pâté store, which sells small gift packs. Then turn right and head down Rue du Vieux Colombier.

You'll pass the ❻ **Théâtre du Vieux-Colombier** (1913), one of three key venues for La Comédie Française, a historic state-run troupe. Enter and find the timeline to the right; take a moment to look for names you recognize. How about the playwright Anton Chekov and poet T. S. Eliot—who both wrote plays performed here—or folk singer John Denver?

In the next two blocks, you'll pass many stores that specialize in just one or two items, but in a variety of colors and patterns. At ❼ Longchamp (#21), you can hunt for a stylish French handbag in any color, and Victoire offers items for the gentleman.

Cross busy Rue de Rennes—glancing to the right at the dreadful Montparnasse Tower in the distance—and continue down Rue du Vieux Colombier.

Here you'll find more specialty boutiques. If the man or *petit-garçon* in your life needs a swimsuit, check out ❽ Vilebrequin (#5). There's ❾ Aubade (#4) for lingerie and Hervé Chapelier (#1) for travel totes and handbags.

Spill into Place St. Sulpice, with its big, twin-tower church. ❿ Café de la Mairie is a great spot to sip a *café crème,* admire the lovely square, and consider your next move. Sightseers can visit St. Sulpice Church (see page 72) or Luxembourg Garden (page 74). Or you can head north on Rue Bonaparte two blocks to Boulevard St. Germain for more shopping and several *grands cafés* (described on page 447).

Our walk continues east, exiting the square (with the church on your right) along what is now called Rue St. Sulpice. ⓫ Estrella is a boutique with excellent teas and coffee beans (including *real* French roast), and a friendly owner, Jean-Claude (closed Sun, 34 Rue St. Sulpice). Pause at ⓬ Marie Mercié's to admire the window display of extravagant and wildly expensive hats (23 Rue St. Sulpice).

Now turn left onto Rue de Seine. What's the best pastry shop in Paris? According to local shopkeepers, it's ⓭ Gérard Mulot's *pâtisserie* (closed Wed, 76 Rue de Seine). That's saying a lot. Ogle the window display and try his chocolate *macarons* and savory quiches—oh, baby. Pick up lunch to go and munch it at nearby Luxembourg Garden. If you need a traditional French picnic knife to cut your quiche, backtrack to the ⓮ Tabac (78 Rue de Seine) for a fine selection of Opinel knives, made in Savoie since 1890. Or if you're missing any other food supplies for the picnic, pop into ⓯ Marché Alimentaire St. Germain (a covered food market on the next block). The English-language bookshop ⓰ San Francisco Book Company is a few blocks east at 17 Rue Monsieur le Prince (used books only, see map on page 407). Around the corner at 10 Rue des Quatre Vents sits Au Gré des Vents, a well-established consignment clothing and accessory shop, where you can rummage through the cast-offs of well-heeled neighborhood residents.

If you'd like more shopping options, you're in the heart of

boutique shopping. Sightseers could take my Left Bank Walk (you're near several points along the route). Or catch the Métro to your next destination at St. Germain, Odéon, or Mabillon. As for me, stick a *fourchette* in me—I'm done.

Rue des Martyrs

As they race from big museum to big museum, visitors often miss the market streets and village-like charm that give Paris a warm

and human vibrancy. Rue Cler remains my favorite market street (see the Rue Cler Walk chapter). But for an authentic, less-touristy market street, serving village Paris, stroll down Rue des Martyrs.

This walk starts at the base of Montmartre, a block from the Pigalle Métro stop, and takes you downhill six blocks along a lively market street, ending at Métro station Notre-Dame-de-Lorette. Like any market street, it's generally quiet on Sunday from 12:00 on, all day Monday, and the rest of the week from about 13:00 to 15:00, when shops close for a break. While Rue des Martyrs is quiet, it's not traffic-free like most other boutique strolls in this chapter.

From the Pigalle Métro stop, head east along Boulevard de Clichy to the first street, where you turn right on Rue des Martyrs. Entering Rue des Martyrs, you pass into a finer neighborhood with broader streets, richer buildings...and signs of the reality of raising a family in an urban setting.

Security can be a concern. The school immediately on your right has barriers to keep possible car bombs at a distance. (Terrorist attacks that rocked Paris decades ago inspired a ban on parking in front of schools or near buildings that serve a predominantly Jewish clientele.) Several side streets are *"voie privée"*—private lanes or high-rise, gated communities. Behind big carriage doors, lanes lead to peaceful inner courtyards serving clusters of apartments.

The carousel at the intersection is a reminder that families live in tight quarters. Along with small children, they have small kitchens, small fridges, and no gardens. They shop daily for small amounts—which helps keep the neighborhood strong.

Slalom past people strolling with dogs and babies. Goods spill out onto the sidewalk. People know their butcher and baker as if they lived in a village. Locals willingly pay more in a shop that's not part of a chain.

Stroll slowly downhill. Notice the variety of small shops. Paris is one of the most densely populated cities in Europe, which makes the streets particularly vibrant. Look up and imagine how population density is great news for fishmongers, flower merchants, and bakers.

The **traditional charcuterie** at #58 still sells various meats, but it has morphed with the times into an appealing *traiteur* with more variety, food to eat in as well as to go, and prepared dishes sold by weight.

Just next door you'll see one of Paris' countless late-night grocery stores. These are generally run by North African immigrants who are willing to work the night shift for the convenience of others. Beware: Produce with the highest prices is often priced by the half-kilo.

At #50, the **cheesemonger** has been serving the neighborhood ever since it actually had goats and cows grazing out back. Notice the marble shelves, old milk jugs, and small artisanal cheeses.

At #46, the English-owned **Rose Bakery** serves a young, affluent, and health-conscious crowd with top-quality organic and vegetarian breakfasts and lunches. Across the street, the baker **Delmontel** (at #39) proudly displays his "best baguette in Paris" award from 2007 and his fresh-baked temptations. At #42 sits **Terra Corsa,** a café/gourmet food shop selling fine foods from Corsica and tasty lunch plates served with wine, beer, or Corsican cola. **Maison Landemaine** (at #26) is another eye-popping bakery.

Continuing your stroll on Rue des Martyrs, take a look at the **traditional butcher** at #21. You know he's good because the ceiling hooks—where butchers once hung sides of beef—now display a red medallion that certifies the slaughtered cow's quality. Like carrots come with greenery intact for the discerning shopper, here the chicken comes with its head on, the rabbit with his heart exposed, and the fish with eyes open. Freshness is expected.

Sebastian Gaudard's *pâtisserie* at #22 is worth popping in to see the typically French edible works of art. Bakers enjoy making special treats in sync with the season: Easter, Christmas, First Communion, and so on.

Nearby, at #20, the **tobacco shop/café** is coping well with the smoking ban by putting out heaters (in cool weather) and as many tables as will fit on the sidewalk. Shops like this—once run by rural people from what was then France's poorest region, Auvergne—are now often managed by Chinese immigrants. Traditionally the corner café was the community's utility sales outlet—where you could pay parking tickets, pick up stamps and Métro tickets, and play the lottery. In spite of the giant letters reading *"fumer tue,"* (smoking kills) cigarettes sell well. Oh...and there's good coffee too.

Down the street (at #9) sit two ultra-specialized food shops: one selling olive oils made exclusively from French olives and **La Chambre à Confiture,** displaying fruity creations like fine jewels that will forever change the way you think of jam (they're generous with samples).

The **"City" Carrefour** at #7 is a small version of a big supermarket chain. With long howwurs daily and more convenience, modern supermarkets are threatening many smaller shops.

Across from Carrefour, browse the long line of produce. Note how price tags come with the place each item was grown. Two more butchers and a cheese shop later, you reach the neighborhood church (the Neoclassical **Notre-Dame-de-Lorette,** circa 1836) and the end of this street.

Our walk is over. The Métro station Notre-Dame-de-Lorette (line 12) awaits. Find the discreet entrance on the opposite (front) side of the church.

MARKETS
Flea Markets

Paris' sprawling flea markets (*marché aux puces;* mar-shay oh-pews; *puce* is French for "flea") started in the Middle Ages, when middlemen sold old, flea-infested clothes and discarded possessions of the wealthy at bargain prices to eager peasants,  allowing buyers to rummage through piles of aristocratic garbage.

Puces St. Ouen: The Flea Market at Porte de Clignancourt

Puces St. Ouen (pews sant-oo-a<u>n</u>), at Porte de Clignancourt, carries on the Parisian flea market tradition, but at a more elevated level—the fleas are gone, as are the bargain prices. This is the mother of all flea markets, attracting interior designers and those who appreciate this ever-changing museum of household goods. More than 2,000 vendors sell everything from flamingos to faucets, but mostly exquisite antiques and vintage silver and art (Sat 9:00-18:00, Sun 10:00-18:00, Mon 11:00-17:00, closed Tue-Fri,

Puces St. Ouen Flea Market

To Ⓜ Garibaldi

ST. OUEN

RUE GAMBETTA

RUE EUGÈNE LUMEAU

RUE MATHIEU

RUE J. FERRY

R. M. BEEK

RUE P. CURIE

RUE LOUIS DAIN

BONS ENFANTS

L'ENTREPOT

IMP. SIMON

RUE DES ROSIERS

RUE MARIE CURIE

BIRON

PAUL BERT

L'USINE

RUE KLÉBER

R. DE LA GAÏTÉ

LECUYER

JULES VALLES

SERPETTE

CAMBO

RUE DE LA VILLA BIRON

RUE BIRON

RUE MICHELET

PIERRE CURIE

RUE JULES VALLES

RUE PLAISIR

ROSIERS #85 Ⓑ

WC

WC

WC

Ⓑ #85

ANTICA

RUE VOLTAIRE

AVENUE MICHELET

⓵

VERNAISON

LE PASSAGE

RUE PAUL BERT

RUE NEUVE

RUE LECUYER

WC

DAUPHINE

MALIK

MALASSIS Ⓑ #85

RUE CHARLES SCHMIDT

RUE JEAN-HENRI FABRE

WC

ELEVATED FREEWAY (PERIPHERIQUE)

LE PLATEAU

100 Meters
100 Yards

⓵ Chez Louisette
⓶ Café Paul Bert
⓷ La Chope des Puces Bar
⓸ Ma Cocotte

MARKET STREETS
COVERED MARKETS

AVENUE DE LA PORTE DE CLIGNANCOURT

To Ⓜ Porte de Clignancourt

pretty dead the first 2 weeks of Aug, tel. 01 58 61 22 90, www.st-ouen-tourisme.com and www.les-puces.com).

Getting to Puces St. Ouen: Take Métro line 4 to the end of the line at Porte de Clignancourt, then carefully follow *Sortie, Marché aux Puces* signs. Walk straight out of the Métro down Avenue de la Porte de Clignancourt, passing leather stores and blocks of tents hawking trinkets and cheap clothing. Ignore street vendors selling knockoff designer bags and fake Marlboro cigarettes. Your destination is just beyond the elevated freeway (white bridge). Cross under the freeway—leaving Paris and entering the suburb of St. Ouen—and veer left on the angled street, Rue des Rosiers, the spine that links the many markets of St. Ouen. To get to the best markets as soon as possible, enter the Vernaison market through an easy-to-miss archway at #129, then use Vernaison's peaceful lanes to get to the others—or continue along Rue des Rosiers. Avoid the crowds along Avenue Jean Henri Fabre, parallel to the freeway, and you'll do fine. If you're considering buying a large item, be aware that shipping is very expensive (Camard company has the best reputation, tel. 01 49 46 10 82, www.antikaparis.com/camard).

Taking bus #85 lets you skip the scruffy stretch between the Métro station and the market, leaving you near the Vernaison or Paul Bert markets on Rue des Rosiers. Catch line #85 (direction: Mairie de St-Ouen) from stops located near the Luxembourg Garden, Hôtel de Ville, or Montmartre. To return to the city, navigate back to Rue des Rosiers and hop on buses heading to Luxembourg.

Visiting the Market: The area around the market shows off Paris' gritty, suburban underbelly and can be intimidating (in Paris, the have-nots live in the burbs, while the haves want to be as central as they can get). No event brings together the melting-pot population of Paris better than this carnival-like market. Some find it claustrophobic, overcrowded, and threatening; others find French *diamants*-in-the-rough and return happy. (Wear your money belt; pickpockets and scam artists thrive in these wall-to-wall-shopper events—and don't use ATM machines here.) The markets actually get downright mellow the farther in you go. You can bargain a bit (best deals are made with cash at the end of the day), though don't expect swinging deals here.

Space for this flea market was created in the 1800s, when the city wall was demolished (its path is now a freeway), leaving large tracts of land open. Eventually the vacuum was filled by street vendors, then antique dealers. The hodgepodge pattern of the market reflects its unplanned evolution. Strolling the stalls can feel more like touring a souk in North Africa—a place of narrow alleys packed with people and too much to see.

The St. Ouen "market" is actually a collection of individual markets. Most of these are covered alleys, each with a different

name and specializing in a particular angle on antiques, bric-a-brac, and junk. You'll find them by walking down the "spine" of the market, Rue des Rosiers—look for a map that tries to explain the general character of each (get it at shops or the TI branch just off Rue des Rosiers on Impasse Simon). Here's a brief rundown of the *marchés:* Vernaison (enter through an easy-to-miss archway at #129, small shops selling a mishmash of stuff from lace doilies to clock parts), Dauphine (a glass-roofed arcade with quiet shops lining its interior-only lanes), Biron and Serpette (classy antiques), and Paul Bert (open lanes of shops selling high-end designs for your home, with clean—and free—WCs).

Even if antiques, African objects, and T-shirts aren't your thing, you may still find this market worth the Métro ride. Pretend you just rented a big, empty apartment...and need to furnish it.

Come for a reality check—away from the beautiful people and glorious monuments of Paris—and get a dose of life in the 'burbs. Time your trip around lunch; there are many lively and reasonable cafés.

Eating at Puces St. Ouen: Buried in Vernaison Market, **$$ Chez Louisette** delivers a rousing lunch experience. Listen to a latter-day Edith Piaf and eat with a Toulouse-Lautrec look-alike. Madame belts out vintage French *chansons* with an accordion and keyboard to back her up, the ramshackle decor is laced with red garlands and big chandeliers, and the jovial crowd sings along. It's popular, so come right at noon or expect to wait (expect to tip the singers, Sat-Mon only, 130 Avenue Michelet, tel. 01 40 12 10 14). **$$ Café Paul Bert** is where locals come for a traditional brasserie meal. The decor is wonderful inside and out, and the cuisine wins rave reviews (closed Tue-Wed, 20 Rue Paul Bert, tel. 01 40 11 90 28). **$$ La Chope des Puces** bar is famous for its live Gypsy music concerts on Saturday and Sunday afternoons, complete with a questionable clientele (open 10:30-19:00, 122 Rue des Rosiers, tel. 01 40 11 28 80). High-end interior designers and costume makers flock to **$$$ Ma Cocotte.** This upscale bistro was designed by living legend Philippe Starck and is tucked into the Paul Bert Market just off Rue des Rosiers (open daily, 106 Rue des Rosiers, tel. 01 49 51 70 00).

Puces de Vanves

Comparatively tiny and civilized with sidewalk stalls and a more traditional flea-market feel, Puces de Vanves is preferred by many market connoisseurs (Sat-Sun 7:00-17:00, best to arrive before 13:00—when the best stalls close, closed Mon-Fri, Mo: Porte de Vanves).

Traffic-Free Shopping and Café Streets

Several traffic-free street markets overflow with flowers, produce, fish vendors, and butchers, illustrating how most Parisians shopped before there were supermarkets and department stores. Shops are open daily except Sunday afternoons, Monday, and lunchtime throughout the week (13:00 to 15:00 or 16:00). Browse these markets for picnics, or find a corner café from which to appreciate the scene.

Rue Cler—a wonderful place to sleep and dine as well as shop—is like a refined street market, serving an upscale neighborhood near the Eiffel Tower (Mo: Ecole Militaire; for details, see the Rue Cler Walk chapter and the Sleeping in Paris and Eating in Paris chapters).

Rue Montorgueil is a thriving and locally popular café-lined street. Ten blocks from the Louvre and five blocks from the

Pompidou Center, Rue Montorgueil (mohn-tor-goy) is famous as the last vestige of the once-massive Les Halles market (just north of St. Eustache Church, Mo: Etienne Marcel). Once the home of big warehouses and wholesale places to support the market, these have morphed into retail outlets to survive. Today you'll find cafés and cute bistros and no food shops, with one important exception—the irresistible creations at **Pâtissier Stohrer,** where the French expression for "window licking" must have started (51 Rue Montorgueil, tel. 01 42 33 38 20). Several traffic-free lanes cross Rue Montorgueil: Don't miss the nearby covered arcade, Passage du Grand Cerf, described later.

Rue Montorgueil leads directly to the **Forum des Halles,** a big modern shopping mall under a vast, yellow, eye-catching (and water-catching) glass-and-steel canopy. The canopy has louvers to maximize the shade and is designed to collect rainwater, which powers a fountain that cascades from its peak down to a babbling man-made brook. The mall, which stands on the former site of the city's main produce market, is the embodiment of 21st-century urban design: It quietly rests over a massive underground transportation hub and faces a delightfully green city park. The park (overlooked by the spindly gothic Church of St. Eustache and the stately old Bourse de Commerce, or stock exchange) has a fun kids' zone. What about actually visiting the mall? If you've never been to a modern American mall, do it.

Rue Mouffetard, originally built by the Romans, is a happening market street by day and does double-duty as restaurant row at night (see page 444). Hiding several blocks behind the Panthéon, it starts at Place Contrescarpe and ends below at St. Médard Church (Mo: Censier Daubenton). The upper stretch is pedestrian and touristic; the bottom stretch is purely Parisian. Pause for a drink on picturesque Place Contrescarpe, then make your descent down this popular street.

Rue Daguerre, near the Catacombs and off Avenue du Général Leclerc, is the least touristy of the street markets listed here, mixing food shops with cafés along a pleasing, traffic-free street (Mo: Denfert-Rochereau; for Catacombs description, see page 79).

Rue de Seine and Rue de Buci combine to make a central, lively, and colorful market within easy reach of many sights (Mo: Odéon; see also "Les Grands Cafés de Paris," on page 447, and my Left Bank Walk). This is a fine place to enjoy a late afternoon drink and observe Parisian shoppers at work (also fun for dinner).

Rue des Martyrs, near Montmartre, makes Paris feel like a village. Consider exploring this lively (though not traffic-free) market scene as part of my Montmartre Walk or my Rue des Martyrs boutique stroll, earlier.

Marché des Enfants Rouges is a compact, covered market for the northern Marais neighborhood. It's also the oldest covered food market in Paris, built when Louis XIII ruled in 1615. It's named for an orphanage where the children wore red uniforms (the name means "Market of the Red Children"). Here you'll find everything under one roof: organic produce; stands offering wine tastings; fun, cheap, international lunch options—and scads of character (Tue-Sat 8:30-20:00, until 18:00 in winter, produce stands closed 13:00-15:00; Sun 9:00-14:00, closed Mon; a 15-minute walk north from the heart of the Marais at 39 Rue de Bretagne, Mo: Filles du Calvaire or Temple, see the East Paris color map at the front of this book). Find the man making *socca*—a chickpea-flour crêpe specialty from Nice, and consider lunch at any of the food stands.

Open-Air Food Markets

Every neighborhood has a *marché volant* ("flying market"), where piles of food stalls take over selected boulevards and squares throughout Paris for one to three mornings each week (for a complete list, visit www.goparis.about.com and search for "food markets"). Expect a lively combination of flea- and street-market atmosphere and items.

Marché d'Aligre, 10 blocks behind the Opéra Bastille down Rue de Faubourg St. Antoine, is a small open-air market where you'll encounter few tourists. You'll find lots of fresh produce, a small but atmospheric market hall, and a swap-meet-like square for trinket shopping (Tue-Sun 9:00-13:30, closed Mon, Place d'Aligre, Mo: Ledru-Rollin). From Métro Ledru-Rollin, walk east (with your back to the Bastille column) and veer right at the second traffic light onto Rue Crozatier.

Marché de la Bastille is the best of the lot, with a vast selection of products extending more than a half-mile north of Place de la Bastille along Boulevard Richard Lenoir (Thu and Sun until 14:30, Mo: Bastille); consider combining either of these two markets with a stroll through Promenade Plantée park (see page 99) and my Marais Walk.

Marché Place Monge is small, with produce, clothing, and a few crafts (Wed, Fri, and Sun 8:00-13:00; near Rue Mouffetard, Mo: Monge).

Marché Boulevard de Grenelle, a few blocks southwest of Champ de Mars park and the Rue Cler area, is packed with produce, nonperishable goods, and Parisians in search of a good value (Wed and Sun 7:00-12:30, between Dupleix and La Motte Picquet-Grenelle Métro stops).

Marché Belleville is big, favored by locals, and very untouristy (Tue and Fri, Mo: Belleville).

Marché Raspail, between Rue du Cherche-Midi and Rue

de Rennes, is where the rich and famous shop for food (Tue and Fri 7:30-14:30, special organic-only market Sun 9:00-15:00, Mo: Rennes).

Marché des Batignolles is Paris' largest organic market, located along Boulevard des Batignolles between Métro stations Place de Clichy and Rome (Sat only 9:00-15:00). Saturdays are also big wedding days in Paris: Sneak up Rue des Batignolles to the neighborhood Hôtel de Ville (16 Rue des Batignolles), have a post-market coffee in a café across the street, and watch as the colorful wedding parties stream by.

ARCADED SHOPPING STREETS *(PASSAGES)*

More than 200 of these covered shopping streets once crisscrossed Paris, providing much-needed shelter from the rain. The first were built during the American Revolution, though the ones you'll see date from the 1800s. Today only a handful remain to remind us where shopping malls got their inspiration, although they now sell things you would be more likely to find in flea markets than at JCPenney. Here's a short list to weave into your sightseeing plan. (They're found on the map in this chapter and on the East Paris color map at the front of this book.)

Galerie Vivienne, behind the Palais Royal off Rue des Petits-Champs and a few blocks from the Louvre (ideal to combine with a visit to the courtyards of Palais Royal), is the most refined and accessible of the *passages* (Mo: Pyramides, Bourse, or Palais Royal). Inside this classy arcade, you'll find a chic wine bar (**Legrand Filles et Fils,** tel. 01 42 60 07 12), tea salon, funky café, and trendy dress shops.

Passage Choiseul and **Passage Ste. Anne,** four blocks west of Galerie Vivienne, are fine examples of most Parisian *passages,* selling used books, paper products, trinkets, and snacks (down Rue des Petits-Champs toward Avenue de l'Opéra, same Métro stops).

Passage du Grand Cerf, up Rue Marie Stuart a block from Rue Montorgueil, is an elegant arcade where small offices and artsy galleries sit side by side. It is easily combined with a visit to the nearby Rue Montorgueil street market described earlier (Mo: Etienne Marcel).

Passage Panoramas and **Passage Jouffroy** are long galleries that connect with several other smaller *passages* to give you the best sense of the elaborate network of arcades that once existed (on both sides of Boulevard Montmartre, between Métro stops Grands Boulevards and Richelieu Drouot).

ENTERTAINMENT IN PARIS

Paris is brilliant after dark. Save energy from your day's sightseeing and experience the City of Light lit. Whether it's a concert at Sainte-Chapelle, a boat ride on the Seine, a walk in Montmartre, a hike up the Arc de Triomphe, or a late-night café, you'll see Paris at its best. Night walks in Paris are wonderful. Any of the self-guided walking tours in this book are terrific after dark. And our DIY taxi/Uber tour of floodlit Paris is a sure memory of a lifetime.

EVENT LISTINGS

Consulting either the weekly *Pariscope* (€0.70, comes out on Wed) or *L'Officiel des Spectacles* (€0.70) is essential if you want to know what's going on in Paris. For help deciphering the all-French listings in these publications, see www.colleensparis.com (hover over the "What's On" drop-down menu, then "How To Find What's On in Paris" until another drop-down appears listing the two publications).

I prefer *Pariscope:* It offers a complete weekly listing of music, cinema, theater, opera, and other special events. Pick one up at a newsstand and page through it. The order of the contents changes periodically, but the basics described below are always there... somewhere.

The magazine begins with a listing of **"Théâtre"** and what's playing at all key theater venues.

The **"Enfants"** section covers children's activities from musicals to treasure hunts. Look for "Spectacles" (events such as magic shows), "Marionettes" (puppet shows), and "Cirques" (circuses). These events usually are offered only in French, but they can be worthwhile even for non-French speakers.

"Cinéma" takes up a third of the magazine. While a code marks films as "Comédie," "Documentaire," "Drame," "Karaté,"

"Erotisme," and so on, the key mark for non-French speakers is "v.o.," for *version originale* (original-language version)—this means the movie hasn't been dubbed in French. Films are listed alphabetically, by neighborhood ("Salles Paris") and by genre. To find a showing near your hotel, simply look for a cinema in the same arrondissement. "Salles Périphérie" means the cinema is located out in the suburbs. Many cinemas offer discounts on Monday or Wednesday nights.

"Arts" gives hours and locations for gallery showings ("expositions," big and small), and up-to-date hours at museums in and near Paris (*tlj* = daily, *sf* = except, *Ent* = entry price, *TR* = reduced price—usually for students and children).

"Musique" lists each day's events, from jazz to classical to dance (program, location, time, price). This section also includes both opera houses if performances are scheduled. Remember that some concerts are free *(entrée libre)*.

"L'Agenda" covers outdoor events and sights, including open-air theater, flea markets, sound-and-light shows *(son et lumières)*, key monuments such as the Eiffel Tower and Arc de Triomphe, river cruises, parks, zoos, and aquariums.

For cancan mischief, look under **"Paris la Nuit."**

Other Resources: Pick up a copy of the free weekly *A Nous Paris* in the Métro and check out the *"L'Agenda de la Semaine"* section, a weekly review of events that is easy to follow even though it's in French. In these pages, this youth-oriented magazine lists what makes their cut for the most interesting event in Paris each day of the week (printed on Monday, www.anous.fr).

Online English Sources: If you prefer your event information in English, the *Paris Voice* website has helpful reviews of Paris art shows, entertainment, and more (www.parisvoice.com). *Time Out*'s English website is another good resource, with listings for the city's most talked-about restaurants, reviews of concerts and stores, and ideas for how to enjoy Paris's nightlife and shopping on a budget (www.timeout.fr/paris/en).

MUSIC AND FILM
Jazz and Blues Clubs

With a lively mix of American, French, and international musicians, Paris has been an internationally acclaimed jazz capital since World War II. You'll pay €12-25 to enter a jazz club (may include one drink; if not, expect to pay €5-10 per drink; beer is cheapest). See *Pariscope* magazine under "Musique" for listings, or, even better, the *Paris Voice* website. You can also check each club's website (all have English versions), or drop by the clubs to check out the calendars posted on their front doors. Music starts after

21:00 in most clubs. Some offer dinner concerts from about 20:30 on. Here are several good bets:

Caveau de la Huchette: This fun, characteristic old jazz/dance club fills an ancient Latin Quarter cellar with live jazz and frenzied dancing every night (admission about €15, €10 for those under 25, drinks from €7, daily from 21:30, no reservations needed, buy tickets at the door, 5 Rue de la Huchette, Mo: St. Michel, tel. 01 43 26 65 05, www.caveaudelahuchette.fr).

Autour de Midi et Minuit: This Old World bistro sits at the foot of Montmartre, above a *cave à jazz*. Eat upstairs if you like (see page 446 for details), then make your way down to the basement to find bubbling jam sessions Tuesday through Thursday and concerts on Friday and Saturday nights (no cover, €5 minimum drink order Tue-Thu; €18 cover Fri-Sat includes one drink; jam sessions at 21:30, concerts usually at 22:00; no music Sun-Mon; 11 Rue Lepic, Mo: Blanche or Abbesses, tel. 01 55 79 16 48, www.autourdemidi.fr).

Other Venues: For a spot teeming with late-night activity and jazz, go to the two-block-long Rue des Lombards, at Boulevard Sébastopol, midway between the river and the Pompidou Center (Mo: Châtelet). **Au Duc des Lombards** is one of the most popular and respected jazz clubs in Paris, with concerts nightly in a great, plush, 110-seat theater-like setting (admission €25-50, €60-90 with dinner, buy online and arrive early for best seats, cheap drinks, shows usually at 19:30 and 21:30, 42 Rue des Lombards, tel. 01 42 33 22 88, www.ducdeslombards.fr). **Le Sunside** is just a block away. The club offers two little stages (ground floor and downstairs): "Le Sunset" stage tends toward contemporary world jazz; "le Sunside" stage features more traditional and acoustic jazz (concerts range from free to €25, check their website; 60 Rue des Lombards, tel. 01 40 26 46 60, www.sunset-sunside.com).

For a less pricey—and less central—concert club, try **Utopia.** From the outside it's a hole-in-the-wall, but inside it's filled with devoted fans of rock and folk blues. Though Utopia is officially a private club (and one that permits smoking), you can pay €3 to join for an evening, then pay a reasonable charge for the concert (usually €12 or under, concerts start about 22:00). It's located in the Montparnasse area (79 Rue de l'Ouest, Mo: Pernety, tel. 01 43 22 79 66, www.utopia-cafeconcert.fr).

Old-Time Parisian Cabaret

Au Lapin Agile, a historic little cabaret on Montmartre, tries its best to maintain the atmosphere of the heady days when bohemians would gather here to enjoy wine, song, and sexy jokes. Today, you'll mix in with a few locals and many tourists (the Japanese love the place) for a drink and as many as 10 different performers—mostly singers with a piano. Performers range from sweet and innocent Amélie types to naughty Maurice Chevalier types. And though tourists are welcome, there's no accommodation for English speakers (except on their website), so non-French speakers will be lost. You sit at carved wooden tables in a dimly lit room, taste the traditional drink (a small brandy with cherries), and are immersed in an old-time Parisian ambience. The soirée covers traditional French standards, love ballads, sea chanteys, and more (€28, €8 drinks, Tue-Sun from 21:00, closed Mon, best to reserve ahead, 22 Rue des Saules, tel. 01 46 06 85 87, www.au-lapin-agile.com, described on page 380).

Classical Concerts

For classical music on any night, consult *Pariscope* magazine (check "Concerts Classiques" under "Musique" for listings), and look for posters at tourist-oriented churches. From March through November, these churches regularly host concerts: St. Sulpice, St. Germain-des-Prés, La Madeleine, St. Eustache, St. Julien-le-Pauvre, and Sainte-Chapelle.

Sainte-Chapelle: Enjoy the pleasure of hearing Mozart, Bach, or Vivaldi, surrounded by 800 years of stained glass (unheated—bring a sweater). The acoustical quality is surprisingly good. There are usually two concerts per evening, at 19:00 and 20:30; specify which one you want when you buy or reserve your ticket. VIP tickets get you a seat in rows 3-10 (€40), Prestige tickets cover the next 10 rows (€30), and Normal tickets are the last five rows (€25). Seats are unassigned within each section, so arrive at least 30 minutes early to get through the security line and snare a good view.

You can book at the box office, by phone, or online. Two different companies present concerts, but the schedule will tell you whom to contact for tickets to a particular performance. The small box office (with schedules and tickets) is to the left of the chapel entrance gate (8 Boulevard du Palais, Mo: Cité), or call 01 42 77 65 65 or 06 67 30 65 65 for schedules and reservations. You can leave your message in English—just speak clearly and spell your name. You can check schedules and buy your ticket at www.euromusicproductions.fr.

Flavien from Euromusic offers last-minute discounts with this book when seats are available (limit 2 tickets per book). VIP tickets are discounted to €30, Prestige tickets to €25, and Normal tickets to €16. The offer applies only to Euromusic concerts and must be purchased with cash only at the Sainte-Chapelle ticket booth close to concert time.

Philharmonie de Paris: This dazzling, 2,400-seat concert hall is situated in the Parc de la Villette complex. It hosts world-class artists, from legends of rock and roll to string quartets to international opera stars. Tickets range from €10 to €150, depending on the artist and seats, and are usually hard to come by, so it's best to buy them in advance (221 Avenue Jean-Jaurès, Mo: Porte de Pantin, tel. 01 44 84 44 84, www.philharmoniedeparis.fr).

Concerts on the Seine: Enjoy live classical music while cruising past Paris' iconic monuments (€30-40, summer months only, board at Vedettes du Pont Neuf, Square du Vert Galant, tel. 01 42 77 65 65, http://vedettesdupontneuf.com/concerts-en-seine).

Other Venues: Look also for daytime concerts in parks, such as the Luxembourg Garden. Even the Galeries Lafayette department store offers concerts. Many of these concerts are free *(entrée libre),* such as the Sunday atelier concert sponsored by the American Church (generally Sept-June at 17:00 but not every week and not in Dec, 65 Quai d'Orsay, Mo: Invalides, RER: Pont de l'Alma, tel. 01 40 62 05 00, www.acparis.org). The Army Museum offers inexpensive afternoon and evening classical music concerts all year round (for programs—in French only—see www.musee-armee.fr).

Opera

Paris is home to two well-respected opera venues. The **Opéra Bastille** is the massive modern opera house that dominates Place de la Bastille. Come here for state-of-the-art special effects and modern interpretations of classic ballets and operas. In the spirit of this everyman's opera, unsold seats are available at a big discount to seniors and students 15 minutes before the show. Standing-room-only tickets for €15 are also sold for some performances (Mo: Bastille).

The **Opéra Garnier,** Paris' first opera house, hosts opera and ballet performances. Come here for grand belle époque decor (Mo: Opéra; generally no performances mid-July-mid-Sept). To get tickets for either opera house, it's easiest to reserve online at www.operadeparis.fr, or call 01 71 25 24 23 outside France or toll tel. 08 92 89 90 90 inside France (office closed Sun). You can also buy tickets in person at their ticket offices,

both of which are open Monday-Saturday (Opéra Bastille 14:30-18:30, Opéra Garnier 11:30–18:30) and an hour before the show, and closed on Sunday.

Movies

The Open Air Cinema at La Villette (Cinéma en Plein Air) is your chance to relax on the grass and see a movie under the stars with happy Parisians. Films, shown in their original language with French subtitles, start at dusk (free, €7 chair rental, mid-July-Aug Wed-Sun, inside Parc de la Villette complex—enter through main entrance at Cité des Sciences et de l'Industrie, 30 Rue Corentin-Cariou, Mo: Porte de la Villette, www.villette.com).

EVENING SIGHTSEEING
Museum Visits

Various museums are open late on different evenings—called *visites nocturnes*—offering the opportunity for more relaxed, less crowded visits: the Louvre, Orsay, Rodin, Pompidou Center, Jacquemart-André, Architecture and Monuments, Quai Branly, and Marmottan museums. See the sidebar on page 69 for hours of these and other night-owl attractions.

Versailles Spectacles: An elaborate sound-and-light show (Les Grandes Eaux Nocturnes) takes place in the gardens at Versailles on some Friday and Saturday evenings in summer (see page 544 for details, www.chateauversailles.fr).

Seine River Cruises

Several companies offer cruises after dark as well as dinner cruises on huge glass-domed boats (or open-air decks in summer) with departures along the Seine, including from the Eiffel Tower; see "Dinner Cruises" on page 447 of the Eating in Paris chapter. Evening concert cruises are also available in summer months; see "Classical Concerts," earlier.

NIGHT WALKS

Go for an evening walk to best appreciate the City of Light. Break for ice cream, pause at a café, and enjoy the sidewalk entertainers as you join the post-dinner Parisian parade. Use any of this book's self-guided walking tours as a blueprint. (They're worth doing twice—once by day with the self-guided tour information and again after dark to enjoy the lively people scene and beautiful lighting.) Consider the following suggestions; most are partial versions of this book's longer walking tours. Don't dilly-dally; lights at many major monuments are turned off at midnight. (Remember to avoid poorly lit areas and stick to main thoroughfares.)

▲▲▲Trocadéro and Eiffel Tower

This is one of Paris' most spectacular views at night. Take the Métro to the Trocadéro stop and join the party on Place du Trocadéro for a magnificent view of the glowing Eiffel Tower (see the "Best Views over the City of Light" sidebar on page 86). It's a festival of hawkers, gawkers, drummers, and entertainers.

Walk down the stairs, passing the fountains and rollerbladers, then cross the river to the base of the tower, well worth the effort even if you don't go up. ☐ See the Eiffel Tower Tour chapter.

From the Eiffel Tower you can stroll through the Champ de Mars park past tourists and romantic couples, and take the Métro home (Ecole Militaire stop, across Avenue de la Motte-Picquet from far southeast corner of park). Or there's a handy RER stop (Champ de Mars-Tour Eiffel) two blocks west of the Eiffel Tower on the river.

▲▲Champs-Elysées and the Arc de Triomphe

The Avenue des Champs-Elysées is best after dark (☐ see the Champs-Elysées Walk chapter). Start at the Arc de Triomphe, then stroll down Paris' glittering grand promenade. A right turn on Avenue George V leads to the Bateaux-Mouches river cruises. A movie on the Champs-Elysées is a fun experience (weekly listings in *Pariscope* under "Cinéma"), and a drink or snack at Renault's futuristic car café is a kick (at #53).

▲Ile St. Louis and Notre-Dame

Do a shortened version of the beautiful Historic Paris Walk after dinner, starting on the island of Ile St. Louis (see the ☐ Historic Paris Walk chapter in this book, or download the ⌂ free audio tour).

To reach Ile St. Louis, take the Métro (line 7) to the Pont Marie stop, then cross Pont Marie to Ile St. Louis. Turn right up Rue St. Louis-en-l'Ile, stopping for dinner—or at least a Berthillon ice cream (at #31) or Amorino Gelati (at #47). At the end of Ile St. Louis, cross Pont St. Louis to Ile de la Cité, with a great view of Notre-Dame. Wander to the Left Bank on Quai de l'Archevêché, and drop down to the river for the best floodlit views. From May through September you'll find several moored barges *(péniches)* that operate as bars. Although I wouldn't eat dinner on one of these barges, the atmosphere is great for a drink, often including live music on weekends (daily until late, closed Oct-April, live music often Thu-Sun from 21:00). End your walk on Place du Parvis Notre-Dame in front of Notre-Dame (sound-and-light shows in summer run twice a week—see page 106), or go back across the river to the Latin Quarter.

Open-Air Sculpture Garden near Jardin des Plantes

Day or night, this skinny riverfront park dotted with modern art makes for a pleasant walk, but it's especially fun on balmy evenings in the summer, when you may encounter rock and salsa dancing or whatever's in vogue. It's on the Left Bank across from Ile St. Louis, running between the Arab World Institute and Jardin des Plantes (free, music around 20:00, very weather-dependent, Quai St. Bernard, Mo: Cardinal Lemoine plus an eight-minute walk up Rue Cardinal Lemoine toward the river).

Place de la Concorde, Place Vendôme, and Place de l'Opéra

These three squares tie together nicely for an elegant post-dinner walk (see page 471 in the Shopping in Paris chapter). Take the Métro to Place de la Concorde and get out to the obelisk for a terrific view of the Champs-Elysées and the beautifully lit, Greek-looking National Assembly building (to your left as you are looking up the Champs-Elysées). Consider a spin around the Paris Ferris Wheel (actually, two spins; see page 84). Then walk up Rue Royale toward La Madeleine, turn right on Rue St. Honoré, then left after several blocks on Rue Castiglione. The sumptuous Place Vendôme makes me wish I were rich. Exit Place Vendôme at the opposite end and walk up Rue de la Paix to find Opéra Garnier, stunning at night (see page 88). End your stroll with a pricey drink at one of Paris' grandest cafés (Café de la Paix), across from Opéra Garnier (the Opéra Métro stop is right there to take you home).

Marais

This artsy neighborhood is a hotbed for nightlife, full of cafés and tiny bars catering to locals and tourists alike. The action centers around Rue Vieille du Temple (Mo: St. Paul), which offers something for every taste and attracts all age groups and sexual persuasions. Look for the Au Petit Fer à Cheval bar and the bookstore/wine bar La Belle Hortense (daily 17:00-24:00, 31 Rue Vieille du Temple), and fan out from there. At the western edge of the Marais, you'll find good boy-meets-girl energy at bars along Rue des Lombards near where it crosses Boulevard de Sebastopol (Mo: Châtelet or Hôtel de Ville, see also "Jazz and Blues Clubs," earlier).

Place St. Germain-des-Prés and Odéon

These areas are close to each other and worth combining for evening fun. The church of St. Germain-des-Prés is usually lit up and open at night, and Parisians sip drinks at two famous nearby cafés: Les Deux Magots and Le Café de Flore (see page 286; Mo: St. Germain-des-Prés). A few blocks toward St. Sulpice Church, night owls prowl along Rues des Canettes and Guisarde, and a few blocks toward the river, they do the same along Rue de Buci (for more on these streets, see page 440 of the Eating in Paris chapter). The Odéon, a few blocks away, is home to several movie theaters and still more lively cafés.

AFTER-DARK TOURS ON WHEELS

Several companies offer evening tours of Paris. You can join a traditional, mass-produced bus tour, or for more money, take a vintage-car tour with a student guide or ride in a pedicab. Do-it-yourself-ers can save money by using Uber or a taxi for a private tour. All options are described below.

▲Deux Chevaux Car Tours

If rumbling around Paris and sticking your head out of the rolled-back top of a funky old 2CV car *à la* Inspector Clouseau sounds like your kind of fun, consider this.

Two enterprising companies have assembled a veritable fleet of these "tin-can" cars for giving tours of Paris day and night: 4 Roues Sous 1 Parapluie (the better choice) and Paris Authentic. Night is best for the tour; skip it in daylight. The informal student-drivers are not professional guides (you're paying for their driving services), though they speak some English. Appreciate the simplicity of the car. It's France's version of the VW "bug" and hasn't been made since 1985. Notice the bare-bones dashboard. Ask your guide to honk the horn, to run the silly little wipers, and to open and close the air vent—*c'est magnifique!*

They'll pick you up and drop you at your hotel or wherever you choose. **4 Roues Sous 1 Parapluie** ("4 wheels under 1 umbrella") offers several tours with candy-colored cars and drivers dressed in striped shirts and berets (for 2 people it's €40/person for 45 minutes and €70/person for 90 minutes; 10 percent tip appropriate if you enjoyed your ride, longer tours available, maximum 3 people/car, tel. 08 00 80 06 31, mobile 06 67 32 26 68, www.4roues-sous-1parapluie.com, info@4roues-sous-1parapluie.com). **Paris Authentic** offers similar options with less personal attention (€50/person for 2 people for a 1-hour tour, €36/person for 3 people, longer trips possible, 23 Rue Jean-Jacques Rousseau, mobile 06 64 50 44 19, www.parisauthentic.com, paris@parisauthentic.com).

Pedicab Tours

Experience the City of Light at an escargot's pace with your private chauffeur pedaling a sleek, human-powered tricycle from TripUp. Call ahead, book online, or flag one down and use our taxi tour (described later) as a road map; they usually work until about 22:00 (www.tripup.fr).

▲Nighttime Bus Tours

City Vision's Paris by Night: City Tour connects all the great illuminated sights of Paris with a 100-minute bus tour in 12 languages. The double-decker buses have huge windows, but the most desirable front seats are sometimes reserved for customers who've bought tickets for the overrated Moulin Rouge. Left-side seats are better. Visibility is fine in the rain. These tours are not for everyone. You'll stampede on with a United Nations of tourists, get a set of headphones, dial up your language, and listen to a recorded spiel (which is interesting, but includes an annoyingly bright TV screen and a pitch for the other, more expensive excursions). Uninspired as it is, the ride provides an entertaining overview of the city at its floodlit and scenic best. Bring your city map to stay oriented as you go. You're always on the bus, but the driver slows for photos at viewpoints (€27, kids-€17, 1.75 hours, departs from 2 Rue des Pyramides at 20:00 Nov-March, at 22:00 April-Oct, reserve one day in advance, arrive 30 minutes early to wait in line for best seats, Mo: Pyramides, tel. 01 44 55 61 00, www.pariscityvision.com). City Vision also offers a Paris by Night tour in a small-group minibus, which follows a similar route to the bus tours. They will pick you up and drop you off at your hotel (€60, kids-€47, 2 hours). For all City Vision tours, buy tickets through your hotel (no booking fee, brochures in lobby) or directly at the City Vision office at 214 Rue de Rivoli, across the street from the Tuileries Métro stop.

You can also take a night tour on L'OpenTour's double-decker buses (see page 37) as extensions of their day-tour program (€48 includes day pass and night tour, €27 for night tour only, April-Oct at 22:00, Nov-March at 18:30, arrive 30 minutes before departure, depart from 13 Rue Auber, tel. 01 42 66 56 56, www.paris.opentour.com).

▲▲▲Floodlit Paris Driving Tour by Taxi or Uber

Seeing the City of Light floodlit is one of Europe's great travel experiences and a great finale to any day in Paris. Sunday is the best night to go, as there's less traffic—you'll get a better value for the time spent in the car. For less than the cost of two seats on a big bus tour, you can hire your own driver and have a glorious hour of illuminated Paris on your terms and schedule. The downside: You don't have the high vantage point and big windows of a bus. The

Floodlit Paris Driving Tour

Stops

1. Notre-Dame View from Pont de la Tournelle
2. Les Invalides View from Place Vauban
3. Eiffel Tower View from Champ de Mars Park
4. Eiffel Tower View from Place du Trocadéro
5. Champs-Elysées View from Place de la Concorde
6. Louvre Museum & Pyramid View

Uber & Taxi Instructions

Bonjour, Monsieur/Madame. Nous voulons faire un circuit de Paris illuminé d'une heure, avec quelques petits arrêts. Nous paierons le montant indiqué sur le compteur. Nous voudrions suivre la route suivante—combien cela va t-il coûter approximativement? Ça marche?

Greetings, Monsieur/Madame. We would like a tour of Paris at night for an hour, with a few short stops. We will pay the metered rate. We would like to take the following route—approximately how much will it cost? Can you do it?

1. Notre-Dame
2. Hôtel de Ville
3. Pont Marie
4. **Pont de la Tournelle (arrêt)**
5. Quai de la Tournelle
6. Musée d'Orsay
7. Esplanade des Invalides
8. Invalides
9. **Place Vauban/Eglise du Dôme (arrêt)**
10. **Champ de Mars (Place Jacques Rueff—arrêt)**
11. Tour Eiffel
12. Pont d'Iena
13. **Place du Trocadéro (arrêt)**
14. Avenue Kléber
15. Arc de Triomphe (2 révolutions)
16. Champs-Elysées
17. **Place de la Concorde (1 ou 2 révolutions)**
18. Quai François Mitterrand
19. **Musée du Louvre/Place du Carrousel/Pyramide (arrêt)**
20. Quai du Louvre
21. Notre-Dame

upside: It's cheaper, you go when and where you like, and you can jump out anywhere to get the best views and pictures.

Tour Overview: This is a circular, one-hour route—from Notre-Dame to the Eiffel Tower along the Left Bank, then back along the Right Bank. Start at Notre-Dame (there's a taxi stand there—just in front, on left), at any convenient point along the route, or from your hotel. Suggested stops are in bold on the list in "Uber & Taxi Instructions" (see page 499; "arrêt" means "stop") though you can make any stops you like. To make it more of a party, bring a bottle of red wine and some chocolate to enjoy each time you hop out (do not consume in the car).

Traffic can be sparse, and lights are shining between 22:00 and 24:00 every night. Complete your tour by midnight when lights are shut off at major monuments. Your only other timing concern: The Eiffel Tower twinkles for only the first five minutes of each hour after dark. If you start at Notre-Dame at half past the hour, you should be right on time for the sparkles.

Taxi Versus Uber: Taxis cost more and drivers can be moody; Uber costs less, with drivers who tend to be more fun and flexible.

Taxis have a strict meter (figure €38/hour plus about €1/kilometer; taxis start with €2.60 on the meter). This suggested loop costs around €50 (more on Sun) via taxi and around €40 by Uber. If your cabbie was easy to work with, add a 10 percent tip; if not, tip just 5 percent. You don't need to tip with Uber (though you can). Drivers can take up to four people in a cab or regular sedan, though this is tight for decent sightseeing (with three, everyone gets a window).

If you enjoy Uber, this is a far better deal than going by taxi. Drivers are fun-loving and you'll save about 20 percent. When ordering your car via the app, you can leave the destination blank, or just choose a random address and then explain your plan when the driver arrives. This is a great gig for an Uber driver and they still make money when you stop and hop out, so that's no problem. And if you win your driver's friendship, he or she will happily snap photos of you at various stops.

The Route: Give the driver the instructions printed on page 499. Before you go, photocopy it (ask at your hotel), or rip the page out (but trace the route on another map so you can follow along). Learn your driver's name and use it (no first names for taxi drivers; use *Monsieur* or *Madame*). Make sure the driver understands the plan—and enjoys the challenge. Review with the driver exactly where you hope to stop before you start. Don't worry about the

Driver Lingo

Use these phrases to communicate with your driver.

English	French
What is your name?	*Quel est votre nom?* (kehl ay voh-truh nohn)
Drive slowly, please.	*Conduisez lentement, s'il vous plaît.* (kohn-dwee-zay lahn-tuh-mahn see voo play)
Slower, please.	*Lentement, s'il vous plaît.* (lahn-tuh-mahn see voo play)
Stop, please.	*Arrêtez, s'il vous plaît.* (ah-reh-tay see voo play)
Wait, please.	*Patientez, s'il vous plaît.* (pah-see-yahn-tay see voo play)
I love Paris!	*J'adore Paris!* (zhah-dor pah-ree)

exact streets the driver takes (as there are necessary deviations); just stick to the overall hit list of stops. Ask the driver to go slowly (or go around again) when you want to enjoy a particular scene.

And you're on your way. Roll the windows down, and turn the dome light on to read if you like (this is no problem for taxi drivers, but better to ask with Uber). Stop when you want (but remember that the meter still runs when stopped). Some drivers might speak a little English; if not, learn and use the key words in the sidebar.

➲ **Self-Guided Tour:** Start at Notre-Dame. Drive over Pont d'Arcole to Hôtel de Ville, then turn right along the Seine (the white stripe of light is a modern bridge connecting the two islands).

Cross the Ile St. Louis on Pont Marie. Stop on the next bridge—**Pont de la Tournelle**—just after the island, get out, and giggle with delight at the city and illuminated Notre-Dame. Then turn right along the Seine on Quai de la Tournelle, motoring scenically past Notre-Dame.

Drive west along the entire length of the river, passing le long Louvre—once the world's biggest building (across the river), then under the Orsay Museum (above you, on left). The National Assembly (on left) faces Place de la Concorde (on right). The ornate Pont Alexandre III comes next (on right).

Turn left down Esplanade des Invalides to the gilded dome of Les Invalides, marking Napoleon's Tomb. As you approach the grand building, watch the illusion of the fancy dome sinking behind the facade. Circle clockwise around Invalides for a close-up view. Get out at **Place Vauban** (behind the dome) and marvel at its symmetry.

Take Avenue de Tourville to Avenue de la Bourdonnais, which runs alongside the **Champ de Mars park** (former military training grounds that now serve as the Eiffel Tower's backyard). Turn left onto Avenue Joseph Bouvard, leading to a circle made to order for viewing the Eiffel Tower. Get out and gasp.

Pont d'Iéna (you can stop directly under the tower at this bridge) leads from directly in front of the tower across the Seine to **Place du Trocadéro** for another grand Eiffel view (get out again and walk toward the tower to get the best photos and to enjoy the night scene here).

Avenue Kléber leads through one of Paris' ritziest neighborhoods to the Arc de Triomphe. Battle twice around the eternal flame marking the Tomb of the Unknown Soldier and Paris' craziest traffic circle: Ask for *"Deux révolutions, s'il vous plaît"* (duh ray-voh-loo-see-yohn see voo play). Notice the rules of the road: Get to the center ASAP, those entering have the right-of-way, and any accidents are no-fault (insurance companies split the costs down the middle). As you circle, notice the uniform boulevards reaching out like spokes from this hub. Try to find the huge and modern La Grande Arche in the distance opposite the Champs-Elysées.

When ready to continue, say the rhyme, "Champs-Elysées, *s'il vous plaît*" (shahnz ay-lee-zay see voo play). Glide down Europe's grandest boulevard—past fancy restaurants, car dealerships, and theaters—to the colorful Paris Ferris Wheel and the bold white obelisk marking the former site of the guillotine, **Place de la Concorde.**

Circle once (maybe twice) around Place de la Concorde, picking out all the famous landmarks near and far. Stop at the center to look up the Champs-Elysées. Then continue east (reminding your driver the next stop is "la Pyramide du Louvre") along the Seine on Quai des Tuileries (the two train-station clocks across the river mark the Orsay Museum) and sneak (via a taxi/bus-only lane if you're in a cab) into the courtyard of the

Louvre for a close look at the magically glowing pyramid. Stop here.

Return to the riverfront along the Right Bank and pass the oldest bridge in Paris, Pont Neuf, and the impressive Conciergerie with its floodlit medieval turrets (this is where Marie-Antoinette was imprisoned during the Revolution). Turn right on Pont de Notre-Dame and you complete the loop back where you (and Paris) started, at Place du Parvis, facing Notre-Dame on the Ile de la Cité. Or you can ask your driver to take you back to your hotel (roughly €10-15 more).

End your night tour by giving your driver a hearty thank you: *"Merci, monsieur/madame/mon ami(e)! Bonne soirée!"*

PARIS IN WINTER

The City of Light sparkles year-round, but Paris has a special appeal in winter. You'll find inexpensive airfares, fewer crowds, and soft prices for hotel rooms and apartments (rent one for a week or more). Sure, the weather can be cold and rainy (average high in Dec is 44°F), but if you dress in layers, you'll keep warm and easily deal with temperature changes as you go from cold streets to heated museums and cafés.

Museums, restaurants, and stores stay open as usual; the concert and arts season is in full bloom; and Paris belongs to the Parisians. So go local, save money, and skip the museum lines that confound peak-season travelers. There are worse ways to spend a wintry day than enjoying world-class art, architecture, and shopping, then lingering over a fine dinner at a cozy corner bistro in the evening. As Cole Porter put it: "I love Paris in the winter, when it drizzles."

Slow down and savor your favorite museums and monuments—spending one-on-one time with Mona and Venus is worth the extra clothes you have to pack. Attend a cooking demonstration, take a short course in art or architecture, or dabble in a wine-tasting class (for details, see the sidebar on page 40). Duck into cafés for a break from sightseeing or shopping and to warm up. Get on a first-name basis with the waiter at your corner café—just because you can now.

Easter marks the start of the tourist season, when locals find they need to make reservations for their favorite restaurants and can no longer find seats on the Métro.

This chapter reviews off-season highlights in Paris, but remember—your reward for traveling in winter is the joy of feeling part of a city, like you almost belong here. That's what you'll find on a trip to Paris from November to March.

NOVEMBER

From late October well into November, leaves tumble from Paris' trees, revealing magnificent building facades and turning parks

into austere yet romantic places. Winter also brings early sunsets and long evenings, ideal for floodlit neighborhood walks, boat rides, and taxi tours that allow you to view the City of Light at a reasonable hour.

If you're in Paris over the Thanksgiving holiday, you can watch with amusement as the entire expat community crams themselves into the tiny food shop aptly named **Thanksgiving** to purchase overpriced cranberries and boxes of stuffing (20 Rue St-Paul, Mo: St-Paul).

Beginning one minute after midnight on the third Thursday of November and running through mid-December, Paris welcomes the arrival of the **Beaujolais Nouveau** with an enthusiasm uncharacteristic for such a coolly indifferent place. The fresh, fruity wine is rushed from vineyards a bit north of Lyon directly to Paris, where wine bars and most cafés serve it happily, buzzing with news of the latest vintage. The first 24 hours are the most fun and raucous, and it's easy to join the party if you don't mind elbowing your way to the *comptoir* for *un verre*. Cafés and bistros continue the celebration for weeks, many offering special dishes with a glass of the Beaujolais Nouveau.

And speaking of wine, the annual *Salon des Vins des Vignerons Indépendents* (independent winemakers' trade show) is held in Paris on the last weekend of November at the Porte de Versailles exhibition center (Mo: Porte de Versailles, line 12). Here, anyone can sample fine wines from more than 1,000 different stands (small entry fee, ask your hotelier for details or check www.france-independent-winegrowers.com).

DECEMBER

One of Europe's greatest treats is strolling down the glowing Champs-Elysées in winter. From late November through early January, **holiday lights** adorn city streets, buildings, and monuments, and the Champs-Elysées beams

WINTER

with a dazzling display of lights on the trees that line the long boule-vard. The city springs for 1,000 fresh-cut fir trees to put up and deco-rate around town, 300 of which ring the Rond-Point roundabout at the lower end of the Champs-Elysées. You'll also find cheerful lighting displays on many traffic-free streets, including Rues Cler, Montorgueil, and Daguerre.

Parisians live to **window shop** (remember that *faire du lèche-vitrines* means "window licking"). Do some licking of your own along Boulevard Haussmann and view the storefront lights and wild window displays at the grand department stores such as Print-emps and Galeries Lafayette. Here you can have your picture taken with Père Noël—France's slimmer version of Santa Claus, dressed in red trimmed with white fur. The seasonal displays in neighbor-hood boutiques around Sèvres-Babylone and in the Marais (among other areas) are more intimate and offer a good contrast to the shows of glitz around the department stores.

Several **ice-skating rinks** open up in festive locations, allowing you to glide and twirl in front of the Hôtel de Ville (Paris' main City Hall, look also for a small sled run) and along a portion of the Champs-Elysées. The rinks are free to use (around €5 to rent skates, generally open late Nov-Jan from noon into the evening).

For the kids, there are **Christmas carousels** (*Manèges de Noël)* that whirl at various locations, including the biggies at Hôtel de Ville, the Eiffel Tower, and at the base of Sacré-Cœur in Montmartre. As soon as school lets out, parks come alive with pony rides, puppet shows, and other activities.

The dazzling château **Vaux-le-Vicomte,** an hour south of Paris, opens for Christmas with special holiday decorations (€20, weekends only Dec-early Jan 10:45-18:00; see page 568 for details on the château).

The Christmas Season

With the arrival of St. Nicholas on December 6, the Christmas season kicks into gear. (Bear in mind, though, that Paris celebrates Christmas with only a fraction of the holiday cheer and commercialism that you'll find in the States.) In mid-December, **Christmas markets** pop up, particularly on the Left Bank (St. Sulpice and St. Germain-des-Prés), along the Champs-Elysées, and clustered around the Abbesses Métro stop in Montmartre. At **Notre-Dame,** a big Christmas tree goes up, and they may have a living *crèche* in front. Parisians pick up tiny and expensive Christmas trees for their homes at flower shops—if you rent an apartment, you could do the same. Be sure to check the *Pariscope* magazine for popular and often free or inexpensive **Christmas concerts.**

Christmas Eve and Christmas Day

The big event is the Christmas Eve dinner, called **La Réveillon**—"the awakening"—when Parisians stay awake late to celebrate the arrival of Jesus. Traditionally, they attend evening Mass (at Notre-Dame, among other churches), then meet with family and friends for a big feast. The meal begins with (what else?) *escargots,* smoked salmon or oysters, and then foie gras. The main dish, similar to American Thanksgiving, is turkey, served with chestnuts and potatoes *(gratin dauphinois).* This evening is normally celebrated at home and with family, though some Paris restaurants (and other businesses) stay open late to accommodate parties indulging in raw oysters, cheese, and the Yule Log *(Bûche de Noël)*—a log-shaped sponge cake iced with chocolate "bark." After dinner the kiddies leave their slippers next to the fireplace for Père Noël to fill with treats.

WINTER

On Christmas Day, Paris is very sleepy—make arrangements ahead of time if you've got a plane to catch, and don't plan on visiting the Louvre (which is closed, along with most museums and businesses). Visitors looking for **religious services in English** will find no shortage of churches to attend—choose between the interdenominational American Church, American Cathedral, Unitarian Church, and St. George's Anglican Church (listed in the appendix). Many of these churches—especially the American Church—also offer Christmas concerts.

JANUARY

All of Paris parties on New Year's Eve, and a table at a restaurant is next to impossible to land (book early or dine at a café). The holidays aren't over yet—Paris celebrates the arrival of the Three Kings on **Epiphany** (Jan 6) with as much fanfare as Christmas itself. Twinkling Christmas lights stay lit through most of the month.

The **after-Christmas sales** *(soldes)* are an even bigger post-holiday tradition, as locals jam boutiques and department stores looking for bargains. These sales, which last until early February, force stores to keep longer hours.

Parisians celebrate the **Chinese New Year** in a big way (usually falls near the end of January) with parades, decorations, and fanfare. Ask your hotelier or a TI for parade locations.

WINTER

Festive Foods

Winter is the season for the hunt, when you'll find game birds and venison on restaurant menus. Seventy percent of France's oysters are eaten in the month of December, most of them raw and on the half-shell. Look for busy shuckers outside big cafés, where most oysters are consumed. On street corners you'll hear shouts of *"Chaud les mar-rons!"* from vendors selling chestnuts roasting on coals. Chocolatiers (including La Maison du Chocolat's five stores) and pastry shops every-where do a bang-up business during the holiday season, serving traditional treats such as Epiphany cakes (flaky mar-zipan cakes called *galette des rois*). Bakeries overflow with these popular cakes starting January 6.

If you like gourmet food, take a spin around Place de la Madeleine, comparing Fauchon's festive displays with Hédiard's, and spring for a truffle omelet at La Maison des Truffe—after all, winter is truffle season (for info on these shops, see page 471). Just because it's cold doesn't mean that outdoor markets are quiet—*au contraire,* you'll find markets alive with shoppers and vendors no matter what the weather (on Place d'Aligre and along Rue de Grenelle, for example).

One of the great pleasures Paris offers is watching the city bustle while you linger at an outdoor table with a *café crème,* a *vin chaud* (hot wine), or, best, a hot chocolate (sim-ply called *chocolat* and *très* popular in winter). Most cafés fire up the braziers and drape blankets over chairs to keep things toasty outside. And with the strict smoking laws, café and res-taurant interiors are wonderfully free of any trace of smoke.

FEBRUARY AND MARCH

These are the quiet months, when Paris is most alone with itself. And though holiday decorations disappear, the City of Light is as beautiful and seductive as ever. Romantics enjoy Paris on Valen-tine's Day, of course, and there is no shortage of romantic places to linger in Paris.

Someday, visit Paris in winter and—for a few days—become a Parisian.

PARIS CONNECTIONS

This chapter covers Paris' two main airports, one smaller airport, seven train stations, the main bus station, parking tips for drivers, and how to reach the city from Le Havre's cruise port.

Whether you're aiming to catch a train or plane, budget plenty of time to reach your departure point. Paris is a big, crowded city, and getting across town or from terminal to terminal on time is a goal you'll share with millions of others. Factor in traffic delays and walking time through huge stations and vast terminals. At the airport, expect lines at ticketing, check-in, baggage check, and security points. Always keep your luggage safely near you. Thieves prey on jet-lagged and confused tourists on public transportation.

By Plane

Here's a rundown of Paris' major airports and the best ways to get into the city from each. For more on flights within Europe, see page 671.

CHARLES DE GAULLE AIRPORT

Paris' main airport (airport code: CDG) has three terminals: T-1, T-2, and T-3 (see map). Most flights from the US use T-1 or T-2. You can travel between terminals on the free CDGVAL shuttle train (departs every 5 minutes, 24/7) or by shuttle bus (on the arrivals level). Allow 30 minutes to travel between terminals and an hour for total travel time between your gates at T-1 and T-2. All three terminals have access to ground transportation.

When leaving Paris, make sure you know which terminal you are departing from (if it's T-2, you'll also need to know which hall you're leaving from—they're labeled *A* through *F*). Plan to arrive at the airport two to three hours early for an overseas flight, and two

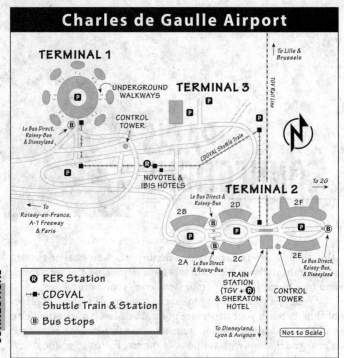

Charles de Gaulle Airport

TERMINAL 1

UNDERGROUND WALKWAYS

TERMINAL 3

CONTROL TOWER

Le Bus Direct, Roissy-Bus & Disneyland

↑ To Lille & Brussels

TGV Rail Line

CDGVAL Shuttle Train

NOVOTEL & IBIS HOTELS

To 2G →

TERMINAL 2

Le Bus Direct & Roissy-Bus

2B   2D   2F

2A   Le Bus Direct & Roissy-Bus   2C

2E   Le Bus Direct, Roissy-Bus, & Disneyland

← To Roissy-en-France, A-1 Freeway & Paris

TRAIN STATION (TGV + ⓡ) & SHERATON HOTEL

CONTROL TOWER

To Disneyland, Lyon & Avignon ↓

Not to Scale

ⓡ RER Station

◼ CDGVAL Shuttle Train & Station

Ⓑ Bus Stops

CONNECTIONS

hours for flights within Europe (particularly on budget airlines, which can have especially long check-in lines). For airport and flight info, visit www.adp.fr.

Services: All terminals have two types of information desks (both bright orange): Airport Information, or ADP (identified with a large I), and Paris Tourisme. ADP counters can help with ground transportation to Paris, bag storage, and airport-related questions. At Paris Tourisme counters you can get city maps, buy a Paris Museum Pass, and get tickets for the RoissyBus or RER train to Paris—a terrific time- and hassle-saver. You'll also find ATMs *(distributeurs)*, free (but slow) Wi-Fi, shops, cafés, and bars. If you are returning home and want a VAT refund, look for tax-refund centers in the check-in area or ask for their location at any ADP information desk.

Terminal 1 (T-1)

This circular terminal has three key floors—arrivals *(arrivées)* on the top floor, and two floors for departures *(départs)* below. The terminal's round shape can be confusing—if you feel like you're going around in circles, you probably are.

Arrival Level *(niveau arrivée):* After passing through

customs, you'll exit between doors *(porte)* 34 and 36. Nearby are orange ADP information desks, a snack stand, and an ATM. Walk counterclockwise around the terminal to find the Paris Tourisme desk (door 6). Walk clockwise to find ground transportation: Le Bus Direct, RoissyBus, and the Disneyland shuttle bus (door 34), car rental counters (doors 24-30), and taxis (door 24).

Departure Levels *(niveaux départ):* Scan the departure screen to find out which hall you should go to for check-in. Halls 1-4 are on floor 2, and 5-6 are downstairs on floor 1. Also on floor 1 are the CDGVAL shuttle train, cafés, a post office (La Poste), pharmacy, boutiques, and a handy grocery. Boarding gates and duty-free shopping are located on floor 3, which is only accessible with a boarding pass.

Terminal 2 (T-2)

This long, horseshoe-shaped terminal is divided into six halls, labeled *A* through *F*. If arriving here, prepare for long walks and, in some cases, short train rides to baggage claim and exits. It's a busy place, but you will have no problem if you take it slow and follow signage carefully. ADP and Paris Tourisme counters are located near gate 6/8 in each hall. Shuttle buses *(navettes)* circulate between T-2 halls A, C, and F, and to terminals T-1 and T-3 on the arrivals level. To locate bus stops for Le Bus Direct and RoissyBus—marked on the map on the previous page—follow *Gare Routière* signs. For the Disneyland shuttle, follow signs to T-2E/F, door 8.

T-2 has a **train station,** with RER suburban trains into Paris (described later), as well as longer-distance trains to the rest of France (including high-speed TGV trains). It's located between T-2C/D and T-2E/F, below the Sheraton Hotel (prepare for a long walk to reach your train). Shuttle buses to **airport hotels** leave from above the RER station at T-2.

Car-rental offices, post offices, pharmacies, and ATMs are all well-signed. T-2E/F has several duty-free shopping arcades, and other T-2 halls have smaller duty-free shops. You can stash your bags at Baggage du Monde, located above the train station in T-2, but it's pricey (€14/12 hours, €18/24 hours, daily 6:00-21:30, tel. 01 34 38 58 90, www.bagagesdumonde.com). Some Paris train stations can store for much less.

Getting Between Charles de Gaulle Airport and Paris

Buses, airport vans, commuter trains, and taxis link the airport's terminals with central Paris. If you're traveling with two or more companions, carrying lots of baggage, or are just plain tired, taxis (or Uber) are worth the extra cost. Total travel time to your hotel should be around 1.5 hours by bus and Métro, one hour by train and Métro, and 50 minutes by taxi. Keep in mind that, at the airport, using buses and taxis requires shorter walks than taking RER trains. Also remember that transfers to Métro lines often involve stairs. For more information, check the "Getting There" tab at www.charlesdegaulleairport.co.uk.

For details on reaching your hotel neighborhood from the various bus/van/train drop-off points, see the "Public Transportation to Recommended Hotels" sidebar.

By RoissyBus: This bus drops you off at the Opéra Métro stop in central Paris (€11, runs 6:00-23:00, 3-4/hour, 50 minutes, buy ticket at airport Paris Tourisme desk, ticket machine, or on bus, tel. 3246, www.ratp.fr). The RoissyBus arrives on Rue Scribe; to get to the Métro entrance or nearest taxi stand, turn left as you exit the bus and walk counterclockwise around the lavish Opéra building to its front. A taxi to any of my listed hotels costs about €12 from here.

By Le Bus Direct (formerly Air France Bus): Several bus routes drop travelers at different points in and near the city (€17 one-way, runs 5:45-22:30, 2/hour, Wi-Fi and power outlets, tel. 08 92 35 08 20, www.lebusdirect.com). **Bus #2** goes to Porte Maillot (with connections to Beauvais Airport, described later), the Arc de Triomphe (Etoile stop, 50 minutes, see map on page 303), the Trocadéro, and ends at the Eiffel Tower/Champ de Mars RER (1.25 hours, see map on page 213). **Bus #4** runs to Gare de Lyon (45 minutes) and the Montparnasse Tower/train station (1.25 hours). **Bus #3** goes to Orly Airport (€21, 1.25 hours). You can book tickets online (must print out and bring with you) or pay the driver (see www.lebusdirect.com for round-trip and group discount details).

To return to the airport from Paris, catch Le Bus Direct coaches at any of these locations: Eiffel Tower/Champ de Mars Métro stop, Trocadéro Métro stop, Arc de Triomphe/Etoile (on Avenue Mac Mahon—the non-Champs-Elysées side), Porte Maillot (on Boulevard Gouvion St-Cyr—east side of the Palais des Congrès), Gare Montparnasse (on Rue du Commandant René Mouchotte—facing the station with the tower behind you, it's around the left side), or Gare de Lyon (look for *Navette-Aéroport* signs, and find the stop on Boulevard Diderot across from Café Les Deux Savoies).

By RER Train: Paris' suburban commuter train is the fastest public transit option for getting between the airport and the city center (€11, runs 5:00-24:00, 4/hour, about 35 minutes). It runs

Public Transportation to Recommended Hotels

You have many options for traveling between Charles de Gaulle Airport and Paris; which alternative makes the most sense depends on where you're staying and your budget. Here are my tips for getting to recommended hotels.

Rue Cler Area: The RoissyBus, RER, and Le Bus Direct coaches all work for Rue Cler accommodations. For hotels near the Ecole Militaire and La Tour Maubourg Métro stops, take the **RoissyBus** directly to the Opéra, then take Métro line 8 (direction: Balard).

For hotels closer to the river, take **RER-B** from the airport, change at the St. Michel stop for the RER-C (direction: Versailles Château Rive Gauche or Pontoise), and get off at Pont de l'Alma.

Le Bus Direct #2 works for most hotels in the area but requires a bit more effort—walk 15 minutes from the Eiffel Tower stop (see below) or get off at the Arc de Triomphe/Etoile stop, walk a few blocks, then grab the #92 city bus and hop off at one of the stops along Avenue Bosquet, shortly after crossing the river (for stop locations near the Arc, see the map on page 303; for stop locations on Avenue Bosquet, see page 390).

Marais and Ile St. Louis: Take **Le Bus Direct** #4 to Gare de Lyon, and find the entrance to Métro line 1 near the bus stop (direction: La Défense). For the Marais, get off at the Bastille or St. Paul stops; for Ile St. Louis, use the Hôtel de Ville stop.

For hotels near Place des Vosges and east of Boulevard Richard Lenoir, you can also take the **RoissyBus** to the Opéra Métro, then transfer to Métro line 8 (direction: Créteil Préfecture) and get off at Bastille. Or, take the **RER-B** from the airport to the Châtelet-Les Halles stop and transfer to Métro line 1 (direction: Château de Vincennes; note this involves a long walk with some stairs in a huge station), and get off at Hôtel de Ville, St. Paul, or Bastille.

Luxembourg Garden: Ride **RER-B** to the Luxembourg stop.

Montmartre: Take the **RER-B** to Gare du Nord, transfer to Métro line 4 (direction: Porte de Clignancourt) and ride three stops to Marcadet-Poissoniers, then transfer to line 12 (direction: Mairie d'Issy). Ride three or four stops and get off at Abbesses or Pigalle.

directly to well-located RER/Métro stations (including Gare du Nord, Châtelet-Les Halles, St. Michel, and Luxembourg); from there, you can hop the Métro to get exactly where you need to go. The RER is handy and cheap, but it can require walking with your luggage through big, crowded stations—especially at Châtelet-Les

Halles, where a transfer to the Métro can take 10-15 minutes and may include stairs.

To reach the RER from the airport terminal, follow *Paris by Train* signs, then *RER* signs. (If you're landing at T-1 or T-3, you'll need to take the CDGVAL shuttle to reach the RER station.) The RER station at T-2 is busy with long ticket-window lines (the other airport RER station, located between T-1 and T-2, is quieter). To save time, buy tickets at a Paris Tourisme counter or from the green machines at the station (labeled *Paris/Ile de France*, coins required, break your bills at an airport shop). For step-by-step instructions on taking the RER into Paris, see www.parisbytrain.com (see the options under "CDG Airport to Paris RER Trains"). Beware of thieves on the train; wear your money belt and keep your bags close.

To return to the airport by RER from central Paris, allow plenty of time to get to your departure gate (plan for a 15-minute Métro or bus ride to the closest RER station serving line B, a 15-minute wait for your train, a 35-minute train ride, plus walking time through the stations and airport). Your Métro or bus ticket is not valid on the RER train to the airport (but a Passe Navigo is); buy the ticket from a clerk or the machines (coins only) at the RER-B station. When you catch your train, make sure the sign over the platform shows *Aéroport Roissy-Charles de Gaulle* as a stop served. (The line splits, so not every line B train serves the airport.) If you're not clear, ask another rider, *"Air-o-por sharl duh gaul?"* Once at the airport, hop out either at T-2 or T-1/3 (where you can connect to T-1 or T-3 on the CDGVAL shuttle).

By Airport Van: Shuttle vans carry passengers to and from their hotels, with stops along the way to drop off and pick up other riders. Shuttles require you to book a precise pickup time in advance—even though you can't ever know if your flight will arrive exactly on time. For that reason, they work best for trips from your hotel to the airport. Though not as fast as taxis, shuttle vans are a good value for single travelers and big families (about €32 for one person, €46 for two, €58 for three; have hotelier book at least a day in advance). Several companies offer shuttle service; I usually just go with the one my hotel uses.

By Taxi or Uber: Taxis charge a flat rate into Paris (€55 to the Left Bank, €50 to the Right Bank—these mandated flat fees have been recently instituted, so confirm with your driver). Taxis are less appealing on weekday mornings as traffic into Paris can be bad—in that case, the train is likely a better option. Taxis can carry three people with bags comfortably, and are legally required to accept a fourth passenger (though they may not like it; beyond that, there's an extra passenger supplement). Larger parties can wait for a larger vehicle. Don't take an unauthorized taxi from cabbies greeting you on arrival. Official taxi stands are well-signed.

For trips from Paris to the airport, have your hotel arrange it. Specify that you want a real taxi *(un taxi normal)*, not a limo service that costs €20 more (and gives your hotel a kickback). For weekday-morning departures (7:00-10:00), reserve at least a day ahead (€7 reservation fee payable by credit card). For more on taxis in Paris, see page 34.

Paris Uber offers airport pickup or drop-off, but since they can't use the bus-only lanes as normal taxis can, expect some added time (€30-80).

By Paris Webservices Private Car: This car service works well from the airport because your driver meets you inside the terminal and waits if you're late (€100 one-way for up to two people, €120-225 round-trip for up to four people, tel. 01 45 56 91 67 or 09 52 06 02 59, www.pariswebservices.com). They also offer guided tours—see page 46.

By Rental Car: Car-rental desks are well signed from the arrival halls. Be prepared for a maze of ramps as you drive away from the lot—get directions from the rental clerks when you do the paperwork. For information on parking in Paris, see page 530.

When returning your car, allow ample time to reach the drop-off lots (at T-1 and T-2), especially if flying out of T-2. Be sure you know your flight's departure hall in T-2 (for example, many Air France and Delta flights for North America leave from T-2E/F). There are separate rental return lots depending on your T-2 departure hall—and imperfect signage can make the return lots especially confusing to navigate.

From Charles de Gaulle Airport to Disneyland Paris

The Magical Shuttle bus to Disneyland leaves from T-2E/F, door 8 or T-1, door 34 (€20, runs about hourly from 9:00-19:45, 45 minutes, www.magicalshuttle.co.uk). TGV trains run to Disneyland from the airport in 10 minutes, but they leave only hourly and require a shuttle bus ride at the Disneyland end.

ORLY AIRPORT

This easy-to-navigate airport (airport code: ORY) feels small, but it has all the services you'd expect at a major airport: ATMs and currency exchange, car-rental desks, cafés, shops, post offices, and more (for airport and flight info, see www.adp.fr). Orly is good for rental-car pickup and drop-off, as it's closer to Paris and far easier to navigate than Charles de Gaulle Airport.

Orly has two terminals: Ouest (west) and Sud (south). Air France and a few other carriers arrive at Ouest; most others use Sud. At both terminals, arrivals are on the ground level (level 0)

CONNECTIONS

and departures are on level 1. You can connect the two terminals with the free Orlyval shuttle train (well signed).

Services: Both terminals have Paris Tourisme desks in the arrivals area (a good spot to buy the Paris Museum Pass and tickets for public transit into Paris). There are also airport information desks (called ADP, near baggage claim) with information on flights, public transit into Paris, and help with other airport-related questions. Both terminals offer free Wi-Fi.

Getting Between Orly Airport and Paris

Shuttle buses *(navettes)*, the RER, taxis, and airport vans connect Paris with either terminal. Bus stops and taxis are centrally located at arrivals levels and are well signed.

By Bus or Tram: Bus bays are found in the Sud terminal outside exits L and G, and in the Ouest terminal outside exit D.

Le Bus Direct route #1 runs to Gare Montparnasse, La Motte-Picquet, Eiffel Tower, Trocadéro, and Arc de Triomphe/ Etoile stops (all except La Motte-Picquet have direct connections to Métro lines). For Rue Cler hotels near the Ecole Militaire Métro stop, take Le Bus Direct to La Motte-Picquet, then walk across the Champ de Mars park to your hotel. Buses depart from the arrivals level—Ouest exit B-C or Sud exit L—look for signs to *navettes* (€12 one-way, 4/hour, 40 minutes to La Motte-Picquet, buy ticket from driver or book online—be sure to print out and bring your tickets with you). See www.lebusdirect.com for details on round-trip and group discounts.

For the cheapest (but slow) access to the Marais area, take **tramway line 7** from outside the Sud terminal (direction: Villejuif-Louis Aragon) to the Villejuif station to catch Métro line 7 (you'll need one Métro ticket for the tram and one for the Métro—buy a *carnet* of 10 tickets at the Paris Tourisme desk in the terminal, 4/ hour, 45 minutes to Villejuif Métro station, then 15-minute Métro ride to the Marais).

By RER: These options take you to the RER suburban train line B, with access to the Luxembourg Garden area, Notre-Dame Cathedral, handy Métro line 1 at the Châtelet stop, Gare du Nord, and Charles de Gaulle Airport. The **Orlybus** goes directly to the Denfert-Rochereau Métro and RER-B stations (€7.50, 3/hour, 30 minutes).

The pricier but more frequent—and more comfortable— **Orlyval shuttle train** takes you to the Antony RER-B station (€10, 6/hour, 40 minutes, buy ticket before boarding). The Orlyval train is well signed and leaves from the departure level at both Orly terminals. Once at the RER-B station, take the train in direction: Mitry-Claye or Aéroport Charles de Gaulle to reach central Paris stops.

For access to RER line C, take the bus marked ***Pont de Rungis***. From the Pont de Rungis station, catch the RER-C to Gare d'Austerlitz, St. Michel/Notre-Dame, Musée d'Orsay, Invalides, and Pont de l'Alma (€7.50, 4/hour, 35 minutes).

By Taxi: Taxis are outside the Ouest terminal exit B, and to the far right as you leave the Sud terminal at exit M. Allow 30 minutes for a taxi ride into central Paris (fixed fare of €30 for Left Bank, €35 for Right Bank).

By Airport Van: From Orly, figure about €23 for one person or €30 for two (less per person for larger groups and kids). For more on airport vans, see page 514.

From Orly Airport to Disneyland Paris

The Magical Shuttle bus to Disneyland departs from the main bus bays at both terminals (€20, runs hourly about 9:00-20:00, 45 minutes, www.magicalshuttle.co.uk).

BEAUVAIS AIRPORT

Budget airlines such as Ryanair use this small airport, offering dirt-cheap airfares but leaving you 50 miles north of Paris. Still, this airport has direct buses to Paris and is handy for travelers heading to Normandy or Belgium (car rental available). The airport is basic, waiting areas are crowded, and services are sparse, but improvements are gradually on the way (airport code: BVA, airport tel. 08 92 68 20 66, www.aeroportbeauvais.paris).

Getting Between Beauvais Airport and Paris

By Bus: Buses depart from the airport when they're full (about 20 minutes after flights arrive) and take 1.5 hours to reach Paris. Buy your ticket (€17 one-way) at the little kiosk to the right as you exit the airport. Buses arrive at Porte Maillot on the west edge of Paris (on Métro line 1 and RER-C). The closest taxi stand is at the Hôtel Hyatt Regency.

Buses heading to Beauvais Airport leave from Porte Maillot about 3.5 hours before scheduled flight departures. Catch the bus in the parking lot on Boulevard Pershing next to the Hyatt Regency. Arrive with enough time to purchase your bus ticket before boarding or buy online at http://tickets.aeroportbeauvais.com.

By Train: Trains connect Beauvais' city center and Paris' Gare du Nord (20/day, 1.5 hours). To reach the Beauvais train station, take the Beauvais *navette* shuttle bus (€5, 6/day, 30 minutes) or local bus #12 (12/day, 30 minutes).

By Taxi: Cabs run from Beauvais Airport to the Beauvais train station or city center (€15-20), or to central Paris (allow €150 and 1.5 hours).

Getting from Beauvais Airport to Disneyland Paris

The Magical Shuttle bus to Disneyland is available by appointment from Beauvais via Charles de Gaulle Airport (price varies with number of passengers, 2-3/day, 2.5 hours, www.magicalshuttle. co.uk).

CONNECTING PARIS' AIRPORTS
Charles de Gaulle and Orly

Le Bus Direct #3 directly and conveniently links Charles de Gaulle and Orly airports (€21, stops at Charles de Gaulle T-1 and T-2 and Orly Ouest exit B-C or Sud exit L, roughly 2/hour 5:45-23:00, 1 hour, www.lebusdirect.com).

RER-B connects Charles de Gaulle and Orly but requires a transfer to the Orlyval train. It isn't as easy as the Le Bus Direct mentioned above, but it's faster when there's traffic (€19, 5/hour, 1.5 hours). This line splits at both ends: Heading from Charles de Gaulle to Orly, take trains that serve the Antony stop (direction: St-Rémy-les-Chevreuse), then transfer to the Orlyval shuttle train; heading from Orly to Charles de Gaulle, take trains that end at the airport—Aéroport Charles de Gaulle-Roissy, not Mitry-Claye.

Taxis take about one hour and are easiest, but pricey (about €80).

Charles de Gaulle and Beauvais

You can connect Charles de Gaulle to Beauvais via train. From Charles de Gaulle, take the **RER-B** to Gare du Nord, catch a train to the town of Beauvais, and then a shuttle or local bus to Beauvais Airport (see above).

Taxis between Charles de Gaulle and Beauvais take one hour and cost about €120.

Orly and Beauvais

To transfer from Orly to Beauvais, you can take the Orlybus or Orlyval shuttle train (described above, under "Orly Airport") to the RER suburban train station, then hop on the **RER-B** to Gare du Nord. From there, catch a train to the town of Beauvais and then a shuttle or local bus to the airport (see "Beauvais Airport," above).

It's about a 1.5-hour **taxi** ride between Orly and Beauvais (about €165).

By Train

In this section, I provide an overview of Paris' major train stations and some specialty train routes from Paris (including the Eurostar). For help on looking up train schedules, buying tickets, and using France's long-distance rail system, see page 664.

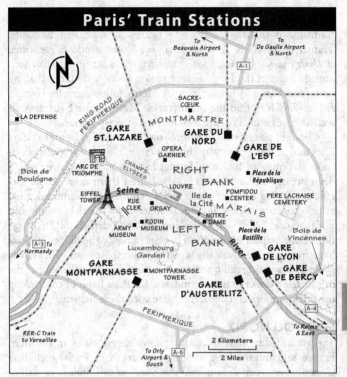

Paris' Train Stations

To Beauvais Airport & North

To De Gaulle Airport & North

A-1

RING ROAD PERIPHERIQUE

LA DEFENSE

SACRE-CŒUR

MONTMARTRE

GARE ST. LAZARE

GARE DU NORD

GARE DE L'EST

OPERA GARNIER

ARC DE TRIOMPHE

CHAMPS-ELYSEES

RIGHT BANK

Place de la République

Bois de Boulogne

EIFFEL TOWER

Seine

RUE CLER

LOUVRE

ORSAY

Ile de la Cité

POMPIDOU CENTER

PERE LACHAISE CEMETERY

MARAIS

NOTRE-DAME

ARMY MUSEUM

RODIN MUSEUM

LEFT BANK

Place de la Bastille

Bois de Vincennes

A-3 To Normandy

Luxembourg Garden

River

GARE DE LYON

GARE MONTPARNASSE

MONTPARNASSE TOWER

GARE D'AUSTERLITZ

GARE DE BERCY

A-4

PERIPHERIQUE

RER-C Train to Versailles

To Orly Airport & South

A-6

To Reims & East

2 Kilometers

2 Miles

CONNECTIONS

Paris is Europe's rail hub, with six major stations and one minor one, and trains heading in different directions:

- Gare du Nord (northbound trains)
- Gare Montparnasse (west- and southwest-bound trains)
- Gare de Lyon (southeast-bound trains)
- Gare de l'Est (eastbound trains)
- Gare St. Lazare (northwest-bound trains)
- Gare d'Austerlitz (southwest-bound trains)
- Gare de Bercy (smaller station with non-TGV southbound trains)

The main train stations all have free Wi-Fi, banks or currency exchanges, ATMs, train information desks, telephones, cafés, newsstands, and clever pickpockets (pay attention in ticket lines—keep your bag firmly gripped in front of you). Because of security concerns, not all have baggage checks.

Any train station has schedule information, can make reservations, and can sell tickets for any destination. Buying tickets can be handier from an SNCF neighborhood office (see the "SNCF Boutiques" sidebar on page 526).

Each station offers two types of rail service: long distance to other cities, called Grandes Lignes (major lines, TGV or TER trains); and suburban service to nearby areas, called Banlieue, Transilien, or RER. You also may see ticket windows identified as *Ile de France*. These are for Transilien trains serving destinations outside Paris in the Ile de France region (usually no more than an hour from Paris). When arriving by Métro, follow signs for *Grandes Lignes-SNCF* to find the main tracks. Métro and RER trains, as well as buses and taxis, are well marked at every station.

Budget plenty of time before your departure to factor in ticket lines and making your way through large, crowded stations. Paris train stations can be intimidating, but if you slow down, take a deep breath, and ask for help, you'll find them manageable and efficient. Bring a pad of paper and a pen for clear communication at ticket/info windows. It helps to write down the ticket you want. For instance: "28/05/17 Paris-Nord → Lyon dep. 18:30." All stations have helpful information booths *(accueil);* the bigger stations have roving helpers, usually wearing red or blue vests. They're capable of answering rail questions more quickly than the staff at the information desks or ticket windows. I make a habit of confirming my track number and departure time with these helpers.

GARE DU NORD

The granddaddy of Paris' train stations serves cities in northern France and international destinations north of Paris, including Copenhagen, Amsterdam, and the Eurostar to London, as well as two of the day trips described in this book (Chantilly and Auvers-sur-Oise).

From the Métro, follow *Grandes Lignes* signs (main lines) to reach the tracks at street level. Grandes Lignes trains depart from tracks 2-21 (tracks 20 and 21 are around the corner), suburban Banlieue/Transilien lines from tracks 30-36 (signed *Réseau Ile-de-France*), and RER trains from tracks 37-44 (tracks 41-44 are one floor below). Glass train-information booths *(accueil)* are scattered throughout the station, and information-helpers circulate (all rail staff speak English).

There's a helpful TI (labeled *Paris Tourisme*) kiosk near track 19 that sells Paris Museum Passes and fast-pass *"coupe-file"* tickets (credit cards only). Information booths for the **Thalys** trains (high-speed trains to Brussels and Amsterdam; see page 527) are opposite track 8. All international and main-line ticket sales are at the windows opposite tracks 8 and 12. The ticket counters are split between trains leaving today *(Departs pour ce Jour)* and departures for another day *(Departs pour un autre Jour)*. Use the touch-screen computers at the entrance (English available) to get your ticket-window number. Tickets for suburban trains are sold at the windows past track 19.

Eurostar trains (to London via the Chunnel) check in on the second level, up the stairs near track 17, or up the glass elevator near track 10. For more on the Eurostar, see page 528.

Pay WCs are down the stairs across from track 10. Baggage check and rental cars are near track 3 and down the steps. Taxis are out the door past track 3. Steps down to the Métro are opposite tracks 10 and 19.

Key Destinations Served by Gare du Nord Grandes Lignes: **Auvers-sur Oise** (hourly, 1.5 hours with transfer, one direct train April-Oct Sat-Sun only at about 9:30, 35 minutes), **Chantilly-Gouvieux** (hourly, fewer on weekends, 25 minutes, also served by slower RER-D lines), **Brussels** (at least hourly, 1.5 hours), **Bruges** (at least hourly, 2.5-3 hours, change in Brussels), **Amsterdam** (9/day direct, 3.5 hours), **Berlin** (4/day, 8.5 hours, change in Cologne or Dortmund), **Koblenz** (4/day, 5 hours, change in Cologne, more from Gare de l'Est that don't cross Belgium), and **London** by Eurostar (1-2/hour, 2.5 hours).

By Banlieue/RER Lines: **Chantilly-Gouvieux** (3/hour, 50 minutes), **Charles de Gaulle Airport** (4/hour, 35 minutes, track 41-44), and **Pontoise** (2/hour, 50 minutes).

GARE MONTPARNASSE

This big, modern station covers three floors, serves lower Normandy and Brittany, and has TGV service to the Loire Valley and southwestern France, as well as suburban service to Chartres.

Baggage check *(consignes)* and WCs are on the mezzanine *(entresol)* level. Most services are provided on the top level (second floor up, Hall 1), where all trains arrive and depart. Trains to Chartres usually depart from tracks 18-24, and the main rail information office *(accueil)* is opposite track 16. As you face the tracks, to the far left and outside are Le Bus Direct buses to Orly and Charles de Gaulle airports (on Rue du Commandant René Mouchotte). Taxis are to the far right as you face the tracks. Car-rental desks are also to the right, along track 24 and up the escalator to Hall 2 (except Hertz, which is outside the station at 15 Rue du Commandant René Mouchotte).

City buses are out front, between the train station and the Montparnasse Tower (down the escalator through the glassy facade). Bus #96 is good for connecting to Marais and Luxembourg area hotels, while #92 is ideal for Rue Cler hotels (both easier than the Métro).

Key Destinations Served by Gare Montparnasse: Chartres (14/day, 1 hour), **Amboise** (8/day in 1.5 hours with change in St-Pierre-des-Corps, requires TGV reservation; non-TGV trains leave from Gare d'Austerlitz), **Pontorson/Mont St-Michel** (5/day, 5.5 hours, via Rennes or Caen), **Dinan** (6/day, 4 hours, change

Key Transportation Phrases

French	English
accueil (ah-kuh-ee)	information/assistance
niveau (nee-voh)	level
billets (bee-yay)	tickets
réservation (ray-zehr-vah-see-oh<u>n</u>)	reservation
départs (day-par)	departures
arrivées (ah-ree-vay)	arrivals
aller simple (ah-lay sa<u>n</u>-pluh)	one-way
aller-retour (ah-lay ruh-toor)	round-trip
à l'heure (ah lur)	on time
côté fenêtre/couloir (koh-tay fuh-neh-truh/ kool-wahr)	window/aisle seat
fenêtre isolée (fuh-neh-truh ee-zoh-lay)	single seat by window (first class only)
voyageurs munis de billets (voy-ah-zhur moo-nee duh bee-yay)	travelers with tickets
navette (nah-veht)	shuttle bus
Grandes Lignes (grah<u>n</u>d leen-yuh)	major domestic and international lines

in Rennes and Dol), **Bordeaux** (20/day, 3.5 hours), **Sarlat** (4/day, 6-6.5 hours, change in Libourne or Bordeaux), **Toulouse** (8/day, 5-7 hours, most require change, usually in Bordeaux), **Albi** (4/day, 6.5-9 hours, change in Montauban or Toulouse), **Tours** (8/day, 1 hour), **Madrid** (2/day, 13-14 hours, 3-4 changes), and **Lisbon** (2/day, 21-24 hours via Irun).

GARE DE LYON

This huge, bewildering station offers TGV and regular service to southeastern France, Italy, Switzerland, and other international destinations. Frequent Banlieue trains serve Fontainebleau.

From the RER or Métro, follow signs for *Grandes Lignes* to reach the street-level platforms (Grandes Lignes and Banlieue lines share the same tracks). Platforms are divided into two areas: Hall 1 (tracks A-N, shaded in light blue on signs) and Hall 2 (tracks 5-23, shaded in yellow). Hall 3 is underground with more ticket offices and services but no trains.

Monitors indicate the hall number well before the track number is posted, so you know in advance which hall your train leaves from. An interior corridor connecting the halls (by track

French	English
RER (ehr-uh-her)	suburban lines
Transilien (trahn-seel-ee-yehn)	suburban lines
RATP (ehr ah tay pay)	Paris' Métro and bus system
SNCF (S N say F)	France's countrywide train system
TGV (tay zhay vay)	high-speed lines
banlieue (bahn-lee-yuh)	suburban
quai (kay)	platform
accès aux quais (ahk-seh oh kay)	access to the platforms
voie (vwah)	track
retard (ruh-tar)	delay
salle d'attente (sahl dah-tahnt)	waiting room
consignes (kohn-seen-yuh)	baggage check (also *espaces bagages*)
consignes automatique (kohn-seen-yuh oh-toh-mah-teek)	storage lockers
première classe (pruhm-yehr klahs)	first class
deuxième classe (duhz-yehm klahs)	second class

CONNECTIONS

A) offers many services, including shops and ticket windows for Grandes Lignes and suburban trains *(billets Ile de France)*. Train information booths are opposite tracks A and M in Hall 1 and near track 11 in Hall 2 (others are downstairs). Hall 2 has the best services—including a pharmacy and a good Monop grocery store. You'll find baggage check *(consignes)* in Hall 2 down the ramp, opposite track 17, and in Hall 1, downstairs by track M. Car rental is out the exit past track M (Hall 1).

Don't leave this station without at least taking a peek at the recommended Le Train Bleu Restaurant in Hall 1, up the stairs opposite tracks G-L (see listing on page 449). Its pricey but atmospheric bar/lounge works well as a quiet waiting area—and there's free (and fast) Wi-Fi. Slip into a leather chair and time travel back to another era.

Taxi stands are well-signed in front of, and underneath, the station. **Le Bus Direct** coaches, to Gare Montparnasse (easy transfer to Orly Airport) and direct to Charles de Gaulle Airport, stop outside the station's main entrance. They are signed *Navette-Aéroport*. To find them, exit Hall 1 with your back to track A. Walk down the ramp with the Café Européen a bit to your right. Turn right at the street (Boulevard Diderot) and find the shelter at the next corner across from Café Les Deux Savoies. (Buses normally depart at :15 and :45 after the hour; see page 512.)

Key Destinations Served by Gare de Lyon: Fontainebleau (nearly hourly, 45 minutes; depart from the Grandes Lignes level), **Disneyland** (RER line A-4 to Marne-la-Vallée-Chessy, at least 3/hour, 45 minutes), **Beaune** (roughly hourly at rush hour but few midday, 2.5 hours, most require change in Dijon; direct trains from Paris' Bercy station take an hour longer), **Dijon** (roughly hourly at rush hour but few midday, 1.5 hours), **Chamonix** (7/day, 5.5-7 hours, some change in Switzerland), **Annecy** (hourly, 4 hours, many with change in Lyon), **Lyon** (at least hourly, 2 hours), **Avignon** (10/day direct, 2.5 hours to Avignon TGV Station, 5/day in 3.5 hours to Avignon Centre-Ville Station, more connections with change—3-4 hours), **Arles** (11/day, 2 direct TGVs—4 hours, 9 with change in Avignon—5 hours), **Nice** (hourly, 6 hours, may require change), **Carcassonne** (8/day, 7-8 hours, 1 change), **Zürich** (4/day direct, 4 hours), **Venice** (4/day, 9.5-11.5 hours with 1-3 changes; 1 direct overnight, 14.5 hours, operated by Thello—which doesn't accept rail passes, important to reserve ahead at www.thello.com), **Rome** (2/day, 10.5-12 hours, 1-3 changes), **Bern** (1/day direct, 6/day with change in Basel, 4-5 hours), **Interlaken** (1/day direct, 4/day with change in Basel, 5-5.5 hours, 8/day more from Gare de l'Est), and **Barcelona** (2-4/day direct, 6.5 hours).

GARE DE L'EST

This two-floor station (with underground Métro) serves northeastern France and international destinations east of Paris. It's easy to navigate: All trains depart at street level from tracks 1-30. Check the departure monitors to see which section your train leaves from: Departures marked with a yellow square leave from tracks 2-12, while those marked with a blue square depart from tracks 23-30 (suburban Banlieue trains depart from tracks 13-22).

The main *billeterie* or ticket office for long-distance trains is in the hall opposite track 9 (nearby yellow ticket machines are handy for those with chip-and-PIN credit cards). A train information office is opposite track 17, and ticket sales are at each end of the station through the halls opposite tracks 8 and 25. White ticket machines between tracks 15-19 are for suburban trains only (coins or credit cards). A TI is opposite track 2 (Mon-Sat 8:00-19:00, closed Sun). Most other services are down the escalator through the hall opposite tracks 12-20 (baggage lockers, car rental, WC, small grocery store, more shops, and Métro access). There's a post office at track level, near the top of the escalators. Access to taxis and buses is in front of the station (exit with your back to the tracks).

Key Destinations Served by Gare de l'Est: Vaux-le-Vicomte

(take train to Verneuil-l'Etang, direction: Provins, 1/hour, 30 minutes, and catch connecting bus from there, see page 568 for details), **Colmar** (12/day with TGV, 3.5 hours, change in Strasbourg), **Strasbourg** (hourly with TGV, 2.5 hours), **Reims** Centre station (12/day with TGV, 50 minutes), **Verdun** (3/day direct via TGV and shuttle bus, 1.5 hours; 3.5 hours by regional train with transfer in Chalôns-en-Champagne), **Interlaken** (8/day, 6.5-8.5 hours, 1-2 changes, faster trains from Gare de Lyon), **Zürich** (12/day, 5-7 hours, 1-2 changes, faster direct trains from Gare de Lyon), **Frankfurt** (4 direct/day, 4 hours; 3 more/day with change in Karlsruhe, 4.5 hours), **Vienna** (7/day, 11-12 hours, 1-3 changes), **Prague** (3/day, 11 hours, 1-2 changes), **Munich** (1/day direct, 6/day with 1 change, 6 hours), and **Berlin** (3/day, 8.5 hours, change in Frankfurt).

GARE ST. LAZARE

This compact station serves upper Normandy, including Rouen and Giverny. All trains arrive and depart one floor above street level.

From the Métro, follow signs to *Grandes Lignes* to reach the tracks (long walk). Grandes Lignes to all destinations listed below depart from tracks 18-27; Banlieue trains depart from 1-16. The ticket office and car rental are near track 27. The main train information office *(accueil)* is near track 21; others are scattered about the station. WCs are opposite track 17. This station has no baggage check, but it does have a three-floor shopping mall (Monop grocery store, pharmacy, clothing stores, and more). Taxis, the Métro, and buses are well signed.

Key Destinations Served by Gare St. Lazare: Giverny (train to Vernon, 8/day Mon-Sat, 6/day Sun, 45 minutes), **Pontoise** (1-2/hour, 45 minutes), **Rouen** (nearly hourly, 1.5 hours), **Le Havre** (hourly, 2.5 hours, some change in Rouen), **Honfleur** (13/day, 2-3.5 hours, via Lisieux, Deauville, or Le Havre, then bus), **Bayeux** (9/day, 2.5 hours, some change in Caen), **Caen** (14/day, 2 hours), and **Pontorson/Mont St-Michel** (2/day, 4-5.5 hours, via Caen; more trains from Gare Montparnasse).

GARE D'AUSTERLITZ

This small station currently provides non-TGV service to the Loire Valley, southwestern France, and Spain (several tracks are being retrofitted to accommodate TGV trains in the future). All tracks are at street level. The information booth and a comfortable waiting room are opposite track 17, and all ticket sales are in the entry hall. Baggage check and car rental are along the side of the station, opposite track 21. You'll find WCs (with €10 showers that include towel and soap) at track 21. To get to the Métro and RER, you must walk outside and along either side of the station. To reach

CONNECTIONS

SNCF Boutiques

You can save time and stress by buying train tickets or making train reservations at an SNCF Boutique. These small branch offices of the French national rail company are conveniently located throughout Paris, with offices near most of my recommended hotels and museums and at Charles de Gaulle and Orly airports. Arrive when they open to avoid lines (generally open Mon-Sat 8:30-19:00 or 20:00, closed Sun).

Historic Core
- 18 Rue du Pont Neuf, Mo: Pont Neuf

Marais
- 2 Rue de Turenne, Mo: St. Paul

Near Major Museums
- Musée d'Orsay RER station, below Orsay Museum
- Forum des Halles shopping mall, basement sublevel -4, returns office (Salle d'Echanges), Mo: Châtelet-Les Halles

Champs-Elysées
- 229 Rue du Faubourg St. Honoré, Mo: St. Philippe-du-Roule

Farther North on the Right Bank
- 53 Rue Chaussée d'Antin, Mo: Chaussée d'Antin (near Opéra Garnier and Galeries Lafayette)
- 32/34 Rue Joubert, Mo: Haussman-St. Lazare (near Gare St. Lazare)
- 71/73 Boulevard Magenta, Mo: Gare du Nord (Gare du Nord)
- 82 Avenue de la Grande Armée, Mo: Porte Maillot (near Hôtel Concorde-Lafayette and Beauvais Airport bus stop)

Eiffel Tower/Rue Cler
- 80 Rue Saint Dominique, Mo: La Tour Maubourg
- 19 Rue de Passy, Mo: Passy (near Marmottan Museum)
- Invalides Métro/RER station

Latin Quarter/Luxembourg Garden
- 54 Boulevard St. Michel, Mo: Cluny-Sorbonne
- 79 Rue de Rennes, Mo: St. Sulpice

Farther South on the Left Bank
- 17 Rue Littré, Mo: Montparnasse-Bienvenüe (near Luxembourg Garden and grand cafés)
- 68 Avenue du Maine, Mo: Montparnasse-Bienvenüe (near grand cafés)
- 30 Avenue d'Italie, in Centre Commerciale Galaxie, Mo: Place d'Italie

You'll also find quieter SNCF Boutiques in train stations of the towns I suggest for day trips from Paris, such as Versailles, Fontainebleau, Melun (for Vaux-le-Vicomte), Chartres, Chantilly, Vernon (for Giverny), and Pontoise (for Auvers-sur-Oise).

Gare de Lyon on foot (a level 10-minute walk), follow signs opposite track 1.

Key Destinations Served by Gare d'Austerlitz: Orly Airport (via RER-C, 4/hour, 35 minutes), **Versailles** (via RER-C, 4/hour, 35 minutes), **Amboise** (3/day direct in 2 hours, more with transfer; faster TGV connection from Gare Montparnasse), **Sarlat** (1/day, 6.5 hours, requires change to bus in Souillac, 3 more/day via Gare Montparnasse), **Carcassonne** (1 direct night train, 7.5 hours, better day trains from Gare de Lyon), and **Cahors** (5/day, 5 hours; slower trains from Gare Montparnasse).

GARE DE BERCY

This smaller station mostly handles southbound non-TGV trains, but some TGV trains do stop here in peak season (Mo: Bercy, one stop east of Gare de Lyon on line 14, exit the Bercy Métro station and it's across the street). Facilities are limited—just a WC and a sandwich-fare takeout café.

SPECIALTY TRAINS FROM PARIS
To Brussels and Amsterdam by Thalys Train

The pricey Thalys train has the monopoly on the rail route between Paris and Brussels. Without a rail pass, for the Paris-Amsterdam train, you'll pay about €80-205 first class, €35-135 second class (compared to €38-50 by bus); for the Paris-Brussels train it's €65-140 first class, €30-100 second class (€20-30 by bus). Even with a rail pass, you need to pay for train reservations (first class-€30-35, includes a meal; second class-€20-25). Book early for the best rates (seats are limited in various discount categories, www.thalys.com).

Thalys also operates a slower, cheaper Paris to Brussels train called IZY (2-3/day, 2.5 hours, tickets from €10 for standing room to €29 full fare, rail passes not accepted, luggage limits, online only at www.izy.com). For another cheap option, try the Eurolines bus or OuiBus operated by SNCF (see "Paris Bus Connections," below).

Low-Cost TGV Trains to Southern France

A TGV train called OuiGo (pronounced "we go") offers a direct connection from Disneyland Paris to select cities in southern France at rock-bottom fares with no-frills service. The catch: These trains leave from the Marne-la-Vallée TGV station, an hour from Paris on RER-A. So you can hang at Disneyland Paris before (or after) your trip south and connect with a direct TGV. You must print your own ticket ahead of time, arrive 30 minutes before departure, and activate your ticket. You can't use a rail pass, and you can only bring one carry-on-size bag plus one handbag for free (children's tickets allow you to bring a stroller). Larger or extra luggage is €5/

bag if you pay when you buy your ticket. If you just show up without paying in advance, it's €20/bag on the train—yikes. There's no food service on the train (BYO), but children under age 12 pay only €5 for a seat. The website explains it all in easy-to-understand English (www.ouigo.com).

To London by Eurostar Train

The fastest and most convenient way to get from the Eiffel Tower to Big Ben is by rail. Eurostar zips you (and up to 800 others in 18 sleek cars) from downtown Paris to downtown London at 190 mph in 2.5 hours (1-2/hour). The tunnel crossing is a 20-minute, silent, 100-mile-per-hour nonevent. Your ears won't even pop.

Eurostar Fares: The Eurostar is not covered by rail passes and always requires a separate, reserved train ticket. Eurostar fares vary depending on how far ahead you reserve and whether you're eligible for any discounts.

A **one-way, full-fare ticket** runs about $225 (Standard), $310 (Standard Premier), and $380 (Business Premier). **Discounts** can lower fares substantially (figure $45-160 for Standard class, one-way) for children under 12, youths under 26, adults booking months ahead or traveling round-trip, and rail-pass holders. The early bird gets the best price. If you're ready to commit, you can book tickets as early as four to nine months in advance.

Buying Eurostar Tickets: Because only the most expensive (Business Premier) ticket is refundable, and other rates have exchange restrictions, don't reserve until you're sure of your plans. But if you wait too long, the cheapest tickets will be gone.

You can buy tickets online using the print-at-home eticket option at www.ricksteves.com/eurostar or www.eurostar.com. You can also order by phone through Rail Europe (US tel. 800-387-6782) for home delivery before you go, or through Eurostar (French tel. 08 92 35 35 39, priced in euros) to pick up at the train station. In continental Europe you can buy your Eurostar tickets at any major train station in any country, at neighborhood SNCF offices (see the "SNCF Boutiques" sidebar, earlier), or at any travel agency that handles train tickets (expect a booking fee). Discount tickets for rail pass holders (which can sell out) are available at Eurostar departure stations, through US agents, or by phone with Eurostar,

Building the Chunnel

The toughest obstacle to building a tunnel under the English Channel was overcome in 1986, when longtime rivals Britain and France reached an agreement to build it together. Britain began in Folkestone, France in Calais, planning a rendezvous in the middle.

By 1988, specially-made machines three football fields long were boring 26-foot-wide tubes under the ground. The dirt they hauled out became landfill in Britain and a hill in France. Crews crept forward 100 feet a day until June 1991, when French and English workers broke through and shook hands midway across the Channel—the tunnel was complete. Rail service began in 1994.

The Chunnel is 31 miles long—24 miles of it under water. It sits 130 feet below the seabed in a chalky layer of sediment. It's segmented into three separate tunnels—two for trains (one in each direction) and one for service and ventilation. The walls are concrete panels and rebar fixed to the rock around it. Sixteen-thousand-horsepower engines pull 850 tons of rail-cars and passengers at speeds up to 100 mph through the tunnel.

The ambitious project—the world's longest undersea tunnel—helped to show the European community that cooperation between nations could benefit everyone.

but they may be harder to get at other train stations and travel agencies.

Taking the Eurostar: Eurostar trains depart from and arrive at Paris' Gare du Nord (see page 520). Check in at least 45 minutes in advance (remember that times listed on tickets are local times—departure from Paris is French time, arrival in London is British time). Pass through airport-like security, show your passport to customs officials, and locate your departure gate (shown on a TV monitor). The currency-exchange booth here has rates about the same as you'll find on the other end. There's a reasonable restaurant before the first check-in point, but there are only a couple of tiny sandwich-and-coffee counters in the cramped waiting area.

Crossing the Channel Without Eurostar: For speed and affordability, look into cheap flights (see page 671). The old-fashioned ways of crossing the Channel are cheaper than Eurostar (taking the bus is cheapest; see below). They're also twice as complicated and time-consuming.

To go by **train and boat** to London, take the TGV train from Paris to Calais, then catch a P&O ferry to Dover, England (hourly, 1.5 hours, www.poferries.com). From Dover's Priory Station, take a train to London's St. Pancras, Charing Cross, or Victoria Station (hourly, 1.5-2 hours).

By Bus, Car, or Cruise Ship

Below I've provided some information for travelers not arriving by plane or train.

PARIS BUS CONNECTIONS

The main bus station, Gare Routière du Paris-Gallieni, is in the suburb of Bagnolet (28 Avenue du Général de Gaulle, Mo: Gallieni). Buses provide cheaper—if less comfortable and more time-consuming—transportation to major European cities. The bus is also the cheapest way to cross the English Channel; book at least two days in advance for the best fares.

Eurolines' buses depart from here (toll tel. 08 92 89 90 91 inside France; from the US, dial 011 33 1 41 86 24 21, www. eurolines.com). Look on their website for offices in central Paris. **OuiBus** also offers cheap, Wi-Fi-equipped bus service with an English-speaking driver from Paris to London (6/day, 8 hours), Amsterdam (7/day, 6.5 hours), Cologne (3/day, 8 hours), and other cities, including many in France (toll tel. 08 92 68 00 68 inside France, www.ouibus.com).

PARKING IN PARIS

Street parking is generally free at night (19:00-9:00) and all day Sunday. To pay for streetside parking, you must go to a *tabac* and buy a parking card *(une carte de stationnement)*, sold in €15 and €45 denominations (figure €2-4/hour in central Paris). Insert the card into the meter (chip-side in) and punch the desired amount of time, then take the receipt and display it in your windshield. Meters limit street parking to a maximum of two hours.

Underground garages are plentiful in Paris. You'll find them under Ecole Militaire, St. Sulpice Church, Les Invalides, the Bastille, and the Panthéon; all charge about €30-45/day (€60/3 days, €10/day more after that, for locations see www.vincipark. com). Some hotels offer parking for less—ask your hotelier.

For a longer stay, park for less at an airport (about €10/day) and take public transport or a taxi into the city. Orly is closer and easier for drivers to navigate than Charles de Gaulle.

LE HAVRE CRUISE PORT

Though it's a landlocked city, Paris is an increasingly popular cruise destination. Ships visiting "Paris" actually call at the industrial city of Le Havre, France's second-biggest port (after Marseille), and the primary French port on the Atlantic. Port information: www. cruiselehavre.com.

To reach Paris from Le Havre, it's about a 2.5-hour train ride each way. To get from the port to the Le Havre train/bus station, you can ride a cruise-line shuttle bus, take a taxi, or walk about 35 minutes. From there, trains leave about every 1-2 hours for the 2.5-hour journey to Paris' St. Lazare Station (fewer on weekends).

If you'd rather stick closer to your ship, consider these alternatives: the harbor town of Honfleur (30 minutes by bus); the historic D-Day beaches (an hour or so to the west); and the pleasant small city of Rouen (one hour by train).

For more details, see my *Rick Steves Northern European Cruise Ports* guidebook.

CONNECTIONS

DAY TRIPS FROM PARIS

Château de Versailles • More Grand Châteaux • Chartres • Giverny & Auvers-sur-Oise

Though there's plenty to see within Paris' ring-road, quick and efficient public transportation expands your sightseeing horizons. The sights covered in this section are about 30 to 60 minutes from central Paris. Do them as day trips, or—for a more relaxed experience—stay overnight.

The granddaddy of them all is the Palace of **Versailles,** 12 miles southwest of Paris. It was the residence of French kings and the cultural heartbeat of Europe for a century. While Versailles is the grandest of the **Grand Châteaux,** fans of these big palaces have plenty of other options, including Vaux-le-Vicomte (the most beautiful), Fontainebleau (thriving town center), or Chantilly (best art). In **Chartres,** an hour southwest of Paris, one of Europe's greatest Gothic cathedrals soars above lively traffic-free lanes and squares. Lovers of Impressionism should make a pilgrimage

to **Giverny** to see Claude Monet's garden, with its pond and lily pads still as picturesque as when he painted them. Fans of Vincent van Gogh can visit **Auvers-sur-Oise,** a modest little town that attracted many Impressionist painters, and where Van Gogh spent his final days gazing at crows over wheat fields.

Day Trips from Paris

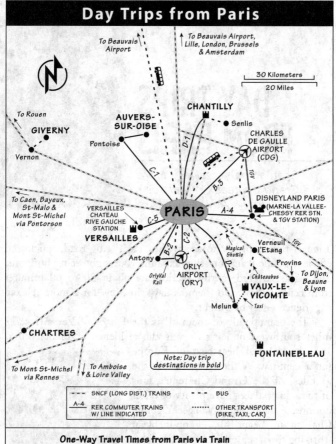

To Beauvais Airport

↑ To Beauvais Airport, Lille, London, Brussels & Amsterdam

30 Kilometers
20 Miles

To Rouen

GIVERNY

AUVERS-SUR-OISE

CHANTILLY

• Senlis

Pontoise

Vernon

CHARLES DE GAULLE AIRPORT (CDG)

D-1

C-1

B-3

TGV

To Caen, Bayeux, St-Malo & Mont St-Michel via Pontorson

VERSAILLES CHATEAU RIVE GAUCHE STATION

PARIS

C-5

A-4

DISNEYLAND PARIS (MARNE-LA VALLEE-CHESSY RER STN. & TGV STATION)

VERSAILLES

B-2

C-2

Antony

Magical Shuttle

Verneuil l'Etang

TGV

OrlyVal Rail

ORLY AIRPORT (ORY)

D-2

Provins

To Dijon, Beaune & Lyon

Châteaubus

VAUX-LE-VICOMTE

CHARTRES

Melun • Taxi

To Mont St-Michel via Rennes

To Amboise & Loire Valley

Note: Day trip destinations in bold

FONTAINEBLEAU

⟶ — — — SNCF (LONG DIST.) TRAINS   - - - BUS

A-4   RER COMMUTER TRAINS W/ LINE INDICATED   ······· OTHER TRANSPORT (BIKE, TAXI, CAR)

DAY TRIPS

One-Way Travel Times from Paris via Train

Day Trip Destinations:
Versailles: 35 min
Vaux-le-Vicomte: 65 min
Fontainebleau: 55 min
Chantilly: 35-60 min
Chartres: 60 min
Vernon (Giverny): 60 min
Auvers-sur-Oise: 35-90 min

Other Destinations:
Charles De Gaulle Airport: 45 min
Orly Airport: 35 min
Disneyland Paris: 45 min
Amboise/Loire Valley: 2 hrs
Bayeux/Caen (D-Day Beaches): 2.5 hrs

VERSAILLES

Château de Versailles

Every king's dream, Versailles (vehr-"sigh") was the residence of French monarchs and the cultural heartbeat of Europe for about 100 years—until the Revolution of 1789 changed all that. The Sun King (Louis XIV) created Versailles, spending freely from the public treasury to turn his dad's hunting lodge into a palace fit for the gods (among whom he counted himself). Louis XV and Louis XVI spent much of the 18th century gilding Louis XIV's lily. In 1837, about 50 years after the royal family was evicted by citizen-protesters, King Louis-Philippe opened the palace as a museum. Today you can visit parts of the huge palace and wander through acres of manicured gardens sprinkled with fountains and studded with statues. Europe's next-best palaces are just Versailles wannabes.

Worth ▲▲▲, Versailles offers three blockbuster sights. The main attraction is the palace itself, called the **Château.** Here you

walk through dozens of lavish, chandeliered rooms once inhabited by Louis XIV and his successors. Next come the expansive **Gardens** behind the palace, a landscaped wonderland crossed with footpaths and dotted with statues and fountains. Finally, at the far end of the Gardens, is the pastoral area called the **Trianon Palaces and Domaine de Marie-Antoinette** (a.k.a. Trianon/Domaine), designed for frolicking blue bloods and featuring several small palaces and Marie's Hamlet—perfect for getting away from the mobs at the Château.

Visiting Versailles can seem daunting because of its size and

Versailles

Petit Canal

Grand Canal

EXIT

GRAND TRIANON

WC

TRIANON TOUR BEGINS

ALLEE DE LA REINE

AVE. DE TRIANON

ALLEE DES MATELOTS

WC

RESTAURANT & SNACKS

T

BOAT RENTAL

ALLEE ST. ANTOINE

BIKE & GOLF CART RENTAL

B

Apollo Basin

ALLEE D'APOLLON

WC

ROUTE DE ST. CYR

(N-10)

KING'S GARDEN

G A R D E N S

COLONNADE

OBELISK GROVE

AVE. DE TRIANON

MIRROR FOUNTAIN

ROYAL DRIVE

STAR GROVE

WC & SNACK KIOSK

WC

QUEEN'S GROVE

Latona Basin

APOLLO'S BATHS GROVE

PORTE DE LA REINE

B

GARDENS TOUR BEGINS

GOLF-CART RENTAL

ORANGERIE

EXIT CHATEAU

ENTRANCE "A"

T

PETIT TRAIN

Neptune Basin

Pièce d'Eau des Suisses

VERSAILLES

CHATEAU

TICKET SALES

CHATEAU TOUR BEGINS

i

See detail map

1ST SECURITY CHECK

GUIDED TOURS

RUE CARNOT

KING'S VEGETABLE GARDEN

Place d'Armes

P

Place Hoche

RUE DE LA PAROISSE

NOTRE DAME

ST. LOUIS

RUE DE SATORY

AVENUE DE SCEAUX

DE PARIS

AVENUE

AVENUE DE ST-CLOUD

STABLES

STABLES

i

AVE. DU GENERAL DE GAULLE

B

RER TRAIN STATION
(VERSAILLES CHATEAU RIVE GAUCHE)

↓ To Paris

AVENUE DE

L'EUROPE

Place du Marché

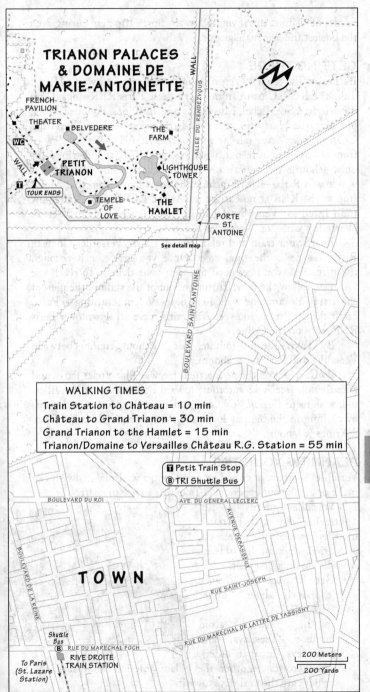

TRIANON PALACES & DOMAINE DE MARIE-ANTOINETTE

FRENCH PAVILION

THEATER

BELVEDERE

THE FARM

WC

WALL

PETIT TRIANON

LIGHTHOUSE TOWER

TOUR ENDS

TEMPLE OF LOVE

THE HAMLET

ALLEE DU RENDEZVOUS

WALL

PORTE ST. ANTOINE

See detail map

BOULEVARD SAINT-ANTOINE

WALKING TIMES
Train Station to Château = 10 min
Château to Grand Trianon = 30 min
Grand Trianon to the Hamlet = 15 min
Trianon/Domaine to Versailles Château R.G. Station = 55 min

T Petit Train Stop
B TRI Shuttle Bus

BOULEVARD DU ROI

AVE. DU GÉNÉRAL LECLERC

AVENUE DE PASSEUX

BOULEVARD DE LA REINE

T O W N

RUE SAINT-JOSEPH

RUE DU MARÉCHAL DE LATTRE DE TASSIGNY

Shuttle Bus

B RUE DU MARÉCHAL FOCH

RIVE DROITE TRAIN STATION

To Paris (St. Lazare Station)

200 Meters

200 Yards

VERSAILLES

hordes of visitors. But if you follow my tips, a trip here during even the busiest times is manageable.

GETTING THERE

By Train: The town of Versailles is 35 minutes southwest of Paris. Take the **RER-C train** from any of these Paris RER stops: Gare d'Austerlitz, St. Michel, Musée d'Orsay, Invalides, Pont de l'Alma, or Champ de Mars. Buy your round-trip ticket—ask for "Versailles Château, *aller-retour* (ah-lay ruh-toor)"—from a ticket window or from an easy-to-figure-out ticket machine (€7.10 round-trip, coins only, 4/hour). You can also buy train tickets at any Métro ticket window in Paris—it will include the connection from that Métro stop to the RER at no extra cost. At the RER station, catch any train listed as "Versailles Château Rive Gauche" (abbreviated to "Versailles Chât" or "Versailles RG").

Board your train and relax. On all trains, Versailles Château Rive Gauche is the final stop. Once you arrive, exit through the turnstiles (you may need to insert your ticket). To reach the Château, follow the flow: Turn right out of the station, then left at the first boulevard, and walk 10 minutes. When returning to Paris, catch the first train you see: All trains serve all downtown Paris RER stops on the C line.

By Taxi: The 30-minute ride (without traffic) between Versailles and Paris costs about €60.

By Car: Get on the *périphérique* freeway that circles Paris, and take the toll-free A-13 autoroute toward Rouen. Exit at Versailles, follow signs to *Versailles Château*, and avoid the hectic Garden lots by parking in the big pay lot at the foot of the Château on Place d'Armes (€4/hour).

PLANNING YOUR TIME

Versailles is all about crowd management; a well-planned visit can make or break your experience. Take this advice to heart.

Versailles merits a full sightseeing day and is much more enjoyable with a relaxed, unhurried approach. Here's what I'd do on a first visit:

- Get a pass in advance (explained later, under "Passes").
- In high season, avoid Sundays, Tuesdays, and Saturdays (in that order), when crowds smother the palace interior. Thursdays and Fridays are the best days to visit.

- Leave Paris by 7:45 and arrive at the palace as it opens at 8:30 (or leave earlier and have breakfast at the Hôtel IBIS across from Versailles' RER station—see page 565).
- In the morning, follow my self-guided tour of the Château's highlights.
- Have a canalside lunch at one of the sandwich kiosks or cafés in the Gardens. Spend the afternoon touring the Gardens, Trianon Palaces, and Domaine de Marie-Antoinette. On weekends from late March to October (and some Tue and Fri), enjoy music and/or flowing fountains in the Gardens. Stay for dinner in Versailles town, or head back to Paris.
- To shorten your visit, focus on the Château and Gardens and skip the Trianon/Domaine, which takes an additional 1.5 hours to see and a 30-minute walk each way.
- An alternate plan that works well is to arrive later in the morning. From Versailles Château Rive Gauche station, catch the shuttle bus (see the "Getting Around the Gardens" sidebar on page 555) to the Trianon Palaces and Domaine de Marie-Antoinette, and see them first (they open at noon). Then work your way back through the Gardens to the Château, arriving after the crowds have died down (usually by 14:00, later on Sun).

In general, allow 1.5 hours each for the Château, the Gardens (includes time for lunch), and the Trianon/Domaine. Add another two hours for round-trip transit, and you're looking at nearly an eight-hour day.

Orientation

Cost: Buy either a Paris Museum Pass or a Versailles Le Passeport Pass, both of which give you access to the most important parts of the complex (see "Passes," next). If you don't get a pass, buy individual tickets for each of the three different sections.

   The Château: €15, includes audioguide, under 18 free. Covers the famous Hall of Mirrors, the king's living quarters, many lesser rooms, and any temporary exhibitions. Free on the first Sunday Nov-March.

   The Trianon Palaces and Domaine de Marie-Antoinette: €10, no audioguide available, under 18 free. Covers the Grand Trianon and its gardens, the Petit Trianon, the queen's Hamlet, and a smattering of nearby buildings. Free on the first Sunday Nov-March.

   The Gardens: Free, except on Spectacle days, when admission is €9 (see "Spectacles in the Gardens," later).

Passes: The following passes can save money and allow you to skip ticket-buying lines (but not security checks). Both passes include the Château audioguide.

The **Paris Museum Pass** (see page 49) covers the Château and the Trianon/Domaine area (a €25 value) and is the best solution for most. It doesn't include the Gardens on Spectacle days.

The **Le Passeport** pass (€18 for one day, €25 for two days) covers the Château and the Trianon/Domaine area. On Spectacle days, it's €25 for one day, €30 for two.

Buying Passes and Tickets: Ideally, buy your ticket or pass before arriving at Versailles. You can purchase Versailles tickets at any Paris TI, FNAC department store (small fee), or at www.chateauversailles.fr (print out your pass/ticket at home or at your hotel). If you arrive in Versailles without a pass or a ticket, you can buy it at the rarely crowded Versailles TI, not far from the train station (10 percent fee—see "Information," later).

Your last and (usually) worst option is to buy a pass or ticket at the busy Château ticket-sales office (to the left as you face the palace). Ticket windows accept American credit cards. If there's a line, you can use the ticket machines at the back of the room (you'll need a chip-and-PIN card or bills).

Hours: The **Château** is open April-Oct Tue-Sun 8:30-19:00, Nov-March Tue-Sun 9:00-17:30, closed Mon year-round.

The **Trianon Palaces and Domaine de Marie-Antoinette** are open April-Oct Tue-Sun 12:00-18:30, Nov-March until 17:30, closed Mon year-round (off-season only the two Trianon Palaces and the Hamlet are open, not other outlying buildings), last entry 45 minutes before closing.

The **Gardens** are open April-Oct daily 8:00-20:30, Nov-March until 18:00, but may close earlier for special events.

Crowd-Beating Strategies: Versailles is packed May-Sept 9:30-13:00, so come early or late. Avoid Sundays, Tuesdays, and Saturdays (in that order), when the place is jammed with a slow shuffle of tourists from open to close. To skip the ticket-buying line, buy tickets or passes in advance, or book a guided tour. Unfortunately, all ticket holders—including those with advance tickets and passes—must go through the often-slow security checkpoint at the Château's courtyard entry and again at the Château entrance (longest lines 10:00-12:00). Consider seeing the Gardens during midmorning and the Château in the afternoon, when crowds die down.

Skip-the-line tickets from **GuidaTours** are hawked with vigor on your arrival at the Versailles RER station. Their €25 ticket gets you into the Château (but not the Gardens) without a wait (so you're paying an extra €10 to save line time, but you still must go through security). I'd consider it on busy days.

Skip their €35 guided tour ticket: You can get the same deal for €22 by booking a tour through the Château directly, with better skip-the-line privileges (see "Tours," later).

Pickpockets: Assume pickpockets are working the tourist crowds.

Information: Check the excellent website for updates and special events—www.chateauversailles.fr. The palace's general contact number is tel. 01 30 83 78 00. You'll pass the city **Tourist Office** on your walk from the RER station to the palace—it's just past the Pullman Hôtel (daily 9:00-19:00, Sun until 18:00, shorter hours in winter, free Wi-Fi, tel. 01 39 24 88 88). The information office at the Château is to the left as you face the Château (WCs, toll tel. 08 10 81 16 14).

Tours: The 1.5-hour English **guided tour** gives you access to a few extra rooms (the itinerary varies) and lets you skip the regular security line (€7, plus €15 palace entry if you don't have it; usually at least five tours in English between 9:00 and 15:00 April-Oct; off-season usually only at 9:30 and 14:00). Book a tour in advance on the palace's website, or reserve immediately upon arrival at the guided-tours office (to the right of the Château—look for yellow *Visites Conferences* signs). Tours can sell out by 13:00, though more are usually available than indicated on the website.

A free **audioguide** to the Château is included in your admission. Other podcasts and digital tours are available in the "multimedia" section at www.chateauversailles.fr.

🎧 Download my free Versailles **audio tour.**

Baggage Check: Free and located just after the Château entry security check. You must retrieve your items one hour before closing (maximum size is same as airlines allow for carry-on bags). Large bags and baby strollers are not allowed in the Château and the two Trianons (use a baby backpack or hire a babysitter for the day; see page 451).

Services: WCs are plentiful and well-signed in the Château. Those in the Gardens are further and fewer between.

Photography: Allowed, but no flash indoors.

Eating: To the left of the Château, the **$** Grand Café d'Orléans offers good-value self-service meals (sandwiches and small salads, great for picnicking in the Gardens). In the Gardens, you'll find several cafés and snack stands with fair prices. One is located near the Latona Fountain (less crowded) and others are in an atmospheric cluster at the Grand Canal (more crowds and more choices, including two restaurants).

Handy McDonald's and Starbucks (both with WCs) are across from the train station. In Versailles town center, the best choices are on the lively Place du Marché Notre-Dame, with a supermarket nearby (listed at the end of this chapter),

Kings and Queens and Guillotines

• *You could read this on the train ride to Versailles. Relax...the palace is the last stop.*

Come the Revolution, when they line us up and make us stick out our hands, will you have enough calluses to keep them from shooting you? A grim thought, but Versailles raises these kinds of questions. It's the architectural embodiment of the *ancien régime,* a time when society was divided into rulers and the ruled, when you were born to be rich or to be poor. To some it's the pinnacle of civilization; to others, the sign of a civilization in decay. Either way, it remains one of Europe's most impressive sights.

Versailles was the residence of the king and the seat of France's government for a hundred years. Louis XIV (r. 1643-1715) moved out of the Louvre in Paris, the previous royal residence, and built an elaborate palace in the forests and swamps of Versailles, 10 miles west. The reasons for the move were partly personal—Louis XIV loved the outdoors and disliked the sniping environs of stuffy Paris—and partly political.

Louis XIV was creating the first modern, centralized state. At Versailles he consolidated his government's scattered ministries so that he could personally control policy. More importantly, he invited France's nobles to Versailles in order to control them. Living a life of almost enforced idleness, the "domesticated" aristocracy couldn't interfere with the way Louis ran things. With 18 million people united under one king (England had only 5.5 million), a booming economy, and a powerful military, France was Europe's number-one power.

Around 1700, Versailles was the cultural heartbeat of Europe, and French culture was at its zenith. Throughout Europe, when you said "the king," you were referring to the French king—Louis XIV. Every king wanted a palace like Versailles. Everyone learned French. French taste in clothes, hairstyles, table manners, theater, music, art, and kissing spread across the Continent. That cultural dominance continued, to some extent, right up to the 20th century.

Louis XIV

At the center of all this was Europe's greatest king. He was a true Renaissance Man, a century after the Renaissance: athletic, good-

or along traffic-free Rue de Satory, on the opposite (south) side as you leave the Château.

Spectacles in the Gardens: The Gardens and fountains at Versailles come alive at selected times, offering visitors a glimpse into Louis XIV's remarkable world. The Sun King had his engineers literally reroute a river to fuel his fountains and feed his plants. Even by today's standards, the fountains are imlooking, a musician, dancer, horseman, statesman, patron of the arts, and lover. For all his grandeur, he was one of history's most polite and approachable kings, a good listener who could put even commoners at ease in his presence.

Louis XIV called himself the Sun King because he gave life and warmth to all he touched. He was also thought of as Apollo, the Greek god of the sun. Versailles became the personal temple of this god on earth, decorated with statues and symbols of Apollo, the sun, and Louis XIV himself. The classical themes throughout underlined the divine right of France's kings and queens to rule without limit.

Louis XIV was a hands-on king who personally ran affairs of state. All decisions were made by him. Nobles, who in other countries were the center of power, became virtual slaves dependent on Louis XIV's generosity. For 70 years he was the perfect embodiment of the absolute monarch. He summed it up best himself with his famous rhyme—*"L'état, c'est moi!"* (lay-tah say-mwah): "The state, that's me!"

Another Louis or Two to Remember

Three kings lived in Versailles during its century of glory. Louis XIV built it and established French dominance. Louis XV, his great-grandson (Louis XIV reigned for 72 years), carried on the tradition and policies, but without the Sun King's flair. During Louis XV's reign (1715-1774), France's power abroad was weakening, and there were rumblings of rebellion from within.

France's monarchy was crumbling, and the time was ripe for a strong leader to reestablish the old feudal order. They didn't get one. Instead, they got Louis XVI (r. 1774-1792), a shy, meek bookworm, the kind of guy who lost sleep over revolutionary graffiti... because it was misspelled. Louis XVI married a sweet girl from the Austrian royal family, Marie-Antoinette, and together they retreated into the idyllic gardens of Versailles while revolutionary fires smoldered.

pressive. Check the Versailles website for current hours and for what else might be happening during your visit.

On nonwinter weekends the Gardens' fountains are in full squirt. The whole production, called **Les Grandes Eaux Musicales,** involves 55 fountains gushing for an hour in the morning, then again for about two hours in the afternoon, all accompanied by loud classical music (€9; late March-Oct Sat-Sun 11:00-12:00 & 15:30-17:00; plus Tue mid-May-June and

Fri late March-early May, same hours). Pay at the entrance to the Gardens, unless you've bought Le Passeport—in which case you've already paid (automatically tacked on to Passeport price on Spectacle days).

On most other in-season Tuesdays you get all-day music, but no water, with the **Les Jardins Musicaux** program (€8, April-mid-May and July-Oct Tue 10:00-18:30).

On certain summer weekend nights you get the big shebang: **Les Grandes Eaux Nocturnes,** which presents whimsical lighted displays leading between gushing fountains and a fireworks show over the largest fountain pool (€20-41, mid-June-mid-Sept Sat plus mid-June-mid-July Fri, 20:30-22:40, fireworks at 22:50).

Starring: Luxurious palaces, endless gardens, Louis XIV, Marie-Antoinette, and the *ancien régime.*

The Tour Begins

On this self-guided tour, we'll see the Château (the State Apartments of the king as well as the Hall of Mirrors), the landscaped Gardens in the "backyard," and the Trianon Palaces and Domaine de Marie-Antoinette, located at the far end of the Gardens. If your time is limited or you don't enjoy walking, I give you permission to skip the Trianon/Domaine, which is a hefty 30-minute hike (each way) from the Château.

The Château

• Stand in the huge courtyard and face the palace. The golden Royal Gate in the center of the courtyard—nearly 260 feet long and decorated with 100,000 gold leaves—is a replica of the original. The ticket-sales office is to the left; guided-tour sales are to the right. The entrance to the Château (once you have your ticket or pass) is marked Entrance A *(where the line usually is). Before entering (or while standing in line at the entrance), take in the Château and the open-air courtyard on the other side of the golden Royal Gate.*

The Original Château and the Courtyard

The section of the palace with the clock is the original château, once a small hunting lodge where little Louis XIV spent his happiest boyhood years. Naturally, the Sun King's private bedroom (the three arched windows beneath the clock) faced the rising sun. The palace and grounds are laid out on an east-west axis.

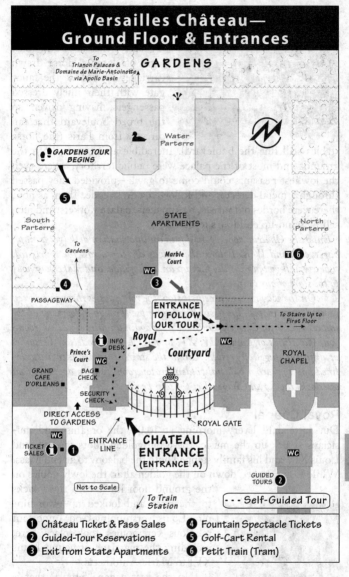

Versailles Château— Ground Floor & Entrances

GARDENS

To Trianon Palaces & Domaine de Marie-Antoinette via Apollo Basin

Water Parterre

GARDENS TOUR BEGINS

5

South Parterre

STATE APARTMENTS

Marble Court

WC

3

North Parterre

T **6**

4

PASSAGEWAY

To Gardens

ENTRANCE TO FOLLOW OUR TOUR

To Stairs Up to First Floor

Royal

INFO DESK

Courtyard

WC

Prince's Court

WC

BAG CHECK

GRAND CAFE D'ORLEANS

SECURITY CHECK

DIRECT ACCESS TO GARDENS

ROYAL CHAPEL

ROYAL GATE

TICKET SALES **1**

ENTRANCE LINE

CHATEAU ENTRANCE (ENTRANCE A)

WC

GUIDED TOURS **2**

Not to Scale

To Train Station

- - - Self-Guided Tour

1 Château Ticket & Pass Sales
2 Guided-Tour Reservations
3 Exit from State Apartments
4 Fountain Spectacle Tickets
5 Golf-Cart Rental
6 Petit Train (Tram)

VERSAILLES

Once king, Louis XIV expanded the lodge by attaching wings, creating the present U-shape. Later, the long north and south wings were built. The total cost of the project has been estimated at half of France's entire GNP for one year.

Think how busy this courtyard must have been 300 years ago. As many as 5,000 nobles were here at any one time, each with an entourage. Riding in sedan-chair taxis, they'd buzz from games to

parties to amorous rendezvous. Servants ran about delivering secret messages and roast legs of lamb. Horse-drawn carriages arrived at the fancy gate with their finely dressed passengers, having driven up the broad boulevard that ran directly from Paris (the horse stables still line the boulevard). Incredible as it seems, both the grounds and most of the palace were public territory, where even the lowliest peasants could come to gawk—provided they passed through a metal detector and followed a dress code. Then, as now, there were hordes of tourists, pickpockets, palace workers, and men selling wind-up children's toys.

• *Enter the Château where you'll find an information desk (get a map), bag check, and WCs. Follow the crowds directly across the courtyard, where you'll go back inside, pick up an audioguide, and make your way to the start of our tour.*

On the way to our tour's first stop, the route passes through a dozen ground-floor rooms. The first offers a glimpse through a doorway at the impressive Royal Chapel, which we'll see again upstairs. You'll see rooms with paintings of Louis XIV, XV, and XVI, and models of Versailles at different stages of growth. Climb the stairs, then wander a statue-lined hall to reach a palatial golden-brown room, with a doorway that overlooks the Royal Chapel. Let the tour begin.

Royal Chapel

Dut-dutta-dah! Every morning at 10:00, the organist and musicians struck up the music, these big golden doors opened, and Louis XIV and his family stepped onto the balcony to attend Mass. While Louis looked down on the golden altar, the lowly nobles on

the ground floor knelt with their backs to the altar and looked up—worshipping Louis worshipping God. Important religious ceremonies took place here, including the marriage of young Louis XVI to Marie-Antoinette.

In the vast pagan "temple" that is Versailles—built to glorify one man, Louis XIV—this Royal Chapel is a paltry tip of the hat to that "other" god...the Christian one. It's virtually the first, last, and only hint of Christianity you'll see in the entire complex. Versailles celebrates Man, not God, by raising Louis XIV to

Versailles Château—First Floor

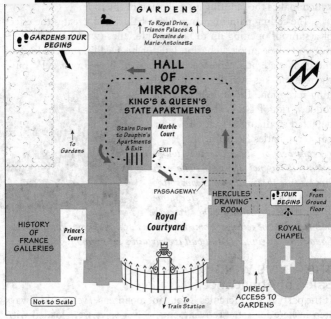

GARDENS

To Royal Drive,
Trianon Palaces &
Domaine de
Marie-Antoinette

GARDENS TOUR
BEGINS

HALL
OF
MIRRORS
KING'S & QUEEN'S
STATE APARTMENTS

Stairs Down
to Dauphin's
Apartments
& Exit

Marble
Court

To
Gardens

EXIT

PASSAGEWAY

HERCULES
DRAWING
ROOM

TOUR
BEGINS

From
Ground
Floor

HISTORY
OF
FRANCE
GALLERIES

Prince's
Court

Royal
Courtyard

ROYAL
CHAPEL

Not to Scale

To
Train Station

DIRECT
ACCESS TO
GARDENS

almost godlike status, the personification of all good human quali-
ties. In a way, Versailles is the last great flowering of Renaissance
humanism and a revival of the classical world.

• *Enter the next room, an even more sumptuous space with a fireplace
and a colorful painting on the ceiling.*

Hercules Drawing Room

Pleasure ruled. The main suppers, balls, and receptions were held
in this room. Picture elegant partygoers in fine silks, wigs, rouge,
lipstick, and fake moles (and that's just the men) as they dance to
the strains of a string quartet.

On the wall opposite the fireplace is an appropriate painting
showing Christ in the middle of
a Venetian party. The work—by
Paolo Veronese, a gift from the Republic of Venice—was one of Louis
XIV's favorites, so the king had the
room decorated around it. Stand by
the fireplace for the full effect: The
room's columns, arches, and frieze

match the height and style of Veronese's painted architecture, which makes the painting an extension of the room.

The ceiling painting, ringed by a balustrade, creates the effect of a sunroof opening up to heaven. Hercules (with his club) hurries up to heaven on a chariot, late for his wedding to the king of the gods' daughter. The scene echoes real life—Louis XIV built the room for his own daughter's wedding reception. The style is pure Baroque, a riot of 142 exuberant figures depicted at all angles by Louis' court painter, Charles Le Brun.

• *From here on it's a one-way tour—getting lost is not allowed. Follow the crowds into the small green room with a goddess in pink on the ceiling. The names of the rooms generally come from the paintings on the ceilings. Some rooms are dark, making it hard to read. Saddle up to a window and pull the curtain a bit to find light.*

THE KING'S WING
Salon of Abundance

If the party in the Hercules Room got too intense, you could always step in here for some refreshments. Silver trays were loaded with liqueurs, exotic stimulants (coffee), juice, chocolates, and, on really special occasions, three-bean salad.

The ceiling painting shows the cornucopia of riches poured down on invited guests.

Around the edges of the ceiling are painted versions of the king's actual treasures and royal dinnerware—golden bowls, urns, and gravy boats. The two black chests of drawers are from Louis' furniture collection (most of it was lost in the Revolution). They rest on heavy bases and are heavily ornamented—the so-called Louis XIV style.

Louis himself might be here. He was a gracious host who enjoyed letting his hair down at night. If he took a liking to you, he might sneak you through those doors there (in the middle of the wall) and into his own private study, or "cabinet of curiosities," where he'd show off his collection of dishes, medals, jewels, or...the *Mona Lisa,* which hung on his wall. Louis' favorite show-and-tell items are now in the Louvre.

The paintings on the walls are of Louis XIV's heirs. He reigned for more than 70 years and outlived three of them, finally leaving the crown to his pink-cheeked, five-year-old great-grandson, Louis XV (on the right).

Venus Room

Love ruled at Versailles. In this room, couples would cavort beneath the goddess of love, floating on the ceiling. Venus sends down

a canopy of golden garlands to ensnare mortals in delicious amour. Another ceiling painting (above the statue, in a rectangular frame) symbolizes the marriage of Louis XIV and Marie-Thérèse, shown in their wedding-limo chariot.

Baroque artists loved to mix their media to fool the eye. Notice how in the paintings at both ends of the room, the painted columns match the room's real ones, extending this grand room into mythical courtyards.

Don't let the statue of a confident Louis XIV as a Roman emperor fool you. He started out as a poor little rich kid with a chip on his shoulder. His father died before Louis was old enough to rule, and, during the regency period, the French *parlements* treated little Louis and his mother like trash. They were virtual prisoners, humiliated in their home, the Royal Palace in Paris (today's Louvre). There they eked by with bland meals, hand-me-down leotards, and pointed shoes. After Louis XIV attained power and wealth, he made Versailles a pleasure palace, with happy hours held in this room every evening.

There was one topic you never discussed in Louis' presence: poverty. Maybe Versailles was his way of saying, "Living well is the best revenge."

Diana Room

Here in the billiards room, Louis and his men played on a table

that stood in the center of the room, while ladies sat surrounding them on Persian-carpet cushions, and music wafted in from next door. Louis was a good pool player, a sore loser, and a king—thus, he rarely lost.

The famous bust of Louis by Giovanni Lorenzo Bernini (in the center) shows a handsome, dashing, 27-year-old playboy-king. His gaze is steady amid his windblown cloak and hair. Young Louis loved life. He hunted animals by day (notice Diana the Huntress, with her bow, on the ceiling) and chased beautiful women at night.

Games were actually an important part of Louis' political strategy, known as "the domestication of the nobility." By distracting the nobles with the pleasures of courtly life, he was free to run the government his way. Billiards, dancing, and concerts were popular, but the biggest distraction was gambling, usually a card game similar to blackjack. Louis lent money to the losers, making them even more indebted to him. The good life was an addiction, and Louis kept the medicine cabinet well-stocked.

As you move into the next room, notice the fat walls that hid thin servants, who were to be at their master's constant call—but out of sight when not needed.

Mars Room

Also known as the Guard Room (as it was the room for Louis' Swiss bodyguards), this red room is decorated with a military flair.

On the ceiling there's Mars, the Greek god of war, in a chariot pulled by wolves. The bronze cupids in the corners are escalating from love arrows to heavier artillery. But it's not all war. Louis loved music and playing his guitar, and enjoyed concerts here in the Mars Room nearly every evening.

Out the window are sculpted gardens in the style of a traditional Italian villa—landscaped symmetrically, with trimmed hedges and cone-shaped trees lining walkways that lead to fountains.

As you wander, the palace feels bare, but remember that entire industries were created to decorate the place with carpets, mirrors, furniture, and tapestries. Most of the furniture we see today is not original, but is from the same period.

Mercury Room

Louis' life was a work of art, and Versailles was the display case. Everything he did was a public event designed to show his subjects how it should be done. This room may have served as Louis' official (not actual) bedroom, where the Sun King would ritually rise each morning to warm his subjects.

From a canopied bed (like this

18th-century one), Louis would get up, dress, and take a seat for morning prayer. Meanwhile, the nobles would stand behind a balustrade, in awe of his piety, nobility, and clean socks. At breakfast they murmured with delight as he deftly decapitated his boiled egg with a knife. And when Louis went to bed at night, the dukes and barons would fight over who got to hold the candle while he slipped into his royal jammies. Bedtime, wake-up, and meals were all public rituals.

Apollo Room

This was the grand throne room. Louis held court from a 10-foot-tall, silver-and-gold, canopied throne on a raised platform placed in the center of the room (the platform is there, though not the throne). Even when the king was away, passing courtiers had to bow to the empty throne.

Everything in here reminds us that Louis XIV was not just any ruler, but the Sun King, who lit the whole world with his presence. On the ceiling the sun god Apollo (representing Louis) drives his chariot, dragging the sun across the heavens to warm the four corners of the world (counterclockwise from above the exit door): 1) Europe, with a sword; 2) Asia, with a lion; 3) Africa, with an elephant; and 4) good ol' America, an Indian maiden with a crocodile. Notice the ceiling's beautifully gilded frame and *Goldfinger* maidens.

The famous portrait by Hyacinthe Rigaud over the fireplace gives a more human look at Louis XIV. He's shown in a dancer's pose, displaying the legs that made him one of the all-time dancing fools of kingery (see a photo of this portrait on page 543). At night they often held parties in this room, actually dancing around the throne.

Louis XIV (who was 63 when this was painted) had more than 300 wigs like this one, and he changed them many times a day. This fashion first started when his hairline began to recede, then sprouted all over Europe, and even spread to the American colonies in the time of George Washington.

Louis XIV may have been treated like a god, but he was not an overly arrogant man. His subjects adored him because he was a symbol of everything a man could be, the fullest expression of the Renaissance Man. Compare the portrait of Louis XIV with the one across the room of his last successor, Louis XVI—same arrogant pose, but without the inner confidence to keep his head on his shoulders.

• *Continue into the final room of the King's Wing.*

War Room

"Louis Quatorze was addicted to wars," and the room depicts his

VERSAILLES

victories—in marble, gilding, stucco, and paint. France's success made other countries jealous and nervous. At the base of the ceiling (in semicircular paintings), we see Germany (with the double eagle), Holland (with its ships), and Spain (with a red flag and roaring lion) ganging up on Louis XIV. But Lady France (center of ceiling), protected by the shield of Louis XIV, hurls thunderbolts down to defeat them. The stucco relief on the wall shows Louis XIV on horseback, triumphing over his fallen enemies.

Versailles was good propaganda. It showed the rest of the world how rich and powerful France was. A visit to the Château and Gardens sent visitors reeling. And Louis XIV's greatest triumph may be the next room, the one that everybody wrote home about.

Hall of Mirrors

No one had ever seen anything like this hall when it was opened. Mirrors were still a great luxury at the time, and the number and size of these monsters was astounding. The hall is nearly 250 feet long. There are 17 arched mirrors, matched by 17 windows letting in that breathtaking view of the Gardens. Lining the hall are 24 gilded candelabra, eight busts of Roman emperors, and eight classical-style statues (seven of them ancient). The ceiling decoration

chronicles Louis' military accomplishments, topped off by Louis himself in the central panel (with cupids playing cards at his divine feet) doing what he did best—triumphing. Originally, two huge carpets mirrored the action depicted on the ceiling.

Imagine this place lit by the flames of thousands of candles, filled with ambassadors, nobles, and guests dressed in silks and powdered wigs. At the far end of the room sits the king, on the canopied throne moved in temporarily from the Apollo Room. Servants glide by with silver trays of hors d'oeuvres, and an orchestra fuels the festivities. The mirrors reflect an age when beautiful people loved to look at themselves. It was no longer a sin to be proud of good looks and fine clothes, or to enjoy the good things in life: laughing, dancing, eating, drinking, flirting, and watching the sun set into the distant canal.

From the center of the hall you can fully appreciate the epic scale of Versailles. The huge palace (by architect Louis Le Vau),

VERSAILLES

the fantasy interior (by Charles Le Brun), and the endless gardens (by André Le Nôtre) made Versailles *le* best. In 1871, after the Prussians defeated the French, Otto von Bismarck declared the establishment of the German Empire in this room. And in 1919, Germany and the Allies signed the Treaty of Versailles, ending World War I (and, some say, starting World War II) right here, in the Hall of Mirrors.

• *Midway down the Hall of Mirrors, you'll be routed to the left through the heart of the palace, to the...*

King's Bedroom and Council Rooms

Pass through a first large room to find Louis XIV's bedroom. It's elaborately decorated, and the decor changed with the season. On

the wall behind the impressive bed, a golden Lady France watched over her king as he slept. The balustrade separated the courtiers from the king. Though this was Louis' actual bedroom, it was also a somewhat public space where he received visitors. The two rooms on either side of the bedroom—right next to where the king slept—were large halls for ambassa-dorial receptions and cabinet meetings.

Look out the window and notice how this small room is at the exact center of the immense horseshoe-shaped building, overlooking the main courtyard and—naturally—facing the rising sun in the east. It symbolized the exact center of power in France. Imagine the humiliation on that day in 1789 when Louis' great-great-great-grandson, Louis XVI, was forced to stand here and acknowledge the angry crowds that filled the square demanding the end of the divine monarchy.

• *The Queen's Wing of the Château is closed for extensive renovation, so from here you'll walk through several unremarkable rooms as you make your way downstairs to the exit. This ends our tour of the Château, but there is more, all described in the free audioguide.*

THE REST OF THE CHATEAU

On the first floor, you can continue into the History of France rooms, lined with paintings of great men and events; find temporary exhibits to explore; or visit the Salon de Thé Angelina, which serves decadent hot chocolate and luscious pastries (most famous is their Mont Blanc—a chestnut-cream meringue with whipped cream).

• *Stairs lead down to the ground floor.*

Downstairs, on the ground floor, are the Dauphin's Apartments. These less-decorated rooms were home to the king's son and daughter-in-law. The dauphin (crown prince) was named for the dolphin on an early family crest. During the reigns of Kings Louis XIV-XVI, five different dauphins played the role of heir apparent without ever becoming king, having been outlived by their aged parents. Also on the ground floor are the Mesdames' Apartments—the rooms set aside for the six daughters of Louis XV.

• *Exit the palace and follow signs to the Gardens* (les Jardins), *located behind the Château.*

Now might be a good time to break for lunch (I prefer lunch in the Gardens—see page 565 for options). You can plan your time in the Gardens with the "Getting Around the Gardens" sidebar on page 555. Don't forget to pick up any checked bags you've left at the Château.

The Gardens

Louis XIV was a divine-right ruler. One way he proved it was by controlling nature like a god. These lavish grounds—elaborately planned, pruned, and decorated—showed everyone that Louis was in total command. Louis loved his gardens and, until his last days, presided over their care. He personally led VIPs through them and threw his biggest parties here. With their Greco-Roman themes and incomparable beauty, the Gardens further illustrated his immense power.

The Gardens are vast. For some, a stroll through the landscaped shrubs around the Château and quick view down the Royal Drive is plenty. But it's worth the ten-minute walk down the Royal Drive to the Apollo Basin and back (even if you don't continue further to the Trianon/Domaine).

• *Entering the Gardens, make your way farther into the king's spacious backyard. You pass by artificial ponds, reclining river-god statues, and cookie-cutter patterns of shrubs and green cones. As you walk, consider that a thousand orange trees were once stored beneath your feet in greenhouses. On sunny days, they were wheeled out in their silver planters and scattered around the grounds. The warmth from the Sun King was so great that he could even grow orange trees in chilly France.*

You soon reach the top step of a staircase overlooking the Gardens. Face away from the palace and take in the jaw-dropping...

View Down the Royal Drive

This, to me, is the most stunning spot in all of Versailles. With the palace behind you, it seems as if the grounds stretch out forever.

VERSAILLES

Getting Around the Gardens

On Foot: It's a solid 45-minute walk from the palace, down to the Grand Canal, past the two Trianon palaces, to the Hamlet at the far end of Domaine de Marie-Antoinette. Allow more time if you stop along the way. After enduring the slow Château shuffle, stretching your legs out here feels pretty good.

By Bike: There's a bike-rental station by the Grand Canal. A bike won't save you that much time (you can't take it inside the grounds of the Trianon/Domaine; park it near an entrance while you tour inside). Instead, simply enjoy pedaling around the greatest royal park in all of Europe (about €8/hour or €18/half-day, kid-size bikes and tandems available, daily 10:00-18:30).

By *Petit Train*: The very slow-moving tram leaves from behind the Château (north side) and makes a one-way loop, stopping at the Petit and Grand Trianons (entry points to Domaine de Marie-Antoinette), then the Grand Canal before returning to the Château (€7.50, round-trip only, free for kids under age 11, 4/hour, runs Tue-Sun 10:00-18:00, Mon 11:00-17:00, shorter hours in winter). Note that you can hop on and off the train and that the one-way loop only goes from the Domaine de Marie-Antoinette to the Grand Canal (not the other way).

By Golf Cart: This makes for a fun drive through the Gardens, complete with music and a relaxing commentary. But you can't go wherever you want—the cart shuts off automatically if you diverge from the prescribed route. You can't drive it in the Trianon/Domaine, but you can park it outside the entrance while you sightsee inside. Be warned: There are steep late fees. To go out to the Hamlet, sightsee quickly, and get back within your allotted hour, you'll need to rent a cart at the Grand Canal and put the pedal to the metal (€32/hour, €8/15 minutes after that, 4-person limit per cart, rent down by the canal or just behind the Château, near the *petit train* stop).

By Shuttle Bus: Phébus runs an hourly "TRI" shuttle bus between three train stations—Versailles Château Rive Gauche, Rive Droite, and Chantiers—and the Trianon/Domaine (shuttle doesn't stop at the Château). This bus can save you 30 minutes of walking time to (and another 30 minutes from) the Trianon/Domaine. It's ideal if you're visiting the Trianon/Domaine first, before the Château. It also works great if you want to return to the station straight from the Trianon/Domaine (€2 or one Métro ticket, mid-April-Oct only, check current schedule for "Ligne TRI" at www.phebus.tm.fr). Buses depart from Versailles Château Rive Gauche train station Tue-Sun at :40 after the hour 8:40-19:40, and from a stop near the Trianon at :08 after the hour 9:08-20:08 (see map on page 559). Schedules are available at the small Phébus office across from the Versailles Château Rive Gauche train station, near McDonald's (closed at lunch and on weekends).

Versailles was laid out along an eight-mile axis that included the grounds, the palace, and the town of Versailles itself, one of the first instances of urban planning since Roman times and a model for future capitals, such as Washington, D.C., and Brasilia.

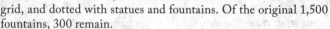

Looking down the Royal Drive (also known as "The Green Carpet"), you see the round Apollo fountain in the distance. Just beyond that is the Grand Canal. The groves on either side of the Royal Drive were planted with trees from all over, laid out in an elaborate grid, and dotted with statues and fountains. Of the original 1,500 fountains, 300 remain.

Looking back at the palace, you can see the Hall of Mirrors—it's the middle story, with the arched windows.

• *Stroll down the steps to get a good look at the frogs and lizards that fill the round…*

Latona Basin

Everything in the garden has a symbolic meaning. The theme of Versailles is Apollo, the god of the sun, associated with Louis XIV.

This round fountain tells the story of the birth of Apollo and his sister, Diana. On top of the fountain are Apollo and Diana as little kids with their mother, Latona (they're facing toward the Apollo fountain). Latona, an unwed mother, was insulted by the local peasants. She called on the king of the gods, Zeus (the children's father), to avenge the insult. Zeus swooped down and turned all the peasants into the frogs and lizards that ring the fountain.

• *As you walk down past the basin toward the Royal Drive, you'll pass by "ancient" statues done by 17th-century French sculptors. You'll see statues of gods, nymphs, mythological heroes, allegories of the seasons, and huge Roman-style vases. A cheap café and WCs are close by. The Colonnade is hidden in the woods on the left side of the Royal Drive, about three-fourths of the way to the Apollo Basin (you'll spot it off the main path through an opening).*

Colonnade

Versailles had no prestigious ancient ruins, so the king built his own. This prefab Roman ruin is a 100-foot circle of 64 red-marble columns supporting pure-white arches. The arches are decorated

with cherubs playing harps. In the center stands a statue of Pluto (Greek god of the Underworld) carrying off Proserpine while her mom gets trampled. Surrounding the whole thing are small birdbath fountains (imagine them all spouting water). Nobles would picnic in the shade to the tunes of a string quartet and pretend that they were the enlightened citizens of the ancient world.

Apollo Basin

The fountains of Versailles were once its most famous attraction, a marvel of both art and engineering. This one was the center-

piece, showing the sun god—Louis XIV—in his sunny chariot as he starts his journey across the sky. The horses are half-submerged, giving the impression, when the fountains play, of the sun rising out of the mists of dawn. Apollo's entourage includes dolphins leading the way and Tritons blowing their conch shells. Most of the fountains were turned on only when the king walked by, but this one played constantly for the benefit of those watching from the palace. Look into the water to see the substantial pipes that feed this powerful fountain.

All the fountains are gravity-powered. They work on the same principle as blocking a hose with your finger to make it squirt. Underground streams (pumped into Versailles by Seine River pressure) feed into smaller pipes at the fountains, which shoot the water high into the air.

Looking back at the palace from here, realize that the distance you just walked is only a fraction of this vast complex of buildings, gardens, and waterways. Be glad you don't have to mow the lawn.

Grand Canal

Why visit Venice when you can just build your own? In an era before virtual reality, this was the next best thing to an actual trip. Couples in gondolas would pole along the waters accompanied by barges with orchestras playing *"O Sole Mio."* The canal is actually cross-shaped; you're looking at the longest part, one mile from end to end. Of course, this, too, is a man-made body of water with no function other than to please. Originally, authentic gondoliers,

VERSAILLES

imported with their boats from Venice, lived in a little settlement next to the canal.

These days, the Grand Canal hosts eateries, rental boats, bike and golf-cart rentals, and a *petit train* tram stop (see sidebar on page 555).

• *The area called the Trianon Palaces and Domaine de Marie-Antoinette is a 10-minute walk from the Grand Canal. You can enter/exit the Trianon/Domaine at three spots: near the palace known as the Grand Trianon (where we'll enter), near the Petit Trianon palace, or way around back on the far side of the Hamlet.*

If you're monitoring your time and energy, note that it's a 1.5-hour time commitment to see the whole Trianon/Domaine, plus a 30-minute walk back to the Château. You can take a bike, golf cart, or petit train *(see sidebar on page 536) as far as the entrance, but you have to walk inside.*

To get to our starting point, the Grand Trianon, veer right just past the restaurants and boat rental (see the map on page 536) and follow the dirt path along a looooong strip of lawn. This leads uphill 500 yards to the Grand Trianon. (Bikers/golf-cart drivers can park their wheels here.)

Trianon Palaces and Domaine de Marie-Antoinette

Versailles began as an escape from the pressures of kingship. But in a short time, the Château became as busy as Paris ever was. Louis XIV needed an escape from his escape, so he built a smaller palace out in the boonies. Later, his successors retreated still farther from the Château and French political life, ignoring the real world that was crumbling all around them. They expanded the Trianon area, building a fantasy world of palaces, ponds, pavilions, and pleasure gardens—the enclosure

called Marie-Antoinette's Domaine. Today, the Trianon/Domaine is a walled-off part of the Gardens accessible only with a ticket.

If you're heading back to Paris from here, note that the TRI bus to Versailles' train stations leaves from near the Trianon buildings at :08 after the hour (see map on next page for stop).

Domaine de Marie-Antoinette

GRAND TRIANON

• *Enter the Grand Trianon and pass through its security checkpoint. Pick up the free palace brochure and follow the simple one-way route through the rooms. Read your flier as you follow this tour to get the most out of your visit.*

Exterior

Delicate, pink, and set amid gardens, the Grand Trianon was the perfect summer getaway. This was the king's private residence

away from the main palace. Louis XIV usually spent a couple of nights a week here (more in the summer) to escape the sniping politics, strict etiquette, and 24/7 scrutiny of official court life.

Louis XIV built the palace (1670-1688) near the tiny peasant village of Trianon (hence the name) and faced it with blue-and-white ceramic tiles. When those began disintegrating almost immediately, the palace was renovated with pink marble. It's a one-story structure of two wings connected by a colonnade, with gardens in back.

Interior—Left Wing

The rooms are a complex overlay of furnishings from many different kings, dauphins, and nobles who lived here over the centuries. Louis

XIV alone had three different bedrooms. Concentrate on the illustrious time of Louis XIV (1688-1715) and Napoleon Bonaparte (1810-1814). Use your map (which has room numbers on it) to find these highlights.

Mirror Room (Salon des Glaces): This spacious living room has the original white walls and mirrors of Louis XIV, and the Empire-style furniture of Napoleon (unornamented, high-polished wood, with

classical motifs). Napoleon inhabited the Grand Trianon with his second wife, Empress Marie-Louise, and his mother—the women in the left wing, the emperor in the right.

Louis XIV's Bedroom (Chambre de l'Impératice): Louis built the Grand Trianon as home for his chief mistress, while his wife lived in the Château. Imagine waking up in this big bed with your lover, throwing back the curtain, and looking out the windows at the gardens. These light, airy, many-windowed rooms were cheery even

when skies were gray, a strong contrast to the heavy-metal decor in the mother Château.

Exit into the open-air **colonnade** (Peristyle) that connects the two wings. Originally, this pink-columned passageway had windows, an enormously expensive luxury that allowed visitors to enjoy the gardens even in bad weather.

Interior—Right Wing

Emperor's Family Drawing Room (Salon de Famille de l'Empereur): This room, immediately to your right upon entering, had many different uses over the years: a theater for Louis XIV, a game room for Louis XV, and Napoleon's family room. After Napoleon was defeated and France's royalty returned, King Louis-Philippe I lived here. Walk through a series of rooms, passing

VERSAILLES

through Louis-Philippe's billiards room, until you reach a room decorated in green malachite.

Malachite Room (Salon des Malachites): This was Napoleon's living room, and his library was next door. You'll see the impressive green basin, vases, and candelabras made of Russian malachite given to Napoleon by Czar Alexander I. Another czar, Peter the Great, who lodged in the Grand Trianon in 1717 and then returned home, was inspired to build the Peterhof—a similarly lavish summer palace near St. Petersburg known as the "Russian Versailles."

Cotelle Gallery (Galerie Cotelle): This white, 170-foot-long room was Louis' reception hall. Later, Marie-Antoinette performed here in theatrical productions for select audiences. The gallery is interspersed with big French doors and lined with paintings of Versailles vistas, peopled by promenading aristocrats. Party guests could admire the gardens in the paintings, then step out into the real thing.

Gardens

Exit into the gardens and look back. The facade of pink, yellow, and white is a welcome contrast to the imposing Baroque facade of the main palace. The flower gardens were changed daily for the king's pleasure—for new color combinations and new "nasal cocktails."

DOMAINE DE MARIE-ANTOINETTE

• *Our next stop is the French Pavilion. To get there from the Grand Trianon gardens, walk clockwise around the perimeter of the Grand Trianon. Make it a tight, 180-degree loop, hugging the palace. A sign will direct you across a footbridge. Directly ahead, you'll see the...*

French Pavilion

This small, white building (generally closed) with rooms fanning out from the center was one more step away from the modern world.

Inside is a circular room with four small adjoining rooms. Big French doors let in a cool breeze. Here Marie-Antoinette spent summer evenings with family and a few friends, listening to music or playing parlor games. She and her friends explored all avenues of *la douceur de vivre,* the sweetness of living.

• *Up ahead is the large, cube-shaped*

Petit Trianon palace—that's where our tour will eventually end. Head toward the Petit Trianon, but midway there, turn left, where you can peek into...

Marie-Antoinette's Theater

Marie-Antoinette adored the theater and was an aspiring performer herself. In this intimate playhouse, far from the rude

intrusions of the real world, the queen and her friends acted out plays. The soft blue decor and upholstered walls and benches give the theater a dollhouse feel. Though small, it has everything you'd find in a major opera house: stage, orchestra pit, balconies, ornate gold ceiling, and raked seating for 100 (photos OK, but no flash).

• *Continue through the oh-so-bucolic gardens until just before the Petit Trianon. Turn left and follow paths uphill to a pond graced with a tiny palace.*

Belvedere, Rock, and Grotto

The octagonal Belvedere palace is as much windows as it is walls. When the doors were open, it could serve as a gazebo for musicians, serenading nobles in this man-made alpine setting. The interior has a marble-mosaic floor and walls decorated with delicate, Pompeii-esque garlands. To the left of the Belvedere is the "Rock," a fake mountain that pours water into the pond. To the right of the Belvedere (you'll have to find it) is the secret Grotto.

• *Facing the Belvedere, turn right (east), following the pond's meandering stream. Continue gamboling along the paths. In the distance you'll spy a complex of buildings, with a round, fanciful tower and a smattering of rustic, half-timbered buildings. Head there to find the Hansel-and-Gretel-like...*

Hamlet

Marie-Antoinette longed for the simple life of a peasant—not the hard labor of real peasants, who sweated and starved around her, but the fairytale world of simple country pleasures. She built this complex of 12 thatched-roof buildings fronting a lake as her own private "Normand" village.

The main building is the Queen's House—actually two

buildings connected by a wooden skywalk. It's the only one without a thatched roof. Like any typical peasant farmhouse, it had a billiard room, library, elegant dining hall, and two living rooms.

This was an actual working farm with a dairy (walk past the lighthouse tower), a water mill, a pigeon coop (in a thatched cottage called Le Colombier), and domestic animals. Beyond the lighthouse tower (La Tour de Marlborough—departure point for boat trips on the pond), you'll see where the queen's servants kept cows, goats, chickens, and ducks. The harvest was served at Marie-Antoinette's table. Marie-Antoinette didn't do much work herself, but she "supervised," dressed in a plain, white muslin dress and a straw hat. Though the royal family is long gone, kid-pleasing animals still inhabit the farm, and beaucoup fat fish swim languid circles in the pond.

• *Head back toward the Petit Trianon. Along the way (in about five minutes), you'll see the white dome of the...*

Temple of Love

A circle of 12 marble Corinthian columns supports a dome, decorating a path where lovers could stroll. Underneath there's a statue of Cupid making a bow (to shoot arrows of love) out of the club of Hercules. It's a delightful monument to a society where the rich could afford that ultimate luxury, romantic love.

• *And, finally, you'll reach the...*

Petit Trianon

Louis XV developed an interest in botany. He wanted to spend more time near the French Gardens, but the Summer House just wasn't big enough. He constructed the Petit Trianon ("Small Trianon") at the urging of his first mistress, Madame de Pompadour, and it later became home to his next mistress, Madame du Barry.

This gray, cubical building is a masterpiece of Neoclassical architecture, built by the same architect who created the Opera House in the main palace. It has four distinct facades, each a perfect and harmonious combination of Greek-style columns, windows, and railings. Walk around it and find your favorite.

You can tour the handsome interior (pick up the helpful flier). English explanations are provided in some rooms, as are interactive screens. The Baroque WC was a head of its time.

When Louis XVI became king, he gave the building to his bride Marie-Antoinette, who made this her home base. On the lawn outside, she installed a carousel. Despite her bad reputation with the public, Marie-Antoinette was a sweet girl from Vienna who never quite fit in with the fast, sophisticated crowd at Versailles. At the Petit Trianon, she could get away and re-create the charming home life that she remembered from her childhood. Here she played, while in the cafés of faraway Paris, revolutionaries plotted the end of the *ancien régime*.

• *The main* **Château** *is a 30-minute walk straight out of the exit to the southeast (allow another 10 minutes to reach the train station). If you've had enough walking, you can ride the* petit train *from here back to the Château.*

Or, you can return directly to **Versailles Château Rive Gauche station** *by catching the TRI line shuttle bus (mid-April-Oct only, leaves at :08 after the hour, see map on page 559 for stop, and read the "Getting Around the Gardens" sidebar, earlier). For a slightly shorter walk back to the train station, and a chance to see the Neptune Basin (an impressive miniature lake with fountains; see map on page 536), walk straight down from the Petit Trianon and turn left on Avenue de la Trianon (the gate here is closed before Spectacle shows). If you stay straight as an arrow, you'll run into the Neptune Basin, where the grand finale takes place on fountain days. Leave Neptune at the far-left corner gate, and you'll pop out onto Rue de la Paroisse, the town's main shopping drag, which takes you into the market square. From here a right on Avenue de l'Europe takes you to the Versailles Château Rive Gauche train station and the RER back to Paris.*

Town of Versailles

For a less expensive and more laid-back alternative to Paris, the town of Versailles can be a good overnight stop, especially for drivers. Park in the palace's main lot while looking for a hotel, or leave your car there overnight (see page 538). Get a map of Versailles at your hotel or at the TI.

SLEEPING IN VERSAILLES

($$$$ = Splurge, $$$ = Pricier, $$ = Moderate, $ = Budget)

$$ Hôtel de France* is in a 17th-century townhouse a peasant's

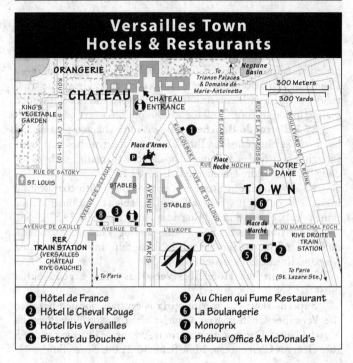

Versailles Town Hotels & Restaurants

ORANGERIE

CHATEAU

CHATEAU ENTRANCE

To Trianon Palaces & Domaine de Marie-Antoinette

Neptune Basin

300 Meters

300 Yards

KING'S VEGETABLE GARDEN

ROUTE DE ST. CYR (N-10)

❶

RUE COLBERT

RUE CARNOT

RUE DE LA PAROISSE

BOULEVARD DE LA REINE

Place d'Armes

P

RUE DE SATORY

ST. LOUIS

STABLES

AVENUE DE SCEAUX

Place Hoche

RUE HOCHE

NOTRE DAME

T O W N

❻

STABLES

AVENUE DE PARIS

AVE DE ST-CLOUD

Place du Marché

R. DU MARECHAL FOCH

RIVE DROITE TRAIN STATION

AVENUE DE GAULLE

❽ ❸ ❶

AVENUE DE

L'EUROPE

❼

❺ ❹ ❷

RER TRAIN STATION (VERSAILLES CHÂTEAU RIVE GAUCHE)

To Paris

To Paris (St. Lazare Stn.)

❶ Hôtel de France
❷ Hôtel le Cheval Rouge
❸ Hôtel Ibis Versailles
❹ Bistrot du Boucher
❺ Au Chien qui Fume Restaurant
❻ La Boulangerie
❼ Monoprix
❽ Phébus Office & McDonald's

toss from the palace. It offers Old World class, mostly air-conditioned, traditional rooms with thick tapestries and rugs, a pleasant courtyard, a bar, and a restaurant (just off parking lot across from Château at 5 Rue Colbert, tel. 01 30 83 92 23, www.hotelfrance-versailles.com, hotel-de-france-versailles@wanadoo.fr).

$$ Hôtel le Cheval Rouge,* built in 1676 as Louis XIV's stables, now boards tourists. Tucked into a corner of Place du Marché, this modest hotel has a big courtyard with free parking and sufficiently comfortable rooms connected by long halls (no aircon, all rooms one floor up, no elevator, 18 Rue André Chénier, tel. 01 39 50 03 03, www.chevalrouge-versailles.fr, chevalrouge@sfr.fr).

$$ Hôtel Ibis Versailles* offers a good weekend value and modern comfort, with 85 air-conditioned rooms (good buffet breakfast open to public and served until 10:00 Mon-Thu, until noon Fri-Sun; pay parking, across from RER station at 4 Avenue du Général de Gaulle, tel. 01 39 53 03 30, www.ibishotel.com, h1409@accor.com).

EATING IN VERSAILLES

In the pleasant town center, around Place du Marché Notre-Dame, you'll find a thriving open market (food market Sun, Tue, and Fri mornings until 13:00; clothing market all day Wed-Thu and Sat), four covered market halls with food stalls (Tue-Sat 7:30-13:00 & 15:30-19:00, Sun 7:30-13:00, closed Mon), a variety of reasonably priced restaurants, cafés, and a few cobbled lanes. The square—a 15-minute walk from the Château (veer left as you leave the Château)—is lined with colorful and inexpensive eateries with good seating inside and out. Troll the various options or try one of these:

$$$ Bistrot du Boucher reeks with fun character inside and has good seating outside. They like their meat dishes best here, though you'll find a full menu of choices (bargain lunch *menu*, daily, 12 Rue André Chénier, tel. 01 39 02 12 15).

$$ Au Chien qui Fume is a good choice, with cozy seating inside and out, a playful staff, and reliable, traditional cuisine (lunch deals, closed Sun, 72 Rue de la Paroisse, tel. 01 39 53 14 56).

$ La Boulangerie has mouthwatering sandwiches, salads, quiches, and more (Tue-Sat until 20:00, Sun until 13:30, closed Mon, 60 Rue de la Paroisse).

Breakfast: The **Hôtel Ibis Versailles** offers a good buffet breakfast (see listing, earlier).

Supermarket: A big **Monoprix** is centrally located between the Versailles Château Rive Gauche train station and Place du Marché Notre-Dame (entrances from Avenue de l'Europe and at 5 Rue Georges Clemenceau, Mon-Sat 8:30-21:00, closed Sun).

MORE GRAND CHATEAUX

Château de Vaux-le-Vicomte •
Fontainbleu • Chantilly

The region around Paris (Ile de France) is studded with sumptuous palaces. The city's booming elite class made it the heartland of European château-building in the 16th and 17th centuries. Most of these châteaux were lavish hunting lodges—getaways from the big city. The only things they defended were aristocratic egos.

If you're planning to visit just one palace in all of Europe, it should be Versailles (see previous chapter). But unlike heavily touristed Versailles, the three châteaux recommended here are quiet (at least on weekdays), letting you enjoy their original pastoral ambience. Consider visiting at least one; they are each very different.

▲▲▲Vaux-le-Vicomte

For sheer beauty and intimacy (open daily, weekends only Nov-mid-March); see page 568.

▲▲Fontainebleau

For its history, fine interior, and pleasant city (château closed Tue, covered by Paris Museum Pass); see page 571.

▲Chantilly

For its beautiful setting and fine collection of paintings (closed Tue, covered by Paris Museum Pass); see page 575.

Mobilis Ticket: Day-trippers using the train to reach Vaux-le-Vicomte or Fontainebleau should purchase a regional Mobilis ticket, which covers a day of travel in the greater Paris region (€16.60, buy at any Métro station, all-day ticket covers zones 1-5). The ticket covers your Métro rides to and from the train station and round-trip train fare (for Fontainebleau, it also includes the bus to and from the château), saving you about €9 total. When you buy the ticket, fill in your name and the date, and then use it like a Métro ticket, validating it on the day you travel in the small gray machines on the train platforms.

Vaux-le-Vicomte

Versailles may be most travelers' first choice for its sheer historic importance, but Vaux-le-Vicomte (voh luh vee-komt) is just flat-out ravishing. With a harmony of architecture, interior decor, and garden design that you won't find anywhere else, it gets my vote for one of the most beautiful châteaux in all of France.

Compared with Versailles, it's also more intimate, better furnished, and comes with a fraction of the crowds. Though getting to Vaux-le-Vicomte requires more effort, it's an absolute joy to tour. Located in a huge forest, with magnificent gardens and no urban sprawl in sight, Vaux-le-Vicomte gives me more than a twinge of palace envy.

GETTING THERE

By Train: Ideally, leave Paris from Gare de l'Est before 12:00, traveling to **Verneuil-l'Etang** (direction: Provins). Buying a Mobilis ticket (see earlier) saves you time and money. Otherwise, buy a round-trip ticket at the white ticket machines between tracks 15-19 or at the SNCF ticket booth opposite track 17. Ile de France (suburban) trains depart from tracks 13-22 (€16.60 round-trip, daily at :46 past the hour, 35 minutes; return trains depart Verneuil-l'Etang's track 2 at :32 past the hour).

Outside the station at Verneuil-l'Etang, a Châteaubus shuttle, timed to train arrivals, takes you to Vaux-le-Vicomte (€5 one-way, cash only, pay driver, daily April-early Nov plus Sat evenings May-Sept). Return shuttles leave the château at 12:05, 13:05, 15:05, and 18:05, with additional Saturday departures at 16:05, 19:05, and 22:05. A 23:05 shuttle (€25) takes you all the way back to Paris's Gare de Lyon.

You can also take the RER-D train to **Melun** from Gare de Lyon, Gare du Nord, or Châtelet-Les Halles (direction: Montereau, 3/hour, 50 minutes). Faster SNCF Banlieue trains to Melun leave from Gare de Lyon (2/hour, 30 minutes, about €9 one-way). The last return train from Melun to Paris departs at about 23:45.

From Melun's scruffy train station, taxis make the 15-minute drive to Vaux-le-Vicomte (€20 one-way Mon-Sat, €26 evenings and Sun, taxi tel. 01 64 52 51 50). Ask a staffer at the château to call a cab for your return, or schedule a pickup time with your driver. Seek others with whom you can split the fare.

By Excursion Bus: The City Vision tour company offers a

Combining Vaux-le-Vicomte and Fontainebleau

These two châteaux can be combined into a full, though manageable, day trip by car, taxi, excursion bus, or train from Paris (except on Tue, when Fontainebleau is closed). Fontainebleau is 12 minutes by train from Melun or a 20-minute drive from Vaux-le-Vicomte (about €30 by taxi). If you want to sleep out here, check into one of my recommended hotels in Fontainebleau (listed on page 574).

handy excursion bus to Vaux-le-Vicomte and Fontainebleau (about €70, includes châteaux entry; departs at 9:15 and returns at 18:15; runs April-Oct Mon, Wed-Sat, and first Sun of the month; tel. 01 42 60 30 01, www.pariscityvision.com; also offers private minibus excursions).

By Car: From Paris, take the A-6 autoroute toward Lyon, then follow signs to Melun. In Melun, follow signs to Meaux, then Vaux-le-Vicomte.

ORIENTATION TO VAUX-LE-VICOMTE

Cost: €15.50; includes entire château, gardens, and carriage museum; family deals available, not covered by Paris Museum Pass.

Hours: Daily 10:00-18:00 except early Nov-March open Sat-Sun only. The impressive fountains run 15:00-18:00 on the second and last Saturdays of each month (April-Oct). For the Christmas season, the château offers special holiday decorations (€17.50, weekends only Dec-early Jan 11:00-18:30).

Information: Tel. 01 64 14 41 90, www.vaux-le-vicomte.com.

Tours: The excellent audioguide is €3.

Services: Parking is easy and free. The gift shop has fine palace guidebooks. Outside the shop are a WC and the **$** L'Ecureuil ("The Squirrel") cafeteria, with a limited but reasonably priced selection (daily 10:00-18:00, until 22:30 during candlelit visits). A leafy **$$$** restaurant, Les Charmilles, is in the garden beyond the château, serving lunch and afternoon tea. Picnics are welcome in designated areas.

Candlelit Visits: Two thousand candles and piped-in classical music illuminate the palace on Saturday evenings in peak season (€19.50, early May-early Oct 20:00-24:00, last entry at 23:00). These *visites aux chandelles* recreate a party thrown in Louis XIV's honor in 1661, but note that the gardens are hard to see by candlelight (although it doesn't get truly dark

GRAND CHATEAUX

until around 22:00 in late May, June, and July). Buses provide service to and from Verneuil-l'Etang's train station during these events (described earlier, under "Getting There"). Fancy dinners are available in the Les Charmilles garden restaurant (€50 *menus*, reservations required, www.vaux-le-vicomte.com).

BACKGROUND

When Vaux-le-Vicomte and Versailles were built, France was slowly heading toward a revolution. Of its 18 million people, 200,000 were clergy ("those who pray"), 150,000 were nobles (those who fight or "carry a sword"), and the rest (17.6 million) were the Third Estate ("those who work"). Of course, there was no democracy—just one king and his ministers who ran the show. Somewhat like modern bankers and financiers, these

people controlled the workings of the economy, amassing almost unfathomable wealth.

One of them was Nicolas Fouquet, France's finance minister during the reign of Louis XIV, in the 17th century. Vaux-le-Vicomte was his home. A brilliant collaboration between three masters—architect Louis Le Vau, artist Charles Le Brun, and landscape designer André Le Nôtre (who pioneered the French formal garden)—this château was the architectural inspiration for Versailles and set the standard for European palaces to come. In fact, after several visits to the château during its construction, a very young Louis XIV found himself impressed that one man could create such magnificence. He was also curious how one man (other than himself) could pay for it. So Louis had the overly ambitious Fouquet arrested, hired his talented trio, and proceeded to have his bigger and costlier (but not necessarily more splendid) palace of Versailles built.

Monsieur Fouquet's arrest features prominently in the third Musketeer book by Alexandre Dumas (and at least two versions of *The Man in the Iron Mask* were filmed here). From the prison cell where he died, Fouquet wrote longingly of his lost home, "This was the estate I regarded as my principal seat and where I intended to leave some traces of the status I had enjoyed."

If the château feels a bit quirky in the way it's run today, remember it's not national property. It's private. The château has been in the same family for five generations and was opened to the public in 1968 by Patrice de Vogüé, who still lives on the grounds (but not in the château).

GRAND CHÂTEAUX

VISITING THE CHATEAU

Start your tour in the stables, at the fine **Museum of Carriages** *(Musée des Equipages)*, where you can gallop through two long halls lined with elegant carriages from a time when horses were a big part of daily life. The exhibit begins with a reminder that when the château was built, France had 2.5 million horses (more than 100 horses per thousand people). Today France has 300,000 horses (just 5 per thousand people). While these stables are worth a look, there is no English info other than the entrance and exit signs.

Next, stroll like a wide-eyed peasant across the **stone bridge** that spans the ornamental moat facing the palace. Take some time to survey the grand design and admire the symmetry and elegance of the grounds, the outbuildings, and the palace itself. The gardens stretch far beyond the palace, but their main axis runs straight through the center of the château.

Next, enter the **palace** and pick up an audioguide if you want to rent one. As you wander through Fouquet's dream home, you'll understand Louis XIV's envy. Versailles was a simple hunting lodge when this was built. Most of the paintings and furniture you'll see here are not original—Louis confiscated what he liked for Versailles.

The one-way route first takes you through lavish rooms, then upstairs to a simple attic for an exhibition on carpentry and a peek at the wood structure of the building. From here, climb 80 steps between the inner and outer **domes** (claustrophobic for some) to a small terrace at the very top, where you can look out to the magnificent gardens—the first French formal gardens.

Continue through the last rooms on the tour route (these are among the best and are explained with concise little histories on the walls), and make your way to the palace's back steps to survey André Le Nôtre's first claim to fame. This **garden** was the cutting edge of sculpted French gardens. The designer integrated ponds, shrubbery, and trees in a style that would be copied in palaces all over Europe. Consider the 30-minute walk (one-way) to the viewpoint atop the grassy hill far in the distance. Rentable golf carts are worth the fee to make the trip easier (€15/45 minutes, 4 passengers maximum, ID and deposit required).

Fontainebleau

When it comes to showing the sweep of French history, the Château of Fontainebleau is unrivaled among French palaces. But don't expect Versailles-like unity here. It's a gangly and confusing series of wings that has grown with centuries of kings.

Its core was built by François I in 1528 over medieval foundations. While Vaux-le-Vicomte and Versailles are French-designed, Fontainebleau was built a century earlier by an Italian. Inspired by his travels through Renaissance Italy, François I hired Italian artists to  build his palaces. He even encouraged one artist—Leonardo da Vinci—to abandon his native Italy and settle in France for the last three years of his life.

It seems every king, queen, and emperor since has loved this place—Louis XIII was born here, Louis XV married here, and Napoleon III was baptized here. And many years later, General George Patton set up headquarters here on his way to Berlin.

Above all, Fontainebleau has more Napoleon Bonaparte connections than any other palace in France. It was here that the pope met Napoleon before the general's 1804 coronation as emperor. And it was from the château's famous horseshoe-shaped staircase that Napoleon gave his stirring abdication speech, trading his rule of France for exile to Elba in 1814.

Tourist Information: There's a small TI at the bus station (on the back side of the train station; follow signs for *gare routiere*). The town of Fontainebleau's larger, helpful TI is two blocks across from the château, just behind Hôtel Londres. It has hiking and biking maps, information on where to rent bikes fit for the forest trails, and posted train/bus schedules (Mon-Sat 10:00-18:00, Sun 10:00-13:00 & 14:00-17:30, Nov-April closed Sun afternoon, 4 Rue Royale, tel. 01 60 74 99 99, www.fontainebleau-tourisme.com).

GETTING THERE

By Train: For a day trip to Fontainebleau, it's best to purchase a Mobilis ticket—see details at the start of this chapter.

From Gare de Lyon, catch a train to Fontainebleau-Avon Station (nearly hourly, 45 minutes, direction: Montereau or Montargis). Trains leave from the Grandes Lignes tracks, typically in Hall 1, but finding the right train can be tricky in huge Gare de Lyon. Check return times before leaving Paris, as there can be big gaps.

From the Fontainebleau-Avon Station, take a bus or taxi to reach the château. Bus line 1 (direction: Les Lilas/Château) leaves from the bus stall marked *#1-Château* and makes the 20-minute trip to the Château stop at a snail's pace (3/hour, €2 if purchased on board, Paris Métro tickets valid, included with Mobilis ticket—validate onboard). To return to the station, board bus #1 (direction: Les Bouleaux/Butte Montceau). The station stop is right in front of the station; confirm when you board the bus by asking, *"Ce bus va à la gare?"* (seh bews vah ah lah gar?).

Taxis from the train station to the château cost about €7 and are worth the convenience (more on Sun and after 19:00, taxi tel. 01 64 22 00 06).

By Car: Follow signs to *Centre*, then *Château*. Park across from the château in the big lot (Parking Boufflers) next to the Hôtel Londres. To reach Vaux-le-Vicomte from Fontainebleau (about 20 minutes), follow signs to *Melun*.

ORIENTATION TO FONTAINEBLEAU

Cost: €11, free for those 17 and under, free first Sun of the month, €7 last hour of the day, covered by Paris Museum Pass.

Hours: Wed-Mon 9:30-18:00, Oct-March until 17:00, closed Tue year-round, last entry 45 minutes before closing, tel. 01 60 71 50 70, www.musee-chateau-fontainebleau.fr. Ballroom often closes one hour before château, and the Papal Apartment is sometimes closed 11:30-2:30.

Tours: The worthwhile videoguide costs €3.

Services: Pay lockers are available to store your bags.

VISITING THE CHATEAU

The château's complex floor plan can seem overwhelming, but visitors have little choice when touring the place, so don't struggle to understand the overall design. Find the entry (inside the main gate on the right), and follow the one-way route through the Napoleon I Museum, special exhibit, and royal apartments.

The **Napoleon I Museum** is fascinating. The first room features grand portraits of Emperor Napoleon and his first wife, Empress Josephine (painted by Gérard after their coronation). Other rooms—each drenched in the Empire style—are dedicated to Napoleon at war (with his battle coat, tent, and camp gear); his second wife, Empress Marie Louise (whom he married for her Habsburg heritage, which Napoleon hoped would color his Corsican blood blue); and to their son, the "King of Rome," Napoleon II (who lived in exile after his dad's defeat and died of tuberculosis at 21).

The hallway is lined with busts and **portraits** of the sprawling imperial family Napoleon created—relatives he put on various thrones across his empire. Looking at the final painting, which depicts Napoleon with symbols of the legal system he gave France, the "Code Napoléon," it's fascinating to consider the mix of idealism, charisma, and megalomania of this leader. This revolutionary hero came out of a movement that killed off the Old Regime—only to create a new Old Regime.

After a swing through the portrait gallery, you'll enter the

royal apartments. The highlights are many. The Papal Apartment was renovated by Napoleon to house Pope Pius VII. The stunning Renaissance hall of François I, which dates from 1528, inspired other royal galleries, including the Hall of Mirrors at Versailles. The opulent ballroom *(salle de bal)* comes with piped-in music and has garden views that evoke royal fêtes. Napoleon's throne room is the only French *salle du trône* that survives with its original furniture. You'll also see the emperor's bathroom, bed, and very important-looking desk.

The palace is slathered in royal and imperial symbolism, and its walls are hung with exquisite tapestries. As you walk its halls, track the artistic shift in style, from Renaissance to Rococo—whose whimsy infuriated the revolutionary mobs—to the more sober, postrevolutionary Neoclassical.

After touring the palace, the **gardens**—designed in the 17th century by landscape architect André Le Nôtre—are worth a stroll.

TOWN OF FONTAINEBLEAU

The town itself has a helpful TI (described earlier), a few hotels, and lots of eating options. The English bookstore **ReelBooks,** at 9 Rue de Ferrare, has a good collection of new, used, and children's books. If you stop in, say hi to Sue and Judy (Tue-Sat 11:00-19:00, open some Sun, closed Mon, tel. 01 64 22 85 85).

Sleeping: $$ Hôtel de Londres*** is run by avid golfer Philippe, who rents 16 immaculate rooms, some with views of the château and most with air-conditioning. He also loans out free golf clubs—one of France's most famous golf courses is close by (some view rooms, no elevator, 1 Place du Général de Gaulle, tel. 01 64 22 20 21, www.hoteldelondres.com, hdelondres1850@aol.com).

$$ Hôtel Ibis Château de Fontainebleau,** a five-minute walk from the château, is central, clean, and easy (18 Rue Ferrare, tel. 01 64 23 45 25, www.ibishotel.com, h1028@accor.com).

Eating: Scads of eating options are in the town center. To reach the center, turn right out of the château courtyard and walk down Rue Denecourt. An appealing collection of pedestrian lanes begins after Place Napoléon Bonaparte. Rue Montebello is restaurant row; you'll find quieter places along the lanes off Rue de la Corne.

$$ La Taverne is a young, happening brasserie with good prices and nonstop service from 6:30 until late at night (daily, 23 Rue Grande, tel. 01 64 22 20 85).

$$ Le Bistrot delivers traditional cooking in a cozy atmosphere with a loyal local clientele (9 Rue Montebello, tel. 01 64 22 87 84).

$$ Le Grand Café, just across from the Chateau entrance, serves good brasserie fare (open daily, 33 Place Napoléon Bonaparte, tel. 01 64 22 20 32).

Chantilly

Chantilly (shahn-tee-yee), 30 minutes north of Paris, floats serenely on a reflecting pond. This extravagant hunting palace delivers great art and formal French gardens with an elaborate moat, but you won't get a feel for château life here. The rooms are 19th-century recreations and can be visited only on a boring tour—in French.

Tourist Information: The TI is located in the linear town of Chantilly, about a half-mile to the left as you exit the train station (halfway between the station and the château). To reach the TI, walk straight out of the station and turn left on busy Avenue Maréchal Joffre, then turn right on Rue du Connétable (Mon-Sat 9:30-12:30 & 13:30-17:30, Sun 10:00-13:00 & 14:30-17:00, closed Tue afternoon May-Sept, 73 Rue du Connétable, tel. 03 44 67 37 37, www.chantilly-tourisme.com).

GETTING THERE

Taking a train to Chantilly is a breeze, but the last mile-and-a-half to the château is a headache unless you spring for a cab or enjoy a good walk. Leave from Paris' Gare du Nord for Chantilly-Gouvieux (on the Creil line, Grandes Lignes). The RER serves Chantilly, but service is twice as fast on the Grandes Lignes main lines. Ask at any information desk for the next departure (hourly, fewer on weekends, 25 minutes by train, 50 minutes by RER, about €10 one-way). Upon arrival in Chantilly, confirm return times and whether the trip is via the faster train or slower RER.

Getting from the Station to the Château: It's a level, 30-minute **walk** to the château through the woods and across a grassy park (maps posted on the exterior of the train station and around town). Walk straight out of the train station and cross the big road that separates the town from the woods. From here, several trails fan out in front of you. All lead to the château, but the most efficient and scenic route is the middle path, marked *Le Tour de l'Hippodrome.* (Midway to the château, a path leads to the left, where you can pop into town and visit the TI en route.) Walking back to the station, cross the big roundabout above the château, find wooden signs marked *Gare,* and follow them along a dirt path (passing behind the racetrack).

Otherwise, the easiest station-to-château trip is by **taxi.** Cabbies prefer longer fares, but they will take you to the château if they're available. Taxi One is one of several options (about €9 one-way, €18 round-trip, mobile 06 42 05 46 79). The free city **bus** (called DUC, Desserte Urbaine Cantilienne) runs from the station to the château but is essentially useless (infrequent, not timed with train arrivals, none on Sun). Returning to the station, taxis and the city bus will pick you up at the château gate.

ORIENTATION TO CHANTILLY

Cost: The château, gardens, horse museum, stables, and dressage horse demonstration are all covered by the Domaine ticket (€17, €9.50 for those under 18) or the Paris Museum Pass. To visit only the gardens, buy the Grounds ticket (€8). Horse enthusiasts can skip the château and buy a ticket that includes the horse museum, stables, dressage demonstration, and the fancier horse show (€21, see below).

Hours: April-Oct daily 10:00-18:00, Nov-March Wed-Mon 10:30-17:00, closed Tue.

Information: Tel. 03 44 27 31 80, www.domainedechantilly.com.

Tours: The free audioguide is worth picking up.

Horse Shows: At the horse museum, the 11:00 daily demonstration of dressage is included in your Domaine ticket. If you're into horses dancing to music and riders in frilly dresses, spring for the show, which takes place daily at 14:30 April-Nov (adds €13 to the Domaine ticket; can also be purchased separately). Confirm demonstration and show times prior to your visit (same contact information as the château).

VISITING THE CHATEAU

Lacking the well-preserved and grandiose interiors of other châteaux, Chantilly lays its claim to fame (and the main reason to visit) with its art collection.

Because of the social upheaval in France during the Revolution of 1848, the château's owner, Prince de Condé, fled to England. Twenty years later, when blue blood was safe again in France, he returned to his château with a fabulous collection of art (800 paintings, including three Raphaels) and priceless books. He turned his palace into the museum you see today and willed it to France on the condition that it would be maintained as he left it and the collections would never be loaned to any other museum.

As most of the château was destroyed during the French Revolution, today's palace is largely rebuilt in a fanciful 19th-century style. It's divided into three parts: apartments, art gallery, and library. The apartments are partially open to the public; to visit the smaller private apartments, you need to pay a €3 supplement and either join a more frequent French-language tour or time your visit for the daily English tour at 15:00.

The **art gallery and library** are the stars (and are included with your entry). Wander the various rooms of the gallery using handheld explanations provided in each room (hunt for an English version). The audioguide adds meaning and context to your visit. Gallery highlights are paintings by Raphael, Titian, Nicolas Poussin, and Eugène Delacroix. Of the 13,000 books in the prince's library, the most exquisite is the 40-page *Book of Hours* by Jean Fouquet (c. 1460).

The **gardens** immediately behind the château are geometric and austere. Drop down the steps from the château, turn right, and

follow the signs for 10 minutes to *le Hameau*, where you'll find a sweet little garden café (limited menu features desserts served with real Chantilly cream, open April-Oct). This little hamlet of three half-timbered, thatched-roofed homes was the prototype for the more famous *hameau* at Versailles. While the homes are peasant-simple on the outside, they are lavishly decorated within: The prince had certain needs when he played peasant. In summer, a shuttle bus occasionally circulates through the gardens (€5, leaves from entry gate).

The prince believed he'd be reincarnated as a horse, so he built an opulent horse château—now a museum (it's the huge building to the right as you look out from the château—allow 10 minutes to walk there from the château). The **horse museum** boasts 15 rooms displaying different bits of horse-related history and art. The museum is beautifully done, with explanations and videos, carved wooden horses from carousels, paintings, and examples of gear used when riding. Entry to the horse museum also includes a walk through the stables, with real-live horses and a demonstration of dressage (daily at 11:00, in French only with an English handout). To get the most from a visit, plan your time to see this demonstration.

TOWN OF CHANTILLY

You'll find many cafés and restaurants in Chantilly town. A lively outdoor **market** runs on Saturday and Wednesday mornings until 12:30 on Place Omer Vallon. Otherwise, a café and a small bakery with sandwiches and drinks are across from the train station.

CHARTRES

Chartres, about 50 miles southwest of Paris, gives travelers a pleasant break in a lively, midsize town with a thriving, pedestrian-friendly old center. But the big reason to come to Chartres (shar-truh) is to see its famous cathedral—arguably Europe's best example of pure Gothic.

Chartres' old church burned to the ground on June 10, 1194. Some of the children who watched its destruction were actually around to help rebuild the cathedral and attend its dedication Mass in 1260. That's astonishing, considering that other Gothic cathedrals, such as Paris' Notre-Dame, took literally centuries to build. Having been built so quickly, the cathedral has a unity of architecture, statuary, and stained glass that captures the spirit of the Age of Faith like no other church.

While overshadowed by its cathedral, the town of Chartres also merits exploration. Discover the picnic-perfect park behind the cathedral, check out the colorful pedestrian zone, and wander the quiet alleys and peaceful lanes down to and along the small river.

PLANNING YOUR TIME

Chartres is an easy day trip from Paris (even if you leave Paris in the afternoon and return later in the evening). But with its statues glowing in the setting sun—and with hotels and restaurants much less expensive than those in the capital—Chartres also makes a worthwhile overnight stop. If you'll be here at night, don't miss the light show—Chartres en Lumières—when dozens of Chartres' most historic buildings are colorfully illuminated, adding to the town's after-hours appeal (mid-April-mid-Oct; details at TI). Chartres' historic center is quiet Sunday and Monday, when most shops are closed.

Chartres is a one-hour ride from Paris' Gare Montparnasse (14/day, about €16 one-way; see page 521 for Gare Montparnasse details). Jot down return times to Paris before you exit the Chartres train station (last train generally departs Chartres around 21:30).

Upon arrival in Chartres, head for the cathedral. Allow an hour to savor the church on your own as you follow my self-guided tour. But don't miss the mesmerizing cathedral tour at noon led by Malcolm Miller; also consider the informative tour at 14:45 by Anne-Marie Woods (details on both tours provided later). Take another hour or two to wander the appealing old city. On Saturday and Wednesday mornings, a small outdoor market sets up a few short blocks from the cathedral on Place Billard.

Orientation to Chartres

Tourist Information: The TI is in the historic Maison du Saumon building (Mon-Sat 9:30-18:30, Sun 10:00-17:30, closes earlier Nov-April, 10 Rue de la Poissonnerie, tel. 02 37 18 26 26, www.chartres-tourisme.com). It offers specifics on cathedral tours and also rents audioguides for the old town (€5.50, €8.50/double set, about 2 hours). The narration offers little more information than my self-guided walk but is relaxing and easy to follow. Skip the Chartres Pass, which is sold here.

The TI has a small map that shows the floodlit Chartres en Lumières sites, and information on the Petit Train you can take to see them all (check the website or ask at the TI for details).

Arrival in Chartres: Exiting Chartres' train station, you'll see the spires of the cathedral dominating the town. It's a 10-minute walk up Avenue Jehan de Beauce to the cathedral. The free mini-bus, called the Filibus, runs to near the cathedral (departs 3/hour Mon-Sat 8:30-19:00), or you can take a taxi for about €7.

The last train to Paris usually leaves around 21:30 (verify for your day of travel).

If arriving **by car,** you'll have fine views of the cathedral and city as you approach from A-11 autoroute.

Helpful Hints: To get online, head to the TI (free Wi-Fi and guest computer) or try the McDonald's (free Wi-Fi, Place des Epars). A **launderette** is a few blocks from the cathedral (by the TI) at 16a Place de la Poissonnerie (daily 7:00-21:00). If you need to call a **taxi,** try tel. 02 37 36 00 00.

Chartres

To Paris
Gare
Montparnasse

To St-Prest
& Paris

TERTRE ST.
NICHOLAS

RUE DES LISSES

BISHOP'S
PALACE
(MUSEE DES
BEAUX ARTS)

Bishop's
Gardens

TRAIN
STATION

Place
Semard

INTERNATIONAL
STAINED GLASS
CENTER

NORTH
PORCH

WALK
BEGINS

CATHEDRAL

❶

Place
Chatelet

SOUTH
PORCH

❽

Place de la
Cathédrale

❻

RUE AU LAIT

WC

❷

❺

❼

POST

Place du
Cygne

PRODUCE
MARKET

MONOPRIX

Pl.
Marceau

RUE DES
CHANGES

RUE DE LA PIE

Place
des
Epars

RUE DU BOIS MERRAIN

RUE R. MARCEAU

RUE TONNELLERIE

R. VOL

ST. FRANCOIS

RUE DU PETIT CHANGE

To Tours
via N-1
& to A-11

Sights in Chartres

▲▲▲CHARTRES CATHEDRAL

The church is (at least) the fourth one on this spot dedicated to
Mary, the mother of Jesus, who has been venerated here for some
1,700 years. There's even speculation that the pagan Romans
dedicated a temple here to a mother-goddess. In earliest times,
Mary was honored next to a natural spring of healing waters (not
visible today).

In 876, the church acquired the torn veil (or birthing gown)
supposedly worn by Mary when she gave birth to Jesus. The
2,000-year-old veil (now on display) became the focus of worship at
the church. By the 11th century, the cult of saints was strong. And
Mary, considered the "Queen of All Saints," was hugely popular.
God was enigmatic and scary, but Mary was maternal and acces-

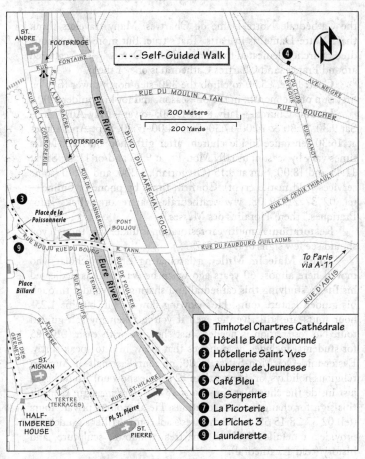

- - - - Self-Guided Walk

200 Meters
200 Yards

1 Timhotel Chartres Cathédrale
2 Hôtel le Bœuf Couronné
3 Hôtellerie Saint Yves
4 Auberge de Jeunesse
5 Café Bleu
6 Le Serpente
7 La Picoterie
8 Le Pichet 3
9 Launderette

sible, providing a handy go-between for Christians and their Creator. Chartres, a small town of 10,000 with a prized relic, found itself in the big time on the pilgrim circuit.

When the fire of 1194 incinerated the old church, the veil was feared lost. Lo and behold, several days later, townspeople found it miraculously unharmed in the crypt (beneath today's choir). Whether the veil's survival was a miracle or a marketing ploy, the people of Chartres were so stoked, they worked like madmen to erect this grand cathedral in which to display it. Thinkers and scholars gathered here, making the small town with its big-city church a leading center of learning in the Middle Ages (until the focus shifted to Paris' university).

By the way, the church is officially called

CHARTRES

the Cathédrale Notre-Dame de Chartres. Many travelers think that "Notre-Dame" is in Paris. That's true. But more than a hundred churches dedicated to Mary—"Notre-Dames"—are scattered around France, and Chartres Cathedral is one of them.

Cost: Free, €5.50 to climb the 300-step north tower (free on first Sun of the month, in the off-season, and for kids under 18).

Hours: Church—daily 8:30-19:30; tower—May-Aug Mon-Sat 9:30-12:30 & 14:00-17:30, Sun 14:00-17:30, Sept-April closes at 16:30 (entrance inside church, after gift shop on left). **Mass** times vary by season: usually Mon-Fri at 9:00 and/or 11:45; Sat at 11:45 and 18:00; Sun at 9:15 (Gregorian), 11:00, and 18:00 (some services held in the crypt). Confirm times by phone or online—tel. 02 37 21 59 08, www.cathedrale-chartres.org (click "Infos Pratiques," then "Horaires des Messes").

Restoration: A multiyear restoration is underway, though you should see few signs of it in 2017.

Tours: Malcolm Miller, a fascinating English scholar who moved here almost 60 years ago when he was 24, has dedicated his life to studying this cathedral and sharing its wonder through his guided lecture tours. He's slowing down a bit, but his 1.25-hour tours are still riveting even if you've taken my self-guided tour. No reservation is needed; just show up with cash (€10, €5 for students, includes headphones that allow him to speak softly, Easter-mid-Oct Mon-Sat at 12:00; no tours last half of Aug, on religious holidays, or if fewer than 12 people show up). Tours begin just inside the church at the *Visites de la Cathédrale* sign. Consult this sign for changes or cancellations. He also offers private tours (tel. 02 37 28 15 58, millerchartres@aol.com). Miller's guidebook provides a detailed look at Chartres' windows, sculpture, and history (sold at cathedral).

Charming American expat **Anne-Marie Woods** is Malcom Miller's understudy and is equally passionate about the cathedral. She leads worthwhile 1.5-hour tours of the cathedral that include the vast crypt (daily at 14:45, tel. 02 37 21 75 02, www.cathedrale-chartres.org).

You can rent **audioguides** inside the cathedral, to the right as you enter. Routes include the cathedral (€4.20, 45 minutes), the choir only (€3.20, 25 minutes), or both (€6.20, 70 minutes). **Binoculars** are a big help for studying the cathedral art (rent at souvenir shops around the cathedral).

Crypt: Beneath the cathedral are extensive remnants of earlier churches, a modern copy of the old wooden Mary-and-baby statue, an amazing 2,000-year-old well, and frescoes from the 12th and 13th centuries. The only way to see the crypt is on a tour. Anne-Marie Woods' tour (see above for details) includes the crypt and helps bring it to life, but I'd avoid the more frequent 30-minute tours in French with English handout (€3, 5/day late June–mid-Sept, fewer on Sun and off-season, start at the gift shop inside the cathedral's north tower, tel. 02 37 21 75 02).

◗ Self-Guided Tour

Historian Malcolm Miller calls Chartres a picture book of the entire Christian story, told through its statues, stained glass, and architecture. In this "Book of Chartres," the text is the sculpture and windows, and its binding is the architecture. The complete narrative can be read—from Creation to Christ's birth (north side of church), from Christ and his followers up to the present (south entrance), and then to the end of time, when Christ returns as judge (west entrance). The remarkable cohesiveness of the text and the unity of the architecture are due to the fact that nearly the entire church was rebuilt in just 30 years (a blink of an eye for cathedral building). The cathedral contains the best and most intact library of medieval religious iconography in existence. Most of the windows date from the early 13th century.

The Christian universe is a complex web of heaven and earth, angels and demons, and prophets and martyrs. Much of the medieval symbolism is obscure today. While it's easy to be overwhelmed by the thousands of things to see, make a point to simply appreciate the perfect harmony of this Gothic masterpiece.
• *Start outside, taking in the...*

❶ Main Entrance (West Facade), c. 1150

Chartres' soaring (if mismatched) steeples announce to pilgrims that they've arrived. For centuries, pilgrims have come here to see holy relics, to honor "Our Lady," and to feed their souls.

The facade is about the only survivor of the intense, lead-melting fire that incinerated the rest of the church in 1194. The church we see today was rebuilt behind this facade in a single generation (1194-1260).

Compare the **towers.** The right (south) tower, with a Romanesque stone steeple, survived the fire. The left (north) tower lost its wooden steeple in the fire. In the 1500s, it was topped with the flamboyant Gothic steeple we see today.

The emaciated column-like statues flanking the three **west doors** are pillars of the faith. These kings of Judah, prophets, and Old Testament big shots foretold the coming of Christ. With solemn gestures and faces, they patiently endure the wait.

What they predicted came to pass. His-

Chartres Cathedral

APSE

8

20 Meters
20 Yards

5

6

TRAN- ☩**4** SEPT

7

12
NORTH
PORCH

11

SOUTH
PORCH

3

10

N
A
V
E

9

2

GIFT
SHOP

★ MEET
TOURS

WEST **1** FACADE

**MAIN
ENTRANCE**

Place de la Cathédrale

1 Main Entrance
(West Facade)
2 Nave
3 Labyrinth
4 View of 3 Rose
Windows
5 Blue Virgin Window
6 Choir Screen
Sculptures
7 Chapel of Our Lady
on the Pillar
8 Mary's Veil
9 Noah Window &
Tower Climb
10 South Exterior –
Flying Buttresses
11 South Porch
12 North Porch

tory's pivotal event is shown above the **right door,** where Mary (seated) produces Baby Jesus from her loins. This Mary-and-baby sculpture is a 12th-century stone version of an even older wooden statue that burned in 1793. Centuries of pilgrims have visited Chartres to see Mary's statue, gaze at her veil, and ponder the mystery of how God in heaven became man on earth, as He passed

through immaculate Mary like sunlight through stained glass.

Over the **central door** is Christ in majesty, surrounded by animals symbolizing Matthew, Mark, Luke, and John. Over the **left door,** Christ ascends into heaven after his death and resurrection.

• *Enter the church (from a side entrance if the main one is closed) and wait for your pupils to enlarge.*

❷ Nave

The place is huge—the nave is 427 feet long, 20 feet wide, and 120 feet high. Notice the height of the entrance doors compared to the tourists...the doors are 24 feet tall!

The long, tall central nave is lined with 12 pillars. These support pointed, crisscrossed arches on the ceiling, which lace together the heavy stone vaulting. The pillars themselves are supported by flying buttresses on the outside of the church (which we'll see later). This skeleton structure was the miracle of Gothic design, making it possible to build tall cathedrals with ribbed walls and lots of stained-glass windows (see the big saints in the upper stories of the nave). Chartres has 28,000 square feet of stained glass. The nave—the widest Gothic nave in France—is flanked by raised side aisles. This design was for crowd flow, so pilgrims could circle the church without disturbing worshippers.

Try to picture the church in the Middle Ages—painted in greens, browns, and golds (like colorful St. Aignan Church in the old town, described later in my self-guided walk). It was packed with pilgrims, and was a rough cross between a hostel, a soup kitchen, and a flea market. The floor of the nave slopes in to the center, for easy drainage when hosing down the dirty pilgrims who camped here. Looking around the church, you'll see stones at the base of the columns smoothed by centuries of tired pilgrim butts. With all the hubbub in the general nave, the choir (screened-off central zone around the high altar) provided a holy place with a more sacred atmosphere.

Taking it all in from the nave, notice that, as was typical in medieval churches, the windows on the darker north side feature Old Testament themes—awaiting the light of Christ's arrival. And the windows on the brighter south side are New Testament. Regardless of which direction they face, the highest windows— way up in the clerestory—are dark from decades of candle soot. As the ongoing cleaning job proceeds, more of the interior will be bright and sparkling like the apse (area behind the front altar).

• *On the floor, midway up the nave, find the...*

❸ Labyrinth

The broad, round labyrinth inlaid in black marble on the floor is a spiritual journey. Labyrinths like this were common in medieval churches. Pilgrims enter from the west rim, by foot or on their

knees, and wind around, meditating, on a metaphorical journey to Jerusalem. About 900 feet later, they hope to meet God in the middle. (The chairs are removed on Fridays from Lent to November 1). To let your fingers do the walking, you'll find a small model of the maze just outside the gift shop, where the tours begin.

• *Walk up the nave to where the transept crosses. As you face the altar and gleaming choir, north is to the left.*

The Chartres Generation—the 1200s

From king to bishop and knight to pawn, French society was devoted to the Christian faith. It inspired knights to undertake the formidable Crusades, artists to recreate the divine in statues and stained glass, and architects to build skyscraping cathedrals filled with the mystic light of heaven. They aimed for a golden age, blending faith and reason. But misguided faith often outstripped reason, resulting in very un-Christian intolerance and violence.

c. 1194 The old cathedral burns down.

1200 The University of Paris is founded, using human reason to analyze Christian faith. Borrowing from the pagan Greek philosopher Aristotle, scholars described the Christian universe as a series of concentric rings spinning around the earth in geometrical perfection.

1202 The pope calls on all true Christians to rescue the Holy Land from Muslim "infidels" in the Fourth Crusade (1202-1204). This crusade ends disastrously in the sacking of Christian Constantinople.

1206 Chartres' cornerstone is laid. The style is *opus francigenum* ("French-style work")—what we now call Gothic. Chartres is just one of several great cathedrals under construction in Europe.

1207 Francis of Assisi, a rebellious Italian youth, undergoes a conversion to a life of Christian poverty and love. His open spirit inspires many followers, including France's King Louis IX (a generation later).

1209 France's King Philip Augustus, based in Paris, invades southern France and massacres fellow Christians (members of the Cathar sect) as heretics.

❹ The Rose Windows—North, South, and West

The three big, round "rose" (flower-shaped) windows over the entrances receive sunlight at different times of day. All three are predominantly blue and red, but each has different "petals," and each tells a different part of the Christian story in a kaleidoscope of fragmented images.

Stained glass was created as a way to teach Bible stories to the illiterate medieval masses...who apparently owned state-of-the-art binoculars. The windows were used in many ways—to tell stories, to allow parents to teach children simple lessons, to help theologians explain complex lessons, to enable worshippers to focus on images as they meditated or prayed...and, of course, to light a dark church in a colorful and decorative way.

The brilliantly restored **north rose window** charts history from the distant past up to the birth of Jesus. On the outer rim, a ring of semicircles, ancient prophets foretell Christ's coming. Then

1212 Thousands of boys and girls idealistically join the Children's Crusade to save the Holy Land. Most die in transit or are sold into slavery.

1220 The external structure of Chartres Cathedral is nearly finished. Work begins on the statues and stained glass.

1226 Eleven-year-old Louis IX is crowned as *rex et sacerdos*, "King and Priest," beginning a 45-year Golden Age combining church and state. His mother, Blanche of Castile (granddaughter of Eleanor of Aquitaine), serves as his regent during his minority and is his lifelong mentor.

1230 Most of Chartres' stained glass is completed.

1244 At age 30, Louis IX falls sick and, while in a coma, sees a vision that changes his life. His personal integrity helps unify the nation. He reforms the judicial system along Christian lines, helping the poor.

1245 The last Albigensian heretics are burned at Montségur, in a crusade ordered by Louis IX and his mother, Blanche.

1248 Louis IX personally leads the Seventh Crusade by walking barefoot from Paris to the port of departure. During the fighting, he is captured and ransomed. He later returns home a changed man. Humbled, he adopts the poverty of the Franciscan brotherhood. His devotion earns him the title of St. Louis.

1260 Chartres Cathedral is dedicated. The church is the physical embodiment of the Age of Faith, with architecture as mathematically perfect as God's Creation, sculpture serving as sermons in stone, and stained glass lit by the light of God.

(circling inward) there's a ring of red squares with kings who are Jesus' direct ancestors. Still closer, circles with white doves and winged angels zero in on the central event of history—Mary, the heart of the flower, with her newborn baby, Jesus.

This window was donated by Blanche of Castile, mother of the future King Louis IX (who would build Paris' stained-glass masterpiece of a church, Sainte-Chapelle). Blanche's heraldry frames the lower edge of the window: yellow fleur-de-lis on a blue background (for France) and gold castles on a red background (for her home kingdom of Castile).

The **south rose window,** with a similar overall design, tells how the Old Testament prophecies were fulfilled. Christ sits in the center (dressed in blue, with a red background), setting in motion radiating rings of angels, beasts, and instrument-playing apocalyptic elders who labor to bring history to its close. The five lancet windows below show Mary flanked by four Old Testament prophets (Jeremiah, Isaiah, Ezekiel, and Daniel) lifting New Testament writers (Luke, Matthew, John, and Mark) on their shoulders. (In the first window on the left, see white-robed Luke riding piggyback on dark-robed Jeremiah.) These demonstrated how the ancients prepared the way for Christ—and how the New Testament evangelists had a broader perspective from their lofty perches.

In the center of the **west rose window,** a dark Christ rings in history's final Day of Judgment. Around him, winged angels blow their trumpets and the dead rise, face judgment, and are sent to hell or raised to eternal bliss. The frilly edge of this glorious "rose" is flecked with tiny clover-shaped dewdrops.

• *Now walk around the altar to the right (south) side and find the window with a big, blue Mary (second one from the right).*

❺ The Blue Virgin Window

Mary, dressed in blue on a rich red background, cradles Jesus, while the dove of the Holy Spirit descends on her. This very old window (mid-12th century) was the central window  behind the altar of the church that burned in 1194. It survived and was reinserted into this frame in the new church around 1230. Mary's glowing dress is an example of the famed "Chartres blue," a sumptuous color made by mixing cobalt oxide into the glass (before cheaper materials were introduced). The Blue Virgin was one of the most popular stops for pilgrims—especially pregnant ones—of the cult of the Virgin-about-to-give-birth. Devotees prayed, carried stones to repair the church, and donated to the church coffers; Mary rewarded them with peace of mind, easy births, and occasional miracles.

Below Mary (bottom panel), see **Christ being tempted** by a red-faced, horned, smirking devil.

The **Zodiac Window** (two windows to the left) shows the 12 signs of the zodiac (in the right half of the window; read from the bottom up—Pisces, Aries, Gemini in the central cloverleaf, Taurus, Cockroach, Leo, Virgo, etc.). On the left side are the corresponding months (February warming himself by a fire, April gathering flowers, and so on).

• *Now turn around and look behind you.*

❻ The Choir Screen—Life of Mary

The choir (enclosed area around the altar where church officials sat) is the heart *(coeur)* of the church. A stone screen rings it with **41 statue groups** illustrating Mary's life. Although the Bible says

Surviving the Centuries

Chartres contains the world's largest collection of medieval stained glass, with more than 150 early 13th-century windows, about 80 percent with the original glass. Through the centuries, much of the rest of France's stained glass was destroyed by various ideologues: Protestant puritans who disapproved of papist imagery (they would never think of it as art), revolutionaries who turned churches into "temples of reason" (or stables), Baroque artists who preferred clear windows and lots of light, and the bombs of World War II.

Chartres was spared many (but not all) of these ravages. During World War II, in anticipation of Nazi destruction, the citizens removed all the windows (burying them in cellars in southwest France) and piled sandbags to protect the statues. Today, Chartres survives as Europe's best-preserved medieval cathedral.

little about the mother of Jesus, legend and lore fleshed out her life. Take some time to learn about the Lady this church is dedicated to.

Scene #1 (south side) shows Mary's dad hearing the news that Mary is on the way. In #4, Mary is born, and maidens bathe the

new baby. In #6, Mary marries Joseph (sculpted with the features of King François I). In scene #7, an angel announces to Mary that she'll be the mother of the Messiah, and (#10) she gives birth to Jesus in a manger. In #12, the Three Kings—looking like the three musketeers—arrive. In #14, Herod orders all babies slaughtered, but Mary's son survives to begin his mission.

Next come episodes from the life of Jesus. On the other side of the choir screen, in #27, Jesus is crucified and, in #28, lies lifeless in his mother's arms. Scene #34 depicts the Ascension, as Jesus takes off, Cape Canaveral-style, while his awestruck followers look up at the bottoms of his rocketing feet. In #39, Mary has died and is raised by angels into heaven, where (#40) she's crowned Queen of Heaven by the Father, Son, and Holy Ghost.

The **plain windows** surrounding the choir date from the 1770s, when the dark mystery of medieval stained glass was replaced by the open light of the French Enlightenment. The plain windows and the choir are some of the only "new" features. Most of the 13th-century church has remained intact, despite style changes, revolutionary vandals, and war bombs.

• *Do an about-face and find the chapel with Mary on a pillar.*

GOD = LIGHT

You can try to examine the details, but a better way to experience the mystery of Chartres is just to sit and stare at these enormous panels as they float in the dark of empty space like holograms or space stations or the Queen of Heaven's crown jewels. Ponder the medieval concept that God is light.

To the Chartres generation, the church was a metaphor for how God brings his creation to life, like the way light animates stained glass. They were heavy into mysticism, feeling a oneness with all creation in a moment of enlightenment. The Gospel of John (as well as a writer known to historians as the Pseudo-Dionysus) was their favorite. Here are select verses from John 1:1-12 (loosely translated):

In the beginning was The Word.
Jesus was the light of the human race.
The light shines in the darkness
and the darkness cannot resist it.
It was the real light coming into the world,
the light that enlightens everyone.
He was in the world, but the world did not recognize Him.
But to those who did, He gave the power
to become the children of God.

❼ Chapel of Our Lady on the Pillar

A 16th-century statue of Mary and baby—draped in cloth, crowned and sceptered—sits on a 13th-century column in a wonderful carved-wood alcove. This is today's pilgrimage center, built to keep visitors from clogging up the altar area. Modern pilgrims (including lots of new moms pushing strollers) honor the Virgin by leaving flowers, lighting candles, and kissing the column.

• *Double back a bit around the ambulatory, heading toward the back of the church. In the next chapel you encounter (Chapel of the Sacred Heart of Mary), you'll find a gold frame holding a fragment of Mary's venerated veil. These days it's kept—for its safety and preservation—out of the light and behind bulletproof glass.*

❽ Mary's Veil

This veil (or tunic) was supposedly worn by Mary when she gave birth to Jesus. It became the main object of adoration for the cult of the Virgin. The great King of the Franks, Charlemagne (742-814), received the veil as a present from Byzantine Empress Irene. Charlemagne's grandson gave the veil to Chartres in 876. In 911,

with the city surrounded by Vikings, the bishop hoisted the veil like a battle flag and waved it at the invaders. It scared the bejeezus out of them, and the town was saved.

In the frenzy surrounding the fire of 1194, the veil mysteriously disappeared, only to reappear three days later (recalling the Resurrection). This was interpreted by church officials and the townsfolk as a sign from Mary that she wanted a new church, and thus the building began. Recent tests confirm that the material itself, and the weaving technique used to make the cloth, date to the first century A.D., lending support to claims of the relic's authenticity.

• *Return to the west end and find the last window on the right (near the tower entrance).*

❾ The Noah Window and Tower Climb

Read Chartres' windows in the medieval style: from bottom to top. In the bottom diamond, God tells Noah he'll destroy the earth.

Next, Noah hefts an axe to build an ark, while his son hauls wood (diamond #2). Two by two, he loads horses (cloverleaf, above left), purple elephants (cloverleaf, right), and other animals. The psychedelic ark sets sail (diamond #3). Waves cover the earth and drown the wicked (two cloverleafs). The  ark survives (diamond #4), and Noah releases a dove. Finally, up near the top (diamond #7), a rainbow (symbolizing God's promise never to bring another flood) arches overhead, God drapes himself over it, and Noah and his family give thanks.

Chartres was a trading center, and its merchant brotherhoods donated money to make 42 of the windows. For 800 years, these panes have publicly thanked their sponsors. In the bottom left is a man making a wheel. More workers are to the right. The panels announce that "these windows are brought to you by..." the wheel-, axe-, and barrelmaking guilds.

• *To climb the north tower, find the entrance nearby. Then exit the church (through the main entrance or the door in the south transept) to view its south side.*

❿ South Exterior—Flying Buttresses

Six flying buttresses (the arches that stick out from the upper walls)

push against six pillars lining the nave inside, helping to hold up the heavy stone ceiling and sloped, lead-over-wood roof. The ceiling and roof push down onto the pillars, of course, but also outward (north and south) because of that miracle of Gothic architecture: the pointed arch. The flying buttresses push back, channeling the stress outward to the six vertical buttresses, then down to the ground. The result is a tall cathedral held up by slender pillars buttressed from the outside, allowing the walls to be opened up for stained glass.

The church is built from large blocks of limestone. Peasants trod in hamster-wheel contraptions to raise these blocks into place—a testament to their great faith.

⓫ South Porch

The three doorways of the south entrance show the world from Christ's time to the present, as Christianity triumphs over persecution.

Center Door—Christ and Apostles: Standing between the double doors, **Jesus** holds a book and raises his arm in blessing. He's a simple, itinerant, bareheaded, barefoot rabbi, but underneath his feet, he tramples symbols of evil: the dragon and lion. Christ's face is among the most noble of all Gothic sculpture.

Christ is surrounded by his **apostles,** who spread the good news to a hostile world. **Peter** (to the left as you face Jesus), with curly hair and beard, holds the keys to the kingdom of heaven. **Paul** (to the right of Jesus) fingers the sword of his martyrdom and contemplates the inevitable loss of his head. In fact, all of these apostles were killed or persecuted, and their faces are humble, with sad eyes. But their message prevailed, and under their feet they crush the squirming rulers who once persecuted them.

The final triumph comes above the door in the **Last Judgment.** Christ sits in judgment, raising his hands, while Mary and John beg him to take it easy on poor humankind. Beneath Christ the souls are judged—the righteous on our left, and the wicked on our right, who are thrown into the fiery jaws of hell. Farther to the right (above the statues of Paul and the apostles), horny demons subject wicked women to an eternity of sexual harassment.

Left Door—Martyrs: Eight martyrs flank the left door. **St. Lawrence** (second from left) cradles the grill (it looks like a book) on which he was barbecued alive. His last brave words to the Romans were: "You can turn me over—I'm done on this side." **St. George** (far right on right flank) wears the knightly uniform of the 1200s, when Chartres was built and King Louis IX was crusading. Depicted beneath the martyrs are gruesome **methods of torture,** such as George stretched on the wheel. Many of these techniques were actually used in the 1200s by Christians against heretics, Muslims, Jews, and Christian Cathars.

• *Reach the north side by circling around the back end of the church. As you walk, enjoy the peaceful park, fine views over the town, and the church's architecture. Ponder the exoskeletal nature of Gothic design and the ability of medieval faith to mobilize the masses.*

⓬ North Porch

In the "Book of Chartres," the north porch is chapter one, from the Creation up to the coming of Christ.

Look between the double doors to see **Baby Mary** (headless), in the arms of her mother, Anne, marking the end of the Old Testament world and the start of the New.

History begins in the tiny details in the concentric arches over the doorway. **God creates Adam** (at the peak of the outermost arch, just to the left of the keystone) by cradling his head in his lap like a child.

Next, look at the statues that flank the doors. **Melchizedek** (farthest to the left of Mary and Anne), with the cap of a king and the cup of communion, is the biblical model of the *rex et sacerdos* (king-priest), the title bestowed on King Louis IX.

Abraham (next to Melchizedek) holds his son by the throat and raises a knife to slit him for sacrifice. Just then, he hears something and turns his head up to see God's angel, who stops the bloodshed. The drama of this frozen moment anticipates Renaissance naturalism by 200 years.

John the Baptist (fourth to the right from Mary/Anne), the last Old Testament prophet, who prepared the way for Jesus, holds a lamb, the symbol of Christ. John is skinny from his diet of locusts and honey. His body and beard twist and flicker like a flame.

All these prophets, with their beards turning down the corners of their mouths, have the sad, wise look of having been around since the beginning of time and having seen it all—from Creation to Christ to Apocalypse. Over the door is the culmination of all this history: **Christ on his throne,** joined by Mary, the Queen of Heaven. These sculptures are some of the last work done on the church, completing the church's stone-and-glass sermon.

Imagine all this painted and covered with gold leaf in preparation for the dedication ceremonies in 1260, when the Chartres generation could finally stand back and watch as their great-grandchildren, carrying candles, entered the cathedral.

CHARTRES WALK

Chartres' old town bustles with activity (except Sun and Mon) and merits exploration. You can rent an audioguide from the TI, or

better, just wander (follow the route shown on the map on page 580).

In medieval times, Chartres was actually two towns—the pilgrims' town around the cathedral, and the industrial town along the river, which was powered by watermills. This self-guided walk takes you on a 45-minute loop around the cathedral, through the old pilgrims' town, down along the once-industrial riverbank, and back to the cathedral.

• *Begin at the square in front of the church.*

Cathedral Close: Around the cathedral was a town within the town. Essentially a precinct run by the church, it was called the "close" of Notre-Dame *(cloître Notre-Dame).* Looking at the square in front of the church, imagine a walled-in cathedral town with nine gates. It was busy, with a hospital, a school (Chartres was a leading center of education in the 12th century), a bishop's palace, markets, fairs, and lots of shops—many of them tucked up against the church between its huge buttresses. Chartres was on the medieval map because of the cathedral and its relic. The town was all about the church. For example, in the medieval mind, the foundation of truth was the number three—the Trinity. Nine (three times three) was also a good number. Chartres consisted of three entities—the town, the close, and the church. And each was sure to have nine gates or doors.

About 20 paces in front of the cathedral's main door, a modern plaque in the pavement points pilgrims to Santiago de Compostela in northwest Spain, home of the tomb of St. James (notice the pilgrim with his walking stick and the stylized scallop shell symbolizing the various routes from all over Europe converging on Santiago). For a thousand years, the faithful have trekked from Paris to Chartres and on to Santiago, a thousand miles away. And for centuries, pilgrims have stoked the economy of Chartres.

• *Circle the cathedral clockwise, passing a fine 24-hour clock as you round the corner, and then find the striking carvings of the north porch (described on page 593). Head under a stately 18th-century wrought-iron gate to the...*

Bishop's Palace and Grounds: The bishop essentially ruled from here until the French Revolution secularized the country. This fine building has housed King Henry IV (here for his coronation), Napoleon, and—since 1939—the city's Museum of Fine Arts (Musée des Beaux Arts). An ivy-covered arcade, running from near the church to the palace, is all that remains of a covered passageway designed to make the bishop's commute more pleasant. Stand close to the banister as you survey the lower levels of the bishop's terraced gardens and enjoy a view of the lower town. From here, you can see why this point has been a strategic choice since ancient times. Beyond the gardens nestles the lower town, which was centered not on the church but on the river, which powered the local industry.

• *From the bishop's garden, continue circling around the cathedral until you reach its south porch (described on page 592). Turn left onto...*

Rue des Changes: This "street of the money changers" runs south from the cathedral. The layout, street names, and building facades of this historic district all date back to a time when businesses catered to the needs of pilgrims rather than tourists. At Rue de la Poissonnerie (where fish were sold), side-trip half a block left, to a fine old half-timbered building called **Maison du Saumon** (House of Salmon). It dates from about 1500, and as you might guess from the carvings, it faced the former fish market. Today it's Chartres' TI.

Back on Rue des Changes, a few more paces brings you to the sky-blue open-air **produce market** on Place Billard (open Sat and Wed until 13:00). Chartres' castle stood here until 1802, when it was demolished with revolutionary gusto to make way for the market.

• *From here, Rue des Changes turns into Rue des Grenets. For a detour into a bigger-than-you-thought pedestrian zone of shops, colorful lanes, and café-dappled squares, turn right up Rue de la Pie to Place Marceau (the hub of this network) and Rue Noël Ballay (the main shopping drag). Return to Rue des Grenets, and continue walking away from the cathedral.*

Rue des Grenets: Farther down the street is the **Church of St. Aignan.** Squat, crumbling, and lopsided, this is the oldest of Chartres' parish churches. Remember: Locals didn't worship in the great cathedral (that was for visitors—like us); they worshipped in the town's simple parish churches. This one is built upon the tomb of a fourth-century bishop of Chartres (his statue stands in front of the choir). Its interior, dating from about 1625, shows how colorful a stone church could be. The vibrant colors, lavish decoration, and vaulted wood ceiling are astonishing, given the plain exterior. The wood ceiling reminds us that churches could burn.

Continue down Rue des Grenets to a tall, skinny **half-timbered house.** As the population grew, so did the fire hazard, and the town required half-timbered buildings to be plastered over for safety. Today, the town government—interested in pumping up the touristic charm—pays folks to peel away the plaster and re-expose those timbers. You can see that this building is one of the oldest—the tilting lintel and the asymmetrical windows are dead giveaways.

Turn left at the house and drop down the *tertre,* a series of **stair-step terraces** that link the upper and lower towns. The well-worn stone benches along the way evoke a day when washerwomen, laden with freshly washed laundry, rested as they climbed the hill after a trip to the river.

• *At the bottom, turn right on Rue St. Pierre, then find the **Church of St. Pierre** (great photo-op of flying buttresses and a delicate yet decrepit interior). Follow Pont St. Hilaire a block below the church, and—bam!—Eure at the river.*

The Eure River: This is another photogenic spot, with old buildings, humpback bridges, and cathedral steeples in the

distance. As in nearly any industrial town back then, waterwheels provided power. The river was once lined with busy mills and warehouses. The worst polluters were kept downstream (dyers, tanners, slaughterhouses). The names of the riverside lanes evoke those times: Rue du Massacre, Rue de la Tannerie, and Rue de la Foulerie (named for a process of cleaning wool).

When the industry moved out to make room for Chartres' growing population, laundry places replaced the old mills. These were two-story structures—the wash cycle downstairs at the river, then the dry cycle upstairs, where vents allowed the wind to blow through. You can still see some of the mechanisms designed to accommodate periodic changes in the river level. The last riverside laundry closed in the 1960s.

• *Turn left on Rue de la Foulerie, and follow the river back toward the cathedral. The bridge at Rue du Bourg was once the town's main bridge. Cross it and climb uphill—you'll see Queen Bertha's Staircase (Escalier de la Reine Berthe), a one-of-a-kind half-timbered spiral staircase. Soon after, turn left up the stairs, and you're back at the cathedral. From here, consider stopping by the...*

International Stained Glass Center (Centre International du Vitrail): This low-key center on the north side of cathedral is worth a visit to learn about the techniques behind the mystery of this fragile but enduring art (€6.50, Mon-Fri 9:30-12:30 & 13:30-18:00, Sat 10:00-12:30 & 14:30-18:00, Sun 14:30-18:00, 5 Rue du Cardinal Pie, 50 yards from cathedral, tel. 02 37 21 65 72, www.centre-vitrail.org).

Here you'll gaze into the eyes of original stained-glass windows from the 12th to the 17th century. The windows you see were gathered from several parish churches around Chartres that were destroyed during the French Revolution. You'll also see several windows from the nearby churches of St. Aignan and St. Pierre (both described earlier). Finish your visit in the 12th-century vaulted wine cellar to enjoy contemporary windows made using modern techniques.

Panels describe the displays, many of which are original windows from area churches. Ask at the entrance about the 25-minute video in English describing the process of blown glass and the 10-minute French-only video explaining how it is turned into stained glass (easy to follow for non-French speakers). The center also offers five-day classes; call ahead or email for topics and dates.

Sleeping in Chartres

($$$$ = Splurge, $$$ = Pricier, $$ = Moderate, $ = Budget)
$$ Timhotel Chartres Cathédrale,*** a block up from the train station, is comfortable and well run. Don't let the facade fool you—inside is a comfy place with a huge fireplace in the lobby and 48 well-kept rooms. Several rooms connect—good for families—and many have partial cathedral views (pricier rooms come with more space and cathedral views, family rooms, good buffet breakfast—extra, but one breakfast per couple free for Rick Steves readers, minibars, air-con, handy and safe pay parking, 6 Avenue Jehan

CHARTRES

de Beauce, tel. 02 37 21 78 00, www.timhotel.com, chartres@
timhotel.fr).

$ Hôtel le Bœuf Couronné*** is more like a vintage two-
star hotel, with 17 colorful, good-value rooms and a handy location
halfway between the station and cathedral (family rooms, elevator,
no air-con, good restaurant with views of the cathedral, reserve
ahead for pay parking, 15 Place Châtelet, tel. 02 37 18 06 06, www.
leboeufcouronne.com, resa@leboeufcouronne.fr).

$ Hôtellerie Saint Yves, which hangs on the hillside just
behind the cathedral, delivers well-priced simplicity with 50
spic-and-span rooms in a renovated monastery with meditative
garden areas. Single rooms have no view; ask for a double room
with views of the lower town (small bathrooms, good breakfast—
extra, 1 Rue Saint Eman, enter via Rue des Acacias, tel. 02 37 88
37 40, www.hotellerie-st-yves.com, contact@hotellerie-st-yves.
com).

Hostel: ¢ Auberge de Jeunesse, a 20-minute walk from the
historic center, is located in a modern building with good views
of the cathedral from its terrace (includes breakfast, dirt cheap
meals, 23 Avenue Neigre, tel. 02 37 34 27 64, www.auberge-de-
jeunesse-chartres.fr, auberge-jeunesse-chartres@wanadoo.fr).

Eating in Chartres

($$$$ = Splurge, $$$ = Pricier, $$ = Moderate, $ = Budget)
Dining out in Chartres is a good deal—particularly if you've
come from Paris. Troll the places basking in cathedral views, and
if it's warm, find a terrace table (several possibilities). Then finish
your evening cathedral-side, sipping a hot or cold drink at Le
Serpente.

$$ Café Bleu offers a great view terrace and an appealing
interior. It serves classic French fare at acceptable prices (closed
Tue, 1 Cloître Notre-Dame, tel. 02 37 36 59 60).

$$ Le Serpente saddles up next door to the cathedral,
with terrific view tables and an adorable collector's interior. The

cuisine is good, basic bistro fare and
fairly priced. Simple dishes and to-go
food are available from the room at the
back (daily, 2 Cloître Notre-Dame, tel.
02 37 21 68 81).

$ La Picoterie serves up a cozy
interior and inexpensive fare (omelets,
crêpes, salads, and such) with efficient
service (daily, 36 Rue des Changes, tel.
02 37 36 14 54).

$$ Le Pichet 3 is run by endearing

Marie-Sylvie and Xavier. This local-products shop and cozy bistro make a fun lunch stop. Sit on the quiet street terrace or peruse the artsy inside. Laura serves lots of fresh vegetables and a good selection of *plats*—try the rabbit with plums (Thu-Tue 11:00-dusk, closed Wed and for dinner off-season, 19 Rue du Cheval Blanc, tel. 02 37 21 08 35).

GIVERNY & AUVERS-SUR-OISE

Paris is the unofficial capital of Impressionism, its museums speckled with sun-dappled paintings. But true Impressionist fans will want to do what the Impressionist painters did: don a scarf and beret, and head for the countryside.

At Giverny and Auvers-sur-Oise, follow in the footsteps of Monet, Van Gogh, Pissarro, Cézanne, and others. See the landscapes and small-town life that inspired these great masters. Little has changed over time: You'll be surrounded by pastoral scenes that still look like an Impressionist painting come to life.

At Giverny, you can visit Monet's home and much-painted garden. (Be warned: the gardens are pretty, but they're filled with tourists, so time your visit carefully.) Auvers-sur-Oise is a quieter village, with Van Gogh's grave, recognizable settings of several of the artist's paintings, and a multimedia museum on Impressionism. Both places are about an hour's journey from Paris and easy to reach by public transportation.

Giverny

Claude Monet's gardens at Giverny are like his paintings—brightly colored patches that are messy but balanced. Flowers were his brushstrokes, a bit untamed and slapdash, but part of a carefully composed design. Monet spent his last (and most creative) years cultivating his garden and his art at Giverny (zhee-vayr-nee), the spiritual home of Impressionism (1883-1926). Visiting the Marmottan and/or the Orangerie museums in Paris before your visit here, or at least reading the chapters on those museums, heightens your appreciation of these gardens.

In 1883, middle-aged Claude Monet, his wife Alice, and their eight children from two families settled into this farmhouse, 50 miles west of Paris (for more on Monet's family, see sidebar on page 272).

Monet, already a famous artist and happiest at home, would spend 40 years in Giverny, traveling less with each passing year. He built a pastoral paradise complete with a Japanese garden and a pond full of floating lilies.

In 1912, Monet—the greatest visionary, literally, of his generation—began to go blind with cataracts. To compensate, he used larger canvases and painted fewer details. The true subject of these later works is not really the famous water lilies but the changing reflections on the pond's surface—of the blue sky, white clouds, and green trees that line the shore.

GETTING TO GIVERNY

Drivers can get in and out of Giverny in a half-day with ease. The trip is also doable in a half-day by public transportation with a train/bus connection, but because trains are not frequent, be prepared for a six-hour excursion.

By Tour: Big tour companies do a Giverny day trip from Paris for around €70. If you're interested, ask at your hotel, but you can easily do the trip yourself by train and bus for about €40.

By Car: From Paris' *périphérique* ring road, follow A-13 toward Rouen, exit at *Sortie 14* to Vernon, and follow *Centre Ville* signs, then signs to *Giverny*. You can park right at Monet's house or at one of several nearby lots.

By Train: Take the Rouen-bound train from Paris Gare St. Lazare Station to Vernon, about four miles from Giverny (normally leaves from tracks 20-25, 45 minutes one-way, about €30 round-trip). The train that leaves Paris at around 8:15 is ideal for this trip, with departures about every two hours after that (8/day Mon-Sat, 6/day Sun). Before boarding, use an information desk in Gare St. Lazare to get return times from Vernon to Paris.

Getting from Vernon's Train Station to Giverny: From the Vernon station to Monet's garden, you have four options: bus, taxi, bike, or hike. If you need to check bags, drop them at L'Arrivée de Giverny café, opposite the train station (€5/bag).

The Vernon-Giverny **bus** meets every train from Paris for the 15-minute run to Giverny (€8 round-trip, pay driver). A bus-and-train timetable is available at the bus stops, on the bus, and online

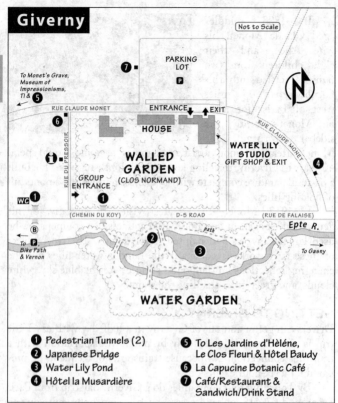

Giverny

Not to Scale

GIVERNY & AUVERS

PARKING LOT
P

To Monet's Grave,
Museum of
Impressionisms,
TI & ⑤

RUE CLAUDE MONET

⑦

ENTRANCE ↓ ↑ EXIT

RUE CLAUDE MONET

HOUSE

⑥

WATER LILY
STUDIO
GIFT SHOP & EXIT

④

RUE DU PRESSOIR

ⓘ

WALLED
GARDEN
(CLOS NORMAND)

GROUP
ENTRANCE
→

WC ①

①

N

(CHEMIN DU ROY)   D-5 ROAD   (RUE DE FALAISE)

Epte R.

Path

Ⓑ
P
To
Bike Path
& Vernon

②

③

To Gasny

WATER GARDEN

① Pedestrian Tunnels (2)
② Japanese Bridge
③ Water Lily Pond
④ Hôtel la Musardière

⑤ To Les Jardins d'Hèléne,
Le Clos Fleuri & Hôtel Baudy
⑥ La Capucine Botanic Café
⑦ Café/Restaurant &
Sandwich/Drink Stand

(www.giverny.org/transpor)—note return times. To reach the bus stop, walk through the station, then follow the tracks—the stop is across from the L'Arrivée de Giverny café. Don't dally in the station—the bus leaves soon after your train arrives. During busy times, a line can form while the driver sells tickets and loads the bus.

The bus leaves Giverny from the same stop where it drops you off (near the pedestrian underpass—see map; good WCs on the north side of the underpass). Buses generally run every hour, with the last one departing at about 19:15 (confirm times by checking schedule upon arrival). Get to the stop at least 15 minutes early to ensure a space. If you miss the return bus and can't wait for the next one, ask any approachable service personnel to call a taxi.

Taxis wait in front of the station in Vernon (allow €15 one-way for up to 3 people, mobile 06 77 49 32 90 or 06 50 12 21 22).

You can also rent a **bike** at L'Arrivée de Giverny café (€14, tel. 02 32 21 16 01) and follow a paved bike path *(piste cyclable)* that runs from near Vernon along an abandoned railroad right-of-way (figure about 30 minutes to Giverny). Get the easy-to-follow map to Giverny when you rent your bike, and you're in business.

Hikers can go on **foot** to Giverny (about 1.5 hours one way) following the bike path (see above) and take a bus or taxi back.

Extension to Rouen: Consider combining your morning Giverny visit with an afternoon excursion to nearby Rouen—together they make an efficient and memorable day trip from Paris. Note that Rouen's museums are closed on Tuesdays. From Vernon (the halfway point between Rouen and Paris), it's about 40 minutes by train to Rouen; the return trip from Rouen back to Paris takes 70-90 minutes. Plan to arrive at Monet's garden when it opens (at 9:30), so you can be back to the Vernon train station by about 13:00. You'll land in Rouen by 14:00 and have just enough time to see Rouen's cathedral and surrounding medieval quarter. In Rouen, the TI is a 15-minute walk from the station and offers an audioguide walking tour (or, better yet, get your hands on the Rouen section from the Normandy chapter of my *Rick Steves France* guidebook). If you leave Rouen around 18:00, you'll pull into Paris about 19:15, having spent a wonderful day sampling rural and urban Normandy.

Orientation to Giverny

All of Giverny's sights and shops string along Rue Claude Monet, which runs in front of Monet's house.

Tourist Information: The TI is located at the intersection of Rue Claude Monet and Rue du Pressoir (daily late March-late Sept 10:00-17:45, closed off-season, 80 Rue Claude Monet, tel. 02 32 64 45 01).

Giverny based taxi: tel. 06 03 30 85 47.

Sights in Giverny

▲MONET'S GARDEN AND HOUSE

All kinds of people flock to Giverny. Gardeners admire the earth-moving landscaping and layout, botanists find interesting new plants, and art lovers can see paintings they've long admired come to life. Fans enjoy wandering around the house where Monet spent half his life and seeing the boat he puttered around in, as well as the henhouse where his family got the eggs for their morning omelets.

There are two gardens, split by a busy road, plus the house, which displays Monet's prized collection of Japanese prints. The gardens are always flowering with something; they're at their most colorful April through July.

Cost: €9.50, not covered by Paris Museum Pass, €16.50 combo-ticket includes nearby Museum of Impressionisms, €18.50

combo-ticket with Paris' Marmottan Museum; daily April-Oct 9:30-18:00, closed Nov-March; tel. 02 32 51 90 31, http://fondation-monet.com.

Crowd-Beating Tips: Though lines may be long and tour groups may trample the flowers, true fans still find magic in the

gardens. Minimize crowds by arriving a little before 9:30, when it opens, or come after 16:00 and stay until it closes. Crowds recede briefly during lunch (12:00-13:30) but descend en masse after lunch. The busiest months here are May and June.

If you're coming at a busy time, your best bet is to buy advance tickets online or at any FNAC store in Paris, which allows you to skip the ticket line and use the group entrance. Another option, if you also plan to visit the Museum of Impressionisms (described later), is to go there first and buy a combo-ticket (*billet couplé*).

Visiting the House and Gardens: After you get in, go directly into the **Walled Garden** (Clos Normand) and work your way around clockwise. Smell the pretty

scene. Monet cleared this land of pine trees and laid out symmetrical beds, split down the middle by a "grand alley" covered with iron trellises of climbing roses. He did his own landscaping, installing flowerbeds of lilies, irises, and clematis. The arched arbors leading to the home's entry form a natural tunnel that guides your eye down the path—an effect exploited in his *Rose Trellis* paintings (on display in Paris at the Marmottan Museum). In his carefree manner, Monet throws together hollyhocks, daisies, and poppies. The color scheme of each flowerbed contributes to the look of the whole garden.

In the southwest corner of the Walled Garden (near the group entrance), you'll find a pedestrian tunnel that leads under the road to the **Water Garden.** Follow the meandering path to the Japanese bridge, under weeping willows, over the pond filled with water lilies, and past countless scenes that leave artists aching for an easel. Find a bench. Monet landscaped like he painted—he built an Impressionist pattern of blocks of color. After he planted the gardens, he painted them, from every angle, at every time of day, in

An Impressionist's Garden

Impressionism was a revolutionary movement and all the rage in European art in the 1880s. Artists abandoned realism in favor of a wispy style that captured light, glimmers, feelings, and impressions. Committed to conveying subtle atmospheric effects, the Impressionists captured nature as a mosaic of short brushstrokes of different colors placed side by side, suggesting shimmering light. And there is no better nature for an Impressionist ready to paint than Monet's delightful mix of weeping willows, luminous clouds, delicate bridges, reflecting ponds...and lush water lilies.

all kinds of weather. Assisted by his favorite stepdaughter, Blanche (also a painter, who married Monet's son Jean, from an earlier marriage), he worked on several canvases at once, moving with the sun from one to the next. In a series of canvases, you can watch the sunlight sweep over the gardens from early dawn to twilight.

Back on the main side, continue your visit with a wander through Monet's mildly interesting **home** (pretty furnishings, Japanese prints, old photos, and a room filled with copies of his paintings). The gift shop at the exit is the actual sky-lighted studio where Monet painted his water-lily masterpieces (displayed at the Orangerie Museum in Paris). Many visitors spend more time in this tempting gift shop than in the gardens themselves.

NEARBY SIGHTS

Museum of Impressionisms (Musée des Impressionnismes)
This bright, modern museum, dedicated to the history of Impressionism and its legacy, houses temporary exhibits of Impressionist art. Check its website for current shows or just drop in. It also has picnic-pleasant gardens in front.

Cost and Hours: €7, daily April-Oct 10:00-18:00, closed Nov-March; to reach it, turn left after leaving Monet's place and walk 200 yards; tel. 02 32 51 94 00, www.mdig.fr.

Claude Monet's Grave

Monet's grave is a 15-minute walk from his door. Turn left out of his house and walk down Rue Claude Monet, pass the Museum of Impressionisms and the Hôtel Baudy, and find it in the backyard of the white church Monet attended (Eglise Sainte-Radegonde). Look for flowers, with a cross above. The inscription says: *Here lies our beloved Claude Monet, born 14 November 1840, died 5 December 1926; missed by all.*

GIVERNY & AUVERS

Vernon Town

If you have time to kill at Vernon's train station, take a five-minute walk into town and sample the peaceful village. Walk between the tracks and the café across the street from the station, and follow the street as it curves left and becomes Rue d'Albuféra. You'll find a smattering of half-timbered Norman homes near Hôtel de Ville (remember, you're in Normandy) and several good cafés and shops—including the killer **$ Boulangerie/Pâtisserie Rose**, which has intense quiche and a good selection of sandwiches (74 Rue d'Albuféra, tel. 02 32 51 03 98).

Sleeping and Eating in Giverny

($$$$ = Splurge, $$$ = Pricier, $$ = Moderate, $ = Budget)

Sleeping: $ Hôtel la Musardière** is nestled in the village of Giverny two blocks from Monet's home (exit right when you leave Monet's). Carole welcomes you with 10 sweet rooms that Claude himself would have felt at home in (family rooms) and a reasonable and homey **$$** *crêperie*-**restaurant** with a lovely yard and outdoor tables (daily with nonstop service, 123 Rue Claude Monet, tel. 02 32 21 03 18, www.lamusardiere.fr, hotelmusardieregiverny@ wanadoo.fr).

$ Les Jardins d'Hèléne *chambres d'hôte* is as lovely as a Monet painting, with floral rooms and a terrific garden. Owner Sandrine Chifman goes out of her way to help her guests have a local experience, including free use of her bikes, and cooks dinner on Sunday and Monday evenings when most restaurants are closed—€20, reserve 2 days ahead (includes breakfast, 15-minute walk from Monet's home at 12 Rue Claude Monet, tel. 02 32 21 30 68 or 06 47 98 14 87, www.giverny-lesjardinsdhelene.com, lesjardinsdhelene@free.fr).

$ Le Clos Fleuri is a family-friendly B&B in a traditional house with three fine rooms, handy cooking facilities, and a lovely garden. It's a 15-minute walk from Monet's place and is run by charming, English-speaking Danielle, who serves up a generous included breakfast (cash only, 5 Rue de la Dîme, tel. 02 32 21 36 51, www.giverny-leclosfleuri.fr, leclosfleuri27@yahoo.fr).

Eating: A flowery **café/ restaurant** and a **sandwich/drink**

stand sit right next to the parking lot across from Monet's home. Enjoy your lunch in the nearby gardens of the Museum of the Impressionisms.

The botanic café by the TI, **$ La Capucine,** is like a self-serve cafeteria, with a pleasant garden and tasty cold or warm soups and quiches (daily 10:00-18:00).

Rose-colored **$$ Hôtel Baudy,** once a hangout for American Impressionists, offers an appropriately pretty setting for lunch or dinner (outdoor tables in front, popular with tour groups, daily, 5-minute walk past Museum of Impressionisms at 81 Rue Claude Monet, tel. 02 32 21 10 03). Don't miss a stroll through the artsy gardens behind the restaurant.

Auvers-sur-Oise

This small, plain town draws Van Gogh pilgrims and those in search of a green escape from the city. Auvers-sur-Oise (oh-vehr soor wahz) is a peaceful place on a bend of the lazy Oise River,

northwest of Paris. A manageable day trip by car, it can be tricky by train (best for the truly devoted). Here you'll get an intimate glimpse into life (and death) during the Impressionist era. Walkers enjoy stretching their legs between the sights in this countryside setting.

Auvers was a magnet for artists in the late 1800s. Charles-François Daubigny, Jean-Baptiste-Camille Corot, Camille Pissarro, and Paul Cézanne all adored this rural retreat (they were also unknown at this time). But Auvers is best known as the village where Vincent van Gogh shot himself. He moved here from southern France to be near his brother Theo (who lived in Paris). Vincent had talked his way out of the asylum in St-Rémy-de-Provence with assurances that he would be under good care from an understanding doctor, Auvers resident Paul Gachet.

Today, this modest little town opens its doors to visitors with a handful of sights and walking trails leading to scenes painted by various artists (some with copies of the paintings posted). Most sights are closed Mondays (some are also closed

Tue) and from November to Easter. Auvers makes a convenient first or last overnight stop for drivers using Charles de Gaulle airport, as it avoids traffic hassles (Auvers is about 20 miles from the airport).

GETTING TO AUVERS-SUR-OISE

By Train: Main-line trains direct to Auvers-sur-Oise run on weekends and holidays from Gare du Nord (one round-trip per day, 45 minutes, departs at about 9:30, returns at about 18:20). This is by far your surest bet for a stress-free trip, but it leaves you there all day. (Take the train at least one direction; see below for other options.) The station in Auvers-sur-Oise is unmanned on weekends, so buy round-trip tickets in Paris, and confirm the return schedule in advance.

Frequent RER trains get you there every day but take 90 minutes each way and require a transfer. Take the RER-C to Pontoise (2/hour, 1 hour to Pontoise, catch in Paris at St. Michel, Musée d'Orsay, Invalides, or Pont de l'Alma stops). Pontoise is the end of the line, where it's easy to transfer to Auvers. Ask at any RER-C station for the best connection or check www.ratp. fr for RER lines. Service from Pontoise back to Paris is frequent, with trains to Gare du Nord, Gare St. Lazare, and points along the RER-C route.

To get from Pontoise to Auvers, a 10-minute ride away, you have three options: You can take the train (direction: Creil), but plan ahead to avoid long waits (before leaving Auvers' train station, get return times to Pontoise, as service is sparse but workable). You can catch bus #9507 (stop to the right of the station, runs hourly, look for the posted schedule—you're at Chemin de la Gare in Pontoise, and you want the Marie stop in Auvers). Or you can go by taxi (about €11; for a bit more money, the same taxi can pick you up in Auvers for the return; tel. 01 30 75 95 95).

By Car: Auvers is about 45 minutes northwest of Paris. Take the A-15 autoroute to A-115, and then exit at Auvers-sur-Oise.

Orientation to Auvers-sur-Oise

Tourist Information: The small but helpful TI is in a white house at the center of the Parc Van Gogh (the park entrance is across from the train station about a block toward town). The TI has good information on all sights, as well as bus, train, and RER schedules (generally open Tue-Sun 9:30-12:30 & 14:00-18:00, Nov-March until 17:00, closed Mon year-round, tel. 01 30 36 71 81, www.

Vincent van Gogh

In the dead of winter in 1888, 35-year-old Vincent van Gogh left big-city Paris for the town of Arles in Provence, hoping to jump-start his floundering career and personal life. Coming from the gray skies and flat lands of the north, Vincent was bowled over by everything Provençal—the sun, bright colors, rugged landscape, and raw people. For two years, he painted furiously, creating a new masterpiece every few days.

The son of disinterested parents, Vincent never found the social skills necessary to sustain close friendships. Lonely Vincent—who dreamed of making Arles a magnet for fellow artists—persuaded Paul Gauguin to join him there. At first, the two got along well, but within a few months, their relationship deteriorated. Gauguin left Arles, leaving Vincent deeply depressed. The local paper reported what happened next: "At 11:30 p.m., Vincent Vaugogh (sic), painter from Holland, appeared at the brothel at no. 1, asked for Rachel, and gave her his cut-off earlobe, saying, 'Treasure this precious object.' Then he vanished." Vincent woke up the next morning at home with his head wrapped in a bloody towel and his earlobe missing.

The bipolar genius (a modern diagnosis) admitted himself to the St. Paul Monastery and Hospital in St-Rémy-de-Provence in the spring of 1889. He spent a year in the hospital, thriving in the care of nurturing doctors and nuns. Painting was part of Vincent's therapy, so they gave him a studio to work in, and he produced more than 100 paintings. Alcohol-free and institutionalized, he did some of his wildest work. With thick, swirling brushstrokes and surreal colors, he made his placid surroundings throb with restless energy.

In the spring of 1890, Vincent left St-Rémy and traveled to Auvers-sur-Oise to enter the care of Dr. Paul Gachet, whom he hoped could help stabilize his mental condition. Gachet advised the artist to throw himself into his work as a remedy for his illness, which he did—Vincent spent the last 70 days of his life in this little town, knocking out a masterpiece each day.

On July 27, Vincent wandered into the famous Auvers wheat field and shot himself, dying of his injuries two days later.

tourisme.fr). Spring for the helpful €1 map showing walking routes, and set the scene for your exploration by watching the 12-minute video on Auvers-sur-Oise and Van Gogh (€1, English version available).

Helpful Hints: There's a handy **supermarket** and **bakery** on your way into town from the station. For a **taxi** in Auvers, call 01 39 60 20 40, or in Pontoise 01 30 30 45 45.

Sights in Auvers-sur-Oise

The best way to spend a few hours in Auvers is to wander the streets and paths of the village. Spot locations where well-known paintings were set, stop by the graves of Vincent and Theo, and visit the Château d'Auvers—the town's most worthwhile sight. It's easy to connect Auvers' sights by following my route or using the TI map.

Musée Daubigny

This skippable museum houses a small collection of works by Charles-François Daubigny and other artists who came to work with him. Daubigny was a big supporter of the Impressionist movement (€4, Wed-Fri 14:00-17:30, Sat-Sun 10:30-12:30 & 14:00-18:00, closed Mon-Tue, Rue de la Sansonne).

• *Leave the museum following signs uphill for* L'Eglise *(10-minute walk). You'll recognize the* **church** *(Notre-Dame d'Auvers) from Van Gogh's paintings (interior open 9:30-19:00). From here, follow signs for* Tombes de Théo et Vincent *up the small street behind the church and walk about 300 yards to the simple cemetery.*

Vincent's Grave

Vincent and his caring brother are buried side by side against the cemetery's upper wall about halfway down (look for the ivy). No one can be sure why Vincent ended his life at 37, but standing at his grave, you can feel the weight of the tragedy and only imagine the paintings he might have created. You can thank Japanese travelers for the gray dust on the ivy that covers Vincent's and Theo's graves: Vincent is wildly popular among the Japanese, some of whom ask to have their ashes spread over his grave. Vincent lies in a coffin made by the same carpenter who built his picture frames.

• *Leave the cemetery and follow the dirt path that bisects a broad* **wheat field** *(any crows swirling on the horizon?), following signs to* Château *via Sente du Montier. Vincent shot himself in this field and died two* *days later in his bedroom at the Auberge Ravoux (described later). His brother was at his side. His last painting was* Wheatfield with Crows, *painted in this very field in 1890.*

Walk to the woods on the far side of the field. There you'll drop down to a street. Turn left when you reach the "T," and pass...

La Maison-Atelier de Daubigny

This well-preserved home/studio once belonged to Charles-François Daubigny, who created the artist colony that Auvers became in the 1880s (€6; Thu-Sun 14:00-18:30, closed Mon-Wed; closed mid-July-mid-Aug and Oct-March; tel. 01 30 36 60 60).

• *Past the Maison-Atelier de Daubigny, veer right at signs to the château. You'll soon pass...*

Musée de l'Absinthe

This small, one-of-a-kind tribute features the highly alcoholic, herb-based beverage popular among artists and writers (including Van Gogh) in the late 1800s. Considered dangerously addictive, absinthe was banned in 1915. Another anise-flavored drink—*pastis*—took its place; it tasted similar but was less toxic. Then, in 2011, absinthe was again declared legal in France. The museum has only minimal English information, but the staff make a good effort to explain the displays.

Cost and Hours: €5, €8 for visit with tasting—in French, bottles for sale; July-Aug Wed-Sun 13:30-18:00, closed Mon-Tue; Sept-mid-June Sat-Sun only 13:30-18:00.

• *From here it's a straight, 300-yard shot to...*

▲Château d'Auvers

This château has been transformed into a splendid recreation of life during the Impressionist years. Elaborate and informative multimedia displays use an audioguide, video screens, and lasers to guide you along the Impressionist route that led from Montmartre west to the sea, giving you a keen appreciation of life's daily struggles and pleasures during this time. You'll experience the cancan and a mock train ride and see more than 500 Impressionist paintings. To maximize your experience, bring your own earphones to use with the included audioguide. The château has a fine café with outdoor seating in the summer.

Cost and Hours: €14.75, family rates, not covered by Paris

Museum Pass; Tue-Sun 10:30-18:00, Oct-March until 16:30, closed Mon; tel. 01 34 48 48 48, www.chateau-auvers.fr.

• *A short walk beyond the château, Van Gogh fans can visit the restored home of Dr. Gachet (well-signed).*

Maison du Docteur Gachet

It was at Camille Pissarro's suggestion that Dr. Gachet agreed to see Van Gogh, who made an immediate connection with the doctor—"I have found a friend in Dr. Gachet...and something of a new brother, since we are so similar both mentally and physically." The home is furnished as it was when Vincent lived in Auvers, and the garden has medicinal plants that the homeopath Dr. Gachet cultivated and used to treat Van Gogh. You'll also find exhibits of contemporary painters. In addition to being Vincent's personal physician in Auvers, Dr. Gachet was an avid painter and entertained famous artists such as Cézanne, Monet, Renoir, and Pissarro. He inherited all of Van Gogh's works from his time in Auvers (those you see at the Orsay Museum were donated by Dr. Gachet's family). As you tour the doctor's simple home, consider that in 1990, one of Vincent's portraits of Gachet fetched over $80 million at auction. Dr. Gachet is buried at Père Lachaise cemetery in Paris.

Cost and Hours: Free, Wed-Sun 10:30-18:30, closed Mon-Tue and Nov-March, 78 Rue du Dr. Gachet.

• *Return to the TI and find...*

Auberge Ravoux

Vincent lived and died in an attic room of this inn (also called "Maison de Van Gogh"). Informative plaques in the courtyard explain Vincent's tragic life. The simple room has been recreated to look exactly as it did when he was here (his few furnishings were burned by church officials shortly after his death, as suicide was considered a sin). Wooden steps lead to Van Gogh's room, where staff give some commentary in English and run a 12-minute slide show.

Cost and Hours: €6, Wed-Sun 10:00-18:00, closed Mon-Tue and Nov-Feb.

• *Your walk is over. Food connoisseurs can enjoy a tasty lunch in the* auberge's *perfectly preserved restaurant.*

Sleeping and Eating in Auvers

($$$$ = Splurge, $$$ = Pricier, $$ = Moderate, $ = Budget)

Sleeping: $$ Hostellerie du Nord*** is small, friendly, and polished—a treat for those who want to sleep in luxury. It has modern, spacious rooms and a seriously good restaurant that requires reservations (*menus* from €65, a block from train station at 6 Rue du Général de Gaulle, tel. 01 30 36 70 74, www.hostelleriedunord.fr).

Eating: The most atmospheric place to eat in Auvers is **$$$ Auberge Ravoux,** unchanged (except for its prices) since 1876, when painters would meet here over a good meal. It's wise to make a reservation for lunch on weekends (closed Mon-Tue, on Place de la Mairie, tel. 01 30 36 60 60, www.maisondevangogh.fr).

If you're visiting the château, its café makes for a logical lunch spot, or you can continue walking past the château to **$$ Le Cadran,** an easy-going café run by a friendly Franco-Dutch couple. They serve up homemade lunches and tasty meat-and-cheese plates all afternoon, accompanied by an interesting selection of wines, artisanal beers, and organic teas (April-Sept Tue-Sat from 11:30, check off-season hours online, tel. 09 52 18 67 81, www.lecadran. eu).

Auvers also has grocery stores, cafés, *crêperies*, restaurants, and bakeries with sandwiches. This place was made for picnics.

FRANCE: PAST AND PRESENT

French History

CELTS AND ROMANS (52 B.C.-A.D. 500)

Julius Caesar conquered the Parisii, turning Paris from a tribal fishing village into a European city. The mix of Latin (southern) and Celtic (northern) cultures, with Paris right in the middle, defined the French character.

Sights
- Cluny Museum (Roman baths)
- Louvre (Roman antiquities)
- Paris Archaeological Crypt (in front of Notre-Dame)

DARK AGES (500-1000)

Roman Paris fell to German pirates known as the Franks (hence "France"), and later to the Vikings (a.k.a. Norsemen, which became "Normans"). During this turbulent time, Paris was just another island-state ("Ile de France") in the midst of many warring kingdoms. The lone bright spot was the reign of Charlemagne (A.D. 768-814), who briefly united the Franks, giving a glimpse of the modern nation-state of France.

Sights
- Cluny Museum (artifacts)
- Statue of Charlemagne (near Notre-Dame)

BORDER WARS WITH ENGLAND (1066-1500)

In 1066, the Norman duke William the Conqueror invaded and conquered England. This united England, Normandy, and much of what is today western France; sparked centuries of border wars; and produced many kings of England who spoke French. In 1328 King Charles IV died without an heir, and the Norman king of England tried to claim the throne of France, which led to more than a century of Franco-Anglo battles, called the Hundred Years' War. Rallied by the teenage visionary Joan of Arc in 1429, the French finally united north and south, and drove the English across the Channel in 1453. Modern France was born, with Paris as its capital.

Sights
- Notre-Dame Cathedral
- Sainte-Chapelle
- Cluny Museum (tapestries)
- Carnavalet Museum
- Sorbonne
- Latin Quarter

RENAISSANCE AND RELIGIOUS WARS (1500s)
A strong, centralized France emerged, with French kings setting Europe's standard. François I made Paris a cultural capital, inviting Leonardo and Mona Lisa to visit. Catholics and Protestants fought openly, with 2,000 Parisians slaughtered in the St. Bartholomew's Day Massacre in 1572. The Wars of Religion subsided for a while when the first Bourbon king, Henry IV, took the throne in 1589 after converting to Catholicism. In 1598, he signed the Edict of Nantes, which instituted freedom of religious worship.

Sights
- Louvre (palace and Renaissance art)
- Pont Neuf
- Place des Vosges
- Fontainebleau

LOUIS XIV, THE ABSOLUTE MONARCH (1600s)
Louis XIV solidified his power, neutered the nobility, revoked the Edict of Nantes, and moved the capital to Versailles, which also became the center of European culture. France's wealth sparked "enlightened" ideas that became the seeds of democracy.

Sights
- Versailles and Vaux-le-Vicomte
- Hôtel des Invalides
- Paintings by Nicolas Poussin and Claude Lorrain

DECADENCE AND REVOLUTION (1700s)
This was the age of Louis XV, Louis XVI, Marie-Antoinette, Voltaire, Jean-Jacques Rousseau, Maximilien de Robespierre, and Na-

Typical Church Architecture

History comes to life when you visit a centuries-old church. Even if you wouldn't know your apse from a hole in the ground, learning a few simple terms will enrich your experience. Note that not every church has every feature, and a "cathedral" isn't a type of church architecture, but rather a designation for a church that's a governing center for a local bishop.

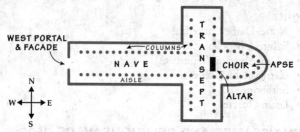

Aisles: The long, generally low-ceilinged arcades that flank the nave.

Altar: The raised area with a ceremonial table (often adorned with candles or a crucifix), where the priest prepares and serves the bread and wine for Communion.

Apse: The space beyond the altar, generally bordered with small chapels.

Barrel Vault: A continuous round-arched ceiling that resembles an extended upside-down U.

Choir: A cozy area, often screened off, located within the church nave and near the high altar, where services are sung in a more intimate setting.

Cloister: Covered hallways bordering a square or rectangular open-air courtyard, traditionally where monks and nuns got fresh air.

Facade: The front exterior of the church's main (west) entrance, generally highly decorated.

Groin Vault: An arched ceiling formed where two equal barrel vaults meet at right angles. Less common usage: term for a medieval jock strap.

Narthex: The area (portico or foyer) between the main entry and the nave.

Nave: The long, central section of the church (running west to east, from the entrance to the altar) where the congregation sits or stands through the service.

Transept: In a traditional cross-shaped floor plan, the transept is one of the two parts forming the "arms" of the cross. The transepts run north-south, perpendicularly crossing the east-west nave.

West Portal: The main entry to the church (on the west end, opposite the main altar).

PAST & PRESENT

poleon. A financial crunch from wars and royal excess drove the French people to revolt. On July 14, 1789, they stormed the Bastille. A couple of years later, the First French Republic arrested and then beheaded the king and queen. Thousands lost their heads—guillotined if suspected of hindering the Revolution's progress. A charismatic commoner promising stability rose amid the chaos: Napoleon Bonaparte.

Sights
- Versailles
- Place de la Concorde and Place de la Bastille
- Conciergerie
- Paintings by Watteau, Boucher, Fragonard, and David (Louvre)

ELECTED EMPERORS AND CONSTITUTIONAL KINGS (1800s)

Napoleon conquered Europe, crowned himself emperor, invaded Russia, was defeated on the battlefields of Waterloo, and ended up exiled to an island in the Atlantic. The monarchy was restored, but rulers toed the democratic line—or were deposed in the popular uprisings of 1830 and 1848. The latter uprising resulted in the Second French Republic, whose first president was Napoleon's nephew. He rewrote the constitution with himself as Emperor Napoleon III, and presided over a wealthy, middle-class nation with a colonial empire in slow decline. The disastrous Franco-Prussian War in 1870 ended his reign, leading to the Third Republic. France's political clout was fading, even as Paris remained the world's cultural center during the belle époque—the "beautiful age."

Sights
- Arc de Triomphe
- Baron Haussmann's wide boulevards
- Eiffel Tower
- Les Invalides and Napoleon's Tomb
- Pont Alexandre III
- Grand Palais and Petit Palais
- Montmartre
- Opéra Garnier
- Paintings by Ingres and Delacroix (Louvre)
- Impressionist and Post-Impressionist paintings (Manet, Monet, Renoir, Degas, Toulouse-Lautrec, Cézanne, and so on) at the Orsay, Marmottan, and Orangerie museums

WAR AND DEPRESSION (1900-1950)

France began the turn of the 20th century as top dog, but two world wars with Germany (and the earlier Franco-Prussian War) wasted the country. France lost millions of men in World War I, sank into an economic depression, and was easily overrun by Hitler in World War II. Paris, now dirt cheap, attracted foreign writers and artists.

This was the age of Pablo Picasso, Maurice Ravel, Claude Debussy, Erik Satie, Igor Stravinsky, Vaslav Nijinsky, Ernest Hemingway, F. Scott Fitzgerald, Gertrude Stein, Ezra Pound, Jean-Paul Sartre, Edith Piaf, and Maurice Chevalier.

Sights
- Army Museum
- Picasso Museum
- Deportation Memorial and Holocaust Memorial
- Pompidou Center (art from this period)

POSTWAR FRANCE (1950-Present)

After the war, France reestablished a democracy with the Fourth Republic. But France's colonial empire dissolved after bitter wars in Algeria and Vietnam, which helped mire an already unsteady government. Wartime hero Charles de Gaulle was brought back in 1958 to assist with France's regeneration. He rewrote the constitution, beginning the Fifth (and current) Republic. Immigrants from former colonies flooded Paris. The turbulent '60s, progressive '70s, socialist-turned-conservative '80s, and the middle-of-the-road '90s bring us to the *début de siècle*, or the beginning of the 21st century.

Sights
- Montparnasse Tower
- La Défense
- Louvre's pyramid
- Pompidou Center (modern art)
- Les Halles

France Today

In 2015, Paris was hit with a double-whammy of Islamist terrorist attacks—at the offices of the satirical magazine *Charlie Hebdo* (January), and then at the Bataclan theater and environs (November). In 2016, there were still more attacks elsewhere in France. The French are still reeling from the realization that many of the attackers were French citizens. The attacks raised serious questions about immigration, policing, class divisions, and what it means to be French.

Despite these attacks, the main political issue in France is the economy. France weathered the 2008 downturn better than the

US, because it was less invested in risky home loans and the volatile stock market. But now France, along with the rest of Europe, is struggling. Growth has flatlined. Unemployment remains high: The overall rate is around 10 percent, but it's a staggering 25 percent for those under 30. France hasn't balanced its books since 1974, and public spending, at over half of GDP, chews up a bigger chunk of output than in any other eurozone country. The challenge for French leadership is to address its economic problems while maintaining the high level of social services that the French people expect from their government.

France has its economic strengths: a well-educated workforce, an especially robust services sector and high-end manufacturing industry, and more firms big enough to rank in the global Fortune 500 than any other European country. Ironically, while France's economy may be one of the world's largest, the French remain skeptical about the virtues of capitalism and the work ethic. Globalization conflicts in a fundamental way with French virtues—many fear losing what makes their society unique in the quest for a bland, globalized world. Business conversation is generally avoided, as it implies a fascination with money that the French find vulgar. (It's considered gauche even to ask what someone does for a living.) In France, CEOs are not glorified as celebrities—chefs are.

The French believe that the economy should support social good, not vice versa, and that people are entitled to secure jobs from which they cannot be fired easily. This has produced a cradle-to-grave social security system of which the French are proud. France's poverty rate is half of that in the US, proof to the French that they are on the right track. On the other hand, if you're considering starting a business in France, think again—taxes are *formidable* (figure a total small-business tax rate of around 66 percent—and likely to increase). French voters are notorious for their belief in the free market's heartless cruelty, and they tend to see globalization as a threat. France is routinely plagued with strikes, demonstrations, and slowdowns as workers try to preserve their rights. During a strike in 2016, oil refineries were blocked—making gas scarce for cars, trucks, and buses—and train workers and air traffic controllers staged walkouts. But strikes usually only last a few days in France, and soon life returned to normal.

France is part of the European Union, a kind of "United States of Europe" that has dissolved borders and implemented a common currency, the euro. France's governments have been decidedly pro-EU. But many French are Euro-skeptics, afraid that EU meddling threatens their job security and social benefits. With the vote in Britain to leave the EU, this view could become even more widespread.

The French political scene is complex and fascinating. France is governed by a president (currently François Hollande), elected by popular vote every five years (2017 is a presidential election year). The president then selects the prime minister, who in turn chooses the cabinet ministers. Collectively, this executive branch is known as the *gouvernement*. The parliament consists of a Senate (348 seats) and the 577-seat Assemblée Nationale.

In France, compromise and coalition-building are essential to keeping power. Unlike America's two-party system, France has a half-dozen major political parties, plus more on the fringes. A simple majority is rare. Even the biggest parties rarely get more than a third of the votes. Since the parliament can force the *gouvernement* to resign at any time, it's essential that the *gouvernement* work with them.

For a snapshot of the current political landscape, look no further than the 2012 elections that brought François Hollande to power. He faced incumbent President Nicolas Sarkozy of the center-right party—the man who had cut taxes, reduced the size of government, limited the power of unions, cut workers' benefits, and (most controversially) raised the retirement age from 60 to 62.

Hollande's Socialist Party (PS) was just one of Sarkozy's challengers. There was the radical Left Front Party (which includes the once-powerful Communists) and the environmental Green Party (Les Verts). On the far-right was the National Front (FN), led by Marine Le Pen. She called for expulsion of ethnic minorities, restoration of the French franc as the standard currency, secession from the EU, and broader police powers.

After several months and one TV debate (yes, the French election season is that short), Hollande emerged victorious. And just one month later, his Socialist Party captured more than half of the 577 seats of the Assemblée Nationale. Nevertheless, Hollande has to work closely with legislators, including a strong minority from opposing parties. Though Hollande is a "Socialist" (a word that spooks Rush Limbaugh), he's in the mainstream of the European political spectrum.

But today Hollande faces many challenges. On the sluggish economy, he favors government expansion and stimulus rather than austerity: hiring thousands of teachers, building hundreds of thousands of homes, and launching countless public works projects (you'll likely experience road work in every region). He favors relaxing hiring and firing rules to spur employment (not popular with the masses). And he's had to abandon his promise to return the retirement age—at least for some workers—to 60. Thanks to the economic mess, Hollande has become the most unpopular French president since World War II: Liberals and conservatives alike are furious over his policies. In the spring of 2016 his approval rating was below 15 percent.

In recent years the French political scene has become as polarized as it is in the United States, although the 2015 terrorist attacks brought some unity, if only for a short period. The government's challenge: to respond with sufficient intensity to deter would-be terrorists without infringing on the rights of its Muslim population. You'll notice tight security at tourist sights and a visible police presence in urban areas.

Another ongoing issue that French leaders must work together to address is immigration, which is shifting the country's ethnic and cultural makeup in ways that challenge French society. Ten percent of France's population is of North African descent, mainly immigrants from former colonies. The increased number of Muslims raises cultural issues in this heavily Catholic society that institutes official state secularism. The French have (quite controversially) made it illegal for women to wear a full, face-covering veil *(niqāb)* in public. They continue to debate whether banning the veil enforces democracy—or squelches diversity.

With a presidential election in May, 2017 will be a fascinating year in French politics. Many seem tired of mainstream parties (sound familiar?) and at this point, there's no clear favorite. The incumbent Hollande and his Socialist Party are suffering from low public approval numbers. The far-right National Front led by Marine le Pen has proven strong, given worries over the economy and immigration, and the general frustration with mainstream parties.

Then there are the personalities. Sarkozy is constantly rumored to be preparing a comeback. Former Prime Minister Alain Juppé is Sarkozy's strongest challenger as leader of the center-right party—which recently changed its name to "The Republicans."

And for the Socialists? Manuel Valls, the Socialist prime minister since 2014, is young, dashing, and ambitious. There's also Ségolène Royal, a leader in the party who lost to Sarkozy in 2007 (and to Hollande in the run-up to the 2012 presidential elections). In 2014, she was appointed France's minister of ecology. As it happens, Royal and Hollande know each other well: They met in college, lived together for 30 years, and raised four children before splitting up in 2007. They never married—French politics makes strange bedfellows. But that's personal...

For more about French history, consider Europe 101: History and Art for the Traveler *by Rick Steves and Gene Openshaw, available at www.ricksteves.com.*

PRACTICALITIES

This chapter covers the practical skills of European travel: how to get tourist information, pay for things, sightsee efficiently, find good-value accommodations, eat affordably but well, use technology wisely, and get between destinations smoothly. To study ahead and round out your knowledge and skills, check out "Resources from Rick Steves."

Tourist Information

The French national tourist office is a wealth of information. **Before your trip,** scan their website—http://us.france.fr. It has particularly good resources for special-interest travel and plenty of free-to-download brochures. Paris' official TI website, www. parisinfo.com, offers practical information on hotels, special events, museums, children's activities, fashion, nightlife, and more. (For other useful websites, see page 20.)

In Paris, TI offices are few and far between. They aren't helpful enough to warrant a special trip, but if you're near one anyway, consider stopping by to confirm opening times, pick up a city map, and get information on public transit (including bus and train schedules), walking tours, special events, and nightlife. For TI locations, see page 20 (the most handy locations may be at the airports).

Travel Tips

Emergency and Medical Help: In France, dial 112 for any emergency. For English-speaking police, call 17. To summon an ambulance (SAMU in French), call 15. If you get sick, do as the locals do and go to a pharmacist for advice. Or ask at your hotel for help—they'll know the nearest medical and emergency services.

Theft or Loss: To replace a passport, you'll need to go in person to an embassy or consulate (see page 676). If your credit and debit cards disappear, cancel and replace them (see "Damage Control for Lost Cards" on page 627). File a police report, either on the spot or within a day or two; you'll need it to submit an insurance claim for lost or stolen rail passes or travel gear, and it can help with replacing your passport or credit and debit cards. For more information, see www.ricksteves.com/help.

Time Zones: France, like most of continental Europe, is generally six/nine hours ahead of the East/West Coasts of the US. The exceptions are the beginning and end of Daylight Saving Time: Europe "springs forward" the last Sunday in March (two weeks after most of North America), and "falls back" the last Sunday in October (one week before North America). For a handy online time converter, see www.timeanddate.com/worldclock.

Business Hours: In Paris, most shops are open Monday through Saturday (10:00-12:00 & 14:00-19:00) and closed Sunday (except in the Marais neighborhood and along the Champs-Elysées). Many small markets, *boulangeries* (bakeries), and street markets are open Sunday mornings until noon.

Saturdays are virtually weekdays, with earlier closing hours at some shops. Banks are generally open on Saturday and closed on Sunday and possibly Monday. Sundays have the same pros and cons as they do for travelers in the US: Special events and weekly markets pop up (usually until about noon) and sightseeing attractions are generally open, while many shops are closed, public transportation options are fewer, and there's no rush hour. Friday and Saturday evenings are lively; Sunday evenings are quiet.

Watt's Up? Europe's electrical system is 220 volts, instead of North America's 110 volts. Most newer electronics (such as laptops, battery chargers, and hair dryers) convert automatically, so you won't need a converter, but you will need an adapter plug with two round prongs, sold inexpensively at travel stores in the US. Avoid bringing older appliances that don't automatically convert voltage;

PRACTICALITIES

instead, buy a cheap replacement in Europe. You can buy low-cost hair dryers and other small appliances at Darty and Monoprix stores, which you'll find in major cities (ask your hotelier for the closest branch).

Discounts: Discounts for sights are generally not listed in this book. However, many sights offer discounts for youths (usually up to age 18), students (with proper identification cards, www.isic. org), families, and groups of 10 or more. Always ask, and have your passport available at sights for proof. Seniors (age 60 and over) may get the odd discount, though these are often limited to citizens of the European Union (EU). To inquire about a senior discount, ask, *"Réduction troisième âge?"* (ray-dewk-see-ohn trwah-zee-ehm ahzh).

Online Translation Tips: Google's Chrome browser instantly translates websites. You can also paste text or the URL of a foreign website into the translation window at http://translate.google. com. The Google Translate app converts spoken English into most European languages (and vice versa) and can also translate text it "reads" with your mobile device's camera.

Money

This section offers advice on how to pay for purchases on your trip (including getting cash from ATMs and paying with plastic), dealing with lost or stolen cards, VAT (sales tax) refunds, and tipping.

WHAT TO BRING

Bring both a credit card and a debit card. You'll use the debit card at cash machines (ATMs) to withdraw local cash for most purchases, and the credit card to pay for larger items. Some travelers carry a third card, in case one gets demagnetized or eaten by a temperamental machine. For an emergency reserve, consider bringing €200 in hard cash in €20 bills (bring euros, as dollars can be hard to change in France).

CASH

Although credit cards are widely accepted in Europe, day-to-day spending is generally more cash-based. I find cash is the easiest—and sometimes only—way to pay for cheap food, bus fare, taxis, and local guides. Having cash on hand can help you avoid a stressful predicament if you find yourself in a place that won't accept your card.

Throughout Europe, ATMs are the easiest and smartest way for travelers to get cash. They work just like they do at home. To withdraw money from an ATM (known as a *distributeur* in France;

Exchange Rate

1 euro (€) = about $1.10

To convert prices in euros to dollars, add about 10 percent: €20=about $22, €50=about $55. (Check www.oanda.com for the latest exchange rates.) Just like the dollar, one euro (€) is broken down into 100 cents. You'll find coins ranging from €0.01 to €2, and bills from €5 to €500 (bills over €50 are rarely used).

---

dee-stree-bew-tur), you'll need a debit card (ideally with a Visa or MasterCard logo), plus a PIN code (numeric and four digits). For increased security, shield the keypad when entering your PIN code, and don't use an ATM if anything on the front of the machine looks loose or damaged (a sign that someone may have attached a "skimming" device to capture account information). Try to withdraw large sums of money to reduce the number of per-transaction bank fees you'll pay.

When possible, use ATMs located outside banks—a thief is less likely to target a cash machine near surveillance cameras, and if your card is munched by a machine during banking hours, you can go inside for help. Stay away from "independent" ATMs such as Travelex, Euronet, YourCash, Cardpoint, and Cashzone, which charge huge commissions, have terrible exchange rates, and may try to trick users with "dynamic currency conversion" (described at the end of "Credit and Debit Cards," next). Although you can use a credit card to withdraw cash at an ATM, this comes with high bank fees and only makes sense in an emergency.

While traveling, if you want to access your accounts online, be sure to use a secure connection (see page 663).

Pickpockets target tourists, particularly those arriving in Paris—dazed and tired—carrying luggage in the Métro and RER trains and stations. To safeguard your cash, wear a money belt—a pouch with a strap that you buckle around your waist like a belt and tuck under your clothes. Keep your cash, credit cards, and passport secure in your money belt, and carry only a day's spending money in your front pocket or wallet.

CREDIT AND DEBIT CARDS

For purchases, Visa and MasterCard are more commonly accepted than American Express. Just like at home, credit or debit cards work easily at larger hotels, restaurants, and shops. I typically use my debit card to withdraw cash to pay for daily purchases. I use my credit card sparingly: to book and pay for hotel rooms, to buy advance tickets for events or sights, to cover major expenses (such as car rentals or plane tickets), and to pay for things online or near

PRACTICALITIES

the end of my trip (to avoid another visit to the ATM). While you could instead use a debit card for these purchases, a credit card offers a greater degree of fraud protection.

Ask Your Credit- or Debit-Card Company: Before your trip, contact the company that issued your debit or credit cards.

Confirm that your **card will work overseas,** and alert them that you'll be using it in Europe; otherwise, they may deny transactions if they perceive unusual spending patterns.

Ask for the specifics on transaction **fees.** When you use your credit or debit card—either for purchases or ATM withdrawals—you'll typically be charged additional "international transaction" fees of up to 3 percent (1 percent is normal). Some banks have agreements with European partners that help save on fees (for example, Bank of America customers don't have to pay the transaction fee when using French Paribas-BNP ATMs). If your card's fees seem high, consider getting a different card just for your trip: Capital One (www.capitalone.com) and most credit unions have low-to-no international fees.

Verify your daily ATM **withdrawal limit,** and if necessary, ask your bank to adjust it. I prefer a high limit that allows me to take out more cash at each ATM stop and save on bank fees; some travelers prefer to set a lower limit in case their card is stolen. Note that foreign banks also set maximum withdrawal amounts for their ATMs.

Get your bank's emergency **phone number** in the US (but not its 800 number, which isn't accessible from overseas) to call collect if you have a problem.

Ask for your credit card's **PIN** in case you need to make an emergency cash withdrawal or you encounter payment machines using the chip-and-PIN system; the bank won't tell you your PIN over the phone, so allow time for it to be mailed to you.

Chip-and-PIN Credit Cards: Europeans use chip-and-PIN credit cards (embedded with an electronic security chip and requiring a four-digit PIN). Major US banks are beginning to offer similar credit cards. Most of these are not true chip-and-PIN cards, but instead are chip-and-signature cards, for which your signature verifies your identity. These cards work in Europe for live transactions and at most payment machines, but won't work for offline transactions such as at self-serve gas pumps.

Older American cards with just a magnetic stripe may not work at unattended payment machines, such as those at train and subway stations, toll plazas, parking garages, bike-rental kiosks, and gas pumps. If you have problems with either type of American card, try entering your card's PIN, look for a machine that takes cash, or find a clerk who can process the transaction manually.

If you're concerned, ask if your bank offers a true chip-and-

PIN card. Andrews Federal Credit Union (www.andrewsfcu.org) and the State Department Federal Credit Union (www.sdfcu.org) offer these cards and are open to all US residents.

No matter what kind of card you have, it pays to carry euros; remember, you can always use an ATM to withdraw cash with your magnetic-stripe debit card.

Dynamic Currency Conversion: If merchants, hoteliers, or ATMs offer to convert your purchase price into dollars (called dynamic currency conversion, or DCC), refuse this "service." You'll pay even more in fees for the expensive convenience of seeing your charge in dollars. Always choose the local currency.

Damage Control for Lost Cards

If you lose your credit or debit card, you can stop people from using your card by reporting the loss immediately to the respective global customer-assistance centers. Call these 24-hour US numbers collect: Visa (tel. 303/967-1096), MasterCard (tel. 636/722-7111), and American Express (tel. 336/393-1111). In France, to make a collect call to the US, dial 08 00 90 06 24, then say "operator" for an English-speaking operator. European toll-free numbers (listed by country) can be found at the websites for Visa and MasterCard. For another option (with the same results), you can call these toll-free numbers in France: Visa (tel. 08 00 90 11 79) and MasterCard (tel. 08 00 90 13 87). American Express has a Paris office, but the call isn't free (tel. 01 47 77 70 00, greeting is in French, dial 1 to speak with someone in English).

If you are the secondary cardholder, you'll need to provide the primary cardholder's identification-verification details (such as birth date, mother's maiden name, or Social Security number). You can generally receive a temporary card within two or three business days in Europe (see www.ricksteves.com/help for more).

If you report your loss within two days, you typically won't be responsible for any unauthorized transactions on your account, although many banks charge a liability fee of $50.

TIPPING

Tipping *(donner un pourboire)* in France isn't as automatic and generous as it is in the US. For special service, tips are appreciated, but not expected. As in the US, the proper amount depends on your resources, tipping philosophy, and the circumstances, but some general guidelines apply.

Restaurants: At cafés and restaurants, a service charge is included in the price of what you order, and it's unnecessary to tip extra, though you can for superb service. For details on tipping in restaurants, see page 645.

Taxis: For a typical ride, round up your fare a bit (for instance, if the fare is €13, pay €14). If the cabbie hauls your bags and zips you to the airport to help you catch your flight, you might want to toss in a little more. But if you feel like you're being driven in circles or otherwise ripped off, skip the tip.

Services: In general, if someone in the tourism or service industry does a super job for you, a small tip of a euro or two is appropriate...but not required. If you're not sure whether (or how much) to tip, ask a local for advice.

GETTING A VAT REFUND

Wrapped into the purchase price of your French souvenirs is a Value-Added Tax (VAT) of about 20 percent. You're entitled to get most of that tax back if you purchase more than €175 (about $195) worth of goods at a store that participates in the VAT-refund scheme. Typically, you must ring up the minimum at a single retailer—you can't add up your purchases from various shops to reach the required amount.

Getting your refund is straightforward and, if you buy a substantial amount of souvenirs, well worth the hassle. If you're lucky, the merchant will subtract the tax when you make your purchase. (This is more likely to occur if the store ships the goods to your home.) Otherwise, you'll need to:

Get the paperwork. Have the merchant completely fill out the necessary refund document, called a *bordereau de détaxe*. You'll have to present your passport. Get the paperwork done before you leave the store to ensure you'll have everything you need (including your original sales receipt).

Get your stamp at the border or airport. Process your VAT document at your last stop in the European Union (such as at the airport) with the customs agent who deals with VAT refunds. Arrive an additional hour before you need to check in for your flight to allow time to find the local customs office—and to stand in line. It's best to keep your purchases in your carry-on. If they're too large or dangerous to carry on (such as knives), pack them in your checked bags and alert the check-in agent. You'll be sent (with your tagged bag) to a customs desk outside security; someone will examine your bag, stamp your paperwork, and put your bag on the belt. You're not supposed to use your purchased goods before you leave. If you show up at customs wearing your chic new shoes, officials might look the other way—or deny you a refund.

Collect your refund. You'll need to return your stamped document to the retailer or its representative. Many merchants work with services, such as Global Blue or Premier Tax Free, that have offices at major airports, ports, or border crossings (either before or after security, probably strategically located near a duty-free shop). At Charles de Gaulle, you'll find them at the check-in area (or ask for help at an orange ADP info desk). These services, which extract a 4 percent fee, can refund your money immediately in cash or credit your card (within two billing cycles). Other refund services may require you to mail the documents from home, or more quickly, from your point of departure (using an envelope you've prepared in advance or one that's been provided by the merchant). You'll then have to wait—it can take months.

CUSTOMS FOR AMERICAN SHOPPERS

You are allowed to take home $800 worth of items per person duty-free, once every 31 days. You can take home many processed and packaged foods: vacuum-packed cheeses, dried herbs, jams, baked goods, candy, chocolate, oil, vinegar, mustard, and honey. Fresh fruits and vegetables and most meats are not allowed, with exceptions for some canned items. As for alcohol, you can bring in one liter duty-free (it can be packed securely in your checked luggage, along with any other liquid-containing items).

To bring alcohol (or liquid-packed foods) in your carry-on bag on your flight home, buy it at a duty-free shop at the airport. You'll increase your odds of getting it onto a connecting flight if it's packaged in a "STEB"—a secure, tamper-evident bag. But stay away from liquids in opaque, ceramic, or metallic containers, which usually cannot be successfully screened (STEB or no STEB).

For details on allowable goods, customs rules, and duty rates, visit http://help.cbp.gov.

Sightseeing

Sightseeing can be hard work. Use these tips to make your visits to Paris' finest sights meaningful, fun, efficient, and painless.

MAPS AND NAVIGATION TOOLS

A good map is essential for efficient navigation while sightseeing. The black-and-white maps in this book are concise and simple, designed to help you locate recommended destinations, sights, and local TIs, where you can pick up more in-depth maps. More detailed maps are sold at newsstands and bookstores.

You can also use a mapping app on your mobile device. Be aware that pulling up maps on the fly or looking up turn-by-turn walking directions requires an Internet connection—to use this feature, it's smart to get an international data plan (see page 659) or only connect using Wi-Fi. With Google Maps or Apple Maps, it's possible to download a map while online, then go offline and navigate without incurring data-roaming charges—though you can't search for an address or get real-time walking directions. A handful of other apps, including City Maps 2Go, OffMaps, and Navfree, also allow you to use maps offline.

PLAN AHEAD

Set up an itinerary that allows you to fit in all your must-see sights. For a one-stop look at opening hours, see "Paris at a Glance" (page 54). Remember, the Louvre and some other museums are closed on Tuesday, and many others are closed on Monday (see "Daily Reminder" on page 20). Most sights keep stable hours, but you can easily confirm the latest by checking their websites or picking up the booklet *Musées, Monuments Historiques, et Expositions* (free at most museums). You can also find good information on many of Paris' sights online at www.parisinfo.com.

Don't put off visiting a must-see sight—you never know when a place will close unexpectedly for a holiday, strike, or restoration. Many museums are closed or have reduced hours at least a few days a year, especially on holidays such as Christmas, New Year's, and Labor Day (May 1). A list of holidays is on page 677; check online for possible museum closures during your trip. In summer, some sights may stay open late; in the off-season, hours may be shorter.

Going at the right time helps avoid crowds. This book offers tips on the best times to see specific sights. Try visiting popular sights very early (arrive at least 15 minutes before opening time) or late. Evening visits are usually peaceful, with fewer crowds. For example, the Louvre and Orsay museums are open selected evenings, while the Pompidou Center is open late every night except Tuesday (when it's closed all day). For a list of sights that are open in the evenings, see "Paris for Early Birds and Night Owls" (page 69).

Most travelers should buy a Paris Museum Pass, which can speed you through lines and save you money. It's also smart to book advance tickets for popular sights (for details, see page 48). For more money-saving tips in pricey Paris, see "Affording Paris' Sights" on page 64.

Study up. To get the most out of the self-guided tours and sight descriptions in this book, read them before you visit. The Louvre is more interesting if you understand why the *Venus de Milo* is so disarming.

AT SIGHTS

Here's what you can typically expect:

Entering: You may not be allowed to enter if you arrive less than 30 to 60 minutes before closing time. And guards start ushering people out well before the actual closing time, so don't save the best for last.

Many sights have a security check, where you must open your

bag or send it through a metal detector. Allow extra time for these lines in your planning. Some sights require you to check daypacks and coats. (If you'd rather not check your daypack, try carrying it tucked under your arm like a purse as you enter.)

At churches—which often offer interesting art (usually free) and a cool, welcome seat—a modest dress code (no bare shoulders or shorts) is encouraged though rarely enforced.

Photography: If the museum's photo policy isn't clearly posted, ask a guard. Generally, taking photos without a flash or tripod is allowed. Some sights ban photos altogether; others ban selfie sticks.

Temporary Exhibits: Museums may show special exhibits in addition to their permanent collection. Some exhibits are included in the entry price, while others come at an extra cost (which you may have to pay even if you don't want to see the exhibit).

Expect Changes: Artwork can be on tour, on loan, out sick, or shifted at the whim of the curator. Pick up a floor plan as you enter, and ask museum staff if you can't find a particular item. Say the title or artist's name, or point to the photograph in this book and ask for its location by saying, *"Où est?"* (oo ay).

Audioguides and Apps: Many sights rent audioguides, which generally offer worthwhile recorded descriptions in English. If you bring your own earbuds, you can enjoy better sound and avoid holding the device to your ear. To save money, bring a Y-jack and share one audioguide with your travel partner. Increasingly, museums and sights offer apps—often free—that you can download to your mobile device (check their websites). I've produced free, downloadable audio tours for my Historic Paris Walk, the Louvre, Orsay Museum, and Versailles; these are indicated in this book with the symbol ∩. For more on my audio tours, see page 8.

Services: Important sights may have a reasonably priced on-site café or cafeteria (handy places to rejuvenate during a long visit). The WCs at sights are free and generally clean.

Before Leaving: At the gift shop, scan the postcard rack or thumb through a guidebook to be sure that you haven't overlooked something that you'd like to see.

Every sight or museum offers more than what is covered in this book. Use the information in this book as an introduction—not the final word.

Sleeping

Accommodations in Paris generally are easy to find and usually cost less than comparable places in other big European cities.

Choose from one- to five-star hotels (two and three stars are my mainstays), bed-and-breakfasts (*chambres d'hôtes*, usually cheaper than hotels), hostels, and apartments.

I favor hotels and restaurants that are handy to your sightseeing activities. Rather than list hotels scattered throughout a city, I choose hotels in my favorite neighborhoods. My recommendations run the gamut, from dorm beds to fancy rooms with all of the comforts.

Extensive and opinionated listings of good-value rooms are a major feature of this book's Sleeping sections. I like places that are clean, central, relatively quiet at night, reasonably priced, friendly, small enough to have a hands-on owner or manager and stable staff, and run with a respect for French traditions. I'm more impressed by a convenient location and a fun-loving philosophy than flat-screen TVs and a fancy gym. Most places I recommend fall short of perfection. But if I can find a place with most of these features, it's a keeper.

Book your accommodations well in advance, especially if you want to stay at one of my top listings or if you'll be traveling during busy times. Reserving ahead is particularly important for Paris—the sooner, the better. Wherever you're staying, be ready for crowds during these holiday periods: Easter weekend; Labor Day; Ascension weekend; Pentecost weekend; Bastille Day and the week during which it falls; and the winter holidays (mid-Dec-early Jan). In August and at other times when business is slower, some Paris hotels offer lower rates to fill their rooms. Check hotel websites for the best deals.

See page 677 for a list of major holidays and festivals in France; for tips on making reservations, see page 638.

RATES AND DEALS

I've categorized my recommended accommodations based on price, indicated with a dollar-sign rating (see sidebar). The price ranges suggest an estimated cost for a one-night stay in a standard double room with a private toilet and shower in high season, don't include breakfast, and assume you're booking directly with the hotel (not through a booking site, which extracts a commission and logically closes the door on special deals). Room prices can fluctuate significantly with demand and amenities (size, views, room class, and so on), but these relative price categories remain constant.

Room rates are especially volatile at larger hotels that use "dynamic pricing" to predict demand. Rates can skyrocket during festivals and conventions, while business hotels can have deep discounts on weekends when demand plummets. For this reason, of the many hotels I recommend, it's difficult to say which will be the best value on a given day—until you do your homework.

Once your dates are set, check the specific price for your preferred stay at several hotels. You can do this either by comparing prices online on the hotels' own websites, or by emailing several hotels directly and asking for their best rate. Even if you start your search on a booking site such as TripAdvisor or Booking.com, you'll usually find the lowest rates through a hotel's own website.

Additionally, some accommodations offer a special discount for Rick Steves readers, indicated in this guidebook by the abbreviation "RS%." Discounts vary: Ask for details when you book. Generally, to qualify you must book directly (that is, not through a booking site), mention this book when you reserve, show the book upon arrival, and sometimes pay cash or stay a certain number of nights. In some cases, you may need to enter a discount code (which I've provided in the listing) in the booking form on the hotel's website. Rick Steves discounts apply to readers with ebooks as well as printed books. Understandably, discounts do not apply to promotional rates.

Hotels in France must charge a daily tax *(taxe du séjour)* of about €1-2 per person per day. Some hotels include it in their prices, but most add it to your bill.

TYPES OF ACCOMMODATIONS
Hotels

In this book, the price for a double room will normally range from €60 (very simple; toilet and shower down the hall) to €400 (grand lobbies, maximum plumbing, and the works), with most clustering around €120-180 (with private bathrooms). Most hotels also offer single rooms and some offer larger rooms for four or more people (I call these "family rooms" in the listings). Some hotels can add an extra bed to a double room to make a triple for a small charge. In general, a triple room is cheaper than the cost of a double and a single. Traveling alone can be expensive: A single room can be close to the cost of a double.

The French have a simple hotel rating system based on amenities and rated by stars

PRACTICALITIES

Sleep Code

Hotels are classified based on the average price of a standard double room without breakfast in high season.

$$$$	**Splurge:**	Most rooms over €200
$$$	**Pricier:**	€150-200
$$	**Moderate:**	€100-150
$	**Budget:**	€50-100
¢	**Backpacker:**	Under €50
RS%	**Rick Steves discount**	
*	**French hotel rating system**	(0-5 stars)

Unless otherwise noted, credit cards are accepted, hotel staff speak basic English, and free Wi-Fi is available. Comparison-shop by checking prices at several hotels (on each hotel's own website, on a booking site, or by email). For the best deal, *book directly with the hotel.* Ask for a discount if paying in cash; if the listing includes **RS%**, request a Rick Steves discount.

(indicated in this book by asterisks, from * through *****). One star is modest, two has most of the comforts, and three is generally a two-star with a fancier lobby and more elaborately designed rooms. Four-star places give marginally more comfort than those with three. Five stars probably offer more luxury than you'll have time to appreciate. Two-star and above hotels are required to have an English-speaking staff, though nearly all hotels I recommend have someone who speaks English.

The number of stars does not always reflect room size or guarantee quality. One- and two-star hotels are less expensive, but some three-star (and even a few four-star hotels) offer good value, justifying the extra cost. Unclassified hotels (no stars) can be bargains...or depressing dumps.

Within each hotel, prices vary depending on the size of room, whether it has a tub or shower, and the bed type (tubs and twins cost more than showers and double beds). If you have a preference, ask for it. Hotels often have more rooms with tubs (which the French prefer) and are inclined to give you one by default. You can save lots by finding the rare room without a private shower or toilet.

Most French hotels now have queen-size beds—to confirm, ask, *"Avez-vous des lits queen-size?"* (ah-vay-voo day lee queen-size). Some hotels push two twins together under king-size sheets and blankets to make *le king* size. If you'll take either twins or a double, ask for a generic *une chambre pour deux* (room for two) to avoid being needlessly turned away. Many hotels have a few family-friendly rooms that open up to each other *(chambres communiquantes)*.

Extra pillows and blankets are often in the closet or available

French Hotel-Room Lingo

Study the price list on the hotel's website or posted at the desk, so you know your options. Receptionists often don't mention the cheaper rooms—they assume you want a private bathroom or a bigger room. Here are the types of rooms and beds:

French	English
une chambre avec douche et WC (ewn shahm-bruh ah-vehk doosh ay vay-say)	room with private shower and toilet
une chambre avec bain et WC (ewn shahm-bruh ah-vehk ban ay vay-say)	room with private bathtub and toilet
une chambre avec cabinet de toilette (ewn shahm-bruh ah-vehk kah-bee-nay duh twah-leht)	room with a toilet (shower down the hall)
une chambre sans douche ni WC (ewn shahm-bruh sahn doosh nee vay-say)	room without a private shower or toilet
chambres communiquantes (shahm-bruh koh-mew-nee-kahnt)	connecting rooms (ideal for families)
une chambre simple, un single (ewn shahm-bruh san-pluh, uhn san-guhl)	a true single room
un grand lit (uhn grahn lee)	double bed (55 in. wide)
deux petits lits (duh puh-tee lee)	twin beds (30-36 in. wide)
un lit queen-size (uhn lee "queen size")	queen-size bed (63 in. wide)
un king size (uhn "king size")	king-size bed (usually two twins pushed together)
un lit pliant (uhn lee plee-ahn)	folding bed
un bérceau (uhn behr-soh)	baby crib
un lit d'enfant (uhn lee dahn-fahn)	child's bed

on request. To get a pillow, ask for *"Un oreiller, s'il vous plaît"* (uhn oh-ray-yay, see voo play).

Old, characteristic, budget Parisian hotels have always been cramped. Don't expect much room to roam. Hotel elevators, while becoming more common, can be tiny—pack light. You may need to send your bags up one at a time.

Hotel lobbies, halls, and breakfast rooms are off-limits to smokers, though they can light up in their rooms. Still, I seldom smell any smoke in my rooms. Some hotels have nonsmoking rooms or floors—ask.

Most hotels offer some kind of breakfast (see page 642), but it's rarely included in the room rates—pay attention when comparing rates between hotels. The price of breakfast correlates with the price of the room: The more expensive the room, the more expensive the breakfast. This per-person charge rises with the number of stars the hotel has and can add up, particularly for families. While hotels hope you'll buy their breakfast, it's optional unless otherwise noted; to save money, head to a bakery or café instead.

Hoteliers uniformly detest it when people bring food into bedrooms. Dinner picnics are particularly frowned upon: Hoteliers worry about cleanliness, smells, and attracting insects. Be tidy and considerate.

If you're arriving in the morning, your room probably won't be ready. Check your bag safely at the hotel and dive right into sightseeing.

Hoteliers can be a good source of advice. Most know their city well, and can assist you with everything from public transit and airport connections to calling an English-speaking doctor, or finding a good restaurant, Wi-Fi hotspot (*point Wi-Fi*, pwan wee-fee), a late-night pharmacy, or a self-service launderette (*laverie automatique*, lah-vay-ree oh-to-mah-teek).

Even at the best places, mechanical breakdowns occur: Sinks leak, hot water turns cold, toilets may gurgle or smell, the Wi-Fi goes out, or the air-conditioning dies when you need it most. Report your concerns clearly and calmly at the front desk. For more complicated problems, don't expect instant results.

To guard against theft in your room, keep valuables out of sight. Some rooms come with a safe, and other hotels have safes at the front desk. I've never bothered using one.

While it's customary to pay for your room upon departure, it can be a good idea to settle your bill the day before, when you're not in a hurry and while the manager's in. That way you'll have time to discuss and address any points of contention.

Above all, keep a positive attitude. Remember, you're on vacation. If your hotel is a disappointment, spend more time out enjoying the place you came to see.

Modern Hotel Chains: France is littered with ultramodern hotels. The clean and inexpensive Ibis Budget chain (about €45-60/room for up to three people), the more attractive and spacious standard Ibis hotels (€80-110 for a double), and the cushier Mercure and Novotel hotels (€130-250 for a double) are all run by the same company, Accor (www.accorhotels.com). Though hardly quaint, these can be a good value (look for deals on their websites), par-

The Good and Bad of Online Reviews

User-generated review sites and apps such as Yelp, Booking.com, and TripAdvisor are changing the travel industry. These sites can give you a consensus of opinions about everything from hotels and restaurants to sights and nightlife. If you scan reviews of a hotel and see several complaints about noise or a rotten location, it tells you something important that you'd never learn from the hotel's own website.

But review sites are only as good as the judgment of their reviewers. And while these sites work hard to weed out bogus users, my hunch is that a significant percentage of user reviews are posted by friends or enemies of the business being reviewed.

As a guidebook writer, my sense is that there is a big difference between this uncurated information and a guidebook. A user-generated review is based on the experience of one person, who likely stayed at one hotel and ate at a few restaurants, and doesn't have much of a basis for comparison. A guidebook is the work of a trained researcher who visited many alternatives to assess their relative value. I recently checked out some top-rated user-reviewed hotel and restaurant listings in various towns; when stacked up against their competitors, some were gems, while just as many were duds.

Both types of information have their place, and in many ways, they're complementary. If something is well-reviewed in a guidebook, and also gets good ratings on one of these sites, it's likely a winner.

ticularly when they're centrally located; I list several in this book. Other chains to consider are Kyriad, with moderate prices and good quality (www.kyriad.com) and the familiar-to-Americans Best Western (www.bestwestern.com). Château and Hotels Collection has more cushy digs (www.chateauxhotels.com).

Bed & Breakfasts

Though B&Bs (*chambres d'hôtes*, abbreviated CH) are generally found in smaller towns and rural areas, some are available in Paris. See page 419 for a list of rental agencies that can help.

Short-Term Rentals

A short-term rental—whether an apartment, house, or room in a local's home—is an increasingly popular alternative to a guesthouse or hotel, especially if you plan to settle in one location for several nights. For stays longer than a few days, you can usually find a rental that's comparable to—or even cheaper than—a hotel room with similar amenities. Plus, you'll get a behind-the-scenes peek into how locals live.

Making Hotel Reservations

Reserve your rooms several weeks or even months in advance—or as soon as you've pinned down your travel dates. Note that some national holidays merit your making reservations far in advance (see page 677).

Requesting a Reservation: It's easiest to book your room through the hotel's website. (For the best rates, use the hotel's official site and not a booking agency's site.) If there's no reservation form, or for complicated requests, send an email (see below for a sample). Most recommended hotels take reservations in English.

The hotelier wants to know:
- the size of your party and type of rooms you need
- your arrival and departure dates, written European-style—day followed by month and year (for example, 18/06/17 or 18 June 2017); include the total number of nights
- special requests (such as en suite bathroom vs. down the hall, cheapest room, twin beds vs. double bed, quiet room)
- applicable discounts (such as a Rick Steves reader discount, cash discount, or promotional rate).

Confirming a Reservation: Most places will request a credit-card number to hold your room. If they don't have a secure online reservation form—look for the *https*—you can email it (I do), but it's safer to share that confidential info via a phone call or fax.

Canceling a Reservation: If you must cancel, it's courteous—and smart—to do so with as much notice as possible, especially for smaller family-run places (which describes most of the hotels

The rental route isn't for everyone. Many places require a minimum night stay, and compared to hotels, rentals usually have less-flexible cancellation policies. Also you're generally on your own: There's no hotel reception desk, breakfast, or daily cleaning service.

Finding Accommodations: Websites such as www.airbnb.com, www.roomorama.com, and www.vrbo.com let you browse properties and correspond directly with European property owners or managers. Or, for more guidance, consider using a rental agency such as www.interhomeusa.com or www.rentavilla.com. Agency-represented apartments may cost more, but this route often offers more help and safeguards than booking directly. For a list of rental agencies in Paris, see page 418.

If you're having trouble locating a hotel or an apartment in Paris, Paris Webservices' staff understands our travelers well and personally inspects every hotel and apartment they work with (see page 389).

Before you commit to a rental, be clear on the details, location,

PRACTICALITIES

From:	rick@ricksteves.com
Sent:	Today
To:	info@hotelcentral.com
Subject:	Reservation request for 19-22 July

Dear Hotel Central,

I would like to stay at your hotel. Please let me know if you have a room available and the price for:

• 2 people
• Double bed and en suite bathroom in a quiet room
• Arriving 19 July, departing 22 July (3 nights)

Thank you!
Rick Steves

I list). Cancellation policies can be strict; read the fine print or ask about these before you book. Many discount deals require pre-payment, with no refunds for cancellations.

Reconfirming a Reservation: Always call or email to recon-firm your room reservation a few days in advance. For B&Bs or very small hotels, I call again on my day of arrival to tell my host what time I expect to get there (especially important if arriving late—after 17:00).

Phoning: For tips on calling hotels overseas, see page 660.

and amenities. I like to virtually "explore" the neighborhood using the Street View feature on Google Maps. Also consider the proximity to public transportation, and how well-connected it is with the rest of the city. Ask about amenities that are important to you (elevator, laundry, coffee maker, Wi-Fi, parking, etc.). Reading reviews from previous guests can help identify trouble spots that are glossed over in the official description.

Apartments: If you're staying somewhere for four nights or longer, it's worth considering an apartment (anything less than that isn't worth the extra effort involved, such as arranging key pickup, buying groceries, etc.). Apartment rentals can be especially cost-effective for groups and families. European apartments, like hotel rooms, tend to be small by US standards. But they often come with laundry machines and small, equipped kitchens, making it easier and cheaper to dine in. If you make good use of the kitchen (and Europe's great produce markets), you'll save on your meal budget.

Private and Shared Rooms: Renting a room in someone's home is a good option for those traveling alone, as you're more likely to find true single rooms—with just one single bed, and a price to match. Beds range from air-mattress-in-living-room basic to plush-B&B-suite posh. Some places allow you to book for a single night; if staying for several nights, you can buy groceries just as you would in a rental house. While you can't expect your host to also be your tour guide—or even to provide you with much info—some may be interested in getting to know the travelers who come through their home.

Other Options: Swapping homes with a local works for people with an appealing place to offer, and who can live with the idea of having strangers in their home (don't assume where you live is not interesting to Europeans). A good place to start is HomeExchange (www.homeexchange.com).

To sleep for free, Couchsurfing.com is a vagabond's alternative to Airbnb. It lists millions of outgoing members, who host fellow "surfers" in their homes.

Hostels

A hostel *(auberge de jeunesse)* provides cheap beds in dorms where you sleep alongside strangers for about €23-35 per night. Travelers of any age are welcome if they don't mind dorm-style accommodations and meeting other travelers. Most hostels offer kitchen facilities, guest computers, Wi-Fi, and a self-service laundry. Hostels almost always provide bedding, but the towel's up to you (though you can usually rent one for a small fee). Family and private rooms are often available.

Independent hostels tend to be easygoing, colorful, and informal (no membership required; www.hostelworld.com). You may pay slightly less by booking directly with the hostel. **Official hostels** are part of Hostelling International (HI) and share an online booking site (www.hihostels.com). HI hostels typically require that you either have a membership card or pay extra per night.

Hip Hop Hostels is a clearinghouse for budget hotels and hostels in Paris. It's worth a look for its good selection of cheap accommodations (tel. 01 48 78 10 00, www.hiphophostels.com).

Eating

The French eat long and well. Relaxed and tree-shaded lunches with a chilled rosé, three-hour dinners, and endless hours of sitting in outdoor cafés are the norm. Here, celebrated restaurateurs are as famous as great athletes, and mamas hope their babies will grow up to be great chefs. Cafés, cuisine, and wines should become a highlight of any French adventure: It's sightseeing for your palate. Even if the rest of you is sleeping in a cheap hotel, let your taste buds

travel first-class in France. (They can go coach in Britain.)

You can eat well without going broke—but choose carefully: You're just as likely to blow a small fortune on a mediocre meal as you are to dine wonderfully for €20. Read the information that follows, consider my restaurant suggestions in this book, and you'll do fine. When restaurant-hunting, choose a spot filled with locals, not the place with the big neon signs boasting, "We Speak English and Accept Credit Cards." Venturing even a block or two off the main drag can lead to higher-quality food for less than half the price of the tourist-oriented places.

In Paris, lunches are a particularly good value, as most places offer the same quality and similar selections for far less than at dinner. If you're on a budget or just like going local, try making lunch your main meal, then have a lighter evening meal at a café.

RESTAURANT PRICING

I've categorized my recommended eateries based on price, indicated with a dollar-sign rating (see sidebar). The price ranges suggest the average price of a typical main course—but not necessarily a complete meal. Obviously, expensive items (steak, seafood, truffles), fine wine, appetizers, and dessert can significantly increase your final bill.

The dollar-sign categories also indicate the overall personality and "feel" of a place:

$ Budget eateries include street food, takeaway, order-at-the-counter shops, basic cafeterias, bakeries selling sandwiches, and so on.

$$ Moderate eateries are typically nice (but not fancy) sit-down restaurants, ideal for a straightforward, fill-the-tank meal. Most of my listings fall in this category—great for getting a good taste of the local cuisine on a budget.

$$$ Pricier eateries are a notch up, with more attention paid to the setting, service, and cuisine. These are ideal for a memorable meal that's still relatively casual and doesn't break the bank. This category often includes affordable "destination" or "foodie" restaurants.

$$$$ Splurge eateries are dress-up-for-a-special-occasion-swanky—Michelin star-type restaurants, typically with an elegant setting, polished service, pricey and intricate cuisine, and an expansive (and expensive) wine list.

I haven't categorized places where you might assemble a picnic,

Restaurant Price Code

I've assigned each eatery a price category, based on the average cost of a typical main course. Drinks, desserts, and splurge items (steak and seafood) can raise the price considerably.

$$$$	**Splurge:** Most main courses over €25
$$$	**Pricier:** €20-25
$$	**Moderate:** €15-20
$	**Budget:** Under €15

In France, a crêpe stand or other takeout spot is **$;** a sit-down brasserie, café, or bistro with affordable *plats du jour* is **$$;** a casual but more upscale restaurant is **$$$;** and a swanky splurge is **$$$$.**

snack, or graze: supermarkets, delis, ice cream-stands, cafés or bars specializing in drinks, chocolate shops, and so on.

BREAKFAST

Most hotels offer an optional breakfast, which is usually pleasant and convenient (generally €10-20). They almost all offer a buffet breakfast (cereal, yogurt, fruit, cheese, ham, croissants, juice, and hard-boiled eggs). Some add scrambled eggs and sausage. Before committing to breakfast, scan the offerings to be sure it's to your liking. Once committed, it's self-service and as much as you want. Coffee is often self-serve from a machine or a thermos. If there's no coffee machine and you want to make your own *café au lait,* find the hot milk and mix it with your coffee. If your hotelier serves your coffee, ask for *café avec du lait.*

If all you want is coffee or tea and a croissant, the corner café offers more atmosphere and is less expensive (though you get more coffee at your hotel). Go local at the café and ask for *une tartine* (ewn tart-teen), a baguette slathered with butter or jam. If you crave eggs for breakfast, drop into a café and order *une omelette* or *œufs sur le plat* (fried eggs). Some cafés and bakeries offer worthwhile breakfast deals with juice, croissant, and coffee or tea for about €7 (for more on coffee and tea drinks, see page 656).

To keep it cheap, pick up some fruit at a grocery store and pastries at your favorite *boulangerie* and have a picnic breakfast, then savor your coffee at a café bar *(comptoir)* while standing, like the French do.

PICNIC DINING AND FOOD TO GO

Whether going all out on a perfect French picnic or simply grabbing a sandwich to eat on an atmospheric square, dining with the city as your backdrop can be one of your most

Picnic Vocabulary

English	French
please	*s'il vous plaît* (see voo play)
a plastic fork	*une fourchette en plastique* (ewn foor-sheht ahn plah-steek)
a plastic cup	*un goblet en plastique* (uhn goh-blay ahn plah-steek)
a paper plate	*une assiette en papier* (ewn ah-see-eht ahn pahp-yay)
napkins	*les serviettes* (lay sehr-vee-eht)
a small box	*une barquette* (ewn bar-keht)
a knife	*un couteau* (uhn koo-toh)
corkscrew	*tire-bouchon* (teer-boo-shohn)
sliced	*tranché* (trahn-shay)
a slice	*une tranche* (ewn trahnsh)
a small slice	*une petite tranche* (ewn puh-teet trahnsh)
more	*plus* (plew)
less	*moins* (mwan)
It's just right.	*C'est bon.* (say bohn)
That'll be all.	*C'est tout.* (say too)
Thank you.	*Merci.* (mehr-see)

PRACTICALITIES

memorable meals. For a list of places to picnic in Paris, see page 430.

Picnics

Great for lunch or dinner, French picnics can be first-class affairs and adventures in high cuisine. Be daring. Try the smelly cheeses, ugly pâtés, sissy quiches, and minuscule yogurts. Shopkeepers are accustomed to selling small quantities of produce. Get a succulent salad-to-go, and ask for a plastic fork. If you need a knife or corkscrew, borrow one from your hotelier (but don't picnic in your room, as French hoteliers uniformly detest this). Though drinking wine in public places is taboo in the US, it's *pas de problème* in France.

Assembling a Picnic: Visit several small stores to put together a complete meal. Shop early, as many shops close from 12:00 or 13:00 to 15:00 for their lunch break. Say *"Bonjour madame/monsieur"* as you enter, then point to what you want and say, *"S'il vous plaît."* For other terminology you might need while shopping, see the sidebar on page 643.

At the **boulangerie** (bakery), buy some bread. A baguette usually does the trick, or choose from the many loaves of bread on display: *pain aux céréales* (whole grain with seeds), *pain de campagne* (country bread, made with unbleached bread flour), *pain complet* (wheat bread), or *pain de seigle* (rye bread). To ask for it sliced, say *"Tranché, s'il vous plaît."*

At the *pâtisserie* (pastry shop, which is often the same place you bought the bread), choose a dessert that's easy to eat with your hands. My favorites are *éclairs* (*chocolat* or *café* flavored), individual fruit *tartes* (*framboise* is raspberry, *fraise* is strawberry, *citron* is lemon), and *macarons* (made of flavored cream sandwiched between two meringues, not coconut cookies like in the US).

At the **crémerie** or **fromagerie** (cheese shop), choose a sampling of cheeses *(un assortiment)*. I usually get one hard cheese (like Comté, Cantal, or Beaufort), one soft cow's milk cheese (like Brie or Camembert), one goat's milk cheese (anything that says chèvre), and one blue cheese (Roquefort or Bleu d'Auvergne). Goat cheese usually comes in individual portions. For all other large cheeses, point to the cheese you want and ask for *une petite tranche* (a small slice). The shopkeeper will place a knife on the cheese indicating the size of the slice they are about to cut, then look at you for approval. If you'd like more, say, *"Plus."* If you'd like less, say *"Moins."* If it's just right, say *"C'est bon!"*

At the **charcuterie** or **traiteur** (for deli items, prepared salads, meats, and pâtés), I like a slice of *pâté de campagne* (country pâté made of pork) and *saucissons sec* (dried sausages, some with pepper crust or garlic—you can ask to have it sliced thin like salami). I get a fresh salad, too. Typical options are *carottes râpées* (shredded carrots in a tangy vinaigrette), *salade de betteraves* (beets in vin-

aigrette), and *céleri rémoulade* (celery root with a mayonnaise sauce). The food comes in takeout boxes, and they may supply a plastic fork.

At a **cave à vin** you can buy chilled wines that the merchant is usually happy to open and re-cork for you.

At a **supermarché, épic-erie,** or **magasin d'alimentation** (small grocery store or minimart), you'll find plastic cutlery and glasses, paper plates, napkins, drinks, chips, and a display of produce. **Daily Monop' and Carrefour City** stores—offering fresh salads, wraps, fruit drinks, and more at reasonable prices—are convenient one-stop places to assemble a picnic. You'll see them all over Paris.

To-Go Food

You'll find plenty of to-go options at *crêperies*, bakeries, and small stands. Baguette sandwiches, quiches, and pizza-like items are tasty, filling, and budget-friendly (about €5).

Sandwiches: Anything served *à la provençale* has marinated peppers, tomatoes, and eggplant. A sandwich *à la italienne* is a grilled *panini*. Here are some common sandwiches:

Fromage (froh-mahzh): Cheese (white on beige).

Jambon beurre (zhahn-bohn bur): Ham and butter (boring for most but a French classic).

Jambon crudités (zhahn-bohn krew-dee-tay): Ham with tomatoes, lettuce, cucumbers, and mayonnaise.

Pain salé (pan sah-lay) or *fougasse* (foo-gahs): Bread rolled up with salty bits of bacon, cheese, or olives.

Poulet crudités (poo-lay krew-dee-tay): Chicken with tomatoes, lettuce, maybe cucumbers, and always mayonnaise.

Saucisson beurre (saw-see-sohn bur): Thinly sliced sausage and butter.

Thon crudités (tohn krew-dee-tay): Tuna with tomatoes, lettuce, and maybe cucumbers, but definitely mayonnaise.

Quiche: Typical quiches you'll see at shops and bakeries are *lorraine* (ham and cheese), *fromage* (cheese only), *aux oignons* (with onions), *aux poireaux* (with leeks—my favorite), *aux champignons* (with mushrooms), *au saumon* (salmon), or *au thon* (tuna).

Crêpes: The quintessentially French thin pancake called a crêpe (rhymes with "step," not "grape") is filling, usually inexpensive, and generally quick. Place your order at the *crêperie* window or kiosk, and watch the chef in action. But don't be surprised if they don't make the crêpe for you from scratch; at some *crêperies*, they might premake a stack of crêpes and reheat them when they fill your order.

Crêpes generally are *sucrée* (sweet) or *salée* (savory). Technically, a savory crêpe should be made with a heartier buckwheat batter, and is called a *galette*. However, many cheap and lazy *crêperies* use the same sweet batter *(de froment)* for both their sweet-topped and savory-topped crêpes. A *socca* is a chickpea crêpe.

Standard crêpe toppings include cheese (*fromage;* usually Swiss-style Gruyère or Emmental), ham *(jambon)*, egg *(œuf)*, mushrooms *(champignons)*, chocolate, Nutella, jam *(confiture)*, whipped cream *(chantilly)*, apple jam *(compote de pommes)*, chestnut cream *(crème de marrons)*, and Grand Marnier.

RESTAURANT AND CAFE DINING

To get the most out of dining out in France, slow down. Allow enough time, engage the waiter, show you care about food, and enjoy the experience as much as the food itself.

French waiters probably won't overwhelm you with friendliness. As their tip is already included in the bill (see "Tipping," below), there's less schmoozing than we're used to at home. Notice how hard they work. They almost never stop. Cozying up to clients (French or foreign) is probably the last thing on their minds. They're often stuck with client overload, too, because the French rarely hire part-time employees, even to help with peak times. To get a waiter's attention, try to make meaningful eye contact, which is a signal that you need something. If this doesn't work, raise your hand and simply say, *"S'il vous plaît"* (see voo play)—"please."

This phrase should also work when you want to ask for the check. In French eateries, a waiter will rarely bring you the check unless you request it. For a French person, having the bill dropped off before asking for it is akin to being kicked out—*très gauche*. But busy travelers are often ready for the check sooner rather than later. If you're in a hurry, ask for the bill when your server comes to clear your plates or checks in to see if you want dessert or coffee. To request your bill, say, *"L'addition, s'il vous plaît."* If you don't ask now, the wait staff may become scarce as they leave you to digest in peace. (For a list of other restaurant survival phrases, see page 650.)

Note that all café and restaurant interiors are smoke-free. Today the only smokers you'll find are at outside tables, which—unfortunately—may be exactly where you want to sit.

For a list of common French dishes that you'll see on menus, see page 650. For details on ordering drinks, see page 655.

Tipping: At cafés and restaurants, a 12-15 percent service charge is always included in the price of what you order (*service compris* or *prix net*), but you won't see it listed on your bill. Unlike in the US, France pays servers a decent wage. Because of this, most locals tip only a very small amount or nothing at all. If you feel the service was good, tip a little—up to 5 percent. If you want the waiter to keep the change when you pay, say *"C'est bon"* (say bohn), meaning "It's good." If you are using a credit card, leave your tip in cash—credit-card receipts don't even have space to add a tip. Never feel guilty if you don't leave a tip.

Cafés and Brasseries

French cafés and brasseries provide user-friendly meals and a relief from sightseeing overload. They're not necessarily cheaper than many restaurants and bistros, and famous cafés on popular squares can be pricey affairs. Their key advantage is flexibility: They offer long serving hours, and you're welcome to order just a salad, a sandwich, or a bowl of soup, even for dinner. It's also OK to share starters and desserts, though not main courses.

Cafés and brasseries usually open by 7:00, but closing hours vary. Unlike restaurants, which open only for dinner and sometimes for lunch, some cafés and all brasseries serve food throughout the day (usually with a limited menu during off hours), making them the best option for a late lunch or an early dinner. *Service Continu* or *Service Non-Stop* signs indicate continued service throughout the day.

Check the price list first, which by law must be posted prominently (if you don't see one, go elsewhere). There are two sets of prices: You'll pay more for the same drink if you're seated at a table *(salle)* than if you're seated or standing at the bar or counter *(comptoir)*. (For tips on ordering coffee and tea, see page 656.)

At a café or a brasserie, if the table is not set, it's fine to seat yourself and just have a drink. However, if it's set with a placemat and cutlery, you should ask to be seated and plan to order a meal. If you're unsure, ask the server before sitting down.

Ordering: A salad, crêpe, quiche, or omelet is a fairly cheap way to fill up. Each can be made with various extras such as ham, cheese, mushrooms, and so on. Omelets come lonely on a plate with a basket of bread.

Sandwiches, generally served day and night, are inexpensive, but most are very plain *(boulangeries* serve better ones). To get more than a piece of ham *(jambon)* on a baguette, order a *sandwich jambon crudités* (garnished with veggies). Popular sandwiches are the croque monsieur (grilled ham-and-cheese) and *croque madame* (*monsieur* with a fried egg on top).

Salads are typically large and often can be ordered with warm ingredients mixed in, such as melted goat cheese, fried gizzards, or roasted potatoes. One salad is perfect for lunch or a light dinner. See page 652 for a list of classic salads.

The daily special—*plat du jour* (plah dew zhoor), or just *plat*—is your fast, hearty, and garnished hot plate for about €12-20. At most cafés, feel free to order only *entrées* (which in French means the starter course); many people find these lighter and more interesting than a main course. A vegetarian can enjoy a tasty, filling meal by ordering two *entrées*.

Regardless of what you order, bread is free but almost never comes with butter; to get more bread, just hold up your basket and ask, *"Encore, s'il vous plaît?"*

Vegetarians, Allergies, and Other Dietary Restrictions

Many French people think "vegetarian" means "no red meat" or "not much meat." If you're a strict vegetarian, be specific: Tell your server what you don't eat—and it can be helpful to clarify what you do eat. Write it out on a card and keep it handy.

But be reasonable. Think of your meal (as the French do) as if it's a finely crafted creation by a trained artist. The chef knows what goes well together, and substitutions are considered an insult to his training. Picky eaters should try their best to just take it or leave it.

However, French restaurants are willing to accommodate genuine dietary restrictions and other special concerns, or at least point you to an appropriate choice on the menu. These phrases might help:

French	English
Je suis végétarien/végétarienne. (zhuh swee vay-zhay-tah-ree-an/vay-zhay-tah-ree-ehn)	I am vegetarian.
Je ne peux pas manger de _____. (zhuh nuh puh pah mahn-zhay duh _____)	I cannot eat _____.
Je suis allergique à _____. (zhuh sweez ah-lehr-zheek ah _____)	I am allergic to _____.
Pas de _____. (pah duh _____).	No _____.

Restaurants

Choose restaurants filled with locals. Consider my suggestions and your hotelier's opinion, but trust your instincts. If a restaurant doesn't post its prices outside, move along. Refer to my restaurant recommendations to get a sense of what a reasonable meal should cost.

Most restaurants open for dinner at 19:00 (some at 18:30). Local favorites get crowded after 21:00. To minimize crowds, go early (by 19:30). Last seating at Parisian restaurants is about 22:00 or later. Many restaurants close Sunday and/or Monday.

Tune into the quiet, relaxed pace of French dining. The French don't do dinner and a movie on date nights; they just do dinner. The table is yours for the night. Notice how quietly French diners speak in restaurants and how this improves your overall experience. Learn from this.

Ordering: In French restaurants, you can choose something off the menu (called the *carte*), or you can order a multicourse, fixed-price meal (confusingly, called a *menu*). Or, if offered, you can get one of the special dishes of the day *(plat du jour)*. If you ask for *un menu* (instead of *la carte*), you'll get a fixed-price meal.

Ordering **à la carte** gives you the best selection. I enjoy going à la carte especially when traveling with others and eating family style (waiters are happy to accommodate this approach and will bring small extra plates). It's traditional to order an entrée (a starter—not a main dish) and a *plat principal* (main course), though it's becoming common to order only a *plat principal*. *Plats* are generally more meat-based, while entrées usually include veggies. Multiple course meals, while time-consuming (a positive thing in France), create the appropriate balance of veggies to meat. Elaborate meals may also have *entremets*—tiny dishes served between courses. Wherever you dine, consider the waiter's recommendations and anything *de la maison* (of the house), as long as it's not an organ meat (tripe, *rognons,* or andouillette).

Two people can split an entrée or a big salad (small-size dinner salads are usually not offered á la carte) and then each get a *plat principal*. At restaurants, it's seen as inappropriate for two diners to share one main course. If all you want is a salad or soup, go to a café or brasserie.

Fixed-price menus—which usually include two, three, or four courses—are generally a better deal than eating à la carte and help you pace your meal like the locals. At most restaurants offering fixed-price *menus,* the price for a two- or three-course *menu* is only slightly higher than a single main course from the à la carte list. With a three-course *menu* you'll choose a starter of soup, appetizer, or salad; select from three or four main courses with vegetables; and finish up with a cheese course and/or a choice of desserts. It sounds like a lot of food, but portions are smaller in France, and what we cram onto one large plate they spread out over several courses. Wine and other drinks are extra, and certain premium items add a few euros to the price, clearly noted on the menu *(supplément* or *sup.).* Most restaurants offer less expensive and less filling two-course *menus,* sometimes called *formules,* featuring an *entrée et plat,* or *plat et dessert.* Many restaurants have a reasonable *menu-enfant* (kid's meal).

Lunch: If a restaurant serves lunch, it generally begins at 12:00 and goes until 14:30, with last orders taken at about 14:00. If you're hungry when restaurants are closed (late afternoon), go to a *boulangerie,* brasserie, or café. Remember that even the fanciest eateries usually have affordable lunch *menus* (often called *formules* or *plat de midi*), allowing you to sample the same gourmet cooking for generally about half the cost of dinner.

PRACTICALITIES

French Specialties by Region

Burgundy: Considered by many to be France's best, Burgundian cuisine is peasant cooking elevated to an art. This wine region excels in *coq au vin* (chicken with wine sauce), *bœuf bourguignon* (beef stew cooked with wine, bacon, onions, and mushrooms), *œufs en meurette* (eggs poached in red wine), *escargots* (snails), and *jambon persillé* (ham with garlic and parsley).

Normandy and Brittany: Normandy specializes in cream sauces, sea salt, organ meats (sweetbreads, tripe, and kidneys—the "gizzard salads" are great), and seafood *(fruits de mer)*. Dairy products are big here. Try the *moules* (mussels) and *escalope normande* (veal in cream sauce). Brittany is famous for its oysters and crêpes. Both regions use lots of *cidre* (hard apple cider) in their cuisine.

Provence: The extravagant use of garlic, olive oil, herbs, and tomatoes makes Provence's cuisine France's liveliest. To sample it, order anything *à la provençale.* Among the area's spicy specialties are ratatouille (a thick mixture of vegetables in an herb-flavored tomato sauce), *brandade* (a salt cod, garlic, and cream mousse), aioli (a garlicky mayonnaise often served atop fresh vegetables), tapenade (a paste of puréed olives, capers, anchovies, herbs, and sometimes tuna), *soupe au pistou* (vegetable soup with basil, garlic, and cheese), and *soupe à l'ail* (garlic soup).

Riviera: The Côte d'Azur gives Provence's cuisine a Mediterranean flair. Local specialties are bouillabaisse (the spicy seafood

FRENCH CUISINE

You can be a galloping gourmet and try several types of French cuisine without ever leaving the confines of Paris. Most restaurants serve dishes from several regions, though some focus on a particular region's cuisine (see the sidebar for a list of specialty dishes by region). Among the listings in this book are restaurants specializing in food from Provence, Burgundy, Alsace, Normandy, Brittany, Dordogne, Languedoc, and the Basque region.

General styles of French cooking include *haute cuisine* (classic, elaborately prepared, multicourse meals); *cuisine bourgeoise* (the finest-quality home cooking); *cuisine des provinces* (traditional dishes of specific regions); and *nouvelle cuisine* (a focus on smaller portions and closer attention to the texture and color of the ingredients). Sauces are a huge part of French cooking. In the early 20th century, the legendary French chef Auguste Escoffier identified five French "mother sauces" from which all others are derived: *béchamel* (milk-based white sauce), *espagnole* (veal-based brown sauce), *velouté* (stock-based white sauce), *hollandaise* (egg yolk-based white sauce), and *tomate* (tomato-based red sauce).

The following list of items should help you navigate a typical

stew/soup that seems worth the cost only for those with a sea-food fetish), *bourride* (a creamy fish soup thickened with aioli), and *salade niçoise* (a tasty salad with tomato, potato, olive, anchovy, egg, green bean, and tuna).

Basque: Mixing influences from the mountains, sea, Spain, and France, it's dominated by seafood, tomatoes, and red peppers. Look for anything *basquaise* (cooked with tomatoes, eggplant, red peppers, and garlic), such as *thon* (tuna) or *poulet* (chicken). Try *piperade,* a dish combining peppers, tomatoes, garlic, and eggs (ham optional), and *ttoro,* a seafood stew and the Basque answer to bouillabaisse.

Alsace: The German influence is obvious—sausages, potatoes, onions, and sauerkraut. Look for *choucroute garnie* (sauerkraut and sausage—although it seems a shame to eat it in a fancy restaurant), the more traditionally Alsatian *Baeckeoffe* (potato, meat, and onion stew), *Rösti* (an oven-baked potato-and-cheese dish), fresh trout, foie gras, and *flammekueche* (a paper-thin pizza topped with bacon, onions, and sour cream).

Languedoc and Périgord: What Parisians call "Southwest cuisine" *(cuisine du sud-ouest)* is hearty peasant fare, using full-bodied red wines and lots of duck. Try *cassoulet* (white bean, duck, and sausage stew), *canard* (duck), *pâté de foie gras* (goose-liver pâté), *pommes sarladaise* (potatoes fried in duck fat), *truffes* (truffles, earthy mushrooms), and anything with *noix* (walnuts).

French menu. Galloping gourmets should bring a menu translator. The most complete (and priciest) menu reader around is *A to Z of French Food* by G. de Temmerman. The *Marling Menu-Master* is also good. The *Rick Steves French Phrase Book & Dictionary*, with a menu decoder, works well for most travelers.

First Course *(Entrée)*

Crudités: A mix of raw and lightly cooked fresh vegetables, usually including grated carrots, celery root, tomatoes, and beets, often with a hefty dose of vinaigrette dressing. If you want the dressing on the side, say, *"La sauce à côté, s'il vous plaît"* (lah sohs ah koh-tay, see voo play).

Escargots: Snails cooked in parsley-garlic butter. You don't even have to like the snail itself. Just dipping your bread in garlic butter is more than satisfying. Prepared a variety of ways, the classic is *à la bourguignonne* (served in their shells).

Foie gras: Rich and buttery in consistency—and hefty in price—this pâté is made from the swollen livers of force-fed geese (or ducks, in *foie gras de canard*). Spread it on bread, and never add mustard. For a real French experience, try this dish with a sweet white wine (such as a muscat).

Huîtres: Oysters, served raw any month, are particularly popular at Christmas and on New Year's Eve, when every café seems to have overflowing baskets in their window.

Œuf mayo: A simple hard-boiled egg topped with a dollop of flavorful mayonnaise.

Pâtés and ***terrines:*** Slowly cooked ground meat (usually pork, though game, poultry liver, and rabbit are also common) that is highly seasoned and served in slices with mustard and *cornichons* (little pickles). Pâtés are smoother than the similarly prepared but chunkier *terrines*.

Soupe à l'oignon: Hot, salty, filling—and hard to find in Paris— French onion soup is a beef broth served with a baked cheese-and-bread crust over the top.

Salads (*Salades*)

With the exception of a *salade mixte* (simple green salad, often difficult to find), the French get creative with their *salades*. Here are some classics:

Salade au chèvre chaud: This mixed green salad is topped with warm goat cheese on small pieces of toast.

Salade aux gésiers: Though it may not sound appetizing, this salad with chicken gizzards (and often slices of duck) is worth a try.

Salade composée: "Composed" of any number of ingredients, this salad might have *lardons* (bacon), Comté (a Swiss-style cheese), Roquefort (blue cheese), *œuf* (egg), *noix* (walnuts), and *jambon* (ham, generally thinly sliced).

Salade gourmande: The "gourmet" salad varies by region and restaurant but usually features cured and poached meats served on salad greens with a mustard vinaigrette.

Salade niçoise: A specialty from Nice, this tasty salad usually includes greens topped with green beans, boiled potatoes, tomatoes, anchovies, olives, hard-boiled eggs, and lots of tuna.

Salade paysanne: You'll usually find potatoes *(pommes de terre),* walnuts *(noix),* tomatoes, ham, and egg in this salad.

Main Course (*Plat Principal*)

Duck, lamb, and rabbit are popular in France, and each is prepared in a variety of ways. You'll also encounter various stew-like dishes that vary by region. The most common regional specialties are described here.

Bœuf bourguignon: A Burgundian specialty, this classy beef stew is cooked slowly in red wine, then served with onions, potatoes, and mushrooms.

Confit de canard: A favorite from the southwest Dordogne region is duck that has been preserved in its own fat, then cooked in its fat, and often served with potatoes (cooked in the same fat). Not for dieters. (Note that *magret de canard* is sliced duck breast and very different in taste.)

Coq au vin: This Burgundian dish is rooster marinated ever so slowly in red wine, then cooked until it melts in your mouth. It's served (often family-style) with vegetables.

Daube: Generally made with beef, but sometimes lamb, this is a long and slowly simmered dish, typically paired with noodles or other pasta.

Escalope normande: This specialty of Normandy features turkey or veal in a cream sauce.

Gigot d'agneau: A specialty of Provence, this is a leg of lamb often grilled and served with white beans. The best lamb is *pré salé*, which means the lamb has been raised in salt-marsh lands (like at Mont St-Michel).

Le hamburger: This American import is all the rage in France. Cafés and restaurants serve it using local sauces, breads, and cheeses. It's fun to see their interpretation of our classic dish.

Poulet rôti: Roasted chicken on the bone—French comfort food.

Saumon and ***truite:*** You'll see salmon and trout *(truite)* dishes served in various styles. The salmon usually comes from the North Sea and is always served with sauce, most commonly a sorrel *(oseille)* sauce.

Steak: Referred to as *pavé* (thick hunk of prime steak), *bavette* (skirt steak), *faux filet* (sirloin), or *entrecôte* (rib steak), French steak is usually thinner and tougher than American steak and is always served with sauces (*au poivre* is a pepper sauce, *une sauce roquefort* is a blue-cheese sauce). Because steak is usually better in North America, I generally avoid it in France (unless the sauce sounds good). You will also see *steak haché,* which is a lean, gourmet hamburger patty served *sans* bun. When it's served as *steak haché à cheval,* it comes with a fried egg on top.

By American standards, the French undercook meats: Their version of rare, *saignant* (seh-nyahn), means "bloody" and is close to raw. What they consider medium, *à point* (ah pwan), is what an American would call rare. Their term for well-done, or *bien cuit* (bee-yehn kwee), would translate as medium for Americans.

Steak tartare: This wonderfully French dish is for adventurous types only. It's very lean, raw hamburger served with savory seasonings (usually Tabasco, capers, raw onions, salt, and pepper on the side) and topped with a raw egg yolk. This is not hamburger as we know it, but freshly ground beef.

Cheese Course *(Le Fromage)*

The cheese course is served just before (or instead of) dessert. It not only helps with digestion, it gives you a great opportunity to sample the tasty regional cheeses—and time to finish up your wine. Between cow, goat, and sheep cheeses, there are at least 350 different ones to try in France. Some restaurants will offer a cheese platter, from which you select a few different kinds. A good platter has at least four cheeses: a hard cheese (such as Cantal), a flowery cheese (such as Brie or Camembert), a blue or Roquefort cheese, and a goat cheese.

Cheeses most commonly served in Paris are Brie de Meaux (mild and creamy, from just outside Paris), Camembert (semicreamy and pungent, from Normandy), chèvre (goat cheese with a sharp taste, usually from the Loire), and Roquefort (strong and blue-veined, from south-central France).

To sample several types of cheese from the cheese plate, say, *"Un assortiment, s'il vous plaît"* (uhn ah-sor-tee-mahn, see voo play). You'll either be served a selection of several cheeses or choose from a large selection offered on a cheese tray. If you serve yourself from the cheese tray, observe French etiquette and keep the shape of the cheese: Shave off a slice from the side or cut small wedges.

A glass of good red wine is a heavenly complement to your cheese course.

Dessert *(Le Dessert)*

If you order espresso, it will always come after dessert. To have coffee with dessert, ask for *"café avec le dessert"* (kah-fay ah-vehk luh day-sayr). See the list of coffee terms on page 657. Here are the types of treats you'll see:

Baba au rhum: Pound cake drenched in rum, served with whipped cream.

Café gourmand: An assortment of small desserts selected by the restaurant, served with an espresso—a great way to sample several desserts and learn your favorite.

Crème brûlée: A rich, creamy, dense, caramelized custard.

Crème caramel: Flan in a caramel sauce.

Fondant au chocolat: A molten chocolate cake with a runny (not totally cooked) center. Also known as *moelleux* (meh-leh) *au chocolat.*

Fromage blanc: A light dessert similar to plain yogurt (yet different), served with sugar or herbs.

Glace: Ice cream—typically vanilla, chocolate, or strawberry.

Ile flottante: A light dessert consisting of islands of meringue floating on a pond of custard sauce.

Mousse au chocolat: Chocolate mousse.

Profiteroles: Cream puffs filled with vanilla ice cream, smothered in warm chocolate sauce.

Riz au lait: Rice pudding.

Sorbets: Light, flavorful, and fruity ices, sometimes laced with brandy.

Tartes: Open-face pie, often filled with fruit.

Tarte tatin: Apple pie like grandma never made, with caramelized apples, cooked upside down, but served upright.

BEVERAGES

In stores, unrefrigerated soft drinks, bottled water, and beer are one-third the price of cold drinks. Bottled water and boxed fruit juice are the cheapest drinks. Avoid buying drinks to-go at streetside stands; you'll pay far less in a shop.

In bars and at eateries, be clear when ordering drinks—you can easily pay €9 for an oversized Coke and €15 for a supersized beer at some cafés. When you order a drink, state the size in centiliters (don't say "small," "medium," or "large," because the waiter might bring a bigger drink than you want). For something small, ask for 25 *centilitres* (vant-sank sahn-tee-lee-truh; about 8 ounces); for a medium drink, order 33 cl (trahnte-twah; about 12 ounces—a normal can of soda); a large is 50 cl (san-kahnt; about 16 ounces); and a super-size is one liter (lee-truh; about a quart—which is more than I would ever order in France). The ice cubes melted after the last Yankee tour group left.

Water, Juice, and Soft Drinks

The French are willing to pay for bottled water with their meal (*eau minérale;* oh mee-nay-rahl) because they prefer the taste over tap water. Badoit is my favorite carbonated water (*l'eau gazeuse;* loh gah-zuhz) and is commonly available. To get a free pitcher of tap water, ask for *une carafe d'eau* (ewn kah-rahf doh). Otherwise, you may unwittingly buy bottled water.

In France *limonade* (lee-moh-nahd) is Sprite or 7-Up. For a fun, bright, nonalcoholic drink of 7-Up with mint syrup, order *un diabolo menthe* (uhn dee-ah-boh-loh mahnt). For 7-Up with fruit syrup, order *un diabolo grenadine* (think Shirley Temple). Kids love the local orange drink, Orangina, a carbonated orange juice with pulp (though it can be pricey). They also like *sirop à l'eau* (see-roh ah loh), flavored syrup mixed with bottled water.

For keeping hydrated on the go, hang on to the half-liter mineral-water bottles (sold everywhere for about €1-2) and refill. Buy juice in cheap liter boxes, then drink some and store the extra in your water bottle. Of course, water quenches your thirst better and cheaper than anything you'll find in a store or café. I drink tap water throughout France, filling up my bottle in hotel rooms.

French Wine-Tasting 101

France is peppered with wineries and wine-tasting opportunities. For some visitors, trying to make sense of the vast range of French wines can be overwhelming, particularly when faced with a no-nonsense winemaker or sommelier. Take a deep breath, do your best to follow my guidance, and don't linger where you don't feel welcome.

Winemakers and sommeliers are usually happy to work with you...especially if they can figure out what you want. It helps to know what you like (drier or sweeter, lighter or full-bodied, fruity or more tannic, and so on). The people serving you may know those words in English, but you're wise to learn the key words in French (see the "French Wine Lingo" section).

French wines usually have a lower alcohol level than American or Australian wines. Whereas many Americans like a big, full-bodied wine, most French prefer subtler flavors. They judge a wine by how well it pairs with a meal—and a big, oaky wine would overwhelm most French cuisine. The French enjoy sampling younger wines and divining how they will taste in a few years, allowing them to buy bottles at cheaper prices and stash them in their cellars. Americans want it now—for today's picnic.

At wine tastings, remember that vintners and wine shops hope you'll buy a bottle or two. If you don't buy, you may be asked to pay a small fee for a tasting. They understand that North Americans can't take much wine with them, but they do hope you'll look for their wines in the US. Some places will ship your purchase home—ask.

French Wine Lingo
Here are some phrases to get you started when wine-tasting:

Hello, sir/madam.
Bonjour, monsieur/madame.
(bohn-zhoor, muhs-yur/mah-dahm)

Coffee and Tea
The French define various types of espresso drinks by how much milk is added. To the French, milk is a delicate form of nutrition: You need it in the morning, but as the day goes on, too much can upset your digestion. Therefore, the amount of milk that's added to coffee decreases as the day goes on. The average French person thinks a *café au lait* is exclusively for breakfast, and a *café crème* is only appropriate through midday. You're welcome to order a milkier coffee drink later in the day, but don't be surprised if you get a funny look.

By law, a waiter must give you a glass of tap water with your coffee or tea if you request it; ask for *"un verre d'eau, s'il vous plaît"* (uhn vayr doh, see voo play).

Here are some common coffee and tea drinks:

We would like to taste a few wines.
Nous voudrions déguster quelques vins.
(noo voo-dree-ohn day-goo-stay kehl-kuh van)

We would like a wine that is _____ and _____.
Nous voudrions un vin _____ et _____.
(noo voo-dree-ohn uhn van _____ ay _____)

Fill in the blanks with your favorites from this list:

English	French
wine	*vin* (van)
red	*rouge* (roozh)
white	*blanc* (blahn)
rosé	*rosé* (roh-zay)
light	*léger* (lay-zhay)
full-bodied	*robuste* (roh-bewst)
fruity	*fruité* (frwee-tay)
sweet	*doux* (doo)
tannic	*tannique* (tah-neek)
fine	*fin, avec finesse* (fan, ah-vehk fee-nehs)
ready to drink (mature)	*prêt à boire* (preh tah bwar)
not ready to drink	*fermé* (fair-may)
oaky	*goût du fût de la chêne* (goo duh foo duh lah sheh-nuh)
from old vines	*de vieille vignes* (duh vee-yay-ee veen-yah)
sparkling	*pétillant* (pay-tee-yahn)

Café (kah-fay): Shot of espresso

Café allongé, a.k.a. *café longue* (kah-fay ah-lohn-zhay; kah-fay lohn): Espresso topped up with hot water—like an Americano

Noisette (nwah-zeht): Espresso with a dollop of milk (best value for adding milk to your coffee)

Café au lait (kah-fay oh lay): Espresso mixed with lots of warm milk (used mostly for coffee made at home; in a café, order *café crème*)

Café crème (kah-fay krehm): Espresso with a sizable pour of steamed milk (closest thing you'll get to an American-style latte)

Grand crème (grahn krehm): Double shot of espresso with a bit more steamed milk (and often twice the price)

Décafféiné (day-kah-fee-nay): Decaf—available for any of the above

Thé nature (tay nah-tour): Plain tea

Thé au lait (tay oh lay): Tea with milk

Thé citron (tay see-trohn): Tea with lemon

Infusion (an-few-see-yohn): Herbal tea

Alcoholic Beverages

The legal drinking age is 16 for beer and wine and 18 for the hard stuff—at restaurants it's *normale* for wine to be served with dinner to teens.

Wine: Wines are often listed in a separate *carte des vins*. House wine at the bar is generally cheap and good (about €3-6/glass). At a restaurant, a bottle or carafe of house wine costs €10-20. To order inexpensive wine at a restaurant, ask for table wine in a pitcher (only available when seated and when ordering food), rather than a bottle. Finer restaurants usually offer only bottles of wine.

Here are some important wine terms:

Vin du pays (van duh pay): Table wine

Verre de vin rouge (vehr duh van roozh): Glass of red wine

Verre de vin blanc (vehr duh van blahn): Glass of white wine

Pichet (pee-shay): Pitcher

Demi-pichet (duh-mee pee-shay): Half-carafe

Quart (kar): Quarter-carafe (ideal for one)

Bouteille (boo-teh-ee): Bottle

Demi-bouteille (duh-mee boo-teh-ee): Half-bottle

Beer: Local *bière* (bee-ehr) costs about €5 at a restaurant and is cheaper on tap (*une pression;* ewn pres-yohn) than in the bottle. France's better beers are Alsatian; try Kronenbourg or the heavier Pelfort (one of your author's favorites). *Une panaché* (ewn pah-nah-shay) is a tasty French shandy (beer and lemon soda). *Un Monaco* is a red drink made with beer, grenadine, and lemonade.

Aperitifs and Digestifs: Champagne is a popular way to start your evening in France. For a refreshing before-dinner drink, order a *kir* (pronounced "keer")—a thumb's level of *crème de cassis* (black currant liqueur) topped with white wine (upgrade to a *kir royale* if you'd like it made with champagne). Also consider a glass of Lillet, a sweet, flowery fortified wine from Bordeaux.

If you like brandy, try a *marc* (regional brandy, e.g., *marc de Bourgogne*) or an Armagnac, cognac's cheaper twin brother. *Pastis,* the standard southern France aperitif, is a sweet anise (licorice) drink that comes on the rocks with a glass of water. Cut it to taste with lots of water.

Staying Connected

One of the most common questions I hear from travelers is, "How can I stay connected in Europe?" The short answer is: more easily and cheaply than you might think. For a very practical one-hour lecture covering tech issues for travelers, see www.ricksteves.com/travel-talks.

The simplest solution is to bring your own device—mobile phone, tablet, or laptop—and use it just as you would at home (following the tips below, such as connecting to free Wi-Fi whenever possible). Another option is to buy a European SIM card for your mobile phone—either your US phone or one you buy in Europe. Or you can travel without a mobile device and use European landlines and computers to connect. Each of these options is described below, and you'll find even more details at www.ricksteves.com/phoning.

USING YOUR OWN MOBILE DEVICE IN EUROPE

Without an international plan, typical rates from major service providers (AT&T, Verizon, etc.) for using your device abroad are about $1.70/minute for voice calls, 50 cents to send text messages, 5 cents to receive them, and $10 to download one megabyte of data. At these rates, costs can add up quickly. Here are some budget tips and options.

Use free Wi-Fi whenever possible. Unless you have an unlimited-data plan, you're best off saving most of your online tasks for Wi-Fi (pronounced *wee-fee* in French). You can access the Internet, send texts, and make voice calls over Wi-Fi.

Many cafés (including Starbucks and McDonald's) have free hotspots for customers; look for signs offering it and ask for the Wi-Fi password when you buy something. You'll also often find Wi-Fi at TIs, city squares, major museums, public-transit hubs, important train stations, airports, and aboard trains and buses.

Sign up for an international plan. Most providers offer a global calling plan that cuts the per-minute cost of phone calls and texts, and a flat-fee data plan. Your normal plan may already include international coverage (T-Mobile's does).

Before your trip, call your provider or check online to confirm that your phone will work in Europe, and research your provider's international rates. Activate the plan a day or two before you leave, then remember to cancel it when your trip's over.

Minimize the use of your cellular network. When you can't find Wi-Fi, you can use your cellular network to connect to the Internet, text, or make voice calls. When you're done, avoid further charges by manually switching off "data roaming" or "cellular data" (in your device's Settings menu; for help, ask your service provider or Google it). Another way to make sure you're not ac-

How to Dial

International Calls

Whether phoning from a US landline or mobile phone, or from a number in another European country, here's how to make an international call. I've used one of my recommended Paris hotels as an example (tel. 01 47 05 25 45).

Initial Zero: Drop the initial zero from international phone numbers—except when calling Italy.

Mobile Tip: If using a mobile phone, the "+" sign can replace the international access code (for a "+" sign, press and hold "0").

US/Canada to Europe

Dial 011 (US/Canada international access code), country code (33 for France), and phone number.

▶ To call the Paris hotel from home, dial 011 33 1 47 05 25 45.

Country to Country Within Europe

Dial 00 (Europe international access code), country code, and phone number.

▶ To call the Paris hotel from Spain, dial 00 33 1 47 05 25 45.

Europe to the US/Canada

Dial 00, country code (1 for US/Canada), and phone number.

▶ To call from Europe to my office in Edmonds, Washington, dial 00-1-425-771-8303.

Domestic Calls

To call within France (from one French landline or mobile phone to another), simply dial the phone number, including the initial 0 if there is one.

▶ To call the Paris hotel from Nice, dial 01 47 05 25 45.

More Dialing Tips

French Phone Prefixes: France doesn't use area codes. French phone prefixes vary by region or type of call. For instance, all Paris landline numbers start with 01, and all landlines in Provence and the Riviera begin with 04.

cidentally using data roaming is to put your device in "airplane" or "flight" mode (which also disables phone calls and texts), and then turn on Wi-Fi as needed.

Don't use your cellular network for bandwidth-gobbling tasks, such as Skyping, downloading apps, and watching YouTube: Save these for when you're on Wi-Fi. Using a navigation app such as Google Maps over a cellular network can take lots of data, so do this sparingly or use it offline.

Limit automatic updates. By default, your device constantly

Any number beginning with 06 or 07 is a mobile phone, and costs more to dial.

Toll and Toll-Free Calls: France's toll-free numbers start with 0800 and are called *numéro vert* (green number); they work only from French phones. Any 08 number without a 00 directly following is a toll call (generally €0.10-0.50/minute; cost announced in French; you can hang up before being billed). International rates apply to US toll-free numbers dialed from France—they're not free.

More Phoning Help: See www.howtocallabroad.com.

PRACTICALITIES

European Country Codes			
Austria	43	Italy	39
Belgium	32	Latvia	371
Bosnia-Herzegovina	387	Montenegro	382
Croatia	385	Morocco	212
Czech Republic	420	Netherlands	31
Denmark	45	Norway	47
Estonia	372	Poland	48
Finland	358	Portugal	351
France	33	Russia	7
Germany	49	Slovakia	421
Gibraltar	350	Slovenia	386
Great Britain	44	Spain	34
Greece	30	Sweden	46
Hungary	36	Switzerland	41
Ireland & N. Ireland	353 / 44	Turkey	90

checks for a data connection and updates apps. It's smart to disable these features so your apps will only update when you're on Wi-Fi, and to change your device's email settings from "auto-retrieve" to "manual" (or from "push" to "fetch").

It's also a good idea to keep track of your data usage. On your device's menu, look for "cellular data usage" or "mobile data" and reset the counter at the start of your trip.

Use Skype or other calling/messaging apps for cheaper calls and texts. Certain apps let you make voice or video calls or send texts over the Internet for free or cheap. If you're bringing a tablet or laptop, you can also use them for voice calls and texts. All you have to do is log on to a Wi-Fi network, then contact any of your friends or family members who are also online and signed into the same service. You can make voice and video calls using Skype, Viber, FaceTime, and Google+ Hangouts. If the connection is bad, try making an audio-only call. You can also make voice calls from your device to telephones worldwide for just a few cents per minute using Skype, Viber, or Hangouts if you buy credit first.

To text for free over Wi-Fi, try apps like Google+ Hangouts, WhatsApp, Viber, Facebook Messenger, and iMessage. Make sure you're on Wi-Fi to avoid data charges.

USING A EUROPEAN SIM CARD IN A MOBILE PHONE

This option works well for those who want to make a lot of voice calls at cheap local rates, and those who need faster connection speeds than their US carrier provides. Either buy a basic cell phone in Europe (as little as $40 from mobile-phone shops anywhere), or bring an "unlocked" US phone (check with your carrier about unlocking it). With an unlocked phone, you can replace the original SIM card (the microchip that stores info about the phone) with one that will work with a European provider.

In Europe, buy a European SIM card. Inserted into your phone, this card gives you a European phone number—and European rates. SIM cards are sold at mobile-phone shops, department-store electronics counters, newsstands, and vending machines. Costing about $5-10, they usually include about that much prepaid calling credit, with no contract and no commitment. A SIM card that also includes data costs (including roaming) will cost $20-40 more for one month of data within the country you bought it. This can be faster than data roaming through your home provider. To get the best rates, buy a new SIM card whenever you arrive in a new country.

I like to buy SIM cards at a mobile-phone shop where there's a clerk to help explain the options and brands. Certain brands—including Lebara and Lycamobile, both of which operate in multiple European countries—are reliable and economical. Ask the clerk to help you insert your SIM card, set it up, and show you how to use it. In some countries you'll be required to register the SIM card with your passport as an antiterrorism measure (which may mean you can't use the phone for the first hour or two).

Find out how to check your credit balance. When you run out of credit, you can top it up at newsstands, tobacco shops, mobile-phone stores, or many other businesses (look for your SIM card's logo in the window), or online.

Tips on Internet Security

Using the Internet while traveling brings added security risks, whether you're accessing the Internet with your own device or at a public terminal using a shared network. Here are some tips for securing your data:

First, make sure that your device is running the latest version of its operating system and security software, and that your apps are up to date. Next, ensure that your device is password- or passcode-protected so thieves can't access it if your device is stolen. For extra security, set passwords on apps that access key info (such as email or Facebook).

On the road, use only legitimate Wi-Fi hotspots. Ask the hotel or café staff for the specific name of their Wi-Fi network, and make sure you log on to that exact one. Hackers sometimes create a bogus hotspot with a similar or vague name (such as "Hotel Europa Free Wi-Fi"). The best Wi-Fi networks require a password. If you're not actively using a hotspot, turn off your device's Wi-Fi connection so it's not visible to others.

Be especially cautious when accessing financial information online. Experts say it's best to use a banking app rather than sign in to your bank's website via a browser (the app is less likely to get hacked). Even if you're using your own mobile device at a password-protected hotspot, there's a remote chance that a hacker who's logged on to the same network could see what you're doing. It's safest to use a hard-wired connection (such as an Ethernet cable in your hotel room). If that's not possible, a cellular network is safer than a Wi-Fi connection, and a password-protected Wi-Fi network is safer than public Wi-Fi. Refrain from logging in to any personal finance sites on a public computer.

Never share your credit-card number (or any other sensitive information) online unless you know that the site is secure. A secure site displays a little padlock icon, and the URL begins with *https* (instead of the usual *http*).

UNTETHERED TRAVEL: PUBLIC PHONES AND COMPUTERS

It's possible to travel in Europe without a mobile device. You can check email or browse websites using public computers and Internet cafés, and make calls from your hotel room.

Phones in your **hotel room** generally charge a fee for placing local and "toll-free" calls, as well as long-distance or international calls—ask for the rates before you dial. Since you're never charged for receiving calls, it's better to have someone from the US call you in your room.

If these fees are low, hotel phones can be used inexpensively for calls made with cheap international phone cards *(carte international).* These cards are not widely used in France, but they can be found at some newsstands, street kiosks, tobacco shops, and train stations. You'll either get a prepaid card with a toll-free number and a scratch-to-reveal PIN code, or a code printed on a receipt.

Public computers are not always easy to find. Some hotels have one in their lobby for guests to use; otherwise you might find one at an Internet café or public library (ask your hotelier or the TI for the nearest location). If typing on a European keyboard, use the "Alt Gr" key to the right of the space bar to insert the extra symbol that appears on some keys. To type an @ symbol on French keyboards, press the "Alt Gr" and "à/0" key. If you can't locate a special character, simply copy it from a Web page and paste it into your email message.

MAIL

You can mail one package per day to yourself worth up to $200 duty-free from Europe to the US (mark it "personal purchases"). If you're sending a gift to someone, mark it "unsolicited gift." For details, visit www.cbp.gov, select "Travel," and search for "Know Before You Go." The French postal service works fine, but for quick transatlantic delivery (in either direction), consider services such as DHL (www.dhl.com). French post offices are referred to as *La Poste* or sometimes the old-fashioned PTT, for "Post, Telegraph, and Telephone." Hours vary, though most are open weekdays 8:00-19:00 and Saturday morning 8:00-12:00. Stamps and phone cards are also sold at *tabacs*. It costs about €1 to mail a postcard to the US. One convenient, if expensive, way to send packages home is to use the post office's Colissimo XL postage-paid mailing box. It costs €50-90 to ship boxes weighing 5-7 kilos (about 11-15 pounds).

Transportation

If your trip covers more of France than just Paris, you may need to take a long-distance train, rent a car, or fly. Below are some specifics on trains and flights. For more detailed information on transportation throughout Europe, including trains, flying, renting a car, and driving, see www.ricksteves.com/transportation.

TRAINS

France's SNCF rail system (short for Société Nationale Chemins de Fer) sets the pace in Europe. Its super TGV (tay zhay vay; Train à Grande Vitesse) system has inspired bullet trains throughout the world. The TGV, which requires a reservation, runs at 170-220 mph. Its rails are fused into one long, continuous track for a faster and smoother ride. The TGV has changed commuting patterns throughout France by putting most of the country within day-trip distance of Paris.

Any staffed train station has schedule information, can make reservations, and can sell tickets for any destination. For more on train travel, see www.ricksteves.com/rail.

Schedules

Schedules change by season, weekday, and weekend. Verify train times shown in this book—online, check www.bahn.com (Germany's excellent all-Europe schedule site), or check locally at train stations. The French rail website is www.sncf.com; for online sales, go to http://en.voyages-sncf.com. If you'll be traveling on one or two long-distance trains without a rail pass, it's worth looking online, as advance-purchase discounts can be a great deal.

Bigger stations may have helpful information agents roaming the station (usually in bright red or blue vests) and at *Accueil* offices or booths. Make use of their help; don't stand in a ticket line if all you need is a train schedule.

Buying Tickets

Online: While there's no deadline to buy any train ticket, the fast, reserved TGV trains get booked up. Buy well ahead for any TGV you cannot afford to miss. Tickets go on sale 90 to 120 days in advance, with a wide range of prices on any one route. The cheapest tickets sell out early and reservations for rail-pass holders also go particularly fast.

To buy the cheapest advance-discount tickets (up to 60 percent less than full fare), visit http://en.voyages-sncf.com, three to four months ahead of your travel date. (A pop-up window may ask you to choose between being sent to the Rail Europe website or staying on the SNCF page—click "Stay.") Next, choose "Train," then "TGV." Under "Book your train tickets," pick your travel dates, and choose "France" as your ticket collection country. The cheapest (nonrefundable) tickets are called "Prems"; be sure it also says "TGV" (avoid iDTGV trains—they're very cheap, but this SNCF subsidiary doesn't accept PayPal). Choose the eticket delivery option (which allows you to print at home), and pay with your PayPal account to avoid credit-card approval issues. These low-rate tickets may not be available from Rail Europe or other US agents.

After the "Prems" rates are sold out, you can buy other fare types on the French site with a US credit card if it has been set up for the "Verified by Visa," "MasterCard SecureCode," or "American Express SafeKey" program. For a credit-card purchase, choose "USA" as your ticket collection country.

Otherwise, US customers can order through a US agency, such as at www.ricksteves.com/rail, which offers both etickets and

France's Rail System

PRACTICALITIES

ENGLAND

London

Eurostar

Dover

To Ireland

Folkstone

Portsmouth

Newhaven

English   Channel

Le
Tréport

Dieppe

Cherbourg

Arro-
manches

Le
Havre

Honfleur

Roscoff

Mont
St-Michel

Caen

Rouen

St-Malo

Bayeux

Brest

Morlaix

Avranches

Lisieux

Versailles

Lamballe

Dinan

Pontorson

Quimper

Dol

TGV

Chartres

Quiberon

Vannes

Rennes

Le Mans

Orléans

Redon

TGV

Blois

Angers

Tours

Amboise

Nantes

Saumur

Chenonceaux

Atlantic

Langeais

Tours
St-Pierre
des Corps
TGV Stn.

Ocean

Chinon

Azay

Vierzon

Poitiers

F R A

La Rochelle

TGV

Oradour-
sur-Glane

Legend

- Rail
- Eurostar Rail
- TGV High-Speed Rail
- Bus
- Boat
- ✈ Airports
  (Not All Shown)

Note: In some cases regular
train lines and TGV lines share
the same track

Saintes

Cognac

Limoges

Angoulême

Perigueux

Brive

Libourne

Sarlat-la-Canéda

Bordeaux ✈

Les Eyzies

Soulliac

St-Emilion

Le
Buisson

Beynac

Cahors

Agen

Montauban

Biarritz

TGV

Dax

Guernica ✈

St-Jean-
de-Luz

Bayonne

Bilbao ✈

Hendaye

Pau

Toulouse ✈

PRIVATE
RAIL

Irun

San
Sebastián

St-Jean
Pied-de-Port

Lourdes

Miranda
de Ebro

Pamplona

Foix

Burgos

La Tour

ANDORRA

SPAIN

50 Kilometers

50 Miles

To Madrid

To Barcelona

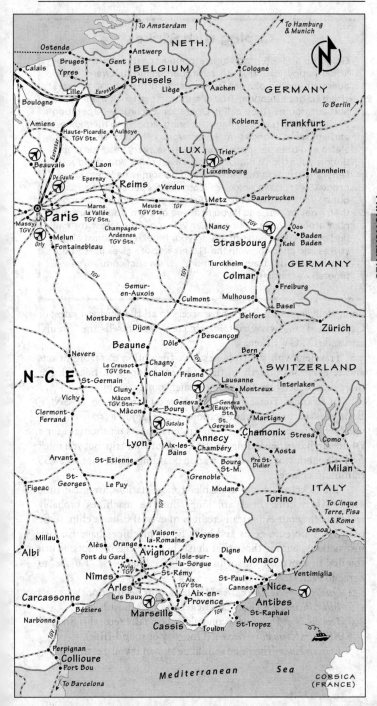

Coping with Strikes

Going on strike *(en grève)* is a popular pastime in this revolution-happy country. Because bargaining between management and employees is not standard procedure, workers strike to get attention. Trucks and tractors block main roads and autoroutes (they call it Opération Escargot—"Operation Snail's Pace"), baggage handlers bring airports to their knees, and museum workers make artwork off-limits to tourists. Métro and train personnel seem to strike every year—probably during your trip. What does the traveler do? You could *jeter l'éponge* (throw in the sponge) and go somewhere less strike-prone (Switzerland's nice), or learn to accept certain events as out of your control. Strikes in France generally last no longer than a day or two, and if you're aware of them, you can usually plan around them. Your hotelier will know the latest (or can find out). Make a habit of asking your hotel receptionist about strikes and checking with the TI. This website gives up-to-date information on train disruptions: www.sncf.com/en/news/timetables-traffic-updates.

home delivery, but may not have access to all the cheapest rates; or Capitaine Train (www.captaintrain.com), which sells the "Prems" fare and iDTGV tickets.

Travelers with smartphones have the option of saving tickets and reservations directly to their phones (choose "m-ticket"). For more details, see http://en.voyages-sncf.com/en/mobile.

In France: You can buy train tickets in person at SNCF Boutiques or at any train station, either from a staffed ticket window or from a machine. You can buy tickets on the train for a €4-10 surcharge depending on the length of your trip, but you must find the conductor immediately upon boarding; otherwise it's a €35 minimum charge.

The ticket machines available at most stations are great time savers when other lines are long. But the machines probably won't accept your American credit card even if it has a chip, so be prepared with euro coins and bills. Some machines have English instructions, but for those that don't, here are the prompts. (Turn the dial or move the cursor to your choice, and press *"Validez"* to agree to each step.)

1. *Quelle est votre destination?* (What's your destination?)
2. *Billet Plein Tarif* (Full-fare ticket—yes for most.)
3. *1ère ou 2ème* (First or second class; normally second is fine.)
4. *Aller simple ou aller-retour?* (One-way or round-trip?)
5. *Prix en Euro* (The price should be shown if you get this far.)

Reservations

Reservations are required for any TGV train, *couchettes* (sleeping berths) on night trains, and some other trains where indicated in timetables. You can reserve any train at any station up to three days before your departure or through SNCF Boutiques. If you're buying a point-to-point ticket for a TGV train, you'll reserve your seat when you purchase your ticket.

Popular TGV routes usually fill up quickly, making it a challenge to get reservations (particularly for rail-pass holders, who are allocated a very limited number of seats). It's wise to book well ahead for any TGV, especially on the busy Paris-Avignon-Nice line. If the TGV trains you want are fully booked, ask about TER trains serving the same destination, as these don't require reservations.

If you're using a rail pass, reservations cost €9-€18 for domestic travel, depending on the kind of train they're for and where you buy them. Seat reservations on Thalys, Artesia, and international TGV trains range from €10-35, but the price also depends on class of service (they can cost up to €50 in first class on TGV trains to Swiss destinations). Eurostar trains to London don't accept rail passes but do offer pass holders some ticket discounts.

Rail-pass holders can book TGV reservations directly at French stations up to three days before departure; reservations, if still available, can be booked anytime as etickets at www.raileurope.com (if lower-priced pass-holder reservations are sold out, try for the "Easy Access" rate). Given the possible difficulty of getting TGV reservations with a rail pass, make those reservations online before you leave home.

If you're taking one of the rare overnight trains in France and need a *couchette,* it can be booked in advance through a US agent (such as www.raileurope.com).

Train Tips
At the Station

- Arrive at the station with plenty of time before your departure to find your platform (platform numbers are posted about 15 minutes prior to departure), confirm connections, and so on. Large stations have separate information *(accueil)* windows; at small stations the ticket office gives information.
- Small stations are minimally staffed; if there is no agent at the station, go directly to the tracks and look for the overhead sign that confirms your train stops at that track.
- Larger stations have platforms with monitors showing TGV layouts (numbered forward or backward) so you can figure out where your car *(voiture)* will stop on the long platform and where to board each car.

Validating Tickets, Reservations, and Rail Passes

- You're required to activate (*composter*, kohm-poh-stay) all train tickets and reservations (when printed on official ticket stock) before boarding any SNCF train. Look for a yellow machine near the platform or waiting area to stamp your ticket or reservation. Reserved tickets that are printed at home on plain paper don't need validation (and won't fit in the machine). You also don't need to activate etickets on your phone.
- If you have a rail pass, activate it at a ticket window before using it the first time (don't stamp it in the machine). If you're traveling with a pass and have a reservation for a certain trip, you must activate the reservation by stamping it.
- If you have a rail flexipass, write the date on your pass each day you travel (before or immediately after boarding your first train).

On the Train

- Before getting on a train, confirm that it's going where you think it is. For example, if you want to go to Chartres, ask the conductor or any local passenger, *"A Chartres?"* (ah shar-truh; meaning, "To Chartres?").
- Some longer trains split off cars en route. Make sure your train car is continuing to your destination by asking, for example, *"Cette voiture va à Chartres?"* (seht vwah-toor vah ah shar-truh; meaning, "This car goes to Chartres?").
- If a non-TGV train seat is reserved, it'll likely be labeled *réservé*, with the cities to and from which it is reserved.
- If you don't understand an announcement, ask your neighbor to explain: *"Pardon madame/monsieur, qu'est-ce qui se passe?"* (kehs kee suh pahs; meaning, "Excuse me, what's going on?").
- Verify with the conductor all of the transfers you must make: *"Correspondance à?"*; meaning, "Transfer to where?"
- To guard against theft, keep your bags in sight (directly overhead is ideal but not always possible—the early boarder gets the best storage space). If you must store them in the lower racks by the doors (available in most cars), pay attention at stops. Your bags are most vulnerable to theft before the train takes off and whenever it stops.
- Note your arrival time, so you'll be ready to get off.
- Use the train's free WCs before you get off (but not while the train is stopped in a station).

FLIGHTS

The best comparison search engine for both international and intra-European flights is www.kayak.com. For inexpensive flights within Europe, try www.skyscanner.com.

Flying to Europe: Start looking for international flights at least four to six months before your trip, especially for peak-season travel. Off-season tickets can usually be purchased a month or so in advance. Depending on your itinerary, it can be efficient to fly into one city and out of another. If your flight requires a connection in Europe, see our hints on navigating Europe's top hub airports at www.ricksteves.com/hub-airports.

Flying within Europe: If you're visiting one or more French cities on a longer European trip—or linking up far-flung French cities (such as Paris and Nice)—a flight can save both time and money. When comparing your options, factor in the time it takes to get to the airport and how early you'll need to arrive to check in.

Well-known cheapo airlines include easyJet (www.easyjet.com), which flies out of Charles de Gaulle and Orly airports, and Ryanair (www.ryanair.com), which flies out of Beauvais Airport. Also check Air France for specials. But be aware of the potential drawbacks of flying with a discount airline: nonrefundable and nonchangeable tickets, minimal or nonexistent customer service, pricey and time-consuming treks to secondary airports, and stingy baggage allowances with steep overage fees. If you're traveling with lots of luggage, a cheap flight can quickly become a bad deal. To avoid unpleasant surprises, read the small print before you book. These days you can also fly within Europe on major airlines affordably—and without all the aggressive restrictions—for around $100 a flight.

Flying to the US and Canada: Because security is extra tight for flights to the US, be sure to give yourself plenty of time at the airport. It's also important to charge your electronic devices before you board because security checks may require you to turn them on (see www.tsa.gov for latest rules).

Resources from Rick Steves

Begin your trip at www.ricksteves.com: My mobile-friendly **website** is *the* place to explore Europe. You'll find thousands of fun articles, videos, photos, and radio interviews organized by country; a wealth of money-saving tips for planning your dream trip; monthly travel news dispatches; a collection of over 30 hours of practical travel talks; my travel blog; my latest guidebook updates (www.ricksteves.com/update); and my free Rick Steves Audio Europe app. You can also follow me on Facebook and Twitter.

Our **Travel Forum** is an immense yet well-groomed collection of message boards, where our travel-savvy community answers questions and shares their personal travel experiences—and our well-traveled staff chimes in when they can be helpful (www.ricksteves.com/forums).

Our **online Travel Store** offers travel bags and accessories that I've designed specifically to help you travel smarter and lighter. These include my popular bags (rolling carry-on and backpack versions, which I helped design...and live out of four months a year), money belts, totes, toiletries kits, adapters, other accessories, and a wide selection of guidebooks and planning maps.

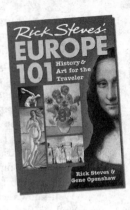

Choosing the right **rail pass** for your trip—amid hundreds of options—can drive you nutty. Our website will help you find the perfect fit for your itinerary and your budget: We offer easy, one-stop shopping for rail passes, seat reservations, and point-to-point tickets.

Tours: Want to travel with greater efficiency and less stress? We organize tours with more than three dozen itineraries and more than 900 departures reaching the best destinations in this book...and beyond. We offer an 11-day Paris and the Heart of France tour (focusing on the best of the north), a 13-day Loire to the South of France tour, a 14-day Best of Eastern France tour, a 7-day in-depth Paris city tour, and a 13-day My Way France tour. You'll enjoy great guides, a fun bunch of travel partners (with small groups of around 24 to 28 travelers), and plenty of room to spread out in a big, comfy bus when touring between towns. You'll find European adventures to fit every vacation length. For all the details, and to get our tour catalog, visit www.ricksteves.com or call us at 425/608-4217.

Books: *Rick Steves Paris 2017* is one of many books in my series on European travel, which includes country guidebooks (including France), city guidebooks (Rome, Florence, London, etc.), Snapshot guidebooks (excerpted chapters from my country guides), Pocket guidebooks (full-color little books on big cities, including Paris), "Best Of" guidebooks (condensed country guidebooks in a full-color, easy-to-scan format), and my budget-travel skills handbook, *Rick Steves Europe Through the Back Door.* Most of my titles are available as ebooks.

My phrase books—for French, Italian, German, Spanish, and Portuguese—are practical and budget-oriented. My other books include *Europe 101* (a crash course on art and history designed for travelers); *Mediterranean Cruise Ports* and *Northern European Cruise Ports* (how to make the most of your time in port); and *Travel as a Political Act* (a travelogue sprinkled with tips for bringing home a global perspective). A more complete list of my titles appears near the end of this book.

TV Shows: My public television series, *Rick Steves' Europe,* covers Europe from top to bottom with over 100 half-hour episodes. To watch full episodes online for free, see www.ricksteves.com/tv.

Travel Talks on Video: You can raise your travel I.Q. with video versions of our popular classes (including my talks on travel skills, packing smart, cruising, tech for travelers, European art for travelers, travel as a political act, and individual talks covering most European countries including France). See www.ricksteves.com/travel-talks.

Audio: My weekly public radio show, *Travel with Rick Steves,* features interviews with travel experts from around the world. A complete archive of 10 years of programs (over 400 in all) is available at www.ricksteves.com/radio. Most of this audio content is available for free through my **Rick Steves Audio Europe** app (see page 8).

PRACTICALITIES

APPENDIX

Useful Contacts

Emergency Needs

Operators at emergency numbers may speak English, but there is no guarantee. Calls to 112 and 114 are received by either the Emergency Medical Assistance Service (called "SAMU") or the fire brigade, who will reroute the call if necessary.

Police: Tel. 17
Fire and Accident: Tel. 18
Emergency Medical Assistance Service (SAMU): Tel. 15
Ambulance for Medical Emergencies: Tel. 15 or 01 45 67 50 50 (message asks for your address and name)
SOS All Services: 112
Hearing-Assisted SOS All Services: 114
American Hospital (with English-speaking staff): Tel. 01 46 41 25 25 (63 Boulevard Victor Hugo, in Neuilly suburb, Mo: Port Maillot, then bus #82, www.american-hospital.org)
English-Speaking Pharmacy (Pharmacie les Champs): Tel. 01 45 62 02 41, open 24 hours every day of the year (84 Avenue des Champs-Elysées, Mo: Georges V)

English-Speaking Doctors: For a good list, search on the US embassy's website: http://france.usembassy.gov

SOS Médicins (SOS Doctors): Tel. 3624, most speak some English, house calls to hotels or homes (€120 or more, www.sosmedecins.fr)

SOS Help: Tel. 01 46 21 46 46, telephone hotline with crisis/suicide prevention listening service in English (daily 15:00-23:00, www.soshelpline.org)

SOS Dentist: Tel. 01 43 37 51 00, contact@1urgencedentaireparis.fr

American Chiropractic Center: Tel. 01 45 51 38 38, open Mon-Sat, closed Sun (119 Rue de l'Université, Mo: Invalides, www.chiropractique.com, contact@chiropractic.fr)

Lost Property (Bureau des Objets Trouvés, at police station): Tel. 08 21 00 25 25; open Mon-Fri 8:30-17:00 (36 Rue des Morillons, Mo: Convention, on south end of line 12)

Embassies and Consulates

US Consulate and Embassy: Tel. 01 43 12 22 22 (2 Avenue Gabriel, to the left as you face Hôtel Crillon, Mo: Concorde, http://france.usembassy.gov)

Canadian Consulate and Embassy: Tel. 01 44 43 29 02, www.amb-canada.fr. For 24/7 emergency assistance, call collect to 613/996-8885 or email sos@international.gc.ca

Australian Consulate: Tel. 01 40 59 33 00 (4 Rue Jean Rey, Mo: Bir-Hakeim, www.france.embassy.gov.au, info.paris@dfat.gov.au)

English-Language Churches in Paris

American Church (interdenominational): Tel. 01 40 62 05 00 (65 Quai d'Orsay, Mo: Invalides, www.acparis.org; for more information, see page 40)

American Cathedral (Episcopalian): Tel. 53 23 84 00 (23 Avenue George V, Mo: George V, www.americancathedral.org)

Unitarian Universalist Fellowship: www.uufp.info

Scots Kirk (Church of Scotland): Tel. 01 48 78 47 94 (17 Rue Bayard, Mo: Franklin D. Roosevelt, www.scotskirkparis.com)

St. George's Anglican Church: Tel. 01 47 20 22 51 (7 Rue Auguste Vacquerie, Mo: George V or Kleber, www.stgeorgesparis.com)

St. Joseph's Church (Roman Catholic): Tel. 01 42 27 28 56 (50 Avenue Hoche, Mo: Etoile, www.stjoeparis.org)

St. Michael's Church (Anglican): Tel. 01 47 42 70 88 (5 Rue d'Aguesseau, Mo: Concorde or Madeleine, www.saintmichaelsparis.org)

Holidays and Festivals

This list includes selected festivals in Paris, plus national holidays observed throughout France. Many sights and banks close on national holidays—keep this in mind when planning your itinerary. Before planning a trip around a festival, verify its dates by checking the festival's website or France's national tourism website (http://us.france.fr).

In Paris, hotels get booked up Easter weekend (note that Easter Monday is a holiday, and the weeks before and after are also busy), Labor Day, V-E Day, Ascension weekend, Pentecost weekend, Bastille Day and the week during which it falls, and the winter holidays (last half of December). Avoid leaving Paris at the beginning of one of these holiday weekends or returning at the end—you'll be competing with Parisians for seats on planes and trains, or fighting them in traffic on the roadways.

Paris is lively with festivals and events throughout the summer and fall. Kicking off the season in late May or early June is the month-long **Festival of St. Denis** in that Parisian suburb, featuring musicians from around the world at various venues (tel. 01 48 13 06 07, www.festival-saint-denis.com).

Paris celebrates the solstice in late June with its **Music Festival** (Fête de la Musique), staging concerts throughout the city.

Bastille Day, France's National Day (July 14), brings fireworks, dancing, and revelry countrywide (see sidebar on page 319). In late July, the **Tour de France** bicycle race ends on the Champs-Elysées (www.letour.fr; see sidebar on page 310).

From mid-July to mid-August, the **Paris Neighborhoods Festival** features theater, dance, and concerts around the city. At the same time, the fun **Paris Plages,** a riverside ersatz beach, is set up in the middle of the city (see page 57).

La Villette Jazz Festival brings a week of outdoor jazz concerts to this Parisian park from late August to mid-September. The first Saturday of October, Montmartre celebrates the **grape harvest** with a parade and festivities. The **Festival of Autumn** (www.festival-automne.com) runs through fall, with theater, dance, film, and opera performances. If you're in Paris during **Christmas,** see the Paris in Winter chapter for information on things to do. (Christmas week is generally quieter than the week of New Year's.)

Here are some major holidays in 2017:

Jan 1	New Year's Day
April 16	Easter Sunday
April 17	Easter Monday
May 1	Labor Day

APPENDIX

May 8	V-E Day (Victory in Europe)
May 25	Ascension
May 28	Mother's Day
June 4	Pentecost
June 18	Father's Day
July 14	Bastille Day
Aug 15	Assumption of Mary
Nov 1	All Saints' Day
Nov 11	Armistice Day
Dec 25	Christmas Day

Recommended Books and Films

To learn more about France past and present, and specifically Paris, check out a few of these books and films. For kids' recommendations, see page 452. To learn what's making news in France, you'll find *France 24 News* online at www.France24.com/en. If you want to experience expat life in Paris virtually, a fun website is www.secretsofparis.com.

Nonfiction

A to Z of French Food, a French to English Dictionary of Culinary Terms (G. de Temmerman, 1995). This is the most complete (and priciest) menu reader around—and it's beloved by foodies.

Almost French: Love and a New Life in Paris (Sarah Turnbull, 2003). Turnbull takes an amusing look at adopting a famously frosty city.

Americans in Paris: Life and Death under Nazi Occupation (Charles Glass, 2009). Using stories from American expatriates, Glass transports readers back to Nazi-occupied Paris in the early 1940s.

The Cambridge Illustrated History of France (Colin Jones, 1995). The political, social, and cultural history of France is explored in detail, accompanied by coffee-table-book pictures and illustrations.

A Corner in the Marais (Alex Karmel, 1998). After buying a flat in the Marais, the author digs into the history of the building—and the evolution of one of Paris' great neighborhoods.

The Course of French History (Pierre Goubert, 1988). Goubert provides a basic summary of French history.

Culture Shock! France (Sally Adamson Taylor, 1991). Demystify French culture—and the French people—with this good introduction.

The Flâneur (Edmund White, 2001). Reading this book is like wandering the streets of Paris with the author, who lived here for 16 years.

French or Foe? (Polly Platt, 1994). This best seller, along with its follow-up, *Savoir-Flair!*, is an essential aid for interacting with the French and navigating the intricacies of their culture.

From Here, You Can't See Paris: Seasons of a French Village and Its Restaurant (Michael S. Sanders, 2002). Foodies may enjoy this book, about a small-town restaurant where foie gras is always on the menu.

How Paris Became Paris: The Invention of the Modern City (Joan DeJean, 2014). DeJean describes how Paris emerged from the Dark Ages to become the world's grandest city.

I'll Always Have Paris (Art Buchwald, 1996). The American humorist recounts life as a Paris correspondent during the 1940s and 1950s.

Into a Paris Quartier: Reine Margot's Chapel and Other Haunts of St. Germain (Diane Johnson, 2005). The author acquaints readers with the sixth arrondissement by recounting her strolls through this iconic neighborhood.

Is Paris Burning? (Larry Collins and Dominique Lapierre, 1964). Set in the last days of the Nazi occupation, this is the story of the French resistance and how a German general disobeyed Hitler's order to destroy Paris.

La Seduction: How the French Play the Game of Life (Elaine Sciolino, 2011). Sciolino, former Paris bureau chief of the *New York Times*, gives travelers a fun, insightful, and tantalizing peek into how seduction is used in all aspects of French life—from small villages to the halls of national government.

A Moveable Feast (Ernest Hemingway, 1964). Paris in the 1920s as recalled by Hemingway.

My Life in France (Julia Child, 1996). The inimitably zesty chef recounts her early days in Paris.

Paris Noir: African Americans in the City of Light (Tyler Stovall, 1996). Stovall explains why African Americans found Paris so freeing in the first half of the 20th century.

Paris to the Moon (Adam Gopnik, 2000). This collection of essays and journal entries explores the idiosyncrasies of life in France from a New Yorker's point of view. His literary anthology, *Americans in Paris,* is also recommended.

A Place in the World Called Paris (Steven Barclay, 1994). This anthology includes essays by literary greats from Truman Capote to Franz Kafka.

Sixty Million Frenchmen Can't Be Wrong (Jean-Benoit Nadeau and Julie Barlow, 2003). This is a must-read for anyone serious about understanding French culture, contemporary politics, and what makes the French tick.

The Sweet Life in Paris (David Lebovitz, 2009). Funny and articulate, pastry chef and cookbook author Lebovitz delivers oodles of food suggestions for travelers in Paris.

Travelers Tales: Paris and *Travelers' Tales: France* (edited by James O'Reilly, Larry Habegger, and Sean O'Reilly, 2002). Notable writers explore Parisian and French culture.

Fiction

City of Darkness, City of Light (Marge Piercy, 1996). Three French women play pivotal roles behind the scenes during the French Revolution.

The Hotel Majestic (Georges Simenon, 1942). Ernest Hemingway was a fan of Simenon, a Belgian writer who often set his Inspector Maigret detective books, including this one, in Paris.

Le Divorce (Diane Johnson, 1997). An American woman visits her stepsister and husband in Paris during a time of marital crisis (also a 2003 movie with Kate Hudson).

Murder in the Marais (Cara Black, 1999). Set in Vichy-era Paris, private investigator Aimée Leduc finds herself at the center of a murder mystery.

Night Soldiers (Alan Furst, 1988). The first of Furst's gripping WWII espionage novels puts you right into the action in Paris.

Suite Française (Irène Némirovsky, 2004). Némirovsky, a Russian Jew who was living in France and died at Auschwitz in 1942, plunges readers into the chaotic WWII evacuation of Paris, as well as daily life in a small rural town during the ensuing German occupation.

A Tale of Two Cities (Charles Dickens, 1859). Dickens' gripping tale shows the pathos and horror of the French Revolution.

A Year in the Merde (Stephen Clarke, 2004). Englishman Paul West takes on life as a *faux* Parisian in this lighthearted novel that relies on some stereotypes.

Film and TV

Amélie (2001). A charming waitress searches for love in Paris.

Before Sunset (2004). Nine years after meeting on a train to Vienna, Jesse and Celine (played by Ethan Hawke and Julie Delpy) are reunited in Paris.

Breathless (1960). A Parisian petty thief (Jean-Paul Belmondo) persuades an American student (Jean Seberg) to run away with him in this classic of French New Wave cinema.

Children of Paradise (1945). This melancholy romance was filmed during the Nazi occupation of Paris.

Dangerous Liaisons (1988). This inside look at sex, intrigue, and revenge takes place in the last days of the French aristocracy in pre-Revolutionary Paris.

The Intouchables (2011). A quadriplegic Parisian aristocrat hires a personal caregiver from the projects, and an unusual and touching friendship ensues.

Jules and Jim (1962). François Truffaut, the master of the French New Wave, explores a decades-long love triangle in this classic.

La Vie en Rose (2007). Marion Cotillard won the Best Actress Oscar for this film about the glamorous and turbulent life of singer Edith Piaf, who famously regretted nothing (many scenes were shot in Paris).

Les Misérables (2012). A Frenchman trying to escape his criminal past becomes wrapped up in Revolutionary intrigues (based on Victor Hugo's 1862 novel).

Marie Antoinette (2006). Kirsten Dunst stars as the infamous French queen (with a Californian accent) at Versailles in this delicate little bonbon of a film about the misunderstood queen.

Midnight in Paris (2011). Woody Allen's sharp comedy shifts between today's Paris and the 1920s mecca of Picasso, Hemingway, and Fitzgerald.

Moulin Rouge! (2001). Baz Luhrmann's fanciful musical is set in the legendary Montmartre nightclub.

Ridicule (1996). A nobleman navigates the opulent court of Louis XVI on his wits alone.

Ronin (1998). Robert De Niro stars in this crime caper, which includes a car chase through Paris and scenes filmed in Nice, Villefranche-sur-Mer, and Arles.

Three Colors trilogy (1990s). Krzysztof Kieślowski's stylish trilogy (*Blue*, *White*, and *Red*) is based on France's national motto— "Liberty, Equality, and Fraternity." Each features a famous French actress as the lead (*Blue*, with Juliette Binoche, is the best).

The Triplets of Belleville (2003). This surreal-yet-heartwarming animated film begins in a very Parisian fictional city.

Conversions and Climate

NUMBERS AND STUMBLERS

- Europeans write a few of their numbers differently than we do: 1 = 1, 4 = 4, 7 = 7.
- In Europe, dates appear as day/month/year, so Christmas 2017 is 25/12/17.
- Commas are decimal points and decimals are commas. A dollar and a half is $1,50, one thousand is 1.000, and there are 5.280 feet in a mile.

- When counting with fingers, start with your thumb. If you hold up your first finger to request one item, you'll probably get two.
- What Americans call the second floor of a building is the first floor in Europe.
- On escalators and moving sidewalks, Europeans keep the left "lane" open for passing. Keep to the right.

METRIC CONVERSIONS

A kilogram is 2.2 pounds, and 1 liter is about a quart, or almost four to a gallon. A kilometer is six-tenths of a mile. I figure kilometers to miles by cutting them in half and adding back 10 percent of the original (120 km: 60 + 12 = 72 miles, 300 km: 150 + 30 = 180 miles).

1 foot = 0.3 meter	1 square yard = 0.8 square meter
1 yard = 0.9 meter	1 square mile = 2.6 square kilometers
1 mile = 1.6 kilometers	1 ounce = 28 grams
1 centimeter = 0.4 inch	1 quart = 0.95 liter
1 meter = 39.4 inches	1 kilogram = 2.2 pounds
1 kilometer = 0.62 mile	32°F = 0°C

CLOTHING SIZES

When shopping for clothing, use these US-to-European comparisons as general guidelines (but note that no conversion is perfect).

Women: For clothing or shoe sizes, add 30 (US shirt size 10 = European size 40; US shoe size 8 = European size 38-39).

Men: For shirts, multiply by 2 and add about 8 (US size 15 = European size 38). For jackets and suits, add 10. For shoes, add 32-34.

Children: For clothing, subtract 1-2 sizes for small children and subtract 4 for juniors. For shoes up to size 13, add 16-18, and for sizes 1 and up, add 30-32.

PARIS' CLIMATE

First line, average daily high; second line, average daily low; third line, average days without rain. For more detailed weather statistics for destinations in this book (as well as the rest of the world), check www.wunderground.com.

J	F	M	A	M	J	J	A	S	O	N	D
43°	45°	54°	60°	68°	73°	76°	75°	70°	60°	50°	44°
34°	34°	39°	43°	49°	55°	58°	58°	53°	46°	40°	36°
14	14	19	17	19	18	19	18	17	18	15	15

Europe takes its temperature using the Celsius scale, while we opt for Fahrenheit. For a rough conversion from Celsius to Fahrenheit, double the number and add 30. For weather, remember that 28°C is 82°F—perfect. For health, 37°C is just right. At a launderette, 30°C is cold, 40°C is warm (usually the default setting), 60°C is hot, and 95°C is boiling. Your air-conditioner should be set at about 20°C.

Fahrenheit and Celsius Conversion

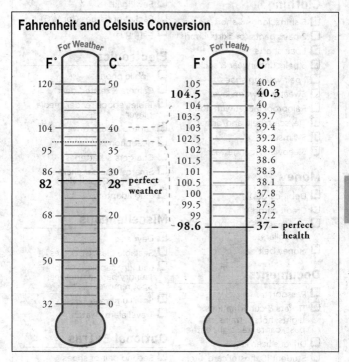

APPENDIX

Packing Checklist

Whether you're traveling for five days or five weeks, you won't need more than this. Pack light to enjoy the sweet freedom of true mobility.

Clothing

- ☐ 5 shirts: long- & short-sleeve
- ☐ 2 pairs pants (or skirts/capris)
- ☐ 1 pair shorts
- ☐ 5 pairs underwear & socks
- ☐ 1 pair walking shoes
- ☐ Sweater or warm layer
- ☐ Rainproof jacket with hood
- ☐ Tie, scarf, belt, and/or hat
- ☐ Swimsuit
- ☐ Sleepwear/loungewear

Money

- ☐ Debit card(s)
- ☐ Credit card(s)
- ☐ Hard cash ($100-200 in US dollars)
- ☐ Money belt

Documents

- ☐ Passport
- ☐ Tickets & confirmations: flights, hotels, trains, rail pass, car rental, sight entries
- ☐ Driver's license
- ☐ Student ID, hostel card, etc.
- ☐ Photocopies of important documents
- ☐ Insurance details
- ☐ Guidebooks & maps
- ☐ Notepad & pen
- ☐ Journal

Toiletries Kit

- ☐ Basics: soap, shampoo, toothbrush, toothpaste, floss, deodorant, sunscreen, brush/comb, etc.
- ☐ Medicines & vitamins
- ☐ First-aid kit
- ☐ Glasses/contacts/sunglasses

- ☐ Sewing kit
- ☐ Packet of tissues (for WC)
- ☐ Earplugs

Electronics

- ☐ Mobile phone
- ☐ Camera & related gear
- ☐ Tablet/ebook reader/media player
- ☐ Laptop & flash drive
- ☐ Headphones
- ☐ Chargers & batteries
- ☐ Smartphone car charger & mount (or GPS device)
- ☐ Plug adapters

Miscellaneous

- ☐ Daypack
- ☐ Sealable plastic baggies
- ☐ Laundry supplies: soap, laundry bag, clothesline, spot remover
- ☐ Small umbrella
- ☐ Travel alarm/watch

Optional Extras

- ☐ Second pair of shoes (flip-flops, sandals, tennis shoes, boots)
- ☐ Travel hairdryer
- ☐ Picnic supplies
- ☐ Water bottle
- ☐ Fold-up tote bag
- ☐ Small flashlight
- ☐ Mini binoculars
- ☐ Small towel or washcloth
- ☐ Inflatable pillow/neck rest
- ☐ Tiny lock
- ☐ Address list (to mail postcards)
- ☐ Extra passport photos

PRONOUNCING PARIS PLACE NAMES

When using the phonetics: Try to nasalize the n sound (let the sound come through your nose). Note that the "ahn" combination uses the "ah" sound in "father," but the "an" combination uses the "a" sound in "sack." Pronounce the "ī" as the long "i" in "light." If your best attempt at pronunciation meets with a puzzled look, just point to the place name on the list.

Arc de Triomphe ark duh tree-ohnf

arrondissement ah-rohn-dees-mohn

Art Nouveau ar noo-voh

Auvers-sur-Oise oh-vehr-sewr-wahz

Bateaux Mouches bah-toh moosh

Bon Marché bohn mar-shay

boulangerie boo-lahn-zheh-ree

Carnavalet kar-nah-val-eh

Champ de Mars shahn duh mar

Champs-Elysées shahn-zay-lee-zay

Chantilly shahn-tee-yee

charcuterie shar-kew-tuh-ree

Chartres shar-truh

château(x) shah-toh

Cité see-tay

Cité des Sciences see-tay day see-ahns

Conciergerie kon-see-ehr-zhuh-ree

Contrescarpe kohn-truh-scarp

droguerie droh-guh-ree

Ecole Militaire ay-kohl mee-lee-tair

Egouts ay-goo

Fauchon foh-shohn

Fontainebleau fohn-tehn-bloh

fromagerie froh-mah-zhuh-ree

Galeries Lafayette gah-luh-ree lah-fay-yet

gare gar

Gare d'Austerlitz gar doh-stehr-leets

Gare de l'Est gar duh lehst

Gare de Lyon gar duh lee-ohn

Gare du Nord gar dew nor

Gare St. Lazare gar san lah-zahr

Giverny zhee-vehr-nee

Grand Palais grahn pah-lay

Grande Arche de la Défense grahnd arsh duh lah day-fahns

Hôtel de Sully oh-tehl duh soo-lee

Ile de la Cité eel duh lah see-tay

Ile St. Louis eel san loo-ee

Jacquemart-André zhahk-mar-ahn-dray

jardin zhar-dan

Jardin des Plantes zhar-dan day plahnt

Jeu de Paume juh duh pohm

La Madeleine lah mah-duh-lehn

Le Hameau luh ah-moh

Les Halles lay zahl

Les Invalides lay-zan-vah-leed

Loire lwahr

L'Orangerie loh-rahn-zhuh-ree

Louvre loov-ruh

Marais mah-ray

Marché aux Puces mar-shay oh pews

Marmottan mar-moh-tahn

Métro may-troh

Monge mohnzh

Montmartre mohn-mart

Montparnasse mohn-par-nas

Moulin Rouge moo-lan roozh

musée mew-zay

Musée de l'Armée mew-zay duh lar-may

Musée d'Orsay mew-zay dor-say

Notre-Dame noh-truh-dahm

Opéra Garnier oh-pay-rah gar-nee-ay

Orangerie oh-rahn-zhuh-ree

Orsay or-say

palais pah-lay

Palais de Justice pah-lay duh zhew-stees

Palais Royal pah-lay roh-yahl

Parc de la Villette park duh lah vee-leht

Parc Monceau park mohn-soh

Père Lachaise pehr lah-shehz

Petit Palais puh-tee pah-lay

Pigalle pee-gahl

place plahs

Place Dauphine plahs doh-feen

Place de la Bastille plahs duh lah bah-steel

Place de la Concorde plahs duh lah kohn-kord

Place de la République plahs duh lah ray-pew-bleek

Place des Vosges plahs day vohzh

Place du Tertre plahs dew tehr-truh

Place St. André-des-Arts plahs san tahn-dray-day-zart

Place Vendôme plahs vahn-dohm

Pompidou pohn-pee-doo

pont pohn

Pont Alexandre III pohn ah-lehks-ahn-druh twah

Pont Neuf pohn nuhf

Promenade Plantée proh-muh-nahd plahn-tay

quai kay

Rive Droite reev drwaht

Rive Gauche reev gohsh

Rodin roh-dan

rue rew

Rue Cler rew klehr

Rue Daguerre rew dah-gehr

Rue des Rosiers rew day roz-ee-ay

Rue Montorgueil rew mohn-tor-goy

Rue Mouffetard rew moof-tar

Rue de Rivoli rew duh ree-voh-lee

Sacré-Cœur sah-kray-kur

Sainte-Chapelle sant-shah-pehl

Seine sehn

Sèvres-Babylone seh-vruh-bah-bee-lohn

Sorbonne sor-buhn

St. Germain-des-Prés san zhehr-man-day-pray

St. Julien-le-Pauvre san zhew-lee-an-luh-poh-vruh

St. Séverin san say-vuh-ran

St. Sulpice san sool-pees

Tour Eiffel toor ee-fehl

Trianon tree-ahn-ohn

Trocadéro troh-kah-day-roh

Tuileries twee-lay-ree

Vaux-le-Vicomte voh-luh-vee-kohnt

Venus de Milo veh-news duh mee-loh

Versailles vehr-sī

French Survival Phrases

When using the phonetics, try to nasalize the n̲ sound.

English	French	Pronunciation
Good day.	Bonjour.	bohn̲-zhoor
Mrs. / Mr.	Madame / Monsieur	mah-dahm / muhs-yuh
Do you speak English?	Parlez-vous anglais?	par-lay-voo ahn̲-glay
Yes. / No.	Oui. / Non.	wee / nohn̲
I understand.	Je comprends.	zhuh kohn̲-prahn̲
I don't understand.	Je ne comprends pas.	zhuh nuh kohn̲-prahn̲ pah
Please.	S'il vous plaît.	see voo play
Thank you.	Merci.	mehr-see
I'm sorry.	Désolé.	day-zoh-lay
Excuse me.	Pardon.	par-dohn̲
(No) problem.	(Pas de) problème.	(pah duh) proh-blehm
It's good.	C'est bon.	say bohn̲
Goodbye.	Au revoir.	oh ruh-vwahr
one / two	un / deux	uhn̲ / duh
three / four	trois / quatre	trwah / kah-truh
five / six	cinq / six	san̲k / sees
seven / eight	sept / huit	seht / weet
nine / ten	neuf / dix	nuhf / dees
How much is it?	Combien?	kohn̲-bee-an̲
Write it?	Ecrivez?	ay-kree-vay
Is it free?	C'est gratuit?	say grah-twee
Included?	Inclus?	an̲-klew
Where can I buy / find...?	Où puis-je acheter / trouver...?	oo pwee-zhuh ah-shuh-tay / troo-vay
I'd like / We'd like...	Je voudrais / Nous voudrions...	zhuh voo-dray / noo voo-dree-ohn̲
...a room.	...une chambre.	ewn shahn̲-bruh
...a ticket to ___.	...un billet pour ___.	uhn̲ bee-yay poor ___
Is it possible?	C'est possible?	say poh-see-bluh
Where is...?	Où est...?	oo ay
...the train station	...la gare	lah gar
...the bus station	...la gare routière	lah gar root-yehr
...tourist information	...l'office du tourisme	loh-fees dew too-reez-muh
Where are the toilets?	Où sont les toilettes?	oo sohn̲ lay twah-leht
men	hommes	ohm
women	dames	dahm
left / right	à gauche / à droite	ah gohsh / ah drwaht
straight	tout droit	too drwah
When does this open / close?	Ça ouvre / ferme à quelle heure?	sah oo-vruh / fehrm ah kehl ur
At what time?	À quelle heure?	ah kehl ur
Just a moment.	Un moment.	uhn̲ moh-mahn̲
now / soon / later	maintenant / bientôt / plus tard	man̲-tuh-nahn̲ / bee-an̲-toh / plew tar
today / tomorrow	aujourd'hui / demain	oh-zhoor-dwee / duh-man̲

In a French Restaurant

English	French	Pronunciation
I'd like / We'd like...	Je voudrais / Nous voudrions...	zhuh voo-dray / noo voo-dree-ohn
...to reserve...	...réserver...	ray-zehr-vay
...a table for one / two.	...une table pour un / deux.	ewn tah-bluh poor uhn / duh
Is this seat free?	C'est libre?	say lee-bruh
The menu (in English), please.	La carte (en anglais), s'il vous plaît.	lah kart (ahn ahn-glay) see voo play
service (not) included	service (non) compris	sehr-vees (nohn) kohn-pree
to go	à emporter	ah ahn-por-tay
with / without	avec / sans	ah-vehk / sahn
and / or	et / ou	ay / oo
special of the day	plat du jour	plah dew zhoor
specialty of the house	spécialité de la maison	spay-see-ah-lee-tay duh lah may-zohn
appetizers	hors d'oeuvre	or duh-vruh
first course (soup, salad)	entrée	ahn-tray
main course (meat, fish)	plat principal	plah pran-see-pahl
bread	pain	pan
cheese	fromage	froh-mahzh
sandwich	sandwich	sahnd-weech
soup	soupe	soop
salad	salade	sah-lahd
meat	viande	vee-ahnd
chicken	poulet	poo-lay
fish	poisson	pwah-sohn
seafood	fruits de mer	frwee duh mehr
fruit	fruit	frwee
vegetables	légumes	lay-gewm
dessert	dessert	day-sehr
mineral water	eau minérale	oh mee-nay-rahl
tap water	l'eau du robinet	loh dew roh-bee-nay
milk	lait	lay
(orange) juice	jus (d'orange)	zhew (doh-rahnzh)
coffee / tea	café / thé	kah-fay / tay
wine	vin	van
red / white	rouge / blanc	roozh / blahn
glass / bottle	verre / bouteille	vehr / boo-tay
beer	bière	bee-ehr
Cheers!	Santé!	sahn-tay
More. / Another.	Plus. / Un autre.	plew / uhn oh-truh
The same.	La même chose.	lah mehm shohz
The bill, please.	L'addition, s'il vous plaît.	lah-dee-see-ohn see voo play
Do you accept credit cards?	Vous prenez les cartes?	voo pruh-nay lay kart
tip	pourboire	poor-bwahr
Delicious!	Délicieux!	day-lee-see-uh

For more user-friendly French phrases, check out *Rick Steves' French Phrase Book and Dictionary* or *Rick Steves' French, Italian & German Phrase Book*.

INDEX

A

Aalto, Alvar: 346
Abbey Mansion: 284–285
Abélard, Peter: 363–364
Absinthe museum, in Auvers: 611
Abstract art: 345–347
Abstract Expressionism: 349–350
Abstract Surrealism: 348
Académie Française: 265, 280
Accommodations: *See* Sleeping
Age of Bronze, The (Rodin): 228
Agoudas Hakehilos Synagogue: 323
Airbnb.com: 638, 640
Air France: 512, 671
Airlines (airfares): 671; budgeting, 5
Airports: 509–518; sleeping near, 417–418; tourist information, 21–22; VAT refunds, 628–629. *See also specific airports*
À La Mère de Famille Confectionery: 210
Alliance Française: 41
Almanac, Paris: 9
Amélie (movie): 383, 680
American Church and Franco-American Center: 40, 41, 264, 388, 676; concerts, 20, 65, 388, 492
American Embassy and Consulate: 313, 676
American Hospital: 675
American Library: 41
American University: 264
Amsterdam: train travel, 527
Amusement parks: 457. *See also* Disneyland Paris
Apartment rentals: 418–419, 637–640
Apollo Basin (Versailles): 557
Apollo Gallery (Louvre): 147–148
Apollo Room (Versailles): 551
Appel, Karel: 349
Apps: audioguides, 631; Gogo Paris, 24; navigation, 24, 629–630
Aquaboulevard: 461
Aquarium: 455
Aquinas, Thomas: 116
Arab World Institute: 87
Arcaded shopping streets *(passages)*: 487

Arcades des Champs-Elysées: 308–309
Arc de Triomphe: 55, 80–81, 86, 300–304; with children, 455; at night, 69, 494
Archaeological Crypt: 53, 56, 109
Architecture and Monuments Museum: 66–67, 69
Arearea, or Joyousness (Gauguin): 186
Army Museum: 67–68, 236–259; concerts, 237, 492; general info, 54, 67–68, 236–237; maps, 239, 256; self-guided tour, 238–259
Arp, Jean: 348
Arrondissements: map, 14; overview, 14–17. *See also* Neighborhoods
Art: *See* Art museums; *And specific artists, artworks and periods*
Art Deco: 139, 308, 477
Art galleries: 281, 284
Artisan Boulangerie: 209–210
Art museums: advance tickets, 52; daily reminder, 20–21; evening hours, 493; Paris Museum Pass, 23, 49–52, 64; planning tips, 630–631; Architecture and Monuments Museum, 66–67, 69; Cluny Museum, 71–72, 291–298; Dalí Museum, 378; Delacroix Museum, 73–74, 283–284; International Stained Glass Center (Chartres), 597; Jacquemart-André Museum, 55, 93–94; Jewish Art and History Museum, 55, 95–98; Louis Vuitton Foundation, 304; Maison-Atelier de Daubigny (Auvers), 611; Marmottan Museum, 70–71, 269–277; Musée Daubigny (Auvers), 610; Musée des Beaux-Arts (Paris), 81–82, 309–310; Musée en Herbe, 456; Museum of Erotic Art, 384–385; Museum of Impressionisms (Giverny), 605; Orangerie Museum, 61, 191–199; Picasso Museum, 95, 328–337; Quai Branly Museum, 62–63, 69; Rodin Museum, 68, 225–235. *See also* Louvre Museum; Orsay Museum; Pompidou Center

INDEX

INDEX

MAP INDEX

Start your trip at

Our website enhances this book and turns

Explore Europe

At ricksteves.com you can browse through thousands of articles, videos, photos and radio interviews, plus find a wealth of money-saving travel tips for planning your dream trip. And with our mobile-friendly website, you can easily access all this great travel information anywhere you go.

TV Shows

Preview the places you'll visit by watching entire half-hour episodes of Rick Steves' Europe (choose from all 100 shows) on-demand, for free.

rickœsteves.com

your travel dreams into affordable reality

Radio Interviews

Enjoy ready access to Rick's vast library of radio interviews covering travel

tips and cultural insights that relate specifically to your Europe travel plans.

Travel Forums

Learn, ask, share! Our online community of savvy travelers is a great resource for first-time travelers to Europe, as well as seasoned pros. You'll find forums on each country, plus travel tips and restaurant/hotel reviews. You can even ask one of our well-traveled staff to chime in with an opinion.

Travel News

Subscribe to our free Travel News e-newsletter, and get monthly updates from Rick on what's happening in Europe.

Audio Europe™

Rick's Free Travel App

Get your FREE **Rick Steves Audio Europe**™ app to enjoy...

- Dozens of self-guided tours of Europe's top museums, sights and historic walks
- Hundreds of tracks filled with cultural insights and sightseeing tips from Rick's radio interviews
- All organized into handy geographic playlists
- For Apple and Android

With Rick whispering in your ear, Europe gets even better.

Find out more at ricksteves.com

Pack Light and Right

Gear up for your next adventure at ricksteves.com

Light Luggage

Pack light and right with Rick Steves' affordable, custom-designed rolling carry-on bags, backpacks, day packs and shoulder bags.

Accessories

From packing cubes to moneybelts and beyond, Rick has personally selected the travel goodies that will help your trip go smoother.

Shop at ricksteves.com

Experience maximum Europe

Save time and energy

This guidebook is your independent-travel toolkit. But for all it delivers, it's still up to you to devote the time and energy it takes to manage the preparation and logistics that are essential for a happy trip. If that's a hassle, there's a solution.

Rick Steves Tours

A Rick Steves tour takes you to Europe's most interesting places with great

great tours, too!

with minimum stress

guides and small groups of 28 or less. We follow Rick's favorite itineraries, ride in comfy buses, stay in family-run hotels, and bring you intimately close to the Europe you've traveled so far to see. Most importantly, we take away the logistical headaches so you can focus on the fun.

travelers—nearly half of them repeat customers— along with us on four dozen different itineraries, from Ireland to Italy to Istanbul. Is a Rick Steves tour the right fit for your travel dreams? Find out at ricksteves.com, where you can also request Rick's latest tour catalog. Europe is best experienced with happy travel partners. We hope you can join us.

Join the fun

This year we'll take thousands of free-spirited

Rick Steves

BEST OF GUIDES

Best of England
Best of France
Best of Germany
Best of Ireland
Best of Italy
Best of Spain

EUROPE GUIDES

Best of Europe
Eastern Europe
Europe Through the Back Door
Mediterranean Cruise Ports
Northern European Cruise Ports

COUNTRY GUIDES

Croatia & Slovenia
England
France
Germany
Great Britain
Ireland
Italy
Portugal
Scandinavia
Scotland
Spain
Switzerland

CITY & REGIONAL GUIDES

Amsterdam & the Netherlands
Belgium: Bruges, Brussels, Antwerp & Ghent
Barcelona
Budapest
Florence & Tuscany
Greece: Athens & the Peloponnese
Istanbul
London
Paris
Prague & the Czech Republic
Provence & the French Riviera
Rome
Venice
Vienna, Salzburg & Tirol

SNAPSHOT GUIDES

Basque Country: Spain & France
Berlin
Copenhagen & the Best of Denmark
Dublin
Dubrovnik
Edinburgh
Hill Towns of Central Italy
Krakow, Warsaw & Gdansk
Lisbon

Nearly all Rick Steves guides are available as ebooks. Check with your favorite bookseller.

Rick Steves guidebooks are published by Avalon Travel, an imprint of Perseus Books, a Hachette Book Group compa